How to become wise

BOOK 5 IN THE REAL CHRISTIANITY SERIES

SEAN KEHOE

realchristianity.com

PUBLISHING DETAILS AND ACKNOWLEDGEMENTS TO BIBLE PUBLISHERS

© Sean Kehoe 2018   Published 2018

How to become wise - Book 5 in the Real Christianity series

Originally published online in much shorter form in May 2014 via our website, under the title *'The wicked, the fool, the simple and the wise'*. This first print edition of the book has been amended from that online version and is copyright 2018.

Sean Kehoe has asserted his right under the Copyright, Designs and Patents Act 1988 to be identified as the author of this work.

Published by realchristianity.com of Philbeach House, Dale, Haverford West, SA62 3QU, United Kingdom

ISBN 978-1-910968-04-8

DEDICATION

This book is dedicated to my wife, who has become the wisest person that I personally know. We have travelled a long way together on the 'narrow path', also known as the 'furnace', or the 'school of hard knocks'. Therefore, like me, she had had to endure the process of having the naivety and foolishness knocked out of her by the painful experiences of life and from the obstacles and opposition, both human and demonic, that we have had to overcome.

I don't doubt that there is more of that turbulence and opposition ahead, because we never stop learning and we never fully 'arrive', at least not in this life. Nevertheless, I can say this – she has changed more than any other person that I know, and all for the better. As a result, she is now my main and best adviser, and the most frequent source of insights and observations that she gleans from reading the Bible each day and which she passes on to me.

i

HOW TO BECOME WISE

BOOK 5 IN THE REAL CHRISTIANITY SERIES

CONTENTS

Page

INTRODUCTION

science

"My people are destroyed for lack of knowledge……..."
Hosea 4:6(a) (RSV)

"….. and a people without understanding shall come to ruin."
Hosea 4:14(b) (ESV)

"For my people are foolish;
  they know me not;
they are stupid children;
  they have no understanding.
They are 'wise'—in doing evil!
  But how to do good they know not."
Jeremiah 4:22 (ESV)

Therefore my people go into exile
  for lack of knowledge;…… (science)
Isaiah 5:13(a) (ESV)

People who have wealth but lack understanding
  are like the beasts that perish.
Psalm 49:20 (NIV)

[6] The stupid man cannot know;
  the fool cannot understand this:
[7] that though the wicked sprout like grass
  and all evildoers flourish,
they are doomed to destruction forever;
Psalm 92:6-7 (ESV)

How much better to get wisdom than gold!
  To get understanding is to be chosen rather than silver.
Proverbs 16:16 (ESV)

If any of you lacks wisdom, let him ask God, who gives to all men generously and without reproaching, and it will be given him.
James 1:5 (RSV)

Behold, you delight in truth in the inward being,
  and you teach me wisdom in the secret heart.
Psalm 51:6 (ESV)

Now set your mind and heart to seek the LORD your God…..
1 Chronicles 22:19 (ESV)

My impression is that most people think of themselves as wise, at least to some degree. They may not say it out loud, but they think it, even if only unconsciously. At any rate, they don't consider themselves to be what the Bible calls simple or naïve, and they certainly don't see themselves as being either fools or wicked. However, that presents a problem, because the Bible indicates that very few people are wise and that the other three groups make up the vast majority of the population.

Even within the Church, the reality is that few people are wise. At best, the majority of us are simple/naïve and many of us, despite the fact that we are members of churches, are fools, or even wicked. So, my first task in this book is a delicate one. It is to seek to convince you that you probably aren't wise at the moment. That's not the way for me to win friends, but it does appear to be what the Bible is saying.

My second task is to persuade you that you ought to make it your aim to *become* wise. To that end, I will set out a host of benefits that come from being wise and try to explain more fully what wisdom really is. Biblical wisdom means thinking, speaking and acting in a godly way, rather than as the world does, or in accordance with your fleshly nature.

The third aim is then to show how such wisdom can be acquired. Although real wisdom is rare, the fact remains that it is fully available to all of us. It is there to be gained and it can be developed by *anybody at all*. You don't have to be naturally clever or educated or have an important job. That is because real wisdom is primarily about developing a Christ-like character and seeing the world, yourself, and those around you *as God sees them*.

It is also about learning the principles by which God operates, and the way He thinks, and then emphasising and valuing the same things that He does. That is why I insist that wisdom really is available to everybody, despite the fact that, in practice, it is so rare. It is only rare because so few people *choose* to pursue it. If they did, they would acquire it, no matter who, or what, they may be at present. You can undoubtedly get it, if you are willing to *seek for it* by studying the Bible with sufficient determination and perseverance.

The problem is that such diligent, long-term study requires effort and commitment. But very few of us are willing to put in the amount of work that is needed to get to know the whole Bible really well and to put it into practice in our day to day lives. Accordingly, wisdom is exceptional, but only because most people, even real Christians, don't want to make that much of an effort. At any rate, they are not sufficiently motivated to keep it up, even if they make a start at it.

That therefore brings us back to the second aim of this book, which is to persuade you that genuine biblical wisdom really is worth making a great effort to obtain. No matter what it requires, or how long it takes, it is worth it. You don't need to take my word for that. The Bible tells us so over and over again. Indeed, the first eight chapters of Proverbs are devoted to trying to convince you of this. The conclusion of those eight chapters is that wisdom should be pursued as if it was gold or precious stones. In fact, it is said to be far more valuable than those things:

13 How blessed is the man who finds wisdom
And the man who gains understanding.
14 For her profit is better than the profit of silver
And her gain better than fine gold.
15 She is more precious than jewels;
And nothing you desire compares with her.
16 Long life is in her right hand;
In her left hand are riches and honor.
17 Her ways are pleasant ways
And all her paths are peace.
18 She is a tree of life to those who take hold of her,
And happy are all who hold her fast.
                    Proverbs 3:13-18 (NASB)

Moreover, we are told all of this by King Solomon, the writer of most of the Book of Proverbs. The Bible says that he was the wisest man who ever lived, other than Jesus. Therefore, he must surely be worth listening to, by anybody's standards. I do hope, therefore, that you will consider very carefully the case that is made for wisdom in this book and then resolve to pursue it for yourself, no matter how high the cost may be, or how great the effort involved, and regardless of how long it takes.

Sean Kehoe
6 April 2018

vii

CHAPTER 1

THE FOUR MAIN TYPES OF PERSON

Stay away from a fool, for you will
not find knowledge on their lips.
Proverbs 14:7 (NIV)

Do not be deceived: "Bad company corrupts good morals."
1 Corinthians 15:33 (NASB)

A wise man is mightier than a strong man,
and a man of knowledge than he who has strength;
Proverbs 24:5 (RSV)

"……. for those who honour me I will honour, and those who despise me shall
be lightly esteemed"
1 Samuel 2:30(b) (RSV)

[6] Yet among the mature we do impart wisdom, although it is not a wisdom of this
age or of the rulers of this age, who are doomed to pass away. [7] But we impart
a secret and hidden wisdom of God, which God decreed before the ages for our
glorification. [8] None of the rulers of this age understood this; for if they had,
they would not have crucified the Lord of glory.
1 Corinthians 2:6-8 (RSV)

The unspiritual man does not receive the gifts of the Spirit of God, for they are
folly to him, and he is not able to understand them because they are spiritually
discerned.
1 Corinthians 2:14 (RSV)

"Many shall purify themselves, and make themselves white, and be refined; but
the wicked shall do wickedly; and none of the wicked shall understand; but
those who are wise shall understand."
Daniel 12:10 (RSV)

Everyone who does evil hates the light, and will not come into the light for fear
that their deeds will be exposed.
John 3:20 (NIV)

And he did evil, for he did not set his heart to seek the LORD.
2 Chronicles 12:14 (ESV)

Like a muddied spring or a polluted fountain
is a righteous man who gives way before the wicked.
                            Proverbs 25:26 (RSV)

……..The LORD is with you while you are with him. If you seek him, he will be
found by you, but if you forsake him, he will forsake you.
                            2 Chronicles 15:2(b) (ESV)

What are the four types of person the Bible speaks of?

In this chapter we shall examine the four broad groups of people, or character types, to which the Bible frequently refers. As with so many other biblical words, these four are widely misunderstood. Every one of us is operating, at any given moment, in ways which place us within one or more of these groups. Therefore, we shall define each of them as accurately as we can. We shall also look at how to identify where we are along the spectrum from wicked to wise and how we can move in the right direction. The four groups are as follows:

a)   the *wicked*

b)   the *fool* (the term *scoffer* is also used, though it can refer either to a fool or a wicked man)

c)   the *simple* (also referred to as being *naive*)

d)   the *wise*

Perhaps one thing which needs to be clarified right at the outset is the difference between being *wicked* and merely *sinful*. The point is that we are all sinful, but we are not all wicked. That has to be so, because God specifically warns us to avoid the wicked and not to follow them or spend time with them, as in this passage:

[14] Do not enter the path of the wicked   Don't respond as they do
And do not proceed in the way of evil men.
[15] Avoid it, do not pass by it;
Turn away from it and pass on.
                    Proverbs 4:14-15 (NASB)

The point is that God is telling us to avoid *"the wicked"* and also *"evil men"*, but common-sense dictates that that must mean that we are not all wicked or evil because, if we were, it would make the instruction absurd, as it would be impossible to obey. It would be like telling us to avoid all people who breathe oxygen. It has to follow, therefore, that God draws a distinction between being a sinner, which all of us are, and being wicked, which only some of us are. We shall seek to identify and explain those differences in chapter 4 below and I also go into much greater detail about the wicked, and how to identify and handle them, in my Book 6.

Although the Bible regularly speaks of people being wicked or fools, one very rarely hears of anybody describing *themselves* by those names. It is almost as rare to hear of anybody classifying themselves as simple or naive. Most people, whether they are Christians or not, automatically assume they belong within the group known as the wise. But that doesn't add up. It means over 90% of people assume themselves to be in the top 5%, or even 1%, whereas the Bible indicates that it is very unusual to be wise, and that simple, foolish and wicked people are to be found in huge numbers.

Therefore, it must follow that most of us are very wrong in the way we see ourselves. Most *real* Christians, as opposed to either nominal or false Christians, are what the Bible calls simple. So, even amongst real Christians, only a minority are wise. A non-Christian, or a false Christian, cannot be wise, because being a genuine Christian and fearing God are the vital first steps on the path to becoming wise. You can't even start the process without those features. Therefore, if you are a non-Christian, or even a nominal Christian, you cannot possibly be wise, at least not in the way the Bible means.

You would have to be somewhere along the spectrum from simple through to wicked. That is the sort of discovery you make when you read the Bible. It is not a complimentary book and never flatters us. On the contrary, it is very frank and tells us the honest truth about ourselves. Moreover, when it speaks in critical terms, it is generally referring to what is wrong with *us*, not just '*other people*'. That is a vital discovery which most of us have not yet made, but we urgently need to grasp it if we are ever to become wise.

The reason the Bible is so frank about the faults and failings of the apostles, prophets and other characters is not so that we can look down on them, or feel good about ourselves in comparison. It is to enable us to see those same faults and sins in ourselves. But we rarely do see such things, even when they are as plain as day to those who know us. Most of us have an excessively favourable view of our own conduct and motives and never examine ourselves at all, let alone conclude, after doing so, that we are at fault in any way:

All a person's ways seem pure to them,
but motives are weighed by the LORD.
                    Proverbs 16:2 (NIV)

3

We are each on a spectrum, somewhere between wicked and wise, but there are no precise boundaries

So, the mere fact that you may have become a real Christian does not, in itself, mean that you are already wise, or even that you will become wise. It is, however, an essential first step. We are commanded, from conversion onwards, to seek for wisdom and to continue doing so for as long as it takes until we get it. It is helpful to think of there being a spectrum, along which we travel in tiny little increments, rather than picturing four distinct groups with precise boundaries and no overlapping. The illustration below may assist in showing how we can move, step by step, in the right direction:

Wicked	Fool	Simple	Wise

In the spectrum above there are no exact boundaries where a person decisively leaves one category and joins another. It is much more indistinct and blurred than that. Yet, there are still broadly identifiable regions. Moreover, nobody is ever 100% wicked, or 100% wise, or 100% anything else. Even the worst of us have some good qualities, and even the best people have their faults, or moments when they let themselves down.

You might say that a person is like a bowl which is filled with thousands of grains of pepper, sand, sugar and salt. Imagine that salt represents wisdom, sugar represents naivety, sand is foolishness and pepper is wickedness. If the bowl represents a person's life, then it will not consist of 100% of any one of those substances. It will always be a mixture. The only question is *in what proportions?* So, if you picture this mixture in the bowl, then to become wiser means adding salt and taking away sand, sugar and pepper. Usually it is only done a few grains at a time.

That is a more realistic way to view the process of becoming wise, rather than seeing it as an overnight transformation. Such a dramatic improvement has never happened to anybody (except Solomon) and it never will. A person can't pick up the 'bowl' at the point when they become a Christian and just empty it all out and refill it with salt all in one go. On the other hand, neither does anyone become entirely foolish, or entirely wicked, in a single moment. Whatever direction we are travelling in, it takes time to change.

However, our objective must always be to keep on and on reducing the 'pepper, sugar and sand' and increasing the 'salt' in our lives. We are to aim to become as salty as possible, and in as many ways as possible. In other words, our task is to

4

keep moving along the spectrum in the correct direction and to become as wise, godly, mature and righteous as we can. Moreover, wisdom is not based on IQ, talent or natural ability. Therefore, it is equally open to any of us to become what the Bible (not the world) calls wise.

Nobody has a head start, because the biblical definition of wisdom is not about cleverness or passing exams. It is nothing to do with being good at maths, or literature, or any other subject. Wisdom in the Bible is mainly about *character*. That, in turn, is primarily defined in terms of our *values, attitudes, beliefs and actions*, not our *ability*. Alternatively, you could say that it is about developing the fruit of the Holy Spirit in our lives. As for how we are meant to *get* wisdom, it mainly comes from:

a) studying and applying the Bible and

b) associating with, and learning from, other people who are already wise, or at least wiser than we currently are.

Our important relationships are meant to be with people we have chosen carefully, and are not to be entered into randomly

Many of us assume that our relationships are meant to be formed randomly and that we don't need to exercise any judgement as to the people with whom we spend our time. The Bible doesn't support that view. The way you spend your time, *and with whom,* is seen as one of your most important areas of stewardship. God will therefore hold you accountable for all the relationship choices you make. Each of those decisions will profoundly affect how your character turns out and whether you end up a wise person, a fool, or even wicked.

There is nothing random about any of that. Whatever we may end up as, it is the *foreseeable* result of the countless choices that we make over the years. Bear in mind also that wisdom is only ever pursued by those who already have at least some of it. Only those who currently have enough understanding to at least realise the importance of wisdom, will be willing to set their face towards acquiring it and to make the effort to develop it further, even though they don't yet fully possess it:

A man of understanding sets his face toward wisdom ....
Proverbs 17:24(a) (RSV)

An intelligent heart acquires knowledge,
and the ear of the wise seeks knowledge.
Proverbs 18:15 (ESV)

Listen to advice and accept instruction,
that you may gain wisdom in the future.
Proverbs 19:20 (ESV)

Such a person will also be willing to pay the price, and to make the necessary sacrifices, in order to acquire wisdom, because it does come at a high cost, not only in terms of time and effort, but in other ways too, sometimes even financial:

Buy truth, and do not sell it;
buy wisdom, instruction, and understanding.
Proverbs 23:23 (ESV)

One of the costs of becoming wise is that it will cause us to be relegated in the opinions of worldly people. What God calls wisdom is foolishness to them and what they call wisdom is foolishness to Him. Therefore, if you want to become wise by God's definition, rather than the world's, it will result in you being considered a fool and sneered at by many who know you. Apostle Paul speaks of this and there is irony in his tone when he refers to *'the wisdom of this world'* and *"the thoughts of the wise"*, by which he means those who wrongly imagine they are wise:

Fool for Christ

[18] *Let no one deceive himself. If anyone among you thinks that he is wise in this age, let him become a fool that he may become wise.* [19] *For the wisdom of this world is folly with God. For it is written, "He catches the wise in their craftiness,"* [20] *and again, "The Lord knows that the thoughts of the wise are futile."*

1 Corinthians 3:18-20 (RSV)

Now let us begin to examine each of the four groups more closely, beginning with the fool. However, the best we can hope to do in this book is to scratch the surface of this huge subject because the Bible has such a vast amount to say about the pursuit of wisdom and God's view of wickedness, foolishness and naivety. Please also be aware that most of what I say about *how* to become wise is not within the early chapters of this book. Those are mostly about what it is to *not* be wise, why that matters, and also persuading you that you are probably not wise at the moment.

If you are eager to see the *'how to'* material, that really gets started from chapter 8 onwards. Do please also be willing to consider topics which you may not have thought had anything to do with being wise, such as work, money, decision-making, marriage, and even obscure concepts like political correctness and human rights.

A wise choice – by their choices you shall know them.

6

I hope that, by the end of this book, you will agree with me that all of these issues are badly misunderstood and neglected in today's churches, and that they are highly relevant areas of study for those who wish to become wise. Indeed, the distinction between the righteous and the wicked, and the profoundly different ways in which God deals with each group, is vital for us to grasp:

16 Then those who feared the LORD spoke with one another. The LORD paid attention and heard them, and a book of remembrance was written before him of those who feared the LORD and esteemed his name. 17 "They shall be mine, says the LORD of hosts, in the day when I make up my treasured possession, and I will spare them as a man spares his son who serves him. 18 Then once more you shall see the distinction between the righteous and the wicked, between one who serves God and one who does not serve him.

Malachi 3:16-18 (ESV)

Wisdom knows it is Nothing without God all that upon God alone it depends for all.

Faith in God is wisdom.

Not Ashamed of Gods word

CHAPTER 2

THE FOOL

The fool says in his heart, "There is no God."
Psalm 14:1(a) (RSV)

For the message of the cross is foolishness to those who are perishing, but to us who are being saved it is the power of God.
1 Corinthians 1:18 (NKJV)

The wise will inherit honour,
but fools get disgrace
Proverbs 3:35 (RSV)

He who commits adultery has no sense;
he who does it destroys himself.
Proverbs 6:32 (RSV)

Fools mock at sin,
But among the upright there is good will.
Proverbs 14:9 (NASB)

A wise man is cautious and turns away from evil,
But a fool is arrogant and careless.
Proverbs 14:16 (NASB)

He who sires a fool does so to his sorrow,
And the father of a fool has no joy.
Proverbs 17:21 (NASB)

The foolishness of man ruins his way,
And his heart rages against the LORD.
Proverbs 19:3 (NASB)

As a ring of gold in a swine's snout
So is a beautiful woman who lacks discretion.
Proverbs 11:22 (NASB)

Man in his pomp yet without understanding is like the beasts that perish.
Psalm 49:20 (ESV)

Who or what is a 'fool'? — Not intellectually stupid

Probably the best definition of a fool is *a man who lives his life as if there was no God.* He might, technically, believe there is a God but, in practice, he *lives* as if there wasn't. To be even more precise, you could say that a fool lives his life as if there was *no Day of Judgment,* and as if God's Word did not matter much. You might think it odd for me to place so much emphasis on these issues.

However, if God has revealed that He intends to judge us, what could be more irresponsible than to ignore or under-emphasise that fact? If true, it is fundamental to the whole of our lives. To deny it, or to be unaware or unconcerned about it, would inevitably cause us to go wrong and to miss the point on just about everything. Viewed in those terms, it would not seem unreasonable to label such a person as a fool. Let's now examine some of the key features of a fool and ask ourselves, very frankly, to what extent we display these.

It is no use just assuming that when the Bible refers to fools it is talking about other people. It is probably referring to us much of the time. Many people consider themselves wise, but have no basis for thinking that. They may be academic, successful, powerful or rich, but still have little or no wisdom. Such people may therefore be making the mistake of imagining themselves to be wise or *"being wise in their own eyes"* when, according to the Bible, they are not:

Woe to those who are wise in their own eyes and clever in their own sight.
Isaiah 5:21 (NIV)

Because of their success in some field, or because of their wealth or their qualifications, they may feel self-sufficient and assume they don't need God. Therefore, Isaiah says *"woe"* to them because their wrong attitude makes it a certainty that they will eventually fall under God's judgment and be brought down. However, before we complacently assume that this warning only refers to others, remember that we are all capable of displaying these proud and foolish attitudes ourselves, and most of us do.

Hardly anybody ever seems to see himself as being a fool

I have never yet met a person who considers himself to be a fool, or at least, who is willing to admit to being one. We are generally incapable of recognising this in ourselves. Ironically, to be capable of seeing the foolishness in yourself, you have to be already well on the way to becoming wise. Consequently, many of us have no idea that God views us as fools and we would be shocked to discover it. We may be clever, highly-qualified, and have a good job. We may go to church

Live with the end in mind

See self for who you really are — as God sees you: weak, foolish, naive, sinful, wicked, incompetent...

and even be a real Christian. But none of that prevents us from being a fool by the biblical definition.

We therefore have to examine ourselves closely and see whether we display any of the characteristics or attitudes of a fool, even if only in part, or only at certain times. It is unlikely that you have ever heard any sermon on what a fool is, let alone been challenged as to whether *you* are one. However, please don't be offended by my suggesting the possibility to you. Be willing to look at this issue with brutal honesty. Then ask God to show you *whether* you are a fool, or are behaving as one, and, if so, *when, where* and *how*? Also ask Him to help you to change.

It may be that you are only foolish in certain ways. Or it may only be at certain times or in particular parts of your life, such as in your marriage, your job, or your finances, and that you are not foolish in every other area. Even if that is so, you would still need to recognise, and admit to, those areas of partial or intermittent foolishness in yourself. If you don't, you are never going to be able to change. Therefore, let's look at some of the key features that fools tend to display. Do any of these features occur in your life or remind you of yourself?

The typical characteristics of a fool

A fully developed fool has no fear of God and *he despises wisdom*. By that I mean that he *under-values* wisdom and that it *does not matter to him*, not that he hates or dislikes it. Therefore, he has no desire to be instructed, or at least not in the things that God wants us to know:

The fear of the LORD is the beginning of knowledge;
Fools despise wisdom and instruction.
             Proverbs 1:7 (NASB)

Wisdom abides in the mind of a man of understanding,
 but it is not known in the heart of fools.
             Proverbs 14:33 (RSV)

Of what use is money in the hand of a fool,
since he has no desire to get wisdom?
             Proverbs 17:16 (NIV)

Many fools are over-confident. They put their trust in themselves and in their own opinions, abilities, status, or possessions. They are self-satisfied and overly self-assured. Instead, they should put their trust in God:

11

[13] This is the fate of those who have foolish confidence,
the end of those who are pleased with their portion. Selah
[14] Like sheep they are appointed for Sheol;
Death shall be their shepherd;
straight to the grave they descend,
and their form shall waste away;
Sheol shall be their home.

Psalm 49:13-14 (RSV)

A fool is also complacent about the things that God wants us to be alarmed about:

For the waywardness of the naive will kill them,
And the complacency of fools will destroy them.

Proverbs 1:32 (NASB)

A fool is not interested in what God says, or concerned about what He wants. Therefore, he is busy with all sorts of things which are of interest to himself, while neglecting or ignoring the things, and the people, that God is interested in. Like the sons of Eli, whom God judged, the fool has *no regard for the LORD:*

Now the sons of Eli were worthless men; they had no regard for the LORD.

1 Samuel 2:12 (RSV)

For the fool speaks folly,
and his heart is busy with iniquity,
to practice ungodliness,
to utter error concerning the LORD,
to leave the craving of the hungry unsatisfied,
and to deprive the thirsty of drink.

Isaiah 32:6 (ESV)

Many fools will go further and even deny the very existence of God. That is a sure sign that a man has become a fully-fledged fool by the biblical definition:

The fool has said in his heart, "There is no God ".........

Psalm 14:1(a) (NASB)

In Romans, Paul explains how God considers His own existence to be completely obvious, because of the complexity, and self-evident design, of all that He has created. Yet, many people ignore the evidence that is all around them and choose not to acknowledge God as the Creator. As a consequence of this they then degenerate further, become increasingly futile in their thinking, and steadily turn into fools. So, the chain of causation works in both directions. A man says there

12

Don't value what God values, don't see as important what God does.

is no God *because* he is already a fool, but he also *becomes* a fool because he rejects and ignores God:

> *19 For what can be known about God is plain to them, because God has shown it to them. 20 Ever since the creation of the world his invisible nature, namely, his eternal power and deity, has been clearly perceived in the things that have been made. So they are without excuse; 21 for although they knew God they did not honor him as God or give thanks to him, but they became futile in their thinking and their senseless minds were darkened. 22 Claiming to be wise, they became fools, 23 and exchanged the glory of the immortal God for images resembling mortal man or birds or animals or reptiles.*
>
> *Romans 1:19-23 (RSV)*

A fool ignores and rejects the true God. He then creates false gods of his own making to put in God's place.

Some fools go so far as to *deny* God's very existence. Others merely *ignore* God, even if they concede that He exists. But fools also create false gods of their own making, which they then put in God's place. We are all capable of that, even if we are real Christians. We need to guard against it, because if we let anything become a god to us we are acting like a fool *in that area of our life*, even if we are not a fool in everything else that we do. The definition of a '*god*' is anything at all which you allow to take God's place. That then begs the questions "*what is God's place?*" One could define it as:

a) to be *worshiped* (no other person or thing may ever receive our worship)

b) to have the *first place in our lives*, ahead of all other people or things

c) to be at the very forefront of our thoughts and plans

If any person or thing in your life ever falls within categories (a)-(c) above then, whatever it is, it has become a god to you and, if you have any such god, then you are a fool. Or, you are at least behaving like a fool in that part of your life. See how God describes those who create idols from wood and metal and then bow down and worship them. He speaks of them in scathing terms as being blind and lacking understanding: *The foolishness of idols*

> *18 What profit is an idol*
> *when its maker has shaped it,*
> *a metal image, a teacher of lies?*
> *For the workman trusts in his own creation*
> *when he makes dumb idols!*
> *19 Woe to him who says to a wooden thing, Awake;*

to a dumb stone, Arise!
Can this give revelation?
Behold, it is overlaid with gold and silver,
and there is no breath at all in it.
                    Habakkuk 2:18-19 (RSV)

⁹ All who make idols are nothing, and the things they delight in do not profit; their witnesses neither see nor know, that they may be put to shame. ¹⁰ Who fashions a god or casts an image, that is profitable for nothing? ¹¹ Behold, all his fellows shall be put to shame, and the craftsmen are but men; let them all assemble, let them stand forth, they shall be terrified, they shall be put to shame together.

¹² The ironsmith fashions it and works it over the coals; he shapes it with hammers, and forges it with his strong arm; he becomes hungry and his strength fails, he drinks no water and is faint. ¹³ The carpenter stretches a line, he marks it out with a pencil; he fashions it with planes, and marks it with a compass; he shapes it into the figure of a man, with the beauty of a man, to dwell in a house. ¹⁴ He cuts down cedars; or he chooses a holm tree or an oak and lets it grow strong among the trees of the forest; he plants a cedar and the rain nourishes it. ¹⁵ Then it becomes fuel for a man; he takes a part of it and warms himself, he kindles a fire and bakes bread; also he makes a god and worships it, he makes it a graven image and falls down before it.

¹⁶ Half of it he burns in the fire; over the half he eats flesh, he roasts meat and is satisfied; also he warms himself and says, "Aha, I am warm, I have seen the fire!" ¹⁷ And the rest of it he makes into a god, his idol; and falls down to it and worships it; he prays to it and says, "Deliver me, for thou art my god!" ¹⁸ They know not, nor do they discern; for he has shut their eyes, so that they cannot see, and their minds, so that they cannot understand. ¹⁹ No one considers, nor is there knowledge or discernment to say, "Half of it I burned in the fire, I also baked bread on its coals, I roasted flesh and have eaten; and shall I make the residue of it an abomination? Shall I fall down before a block of wood?" ²⁰ He feeds on ashes; a deluded mind has led him astray, and he cannot deliver himself or say, "Is there not a lie in my right hand?"
                    Isaiah 44:9-20 (RSV)

You might feel complacent about this, because you have not made any literal physical idols from wood or metal. If so, think again. We can create just as many gods as the Israelites. The only difference is that our gods tend to be money, career, status, ambition, popularity, fame, celebrities, sports, possessions, houses, cars etc. Any of those can become a god to you if you let it take places at (a)-(c) above, which only God can have. The Chaldeans even made a god out of their

high esteem
(A Source of Pride to you?)
Depend upon?

14

What drives you?
Who do you serve?
What is your passion, motivation?
What are you in love with?

own power and might. They were famous for their military prowess and that strength, in itself, become a god to them:

> [9] *They all come for violence;*
>   *terror of them goes before them.*
>   *They gather captives like sand.*
> [10] *At kings they scoff,*
>   *and of rulers they make sport.*
> *They laugh at every fortress,*
>   *for they heap up earth and take it.*
> [11] *Then they sweep by like the wind and go on,*
>   *guilty men, whose own might is their god!*
>   *Habakkuk 1:9-11 (RSV)*

We boast in the cross of Christ

You might think this last point does not affect you either, but don't be too sure. For centuries, the United Kingdom was, overwhelmingly, the most powerful nation on Earth. Its army, and especially its navy, won war after war and built by far the largest empire the world has ever seen. Even until shortly before World War Two, it was the UK's policy always to ensure that its navy was stronger than the next two biggest navies in the world *combined,* in case they ever formed an alliance against us.

Many British people were therefore proud of their military strength and it became a god to some. The same is true today for some Americans, now that they are the world's only super-power. It is difficult not to take pride in such things and to begin to rely on them, to such an extent that they become gods to us. We therefore need to be alert to see our own potential for creating *any kind* of gods for ourselves, and in *any area* of our lives. Above all, we need to grasp that it is something which we ourselves are capable of, not merely something that *other people* do.

Even Christians can 'adjust' God, so as to make Him into the kind of God they want Him to be, rather than as He describes Himself in the Bible

Another problem, which affects many Christians, even real ones, is to take the God of the Bible and *'adjust' Him,* such that you end up creating a false god to put in His place. I have seen many people either do this or come close to it. This happens where we, consciously or unconsciously, reject or ignore what God says about Himself in the Bible. We may dislike certain aspects of His nature or character and edit those features out and focus instead on other characteristics of God which we prefer, or are willing to accept.

We may even go so far as to invent new, or additional, or alternative characteristics for God, which He does not have. We then decide for ourselves

15

'I am who I am' - not who you want me to be
AND - the gospel - dilute it - to sell it

that that is what He is like, rather than simply accept that He is *how He describes Himself* in the Bible. The classic example of this is where liberals *redefine* God and eliminate from Him any features to which they object, such as His holiness, judgment or wrath. They will usually do the same with His love for Israel and the Jewish people.

The people who do this are in severe danger of creating a false god of their own making and putting that invented god in place of the real God of the Bible. When people do this, they invariably produce a god who just happens to share all their own opinions and preferences. Indeed, their god sounds remarkably like themselves. The things that the real God says about Himself in the Bible are brushed aside and they end up worshiping a new god which is just a reflection of themselves in a mirror.

A person who does this is no less foolish than a man who worships a statue made of wood or stone. Their god is equally false and equally home-made. Therefore, we must not imagine ourselves to be immune to this kind of error. We are all in danger of creating false gods for ourselves if we do not have what the Bible calls *'the love of the truth'*. A person who has that quality is determined to believe whatever is true, and to reject whatever is false, regardless of their own personal preferences, and also regardless of whether it is convenient, or is in their financial interest.

Therefore, make up your mind to accept and believe *whatever God says about Himself* in the Bible, *irrespective of whether it suits you*. Never impose upon God other features which you would prefer Him to have. God classified the majority of the Jewish people of Jeremiah's day as fools, not because they did not *believe* in Him, but because they did not *know* Him. They also ignored or undervalued His written Word and also His verbal warnings via the prophet Jeremiah. In other words, they lived in a way which showed that God, and His commands, did not matter much to them:

"For My people are foolish,
They know Me not;
They are stupid children
And have no understanding
They are shrewd to do evil,
But to do good they do not know."
Jeremiah 4:22 (NASB)

The same applied to the leaders, both religious and civil. They ignored God's Word, disobeyed His commands, and even prophesied under the influence of demons:

The priests did not say, 'Where is the LORD?'
 Those who handle the law did not know me;
the shepherds transgressed against me;
 the prophets prophesied by Baal
 and went after things that do not profit.
                    Jeremiah 2:8 (ESV)

For the shepherds are stupid
 and do not inquire of the LORD;
therefore they have not prospered,
 and all their flock is scattered.
                Jeremiah 10:21 (ESV)

And the LORD said to me: "The prophets are prophesying lies in my name. I did not send them, nor did I command them or speak to them. They are prophesying to you a lying vision, worthless divination, and the deceit of their own minds.
                            Jeremiah 14:14 (ESV)

The main problem with the fool is not his IQ, but his heart attitude

A fool's main problem is his heart-attitude, not his IQ. He basically does not value what God values and does not care about what God says. He will not respond well to instruction or correction, especially on moral or spiritual matters. Generally speaking, a fool will not stop being a fool. Therefore, most fools never come to their senses, or change for the better, whatever is done to them, or for them:

Though you pound a fool in a mortar
with a pestle along with crushed grain,
Yet his foolishness will not depart from him.
                Proverbs 27:22 (NASB)

The main reason a fool does not learn from instruction is that he does not value knowledge, understanding or wisdom in the first place. Therefore, he has no motivation to make the effort to seek those things. He also has no desire to find out the real truth about himself, or to change. He assumes he already knows it all and therefore needs nothing more. By contrast, a wise man is painfully aware that he does *not* already know everything. Consequently, he is eager to listen, and even to be corrected and rebuked:

The way of a fool is right in his own eyes,
but a wise man listens to advice.
                Proverbs 12:15 (RSV)

17

A rebuke goes deeper into a man of understanding
than a hundred blows into a fool
Proverbs 17:10 (ESV)

Whoever loves discipline loves knowledge,
But he who hates reproof is stupid.
Proverbs 12:1 (NASB)

A fool over-estimates himself and is content to stay as he is. He sees little or nothing wrong with himself and does not recognise his own faults. Even if those are pointed out, they don't bother him, and he does not see any need to change. On the contrary, once a person becomes a fool, he usually just becomes more and more foolish. That is he becomes an ever more concentrated version of what he already is, like a sugary drink evaporating in a glass on a hot day and becoming increasingly thick and viscous. He also feeds on other people's foolishness and adds their folly to his own:

The mind of the intelligent seeks knowledge,
But the mouth of fools feeds on folly.
Proverbs 15:14 (NASB)

When was the last time you ever thought about your own faults? Indeed, have you ever done so at all? Foolishness is in all of us, at least to some extent, and in some areas of our life. Moreover, it will remain in us, and keep on increasing, unless we resolve to get rid of it by taking active steps. It won't ever go away by itself. So, unless you are taking such steps, the chances are that you are currently a fool and will continue to be one, at least in some areas of your attitude, conduct or character.

What do fools do and how else do they display their foolishness?

A fool prefers to maintain and express his own opinions, instead of simply finding out what God thinks and then agreeing with Him:

A fool takes no pleasure in understanding,
but only in expressing his opinion.
Proverbs 18:2 (RSV)

A fool is also careless about what he says and may casually make vows to God or promises to other people that he has no intention of keeping. A fool will also curse others, which then brings God's curse down on him in return. A fool will also condemn or criticise others without having any adequate evidence, let alone proof. For all such careless words, we will be held accountable and brought into judgment:

36 I tell you, on the day of judgment men will render account for every careless word they utter; 37 for by your words you will be justified, and by your words you will be condemned."

Matthew 12:36-37 (RSV)

A fool's speech will not only bring him into deeper trouble. His voice is also an outlet for the folly that is already within him:

A fool's mouth is his ruin,
and his lips are a snare to himself.
Proverbs 18:7 (RSV)

The talk of a fool is a rod for his back,
but the lips of the wise will preserve them.
Proverbs 14:3 (RSV)

One of the classic identifying features of a fool is that he does not learn from his mistakes, even when things go badly wrong and end in failure. Therefore, time and time again, a fool will repeat the same behaviour pattern, or display the same attitude, which led to things going so badly wrong in the past:

Like a dog that returns to his vomit
is a fool that repeats his folly
Proverbs 26:11 (RSV)

Another hallmark of a fool is that he doesn't see that it is his own conduct, attitudes, ways and habits which are repeatedly leading him into trouble and failure. On every occasion, he attributes his problems to other people, circumstances, or bad luck. What he won't do is ask whether *he himself* might be the cause of what is going wrong. If he paused for a moment and asked himself that obvious question he would make a series of discoveries about himself and could even cease to be a fool. Sadly, very few fools ever do ask that question, due to complacency and their inflated view of themselves:

A wise man is cautious and turns away from evil,
But a fool is arrogant and careless.
Proverbs 14:16 (NASB)

To be angry is not necessarily sinful, but to be bad-tempered is both sinful and foolish

A fool is also quick-tempered and lacks self-control and restraint. Yet, far from seeing that as a fault, he will often even see his own forthrightness as a quality. Thus, he will express his views too quickly, or too stridently, and antagonise others unnecessarily:

The vexation of a fool is known at once,
but the prudent man ignores an insult.
                    Proverbs 12:16 (RSV)

A hot-tempered man stirs up strife,
but he who is slow to anger quiets contention.
                    Proverbs 15:18 (ESV)

Whoever is slow to anger is better than the mighty.
and he who rules his spirit than he who takes a city
                    Proverbs 16:32 (ESV)

He who is slow to anger has great understanding,
But he who is quick-tempered exalts folly.
                    Proverbs 14:29 (NASB)

A man without self-control
is like a city broken into and left without walls
                    Proverbs 25:28 (ESV)

A fool gives full vent to his anger,
but a wise man quietly holds it back.
                    Proverbs 29:11 (RSV)

Now we see why God's anger is held back for so long, even for centuries, before He eventually brings nations to judgment. God feels anger, but He does not have a *temper*. Therefore, He never loses it. Anger can be a godly emotion, but to lose one's temper is just a display of our fleshly nature. Therefore, it is sin. God's wisdom is so infinite He can restrain His anger for as long as He chooses. We need to develop some of that patient self-control that God has. Then we would not be so quick to form, or express, our own opinions before hearing what others have to say, and before we know the full facts:

[19] Know this, my beloved brethren. Let every man be quick to hear, slow to speak, slow to anger, [20] for the anger of man does not work the righteousness of God.
                    James 1:19-20 (RSV)

If one gives answer before he hears,
it is his folly and shame.
                              Proverbs 18:13 (RSV)

We should also ask God to help us to maintain a rigorous self-control and to be careful how we react to vexation and especially what we say to others:

Set a guard, O LORD, over my mouth;
Keep watch over the door of my lips
                              Psalm 141:3 (ESV)

Even if we are right, and even if what we propose to say is true, it is not always appropriate to display our knowledge or tell people what we think. A wise person knows when to stay silent, but a fool doesn't, thus adding to his problems and also making it all the more apparent that he is a fool:

The prudent keep their knowledge to themselves,
  but a fool's heart blurts out folly.
                              Proverbs 12:23 (NIV)

Fools also have a craving to be seen as important. Therefore, if they see an opportunity to appear important, or gain approval in the eyes of others, by disclosing private or confidential information, they will do so. Therefore, a fool can't be trusted with secrets, whether personal or commercial, so don't ever confide in a fool, or share any sensitive information with him:

He who goes about gossiping reveals secrets;
therefore do not associate with one who speaks foolishly.
                              Proverbs 20:19 (RSV)

A fool will not accept correction or listen to advice

Unwillingness to take advice or be corrected is another key characteristic of a fool. It is also one reason why he tends to remain a fool, rather than change. There are traces of that unwillingness in all of us, whether we are Christians or not. However, in the fully-developed fool, it is particularly evident. Therefore, if you rebuke a fool, or a scoffer, he will only hate you for doing so. By contrast, a wise man will appreciate you for correcting him:

[7]He who corrects a scoffer gets himself abuse,
and he who reproves a wicked man incurs injury.
[8]Do not reprove a scoffer, or he will hate you;
 reprove a wise man, and he will love you.

The need to know identify who it is you are speaking to

21

⁹Give instruction to a wise man,
and he will be still wiser;
teach a righteous man and he will increase in learning.
Proverbs 9:7-9 (RSV)

³¹ The ear that listens to life-giving reproof
will dwell among the wise.
³² Whoever ignores instruction despises himself,
but he who listens to reproof gains intelligence.
Proverbs 15:31-32 (ESV)

A wise son hears his father's instruction,
but a scoffer does not listen to rebuke.
Proverbs 13:1 (ESV)

A fool despises his father's instruction,
but he who heeds admonition is prudent.
Proverbs 15:5 (RSV)

A scoffer does not like to be reproved;
he will not go to the wise.
Proverbs 15:12 (RSV)

Do you dislike being rebuked or corrected and react badly to it, even when what is said is true? In fact, do you resent it all the more precisely *because it is true*? Do you also object to being given advice? If so, it is evidence of your own foolishness. Therefore, ask God to help you to change, so as to become not only willing, but *eager* to be corrected. Wise people positively look for correction and value it. That is one reason why they become wise, but it is also the result of their having already started to become wise, and is thus a very good sign in itself.

One of the features of a wise boss or leader is that he will deliberately gather people around him who are brave enough to stand up to him and to constructively criticise him. He will not resent their doing so. On the contrary, a wise man will go out of his way to look for such criticism, and will even ask for it, so as to get his policies and decisions as right as he can and to avoid all unnecessary errors. We should all do the same, though the truth is that the vast majority of us don't, even if we are Christians, and won't listen to advice or criticism even when it is offered, let alone invite people to give it.

If we are wrong on a point of doctrine, or in our attitude or behaviour, most of us would prefer to remain wrong rather than be corrected, even if we now know that the other person is correct. That is especially so if that correction has to take place in front of other people. However, if we have the love of the truth, then we will

22

prefer to be corrected, and thus to find the real truth, even if it means being embarrassed in front of others or diminished in their estimation. It is not only about rebuke and correction. A wise person listens to advice even when he hasn't yet gone wrong or behaved badly.

In fact, he goes out looking for advice and values it highly. In stark contrast to that, a fool either takes no advice at all, or he only ever takes it from the wrong people, whose opinions are so worthless that it would be better if they said nothing at all. He prefers to ask those who are foolish themselves and thus likely to agree with him, rather than going to those who are further ahead than him, and who therefore don't agree with him. Consequently, the Bible repeatedly urges us to take advice and points out the great benefits that flow from doing so:

Listen to advice and accept instruction,
that you may gain wisdom in the future.
Proverbs 19:20 (ESV)

Where there is no guidance, a people falls,
but in an abundance of counsellors there is safety.
Proverbs 11:14 (ESV)

Without counsel plans fail,
but with many advisers they succeed.
Proverbs 15:22 (ESV)

Better was a poor and wise youth than an old and foolish king who no longer knew how to take advice.
Ecclesiastes 4:13 (ESV)

If you want an example of a fool, who resented truthful advice from a genuine prophet, consider King Ahab of the Northern Kingdom of Israel. He liked to gather around himself false prophets who would flatter him, give him positive messages, and tell him nice things that he wanted to hear. There was a genuine prophet at that time, who always told him the truth, but Ahab hated him for that very reason, because telling Ahab the truth unavoidably involved giving bad news, rebukes and warnings. This prophet's name was Micaiah and King Jehoshaphat of Judah urged Ahab to listen to him:

[5] Then the king of Israel gathered the prophets together, four hundred men, and said to them, "Shall we go to battle against Ramoth-gilead, or shall I refrain?" And they said, "Go up, for God will give it into the hand of the king." [6] But Jehoshaphat said, "Is there not here another prophet of the LORD of whom we may inquire?" [7] And the king of Israel said to Jehoshaphat, "There is yet one man by whom we may inquire of the LORD, Micaiah the son of Imlah; but I

hate him, for he never prophesies good concerning me, but always evil." And Jehoshaphat said, "Let not the king say so."

2 Chronicles 18:5-7 (ESV)

So, Ahab reluctantly called Micaiah and asked him whether he should go to war with the King of Syria at Ramoth-gilead and whether it would result in victory. Micaiah gave a truthful answer and told him it would result in defeat and in Ahab's own death if he was to attack the King of Syria. However, yet again, Ahab resented the advice and ordered that Micaiah be put in prison and fed only meagre rations of bread and water for having given him bad news. So, Micaiah was put in prison and Ahab went off to the war in which, as Micaiah had warned him, his army was defeated and he himself was killed:

25 And the king of Israel said, "Seize Micaiah and take him back to Amon the governor of the city and to Joash the king's son, 26 and say, 'Thus says the king, Put this fellow in prison and feed him with meager rations of bread and water until I return in peace.'" 27 And Micaiah said, "If you return in peace, the LORD has not spoken by me." And he said, "Hear, all you peoples!"

2 Chronicles 18:25-27 (ESV)

33 But a certain man drew his bow at random and struck the king of Israel between the scale armor and the breastplate. Therefore he said to the driver of his chariot, "Turn around and carry me out of the battle, for I am wounded." 34 And the battle continued that day, and the king of Israel was propped up in his chariot facing the Syrians until evening. Then at sunset he died.

2 Chronicles 18:33-34 (ESV)

A fool automatically assumes that his own position is right and that his own needs are the most important

A fool is "*wise in his own eyes*". He therefore tends to see himself as being already right and not needing any advice:

"A sluggard is wiser in his own eyes
than seven people who answer discreetly."
Proverbs 26:16 (NIV)

A fool also tends to trust in his own abilities and especially his own mind:

"He who trusts in his own mind is a fool......."
Proverbs 28:26(a) (RSV)

24

When there is a dispute, or conflicting needs and insufficient resources to go round, a fool will automatically assume, without even pausing to think about it, that:

a) he is obviously in the right,

b) his own need, or his own activity or project, is obviously the most important, and the most urgent,

c) if any wrong has been done, it has only ever been done *to* him, never *by* him.

Are any of these points true of you? Are you programmed with default-settings which immediately assume (a)-(c) about yourself? Or, when you are in a conflict, do you genuinely cross-examine yourself to find out *whether* you are actually right? Do you force yourself to admit unpalatable facts to yourself, and to others, which would put you in the wrong, or show that your need, or your role, is less important than someone else's? Such probing interrogation of oneself is rare and only ever happens at all if you force yourself to do it.

Such an approach will never be taken by what the Bible calls your *old man*, i.e. your sinful, flesh nature. (See my Book 7) The old man always puts himself first and will never change. If we are to avoid leaping automatically to these selfish assumptions and reactions, we must choose to *act in the opposite spirit*. That means to force yourself to say and do the opposite of what your own flesh nature wants. It can also mean doing the opposite of what the other person is doing to you, because they have a sinful, fleshly nature too.

Unless we intervene to stop ourselves, we will instinctively respond in the same way and *give as good as we get*. When we choose to act in the opposite spirit it is as if we are grabbing the 'microphone', or the 'steering wheel', from our old man and handing it to our *new man*. That is the part of us which was reborn when we were saved. Our new man cannot sin and will always react well. However, he is not always the one making the decisions, or *holding the microphone* and speaking for us.

Such righteous responses will only occur if, with our *will*, we consciously *insist* that our new man has his way, rather than letting our old man or flesh speak for us. That choice to adopt the manner and approach of our new man will never come naturally, but it does gradually get less difficult the more we practice it. Where there is conflict, or where blame is being allocated, take note how few people, (probably including you), are genuinely willing to see themselves as being at fault.

The same trait is in all of us, to one extent or another. That reluctance even to consider the possibility of being in the wrong is still very strong, even when the

25

facts are laid out plainly for all to see. The automatic reaction, when we are operating in our flesh nature, is to deny all blame, regardless of the facts. Many of us do so even if it means adopting a position of wilful blindness, such that we are the only person in the room who cannot see what is as plain as day to everyone else.

Our flesh also regards it as inherently wrong, and objectionable, for anybody to criticise us, however validly they may do so. The absolute assumption that we are in the right is almost universal. But that self-justifying attitude will do us a lot of damage. It will also prevent us from learning or changing, because we will assume that we have no need to do either of those things. So, being wise in our own eyes will bring us down and cause us to fail:

> *"Woe to those who are wise in their own eyes,*
> *and shrewd in their own sight!"*
> ### Isaiah 5:21 (RSV)

I can think of a meeting which I was told of, involving persons A, B, C and D. Person A was obviously partly at fault, but spoke only of the wrong which person D had done. Person A would not tolerate anybody saying anything to contradict that, or to suggest that they bore any responsibility. In fact, person A had plainly contributed to the difficult situation, but would not allow that to be said. The very idea of being at fault in any way was unthinkable to person A and certainly 'unsayable' by anybody else.

A fool has the fear of *man*, instead of the fear of *God*. He fears the disapproval of others and allows peer pressure to dictate how he lives

Few of us are brave enough, or wise enough, to live our lives without seeking continually for the approval of others. Obviously, we should not deliberately seek to antagonise people. On the contrary, we should try hard to avoid doing so. But it is not right for us to *want* their approval so strongly that we are willing to do wrong in order to get it. Many of us, even in the Church, would prefer to do wrong, but be approved of by those around us, than to do what is right, if that would mean being disapproved of.

However, how can it make any sense to do wrong, and thereby receive God's disapproval and eternal judgment, merely to gain the temporary (and misguided) approval of those around us? King Saul of Israel was judged to be a failure, and was rejected by God, despite all his abilities. He failed because he feared the opinions of the people instead of fearing God. That fear of public opinion led to him making a series of wrong choices and eventually ended with him being deposed by God:

people pleaser

Athaned of the gospel

23 For rebellion is as the sin of divination,
and presumption is as iniquity and idolatry.
Because you have rejected the word of the LORD,
he has also rejected you from being king."
24 Saul said to Samuel, "I have sinned, for I have transgressed the
commandment of the LORD and your words, because I feared the people and
obeyed their voice.

1 Samuel 15:23-24 (ESV)

The approval, or disapproval, of our fellow human beings has no eternal significance. It is only God's view of us that really counts. Many of us therefore end up with our lives shipwrecked simply because we wanted to be approved of by others. The Bible calls this craving for approval "*the fear of man*". If we are foolish enough to let this fear influence us it will become a *snare* which will trap us and paralyse us. In the end it will ruin us. Instead, we should focus solely on what God wants, seek only for His approval, and never let anybody pressurise us into doing otherwise:

The fear of man lays a snare,
but he who trusts in the LORD is safe.
Proverbs 29:25 (RSV)

The craving for people's approval, or the fear of their disapproval, not only leads us into sin, but also into foolish, unnecessary decisions and activities. It therefore causes people to do things they don't actually enjoy, and to be in places where they don't really want to be, and with people they don't even like, merely to avoid the criticism of others. Even if those situations don't involve outright sin, they still involve, at the very least, wasting your own time, and doing things that don't profit you.

And it is done solely to please others, even where those others, whose approval you seek, are people of whom you *don't actually approve yourself!* What could be sillier, and sadder, than that? You only have one shot at this life, and each day can only be lived once. Therefore, it is utter folly to feel obliged to please others, and therefore not to do what you really want, *and need,* to do merely because they might disapprove.

When I was a teenager and beginning to go out to pubs with my friends, who were all non-Christians, my Dad advised me never to let myself be pressured into drinking at the same pace as any other man, or to match how much they drink. He said I should only ever drink *what I wanted to drink,* and only ever at my *own pace,* no matter what everybody else was drinking, and no matter what they thought of me. That might be easy enough for a mature adult, but for a teenager, mixing in groups which applaud laddish behaviour, and where drinking is treated as a race, that was harder to do.

I took my Dad's advice and when others had pints of beer, I had halves. I also made those last, such that I did not get another glass every time they did. Therefore, during an evening, I would drink about half, or even a third, of what the others drank. I refused to be a follower, or to accept the idea that 'real men' are those who drink the most, or the fastest. I insisted on only ever doing what *I wanted to do*, never what *others* thought I should do. I recommend that resolute approach, not only in relation to drinking, but every aspect of life. It is liberating not to be ruled by the opinions or practices of others.

We must not yield to peer pressure, even where doing so would not be sin

Let me give another example of how peer pressure arises, and how it needs to be resisted, even where it doesn't involve sin. I was once a member of a YMCA committee. The Chairman was keen on money-raising activities, whereby committee members were urged to spend evenings, and even whole days, doing things to raise cash for the YMCA. One such activity was going round all day gathering old newspapers to sell for recycling. They didn't make much money from it and I felt that spending a whole day of my precious time just to raise a modest sum was not a good idea.

At any rate, I simply *didn't want to do it,* even if they were to make a good profit, because I valued my free time. So, in one particular committee meeting, the Chairman proposed a newspaper-gathering day and went round each committee member, one by one, asking us to confirm that we would come. He intentionally put them on the spot and most of them caved in, even though they may not have wanted to spend a whole Saturday doing that. A few made excuses about other prior engagements, probably because they knew how he operated, and they had come prepared with ready-made excuses.

When they did try to wriggle out of it, the Chairman acted even more manipulatively and put pressure on them to rearrange their diaries, or to drop out of the other things in order to do this. He was really quite pushy and the whole committee seemed to be too afraid to say openly, in front of everybody else, that they just *didn't want to do it.* They all assumed they had to do what he wanted unless they had some compelling excuse, or an important and immovable prior engagement. I was the last one to be asked whether I was coming and I replied, calmly, and *completely unapologetically*, that I was not.

However, he didn't leave it at that. He asked me what prior engagement I had which prevented me from coming. I then replied, again without any apology,

"Nothing whatsoever. I just intend to enjoy that Saturday as a day off and relax." When I said that the whole committee fell silent and the Chairman was stunned. Some members looked at me with a mixture of envy, regret and pained admiration for having the boldness to say what they felt, but were afraid to say. One member approached me afterwards and said he was kicking himself for not having the nerve to do as I had. But, by then, he felt trapped into doing it.

Another example involves something my Dad did on his first day as a coalminer. He and several other brand new recruits were placed under the care of an old miner who was given the soft duty of showing them around the pit. The old miner had to tell them what to do and point out safety hazards. He was in his sixties with a group of lively youngsters to look after. At some point the old man had to do something for a few minutes and he left the youngsters unaccompanied deep underground.

While he was away, some of them had the idea of playing a trick on him by pretending to have got lost. So they each hid in shadowy corners, or behind machinery, and made no noise. When the old man came back a few moments later they were nowhere to be found. He then began to call out to them and, when there was no reply, he started to panic, fearing that some harm may have come to them or that they had wandered off into a dangerous zone.

My Dad told me, decades later, that he could not bear to hear the anxious shouts of the old man as he searched for them in his distress. So, my Dad emerged from the shadows and shouted: *"It's alright. We are all here. We have just been hiding."* The joke was then over, due to my Dad's intervention, and the others all emerged too. Speaking up in that way, and being willing to stand alone, and maybe to be disapproved of, or considered *'not one of the boys'*, is very difficult.

However, it is also right, and absolutely necessary, if you want to live successfully, operate freely, and do what you believe in, rather than what others think you should do. Ironically, in the end, people will actually admire you more for *not* fearing them, and for not slavishly seeking their approval, than if you had chosen to conform. I am proud of what my Dad did that day as a young man, and for his courage and independence of mind. It was typical of how he always acted.

The fool tends to lives for pleasure and he is often a mocker and a scoffer.

A fool generally lives for the moment and has his heart set on pleasure and amusement. The things that ought to grieve him have no effect upon him and are even sneered at:

Wisdom is brave –
it will not bend to
peer pressure – herdmentality – social proof
True to true self
True to the New man

The heart of the wise is in the house of mourning,
but the heart of fools is in the house of pleasure.
Ecclesiastes 7:4 (NIV)

There is little point in a wise person trying to argue with a fool, or at least not if the aim is to enlighten him. It won't succeed. The fool will either get angry or mock what is said. He will not listen, or learn anything from it:

When a wise man has a controversy with a foolish man,
The foolish man either rages or laughs, and there is no rest.
Proverbs 29:9 (NASB)

As an employer I wasted a vast amount of time for many years trying to rebuke and correct fools. But they had no interest in listening to any corrections, and no desire to learn or change. It took me years to realise that what I was doing was futile. Now I don't even attempt it. If I come to the conclusion that an employee is a proper fool, not just partially and intermittently foolish, as we all are, then I no longer make any attempt to improve him or challenge him. I just get rid of him.

I eventually realised that I need to focus all my energy on training those staff who genuinely want to learn and who are open and willing to be instructed. That discovery changed my life and altered the whole atmosphere of my business. I decided to aim to create a *fool-free zone* in my firm. If ever a fool managed to get recruited, I did not let him stay for long. That may sound harsh, especially in the UK, where sacking people is frowned upon and assumed to be wrong. However, it is the only sensible way to operate, for the sake of the business, its clients, and the other staff.

Fools live their lives as if actions don't have consequences.

All actions have consequences, whether good or bad. This is closely linked to the law of sowing and reaping, which we will look at in closer detail in chapter 12 below. Each of the thousands of steps that we take and decisions that we make have consequences. Some are easily foreseeable and others less so. However, much of the time, they are at least reasonably foreseeable. Wise people are acutely conscious of those potential consequences, and bear them in mind whenever they take any action or make any decision. *What did you expect?*

But fools don't. They mistakenly suppose that they can do whatever they want and that no adverse consequences will follow. Or they give it no thought at all. Above all, they imagine that they can sin and that nothing will happen to them as a result. They also imagine that they will never have to face God's judgment for their actions or omissions, whether here and now, or later in life, or even at the final judgment. Therefore, a fool assumes, usually without giving it any thought, that he can get away with things.

Sadly, that is not so. Even when a person later repents and is forgiven by God, and even if he goes on to become a mature disciple, he will still have to live with the results of his past actions, even if those took place before his conversion. Becoming a Christian wipes away the *guilt and penalty* of our sins, but it does not remove their *consequences*. A wise person bears that fact in mind and takes it into account when deciding what he can and cannot, and what he should and should not, do. But the fool presses ahead with indifference.

For example, if we sin sexually and pregnancy results, then a child has come into the world, for whom we are responsible. That child's existence will lead to long term, indeed eternal, consequences, even if we did not foresee those when we sinned sexually. Even if we try to prevent those consequences by asking an abortionist to kill the child for us, there is still no escape. The only difference is that we will have to face the consequences of having murdered our own son or daughter rather than of having to look after them.

Such a step cannot be taken without consequences of some kind, whether spiritual, emotional, or physical. Regardless of your own personal opinions as to whether abortion is wrong, those will still follow. In fact, they will pursue you, and for as long as you live. A wise person knows all this, and regulates his conduct and choices accordingly. But a fool doesn't, and he therefore suffers for it. The same principle applies, not only in the context of sexual sin or abortion, but right across the board.

Therefore, if we lie, steal, gamble, borrow, skive in our job or our studies, mix with the wrong people, marry the wrong person, watch the wrong TV programmes, or sin in any other way whatsoever, then consequences will inevitably flow from it. Conversely, if we act rightly, love others, obey God, study the Bible, bless Israel and the Jewish people, and so on, then positive consequences will follow, whether sooner or later, and whether we foresee them or not.

ideas have consequen—

The fool reveals his nature through his words.

The Bible says "*...out of the abundance of the heart the mouth speaks*". It means that whatever we are on the inside will inevitably be revealed in the way we speak, whether we are foolish, wicked, wise or simple. Sooner or later, our character will display itself through our mouths:

31

³⁴Brood of vipers! How can you, being evil, speak good things? For out of the abundance of the heart the mouth speaks. ³⁵A good man out of the good treasure of his heart brings forth good things, and an evil man out of the evil treasure brings forth evil things.

Matthew 12:34-35 (NKJV)

It is rare for anything valuable to come out of the mouth of a fool, at least not during the times when he is operating as a fool. What he has to say is usually just worthless noise:

The tongue of the wise dispenses knowledge,
but the mouths of fools pour out folly.
Proverbs 15:2 (RSV)

For as the crackling of thorn bushes under a pot,
So is the laughter of the fool;
And this too is futility.
Ecclesiastes 7:6 (NASB)

A foolish woman is noisy;
she is wanton and knows no shame.
Proverbs 9:13 (RSV)

The fool is lazy and does not plan ahead or work to achieve his future goals

Many fools (not all) see no point in working hard and take no pleasure from it. They will therefore try to avoid effort. It is linked to the fact that the fool does not look ahead. He thinks only of the present, whereas a wise person focuses on the future. The fool wants gratification now and is not willing to wait for it. The idea of working now, and only being rewarded later, doesn't appeal to him. But he will lose out later in life when he has nothing to show for the times when he wasted his opportunities:

Instant gratification

The sluggard does not plow in the autumn;
he will seek at harvest and have nothing.
Proverbs 20:4 (RSV)

Like vinegar to the teeth and smoke to the eyes,
So is the lazy one to those who send him.
Proverbs 10:26 (NASB)

Please also refer to chapter 11 below in which I look much more closely at the subject of work and the workplace, and why so many employees are not good workers.

The fool has no regard for the concept of eternity.

A fool rarely thinks about eternity, if at all, and has no regard for the Day of Judgment. Therefore, if you don't currently spend much time considering eternity in general, and judgment in particular, then, at least in that regard, you are being foolish. Accordingly, one way to become wiser is to force yourself to reflect on your own death and on the judgment which will then follow as you enter into eternity. Considering those momentous future events will profoundly affect how you live *now* and alter all your priorities. This is one of the best ways that we can grow in wisdom and rid ourselves of foolishness. *Live with the end in mind*

A fool is self-centred. He automatically sees himself as being at the centre of the universe, with all other people and situations orbiting around him.

A fool is always positioned at the centre of his own universe. It is actually difficult for any of us to avoid this, not just fools. Obsession with oneself, and focusing excessively, or even exclusively, on one's own needs, is the natural attitude of our *old man,* which we all continue to have, even after we are saved. Therefore, this is deeply ingrained in all of us. I trained my staff about this tendency to be self-centred and referred to it as having a *wrong astronomy*. That means automatically assuming we are at the centre of the universe and that clients, colleagues, bosses etc. are all in orbit around us.

If we think that way we will inevitably go wrong. Instead, we have to make a decision to go against all our ingrained fleshly instincts and start to see ourselves as being in orbit around whoever we are dealing with or working for, not to see them as being in orbit around us. So, if we are a lawyer, the client is at the centre and we must always be on the periphery, in orbit around him. If we are a nurse, the patient's needs should always be at the centre, never our own needs. That is easy enough to say as a slogan, but hard to do and even harder to get your staff to do it.

My personal belief is that fewer than 10% of British people genuinely think that way about their jobs, or indeed about any part of their lives. Actually, it's probably fewer than 2%. However, if you will force yourself to adopt this attitude it will have a knock-on effect on all your actions, decisions and priorities. Everything changes when you realise that you are not even the centre of your own workplace, let alone the universe. Keep on reminding yourself of your correct place, which must always be at the *edge* of any situation you are in, *not the centre*.

You are not meant to be at the centre of anything and if that is where you think you are, then you have a wrong view of yourself and of the world. I once interviewed a young woman aged 22 named Emily who had just graduated in law and wanted to become a trainee solicitor. She did quite well in the interview, so I invited her in for an open-ended trial period. My policy was always to pay candidates a full daily wage if they were invited to have a short trial period with us, even though they never did anything of any value for us. That approach is unusual. Many firms treat it as unpaid work experience.

The purpose of the trial was just for us to assess them, not for them to actually help us, or to do any useful work. Emily did quite well on her first trial day, so I invited her to stick around and go onto a more extended trial period, during which we would continue to review her daily. After 4 days on trial I told her that she was still doing well and that I was therefore going to extend her *(fully paid)* trial period even longer. This was in the middle of a deep recession, when such jobs were hard to get.

To my surprise she began to cry and complained that she had already been on trial for 4 days and that we "*ought to be able to decide by now*". She said it was "*not fair*" to keep her on trial! I would have been amazed by that reaction years ago, but I have learned that it is a very common attitude. Her problem was she was profoundly self-centred and also proud. Therefore, it was intolerable to her that she had not been accepted immediately. *Must allow them to test you - v.r*

The trial period was actually a privilege, but she could only see it as an imposition, which was delaying her in getting what she wanted. Her self-centeredness had never been challenged before by her parents or teachers. They had therefore helped to make her into a fool. I brought her trial period to a swift end and sent her home that day. However, she saw nothing wrong in what she had said. Her focus was so entirely upon herself that she thought she was being mistreated and that we had wronged her by not approving of her immediately and appointing her to a permanent job.

A fool is self-absorbed and is guided almost entirely by self-interest, not by duty or by the wish to act rightly.

When a fool is choosing what to do, or how to react to a situation, self-interest will usually be his only guiding principle. One sees this at elections, where most people vote primarily, or even solely, on the basis of what they imagine to be best for themselves. They have no regard for, and don't even give any thought to, the question of what God wants, or what is best for their local community or for the nation. Such considerations rarely come into it. Thus, few politicians today even bother appealing to our generosity or our sense of civic duty.

They know that most of us are only interested in ourselves. Therefore, they are realistic enough to focus on what interests us and they carefully avoid telling us any home truths. We can't blame them. It's mainly our fault, not theirs. We are bigger fools than them. They are just responding rationally to the facts of what kind of an electorate we really are. If our thinking is self-centred, we need, first of all, to acknowledge that fact and then take active steps to change. When we vote we must focus on our duty, on what God wants, and on what is inherently right, not just on what we think is best for ourselves.

The same applies to all areas of life and to all the choices we have to make in our work life or family life, not just how we use our vote. However, as with all the other changes we need to make, it won't even begin to happen unless we force ourselves to think differently. One of the features of self-absorption is that it makes you forgetful of others, and of their needs. Instead, what we actually need is to be forgetful of ourselves and mindful of others.

That is part of what it means to *"die to self"* and *"crucify the flesh"*. Doing so helps us to wrench our attention away from ourselves and apply it elsewhere, contrary to all our sinful habits and ways. That is one of the good things about pursuing *'the Great Commission'* which Jesus instituted in Matthew 28:19-20, when He commanded us to make disciples of all nations. The process of doing that helps us to redirect our focus away from ourselves and towards others, which would never happen naturally.

The world's wisdom, which is actually just folly, is all about looking after number one and putting yourself first. Approaching life in that way, as the unsaved world, and too much of the Church, does, will only cause you to become more self-absorbed and thus, more of a fool. But obeying Jesus's words and applying yourself to the task of making disciples, will help to cure you of that. It will 'recalibrate' you, until focusing on others begins to become normal, and even your preference.

God commands us not to waste our time with fools as we will only become like them.

There are a number of reasons why we are told not to associate with fools. Firstly, one cannot learn much from a fool, except by noting his bad habits and seeking to avoid them in yourself. Other than that, he has very little to offer. But he will not learn from you either, because he has *no desire to*. Secondly, whatever group we

35

currently belong to, we will inevitably become like the people with whom we spend most of our time. Whatever group they may be in, we will move in their direction. That law applies just the same if we spend time with fools as it does with people from any other group:

He who walks with wise men will be wise,
but the companion of fools will suffer harm.
Proverbs 13:20 (NASB)

[24]Do not associate with a man given to anger;
Or go with a hot-tempered man,
[25]Or you will learn his ways and find a snare for yourself.
Proverbs 22:24-25 (NASB)

Do not be deceived: "Bad company ruins good morals."
1 Corinthians 15:33 (ESV)

Leave the presence of a fool,
for there you do not meet words of knowledge.
Proverbs 14:7 (ESV)

Be not envious of evil men,
nor desire to be with them,
Proverbs 24:1 (ESV)

[To repent is an act of wisdom]

[21] My son, fear the LORD and the king,
and do not join with those who do otherwise,
[22] for disaster will arise suddenly from them,
and who knows the ruin that will come from them both?
Proverbs 24:21-22 (ESV)

If a fool was to spend a lot of time with wise men then, over a period of time, he too would change and become wiser. However, that rarely happens because fools *don't want* to be with wise people and try hard to avoid them. Wise people make fools feel uncomfortable, just by being there, even if they say nothing to rebuke them. So you will never become wise unless you are willing to be made to feel uncomfortable, for a time, by being with people who are wiser, and godlier, than you.

The process of being influenced by those people, and changing for the better, will always feel difficult while it is happening. Moreover, the benefit only becomes apparent later, which is another reason why it does not appeal to fools. Therefore, a wise man will not usually be able to influence a fool. If he engages him in a

36

meaningful conversation, about anything that really matters, the fool will usually only despise what is said and will not listen:

Do not speak in the hearing of a fool,
For he will despise the wisdom of your words.
Proverbs 23:9 (NASB)

Therefore, if you aren't yet a fully-developed fool, and don't want to become one, avoid spending time with fools. Likewise, if you are behaving foolishly in some ways already, but don't want to continue doing so, or to get even worse, then keep away from other fools. Avoid their influence and break off your contact with them. However, there are some people whom we have no choice but to be with. They may be our neighbours or work colleagues, such that contact with them can't be avoided.

Those are not the people we are told to avoid. The Bible is referring to the *voluntary* choices we make as to whom we spend our time with. God only wants us to associate, where possible, with those who are likely to be a good influence upon us, or whom we can realistically hope to influence for good. In this next pair of linked verses from Proverbs we are given advice that sounds like a contradiction. Verse 4 says:

Answer not a fool according to his folly,
lest you be like him yourself.
Proverbs 26:4 (RSV)

But verse 5 says:

Answer a fool according to his folly,
lest he be wise in his own eyes.
Proverbs 26:5 (RSV)

In fact, there is no contradiction. The two verses go together and what they mean is:

a) Do *not* sink to the same level as a fool by answering him in the same foolish, carnal, scoffing manner in which *he speaks to you*. If you do, you will just become like him. But,

b) *Do* answer him in the way he *deserves*, i.e. by side-stepping or ignoring him. Don't waste any time trying to influence or educate a fool. Just avoid him. Spend your time with wise or simple people instead, so far as you can.

37

It is both foolish and sinful to drink alcohol excessively, to smoke tobacco, and to take drugs.

Contrary to many denominational traditions, it is *not* a sin to drink alcohol. Alcohol, in itself, is not an evil and we are free to drink it. The Bible makes that very clear. Admittedly, some people in the Bible are told not to drink, and not to do various other things either. But the rest of us are never forbidden to drink, as such, but only forbidden to get drunk.

For example, look at the *'Nazarite vow'* which a small minority of Jews took, with John the Baptist being the most famous example. Those who took this vow separated themselves to the LORD and, as part of that, they separated themselves from wine and strong drink, but also even from the very grapes themselves, or even the seeds:

¹ And the LORD said to Moses, ² "Say to the people of Israel, When either a man or a woman makes a special vow, the vow of a Nazirite, to separate himself to the LORD, ³ he shall separate himself from wine and strong drink; he shall drink no vinegar made from wine or strong drink, and shall not drink any juice of grapes or eat grapes, fresh or dried. ⁴ All the days of his separation he shall eat nothing that is produced by the grapevine, not even the seeds or the skins.

Numbers 6:1-4 (RSV)

Therefore, those who took this vow, whom we refer to as *'Nazirites'*, were the exception, not the norm. I stress that fact because some people oppose alcohol in and of itself, and they refer to the command given to the Nazirites as if it applied to all of us when it plainly doesn't. It only applies to those who are called by God to that special ministry, which was always a small minority. Moreover, note how, in the above passage, both wine *and* strong drink are referred to, but also *the very grapes themselves*, and their *juice* and even their *seeds*.

If, therefore, God intended the Nazirite vow to apply to all of us, which He doesn't, then we would all be forbidden to drink grape juice either, or even to eat grapes. But those who wish to abolish alcohol, and who tell us that God forbids its consumption, never say that we can't drink grape juice or eat grapes. They know that would be absurd and that the Bible makes no such command. They also know, deep down, as we all know, that wine means wine and grape juice means grape juice and that they are two different things.

The very fact that God refers to both in the above passage proves that wine and grape juice are not the same things and that when God refers to wine, He means wine, i.e. fermented, alcoholic wine, not grape juice. I stress that point too, because there are many people who point to passages in the Bible where godly characters drink wine, including the prophets and apostles, and even Jesus

Himself, and they explain it away by saying that they were all drinking unfermented, non-alcoholic grape juice. But, as we saw, those are two different things and God does not confuse the two words in the Bible.

Therefore, although wine, and everything else associated with the grape, plus various other things such as cutting their hair, were forbidden to the Nazirites, they are not forbidden to the rest of us. Perhaps the most compelling proof of that point is that Jesus Himself produced wine for the wedding at Cana. Moreover, it was not mere non-alcoholic 'grape juice', as some people implausibly claim. It was real wine. If wine was forbidden to us, why would God Himself speak favourably of it, and cause the ground to provide it to us as He speaks of in these verses?

> *¹⁴ You cause the grass to grow for the livestock*
> *and plants for man to cultivate,*
> *that he may bring forth food from the earth*
> *¹⁵ and wine to gladden the heart of man,*
> *oil to make his face shine*
> *and bread to strengthen man's heart.*
> *Psalm 104:14-15 (ESV)*

In any case, how can a person's heart be *'gladdened'* by drinking mere unfermented grape juice? It is ridiculous to suggest, as so many do, that that is what is meant. If you take that approach, why not also suggest that the verses which refer to bread or olive oil are not referring to real bread or real olive oil? Why single out wine alone when making that claim? Also, why would we be told in the Bible not to get *drunk* on wine if wine is just unfermented grape juice? It would not be possible to do so.

We cannot have it both ways and interpret the meaning of the word *'wine'* differently, according to whatever suits our argument at any given time. The suggestion that God means non-alcoholic wine is absurd and the only limitation which the Bible puts upon us is that our drinking should not be *excessive*. In other words, we must not get *drunk*. So moderate, sensible, responsible drinking is fine and involves no sin at all.

Although drinking alcohol is not a sin, drunkenness is, and we must avoid it

However, having said all of that, the fact is that getting drunk is a sin, in itself, even if it does not lead to other things such as violence or promiscuity. The main reason why God forbids drunkenness, as opposed to Him forbidding any drinking at all, even when it is done moderately, is that when a person is drunk they lose some or all of their *self-control*. Therefore, the person becomes vulnerable and is at increased risk *from their own sin nature* which, while they are drunk, has far greater power over them. That is because their mind, and especially their will, cease to function as effectively as they should.

Therefore, quite foreseeably, a person who is drunk is likely to do or say things to others, or allow things to be done to them, which would never have happened if they had not been drunk. That is surely obvious. We see the evidence for it all around us. Drunken people often behave appallingly and destroy many lives, including our own. This arises, directly or indirectly, through the effects of their drunkenness, either on themselves, or their families, or on others with whom they come into contact. Therefore, the Bible warns us against drunkenness:

Wine is a mocker, strong drink a brawler;
* and whoever is led astray by it is not wise.*
*   Proverbs 20:1 (RSV)*

20 Be not among drunkards
* or among gluttonous eaters of meat,*
21 for the drunkard and the glutton will come to poverty,
* and slumber will clothe them with rags.*
*   Proverbs 23:20-21 (ESV)*

11 Woe to those who rise early in the morning,
* that they may run after strong drink,*
* who tarry late into the evening*
* till wine inflames them!*
12 They have lyre and harp,
* timbrel and flute and wine at their feasts;*
* but they do not regard the deeds of the LORD,*
* or see the work of his hands.*
*   Isaiah 5:11-12 (RSV)*

13let us conduct ourselves becomingly as in the day, not in reveling and drunkenness, not in debauchery and licentiousness, not in quarreling and jealousy. 14 But put on the Lord Jesus Christ, and make no provision for the flesh, to gratify its desires.

*   Romans 13:13-14 (RSV)*

19 Now the works of the flesh are plain: fornication, impurity, licentiousness, 20 idolatry, sorcery, enmity, strife, jealousy, anger, selfishness, dissension, party spirit, 21 envy, drunkenness, carousing, and the like. I warn you, as I warned you before, that those who do such things shall not inherit the kingdom of God.
*   Galatians 5:19-21 (RSV)*

So, we have very clear biblical commands not to get drunk and the wisdom of that is corroborated by the evidence of our own eyes as to what happens to people when they do. Therefore, we need to make sure that we never get drunk. If we do, we are effectively abdicating our responsibility for maintaining our control of ourselves and allowing it to be taken away from us. Indeed, much of the time, people positively *want* to lose their 'inhibitions', which is a negative alternative word for 'self-control'.

Therefore, they get drunk deliberately, to help themselves cast off restraint and to do things, including sinful things, which they would never do otherwise. Accordingly, from God's perspective, to deliberately drink alcohol to the extent that we lose some or all of our self-control, is a serious sin in itself. It would be like tampering with the brakes and steering of your car, thereby reducing or removing your ability to control it or stop it, but then getting in and driving it on the road.

Drink Driving

Everyone would see that as an act of great recklessness, and even wickedness, given the obvious potential that your car has to injure yourself or others. In the same way, doing anything to deliberately reduce your own restraints, and knowingly rendering yourself more *likely to sin*, or to sin in *more serious ways,* is a sinful act in itself. That would still be so, even if it was not your express intention for it to result in any harm. Merely to expose yourself, and others, to an increased risk that such things *might* occur is sinful.

After all, weakening the brake pipes on your car does not guarantee that an accident will occur. It does, however, foreseeably increase the chances of it happening and the point is that to take such an additional risk is blameworthy. Firstly, you have no right to take risks with other people's lives. But, secondly, you don't even have the right to take risks with your own life. Neither do you have any right to take risks with your own propensity to sin, because you *do not own yourself.* You, and your body, belong to God. You are only a *steward* of His property, not the owner. *You belong to another*

You cannot therefore tell Him that what you do with your own body is exclusively your own affair, even if you could be sure, which you can't, that nobody else would ever be harmed by your drinking. The point is that God owns you and your body, and He is fully entitled to tell you what you can and cannot do with it. That fact alone is conclusive, quite apart from the additional point that drunkenness also *increases the chances of your sinning against Him* in lots of other ways as well, by reducing your self-control in all areas.

I am warning against the danger, and the sinfulness, of drunkenness because it is on the increase, at least in the UK. Amongst older people, especially those in professional jobs or from educated, wealthier backgrounds, a high proportion are

(Risks, Danger – level)

now quietly sitting at home most evenings and drinking themselves into a numb forgetfulness. They are seeking to calm their nerves, or to mask their unhappiness, or to reduce the dullness of their lives.

Amongst young people this is occurring more publicly, as they go out drinking into the small hours, including engaging in 'drinking games'. Many drink cheap vodka from the supermarket, even before they go out, so as to get drunk less expensively. Their excessive drinking not only results in sin, violence and promiscuity, but also in serious damage to their own *health*. Doctors are reporting that many people in their twenties or thirties now have the kind of unhealthy livers that were previously associated with people in their seventies. Isaiah has something to say to those who turn drinking into a contest:

Woe to those who are heroes at drinking wine,
  and valiant men in mixing strong drink,
                   Isaiah 5:22 (RSV)

However, it is not only a person's health which will be damaged by drunkenness. There is a clear pattern that drunkards also tend to end up in *poverty* for all sorts of direct and indirect reasons:

He who loves pleasure will be a poor man;
  he who loves wine and oil will not be rich.
                   Proverbs 21:17 (RSV)

Unlike alcohol, tobacco and illegal drugs are sinful in themselves and should not be used except on medical advice

All the same points apply, with even greater force, to those who take illegal drugs, or even the so-called 'legal highs', to produce the kind of euphoria and reduced inhibitions that excessive alcohol produces. Such drugs are not only a cause of increased sin, due to reduced self-control. They also damage health, destroy families and even render people effectively unemployable. Again, only a fool would take such drugs. At any rate, anyone who does so will soon *become* a fool, even if he isn't already one when he begins.

Concerning tobacco, only a fool would *continue* to smoke by choosing not to take steps to overcome his addiction. However, to intentionally *start* to smoke when one isn't yet addicted, makes one an even bigger fool. One might partially excuse those who are now addicted, due to having started in the past, such that they now find it difficult to stop. But for a person who is *not addicted* to deliberately *create* an addiction and then continue to smoke merely to satisfy a craving which they

42

only have because they *chose to create it*, is utter folly, quite apart from the damage they inflict on their health.

There surely cannot be any person, at least in the West, who is not aware that smoking causes lung cancer, heart disease, and many other illnesses. Thus, to start to inflict those on oneself, or to continue to do so, is foolishness, and sin as well, since one is wilfully damaging one's own body which, as we saw, is not one's own property. It is also desecrating a temple of the Holy Spirit in the case of a believer.   *Tatoos ?*

Some guidelines on how to drink alcohol sensibly rather than foolishly

Returning to the theme of alcohol, which is the only drug that is legitimate, i.e. when used moderately, I suggest some simple guidelines to prevent it getting control over you;

a) Never drink alcohol when you are *alone*. It was given to us as a gift from God and is meant to be used as part of *social interaction*, when dining or relaxing with others in fellowship and friendship, not for when we are by ourselves.

b) Never drink when you feel *sad*. Do so only when you are happy. As above, alcohol is only meant for fellowship, not for "drowning your sorrows". Besides, alcohol is actually a *depressant* and it only lifts the mood of those who are *already happy*. Contrary to what many assume, it actually further depresses those who are feeling down to begin with.

c) Don't drink in the *daytime* unless it is a very special occasion, such as a wedding, or in some other exceptional situation. Due to the way the human liver was created, it processes alcohol twice as effectively in the evening than in the morning or afternoon. Thus, alcohol consumed before about 7pm will be twice as potent and will make you drunk far more quickly.

d) Have at least two whole days per week when you don't drink at all. This will give your liver some recovery time. It will also prove that you are not dependent on alcohol, which you should never allow yourself to become. If you feel any withdrawal symptoms when you have a day off from drinking, or if you *crave* for a drink, or feel that you *"need it"*, then stay off it even longer, or even permanently. Force your body to do without it and reassert the authority that your will has over your body and emotions. They need to be shown who the boss is.

e) Never drink *to please others* or because *they want you to*, especially if they try to pressurise you. Only drink when *you* want to, and only with the type,

43

quantity, strength and frequency of drink that you want. Therefore, never try to *"keep up"* or *"fit in"* or to meet others' expectations or satisfy peer pressure. What you drink, and when, and how much, is entirely a matter for you, not other people.

f) Be sensitive to others who are present who might have a 'drink problem', even where you aren't sure, but only suspect it to be so. In such situations don't drink anything yourself, so as to avoid putting temptation in their way and also to show solidarity if they are struggling to exercise self-control.

g) Never drink to the extent that your speech, reaction time or motor skills, are in any way affected. Ideally, except on special occasions, stay within the drink driving limits for England and Wales. (not Scotland or the EU - their limits are needlessly strict)

These simple guidelines will make sure that you never have any problems with alcohol or allow yourself to become dependent on it. Above all, they will greatly reduce the chances of you ever becoming drunk, which is the key thing to avoid.

Fools are useless and unreliable, especially as employees.

We should avoid employing fools to work for us, i.e. those who have a substantial amount of foolishness in their character. I am not referring to people who in any way, or at any time, display even traces of foolishness. Otherwise, none of us could ever employ anybody at all, not even ourselves. Fools make ineffective and unreliable staff and will cause us grief. I have never had a profitable experience employing a fool. They are always a disappointment and it always ends badly:

⁶He cuts off his own feet and drinks violence
Who sends a message by the hand of a fool.
⁷Like the legs which are useless to the lame,
So is a proverb in the mouth of fools.
⁸Like one who binds a stone in a sling,
So is he who gives honour to a fool.
⁹Like a thorn which falls into the hand of a drunkard,
So is a proverb in the mouth of fools.
¹⁰Like an archer who wounds everyone,
So is he who hires a fool or who hires those who pass by.
                    Proverbs 26:6-10 (NASB)

I learned, from a series of bitter experiences, that it is useless trying to train or discipline staff who are fools. They were not interested in learning how to do their jobs better, or raising their standards or serving clients properly. Therefore, everything I tried to do to train and improve them was unsuccessful, as they paid no attention. Conversely, with wise and teachable staff, one only needed to have a quiet word with them and they would listen and benefit from it. King Solomon obviously had the same experiences in trying to manage fools:

"The words of the wise heard in quiet are better than the shouting of a ruler among fools."

Ecclesiastes 9:17 (ESV)

What are you really like as an employee? Are you thoroughly reliable? Are you sensible? Do you put the client/patient/customer ahead of yourself? Do you serve your boss faithfully and loyally, even if he doesn't treat you well? Do you treat colleagues fairly? Can they always count on you, or do you let the side down? Are you emotionally stable? Does your firm make a profit or a loss from employing you? Do you save management time or waste it? Are you an asset or a liability? Have you ever asked yourself any of these blunt questions? If not, it is unlikely that you are a good employee.

Many people in churches are fools.

One might ask how a real Christian, or even a mere churchgoer, can be a fool. Aren't fools meant to say *"there is no God"*? Or, at least, aren't they meant to live as if there was no God? Therefore, how can people do either of those things and still go to church? How can they be so inconsistent, or hypocritical, as to act the way they do, where they are real Christians? The short answer is that it's actually not difficult at all to behave inconsistently. At any rate, it is certainly not unusual. Millions of people find it very easy indeed.

Many fools, and even wicked people, belong to churches but live in a worldly way. Yet they are usually completely unchallenged by the leaders. Indeed, many such foolish, and even wicked, people are leading churches themselves. Another reason why foolish people claim to believe in God and yet behave wrongly is that, as we saw above, many redesign or redefine God so as to make Him into someone more acceptable to themselves, indeed, usually into a replica of themselves.

So, a liberal might want to focus on God's love because, that feature (as they wrongly understand it) happens to appeal to them. They like the sound of those aspects of God's nature, at least as they imagine them to be. However, they dislike any talk of God's wrath or judgment. To deal with that problem of Him having attributes which they don't like, they simply 'rebrand' God, or redefine Him, to remove any mention of His judgment or holiness. Then they focus solely on the features they do like, as if the Bible was a self-service buffet bar.

45

They then put onto their 'plate' whatever they like, but leave off it anything that sounds uncomfortable, or is convicting. They simply pick and choose what they *want to believe* and ignore or reject the rest, and see nothing wrong in doing so. I have pointed out this practice to a number of people. Some appear to be unaware, and even unconcerned, that they do this. Others are aware, but try to justify it. Such a person does not want the real God of the Bible. They want a false god that they can design and build for themselves. *Cherry Picking*

That being so, what God, or rather what *god*, do they actually have? It depends on the precise circumstances and on how far they go in editing out those parts of God's character that they don't like. However, they may easily end up with a completely false god, who is entirely of their own making instead of the real God who is revealed in the Bible. That may sound a harsh thing to say, but isn't it clearly true? Many say, for example, that the god they believe in:

a) is not angry at sin

b) is not going to judge anyone

c) will not condemn anyone

d) will not send anyone to the Lake of Fire

e) did not create us and does not own us

f) does not have the right to tell us how to live

g) has entirely changed his mind on issues of sexuality and gender since the Bible was written

Sometimes the god they manufacture is angry about sin, but only at certain types of sin, i.e. the ones which *they personally disapprove of*, such as financial corruption, racism, or *'homophobia'*, as they call it. Their god is never angry about other sins such as abortion, promiscuity or homosexuality, which the Bible condemns, but which *they* don't consider to be wrong. It is remarkable how many people design a god who shares all their own personal opinions and preferences, instead of allowing the real God to *describe Himself* through the pages of the Bible.

If a person has any of the false beliefs listed above, then how can the god they believe in possibly be the real God of the Bible? So, if they do hold those wrong beliefs about God, then what does that make that person? Are they a fool? Are they even a real Christian? Again, it depends on all the circumstances and on how far they go in their errors and unbelief. Merely to lack some particular piece of knowledge, or to make an error about God's character or intentions, does not

46

necessarily mean that we therefore have a false god or that we are a fool. That must be so because none of us has a complete understanding of God.

However, many go far beyond mere gaps in their knowledge and end up with such a distorted view of God that what they have is not even remotely like the true God of the Bible. For some their perception of God is so false that they must either be fools, or close to it. At any rate, whether they are fools or not, what they believe in may well be a false god, because it is such a misrepresentation, or caricature, of the real God. That helps to explain why so many people's lives are in such a mess. They reject what the real God says and follow their own home-made god who shares all their own opinions.

Nobody is 100% foolish. We are all a mixture.

People do not fit into neatly defined groups, such that wise people are wise all the time and are never foolish or naïve. Therefore, it is wrong to assume that if a person is a fool that must mean he thinks and acts in a foolish way all the time, in every part of his life. If that was true it would mean that if a person ever does or says anything wise they cannot be a fool, and if they ever say anything naïve or foolish then they can't be wise. That's the wrong way to see this.

The reality is much more complicated and changeable. None of us are ever 100% anything. We are all a blend of wise, simple, foolish and wicked characteristics. The real question is in what proportions? Are we mainly foolish or mainly wise? And, more importantly, in which direction are we travelling? Moreover, are we wiser in some parts of our lives but more foolish in others? For example, we might be relatively wise in the way we do our job, or run a business, but relatively foolish in the way we treat our wife or children. Or it could be the other way round.

Alternatively, we might be wise in our drinking habits, but foolish when it comes to gambling. We each have stronger and weaker areas of our lives, where we show more or less wisdom, maturity or sense. So, we need to be a good deal more flexible and sophisticated when deciding who is wise, and who is foolish or simple etc. A better way to put the question would be *"Is that person generally/mainly foolish?"* Or *"Is that person mainly/usually wise?"* Or, concerning specific incidents, we could say *"Is that person thinking/behaving in a foolish way at the moment?"* Exception?

That is a more meaningful and realistic way in which to approach this subject. It will also help to prevent us from being overly simplistic and from categorising other people, and ourselves, too glibly and hastily. Another vital point is that when the Bible refers to fools, and to foolish thoughts or behaviour, *it is referring to you and me, not just to others.* There is not a person on this Earth, not even the

47

most mature Christian, who has not been naïve, foolish, and perhaps even wicked, on many occasions. *learn from mistakes*

Moreover, we still display those traits, even now, and will continue to do so until the day we die and are at last set free from our sinful, flesh nature. The reason the Bible says so much about naivety, foolishness and wickedness is because those descriptions are frequently applicable *to us*, not just to other people. The foolish people are not *"that group over there"*. At times they are you, me, and all the people we know. So, when God speaks of these faults He is speaking to you and me, not just to other people.

We cannot therefore switch off and skim-read those parts of the Bible which address these character faults, as if they were only of relevance to other people. Some of us think, without ever saying it out loud, *"I am a Christian, so that automatically means I am wise, unlike those non-Christians over there who are foolish and wicked. Thank goodness I'm not like them."* Therefore, what the Bible has to say about foolishness, naivety and wickedness *is* of relevance to you. Those traits *are* present in you, at least from time to time, and need to be removed.

Realistically, however, our aim should not be to change overnight from a fool into a wise person, but to bring gradual change to each of the parts of our character, like renovating a derelict old house. You may get to the point where one of the rooms is starting to look quite good, but the others still aren't any better. That is a more accurate reflection of how we really are. So we need to keep on pursuing wisdom until every 'room', or every part of us, is mainly/usually wise, or at least wiser than it was, or more frequently than it was.

A wise person can learn valuable lessons from absolutely anyone, even if they are a fool, and indeed, even if they are wicked. At the very least, one can learn how *not to think,* how *not to behave,* and how things should *not be done.* Therefore, if you are beginning to be wise and want to be wiser still, you can learn almost as much from bad colleagues, bad bosses, and even bad pastors, as you can from good ones. They are all there to be watched and heard, and can all be treated as living demonstrations, illustrating what goes wrong when a person thinks, speaks or behaves foolishly.

In a certain sense, therefore, it can be a blessing when God allows foolish people to come into our lives as colleagues, bosses or fellow church members. It gives us an opportunity, albeit one we did not seek, to learn from observation how *not* to live and what *not* to do. If it were not for being able to observe such people at close quarters you would either have to learn those lessons directly from Scripture, or from taking advice, which can be hard to find. Or we would have to do so from making those same foolish errors and bad decisions ourselves.

48

But that would mean learning from our own pain and suffering, rather than from other people's, which is far easier. Accordingly, look for events and situations arising in the lives of others. That way we can learn valuable life lessons at *their expense,* rather than our own. That is not an argument for seeking to make friends with fools or to spend more time with them by choice. But it is an argument for taking every opportunity to learn lessons from the things that are said and done by those fools whom we have *no choice but to be with.*

Counterproductive - self defeating behaviours

CHAPTER 3

THE SIMPLE (OR NAIVE)

"How long, O simple ones, will you love being simple?...."
Proverbs 1:22(a) (RSV)

The naive believes everything,
But the sensible man considers his steps.
Proverbs 14:15 (NASB)

The naive inherit foolishness,
But the sensible are crowned with knowledge.
Proverbs 14:18 (NASB)

O simple ones, learn prudence;
O foolish men, pay attention.
Proverbs 8:5 (RSV)

.....for the sons of this world are more shrewd in dealing with their own
generation than the sons of light.
Luke 16:8(b) (RSV)

My son, if sinners entice you,
do not consent.
Proverbs 1:10 (ESV)

The law of the LORD is perfect,
reviving the soul;
the testimony of the LORD is sure,
making wise the simple;
Psalm 19:7 (RSV)

The unfolding of thy words gives light;
it imparts understanding to the simple.
Psalm 119:130 (RSV)

"Strike a scoffer and the naïve may become shrewd....
Proverbs 19:25(a) (NASB)

"When a scoffer is punished, the simple becomes wise....."
Proverbs 21:11(a) (RSV)

The fear of the LORD is the beginning of wisdom;
all those who practice it have a good understanding......
Psalm 111:10(a) (ESV)

Who are the simple or the naïve?

The words *simple* and *naive* mean the same and can be used interchangeably. The simple or naive person falls in between the categories of the fool and the wise. They are in the middle and are not fools, but they are not wise either. They do not deny or ignore God's existence or reject His values. Neither do they generally live as if God didn't exist. Therefore, overall, they have quite a bit to commend them.

However, they still cannot be classified as wise, as they have not yet acquired knowledge, understanding, prudence, insight, discernment, discretion or the fear of the LORD. At least, they do not yet have *enough* of those things to be considered wise, even if they are Christians. Thus, the naïve do not yet have the habits and attitudes that this book seeks to help you to develop.

The majority of Christians, even genuine ones, fall into this category because very few people are wise, even within the real Church. That is one reason why there is so much apostasy and false teaching today. There are too few wise people in our churches to challenge it and the naïve, although numerous, cannot see what is going on.

The main problem of the simple is that they lack discernment. In particular they are unable to judge accurately the character of other people.

The simple person is too gullible, naive and trusting. Therefore, as well as being unable to identify false teaching in the churches, he regularly misjudges the nature, motives and intentions of others. He will believe what people say, and trust them, whoever they may be. He does not realise that there are different types of person in this world, and that he is meant to try to differentiate or judge between them.

However, let me make clear that there are two main words for *'judge'* or *'judging'* in the New Testament, *diakrino* and *kreetace*, and they have very different meanings. There is one kind of judging which we are *commanded* to do and another kind which is *forbidden*. So, when I say that we *must* judge other people, I mean in the sense of *'diakrino'*. That means to distinguish, assess or differentiate, all of which we are commanded to do.

I do not mean *'kreetace'* type judgment. To 'kreetace' others would mean assuming a position of superiority, acting hypocritically, and usurping Jesus' role as the judge of the whole world. It therefore involves condemning others and doing so invalidly and self-righteously. For much more detail on the important distinction between these two Greek words, please listen to my audio teaching on Matthew's gospel or see my written commentary on Matthew which I hope to write shortly.

However, the naïve person doesn't know *how* to assess people anyway, or how tell them apart, even if he knew that he was supposed to try to do so. In particular, he does not understand the way in which the wicked operate. Therefore, he tends to believe everything he is told because he is unaware that there are people out there who would actually want to deceive him, or who are deceived themselves. Above all, he has no idea that such deceivers are so numerous:

The naive believes everything,
But the sensible man considers his steps.
Proverbs 14:15 (NASB)

There is nothing virtuous about trusting people whom we do not yet know and whose character and fruit we have not yet measured. In fact, the Bible positively tells us *not* to trust them. We are commanded instead to critically appraise *everything* we see and hear and to form a judgement, in the sense of *'diakrino'*, not *'kreetace'*. That applies to *everyone* we deal with. We have to find out exactly whom, and what, we are dealing with before we even considering trusting anybody. (See my Book 6, concerning the wicked, for a much fuller discussion of this.)

Naivety is a fault, not a quality. Jesus does *not* want us to automatically trust everybody - not even fellow Christians.

The simple person's excessive and premature willingness to trust others and to *"see good in everyone"* may seem endearing. I have often heard that approach praised, as if it was a virtue. However, it is not something that God ever praises. God views it as *gullibility* and regards that as a major fault. It will lead the simple person into a great deal of trouble, such that he will regularly become prey for others, especially the wicked.

Apostle Paul therefore tells us to be innocent *ourselves*. But, at the same time, we are meant to be completely realistic about the evil that is in *other people*, or likely to be in them, or even that might possibly be in them. That must be our approach, however unlikely it may seem to us that the person is bad, based on what we currently know and believe:

Brothers and sisters, stop thinking like children. In regard to evil be infants, but in your thinking be adults.

1 Corinthians 14:20 (NIV)

Jesus did not trust everybody. Far from it. He was entirely realistic and knew all about the hidden malice in men's hearts:

[23]Now while he was in Jerusalem at the Passover Feast, many people saw the miraculous signs he was doing and believed in his name.[24]But Jesus would not entrust himself to them, for he knew all men. [25]He did not need man's testimony about man, for he knew what was in a man.

John 2:23-25 (NIV)

If a simple/naive person does not take steps to acquire wisdom, he is in danger of going the other way and descending into being a fool himself. The membership of each of these four groups is not static. People move up and down, and it is rare to stay in the same place, at the same level. We are all travelling along the spectrum, either upwards from simple to wise, or downwards from simple to fool and then on to being wicked. That said, for most people, the direction of travel is downward, i.e. from naive to foolish, rather than for fools to move up to become simple and then wise:

The naive inherit foolishness,
But the sensible are crowned with knowledge.

Proverbs 14:18 (NASB)

Having become a fool, a man can easily degenerate even further, until he becomes wicked.

If we are currently simple, but do nothing to try to become wise, we are likely to end up as a fool. The very act of choosing not to pursue wisdom is foolish in itself. It is also *disobedience*, since the Bible commands it. Going downwards is easy and automatic, like drifting downstream, but we will never go up unless we *consciously* try to do so. Upward movement is not automatic, whereas we will inevitably descend unless we actively seek not to. We have to be moving in some direction, as the option of standing still is not available. Thus, if a fool does nothing to try to change, he is likely to end up wicked:

For a fool speaks nonsense,
And his heart inclines toward wickedness ....

Isaiah 32:6(a) (NASB)

Simple people lack prudence and caution so they 'sleepwalk' into danger or into being deceived, used or manipulated.

Because the simple don't understand other people, especially the wicked, they are generally unaware of the danger they are in. They do not see others as a threat, even when the danger would be obvious to a wise person. The simple go through life with their guard down and their 'carbon monoxide detectors' switched off. Unlike Jesus, they are not alert to the falseness in other people's hearts and are generally unaware that it exists at all. Accordingly, they are not expecting to be deceived today, or by whoever they are with at the moment.

Therefore, they are not being careful and vigilant because they do not even realise that they need to be. A man who does not realise there is any danger is not going to brace himself or be ready for it. Therefore, the simple sleepwalk into situations in which they are then used or exploited. Even afterwards, they are slow to realise what happened to them. They still can't see the manipulation, even after it has become obvious to others. The simple/naive person therefore walks into the traps that are set for him:

A prudent man sees evil and hides himself,
The naive proceed and pay the penalty.
Proverbs 27:12 (NASB)

The simple person generally doesn't learn, even from repeated bad experiences and mistreatment by others. Therefore, even after those experiences are over, he still doesn't know what went wrong or how he got into the mess. He doesn't realise that he was deceived or manipulated and makes little or no attempt to figure it out. Therefore, he often emerges from the fiasco still trusting, and even confiding in, the very person who has deceived or used him. I know, because I have done so myself a number of times.

That inability to see how the deception or manipulation occurred prevents the simple man from learning from his errors. Thus, he is doomed to repeat them over and over again. He may never come to understand the nature of the problem, because he doesn't even know he has got a problem. At any rate, it doesn't occur to him that his own naivety is one of the causes of his difficulties. He assumes he is just unlucky. Therefore, being naive is obviously less damaging than being wicked or foolish, but it is still likely to result in us being harmed.

God is very sensible, and He knows how much grief is caused merely by naivety, i.e. the absence of wisdom, even where there is no sin or transgression. That's why it's so crucial to pursue wisdom. You can't just wait for it to come to you automatically, as you get older, merely by the passage of time. It has to be actively pursued. Proverbs portrays wisdom as if it was a person who is calling to you and

We forget what in man's heart
that this is a fallen world - fallen condition

to whom *you must go,* because wisdom never comes to you, no matter how much time passes:

¹Does not wisdom call,
does not understanding raise her voice?
²On the heights beside the way,
in the paths she takes her stand;
³beside the gates in front of the town,
at the entrance of the portals she cries aloud:
⁴"To you, O men, I call,
and my cry is to the sons of men.
⁵ O simple ones, learn prudence;
O foolish men, pay attention.
⁶Hear, for I will speak noble things,
and from my lips will come what is right;
⁷for my mouth will utter truth;
wickedness is an abomination to my lips.
⁸All the words of my mouth are righteous;
there is nothing twisted or crooked in them.
⁹They are all straight to him who
understands and right to those who find knowledge.
¹⁰Take my instruction instead of silver,
and knowledge rather than choice gold;
¹¹for wisdom is better than jewels,
and all that you may desire cannot compare with her.
¹²I, wisdom, dwell in prudence,
and I find knowledge and discretion.
Proverbs 8:1-12 (RSV)

I love those who love me,
and those who seek me diligently find me.
Proverbs 8:17 (RSV)

Again in Proverbs chapter 9, wisdom is spoken of as if it was a person. Here it is portrayed as a woman calling to the simple/naive person and urging him to spend time with her and, thereby, to gain understanding. We are to pursue this 'person' called wisdom and to become thoroughly acquainted:

¹Wisdom has built her house,
She has hewn out her seven pillars;
²She has prepared her food, she has mixed her wine;
She has also set her table;
³She has sent out her maidens, she calls
From the tops of the heights of the city:

4"Whoever is naive, let him turn in here!"
To him who lacks understanding she says,
5"Come, eat of my food
And drink of the wine I have mixed.
6"Forsake your folly and live,
And proceed in the way of understanding."
Proverbs 9:1-6 (NASB)

Absolutely anybody can stop being simple and start to become wise if they really want to

There is always hope for the simple person. He can stop being naive and start to become wise if he really wants to. His condition is not unchangeable. If he pursues wisdom he can fully expect to get it. Moreover, he can get as much of it as he wants, and is willing to work for. God would not command us to stop being naive and to become wise if it could not be done. Therefore, being wise is entirely a matter of *choice*, not something which randomly happens to you, or a natural ability you are born with. It is something you build or grow as a matter of your own *decisions:*

Leave simpleness, and live,
and walk in the way of insight."
Proverbs 9:6 (RSV)

There is a way for even the most naive person to become shrewd and discerning, provided he realises his need to change, and is determined to do so. Being naïve is nothing to boast about, as it is only one step up from being a fool. God is therefore urging us all to wake up, to leave our naivety and gullibility behind, and to get wisdom:

"How long, O naive ones,
will you love being simple-minded?
Proverbs 1:22(a) (NASB)

Hear instruction and be wise,
and do not neglect it.
Proverbs 8:33 (RSV)

5 do not forget, and do not turn away from the words of my mouth.
Get wisdom; get insight.
6 Do not forsake her, and she will keep you;
love her, and she will guard you.
7 The beginning of wisdom is this: Get wisdom,

and whatever you get, get insight.
⁸ Prize her highly, and she will exalt you;
* she will honor you if you embrace her.*
⁹ She will place on your head a fair garland;
she will bestow on you a beautiful crown."
                                    Proverbs 4:5-9 (RSV)

The simple also lack knowledge.

Another major problem for the simple person is sheer lack of knowledge. There are so many things that he just doesn't know. He doesn't know how wicked people operate, or what the Bible warns us of. He doesn't know the techniques that people use to control and manipulate us, or the tell-tale signs of deception and malice. Therefore, he isn't looking for them. Lack of knowledge alone can cause us to be destroyed, quite apart from lack of wisdom. Our lives may be damaged or even ruined, simply because we lack knowledge of the Bible and of other people's evil characters and schemes:

"My people are destroyed for lack of knowledge..."
                    Hosea 4:6(a) (RSV)

Perhaps you are now beginning to realise that you belong to this group called the simple and not to the wise and are even willing to admit that you are prone to being deceived, used and manipulated. If so, then resolve to see these things as faults, and to start to address them. Begin by recognising what you really are at present. Then set your face to seek the knowledge that you lack, and to keep searching until you have it. Even then, continue pursuing knowledge permanently, because you can never really finish the job or get too much of it:

"Wise men lay up knowledge ..."
          Proverbs 10:14(a) (RSV)

The simple are easily used and manipulated by the wicked.

One of the hallmarks of Satan and his demons, and also of wicked people, is that they seek to *dominate, manipulate* and *control* others. To succeed in that they have to go in search of suitable victims who are likely to fall for their devious tactics. The wicked know that other wicked people will rarely allow themselves to be used, manipulated or controlled, as they themselves are seeking to do all those things to others. Therefore, they can easily see through anybody who is using the same methods against them.

Therefore, albeit for different reasons, neither the demons nor the wicked will get very far by seeking their victims from among the wise. The wise do not use such devious tactics themselves but they have, nevertheless, learned how to see through the wicked when they engage in them. So, the only groups left for the wicked to prey upon are the foolish and the simple. That said, a high proportion of the foolish are already well on the way to becoming wicked themselves and so they often have at least some understanding of the crafty schemes that the wicked use.

That means, therefore, that the prime target group that the wicked have left to focus on is the simple. They are easy prey, even when the same tricks are used against them repeatedly. Any contest between the wicked and the simple generally results in victory for the wicked man, mainly because he is the only one who even knows that there is a contest going on. There is therefore an inbuilt inequality, because the wicked can understand and recognise the simple, but the simple cannot do the same with the wicked. *know your enemy*

The simple are easily recognised by the wicked. It is as if they have a neon sign on their head advertising what they are.

The tricks that are played on the simple are remarkably repetitive. They are deceived, manipulated and used over and over again and in the same ways, even by the same people. That is not just a coincidence. One reason for it is that the wicked are very skilled at recognising the simple and can immediately spot them, even across a crowded room. In part, the wicked person's ability to see a victim so quickly is because they have their own native cunning, also aided by years of experience.

However, on top of all that, they also have the help of demons. The overall effect is that it is as if the simple have a neon sign on their heads saying "*easily deceived*". I have a particular person in mind as an example of this, but I could also think of many others who are repeatedly manipulated. In fact, I was in that group myself, when I was younger. The particular person I am thinking of used to live in one part of the country where he was repeatedly deceived, used and taken advantage of.

He was tricked into helping false, unworthy people, for example by lending them money. He kept falling for the same old tricks again and again. Then he moved to a different part of the country, but within a matter of days, he had fallen into the clutches of two new manipulators, quite separately, neither of whom knew each other. It was no coincidence. It was due to the 'neon sign' on his head. He had brought that with him when he moved towns and the wicked saw it.

Too trusting!

59

to not a victim it's a sin

Therefore, he immediately stood out to the wicked as someone who would be easy prey. So, one of our first tasks, if we want to stop being simple, is to remove that neon sign from our heads. We must stop sending out those signals which tell the wicked that we are gullible and available to be used and deceived. As soon as we realise this problem, and start to send out a different kind of signal, the wicked will notice straight away. You can be quite sure of that, because they notice everything.

The simple allow themselves to be walked on

The simple are easily walked on and pushed around by others. Fools and wicked people develop a thick, leathery skin, and are brass-faced when challenged. Simple people do not have that thick skin, and find it hard to grasp the fact that other people do. That being so, they tend to try too hard to avoid giving offence. In fact, they need not be so concerned about it, because the wicked, and also fools, are not easily hurt whatever one does. *what did you expect in a fuller...*

They can certainly be *angered* at being challenged, resisted or caught out in a lie or a scheme. But it would be wrong to think of them being *hurt*. That is the reaction of simple people. Fools, and especially wicked people, feel outrage, fury, temper etc, but rarely hurt feelings. Therefore, in their effort to avoid offending others, the simple frequently fail to show enough assertiveness and are insufficiently direct. *Tolerate the intolerable - virtue of tolerance*

Their wish to avoid offending others, causes them to stay silent when they should defend themselves and to tolerate things which ought not to be tolerated. However, that concern for the feelings of others is not shared by the wicked, or even by fools. Thus, the simple often end up going through the battles of life with one hand, or even both hands, tied behind their backs, while the wicked use both hands, elbows, and their feet as well.

The simple can't discern what the 'time' is.

Even if we are beginning to wake up and to discover some facts and principles that we did not previously know about, there is still a difficulty in knowing *when* to apply a particular principle and when not to. Timing is vitally important. One might learn of a new factor which may need to be considered, but still be unsure as to whether or not it is applicable at this *specific time*. For example, there is a time to be firm and a time not to be.

There is also a time to ask probing questions and a time not to, a time to give or to lend money and a time not to, a time to confront and a time not to. The same

60

can be said of every principle that we see in Scripture. For each one, wisdom is needed to work out *whether*, *when*, *how*, and to *what extent*, it ought to be applied *in the particular situation that you face.* Solomon identified this vexed problem when, as an old man, he wrote the book of Ecclesiastes:

¹For everything there is a season,
and a time for every matter under heaven:
²a time to be born, and a time to die;
a time to plant,
and a time to pluck up what is planted;
³a time to kill, and a time to heal;
a time to break down,
and a time to build up;
⁴a time to weep, and a time to laugh;
a time to mourn, and a time to dance;
⁵ a time to cast away stones,
and a time to gather stones together;
a time to embrace,
and a time to refrain from embracing;
⁶a time to seek, and a time to lose;
a time to keep,
and a time to cast away;
⁷a time to rend,
and a time to sew;
a time to keep silence,
and a time to speak;
⁸a time to love,
and a time to hate;
a time for war,
and a time for peace.
Ecclesiastes 3:1-8 (RSV)

Appropriate

If we have been simple, or still are, we may not have been aware until now that certain principles even existed. Now we might know of them, but still be unsure as to when to apply them and when not to. On many occasions I have come to learn of some principle but have then applied it prematurely. Other times I have applied it too late, or with the wrong people, for whom it was not applicable. This is something we just have to learn gradually, from painful experience. There is no other way.

However, we can speed up the learning process by praying on each occasion and asking God to guide us as to timing and as to whether or not the principle is applicable at this time and in this particular situation. I know of no short cuts. It inevitably takes years to learn. I have therefore discovered many new factors or considerations over the years that may potentially be of relevance to a situation I am facing. But deciding whether and when to apply principle A, or whether and when to apply principle B instead, can be quite bewildering.

One can find that one was too vigilant in one situation and/or that one acted too hastily, and/or went too far. Therefore, on the next occasion one adjusts, only to find, in that different situation, that one has over-compensated and therefore was not vigilant enough, and/or was too slow to act, and/or did not go far enough. It is due to having misread the timing or wrongly assessing the nature and gravity of the circumstances, or because one is not yet experienced enough at applying the various principles one has learned.

It is just as with learning any new skill. We might learn a new recipe, but the first time we try it, the dinner is overcooked. Then the next time it is undercooked until, eventually, after several attempts, we get the hang of it. The precise timing of difficult situations, knowing when to start, how far to go, and how vigorous to be, especially when handling the wicked, is rather like that. Realistically, the only way to learn is by trial and error, which means being willing to risk making mistakes. If you are not willing to make those you will never get anywhere and will certainly never learn the art of 'telling the time'.

A simple person is often humble enough to be willing to be corrected without resenting it. Thus, they are much more open to the Gospel than fools or wicked people are.

In my experience, most people who get saved seem to come from among the simple. They tend to have tender hearts and are not too proud to be corrected or to see that they are at fault. We see an example of this in the case of the Samaritan women whom Jesus met by the well:

⁵ So he came to a city of Samar'ia, called Sy'char, near the field that Jacob gave to his son Joseph. ⁶ Jacob's well was there, and so Jesus, wearied as he was with his journey, sat down beside the well. It was about the sixth hour. ⁷ There came a woman of Samar'ia to draw water. Jesus said to her, "Give me a drink." ⁸ For his disciples had gone away into the city to buy food. ⁹ The Samaritan woman said to him, "How is it that you, a Jew, ask a drink of me, a woman of Samar'ia?" For Jews have no dealings with Samaritans. ¹⁰ Jesus answered her, "If you knew the gift of God, and who it is that is saying to you, 'Give me a drink,' you would have asked him, and he would have given you living water." ¹¹ The woman said to him, "Sir, you have nothing to draw with, and the well is deep; where do you get that living water? ¹² Are you greater than our father Jacob, who gave us the well, and drank from it himself, and his sons, and his cattle?" ¹³ Jesus said to her, "Every one who drinks of this water will thirst *again, ¹⁴ but whoever drinks of the water that I shall give him will never thirst; the water that I shall give him will become in him a spring of water welling up to eternal life." ¹⁵ The woman said to him, "Sir, give me this water, that I may not thirst, nor come here to draw."*

John 4:5-15 (RSV)

Note how open the Samaritan women was. When Jesus spoke of this living water her immediate reaction was to take Him seriously and to ask Him for it. A hardened person would have sneered at Jesus' words, but she wanted what He was speaking of, and did not try to pretend that she already had it. Moreover, she did not object when Jesus pointed out some of the sins in her life, in particular that she had lived immorally with many different men. A fool or a wicked person would have been enraged, but she just continued to question Jesus and was not at all resentful:

¹⁶ Jesus said to her, "Go, call your husband, and come here." ¹⁷ The woman answered him, "I have no husband." Jesus said to her, "You are right in saying, 'I have no husband'; ¹⁸ for you have had five husbands, and he whom you now have is not your husband; this you said truly." ¹⁹ The woman said to him, "Sir, I perceive that you are a prophet. ²⁰ Our fathers worshiped on this mountain; and you say that in Jerusalem is the place where men ought to worship." ²¹ Jesus said to her, "Woman, believe me, the hour is coming when neither on this mountain nor in Jerusalem will you worship the Father. ²² You worship what you do not know; we worship what we know, for salvation is from the Jews. ²³ But the hour is coming, and now is, when the true worshipers will worship the Father in spirit and truth, for such the Father seeks to worship him. ²⁴ God is spirit, and those who worship him must worship in spirit and truth." ²⁵ The woman said to him, "I know that Messiah is coming (he who is called Christ); when he comes, he will show us all things." ²⁶ Jesus said to her, "I who speak to you am he."

John 4:16-26 (RSV)

She also took Jesus perfectly seriously when He told her that He was the Messiah. In fact, she not only believed Him, she went immediately to tell others:

²⁸ So the woman left her water jar, and went away into the city, and said to the people, ²⁹ "Come, see a man who told me all that I ever did. Can this be the Christ?" ³⁰ They went out of the city and were coming to him.

John 4:28-30 (RSV)

Do not build your life on sand.

Here is one of Jesus' statements which has entered into the English language:

24 "Everyone then who hears these words of mine and does them will be like a wise man who built his house on the rock. 25 And the rain fell, and the floods came, and the winds blew and beat on that house, but it did not fall, because it had been founded on the rock. 26 And everyone who hears these words of mine and does not do them will be like a foolish man who built his house on the sand. 27 And the rain fell, and the floods came, and the winds blew and beat against that house, and it fell, and great was the fall of it."

Matthew 7:24-27 (ESV)

The just shall live by faith in the faithful God

Jesus commands us to build our lives on *Him*. He, and His Word, are solid rock, and can be depended on, whereas *everything else is sand*. That, in a nutshell, is what wisdom is all about. We have to make Jesus, and *obedience to His commands*, the very foundation of our lives, upon which everything else has to be built. If you don't then you cannot claim to be His disciple, in which case, you cannot hope to become wise either, as that is a pre-condition to doing so. Therefore, Jesus asks this stark question in the parallel passage in Luke about building on the rock:

"Why do you call me 'Lord, Lord,' and not do what I tell you?
Luke 6:46 (ESV)

Jesus is even blunter in Matthew's gospel where He makes clear that those who do not do the Father's will are not going to enter the Kingdom of heaven:

21 "Not everyone who says to me, 'Lord, Lord,' will enter the kingdom of heaven, but the one who does the will of my Father who is in heaven. 22 On that day many will say to me, 'Lord, Lord, did we not prophesy in your name, and cast out demons in your name, and do many mighty works in your name?' 23 And then will I declare to them, 'I never knew you; depart from me, you workers of lawlessness.'

Christianity Christ's way - or our own, cultural, denominal way... Its not what you DO - its the WAY that you do it

Matthew 7:21-23 (ESV)

Don't build your life on unrighteousness – the means are more important than the ends

Building your life on unrighteousness means doing things, and making decisions, which are motivated by, or based on, some kind of sin rather than on obedience to what Jesus has said. So, for example, we might be motivated by pride or greed or envy. Or we might cut corners in our lives and seek to build our career, business or relationships with the 'help' of lies or sharp practices or by manipulating or dominating others. The potential list of such sinful methods or techniques is endless. But they are all the opposite of what God wants us to do.

Preaching God's gospel
God's way - not the newest human model way
'Short cut' fast-track discipleship...

Anything we build by using such carnal or worldly methods is built upon a foundation of iniquity. It might appear to succeed in the short term, but it will not last, because God was not involved in it and it was not achieved in *His way*. God is far more interested in *how we go about things* than in *how much we succeed or achieve*. To Him, the means are more important than the ends. He will only bless and give His approval to those who build things *His way*, based on godliness and righteousness, not in their own way, or in the flesh, or by using worldly practices:

⁹Woe to him who gets evil gain for his house, to set his nest on high, to be safe from the reach of harm! ¹⁰You have devised shame to your house by cutting off many peoples; you have forfeited your life. ¹¹For the stone will cry out from the wall, and the beam from the woodwork respond. ¹²Woe to him who builds a town with blood, and founds a city on iniquity!

Habakkuk 2:9-12 (RSV)

It is therefore stupidly short-sighted to try to cheat in this life by doing things in an unfair or dishonest way. Likewise, being wilful and impulsive and going faster than God wants you to go, or doing more than He wanted, is carnal and He won't support it. It may bring the appearance of success, in the short term, but it will produce nothing in the long term, and certainly not in eternity. Dishonesty, in particular, will only bring woe upon yourself, i.e. God's curse. Then He will dismantle everything that was built by any other means than *obedience to Him* and *in accordance with His principles.*

Like the partridge that gathers a brood that she did not hatch, so is he who gets riches but not by justice; in the midst of his days they will leave him, and at his end he will be a fool.　　　　*Jeremiah 17:11 (ESV)*

⁵ The plans of the diligent lead surely to abundance,
*　　but every one who is hasty comes only to want.*
⁶ The getting of treasures by a lying tongue
*　　is a fleeting vapor and a snare of death.*
*　　　　　　　Proverbs 21:5-6 (RSV)*

Wealth hastily gotten will dwindle,
*　　but he who gathers little by little will increase it.*
*　　　　　　　Proverbs 13:11 (RSV)*

In fact, do not build anything at all unless God is building it. If you do, it will just be a work of the flesh.

Another lesson I have learned through many bitter experiences is that we should never do, or build, or join, anything at all *unless God is in it*. Over the years I

65

have initiated, or got involved in, all sorts of apparently good causes or worthy sounding activities that seemed good to me. But I later realised they were just my own 'bright ideas', and that God was never in them, or at least that He never told *me* to get involved in them.

God has never promised to assist us with tasks or projects which are merely our own ideas, or which we have embarked on solely by our own initiative, due to our own wilfulness or impulsiveness. If we attempt such things we may find that God will leave us to do them on our own, without His help. If so, they will inevitably come to nothing and we will find that we have laboured in vain:

Unless the LORD builds the house,
those who build it labour in vain.
Unless the LORD watches over the city,
the watchman stays awake in vain.
Psalm 127:1 (RSV)

Therefore, even if a thing sounds good, always ask God whether *He* is involved in it, and whether He wants *you* to be doing it, before you get involved. This simple measure will save you from a lot of wasted stress and effort and enable you to focus exclusively on those things which God *is* calling you to. That is very liberating and will also greatly increase your effectiveness. One would imagine this to be obvious, but how many of us actually think and act in this way, rather than just pressing full steam ahead, pursuing our own ideas, opinions, and even pipe dreams?

¹"Woe to the rebellious children," declares the LORD,
"Who execute a plan, but not Mine,
And make an alliance, but not of My Spirit,
In order to add sin to sin;
² Who proceed down to Egypt
Without consulting Me,
To take refuge in the safety of Pharaoh
And to seek shelter in the shadow of Egypt!
³ "Therefore the safety of Pharaoh will be your shame
And the shelter in the shadow of Egypt, your humiliation.
Isaiah 30:1-3 (NASB)

The difference between a '*dream*' and a '*pipedream*' is that a dream is valid and is planted in your mind by God because He wants you to pursue it. By contrast, a pipedream is something of your own making, which you have imagined or invented, and which did not come from God. It is an ambition, or even a fantasy, which you pursue in your own strength, as a work of the flesh. That is why it is essential to know whether any idea or project is from God, or from yourself, or

66

even from a demon. That is often difficult to tell, but we need to try hard to get it right, because there is a lot at stake.

If you have now realised that you are not wise, but simple, and that you need to change, then start to seek wisdom now, in every possible way

This book is not intended to flatter you. Neither is the Bible. The aim is to tell the truth and to help you to see the truth about yourself and about your lack of wisdom, your naivety, and perhaps even your foolishness. Wherever you may currently be on the wickedness to wisdom 'spectrum', if you have made some discoveries about what you really are, then resolve to *do something about it,* not just as a one-off exercise, but as a life-long project.

From now on seek to identify all the areas in which you are naïve, or foolish, or where you currently lack knowledge, understanding, discernment, prudence, insight, discretion or the fear of the LORD. Then set about putting things right and plugging all of the gaps. This book sets out many of the ways in which you can do that. However, I suggest that you begin by praying, as Paul prayed for the people in Ephesus, that God would grant you wisdom and revelation and help you to change:

¹⁵ For this reason, because I have heard of your faith in the Lord Jesus and your love toward all the saints, ¹⁶ I do not cease to give thanks for you, remembering you in my prayers, ¹⁷ that the God of our Lord Jesus Christ, the Father of glory, may give you the Spirit of wisdom and of revelation in the knowledge of him, ¹⁸ having the eyes of your hearts enlightened, that you may know what is the hope to which he has called you, what are the riches of his glorious inheritance in the saints, ¹⁹ and what is the immeasurable greatness of his power toward us who believe, according to the working of his great might
Ephesians 1:15-19 (ESV)

Ask God to give you the wisdom that you lack and to build in you the right attitudes and habits. But you must also keep on and on asking Him, in your devotional times, but also as you face difficulties, trials and tests that you have not faced before. Above all, ask Him every time you read the Bible. Ask Him to open it up to you and to enable you to see its real meaning, to realise where it is speaking of faults that you have, or areas where your doctrines are mistaken. Also ask Him generally to give you new insights, of various kinds, that you have not previously seen.

I have done that for many years and God has answered my prayers remarkably. Often He does it by allowing me to see things in the Bible for the first time, or to see connections between passages. Or, He will give me insights into matters of doctrine or practice, or into my own character faults, or someone else's, that I had not previously noticed. That is largely how my books have been written. I ask God to teach me things, mainly from Scripture, which I can then teach others, and He does. Indeed, He is glad to do so, as James told us He would be:

If any of you lacks wisdom, let him ask God, who gives to all men generously and without reproaching, and it will be given him.

James 1:5 (RSV)

However, when God gives you those insights, as He will if you sincerely ask Him to, and if you really want to know, then don't waste those discoveries by allowing yourself to forget them. Write them down *at the time* in a journal, or notebook, or in your Bible. Then you will have a permanent record and reminder of the lesson that God has just given to you, or the insight He has revealed. Don't leave it until later, or you will forget it, partly because it is in our nature to forget, but also because the demons will try hard to make sure that you do, by distracting you.

So, foresee all that and act sensibly by recording all such insights there and then. God also wants to know what you will *do* about any insight that He has given you before He will give you further ones. Therefore, don't despise, neglect, ignore or disobey anything that God has shown you, however small it might seem. Take it seriously, note it down and remember it. Above all, *act upon it* by immediately obeying it or putting it into practice in your life.

As God sees you doing that, and thus honouring Him, He will honour you in return by continuing to give you more and more insights, and on an ever larger scale. He will also correct your errors and misunderstandings about His Word and show you your own personal faults and character failings. That may not sound like a privilege, but I can assure you it is, and that it is one that you must not allow yourself to miss. If you don't do this, and instead you ignore or disobey God's insights and revelations, or even delay in obeying them, then they will dry up.

The Bible will then become for you a difficult, impenetrable book which you do not enjoy reading and get little from. That happens to people not because there is something wrong with the Bible, but because there is something wrong with their *attitude towards it*. In particular it is due to their failure to take seriously, and to act upon, the insights and revelations they have *already had*. In short, if you obey what you now know, then God will tell you more. But if you don't, then He won't. Or at least He will not do so until you repent and change your attitude.

CHAPTER 4

THE WICKED

All wrongdoing is sin, but there is sin which is not mortal.
1 John 5:17 (RSV)

14 Do not enter the path of the wicked
And do not proceed in the way of evil men.
15 Avoid it, do not pass by it;
Turn away from it and pass on.
Proverbs 4:14-15 (NASB)

Everyone who is proud in heart is an abomination to the LORD;
Assuredly, he will not be unpunished.
Proverbs 16:5 (NASB)

Pride goes before destruction,
And a haughty spirit before stumbling.
Proverbs 16:18 (NASB)

He who justifies the wicked and he who condemns the righteous,
Both of them alike are an abomination to the LORD.
Proverbs 17:15 (NASB)

On every side the wicked prowl,
as vileness is exalted among the children of man.
Psalm 12:8 (ESV)

Haughty eyes and a proud heart,
the lamp of the wicked, are sin.
Proverbs 21:4 (RSV)

"Scoffer" is the name of the proud, haughty man
who acts with arrogant pride.
Proverbs 21:24 (RSV)

He who digs a pit will fall into it,
and a stone will come back upon him who starts it rolling.
Proverbs 26:27 (RSV)

If favour is shown to the wicked,
he does not learn righteousness;
Isaiah 26:10(a) (RSV)

Who are the wicked?

Before we look at the wicked more closely, firstly in this chapter and then, in much greater detail, in Book 6, we need to make clear at the start that the wicked can be divided into two main sub-groups:

a) the non-religious wicked

These are the people who *openly reject God*, despise His Word, and live for themselves. They are dishonest and hard-faced and would never be mistaken for Christians: *Clear disregard disrespect for Gods word always!*

Defiant

³ For the wicked boasts of the desires of his soul,
  and the one greedy for gain curses and renounces the LORD.
⁴ In the pride of his face the wicked does not seek him;
  all his thoughts are, "There is no God."

                                        Psalm 10:3-4 (ESV)

b) the religious wicked

These believe in God, *or say they do,* and may be *'churchgoers'*. However, they are not sincere or genuine and have not been born again. They are false, and their hearts are hard and unrepentant. They don't have reverence for the Bible and don't regard it as infallible or as having authority over them. Many don't even read it at all and prefer to get their beliefs from the secular world, the media, denominational traditions, or their own opinions. They may look and sound like Christians, but they are not real:

They profess to know God, but they deny him by their deeds; they are detestable, disobedient, unfit for any good deed.

                                        Titus 1:16 (RSV)

The same kind of people existed in the Old Testament. Some Jewish people were not sincere and did not truly believe, even though they sounded and acted as if they were believers:

Hear this, O house of Jacob,
who are called by the name of Israel,
  and who came forth from the loins of Judah;
who swear by the name of the LORD,
  and confess the God of Israel,
  but not in truth or right.

                                        Isaiah 48:1 (RSV)

70

God recognises that such people are wicked, no matter how much time they spend in religious rituals and liturgy. He does not accept them, or their prayers, because He knows they are *false* and have no regard for the Bible and that they "cast His words" behind them:

[21] "I hate, I despise your feasts,
and I take no delight in your solemn assemblies.
[22] Even though you offer me your burnt offerings and cereal offerings,
I will not accept them,
and the peace offerings of your fatted beasts
I will not look upon.
[23] Take away from me the noise of your songs;
to the melody of your harps I will not listen.
Amos 5:21-23 (RSV)

[16] But to the wicked God says:
"What right have you to recite my statutes,
or take my covenant on your lips?
[17] For you hate discipline,
and you cast my words behind you.
[18] If you see a thief, you are a friend of his;
and you keep company with adulterers.
[19] "You give your mouth free rein for evil,
and your tongue frames deceit.
Psalm 50:16-19 (RSV)

So, the label 'wicked' is not limited only to those who do not believe in God or who even hate Him. Those who believe in God, or claim to, can also be wicked, or become so, if they disregard Him. Even to think such things of God, they would have to believe in Him in the first place. But, although they know He exists, *they do not honour Him or fear Him.* That is true of many people in churches who have no fear of God and, in particular, no fear of being judged by Him. They do not believe that God sees what they do and they don't care what He thinks anyway:

He says to himself, "God has forgotten;
He has hidden His face; He will never see it."
Psalm 10:11 (NASB)

Why does the wicked renounce God,
and say in his heart, "Thou wilt not call to account"?
Psalm 10:13 (RSV)

Woe to those who go to great depths
to hide their plans from the LORD,

who do their work in darkness and think,
"Who sees us? Who will know?"
                                            Isaiah 29:15 (NIV)

If a person believes in God, and knows at least some of the Bible, then their responsibility for their sin is much greater than that of a person who does not. To know what God has said, *but then to ignore it,* is worse, and more wicked, than the sins of those who don't know anything about God or His Word. That is why God's judgment on Israel has been so severe, because they knew more, and had been given more, than the Gentile nations:

⁵ *"Thus says the Lord GOD, 'This is Jerusalem; I have set her at the center of the nations, with lands around her.* ⁶ *But she has rebelled against My ordinances more wickedly than the nations and against My statutes more than the lands which surround her; for they have rejected My ordinances and have not walked in My statutes.'*
                                            Ezekiel 5:5-6 (NASB)

King Solomon tells us that even where there is justice and righteousness, there is also wickedness. We are all a mixture and, therefore, there is an element of wickedness, or the potential for wickedness, in every one of us:

Moreover I saw under the sun that in the place of justice, even there was wickedness, and in the place of righteousness, even there was wickedness.
                                            Ecclesiastes 3:16 (RSV)

Solomon also says that it is even possible to offer a sacrifice to God, but for it still to be viewed as evil, because it is a *"sacrifice of fools"*:

Guard your steps when you go to the house of God; to draw near to listen is better than to offer the sacrifice of fools; for they do not know that they are doing evil.
                                            Ecclesiastes 5:1 (RSV)

Even though they believed in Him, God viewed most of the Exodus generation as wicked

A sobering passage in Numbers speaks of almost an entire generation of Israelites whom God describes as wicked. They were those who were adults when God miraculously rescued them from slavery in Egypt, bringing them through the Red Sea and into the wilderness. However, He declares that the vast majority of them will not be allowed to enter the Promised Land. They therefore lost their *inheritance*, though not necessarily their *salvation*. God then kept them wandering in the desert for 38 years waiting for all of those who were over the age of 20 at the time of the Exodus to die of disease or old age:

26 And the LORD spoke to Moses and to Aaron, saying, 27 "How long shall this wicked congregation grumble against me? I have heard the grumblings of the people of Israel, which they grumble against me. 28 Say to them, 'As I live, declares the LORD, what you have said in my hearing I will do to you: 29 your dead bodies shall fall in this wilderness, and of all your number, listed in the census from twenty years old and upward, who have grumbled against me, 30 not one shall come into the land where I swore that I would make you dwell, except Caleb the son of Jephunneh and Joshua the son of Nun.
31 But your little ones, who you said would become a prey, I will bring in, and they shall know the land that you have rejected. 32 But as for you, your dead bodies shall fall in this wilderness. 33 And your children shall be shepherds in the wilderness forty years and shall suffer for your faithlessness, until the last of your dead bodies lies in the wilderness. 34 According to the number of the days in which you spied out the land, forty days, a year for each day, you shall bear your iniquity forty years, and you shall know my displeasure.' 35 I, the LORD, have spoken. Surely this will I do to all this wicked congregation who are gathered together against me: in this wilderness they shall come to a full end, and there they shall die."

Numbers 14:26-35 (ESV)

God was angry with almost all of that generation because they had behaved wickedly. That is how He viewed their attitudes and their unbelief. Yet, what had they done? And why did their attitude anger God so much? This is the alarming part, because they actually sound rather like our modern Western churches. These are the kind of things they did:

a) They *grumbled* against God because of their circumstances. They complained about their food and the initial lack of water and about being in the wilderness. But most of us grumble and complain about far smaller things than those and we can be equally ungrateful, if not more so.

b) They *had a lot of knowledge,* for which God held them accountable. They had personally seen a series of extraordinary miracles such as walking through the Red Sea with the water stacked up as a wall to their left and right. Then they saw that water come crashing down on the Egyptian army. Yet once that series of miracles was over they quickly began to *doubt God's promises* and to question whether He would even provide food and water. But the truth is most of us have had similar doubts. We have not seen such spectacular miracles, but we do have the Bible, in which these are written about. So, we have at least indirect knowledge, for which we are going to be held equally accountable, if not more so.

c) They *criticised and blamed God* for their circumstances. They also slandered and misrepresented Him. Some even said that God must hate them because He was exposing them to such hardship and inconvenience. In saying such things they defamed God's character. They also discouraged and misled younger people and tarnished their view of God.

d) They *did not sufficiently value the promises* that God had made to Abraham, Isaac and Jacob, of which they, as the Hebrew nation, were all beneficiaries. Like Esau, most of them had failed to value the promises and they did not appreciate the great privilege of being included within God's Chosen People. Again, many of us do exactly the same, despising our birthright as Christians, and failing to value God's promises in particular, and the Bible in general.

The point is that when the people of Israel behaved in these ways, or displayed these attitudes, God viewed them as wicked, especially that particular generation which came out of Egypt as adults. They had heard God's Word through Moses and had directly witnessed God's miraculous power. Therefore, they were judged very severely and held more strongly accountable for their attitudes in the light of the enormous *knowledge* and other *privileges* they had been granted. Few of us would think of them as an example of wicked people.

We would be more likely to have in mind drug-dealers and paedophiles. But that is not necessarily how God sees it. In His eyes, it is also wicked, and possibly more wicked, for us to have been given knowledge, understanding, blessings and advantages and yet to *ignore those things* and act like an unbeliever instead. God might well see such attitudes as more serious, and more wicked, than the actions of those who lie and steal. There is no basis for us to be complacent about any of this, because we have been given far more access to God's Word than the Israelites of that generation ever had.

At any rate, the point is that none of us can assume that because we know the Bible, and believe in God, we cannot therefore be viewed as wicked. Many of us may be surprised, and even appalled, when we face Jesus in judgment, to find that His appraisal of us is far worse than the way we see ourselves. That needs to concern all of us as we contemplate the Judgment that is coming which, by the way, we should all be thinking of regularly.

Likewise, God viewed it as wickedness when the people of Israel asked Samuel to give them a King, rather than have God as their King.

Another surprising example of where a group of people are described by God as being wicked is the generation of Israelites which asked Samuel to give them a King. God wanted for Himself to be their King. But the people wanted a man, so they could be like all the other nations. God considered their request for a king, and their implicit rejection of Him, to be wickedness:

And Samuel said to all Israel, "Behold, I have obeyed your voice in all that you have said to me and have made a king over you.

1 Samuel 12:1 (ESV)

[6] And Samuel said to the people, "The LORD is witness, who appointed Moses and Aaron and brought your fathers up out of the land of Egypt. [7] Now therefore stand still that I may plead with you before the LORD concerning all the righteous deeds of the LORD that he performed for you and for your fathers. [8] When Jacob went into Egypt, and the Egyptians oppressed them, then your fathers cried out to the LORD and the LORD sent Moses and Aaron, who brought your fathers out of Egypt and made them dwell in this place. [9] But they forgot the LORD their God. And he sold them into the hand of Sisera, commander of the army of Hazor, and into the hand of the Philistines, and into the hand of the king of Moab. And they fought against them. [10] And they cried out to the LORD and said, 'We have sinned, because we have forsaken the LORD and have served the Baals and the Ashtaroth. But now deliver us out of the hand of our enemies, that we may serve you.' [11] And the LORD sent Jerubbaal and Barak and Jephthah and Samuel and delivered you out of the hand of your enemies on every side, and you lived in safety. [12] And when you saw that Nahash the king of the Ammonites came against you, you said to me, 'No, but a king shall reign over us,' when the LORD your God was your king. [13] And now behold the king whom you have chosen, for whom you have asked; behold, the LORD has set a king over you.

1 Samuel 12:6-13 (ESV)

[16] Now therefore stand still and see this great thing that the LORD will do before your eyes. [17] Is it not wheat harvest today? I will call upon the LORD, that he may send thunder and rain. And you shall know and see that your wickedness is great, which you have done in the sight of the LORD, in asking for yourselves a king." [18] So Samuel called upon the LORD, and the LORD sent thunder and rain that day, and all the people greatly feared the LORD and Samuel.

1 Samuel 12:16-18 (ESV)

The way God viewed this was that the Israelites were rejecting Him. To do that, despite knowing who He is, what He had done for them, and their unique role as the Chosen People, was seen by God as wickedness. He saw the Israelites of Samuel's day as being accountable for all the knowledge they had and for all their other privileges. So, for people in their position to prefer to have a human king, and to be like all the other nations instead of being God's special people, was a gross insult to God.

Backsliding
Apostasy

Again, that has got to make us consider our own position. Many of us are at least equally guilty of the same attitudes they had, and of rejecting God in favour of some other person or thing. Some of the religious wicked *know* that they are false. However, some of them are deceived about it themselves and are not necessarily aware of how wicked they are. Many do not even realise they are not real Christians and completely assume that they are saved when they aren't, or even that everybody will be saved. They will get a terrible shock when they die.

The religious wicked may seem to be saved, but God knows those who are His and those who are not.

This group can therefore be mistaken for Christians and they frequently are. However, *God knows those who are His, and those who aren't.* He makes no mistakes and cannot be deceived. In some ways, the religious wicked are actually the larger threat to the real Church as they are more likely to be listened to and believed by others when they preach myths and false doctrines of their own making. They then cause others to follow them and to reject the truth.

The judgment of God is going to fall heavily on those false teachers who reject the truth, and who lead so many others to do the same. However, His judgment will also come upon those members of lukewarm and apostate churches who prefer to hear false teaching and pleasant, positive sermons about things like prosperity rather than being taught the real truth from the Bible by genuine leaders and teachers:

⁹ For this is a rebellious people, false sons,
Sons who refuse to listen
To the instruction of the LORD;
¹⁰ Who say to the seers, "You must not see visions";
And to the prophets, "You must not prophesy to us what is right,
Speak to us pleasant words,
Prophesy illusions.
¹¹ "Get out of the way, turn aside from the path,
Let us hear no more about the Holy One of Israel."

¹² Therefore thus says the Holy One of Israel,
"Since you have rejected this word
And have put your trust in oppression and guile, and have relied on them,
¹³ Therefore this iniquity will be to you
Like a breach about to fall,
A bulge in a high wall,
Whose collapse comes suddenly in an instant,
¹⁴ Whose collapse is like the smashing of a potter's jar,

So ruthlessly shattered
That a sherd will not be found among its pieces
To take fire from a hearth
Or to scoop water from a cistern."
                    Isaiah 30:9-14 (NASB)

Please see below, and also in my Book 6, a discussion of some passages from the letter to the Hebrews. From these it emerges that even *real* Christians, who have been genuinely saved and *have begun to be sanctified*, can fall away, *i.e. become apostate*, and join the ranks of the religious wicked. It is also made clear that they will end up in the Lake of Fire. Even more alarmingly, we are told that it is virtually impossible for such apostates to repent, and to regain a real faith, once they have degenerated in this way.

That is how seriously God takes all of this, and therefore it needs to make us tremble. We need to be clear then, that when we speak of the wicked, we are not always referring to outright *unbelievers*. Sometimes we mean people *who look and sound like Christians*, and who *may once have been real Christians*, but have since fallen away and become apostate.

Either way, whether they *ceased to be real* Christians, or *never were real* to begin with, they are now false, and are a danger to the real Church. In the pages that follow, and within Book 6 too, we shall repeatedly refer to 'the wicked', but you need to be aware, in each case, which type is being spoken of, i.e. the religious wicked, or the non-religious wicked, or both.

The wicked in general, whether religious or not

Another name which is frequently applied to the wicked in the Bible, and also to fools, is the *scoffer*. Such a person mocks and belittles the things that God considers precious. Therefore, at the very least, a scoffer is automatically a fool, but many of them are wicked as well:

"Scoffer" is the name of the proud,
haughty man who acts with arrogant pride.
                    Proverbs 21:24 (RSV)

Another feature of the wicked, which they also share with fools, is that *they do not fear God*. In particular, *they do not fear His judgment* and do not expect ever to be found out, caught or punished. They believe that they can do whatever they wish and that there will be no adverse consequences for them, either now or in eternity:

¹ Transgression speaks to the wicked
deep in his heart;
there is no fear of God
before his eyes.
² For he flatters himself in his own eyes
that his iniquity cannot be found out and hated.
Psalm 36:1-2 (ESV)

We hear of the wicked even as far back as Genesis chapter six. By that time in the Earth's history God had become dismayed and regretted making mankind. Things had degenerated to such a low point that almost the whole population of the world was classified by Him as wicked. The only exceptions were Noah and his family:

Then the LORD saw that the wickedness of man was great on the earth, and that every intent of the thoughts of his heart was only evil continually.
Genesis 6:5 (NASB)

The situation became so grave that God solved it by wiping out almost all of the people on the Earth, using a worldwide flood. That indicates how seriously God takes wickedness and shows that we cannot afford not to take it seriously ourselves. Moreover, He is going to judge the whole world again, albeit by fire next time, not water. To begin with, Jesus Himself will destroy all the wicked when He returns at His second coming:

For the ruthless will come to an end and the scorner will be finished,
Indeed all who are intent on doing evil will be cut off;
Isaiah 29:20 (NASB)

¹ For behold, the day is coming, burning like a furnace; and all the arrogant and every evildoer will be chaff; and the day that is coming will set them ablaze,"
says the LORD of hosts, "so that it will leave them neither root nor branch."
² "But for you who fear My name, the sun of righteousness will rise with healing in its wings; and you will go forth and skip about like calves from the stall. ³ You will tread down the wicked, for they will be ashes under the soles of your feet on the day which I am preparing," says the LORD of hosts.
Malachi 4:1-3 (NASB)

After the 1000 year Millennial reign of King Jesus is over, the very surface of the Earth itself will be burned up and all wickedness will then be fully and finally removed:

But the day of the Lord will come like a thief, and then the heavens will pass away with a loud noise, and the elements will be dissolved with fire, and the earth and the works that are upon it will be burned up.

2 Peter 3:10 (RSV)

Moreover, all those who have rejected the Gospel will face their complete and eternal judgment at the Great White Throne Judgment, after which they will all be cast into the Lake of Fire:

[11] Then I saw a great white throne and him who sat upon it; from his presence earth and sky fled away, and no place was found for them. [12] And I saw the dead, great and small, standing before the throne, and books were opened. Also another book was opened, which is the book of life. And the dead were judged by what was written in the books, by what they had done. [13] And the sea gave up the dead in it, Death and Hades gave up the dead in them, and all were judged by what they had done. [14] Then Death and Hades were thrown into the lake of fire. This is the second death, the lake of fire; [15] and if any one's name was not found written in the book of life, he was thrown into the lake of fire.

Revelation 20:11-15 (RSV)

But as for the cowardly, the faithless, the polluted, as for murderers, fornicators, sorcerers, idolaters, and all liars, their lot shall be in the lake that burns with fire and sulphur, which is the second death."

Revelation 21:8 (RSV)

God scorns, abhors, curses, and even hates, the wicked and He intends to wipe them all out

The wicked are at the bottom end of the spectrum. Not only are they fools, they go even further and are also arrogant, dishonest and *hard-hearted*. Many of them hate God, or at least despise Him, which is to say that they under-value Him, whether they realise it or not. That is the case whether they are religious or not. God actually hates the wicked, and all that they stand for. He considers them an *abomination* and treats them as His *enemies*.

If you are not convinced of all that, consider the following passages and note how strongly God feels and how resolved He is to confront and punish the wicked. I have included several such passages because so many people find it hard to believe that God really will deal with the wicked in this way. They have been told that He loves everyone, and hates nobody, and that He will forgive everyone and punish nobody. But there is no basis for those views in the Bible. God's hatred for sin, *and of the wicked*, emerges clearly, however much our apostate generation might deny those facts:

79

⁴ For you are not a God who delights in wickedness;
   evil may not dwell with you.
⁵ The boastful shall not stand before your eyes;
   you hate all evildoers.
⁶ You destroy those who speak lies;
   the LORD abhors the bloodthirsty and deceitful man.
                                        Psalm 5:4-6 (ESV)

³¹Do not envy a man of violence
and do not choose any of his ways,
³²for the devious person is an abomination to the LORD,
but the upright are in his confidence.
³³The LORD's curse is on the house of the wicked,
but he blesses the dwelling of the righteous.
³⁴ Toward the scorners he is scornful,
but to the humble he gives favour.
                                        Proverbs 3:31-34 (ESV)

²⁰Men of perverse mind are an abomination to the LORD,
but those of blameless ways are his delight.
²¹Be assured, an evil man will not go unpunished,
but those who are righteous will be delivered.
                                        Proverbs 11:20-21 (RSV)

²The LORD is a jealous and avenging God; the LORD is avenging and wrathful; the LORD takes vengeance on his adversaries and keeps wrath for his enemies. ³The LORD is slow to anger and great in power, and the LORD will by no means clear the guilty. His way is in whirlwind and storm, and the clouds are the dust of his feet.
                                        Nahum 1:2-3 (ESV)

⁷The LORD is good, a stronghold in the day of trouble; he knows those who take refuge in him. ⁸But with an overflowing flood he will make a full end of his adversaries, and will pursue his enemies into darkness.
                                        Nahum 1:7-8 (RSV)

God scorns the wicked,
but the upright enjoy his favour.
            Proverbs 14:9 (RSV)

The thoughts of the wicked are an abomination to the LORD,
the words of the pure are pleasing to him.
                                        Proverbs 15:26 (RSV)

8Your hand will find out all your enemies;
your right hand will find out those who hate you.
9You will make them as a blazing oven
when you appear.
The LORD will swallow them up in his wrath;
and fire will consume them.
Psalm 21:8-9 (RSV)

All the wicked of the earth thou dost count as dross;
therefore I love thy testimonies.
Psalm 119:119 (RSV)

But God will strike the heads of his enemies,
the hairy crown of him who walks in his guilty ways.
Psalm 68:21 (ESV)

He will bring back on them their iniquity
and wipe them out for their wickedness;
the LORD our God will wipe them out.
Psalm 94:23 (RSV)

1God shall arise, his enemies shall be scattered;
and those who hate him shall flee before him!
2As smoke is driven away,
so you shall drive them away;
as wax melts before fire,
so the wicked shall perish before God!
Psalm 68:1-2 (ESV)

To be classified as 'wicked' does not require us to be famous or to do spectacularly evil things

Do not make the mistake of assuming that when the Bible speaks of the wicked it means only spectacularly evil people, such as murderers, drug-dealers and dictators. It also includes many people who are *entirely ordinary*, but who have *proud, hard, dishonest hearts*. In particular they have *no willingness to listen to God or to repent*. They obstinately close their ears until, eventually, they become deaf to God's convicting voice. That includes the religious wicked who are not sincere, or who are even outright apostates.

They have no love for the truth, no genuine repentance and no fear of God. In fact, such falsely religious people are often the proudest and most hard-hearted of all. They are frequently also the most antagonistic to real Christians. The wicked

81

are very willing to lie, whether they are religious or non-religious. They are also mean and selfish, and they have a contempt for God, i.e. for the real God, as opposed to the false god they create for themselves.

The wicked also have contempt for genuine Christians, who are hated by all of the wicked, but with particular venom by the falsely religious. Perhaps the main reason for the increased antagonism that the religious wicked display is that genuine Christians make false Christians feel convicted. Their very lives are a rebuke to them, even when they aren't saying anything, and the wicked do not like to be rebuked, however politely or sensitively it is done.

Wicked people exist at every level of the social scale and make up perhaps 20% to 30% of the population. It may be a lot more. I don't know, as only God knows their exact number. It will also vary from country to country, and from one generation to the next, but that is my personal guess. God is determined to resist the wicked and to bring them to judgment. Ultimately, He will destroy them all i.e. end their lives, because He classes them as His enemies. I emphasise that fact again, for the sake of those who still find it hard to believe. Consider these further verses:

The LORD preserves all who love him;
but all the wicked he will destroy.
Psalm 145:20 (RSV)

God is a just judge,   sinners
And God is angry with the wicked every day.
Psalm 7:11 (NKJV)

The face of the LORD is against evildoers,
to cut off the remembrance of them from the earth.
Psalm 34:16 (RSV)

Evil shall slay the wicked; and those who   Is evil & wicked the same?
hate the righteous will be condemned.
Psalm 34:21 (RSV)

[1]Why do you boast, O mighty man,
of mischief done against the godly?
All the day [2]you are plotting destruction.
Your tongue is like a sharp razor,
you worker of treachery.
[3]You love evil more than good,
and lying more than speaking the truth.
[4]You love all words that devour,

O deceitful tongue.
⁵But God will break you down for ever;
he will snatch and tear you from your tent;
he will uproot you from the land of the living.
Psalm 52:1-5 (RSV)

Some readers may be surprised that I spoke of false Christians as having *contempt* for God, or at least that they *despise*, i.e. devalue, the real God. I also spoke of them constructing a false god of their own because every false Christian I have ever met has *redefined* or *rebranded* God in some way to suit their own beliefs, opinions, preferences, likes and dislikes. Above all, they do it to make Him fit in with their own *denominational traditions, customs and practices*.

Any person whose focus is on *tradition* rather than on the Bible, and who seeks to uphold their own *denomination* rather than the truth, is in danger of creating their own false god in place of the real God. Such a false god is then likely to tell them that real Christians, who don't redefine God, but accept what He says about Himself in the Bible, need to be persecuted, and even killed, for the sake of defending that tradition or denomination. Throughout history, and also today, falsely religious people have found it easy to justify such persecution.

There was also wickedness amongst those who claimed to be believers in the days of the prophet Jeremiah. In the passages below, note the kinds of things which God regards as wicked. The sins described are not spectacular ones. They include things like not having any fear of God, being stubborn and rebellious, telling lies, and giving (and also accepting) false prophecies. The problem is that all of those things, and more besides, *are being done regularly in very many churches today* and on an even larger scale than in Jeremiah's time:

²¹ 'Now hear this, O foolish and senseless people,
Who have eyes but do not see;
Who have ears but do not hear.
²² 'Do you not fear Me?' declares the LORD.
'Do you not tremble in My presence?
For I have placed the sand as a boundary for the sea,
An eternal decree, so it cannot cross over it.
Though the waves toss, yet they cannot prevail;
Though they roar, yet they cannot cross over it.
²³ 'But this people has a stubborn and rebellious heart;
They have turned aside and departed.
²⁴ 'They do not say in their heart,
"Let us now fear the LORD our God,
Who gives rain in its season,
Both the autumn rain and the spring rain,

83

Who keeps for us
The appointed weeks of the harvest."
[25] 'Your iniquities have turned these away,
And your sins have withheld good from you.
[26] 'For wicked men are found among My people,
They watch like fowlers lying in wait;
They set a trap,
They catch men.
[27] 'Like a cage full of birds,
So their houses are full of deceit;
Therefore they have become great and rich.
[28] 'They are fat, they are sleek,
They also excel in deeds of wickedness;
They do not plead the cause,
The cause of the orphan, that they may prosper;
And they do not defend the rights of the poor.
[29] 'Shall I not punish these people?' declares the LORD,
'On a nation such as this
Shall I not avenge Myself?'
[30] "An appalling and horrible thing
Has happened in the land:
[31] The prophets prophesy falsely,
And the priests rule on their own authority;
And My people love it so!
But what will you do at the end of it?
                    Jeremiah 5:21-31 (NASB)

To whom shall I speak and give warning
That they may hear?
Behold, their ears are closed
And they cannot listen.
Behold, the word of the LORD has become a reproach to them;
They have no delight in it.
                    Jeremiah 6:10 (NASB)

The wickedness that has always been, and still is, within the Roman Catholic Church

Consider what the Roman Catholic church has done over many centuries, *and is still doing*, to oppose genuine, biblical Christianity. Their power was at its peak for over a thousand years, from the fifth century until the sixteenth. During that time they dominated all of Europe and even kings submitted to the popes. All real

84

Christianity was driven underground, reading the Bible was forbidden, and they hunted, persecuted and killed genuine Christians, all over Europe.

Such real Christians have always existed, in every century, and the Roman Catholic church has *always* persecuted them, wherever and whenever it had the power to do so. However, it was in the years before and during the Reformation, when the popes were fighting to preserve their power over the people, that we saw them at their most brutal, arrogant and devious. *John Wycliff*, who lived in the fourteenth century, from 1320 to 1384, was originally a Roman Catholic priest but he then began to study the Bible. That was strictly forbidden for lay people, but very few priests ever did so either.

Indeed, priests still don't study it much today. Most of the priests I have known, which is a lot, barely know the Bible at all, even at the shallowest level. As usually happens when Catholics begin to read the Bible, Wycliff saw that what he was reading did not match the doctrines, practices, traditions or standards of behaviour, that he had grown up with. From what he read, he began to understand the real Gospel, was born again, and became a true Christian. That did not go down well with those in authority, so they tried to silence him, using various forms of pressure, *including violence.*

But Wycliff refused to be silenced. Instead he trained up hundreds of lay preachers who came to be called '*Lollards*. They went round the UK, and also into Europe, preaching the real Gospel and telling people the truth about the Bible and also about the corruption in the Catholic church. Many of those men were then put to death simply because they preached the real Gospel, told the truth about Catholicism, and read the Bible out loud in public to the ordinary people. Those were three activities which the Catholic hierarchy were determined to stamp out.

The popes and bishops did not want any member of the public to read the Bible. They knew that if people did start to read it, they would soon realise that what Catholicism had *become* was totally different from what the Bible says the Church *should be.* Their entire power structure, and all of their pomp and vast wealth, would then have been threatened. There was no way they would ever permit that and they still don't today. However, Wycliff continued to defy them and went ahead and translated the New Testament into English in the face of all their threats.

Wycliff had a huge influence, both in England and in Europe, where his ideas and teaching had spread. His influence even went as far as what we now call the Czech Republic and reached another great man called *Jan Hus*. Wycliff also laid the foundations for the work of *Martin Luther, John Calvin* and many others who later played key roles in the Reformation of the sixteenth century. That is why Wycliff is now referred to as *"the morning star of the Reformation"*. He would undoubtedly have been put to death were it not for the protection of a very powerful man called *John of Gaunt*.

He was a wealthy aristocrat, and was related to royalty, but he was also a Bible-believing Christian, and he arranged for Wycliff to be accompanied by armed soldiers everywhere he went. They were needed to protect him from being assassinated. Without them, the Pope would certainly have killed him. That is how venomous they were towards him and the real Gospel. One day Wycliff was discussing the question of martyrdom, which many of his followers had suffered, and he said: *"Why do you talk of seeking the crown of martyrdom afar? Just preach the gospel of Christ to haughty prelates and martyrdom will not fail you"*.

So, moving back to our main point, would it be right to describe as *wicked* the Roman Catholic popes and bishops, and those working for them, who opposed Wycliff and killed his followers? Am I exaggerating if I do? I don't think so. Let's summarise just some of what they did and then you can decide for yourself:

a) They forbade the translation of the Bible into any language other than Latin, so that only educated priests could read it (not that many of them ever bothered to read it either, and very many priests were not educated men anyway).

b) They destroyed any English Bibles they found.

c) They put the Lollards to death for preaching the real Gospel and telling the truth about Roman Catholicism.

d) They wanted to put Wycliff himself to death and tried hard to do so.

It would surely be difficult to describe the actions and attitudes of those popes and bishops as anything other than wicked. They were proud, arrogant, devious and cruel. They were also selfish, greedy for money and power, and had no respect at all for the truth, or the Bible. It was not just *Wycliff* and his followers that were persecuted. They did the same, and worse, to the Czech reformer, *Jan Hus,* who preached the true Gospel fearlessly and was burned alive at the stake for doing so.

Likewise, in the early sixteenth century, *William Tyndale* (1494-1536) translated a large part of the Bible into English from Greek and Hebrew, despite the violent opposition of the Pope and bishops of his day. He also preached the truth about the Gospel and about the corrupt nature of the Roman Catholic church and its leaders. One day a Roman Catholic bishop said to Tyndale:

"Well then, it [is] better to be without God's laws than the Pope's".

Tyndale boldly replied:

"I defy the Pope and all his laws. If God spares my life I will take care that a ploughboy knows more of the Scriptures than [you do]!"

That aim was not as hard as it sounds, because Catholic clergy, both then and now, know very little about the Bible and do not read much of it. *Tyndale* was eventually lured to his death by tricks and lies. His only 'crimes' were to speak the truth, to preach the real Gospel, and to translate the Bible into English. How can we call what they did to him anything other than wicked? This brutality did not only occur at the time of the Reformation. It is the way the Roman Catholic church *has always behaved, throughout its entire history* and it still does, wherever it has the power to do so.

One common response, if one speaks of these atrocities, is for Catholics to say *"That was all in the past. Things have changed now, especially since the 2nd Vatican Council of the 1960s".* However, Roman Catholicism *has not changed* in any material sense. Its essential *character and nature* are just as they have always been. Moreover, they have never, at any stage, renounced or condemned any of the wicked things they have ever done, or the actions of any of their present or former leaders.

The only real change that has taken place is that the Reformation freed many European nations from the *power* of the Popes and thus reduced the influence of Catholicism over them. But that was contrary to their wishes and, if they still had the power today to put people to death, they would assuredly do so, *as they always did when they had got that power.* If you aren't convinced that the character of the Roman Catholic leadership is the same as it always was, you need only look at the worldwide scandal of the sexual abuse of children by paedophile priests.

On top of that there is also the systematic cover-up of that abuse by the bishops, cardinals and popes. Most of them, and probably all of them, were *well aware of what was going on*, and of the extent and gravity of what was being covered up. Yet they all looked after their institution and did whatever was needed to protect it, rather than the thousands of children who were being abused, on an industrial scale, by priests. For example, Pope John-Paul II, who 'reigned' from 1978 to 2005, and was recently made what they call a 'saint', consistently covered up reports of child abuse and took no action against his clergy.

When anyone spoke out about paedophile priests, they were silenced rather than helped, and the priests concerned went completely unpunished. If there was any trouble locally, the offending priests were simply moved to another parish, where they could continue, as before, unchallenged and unsupervised. If we look at just one very small country, Austria, we see that, at the time of writing, the Roman

Catholic church there has paid out token compensation to 1800 victims of abuse. However, they did so on the strict condition that those victims *must remain silent* about what was done to them.

Moreover, *not even one Austrian priest or bishop has been removed from his position*, either for the abuse itself, or for failing to tackle the abusers. How can one find that anything other than appalling, not only the initial abuse, but also the way it was then covered up? And how can they possibly justify taking no action whatsoever against *any* of the guilty priests? And why should the victims be required to stay silent when it might well help them to speak about it?

The way the Catholic authorities have acted proves conclusively that there is no genuine repentance on their part, or even remorse. They care only for their own reputation, the preservation of the institution, and maintaining their own power base. However, I am not just picking on Austria, as if they were somehow worse than the rest. What happened there is entirely typical of how this scandal has been handled. This paedophilia and its subsequent cover-up has not just happened once or twice, here and there.

It has been *happening systematically, in thousands of places, all over the world*. In fact, even now, we are generally only getting to hear of a fraction of the abuse that went on, and is still going on. The organisation called SNAP – *Survivors Network of those Abused by Priests*, represents 18,000 people from 79 countries who were sexually abused by priests. But those who have chosen to do something about it are only a small fraction of the true number of victims who are still alive today.

Even that huge number, 18,000, is just the tip of a vast iceberg that remains hidden. Moreover, we are only really getting to hear of it in countries in which the majority of the population is *not* Roman Catholic. In the countries where they do have a majority, and especially in the developing world, they find it much easier to cover things up, suppress criticism, undermine witnesses and stop the police enquiring effectively into complaints.

The wickedness that has been, and still is, within the Reformed, Lutheran and other Protestant churches and in the Pentecostal and Charismatic churches too

If anyone thinks I am singling out the Roman Catholic church alone for criticism, I assure you I am not. It simply contains more doctrinal errors, has a false gospel, has more paedophiles, and has done more wicked things, than any other denomination. But, it is far from being alone in any of these things. Many other churches have also acted in ways which can only be called wicked, albeit on a smaller scale. For example, some of the Reformers (by no means all) oppressed those people who wanted to take the Reformation even further.

Those reformers promoted their own opinions and practices by punishing and even executing those who disagreed with them. They displayed the very same pride, haughtiness and cruelty that the Popes had shown to them. Some of the leadership of the new Protestant denominations began very quickly to impose their views by force. They abused their positions of power in very similar ways to how the popes and bishops had always operated. One example is their oppressive treatment of the Anabaptists, who preached believers' baptism instead of baptism for babies, which most Reformed leaders continued to practise.

Likewise, in Geneva, *John Calvin* and his followers were creating a city which was supposedly *made up entirely of 'the elect'*, an absurd idea which they invented. They therefore became the leaders not only of the church in Geneva, but also of the city itself. They took over the councils, and also the civil and criminal courts, and began to make the laws and to enforce them brutally. They became appallingly domineering and forced people to go to church, as well as imposing dictatorial rules about conduct and speech.

They were proving, by their own oppressive actions, that the craving to control and dominate other people is deeply ingrained in the fallen human nature. It is by no means limited to Roman Catholicism, or to any other denomination. Any person who achieves absolute power, as some of the reformers did, just as the popes and bishops had done, is likely to end up a dictator. One of the many savage things which happened in Geneva, was that *John Calvin* had a part to play in the execution of a good man, *Michael Servetus*, who was put to death merely because he would not accept Calvin's teachings.

Today, the supporters of Calvin try to play down the extent of his personal involvement in Servetus being *burned alive at the stake for his beliefs*. However, it is clear that Calvin was *personally* involved and that he acted just like a pope. An even starker example is Martin Luther. He began well and said many true things as he stood up to the Roman Catholic church and its false practices and teachings. Consequently, he is revered by those who admire his early actions and beliefs and there is therefore a reluctance to hear about how he ended up.

However, the truth is that, in many ways, even Luther became a heretic. He rejected the book of James, calling it a *"letter of straw"* and taught that it should not even be in the Bible. He did the same with the book of Revelation and urged people not to bother with it. However, the lowest point for Luther came at the end of his life when he turned against the Jews and publicly taught, and wrote, *that they should be persecuted and killed*. These were not just unscripted off-the-cuff remarks, which he did not really mean, and later regretted.

89

He *deliberately and clearly taught that people everywhere should kill the Jews*. Therefore, the sermons and writings of Martin Luther were later used as the theological justification for the Nazi holocaust. Indeed, *Adolf Hitler* quoted Luther's teachings in his book, *'Mein Kampf'*, in which he set out the manifesto of the Nazi Party. Moreover, Hitler was not misquoting, misunderstanding or exaggerating any of Luther's words. Neither was he taking them out of context. It was an *accurate* representation of what Luther had said and was in its *proper context*.

One very rarely hears about any of this, because it is not considered polite to speak ill of a "great man" like Luther, who is an idol for many. But the facts are what the facts are. What Luther taught, at least in his later years, was evil, quite apart from his heretical views about the authority of some of the Scriptures. Therefore, if we have any regard for the truth, we need to be willing to admit such facts and to speak of them openly, without hiding anything. We must not make an idol of any man, however famous he might be, and no matter how much good he might also have done in other ways.

What therefore, do the brutal actions and policies of men like Luther and Calvin amount to? Would it be fair to call it wickedness? I think it would. Some of the reformers (not all) took on the very same haughty, autocratic ways as the popes and bishops, albeit not to the same extent. However, that was probably only because they never achieved the same levels of unlimited *power* that the popes had. If the reformers had had more power, some of them would have used it and would have been even more vicious than they already were.

We see the same dictatorial features today, although in less dramatic ways, but that is probably only because the churches no longer have the power to execute anybody. However, there are still controlling, manipulative and dominating leaders in almost all the denominational churches, at least in all the ones I have ever been in. In some cases that abuse of authority is only at a low level. Fleshly, insecure men jockey for position and do whatever they feel they need to do to preserve their own position.

However, that behaviour often reaches the level of outright wickedness. For example, many church leaders lie. Moreover, they do so entirely deliberately, and regularly, not just by mistake or only on rare occasions. They also manipulate and dominate people to get their own way. I know several Evangelical and Charismatic church leaders who have gone way beyond just being carnal. Some have undoubtedly acted wickedly and with deliberate intent. Yet that is just my own experience. Far worse things have been done elsewhere, that I have only read of or heard about.

The religious wicked have the same desire to rule, in every denomination, and are not willing to be questioned or contradicted.

All of the religious wicked, of whatever denomination, are proud and haughty, especially those who are *'ordained'* as *'clergy'*. They display this in many ways, for example by their love of the trappings of office and the power it gives them. They like their special clothes and to be set apart, deferred to, and held in honour. In particular they hate to be challenged or questioned, especially by 'lay' people. I describe such leaders as having a *'clergy mentality'*.

They come to believe that God has elevated them to a special status above ordinary members of the church, and that He has appointed them to rule. They see it as their natural place to *teach, not to be taught*, and to *correct, not to be corrected*. Few ever say any of that out loud, in express words, but that is how they think, and it shows in their actions and tone, especially when you begin to look for it. An example of this kind of haughtiness can be seen in the Pharisees who spoke to the man born blind, whose sight Jesus had restored:

[24] So for the second time they called the man who had been blind, and said to him, "Give God the praise; we know that this man is a sinner." [25] He answered, "Whether he is a sinner, I do not know; one thing I know, that though I was blind, now I see." [26] They said to him, "What did he do to you? How did he open your eyes?" [27] He answered them, "I have told you already, and you would not listen. Why do you want to hear it again? Do you too want to become his disciples?" [28] And they reviled him, saying, "You are his disciple, but we are disciples of Moses. [29] We know that God has spoken to Moses, but as for this man, we do not know where he comes from."
[30] The man answered, "Why, this is a marvel! You do not know where he comes from, and yet he opened my eyes. [31] We know that God does not listen to sinners, but if any one is a worshiper of God and does his will, God listens to him. [32] Never since the world began has it been heard that any one opened the eyes of a man born blind. [33] If this man were not from God, he could do nothing." [34] They answered him, "You were born in utter sin, and would you teach us?" And they cast him out.

John 9:24-34 (RSV)

These Pharisees were incensed at the idea of an ordinary man having the impertinence to tell *them* something. They were not willing even to be questioned, let alone instructed or corrected, by *'non-clergy'*. I have come across that attitude consistently, in *virtually every church I have ever attended*. There has been that same assumption of superiority wherever I have tried to question leaders, and even more so if I have tried to tell them something. They have seen it as *their role to teach me, not mine to teach them*.

91

Moreover, the more accurate my point was, the more bitterly they resented it. So, they were not objecting to me making *inaccurate or unjustified* remarks, but to the fact that they were *true*. However, they were mainly objecting to the idea that someone would have the nerve to '*answer back*' at all and not to show them the deference that they expected to receive. Yet, the truth is that we are *all* supposed to teach, correct, question, challenge and inform each other. It is meant to be done *by everybody and to everybody*, regardless of rank, role or status.

The only position of authority the Bible recognises within a *local* church is that of an '*elder*' *(presbuteros)*. But that just means a mature man, who is recognised as a leader within a local church. They were not '*clergy*' of the kind that we have today. They were not '*ordained*' either, and they did not wear fancy clothes, or have any special status or powers. Therefore, they were not considered to be high and lifted up. *The Nicolaitans*

On the contrary, an elder was meant to submit, defer, and listen to, *all other members of the church*, not just to those of a particular role or status. In short, we are *all* meant to submit to *all* other believers and *to all* fellow workers whenever they have something to say to teach or correct us. Thus, when the circumstances require it, an elder is just as much under a duty to submit to non-elders as they are to submit to him. We are all meant to be humble, gentle and cooperative and also to be open to being corrected, questioned and instructed, whether we are leaders or not.

Therefore, from time to time, we are all called upon to submit to each other, *"and to every fellow worker and labourer"*, even to the youngest and lowliest of Christians. Age, status and rank don't come into it. For example, if a 16 year old is in charge of the sound desk at church, then we would all be under a duty to submit to him and to cooperate *while he attends to those tasks*. The same applies to the man who puts out the chairs, or those who serve tea and coffee afterwards. Submit to *all* of them, when they have some request to make or some instruction to give. Consider these verses:

15 Now, brethren, you know that the household of Steph'anas were the first converts in Acha'ia, and they have devoted themselves to the service of the saints; 16I urge you to be subject to such men and to every fellow worker and laborer.

1 Corinthians 16:15-16 (RSV)

submitting to one another out of reverence for Christ.

Ephesians 5:21 (ESV)

It is interesting also to note apostle Peter's attitude, not only to himself, but also to every other Christian. Firstly, he saw himself as a *servant*, rather than as a

The upside down kingdom 92

celebrity or superstar. Secondly, he saw other Christians as having a faith *"of equal standing with [his]"*. There was not even a trace of pride, arrogance or what I call 'clergy mentality' in him:

Simeon Peter, a servant and apostle of Jesus Christ, To those who have obtained a faith of equal standing with ours by the righteousness of our God and Savior Jesus Christ:

2 Peter 1:1 (ESV)

Having said all that, there is still a valid role for elders as leaders and 'shepherds' and we are also meant to submit to them, or be subject to them. That means we are to make their role of leadership easier by cooperating and not being stubborn, awkward or argumentative. Anyone who has been appointed as an elder has an important job to do in the local church but they are meant to do it honestly, unselfishly, humbly and unpretentiously, without seeking to gain anything financially, and without being domineering or controlling.

So, the elder cares for the people, and he also leads, but he must do so in the right way and with the right attitude. The members of the church are then to "be subject" to such elders, but only in the sense of honouring them and cooperating, not with any kind of unquestioning obedience or subservience. At the same time, as we saw above, we are all meant to act with humility towards one another, i.e. to everyone whether we, or they, are elders or not. Apostle Peter also writes helpfully on this:

[1] So I exhort the elders among you, as a fellow elder and a witness of the sufferings of Christ, as well as a partaker in the glory that is going to be revealed: [2] shepherd the flock of God that is among you, exercising oversight, not under compulsion, but willingly, as God would have you; not for shameful gain, but eagerly; [3] not domineering over those in your charge, but being examples to the flock. [4] And when the chief Shepherd appears, you will receive the unfading crown of glory. [5] Likewise, you who are younger, be subject to the elders. Clothe yourselves, all of you, with humility toward one another, for "God opposes the proud but gives grace to the humble." [6] Humble yourselves, therefore, under the mighty hand of God so that at the proper time he may exalt you,

1 Peter 5:1-6 (ESV)

Whenever you come across haughtiness and pride in a leader it should immediately put you on your guard. It does not necessarily mean that that leader is wicked. He may just be foolish, immature and carnal. Perhaps he will grow out of such attitudes as he gets older. That is possible, though unlikely. It is far more likely that such a leader, having already developed an attitude of seeing himself as being above correction or instruction, may degenerate further and eventually become properly wicked.

That is one reason why you need to beware of, and draw back from, proud, arrogant, *clergy-minded* leaders. For more detail on this theme please refer to Book 8 in this series, entitled *'Biblical and unbiblical churches'*. Also see Book 6, entitled *"How to identify and handle wicked people"*. This is a very important issue, and one which you are bound to come across, especially if you ever start to question their teaching or decisions.

The wicked are brass-faced, defiant and bold, even when they are exposed and ought to be ashamed.

One of the most consistent features of the wicked is that they are *brass-faced*, even when it has been proved that they were lying or acting wrongly. Indeed, that is usually when they are at their most defiant. Therefore, brazen, unrepentant defiance and petulance are some of the classic signs of wickedness that we should be looking out for:

A wicked man puts on a bold face,
but the upright gives thought to his ways.
Proverbs 21:29 (ESV)

Shameless liars
incapable of blushing

This is the way of an adulterous woman:
She eats and wipes her mouth,
And says, "I have done no wrong."
Proverbs 30:20 (NASB)

O LORD, do not thy eyes look for truth?
Thou hast smitten them,
but they felt no anguish;
thou hast consumed them,
but they refused to take correction.
They have made their faces harder than rock;
they have refused to repent.
Jeremiah 5:3 (RSV)

I have confronted many wicked people, both religious and non-religious ones, partly because God gave me jobs that required it. I was a police officer and then a solicitor (lawyer) and I have also been an employer of a great many staff over the years. So I often needed to confront wicked people, firstly criminals, and then employees, who had been behaving badly. However, I had to do the same *within churches*, and was appalled to discover that *exactly the same techniques and attitudes* are found in wicked, false churchgoers, and even wicked church leaders, as in wicked staff, or even criminals.

If anything, the dishonesty and pride of falsely religious people is worse than that of the non-religious, which is actually not surprising, if one thinks about it. Their greater knowledge of God, and of the Bible, makes their behaviour all the more blameworthy, and makes them all the more accountable. It is also indicative of *hypocrisy* rather than just *ignorance*. The hardest thing to get used to is their inability to feel shame, even when they are publicly exposed. Not only do they not repent, *they do not even feel embarrassed.*

The only emotions they are likely to feel when they are caught red-handed are anger and resentment, not shame. They do not blush or hide themselves away in disgrace. On the contrary, most of the wicked people I confront, whether religious or non-religious, go the other way. Even after being exposed in their wrongdoing, they show their faces immediately, without any embarrassment at all, and continue to strut about as if nothing had happened. They also socialise openly, even amongst those who know what they have done, and display no trace of shame:

"...but the unjust knows no shame".
Zephaniah 3:5 (b) (RSV)

Were they ashamed when they committed abomination?
No, they were not at all ashamed;
they did not know how to blush.
Therefore they shall fall among the fallen;
when I punish them, they shall be overthrown,
says the LORD.
Jeremiah 8:12 (RSV)

The difference between being wicked and merely being sinful, as we all are

When the Bible speaks of the wicked it does not mean that those who are not *wicked* are therefore not *sinful*. Everybody is sinful, even the godliest, wisest person you know. King David makes it quite clear that no one is righteous or, in other words, that we are all sinners:

Enter not into judgment with your servant,
for no one living is righteous before you.
Psalm 143:2 (ESV)

the wicked is a
psychopath
sociopath

95

Therefore, even the prophet Daniel was a sinner, as were Moses, Job, Joseph, David and the apostle Paul. We all continue to have a flesh nature, even if we are a real Christian, and anything that we do in, or through, our flesh nature is sin:

5 For those who live according to the flesh set their minds on the things of the flesh, but those who live according to the Spirit set their minds on the things of the Spirit. 6 To set the mind on the flesh is death, but to set the mind on the Spirit is life and peace. 7 For the mind that is set on the flesh is hostile to God; it does not submit to God's law, indeed it cannot; 8 and those who are in the flesh cannot please God.

Romans 8:5-8 (RSV)

Basically, anything we do that does not proceed from faith is sin and therefore cannot please God, because it falls short of His perfect standard. Also, if it does not come from faith, then it must come from our own flesh, which automatically makes it sin, even if it looks good to us:

"......for whatever does not proceed from faith is sin"
Romans 14:23 (b) (RSV)

However, there are some levels and categories of sin which go farther than the ordinary sins we all commit, and which would require us to be reclassified as wicked, rather than ordinary sinners:

All wrongdoing is sin, but there is sin which is not mortal.
1 John 5:17 (RSV)

So, when we speak of wickedness we do not mean the ordinary sin, of which we are all guilty. It goes beyond that. The wicked sink to a lower level and yet, having said that, the things they do are still not necessarily spectacular. Most of the wicked look and sound very ordinary. Their key features are that they are *hard-hearted* and *devious* and that their *consciences are seared*. Moreover, they are not moved by pity, and they speak arrogantly:

They close their hearts to pity;
with their mouths they speak arrogantly.
Psalm 17:10 (RSV)

The wicked are dishonest and devious and tend also to be two-faced flatterers. They often say one thing to a person's face and another thing behind their back:

They speak falsehood to one another;
With flattering lips and with a double heart they speak.
Psalm 12:2 (NASB)

The wicked oppose both God and real Christians and they will react adversely to the Gospel, or even to being in the presence of a godly person. Frequently the wicked have no conscious understanding of *why* they do that. Their flesh nature, or 'old man', simply doesn't like the reborn human spirit in the godly person and therefore reacts against it by lashing out. However, it goes beyond just the flesh. A wicked person is also likely to be strongly influenced by demons.

The more wicked they become, the more they open themselves up to be influenced by demons. Therefore, when a wicked man meets a godly person then, even as they enter the room, before anyone says a word, irrational hostility may spring up in him. The demon accompanying him, or living within him, alerts him to the nature of that godly person and whips up his antagonism by getting his flesh to react more than it would ordinarily.

The wicked therefore go further in their sin than ordinary sinners and are much more hostile to the godly. Another key identifying feature is they are *not ashamed* of their sins, so they display them brazenly. In the end, if the wicked gain the upper hand in a society, their sin will be paraded openly, as we see in our day, where homosexuality is thrust at us aggressively and treated as if it was something to be proud of, rather than unnatural and perverted:

26 For this reason God gave them up to dishonorable passions. Their women exchanged natural relations for unnatural, 27 and the men likewise gave up natural relations with women and were consumed with passion for one another, men committing shameless acts with men and receiving in their own persons the due penalty for their error.

Romans 1:26-27 (RSV)

Likewise, abortion is aggressively and shamelessly proclaimed as a so-called '*human right*' when it is actually a terrible crime in God's eyes. The wicked therefore strut about assertively at times in history, such as our own day, when their evil values prevail and vileness is exalted. They can quickly sense when they are in the ascendant and that realisation emboldens them to go further, and do more, than they would in less wicked times:

The wicked strut about on every side
When vileness is exalted among the sons of men.
Psalm 12:8 (NASB)

If evil is on the rise in a nation, or in a business, the wicked have the confidence to show themselves openly, but in better times, the influence of godly people and of righteous laws restrains them and they keep a lower profile. So the wicked tend to come out when it is 'dark', like cockroaches, as the more committed Nazis, and their sympathisers, did in Germany in the 1930s and 1940s. When it was evil's hour in Germany, the wicked developed a greater willingness to come out into the open.   *(NB) Covid Correct - who does this job/state attract?*

They therefore joined the Nazi Party, SS, Gestapo and so on and publicly embraced Nazi ideology because they saw advantage in doing so and that they could gain from it. However, in May 1945, they all vanished overnight when Germany lost the war. It then became impossible to find anybody who would admit that they had ever been a Nazi, as if Germany had always been a nation of Hitler-opposers. The reality was that, from 1933-1945, there were advantages to being openly wicked, so those whose hearts were already wicked, or going that way, seized their opportunity.

The wicked are also recognisable by their capacity for hatred

Another identifying feature of the wicked is the fact that they have such a strong tendency to *hate*:

Consider how many are my foes, and with what violent hatred they hate me.
Psalm 25:19 (RSV)

Those who hate me without a cause are more than the hairs of my head......
Psalm 69:4(a) (NASB)

The wicked particularly hate the real God, the real Gospel, any real Christian and anything else which is genuinely biblical. Therefore, when any person is telling the truth about God or the Bible the wicked will instinctively lash out with irrational hatred and anger. You need to watch out for that, because it is one of the main ways in which you can identify them:

[19] But my foes are vigorous, they are mighty,
and many are those who hate me wrongfully.
[20] Those who render me evil for good
accuse me because I follow after good.
Psalm 38:19-20 (ESV)

The wicked draw the sword and bend their bows,
to bring down the poor and needy,
to slay those who walk uprightly;
Psalm 37:14 (RSV)

The wicked watches the righteous, and seeks to slay him.
Psalm 37:32 (RSV)

Ordinary sinners tend to be opportunistic, whereas the wicked conspire, scheme and plan their wicked deeds in advance.

The wicked also go beyond the ordinary sin that we all display in that they tend to *scheme and conspire* and much of their wrongdoing is *premeditated*. They plan their sins in advance and come to situations with a plot already worked out, by which they can more effectively lie, cheat or do harm. An ordinary sinner, who is not wicked but only foolish, simple, or even wise, tends to sin spontaneously, in unplanned ways, as and when opportunities or temptations arise. That is still sin, but it does not have the same devious or conspiratorial quality that the wicked display:

For, behold, the wicked bend the bow,
They make ready their arrow upon the string
To shoot in darkness at the upright in heart.
Psalm 11:2 (NASB)

14Behold, the wicked man conceives evil,
and is pregnant with mischief, and brings forth lies.
15He makes a pit, digging it out,
and falls into the hole which he has made.
Psalm 7:14-15 (RSV)

The wicked are hostile to the godly, partly due to the hatred they feel for them, but also because it suits the purposes of their demon guides to harm God's people. That is one reason why we need to pray for God's protection from the wicked. In the Psalms this is a frequent subject for prayer, especially in those that David wrote. He was a mighty man, but fully aware of the harm the wicked can do and of his need for God's protection from them. Accordingly, we need to pray as David did:

1Deliver me, O LORD,
from evil men; preserve me from violent men,
2 who plan evil things in their heart,
and stir up wars continually.
3They make their tongue sharp as a serpent's,
and under their lips is the poison of vipers.
4Guard me, O LORD, from the hands of the wicked;
preserve me from violent men,
who have planned to trip up my feet.
5Arrogant men have hidden a trap for me,
and with cords they have spread a net,
by the wayside they have set snares for me.
Psalm 140:1-5 (RSV)

99

Rescue me, O my God, from the hand of the wicked,
from the grasp of the unjust and cruel man.
                              Psalms 71:4 (ESV)

Vindicate me, O God, and defend my cause
    against an ungodly people,
from the deceitful and unjust man
    deliver me!
                              Psalm 43:1 (ESV)

It is far from obvious who the wicked are, especially those who are inside churches

The wicked are not always easy to recognise, especially if you are not yet a mature Christian, but even if you are. I have come across many people in my work as a policeman, and then as a lawyer, who were crude and foul-mouthed. Some were even persistent criminals. *Yet, they were not necessarily wicked*, contrary to what one might assume. As I got to know them better, underlying qualities of kindness, generosity and decency often emerged.

Conversely, there have been others who seemed respectable at first, such that I never guessed that they were wicked. But it later emerged that they were, because they were so hard-hearted, stingy, devious, malicious, and contemptuous towards God. Ironically, some of the criminals I have prosecuted have actually had better attitudes, and been more genuine, and certainly more humble, than some of the 'respectable', professional people I have dealt with.

You have to look beneath the surface and not be misled by mere appearances based on the person's status, wealth, education or cultured manners. Such things can easily cause you to misjudge them. One's view of a person can therefore alter, in either direction, as more facts emerge, and one certainly cannot judge by mere appearances, such as by a person's *job,* or *where they live.* Those things are irrelevant, and Jesus warned us against judging by such superficial factors:

Do not judge by appearances, but judge with right judgment."
                              John 7:24 (RSV)

Thus, one cannot just assume that a criminal or a prostitute is necessarily wicked. They might well be, but equally, *they may well not be.* On the other hand, we could meet a lawyer or banker, or even a church leader, and assume, by virtue of his role and status, that he cannot possibly be wicked, only to find out later that he is. Indeed, I can think of a number of church leaders I have known who turned out to be extremely wicked.

They were insecure and even paranoid, were motivated by personal ambition, had cold, hard hearts, and a lying tongue, and they regularly manipulated others. Moreover, so far as I could see, they had no fear of God. Thus they could comfortably preach a sermon, or lead worship, and then go on to lie, use and control people, and abuse their leadership position, without feeling any shame, or being the least bit uncomfortable. It is nothing new. Such men did exactly the same in Jeremiah's day:

11 "Both prophet and priest are ungodly; even in my house I have found their wickedness, says the LORD. 12 Therefore their way shall be to them like slippery paths in the darkness, into which they shall be driven and fall; for I will bring evil upon them in the year of their punishment, says the LORD. 13 In the prophets of Sama'ria I saw an unsavory thing: they prophesied by Ba'al and led my people Israel astray. 14 But in the prophets of Jerusalem I have seen a horrible thing: they commit adultery and walk in lies; they strengthen the hands of evildoers, so that no one turns from his wickedness; all of them have become like Sodom to me, and its inhabitants like Gomor'rah." 15 Therefore thus says the LORD of hosts concerning the prophets: "Behold, I will feed them with wormwood, and give them poisoned water to drink; for from the prophets of Jerusalem ungodliness has gone forth into all the land."

Jeremiah 23:11-15 (RSV)

Such carnal and apostate believers fall very clearly into the camp of the wicked, however 'respectable' they may appear to be and whatever leadership position they may occupy. Indeed, their wickedness is all the more intense, given that they know so much more than others and they are, therefore, more accountable, because they have transgressed more directly. In other words, they have sinned more in *knowingly disobeying God's Word* than an unbeliever does, who possibly had no knowledge to begin with, and had never even seen a Bible.

The sins of an outright unbeliever might well be more visible and obvious, but the sins of a false Christian or an apostate are probably more serious, from God's perspective. Therefore, we need to be more discerning and try to see people *as God sees them*. Otherwise we will miss the signs. For example, the gospel accounts show that not one of the other disciples of Jesus ever realised that Judas Iscariot was false. Not only did they not realise the scale of the problem, they did not seem to notice any problem with him at all:

21 When Jesus had said this, He became troubled in spirit, and testified and said, "Truly, truly, I say to you, that one of you will betray Me." 22 The disciples began looking at one another, at a loss to know of which one He was speaking.

John 13:21-22 (NASB)

101

One cannot even say that Judas had only degenerated into that condition of wickedness very shortly beforehand. On the contrary, we are told that he was already a thief, and had been stealing regularly since long before the time when he betrayed Jesus:

⁴But Judas Iscariot, one of His disciples, who was intending to betray Him, said, ⁵"Why was this perfume not sold for three hundred denarii and given to poor people?" ⁶Now he said this, not because he was concerned about the poor, but because he was a thief, and as he had the money box, he used to pilfer what was put into it.

John 12:4-6 (NASB)

The clear impression from Scripture is that Judas Iscariot had been false from the very outset and had never been a genuine believer at any stage. If so, we have to face the fact that he was, nevertheless, able to *appear* to be a believer and a disciple, and to keep up the act for three and a half years. And he was able to do that so convincingly that none of the disciples suspected him of anything. Note that when Jesus said that one of them would betray Him, none of them said or thought *"I bet it's Judas – I've always thought there was something not quite right about him".*

Far from it. We are told above that the disciples were *"at a loss to know of which one He was speaking".* Thus, we can conclude that they saw nothing wrong or unusual about Judas' speech or actions. He seemed to be one of them, and to be genuine. Therefore, if even the apostles could be so effectively deceived by Judas for three and a half years, and so unable to see that he was false, why should you assume that you are going to be able to identify false/bogus/apostate Christians easily? Sometimes they can be spotted straight away, because they stand out a mile. But very often they don't.

Perhaps the clearest indication of all that we see in Scripture as to the real nature of Judas is seen in John 6:70 when Jesus refers to him as *"a devil".* That was said approximately two years into Jesus' public ministry. So there was still at least a year left to go and yet, even at that early stage, Jesus plainly considered Judas to be false:

⁶⁶ After this many of his disciples drew back and no longer went about with him. ⁶⁷ Jesus said to the twelve, "Do you also wish to go away?" ⁶⁸ Simon Peter answered him, "Lord, to whom shall we go? You have the words of eternal life; ⁶⁹ and we have believed, and have come to know, that you are the Holy One of God." ⁷⁰ Jesus answered them, "Did I not choose you, the twelve, and one of you is a devil?" ⁷¹ He spoke of Judas the son of Simon Iscariot, for he, one of the twelve, was to betray him.

John 6:66-71 (RSV)

We cannot always easily, or immediately, discern the real nature of those with whom we are dealing, whether in churches or outside in the world. If we think we can then we are deluding ourselves. We can all get it very wrong, especially if we are too quick to form a view. Sometimes it takes a long time to correctly weigh up a person's character. Nevertheless, that is still what we need to *aim* to do and to begin to *learn how* to do. The only sure way of knowing what someone is like is to assess the *fruit* that their lives produce, and over a period of time, not a single day.

When you are eventually in a position to do that, you can end up being surprised in either direction. In the end, a man's wickedness shows itself in every part of his life. It is what he is. It defines him and the fruit that he produces can be identified and assessed, *provided you are looking for it.* If you aren't looking at all, then you won't see anything. But if you are sufficiently alert and vigilant you will eventually see the evidence, because the wicked cannot stop themselves from producing fruit that reflects what they really are. Their nature inevitably manifests itself in their actions:

"As the proverb of the ancients says, 'Out of the wicked comes forth wickedness';

1 Samuel 24:13(a) (NASB)

As with the fool, the wicked man ignores, and even rejects, God. Every wicked man starts off simple, even if only when he is a child, and then he gradually becomes a fool. But his decision to ignore God eventually leads him to slide further and further downwards into other kinds of sin. Eventually he moves into open and blatant rebellion. That is how a fool eventually 'graduates' into being a wicked man, which is where every man's life is heading if he ignores or rejects God, as it will always lead to degeneration.

For some people the pace of that decline intensifies at the point when God *"gives them up"* A time may come where they become so hardened and unresponsive that He effectively hands them over and allows them to sink as low as they wish to go. God eventually does that when He sees, after trying repeatedly to get them to repent, that they are determined not to acknowledge Him or to turn from their sin:

Therefore God gave them up in the lusts of their hearts to impurity, to the dishonoring of their bodies among themselves,

Romans 1:24 (RSV)

[28]And since they did not see fit to acknowledge God, God gave them up to a base mind and to improper conduct. [29] They were filled with all manner of

103

wickedness, evil, covetousness, malice. Full of envy, murder, strife, deceit, malignity, they are gossips,

Romans 1:28-29 (RSV)

These types of behaviour set out above are, in brief, the kind of things that the wicked do. But the point is *it all begins with ignoring God* and not *acknowledging* Him. That is all it takes for any of us to get on to this terrible downward spiral from being simple, to being a fool, and then eventually becoming wicked.

The non-religious wicked very rarely become Christians.

Experience indicates that there is very little hope for the wicked to be saved. By the time they have sunk to that level, they rarely ever choose to repent, because they have already travelled a long way downhill by then. However, no matter how low they sink, they could still repent *if they wished to*. They just *don't usually want to*. Therefore, the people who do choose to repent are mostly drawn from the ranks of the simple and, to a lesser extent, fools. But those who have gone so far as to join the ranks of the wicked seldom repent or change their ways. Neither will they understand God's Word, especially prophecy:

"Many will be purged, purified and refined, but the wicked will act wickedly; and none of the wicked will understand, but those who have insight will understand.

Daniel 12:10 (NASB)

Also, their lack of receptivity to the Gospel is partly because the wicked have no interest in, or respect for, the Bible, such that *"their ears are closed"*:

Salvation is far from the wicked,
for they do not seek thy statutes.
     Psalm 119:155 (RSV)

To whom shall I speak and give warning,
that they may hear?
Behold, their ears are closed,
they cannot listen;
behold, the word of the LORD is to them an object of scorn,
they take no pleasure in it.
     Jeremiah 6:10 (RSV)

The wicked man does not often choose to listen or respond, even when he is shown God's kindness, partly because he does not understand or respect goodness or mercy. These are alien concepts to him and he despises them. He wrongly assumes that they are signs of weakness and thus he will mistreat and disrespect those who show him kindness or generosity. The wicked man therefore deals wickedly, even when he is with the upright (the wise and godly) and he is oblivious to God's majesty, even when it is straight in front of him, as when we see the beauty of His Creation, or of His written Word:

Though the wicked is shown favour,
He does not learn righteousness;
He deals unjustly in the land of uprightness,
And does not perceive the majesty of the LORD.
                    Isaiah 26:10 (NASB)

Because of the way the wicked think and act, they are far away from God. However, it is also true to say that He is far from them, as He keeps the wicked at arm's length. That makes it even less likely that they will ever find God and be saved:

For though the LORD is high,
he regards the lowly;
but the haughty he knows from afar.
                    Psalm 138:6 (RSV)

Nevertheless, the fact remains that, until the moment we die, the offer of the Gospel is always available, even to the wickedest of people. If they want to, they can still repent and be saved, no matter how evil they have become. So, even though very few of them ever actually choose to accept that offer, it is still made. Therefore, we do need to share the Gospel with the wicked and must not keep it from them or assume that they would never respond. Occasionally they do repent and God is entirely willing to receive them, and save them, if they do. In fact, He is very eager to do so:

Let the wicked forsake his way
And the unrighteous man his thoughts;
And let him return to the LORD,
And He will have compassion on him,
And to our God,
For He will abundantly pardon.
                    Isaiah 55:7 (NASB)

[21] "But if the wicked man turns from all his sins which he has committed and observes all My statutes and practices justice and righteousness, he shall surely live; he shall not die. [22] All his transgressions which he has committed will not be remembered against him; because of his righteousness which he has practiced, he will live. [23] Do I have any pleasure in the death of the wicked,"

declares the Lord GOD, "rather than that he should turn from his ways and live?

Ezekiel 18:21-23 (NASB)

[30] "Therefore I will judge you, O house of Israel, each according to his conduct," declares the Lord GOD. "Repent and turn away from all your transgressions, so that iniquity may not become a stumbling block to you. [31] Cast away from you all your transgressions which you have committed and make yourselves a new heart and a new spirit! For why will you die, O house of Israel? [32] For I have no pleasure in the death of anyone who dies," declares the Lord GOD. "Therefore, repent and live."

Ezekiel 18:30-32 (NASB)

Perhaps the most famous example of wicked people being willing to repent comes from the book of Jonah. He went to Ninevah to tell the people of that city that God was about to destroy their city because of their wickedness. Surprisingly, the King of Ninevah chose to listen and to repent and he urged the whole city to do so as well. Amazingly, many of them did:

[4] Then Jonah began to go through the city one day's walk; and he cried out and said, "Yet forty days and Nineveh will be overthrown." [5] Then the people of Nineveh believed in God; and they called a fast and put on sackcloth from the greatest to the least of them. [6] When the word reached the king of Nineveh, he arose from his throne, laid aside his robe from him, covered himself with sackcloth and sat on the ashes. [7] He issued a proclamation and it said, "In Nineveh by the decree of the king and his nobles: Do not let man, beast, herd, or flock taste a thing. Do not let them eat or drink water. [8] But both man and beast must be covered with sackcloth; and let men call on God earnestly that each may turn from his wicked way and from the violence which is in his hands. [9] Who knows, God may turn and relent and withdraw His burning anger so that we will not perish."
[10] When God saw their deeds, that they turned from their wicked way, then God relented concerning the calamity which He had declared He would bring upon them. And He did not do it.

Jonah 3:4-10 (NASB)

The *religious* wicked rarely become real Christians, or regain their faith if they become apostate. They like their positions of power within churches and are too proud to repent.

In all my personal experience, I cannot think of even one falsely religious or apostate person that I have dealt with who has ever repented, changed and become a real Christian. The chances of a genuine repentance seem to be even lower amongst the religious wicked than with the unbelieving wicked. However, that ought not to surprise us. The writer to the Hebrews tells us that false religious people very rarely repent, or find their way back to having a real faith after having become apostate:

⁴For it is impossible to restore again to repentance those who have once been enlightened, who have tasted the heavenly gift, and have become partakers of the Holy Spirit, ⁵and have tasted the goodness of the word of God and the powers of the age to come, ⁶if they then commit apostasy, since they crucify the Son of God on their own account and hold him up to contempt. ⁷For land which has drunk the rain that often falls upon it, and brings forth vegetation useful to those for whose sake it is cultivated, receives a blessing from God. ⁸But if it bears thorns and thistles, it is worthless and near to being cursed; its end is to be burned.

Hebrews 6:4-8 (RSV)

In case anybody thinks that the wickedness of the religious wicked is less serious than that of the unbelieving wicked, or that God will not punish the religious wicked, consider this passage from Hebrews:

²⁶For if we sin deliberately after receiving the knowledge of the truth, there no longer remains a sacrifice for sins, ²⁷but a fearful prospect of judgment, and a fury of fire which will consume the adversaries. ²⁸A man who has violated the law of Moses dies without mercy at the testimony of two or three witnesses. ²⁹ How much worse punishment do you think will be deserved by the man who has spurned the Son of God, and profaned the blood of the covenant by which he was sanctified, and outraged the Spirit of grace? ³⁰ For we know him who said, "Vengeance is mine, I will repay." And again, "The Lord will judge his people." ³¹ It is a fearful thing to fall into the hands of the living God.

Hebrews 10:26-31 (RSV)

The passage above is clearly speaking of the Lake of Fire as being the punishment that awaits these people. Yet it is referring to people who *used to be Christians*. Indeed, there is every reason to conclude that they were *real* Christians, because we are told that they had '*receive[d] the knowledge of the truth*' and also that they had '*profaned the blood covenant by which he was sanctified*'. That last point is crucial. Nobody can even begin to be 'sanctified' until after they have previously been justified, i.e. forgiven and made righteous.

So the person being spoken of in Hebrews 10 must have been genuinely saved or born again to begin with. The point is that, even after they had received God's grace and blessing in that way, they then '*spurned the Son of God*' and '*outraged the Spirit of grace*'. Therefore we are dealing here with a situation where a genuinely saved Christian chooses to turn away from the truth and to become

107

apostate by speaking and acting in a manner which despises God's grace and dishonours His name.

But what makes it even more alarming is that there is nothing unusual or rare about this. *It is happening on a massive scale today in the Western churches.* More than any other thing, the falsely religious harden their hearts towards the Bible. Many of them ignore it and even those who do read parts of it are unmoved by it. They cannot see, or do not care, that it is calling on *them* to repent and change. They probably assume it is aimed at someone else. Then they harden their own hearts towards it, so that God's Word bounces off them and is not understood, or even noticed:

[12] They made their hearts like adamant lest they should hear the law and the words which the LORD of hosts had sent by his Spirit through the former prophets. Therefore great wrath came from the LORD of hosts. [13] "As I called, and they would not hear, so they called, and I would not hear," says the LORD of hosts,

Zechariah 7:12-13(RSV)

This passage too is clearly *speaking of people who claim to be believers.* That must be so, because we are told that their hardness towards God's Word results in Him refusing to hear their *prayers.* But they would not even attempt to pray in the first place unless they were religious, at least in some sense of the word, either genuinely or falsely.

What God will do to the wicked, both the falsely religious and the non-religious, in the present and in the future

Whether the wicked are falsely religious or non-religious, they will all come under God's judgment in this life. He will intervene in their lives to oppose them and to bring judgment and retribution on them, even while they are still alive:

[5] Him who slanders his neighbour secretly
I will destroy.
The man of haughty looks and arrogant heart
I will not endure.
[6] I will look with favour on the faithful in the land,
that they may dwell with me;
he who walks in the way that is blameless
shall minister to me.
[7] No man who practices deceit
shall dwell in my house;
no man who utters lies

shall continue in my presence.
⁸ Morning by morning I will destroy
all the wicked in the land,
cutting off all the evildoers
from the city of the LORD.
Psalm 101:5-8 (RSV)

¹Woe to those who devise wickedness and work evil on their beds! When the morning dawns, they perform it, because it is in the power of their hand. ²They covet fields and seize them, and houses, and take them away; they oppress a man and his house, a man and his inheritance. ³Therefore thus says the LORD: behold, against this family I am devising disaster, from which you cannot remove your necks, and you shall not walk haughtily, for it will be a time of disaster.

Micah 2:1-3 (ESV)

The wicked will inevitably receive God's opposition, but they generally have no idea that it is Him who is opposing them and bringing them to ruin and disaster. So, the wicked will eventually fall, in all sorts of ways, but they do not usually realise *why* they are stumbling:

But the way of the wicked is like deep darkness;
they do not know what makes them stumble.
Proverbs 4:19 (NIV)

To a very large extent it is the wicked person's own evil deeds which ensnare him and keep him trapped. In other words, he brings judgment upon himself by his own actions. I have witnessed that on countless occasions with people I have dealt with, especially employees. The things they do build up and eventually catch up with them and they are then ruined:

²² The evil deeds of the wicked ensnare them;
the cords of their sins hold them fast.
²³ For lack of discipline they will die,
led astray by their own great folly.
Proverbs 5:22-23 (NIV)

But a man who commits adultery has no sense;
whoever does so destroys himself.
Proverbs 6:32 (NIV)

Although very few people realise this, and even fewer speak of it, God also specifically *curses* those who steal and lie. He makes sure that they are opposed

109

and obstructed. In the end they will be cut off completely as a result of God's intervention in their lives:

³ Then he said to me, "This is the curse that goes out over the face of the whole land; for everyone who steals shall be cut off henceforth according to it, and everyone who swears falsely shall be cut off henceforth according to it. ⁴ I will send it forth, says the LORD of hosts, and it shall enter the house of the thief, and the house of him who swears falsely by my name; and it shall abide in his house and consume it, both timber and stones."

Zechariah 5:3-4 (RSV)

With some wicked people, God even chooses to end their lives early. An example of this is a man called Er, who was Judah's son. He was wicked and the Bible says the LORD "*slew him*":

But Er, Judah's first-born, was wicked in the sight of the LORD; and the LORD slew him

Genesis 38:7 (RSV)

We are not told what Er did, or how wicked he was, or how exactly God killed him. Perhaps it was through some illness. But the point is that *God did it* and He might choose to do the same with others too. It is certainly true that the wicked have shorter lives on average, because God deliberately shortens their lives, whereas He says that He prolongs the lives of those who fear Him and keep His commandments:

The fear of the LORD prolongs life,
But the years of the wicked will be shortened.
Proverbs 10:27 (NASB)

¹ My son, do not forget my teaching,
*   but let your heart keep my commandments,*
² for length of days and years of life
*   and peace they will add to you.*
Proverbs 3:1-2 (ESV)

That reduction of life span is partly a direct judgment upon them, but also it is a natural consequence of the ways in which they choose to live. For example, those who are violent will also encounter violence against themselves. People's own *lifestyle choices* have a major bearing on their life expectancy. We can clearly see that *sexual sin* is highly correlated with the contracting of serious diseases and cancers which can be fatal in themselves or shorten lives indirectly. The most striking example of all is *homosexual activity between men.*

110

The data gathered by insurance companies, based on health service figures, shows unmistakably that, on average, men who engage in homosexual sex have over 20 years taken off their life expectancy. Many die in their twenties, thirties and forties, such that, *on average* they tend not to live beyond their late fifties or early sixties. You might imagine that would be spoken about continually in the media, together with public information campaigns, just as we hear of research projects and surveys on the dangers of white sugar, fat, aspartame or smoking.

However, politicians and the media, and even doctors, do not have enough courage or integrity to say *anything* about the health consequences for homosexuals of their chosen lifestyle. There is a wall of silence and a news blackout, especially about their reduced life expectancy. These alarming statistics do not fit in with the politically correct ideology of the media or our governments and so they are simply not willing to publicise it. However, apostle Paul spoke of it very directly and identified it as a judgment from God. Paul says that homosexuals are:

"….receiving in their own persons the due penalty for their error"
Romans 1:27(b) (RSV)

We can do the maths for ourselves and see how the life expectancy of the wicked is shortened by simply adding up the average length of reigns of the wicked Kings of Israel and Judah, as compared to those of the good kings. There is a stark difference. The wicked ones almost all had short reigns and died young. It would seem that one of God's reasons for shortening their lives was to limit the amount of harm that they could do.

The biggest exception to that general rule was the wicked King Manasseh of Judah, who reigned for 52 years. However, he repented close to the end of his reign and was saved. He was also the grandfather of Josiah, the most faithful King of Judah. Those two facts may help to explain why God spared his life during the many years when he was doing so much evil. As we watch them now, it may not seem to us that the wicked are doing badly or suffering much in this life. In fact, it often seems that the opposite is the case:

³For I was envious of the arrogant,
when I saw the prosperity of the wicked.
⁴For they have no pangs;
their bodies are sound and sleek.
⁵ They are not in trouble as other men are;
they are not stricken like other men.
⁶ Therefore pride is their necklace;
violence covers them as a garment.
⁷Their eyes swell out with fatness,

111

their hearts overflow with follies.
[8] They scoff and speak with malice
; loftily they threaten oppression.
[9] They set their mouths against the heavens,
and their tongue struts through the earth.
[10] Therefore the people turn and praise them;
and find no fault in them.
[11] And they say, "How can God know?
Is there knowledge in the Most High?"
[12] Behold, these are the wicked;
always at ease, they increase in riches.
[13] All in vain have I kept my heart clean
and washed my hands in innocence.

Psalm 73:3-13 (RSV)

However, it is the way that things work out *in the end* that really counts. Whatever may happen in the short term, while God's judgment is being delayed, the end result is inevitably the same, and the wicked are swept away. Again, I will set out several passages, because so many Christians, even real ones, find it very hard to believe that God could really be so severe:

[16]But when I thought how to understand this,
it seemed to me a wearisome task,
[17] until I went into the sanctuary of God;
then I perceived their end.
[18] Truly thou dost set them in slippery places;
thou dost make them fall to ruin.
[19] How they are destroyed in a moment,
swept away utterly by terrors!
[20] They are like a dream when one awakes,
on awaking you despise their phantoms.

Psalm 73:16-20 (RSV)

For lo, those who are far from thee shall perish;
thou dost put an end to those who are false to thee.

Psalm73:27 (RSV)

[11] I will punish the world for its evil,
and the wicked for their iniquity;
I will put an end to the pomp of the arrogant,
and lay low the pompous pride of the ruthless.
[12] I will make people more rare than fine gold,
and mankind than the gold of Ophir.
[13] Therefore I will make the heavens tremble,

and the earth will be shaken out of its place,
at the wrath of the LORD of hosts
  in the day of his fierce anger.
                    Isaiah 13:11-13 (ESV)

For the LORD is enraged against all the nations,
  and furious against all their host;
  he has devoted them to destruction, has given them over for slaughter.
                    Isaiah 34:2 (ESV)

[31] The clamour will resound to the ends of the earth,
for the LORD has an indictment against the nations;
he is entering into judgment with all flesh,
and the wicked he will put to the sword,
declares the LORD.'
[32] "Thus says the LORD of hosts:
Behold, disaster is going forth
from nation to nation,
and a great tempest is stirring
from the farthest parts of the earth!
[33] "And those pierced by the LORD on that day shall extend from one end of the
earth to the other. They shall not be lamented, or gathered, or buried; they shall
be dung on the surface of the ground.
                    Jeremiah 25:31-33 (ESV)

[23] Behold the storm of the LORD!
Wrath has gone forth,
a whirling tempest;
it will burst upon the head of the wicked.
[24] The fierce anger of the LORD will not turn back
until he has executed and accomplished
the intentions of his mind.
In the latter days you will understand this.
                    Jeremiah 30:23-24 (ESV)

However, much it may seem that the wicked get away with things, and even profit
from their wrongdoing, there will inevitably come a time when God will confront
them and give back to them what they did to other people:

Woe to you, destroyer,
who yourself have not been destroyed;
you treacherous one,
with whom none has dealt treacherously!
When you have ceased to destroy,

you will be destroyed;
and when you have made an end of dealing treacherously,
you will be dealt with treacherously.

Isaiah 33:1 (RSV)

There is a 'cup of judgment' which is being prepared for the wicked. Usually they get to drink at least some of it in this life, though not always. However, absolutely all wicked people will, in the end, have to drink every last drop of it:

²At the set time which I appoint
 I will judge with equity.
³When the earth totters, and all its inhabitants,
it is I who keep steady its pillars.
⁴ I say to the boastful, "Do not boast,"
and to the wicked, "Do not lift up your horn;
⁵ do not lift up your horn on high,
or speak with insolent neck."
⁶ For not from the east or from the west
and not from the wilderness comes lifting up;
⁷ but it is God who executes judgment,
putting down one and lifting up another.

⁸ For in the hand of the LORD there is a cup,
with foaming wine, well mixed;
and he will pour a draught from it,
 and all the wicked of the earth
shall drain it down to the dregs.
⁹ But I will rejoice for ever,
I will sing praises to the God of Jacob.
¹⁰ All the horns of the wicked he will cut off,
but the horns of the righteous shall be exalted.

Psalm 75:2-10 (RSV)

The Bible is even blunter than that about what will happen to the wicked in the end. They will be sent to Sheol/Hell when they die. Moreover, there is no reason to suppose that that this is only referring to the non-religious wicked. It would seem clear that false, unrepentant, hard-hearted, apostate churchgoers, and especially insincere church leaders, will also face this dreadful fate:

¹³This is the fate of those who have foolish confidence,
 the end of those who are pleased with their portion.
 ¹⁴ Like sheep they are appointed for Sheol;
Death shall be their shepherd;
straight to the grave they descend,

114

and their form shall waste away;
Sheol shall be their home.
Psalm 49:13-14 (RSV)

The wicked shall be turned into hell,
And all the nations that forget God.
Psalm 9:17 (NKJV)

They will then be sent onwards from Hell to the Lake of Fire:

[11]Then I saw a great white throne and him who was seated on it. From his presence earth and sky fled away, and no place was found for them. [12]And I saw the dead, great and small, standing before the throne, and books were opened. Then another book was opened, which is the book of life. And the dead were judged by what was written in the books, according to what they had done.

[13]And the sea gave up the dead who were in it, Death and Hades gave up the dead who were in them, and they were judged, each one of them, according to what they had done. [14]Then Death and Hades were thrown into the lake of fire. This is the second death, the lake of fire. [15]and if anyone's name was not found written in the book of life, he was thrown into the lake of fire.
Revelation 20:11-15 (ESV)

Having said that, unless we repent and believe in Jesus Christ, that same end awaits *all of us, whatever category we may currently be in*. We are all sinners, even if we aren't wicked. It is a man's sin, and his rejection of Jesus, that takes him to Hell, and from there to the Lake of Fire. Nevertheless, the wicked are in that group and are all on their way to Hell, unless and until they repent. Their problem is that they do not care about that fact, even if they are told of it.

The wicked do not generally enjoy their lives, especially in middle age and old age, and they usually end up miserable. Though a wicked man's life may bring him some temporary pleasure, it never brings joy or peace, because a man's wickedness provokes God into opposing him. Therefore, God will not allow the wicked to have any real peace and deliberately intervenes in their lives to ensure that they don't:

"There is no peace for the wicked," says the LORD.
Isaiah 48:22 (NASB)

The LORD has made himself known; he has executed judgment;
the wicked are snared in the work of their own hands…….
Psalm 9:16 (ESV)

115

Many are the pangs of the wicked;
but steadfast love surrounds him who trusts in the LORD

Psalm 32:10 (RSV)

God is watching everything and testing everybody and He will make sure that the wicked encounter His opposition and judgment, either in this life, or after death, or both:

[4]The LORD is in his holy temple,
the LORD's throne is in heaven;
his eyes behold, his eyelids test,
the children of men.
[5]The LORD tests the righteous and the wicked,
and his soul hates him that loves violence.
[6]On the wicked he will rain coals of fire and brimstone;
a scorching wind shall be the portion of their cup.
[7]For the LORD is righteous, he loves righteous deeds;
the upright shall behold his face.

Psalm 11:4-7 (RSV)

I will punish the world for its evil, and the wicked for their iniquity; I will put an end to the pride of the arrogant, and lay low the haughtiness of the ruthless.

Isaiah 13:11 (RSV)

[10]The righteous will rejoice when he sees the vengeance;
he will bathe his feet in the blood of the wicked.
[11] Men will say, "Surely there is a reward for the righteous;
surely there is a God who judges on earth."

Psalm 58:10-11 (RSV)

Righteous Job, when speaking to his friends about the fate of the wicked, put it this way:

[13]"This is the portion of a wicked man with God, and the heritage that oppressors receive from the Almighty: [14]If his children are multiplied, it is for the sword, and his descendants have not enough bread. [15]Those who survive him the pestilence buries, and his widows do not weep. [16]Though he heap up silver like dust, and pile up clothing like clay, [17]he may pile it up, but the righteous will wear it, and the innocent will divide the silver. [18]He builds his house like a moth's, like a booth that a watchman makes. [19]He goes to bed rich, but will do so no more; he opens his eyes, and his wealth is gone. [20]Terrors overtake him like a flood; in the night a whirlwind carries him off. [21]The east wind lifts him up and he is gone; it sweeps him out of his place. [22]It hurls at him

without pity; he flees from its power in headlong flight. ²³*It claps its hands at*
him and hisses at him from its place.

Job 27:13-23 (ESV)

The wicked will tend to hate people who are righteous and godly.

The wicked frequently have a hatred for the wise and godly:

Bloodthirsty men hate one who is blameless,
and the wicked seek his life.
> *Proverbs 29:10 (RSV)*

They hate him who reproves in the gate,
And they abhor him who speaks with integrity.
> *Amos 5:10 (NASB)*

This hatred is often unconscious, because there is something about a godly person that sets a wicked person's teeth on edge, without him even knowing why he feels like that. A wicked man will often take an instant dislike to a godly person, for no apparent reason. In fact, a wicked man sees a righteous, godly person as an abomination, in just the same way as a righteous man sees an unjust or wicked man as an abomination:

An unjust man is an abomination to the righteous,
but he whose way is straight is an abomination to the wicked.
> *Proverbs 29:27 (RSV)*

Therefore, ironically the more blameless and innocent a person is, *the more they will be hated* by the wicked. Moreover, a wicked man cannot usually be won over or softened by kindness. On the contrary, he will have contempt for it. Goodness makes no sense to the wicked. They see it as weakness and it only increases their malice.

The wicked plots against the righteous
And gnashes at him with his teeth.
> *Psalm 37:12 (NASB)*

The starkest example of how the wicked hate the righteous is the treatment given to Jesus as He died on the cross. He was surrounded by wicked men and He could see their malice towards Him, even as He was giving His life for them. No person has ever been more blameless, but nobody has ever been more hated than He was. If they treated Jesus that way, they will hate you too. If even His goodness could not melt their hard hearts, yours is unlikely to. In my own life I have treated some people well, and have helped them, but they hated me in return.

Part of that could be explained by my being an employer and a boss, but not all of it, and certainly not the extreme intensity. Besides, it had already arisen many times, long before I ever became a boss. It comes from deep within the heart of the wicked person. They *"hate the light"* because it exposes their own evil nature and because the very life of a godly person transmits an unspoken rebuke to them. Therefore, if a person is wicked they will react against anybody whose life is a light.

However, every Christian is meant to be a source of salt and light. If they are, then the way they live lights up the darkness, whether at home or at work. The light that their life gives off is, in itself, a kind of unspoken rebuke to the wicked. It convicts him of his wickedness and he sees that as an affront. The wicked do not want their evil deeds to be exposed, or for them to be shown to be in the wrong. Therefore, they avoid Christians if they can, and attack them if they can't:

[19]And this is the judgment: the light has come into the world, and people loved the darkness rather than the light because their works were evil. [20]For everyone who does wicked things hates the light and does not come to the light, lest his works should be exposed. [21]But whoever does what is true comes to the light, so that it may be clearly seen that his works have been carried out in God."
John 3:19-21 (ESV)

[15]But at my stumbling they gathered in glee,
they gathered together against me;
cripples whom I knew not slandered me without ceasing;
[16]they impiously mocked more and more,
gnashing at me with their teeth.
Psalm 35:15-16 (RSV)

A righteous person being in the room can cause the wicked man to feel rebuked, *even if he doesn't say a word*. The wicked man feels told off because the contrast between his own life and that of the godly person is so apparent that it irritates him and he may therefore lash out in an unprovoked verbal blast.

A false, apostate Christian hates the true Gospel and any real Christian who speaks of it, or demonstrates it in his life.

If anything, the hostility manifested towards real Christians by false Christians is greater than that which comes from outright unbelievers. I have been in many discussions and debates with unbelievers, including atheists and I have generally found them to be less discourteous. When I was involved in an evangelistic ministry to students, in my twenties, I knocked on literally hundreds of doors on campus and had countless conversations.

Most atheists were quite happy to talk and argue, whereas I have often found that falsely religious and apostate people cannot cope with any debate. They are more likely to lose their temper and shut the discussion down than unbelievers are, especially where they are out of their depth or are losing the argument. Falsely religious people also cannot cope with being challenged or corrected about what they believe. Therefore, in the main, I have found them less open-minded, and more proud, than atheists are.

That said, things have been changing over the past 20 years or so and there is a growing wave of militant political correctness which has the same aim of silencing any opposition to itself. But those who act in that way, even if they are not religious, are only doing the same as the religious wicked have always done. Even the worst of them are no worse than the popes who burned the evangelical believers who chose to leave the Roman Catholic church when they realised how corrupt and unbiblical it is.

Do not 'cast your pearls before swine'.

Here is a hard lesson about dealing with fools, and especially the wicked, that I have had to learn. This is how Jesus put it:

"Do not give what is holy to dogs, and do not throw your pearls before swine, or they will trample them under their feet, and turn and tear you to pieces.
Matthew 7:6 (NASB)

Though it sounds a little harsh, this is a practical and realistic statement. Jesus is telling us to recognise that some of the people with whom we come into contact are going to be callous scoffers and mockers, with no sensitivity or respect. They care nothing for God, or the Bible, or for the precious things that Jesus came to do for us or to teach us. They are therefore fools, and Solomon tells us that fools will despise your words of wisdom:

Do not speak in the hearing of a fool,
for he will despise the wisdom of your words.
Proverbs 23:9 (RSV)

So, we must not go out into the unbelieving world in a naïve manner, sharing every precious truth with wicked people whose hearts are as hard as stone and who have no respect for the Bible. They will take the truth that we speak and

119

trample it under their feet, as a pig would do if we threw pearls on the ground in front of it. So how does this principle work out in practice? What should we say and what should we avoid saying and to whom? It doesn't mean that we should never discuss Jesus or never share the Gospel with unbelievers. We need to do that, or they can never be saved.

It means that there are certain truths or experiences which are *so intimate and precious,* we should not discuss them in front of scoffers whose hearts are hard and flippant. Reserve such precious things for that minority of people who are wise, or at least simple. When speaking to scoffers, whether wicked or foolish, our message needs to be less intimate. It needs to focus on sin, judgment and the Lake of Fire, and on how to repent and be saved through what Jesus did on the cross. Unless people are willing to listen to such things as those, don't go any further. Don't share more intimate truths unless the situation is exceptional.

If you do so, they will only abuse you, disrespect what you say, and even leave you feeling violated. However, we certainly *should* share the Gospel with the wicked and tell them of their need to repent and be saved. Never write them off or assume they will never respond. There is always that chance, however small, that they might. Neither should we ever fear them or be intimidated into silence. On the contrary, the wicked need to hear the Gospel just as much as every other person does. Moreover, God will hold us accountable if we do not warn the people whom He wants us to warn, which includes the wicked:

[8] When I say to the wicked, 'O wicked man, you will surely die,' and you do not speak to warn the wicked from his way, that wicked man shall die in his iniquity, but his blood I will require from your hand. [9] But if you on your part warn a wicked man to turn from his way and he does not turn from his way, he will die in his iniquity, but you have delivered your life.

Ezekiel 33:8-9 (NASB)

How should we handle the wicked and in what ways should we pray about, or even against, them?

In this chapter we have merely begun to examine and define the wicked, and to describe how they operate. The question then is how to handle them, and defend ourselves from them, without becoming like them ourselves. In particular, one question I have grappled with for years is how we ought to pray about the wicked. Can we pray *against* them using *'imprecatory'* prayers, whereby we ask God to defeat, and even destroy, them as Moses and many others did? Here is an example of how Moses did this, but King David also prayed in the same way, as did many others:

120

And whenever the ark set out, Moses said, "Arise, O LORD, and let thy enemies be scattered; and let them that hate thee flee before thee."

Numbers 10:35 (RSV)

These are all very big questions which require detailed responses. I have attempted to provide some answers in Book Six entitled *"How to identify and handle wicked people"* and would refer you to that to take this subject further. It sets out a fuller explanation of what the Bible says about dealing with the wicked, as well as a lot of practical examples and advice from my own personal experience. There is also a lengthy chapter on 'imprecatory' prayer, which is yet another of the many taboo subjects that are hardly ever mentioned, let alone taught on, in most churches today.

CHAPTER 5

THE WISE

There was a man in the land of Uz whose name was Job, and that man was blameless and upright, one who feared God and turned away from evil.
Job 1:1 (ESV)

The merciful man does himself good,
But the cruel man does himself harm.
Proverbs 11:17 (NASB)

A wise son accepts his father's discipline,
But a scoffer does not listen to rebuke.
Proverbs 13:1 (NASB)

Folly is a joy to him who lacks sense,
but a man of understanding walks straight ahead.
Proverbs 15:21 (ESV)

Listen to advice and accept instruction,
that you may gain wisdom for the future.
Proverbs 19:20 (RSV)

A good name is to be more desired than great wealth,
Favor is better than silver and gold.
Proverbs 22:1 (NASB)

Wisdom strengthens a wise man more than ten rulers who are in a city.
Ecclesiastes 7:19 (NASB)

".... Do not be wise in your own estimation."
Romans 12:16(b) (NASB)

A rebuke goes deeper into a man of understanding
than a hundred blows into a fool.
Proverbs 17:10 (RSV)

The beginning of wisdom is this: Get wisdom.
Though it cost all you have, get understanding.
Proverbs 4:7 (NIV)

And he said to man,
'Behold, the fear of the Lord, that is wisdom,
and to turn away from evil is understanding.'"
Job 28:28 (ESV)

Nobody is 100% wise, or 100% anything else

Nobody is ever 100% wise. Even those whom the Bible would classify as wise are not wise all the time, or in every aspect of their character or conduct. Therefore, in general terms, the wise are those people who:

a) are genuine Christians - this is the first and most vital requirement, on which all the others depend

b) fear God and take the Bible seriously - we cannot get any further up the wisdom scale if we don't

c) try to think the same way God thinks

d) value what God values

e) want what God wants

f) pursue knowledge and understanding

g) spend time with wise people and imitate them

Alternative descriptions of the wise - the 'godly', 'upright', 'blameless', 'God-fearing' and 'righteous'

The wise are also referred to in the Bible as the *godly*, the *upright*, the *blameless* the *God-fearing* and the *righteous*. These alternative phrases are used interchangeably as different names for, or characteristics of, the same group. They express different aspects of what it means to be wise. God sees this group as precious and He protects and blesses them:

But know that the LORD has set apart the godly for himself;
the LORD hears when I call to him.
Psalm 4:3 (RSV)

For you bless the righteous, O LORD;
you cover him with favor as with a shield.
Psalm 5:12 (ESV)

Cast your burden on the LORD,
and he will sustain you;
he will never permit the righteous to be moved.
                    Psalm 55:22 (RSV)

[10]His delight is not in the strength of the horse,
nor his pleasure in the legs of a man;
[11]but the LORD takes pleasure in those who fear him,
in those who hope in his steadfast love.
                    Psalm 147:10-11 (RSV)

[11]But let all who take refuge in thee rejoice,
let them ever sing for joy; and do thou defend them,
that those who love thy name may exult in thee.
[12]For thou dost bless the righteous, O LORD;
thou dost cover him with favour as with a shield.
                    Psalm 5:11-12 (NIV) ? No!

[18]The LORD is near to all who call upon him,
to all who call upon him in truth.
[19]He fulfils the desire of all who fear him,
he also hears their cry, and saves them.
[20]The LORD preserves all who love him;
but all the wicked he will destroy.
                    Psalm 145:18-20 (RSV)

For the eyes of the Lord are upon the righteous,
and his ears are open to their prayer.
But the face of the Lord is against those that do evil."
                    1 Peter 3:12 (RSV)

Wise people seek to acquire ever more knowledge and understanding of God and His Word by diligently and persistently studying the Bible and putting it into practice. Anyone prepared to do that, for a sufficiently long period, will inevitably become wise. In fact, even our natural cleverness or IQ will increase if we study the Bible. It has a way of elevating people in every sense, including intellectually. That is why there has been such an explosion of learning and scientific achievement since the Reformation of the sixteenth century.

At that time study of the Bible began to take place on a much wider basis in countries such as Britain, Holland, Germany, Czechoslovakia, Scandinavia and Switzerland (and later America). The growing knowledge of the Bible literally transformed those nations in a host of ways. It was even the foundation for the industrial revolution of the eighteenth and nineteenth centuries and for the

125

technological and communications revolution of the twentieth century. However, for the same reasons, the widespread abandonment of the Bible in recent decades has resulted in the catastrophic 'dumbing down' of our generation, which we are now witnessing.

What does wisdom consist of?

Let's look at just a few of the many passages from the book of Proverbs in which the general subject of wisdom is discussed. Note the various words used to define or illustrate what it is and what it consists of. Those are all needed because wisdom is a multi-faceted thing:

[1]The proverbs of Solomon,
son of David, king of Israel:
[2]To know wisdom and instruction,
to understand words of insight,
[3]to receive instruction in wise dealing,
in righteousness, justice, and equity;
[4]to give prudence to the simple,
knowledge and discretion to the youth--
[5]Let the wise hear and increase in learning,
and the one who understands obtain guidance,
[6]to understand a proverb and a saying,
the words of the wise and their riddles.
[7]The fear of the LORD is the beginning of knowledge;
fools despise wisdom and instruction.
[8]Hear, my son, your father's instruction,
and forsake not your mother's teaching,
[9]for they are a graceful garland for your head
and pendants for your neck.
                    Proverbs 1:1-9 (ESV)

[1]My son, do not forget my teaching,
but let your heart keep my commandments,
[2]for length of days and years of life and peace they will add to you.
[3]Let not steadfast love and faithfulness forsake you;
bind them around your neck;
write them on the tablet of your heart.
[4]So you will find favour and good success
in the sight of God and man.
[5]Trust in the LORD with all your heart,
and do not lean on your own understanding.
[6]In all your ways acknowledge him,

and he will make straight your paths.
7Be not wise in your own eyes; fear the LORD,
and turn away from evil.
8It will be healing to your flesh and refreshment to your bones.

Proverbs 3:1-8 (ESV)

12"I, wisdom, dwell with prudence,
And I find knowledge and discretion.
13"The fear of the LORD is to hate evil;
Pride and arrogance and the evil way
And the perverted mouth, I hate.

Proverbs 8:12-13 (NASB)

The main ingredients of wisdom are knowledge, understanding, insight, discretion, prudence, discernment and the fear of God.

These seven words or concepts are mentioned again and again, whenever the Bible speaks about what wisdom is. The word *wisdom* is an umbrella term and is made up of all of these seven ingredients or factors combined. Let us therefore examine each word in turn and attempt to define them.

Knowledge

By this we mean factual information of almost every kind, particularly knowledge of what the Bible says, from beginning to end, on every theme, issue, doctrine or point. The most important knowledge is of who God is, what He is like, what He thinks, and what He requires of us. If we learn about Him and His holiness, goodness, righteousness and so on, then we will then be in the right position to start to learn the truth about ourselves, especially in regard to our sin. We will also learn how to deal with other people and with the situations we face in life. Therefore, the Psalmist asked God to give him knowledge:

Teach me good judgment and knowledge,
* for I believe in your commandments.*

Psalm 119:66 (ESV)

The starting point is that we need knowledge of *what God says* on all these things, rather than what the unsaved world says, or our own opinions. I have always had an insatiable desire for knowledge and information. This intensified when I became a Christian. I studied the Bible and read huge numbers of books and commentaries. When older Christians saw me doing this some tried to put me down and advised me not to be so diligently studious. They even tried to quote apostle Paul in support of their argument, saying that *"knowledge puffs up"*:

Now concerning food offered to idols: we know that "all of us possess knowledge." "Knowledge" puffs up, but love builds up.

1 Corinthians 8:1 (RSV)

I felt deflated by their remarks, which they probably intended me to be, because an insecure Christian can get very threatened by a younger believer who is rapidly gaining knowledge. Therefore, they wanted to bring me down a peg or two. They had a point, in one sense, as knowledge *by itself,* if not accompanied by love, and the other 'ingredients' of wisdom, can cause a person to puff up with pride. However, the remedy for that is not to avoid knowledge, but to grow in love, and other aspects of wisdom, *in addition* to acquiring knowledge, not *instead of* doing so.

The way they spoke suggested that they saw knowledge and love as being mutually exclusive alternatives, as if we can choose to have either one, or the other, but not both. That is not what apostle Paul meant and he would be horrified at the idea of anybody taking him to mean that, or assuming that he was speaking against knowledge in any way. Knowledge is good, which is why Paul and all the apostles and prophets spent their lives dispensing it and urging us to acquire it.

The point is simply that we are not meant to pursue knowledge *alone,* and then to stop there, without *also* seeking to develop many other qualities and features in our character. We obviously need other things in addition. Nevertheless, knowledge is the first ingredient which God gives us as He seeks to develop our wisdom. Therefore we have to begin there, as there is no other place to begin.

Understanding

— Not simply 'know' but comprehend at a deep level — having 'thought through' - Perspective & Proportion PLACE/Position

Understanding is the next stage. It means to take that knowledge and to begin to absorb it more deeply because, in addition to knowing objective facts, we also need to see *why* those things are true, *how* they operate, and why they matter. In addition to that, it means having a grasp of the meaning, significance, and practical application of the information that we have learned about God, ourselves and others and then supplementing our knowledge with love and also with all the other fruit of the Holy Spirit.

We can then see facts, and also other people, in a deeper, wider, and more rounded context. Then the truths and principles that we learn from God's Word, and also from our experience, will fit together better, make more sense, and be held in a proper balance. Moses speaks of how we can gain understanding from learning and obeying God's commands. Therefore, *obeying* is an essential part of the process. We can't get understanding by merely reading God's Word, without putting it into practice:

⁵ See, I have taught you statutes and rules, as the LORD my God commanded me, that you should do them in the land that you are entering to take possession of it. ⁶ Keep them and do them, for that will be your wisdom and your understanding in the sight of the peoples, who, when they hear all these statutes, will say, 'Surely this great nation is a wise and understanding people.'
Deuteronomy 4:5-6 (ESV)

So, obeying God's commands will increase our understanding even if, to begin with, we have no desire to obey but do it solely by willpower and resolve. However, obedience leads to increased understanding, and as our understanding increases, so too will our willingness, and even our desire, to obey. The writer of Psalm 119 ended up with such a longing for understanding that he asked God for it, even though it is plain that he already had a great deal of understanding. That must be so, or he could not have written Psalm 119:

Give me understanding, that I may keep your law
and observe it with my whole heart.
Psalms 119:34 (ESV)

Insight

Insight is a form of understanding, but one which operates in a more specific way. We will be given *a flash of inspired understanding* which enables us to take the knowledge and understanding that we have learned, and apply them to the particular situation or issue that we are dealing with. Or a person might suddenly see a deeper meaning to a particular verse in the Bible, or realise how it relates to some other verse. That may form a connection which reveals something else, or a deeper level of meaning.

One might also be given an insight into the nature of another person, or a difficulty that we face, or how best to approach them or it. I found that regularly in my work as a lawyer. There would be a problem, either for a client, or a colleague, and it seemed insoluble. Then I would suddenly get an insight or a flash of inspiration, which seemed to come from nowhere. It probably comes from a sudden realisation of how to apply my accumulated reservoir of knowledge and understanding to the specific person or situation that I am dealing with.

That insight then unlocks or solves the problem. However, insights can also be *given* to us because, in addition to those that we acquire through study, reflection

129

and meditating on Scripture, God Himself will speak into the mind of a person who has taken the trouble to study the Bible. He will provide the necessary flashes of inspiration, or connections, so as to 'join up the dots' and enable that person to understand a point more deeply, especially in relation to an issue or problem they are studying.

Another vital form of insight is where God gives us specific understanding of our own sinfulness or of deficiencies in our character, of which we were previously unaware. Indeed, we may well have been blind to it until now, but then God suddenly provides illumination, like a camera flash, which reveals the sin or fault and enables us to see it at last. This is a precious discovery and can enable us to begin to take steps to change. Therefore, we should keep asking God to give us such insights, and on a regular basis.

Discretion

Appropriateness

Discretion involves having a sensitivity and awareness about whether, and also when, to say a thing, or to take action, or to become involved in something. One learns over the years how right King Solomon was when he said:

For everything there is a season, and a time for every matter under heaven.
Ecclesiastes 3:1 (ESV)

In particular, he goes on to say that there is:

[7]a time to tear, and a time to sew; a time to keep silence, and a time to speak; [8]a time to love, and a time to hate; a time for war, and a time for peace.
Ecclesiastes 3:7-8 (ESV)

Discretion is primarily that part of wisdom which has to do with *knowing what the time is* and whether it is a *"time to kill"* or a *"time to heal"*, a *"time to plant"*, or a *"time to pluck up what is planted"*. The hardest one of all is knowing the difference between *"a time to keep silence"* and *"a time to speak"*. Which of us has not got that wrong countless times, speaking when it would have been wiser to say nothing, and saying nothing when it would have been wiser to speak? As we grow in discretion we make fewer mistakes and also gain more tact and a better sense of timing.

We also develop a sensitivity as to what is appropriate and what biblical principles are applicable to that specific situation or issue. A large part of the book of Proverbs consists of advice which is along the lines of *"On the one hand, bear this principle in mind. But, on the other hand, also bear this opposite, counter-balancing principle in mind. Then hold them both in a healthy tension and apply*

Wisdom is under NO Illusion 130

about the wickedness of man;
is unsurpassed by even extreme evil
Expect evil always from any & every quarter

one, or other, or both, at the right time and in the right proportions". That's not what the Bible actually says, but it's my own paraphrase of Solomon's general approach.

We are meant to look at issues from every angle and examine all the pros and cons as to whether we should take a particular approach or some other approach instead, which might even be the very opposite, depending on the circumstances of the case. We also need to consider whether to say or do that thing openly, or more quietly and discreetly. Discretion was something I used to lack. I had a default-setting to speak frankly all the time, even when it was unwise to do so. I have a lot more discretion now, but I need even more.

Prudence

By prudence we mean carefulness, caution and a proper appreciation of the risks and hazards that may lie ahead for ourselves, or others, if we take a particular route. It involves being able to figure out, ahead of time, the possible unintended consequences and side-effects of a particular course of action. Then, by foreseeing them, we may be able to prevent them happening. Alternatively, if such things cannot be prevented by timely intervention, a prudent person will delay taking action until the time is more suitable. Or he may even refrain from acting altogether. Solomon makes these observations:

O simple ones, learn prudence;
O foolish men, pay attention.
Proverbs 8:5 (RSV)

The prudent sees danger and hides himself,
but the simple go on and suffer for it.
Proverbs 22:3 (ESV)

The vexation of a fool is known at once,
but the prudent man ignores an insult.
Proverbs 12:16 (RSV)

[15] The simple believes everything,
but the prudent gives thought to his steps.
[16] One who is wise is cautious and turns away from evil,
but a fool is reckless and careless.
[17] A man of quick temper acts foolishly,
and a man of evil devices is hated.
[18] The simple inherit folly,
but the prudent are crowned with knowledge.
Proverbs 14:15-18 (ESV)

131

A prudent person on a team or committee can make a tremendously valuable contribution. They can often foresee, and then prevent, issues and outcomes which the others on that committee would never have considered. Others, who lack this quality, may wrongly regard a prudent person as negative, or even obstructive, and be exasperated by them. Nevertheless, provided it is genuine prudence, and not mere pessimism or cynicism, it is a highly valuable quality and is one of the component parts of wisdom. As for how we get prudence, the main source is God's Word.

The Bible alerts us, ahead of time, to countless issues and hazards. It also warns us of various character-types and the kinds of people we are likely to meet, including fools and also the wicked. That enables us to be under no illusions about the nature of other people's hearts and what we can expect of them. That gives us general material to bear in mind as we ponder a specific situation. However, prudence also comes from living in close fellowship with God and hearing the still, small voice of the Holy Spirit, nudging and warning us about the dangers we face and difficulties that lie ahead.

Discernment

Discernment means the ability to tell the difference between two things which may look or sound similar, but are actually different. It also enables us to gauge the real nature of a person, situation, proposal or idea and to sense whether it is from God, men, or a demon. We are presented daily with people, opportunities and proposals which may look good and claim to be good. But are they really? They could just be based on misguided human reasoning. You could even be being enticed into a trap which a person or a demon has set up for you.

Then again, it could be a God-given opportunity and the person concerned could be a genuine friend, whom God has provided for you. An example of a person displaying discernment is Nehemiah, when he was being deceived by Shemaiah. It was at a time when enemies, led by Sanballat and Tobiah, were doing everything they could to stop Nehemiah and his men from rebuilding the walls of Jerusalem. They tried one trick after another and various threats. But, each time, Nehemiah saw through them and refused to be intimidated or diverted from his task.

Then they sent Shemaiah, a supposedly friendly figure, and paid him to try to persuade Nehemiah to take shelter in the Temple. They wanted him to hide away rather than continue the rebuilding work. However, Nehemiah also saw through Shemaiah, just as he had the others. He discerned that his motives were false and that he had been hired by Sanballat and Tobiah to try to get him to stop the work. Nehemiah also realised that Shemaiah was trying to discredit his good name, hoping to be able to accuse him afterwards of having run away from danger:

132

¹⁰ Now when I went into the house of Shemaiah the son of Delaiah, son of Mehetabel, who was confined to his home, he said, "Let us meet together in the house of God, within the temple. Let us close the doors of the temple, for they are coming to kill you. They are coming to kill you by night." ¹¹ But I said, "Should such a man as I run away? And what man such as I could go into the temple and live? I will not go in." ¹² And I understood and saw that God had not sent him, but he had pronounced the prophecy against me because Tobiah and Sanballat had hired him. ¹³ For this purpose he was hired, that I should be afraid and act in this way and sin, and so they could give me a bad name in order to taunt me.

Nehemiah 6:10-13 (ESV)

Nehemiah discerned Shemaiah's real motives, despite the fact that he was a fellow Jew and purported to be a friend. He ought, therefore, on the face of it, to have been trustworthy. But Nehemiah did not rely on appearances and neither can you if you want to develop discernment. Like him, we need to be able to know the real facts of the situation we are in and the real nature and motives of the person we are dealing with. We cannot afford to go through life taking random chances and hoping for the best.

Discernment is not just a useful optional extra for those who want it. God *commands* us to develop it and has also given us what we need in order to do so. We therefore need to saturate ourselves in the Bible so that we have a sound knowledge of Scripture. But, in addition to that general form of discernment, which can be learned, we also need the gift of the *discerning of spirits*. Or you could call it the ability to *distinguish between spirits*, one of the gifts of the Holy Spirit, of which apostle Paul speaks:

⁸For to one is given the word of wisdom through the Spirit, and to another the word of knowledge according to the same Spirit; ⁹to another faith by the same Spirit, and to another gifts of healing by the one Spirit, ¹⁰and to another the effecting of miracles, and to another prophecy, and to another the distinguishing of spirits, to another various kinds of tongues, and to another the interpretation of tongues.

1 Corinthians 12:8-10 (NASB)

We therefore need *both* thorough knowledge of the Bible *and* also to receive the gifts of the Holy Spirit (See chapter 17 in Book 1). Sadly, many Christians in the West have neither. Or, at most, they only have one. Their denominational traditions ignore, or even oppose, either the Scriptures, or the gifts of the Holy Spirit, or both. Many Evangelicals honour the Bible, up to a point, but are wary of the gifts of the Holy Spirit. Conversely, many Charismatics accept the gifts of the Holy Spirit, but neglect the Bible. Both of those approaches are incomplete and misguided.

The Fear of God — *Submission to God !*

I could have put this first in the list of ingredients of wisdom, because the Bible describes the *fear of God*, or the *fear of the LORD*, as the vital first requirement that we need if we are to become wise. That's because if we don't respect God properly we will not give Him, or His Word, the devoted attention that we need to give. It is no exaggeration therefore to say that we must *fear* God. Neither is it just poetic language. That really is what God means, because nothing less than fear will produce the right attitude in us. Note what Job says about this:

And he said to man,
'Behold, the fear of the Lord, that is wisdom;
and to depart from evil is understanding.'
Job 28:28 (RSV)

The Psalmist also says that the mountains, seas and rivers, and even the very Earth itself, fear God and tremble because of Him:

⁵ Why was it, sea, that you fled?
Why, Jordan, did you turn back?
⁶ Why, mountains, did you leap like rams,
you hills, like lambs?
⁷ Tremble, earth, at the presence of the Lord,
at the presence of the God of Jacob,
Psalm 114:5-7 (NIV)

fear & trembling

Likewise, the Psalmist himself felt fear towards *God* and His *judgment* and towards His *Word* in particular:

My flesh trembles for fear of you,
and I am afraid of your judgments.
Psalm 119:120 (ESV)

Rulers persecute me without cause,
but my heart trembles at your word.
Psalm 119:161 (NIV)

Mere respect alone is not enough. There must also be genuine reverence and awe. King David literally feared God. It was not just metaphorical. He actually feared God's judgment coming upon him. We see an example of that fear after Uzzah was struck dead by God for having put out his hand to touch the Ark of the Covenant, which he ought not to have done:

⁹ And when they came to the threshing floor of Chidon, Uzzah put out his hand to take hold of the ark, for the oxen stumbled. ¹⁰ And the anger of the LORD was kindled against Uzzah, and he struck him down because he put out his hand to the ark, and he died there before God.

1 Chronicles 13:9-10 (ESV)

¹² And David was afraid of God that day, and he said, "How can I bring the ark of God home to me?" ¹³ So David did not take the ark home into the city of David, but took it aside to the house of Obed-edom the Gittite.

1 Chronicles 13:12-13 (ESV)

Another example of King David having a literal fear of God was when he, and others, saw *the angel of the LORD* at the site of the threshing floor of Ornan the Jebusite. This was a pre-appearance, in bodily form, of the *Son of God Himself,* the Second Person of the Trinity, also known as the angel of the LORD, which explains why David feared Him:

¹⁴ So the LORD sent a pestilence on Israel, and 70,000 men of Israel fell. ¹⁵ And God sent the angel to Jerusalem to destroy it, but as he was about to destroy it, the LORD saw, and he relented from the calamity. And he said to the angel who was working destruction, "It is enough; now stay your hand." And the angel of the LORD was standing by the threshing floor of Ornan the Jebusite. ¹⁶ And David lifted his eyes and saw the angel of the LORD standing between earth and heaven, and in his hand a drawn sword stretched out over Jerusalem. Then David and the elders, clothed in sackcloth, fell upon their faces.

1 Chronicles 21:14-16 (ESV)

²⁸ At that time, when David saw that the LORD had answered him at the threshing floor of Ornan the Jebusite, he sacrificed there. ²⁹ For the tabernacle of the LORD, which Moses had made in the wilderness, and the altar of burnt offering were at that time in the high place at Gibeon, ³⁰ but David could not go before it to inquire of God, for he was afraid of the sword of the angel of the LORD.

1 Chronicles 21:28-30 (ESV)

Consider also Job's attitude. He feared God greatly and yet God did not disapprove of that fear or consider it inappropriate or excessive. On the contrary, He described Job, and his fear, in glowing terms, saying:

And the LORD said to Satan, "Have you considered my servant Job, that there is none like him on the earth, a blameless and upright man, who fears God and turns away from evil?"

Job 1:8 (RSV)

135

This is how Job described his own fear towards God, even using words like *'terrified'* and *'dread'* to express it:

> *¹⁵ Therefore I am terrified at his presence;*
>   *when I consider, I am in dread of him.*
> *¹⁶ God has made my heart faint;*
>   *the Almighty has terrified me;*
> > *Job 23:15-16 (RSV)*

We also get a glimpse at how awesome God is, and of the fear generated by meeting Him, by seeing how apostle John reacts when he sees Jesus, face to face, in all His glory. John is so terrified he falls on the floor in front of Him, even though, during Jesus' earthly ministry, he was Jesus' best friend:

> *¹² Then I turned to see the voice that was speaking to me, and on turning I saw seven golden lampstands, ¹³ and in the midst of the lampstands one like a son of man, clothed with a long robe and with a golden girdle round his breast; ¹⁴ his head and his hair were white as white wool, white as snow; his eyes were like a flame of fire, ¹⁵ his feet were like burnished bronze, refined as in a furnace, and his voice was like the sound of many waters; ¹⁶ in his right hand he held seven stars, from his mouth issued a sharp two-edged sword, and his face was like the sun shining in full strength.*
> *¹⁷ When I saw him, I fell at his feet as though dead. But he laid his right hand upon me, saying, "Fear not, I am the first and the last, ¹⁸ and the living one; I died, and behold I am alive for evermore, and I have the keys of Death and Hades.*
> > *Revelation 1:12-18 (RSV)*

Ezekiel reacted in a very similar way when he saw God, i.e. a bodily pre-appearance by the Son of God, centuries before His incarnation as Jesus:

> *²⁶ And above the firmament over their heads there was the likeness of a throne, in appearance like sapphire; and seated above the likeness of a throne was a likeness as it were of a human form. ²⁷ And upward from what had the appearance of his loins I saw as it were gleaming bronze, like the appearance of fire enclosed round about; and downward from what had the appearance of his loins I saw as it were the appearance of fire, and there was brightness round about him. ²⁸ Like the appearance of the bow that is in the cloud on the day of rain, so was the appearance of the brightness round about.*
> *Such was the appearance of the likeness of the glory of the LORD. And when I saw it, I fell upon my face, and I heard the voice of one speaking.*
> > *Ezekiel 1:26-28 (RSV)*

The Israelites also felt real fear when God descended upon Mount Sinai with much thunder and lightning:

¹⁶ On the morning of the third day there were thunders and lightnings, and a thick cloud upon the mountain, and a very loud trumpet blast, so that all the people who were in the camp trembled. ¹⁷ Then Moses brought the people out of the camp to meet God; and they took their stand at the foot of the mountain. ¹⁸ And Mount Sinai was wrapped in smoke, because the LORD descended upon it in fire; and the smoke of it went up like the smoke of a kiln, and the whole mountain quaked greatly. ¹⁹ And as the sound of the trumpet grew louder and louder, Moses spoke, and God answered him in thunder. ²⁰ And the LORD came down upon Mount Sinai, to the top of the mountain; and the LORD called Moses to the top of the mountain, and Moses went up.

Exodus 19:16-20 (RSV)

What the Israelites saw and heard that day was so awe-inspiring they feared that God might be going to kill them. Moses told them that God was not going to do so, but that there was, nonetheless, benefit from fearing God because that fear would keep them from sinning:

¹⁸ Now when all the people perceived the thunderings and the lightnings and the sound of the trumpet and the mountain smoking, the people were afraid and trembled; and they stood afar off, ¹⁹ and said to Moses, "You speak to us, and we will hear; but let not God speak to us, lest we die." ²⁰ And Moses said to the people, "Do not fear; for God has come to prove you, and that the fear of him may be before your eyes, that you may not sin."

Exodus 20:18-20 (RSV)

There cannot be any genuine reverence without the fear of the LORD

We can't have genuine reverence unless we feel a real sense of fear towards God arising out of His holiness, His righteousness and, above all, His impending judgment. My apprehension at that prospect is what causes me to fear God most. When I say that, I am primarily referring to the Judgment Seat of Christ, not the Great White Throne. (See Book Four).

Consider this selection of verses which indicate how strongly, *and frequently,* the Bible emphasises this theme of fearing God and be aware that I could actually have added very many more:

The fear of the LORD is the beginning of knowledge;
Proverbs 1:7(a) (NASB)

[7]Do not be wise in your own eyes;
Fear the LORD and turn away from evil.
[8]It will be healing to your body
And refreshment to your bones.
Proverbs 3:7-8 (NASB)

But the LORD of hosts, him you shall regard as holy;
let him be your fear, and let him be your dread.
Isaiah 8:13 (RSV)

"The fear of the LORD is to hate evil;
Pride and arrogance and the evil way
And the perverted mouth, I hate.
Proverbs 8:13 (NASB)

The fear of the LORD is the beginning of wisdom,
And the knowledge of the Holy One is understanding.
Proverbs 9:10 (NASB)

Better is a little with the fear of the LORD
Than great treasure and turmoil with it.
Proverbs 15:16 (NASB)

As a father shows compassion to his children,
so the LORD shows compassion to those who fear him.
Psalm 103:13 (ESV)

The fear of the LORD is the instruction for wisdom,
And before honour comes humility.
Proverbs 15:33 (NASB)

The angel of the LORD encamps
around those who fear him, and delivers them.
Psalm 34:7 (ESV)

"...and by the fear of the LORD one keeps away from evil.
Proverbs 16:6(b) (NASB)

[18] Behold, the eye of the LORD is on those who fear him,
on those who hope in his steadfast love,
[19] that he may deliver their soul from death
and keep them alive in famine.
Psalm 33:18-19 (ESV)

Do not let your heart envy sinners,
But live in the fear of the LORD always.
                        Proverbs 23:17 (NASB)

Oh, fear the LORD, you his saints,
or those who fear him have no lack!
                        Psalm 34:9 (ESV)

he will bless those who fear the LORD,
both small and great.
                        Psalm 115:13 (RSV)

Note also this stark passage from Psalm 2 in which the Messiah is described. Many people wrongly imagine that Jesus is not to be feared, and that only the Father should be feared. That is absolutely wrong, and this passage shows why we should also fear Him. Observe how frank it is about His severity in the future, when He operates as the King and Judge of the whole Earth:

[6] *"As for me, I have set my King*
on Zion, my holy hill."
[7] *I will tell of the decree:*
The LORD said to me, "You are my Son;
today I have begotten you.
[8] *Ask of me, and I will make the nations your heritage,*
and the ends of the earth your possession.
[9] *You shall break them with a rod of iron*
and dash them in pieces like a potter's vessel."

[10] *Now therefore, O kings, be wise;*
be warned, O rulers of the earth.
[11] *Serve the LORD with fear,*
and rejoice with trembling.
[12] *Kiss the Son,*
lest he be angry, and you perish in the way,
for his wrath is quickly kindled.
Blessed are all who take refuge in him.
                        Psalm 2:6-12 (ESV)

How and why do we benefit from having the fear of the LORD?

You might wonder why the fear of the LORD should produce all these benefits and make so much difference in our lives. There are a number of reasons why it does:

139

a) It causes us to give greater honour to God's Word and to study it more closely.

b) It gives us a stronger motivation, to resist peer pressure and the fear of other people is outweighed, or even completely displaced, by the fear of the LORD. We are therefore more likely to end up doing what God wants, rather than what public opinion dictates.

c) It keeps us from sin and spurs us on to holy living, especially when we focus on God's judgment.

Therefore, contrary to what many people assume, those who fear God will actually end up *closer to Him,* not farther away, and also have their wisdom increased:

The fear of the LORD is the beginning of wisdom;
a good understanding have all those who practice it.
His praise endures for ever!
                              Psalm 111:10 (RSV)

Moreover, God will reveal the secrets of His plans and intentions to those who fear Him:

The LORD confides in those who fear him;
*   he makes his covenant known to them.*
                      Psalm 25:14 (NIV)

In addition to all its other benefits, the fear of the LORD therefore helps us to become wise. That being so, a good place to start in cultivating that fear is to focus on the fact that His judgment is coming, as that is the main thing we need to fear. Think long and hard about the reality of that. In fact, ask God to make the prospect of His judgment ever more real and vivid to you. You might wish to consider the following verses to start with, but go on from there and make the subject of judgment a lifelong study:

Be happy, young man, while you are young, and let your heart give you joy in the days of your youth. Follow the ways of your heart and whatever your eyes see, but know that for all these things God will bring you to judgment
                              Ecclesiastes 11:9 (RSV)

[13] The end of the matter; all has been heard. Fear God, and keep his commandments; for that is the whole duty of everyone. [14] For God will bring every deed into judgment, including every secret thing, whether good or evil.
                              Ecclesiastes 12:13-14 (RSV)

[3] Do you suppose, O man—you who judge those who practice such things and yet do them yourself—that you will escape the judgment of God? [4] Or do you

presume on the riches of his kindness and forbearance and patience, not knowing that God's kindness is meant to lead you to repentance? ⁵ But because of your hard and impenitent heart you are storing up wrath for yourself on the day of wrath when God's righteous judgment will be revealed.

⁶ He will render to each one according to his works: ⁷ to those who by patience in well-doing seek for glory and honor and immortality, he will give eternal life; ⁸ but for those who are self-seeking and do not obey the truth, but obey unrighteousness, there will be wrath and fury. ⁹ There will be tribulation and distress for every human being who does evil, the Jew first and also the Greek, ¹⁰ but glory and honor and peace for everyone who does good, the Jew first and also the Greek. ¹¹ For God shows no partiality.

Romans 2:3-11 (ESV)

¹⁰You, then, why do you judge your brother? Or why do you look down on your brother? For we will all stand before God's judgment seat. ¹¹It is written: " 'As surely as I live,' says the Lord, 'every knee will bow before me; every tongue will confess to God.' "¹² So then, each of us will give an account of himself to God.

Romans 14:10-12 (RSV)

Therefore do not pronounce judgment before the time, before the Lord comes, who will bring to light the things now hidden in darkness and will disclose the purposes of the heart. Then every man will receive his commendation from God.

1 Corinthians 4:5 (RSV)

⁹So we make it our goal to please him, whether we are at home in the body or away from it. ¹⁰For we must all appear before the judgment seat of Christ, that each one may receive what is due him for the things done while in the body, whether good or bad.

2 Corinthians 5:9-10 (RSV)

Nothing in all creation is hidden from God's sight. Everything is uncovered and laid bare before the eyes of him to whom we must give account.

Hebrews 4:13 (NIV)

For nothing is hid that shall not be made manifest, nor anything secret that shall not be known and come to light.

Luke 8:17 (RSV)

But I tell you that every careless word that people speak, they shall give an accounting for it in the day of judgment.

Matthew 12:36 (NASB)

For the Son of man is to come with his angels in the glory of his Father, and then he will repay every man for what he has done.

Matthew 16:27 (RSV)

In the longer term, a person who fears the LORD will find that their life becomes filled with all sorts of blessings and privileges and God will honour them in many different ways. Of course, that does not mean they can escape from the pressures and trials that all disciples have to face. However, the person who fears the LORD will overcome those trials and be blessed by God, even while he is going through them. Consider these psalms which set out some of the many advantages that will come to a person who fears the LORD:

¹Praise the LORD!
Blessed is the man who fears the LORD,
who greatly delights in his commandments!
² His descendants will be mighty in the land;
the generation of the upright will be blessed.
³ Wealth and riches are in his house;
and his righteousness endures for ever.
⁴ Light rises in the darkness for the upright;
the LORD is gracious, merciful, and righteous.
⁵ It is well with the man who deals generously and lends,
who conducts his affairs with justice.

⁶ For the righteous will never be moved;
he will be remembered for ever.
⁷ He is not afraid of evil tidings;
his heart is firm, trusting in the LORD.
⁸ His heart is steady, he will not be afraid,
until he sees his desire on his adversaries.
⁹ He has distributed freely, he has given to the poor;
his righteousness endures for ever;
his horn is exalted in honour.
¹⁰ The wicked man sees it and is angry;
he gnashes his teeth and melts away;
the desire of the wicked man comes to nought.

Psalm 112:1-10 (RSV)

¹ Blessed is every one who fears the LORD,
who walks in his ways!
² You shall eat the fruit of the labour of your hands;
you shall be happy, and it shall be well with you.
³ Your wife will be like a fruitful vine within your house;
your children will be like olive shoots

around your table.
4 Lo, thus shall the man be blessed who fears the LORD.
                                Psalm 128:1-4 (RSV)

Wise people are loyal, steadfast and faithful. They show courage, stick to their principles, and do their duty even when under pressure.

Most of the time we are not clever enough to be able to know exactly how to do our duty while, at the same time, entirely avoiding all risks and hazards. Sometimes that would not even be possible for King Solomon, or the prophet Daniel, as we see vividly illustrated by his being cast into the lions' den. However, one thing which is easier to see, provided you are looking for it, is what your *duty* is in a given situation, even where one cannot find any way to remove the risk. Duty is a broad concept and covers all of your many and varied obligations to:

a) God, so as to obey all His commands, as set out in the Bible

b) your family, with your greatest duty being owed to your wife or husband, then your children, then your parents, and then your wider family, in descending order

c) the law of the land

d) your employer

e) your church

f) your community

When faced with a difficult situation, decision or confrontation, where doing the right thing may be costly, or even dangerous, a faithful man will set his face to do that right thing, *regardless of what it means for him.* Sadly, such people are very rare, as Solomon says:

Many a man proclaims his own loyalty,
 but a faithful man who can find?
                Proverbs 20:6 (RSV)

Therefore, if you want to be wise, then be faithful. Do what is right, *even when you are afraid*, and even when you know it will cost you. Having the courage to force yourself to do what you know is right, even where doing it will be hard, is a vital part of wisdom. There is no use in knowing God's Word, and the many commands and principles it contains, if you do not choose to have the courage to implement them. Moreover, I say *choose* deliberately, because we can always

143

summon up the courage we need, or ask God to give us more, provided we actually *want it*.

Most people who take the easy option and shirk their duty do so not because they do not have the courage, or cannot get it. It is because they do not *choose* to exercise it and do not *want* to ask God to give it to them. Therefore, make it your practice, starting with small things, to force yourself to do your duty and to be faithful to God's Word, and faithful to other people. Choose to have the courage to do the things that you know are right, even if you fear doing so. That way your 'courage muscle' will grow, ready to face even bigger tests ahead.

The difference between God's wisdom and mere human wisdom

In his second letter to the Corinthians apostle Paul refers to "*earthly wisdom*". He might equally have called it "*worldly wisdom*" or even "*carnal*" or "*fleshly wisdom*". Paul contrasts this earthly wisdom with the way that he conducts himself:

For our boast is this, the testimony of our conscience that we have behaved in the world, and still more toward you, with holiness and godly sincerity, not by earthly wisdom but by the grace of God.

2 Corinthians 1:12 (RSV)

Likewise, Jesus' half-brother, James, contrasts 'earthly wisdom', which is "*unspiritual and demonic*" with the wisdom which comes from God. He says that is "*pure, then peaceable, gentle, open to reason, full of mercy and good fruits, impartial and sincere*":

[13] Who is wise and understanding among you? By his good conduct let him show his works in the meekness of wisdom. [14] But if you have bitter jealousy and selfish ambition in your hearts, do not boast and be false to the truth. [15] This is not the wisdom that comes down from above, but is earthly, unspiritual, demonic. [16] For where jealousy and selfish ambition exist, there will be disorder and every vile practice. [17] But the wisdom from above is first pure, then peaceable, gentle, open to reason, full of mercy and good fruits, impartial and sincere.

James 3:13-17 (ESV)

Earthly or worldly wisdom is not really wisdom at all. It is actually foolishness, or even wickedness. But it is what this lost and blind world misguidedly regards as wisdom. It is largely about "*looking after number one*" and making sure you *get what you want from people*. It is also about self-promotion and self-preservation and has nothing at all to do with knowing or obeying God's will or

144

serving His purposes. So, it is actually the reverse of real wisdom, but it is all that this unsaved world has to offer. Therefore, that kind of 'wisdom' is not for us.

In fact, the very word is used ironically in the Bible, because it is so far removed from the biblical definition of wisdom. There is a huge difference between godly wisdom, of the kind which God gives to us via the Bible, and ordinary human wisdom, which is based on men's ideas and experiences. Such human wisdom reflects the carnal, sinful thinking of this world rather than God's thinking. Therefore, even the best logic and reasoning that human beings have to offer is only foolishness in comparison to God's. *Its not logic or reason - but ones starting premise, frame, objective that*

The beliefs and values of every philosopher, and of every man-made religion, are all futile. None of them will ever guide you into the truth. On the contrary, they will all lead you away from it. Apostle Paul writes in some detail about these issues in his first letter to the Corinthians. He explains why the Gospel doesn't make any sense to worldly people and why it cannot be explained in terms of the *"wisdom of this world"*: *① Frame First - The Fear Frame ①*

[17] For Christ did not send me to baptize but to preach the gospel, and not with eloquent wisdom, lest the cross of Christ be emptied of its power. [18] For the word of the cross is folly to those who are perishing, but to us who are being saved it is the power of God. [19] For it is written, *(fear this who is perishing)*
"I will destroy the wisdom of the wise,
and the cleverness of the clever I will thwart."
[20] Where is the wise man? Where is the scribe? Where is the debater of this age? Has not God made foolish the wisdom of the world? [21] For since, in the wisdom of God, the world did not know God through wisdom, it pleased God through the folly of what we preach to save those who believe. [22] For Jews demand signs and Greeks seek wisdom, [23] but we preach Christ crucified, a stumbling block to Jews and folly to Gentiles, [24] but to those who are called, both Jews and Greeks, Christ the power of God and the wisdom of God. [25] For the foolishness of God is wiser than men, and the weakness of God is stronger than men.

[26] For consider your call, brethren; not many of you were wise according to worldly standards, not many were powerful, not many were of noble birth; [27] but God chose what is foolish in the world to shame the wise, God chose what is weak in the world to shame the strong, [28] God chose what is low and despised in the world, even things that are not, to bring to nothing things that are, [29] so that no human being might boast in the presence of God. [30] He is the source of your life in Christ Jesus, whom God made our wisdom, our righteousness and sanctification and redemption; [31] therefore, as it is written, "Let him who boasts, boast of the Lord."

1 Corinthians 1:17-31 (RSV)

145

Therefore, when apostle Paul preached, he didn't attempt to sound impressive by using the fashionable and complicated jargon of secular philosophy or literature. Neither did he attempt to impress people with his academic credentials. In fact, he did not try to sound intellectual at all, as so many preachers try to do today. Apostle Paul had no time for such pretentions. He stuck firmly to the truth of what the Bible says. Then he relied on the power of the Holy Spirit to convict people of the truth of it, rather than relying on his own cleverness or persuasiveness:

¹ When I came to you, brethren, I did not come proclaiming to you the testimony of God in lofty words or wisdom. ² For I decided to know nothing among you except Jesus Christ and him crucified. ³ And I was with you in weakness and in much fear and trembling; ⁴ and my speech and my message were not in plausible words of wisdom, but in demonstration of the Spirit and of power, ⁵ that your faith might not rest in the wisdom of men but in the power of God.
⁶ Yet among the mature we do impart wisdom, although it is not a wisdom of this age or of the rulers of this age, who are doomed to pass away. ⁷ But we impart a secret and hidden wisdom of God, which God decreed before the ages for our glorification. ⁸ None of the rulers of this age understood this; for if they had, they would not have crucified the Lord of glory. ⁹ But, as it is written,
"What no eye has seen, nor ear heard,
nor the heart of man conceived,
what God has prepared for those who love him,"
¹⁰ God has revealed to us through the Spirit. For the Spirit searches everything, even the depths of God. ¹¹ For what person knows a man's thoughts except the spirit of the man which is in him? So also no one comprehends the thoughts of God except the Spirit of God. ¹² Now we have received not the spirit of the world, but the Spirit which is from God, that we might understand the gifts bestowed on us by God. ¹³ And we impart this in words not taught by human wisdom but taught by the Spirit, interpreting spiritual truths to those who possess the Spirit. ¹⁴ The unspiritual man does not receive the gifts of the Spirit of God, for they are folly to him, and he is not able to understand them because they are spiritually discerned. ¹⁵ The spiritual man judges all things, but is himself to be judged by no one. ¹⁶ "For who has known the mind of the Lord so as to instruct him?" But we have the mind of Christ.

1 Corinthians 2:1-16 (RSV)

Too many church leaders are trying to sound intellectual, rather than being wise, but that can actually cause them to become foolish in God's eyes

Too many church leaders and writers are trying to sound impressive or intellectual, rather than simply telling the truth of what the Bible says as clearly as they can. I read a theology book a while ago and the author referred to the

146

gospel and letters written by apostle John as "*the Johannine corpus*". He could just as easily have said "*John's writings*", but I suspect that he did not feel that such a simple phrase would have impressed his readers. He appeared overly concerned to establish his academic credibility, probably due to his own feelings of insecurity and lack of confidence.

Ironically, the more truly intellectual a writer is, the less he feels the need to try to impress us by using big words or long sentences. John Maynard Keynes had glittering credentials as a mathematician at Cambridge and also knew himself to be one of the greatest economists in the world. Yet he wrote in clear, simple, short sentences and used very little maths or algebra to illustrate his points. C S Lewis was similar. He was an eminent authority on English Literature and also a famous part-time theologian. Yet he wrote very simply, so that the greatest possible number of ordinary people could understand him.

Sadly, one sees a lot of academic snobbery in churches. I can think of a big church I used to go to in a university city with a large teaching hospital. Many of the congregation were either students, lecturers or medical doctors. Some preachers went out of their way to try to speak in a sophisticated and complicated way, so as to be impressive. They were concerned about not being considered to be intellectual.

But why did they want to sound intellectual anyway? In fact, why try to be impressive in any other way? Whom were they seeking to impress? It certainly wouldn't work with God. He isn't impressed by pseudo-intellectualism, or by showing off of any other kind. Therefore, it was plainly the people in the congregation whose admiration they were craving for, not God's approval. However, when we teach or preach it should never be our aim to impress anybody at all, but only to be:

a) faithful to God's Word

b) truthful

c) as accurate as possible

d) as clear as possible

e) as helpful as possible

If we are to do all of the above then, as Paul found, it will be necessary to be willing to be considered a fool in the eyes of worldly people. That is what they will inevitably think of us if we preach the Word of God *faithfully*, without editing it, adding to it, or watering it down:

¹⁸ Let no one deceive himself. If anyone among you thinks that he is wise in this age, let him become a fool that he may become wise. ¹⁹ For the wisdom of this world is folly with God. For it is written, "He catches the wise in their craftiness," ²⁰ and again, "The Lord knows that the thoughts of the wise are futile." don't admire their pretentions

1 Corinthians 3:18-20 (RSV)

If you reject evolution and preach what the Bible says about creation, you will be considered simplistic and unsophisticated and will be patronised, and despised, *even within churches.* The same will apply if you take seriously what the Bible says about demons and say openly that you believe in their existence and their active involvement in our lives. Many churches treat demons as myths and assume that what the Bible refers to was actually mental illness, as if the writers of the Bible were incapable of distinguishing between brain injuries, mental illnesses, and demonisation.

The Cambridge don (professor) and Bible-teacher, Derek Prince, got a lot of abuse because he took seriously what the Bible says about demons and the problems they cause, even in the lives of real Christians. Many people, including sincere friends of his, warned him that he was putting his academic reputation at risk, and making himself an object of ridicule, by speaking so openly. They said he should avoid teaching about deliverance, or even saying that demons are actively involved in people's lives today.

He was especially warned not to actually cast demons out of people, especially believers, or it would make him look primitive and undignified, and arouse criticism. However, Derek Prince refused to be silenced or to alter, or tone down, what the Bible clearly teaches. Having said all that, I do not agree with everything Derek Prince taught about demonology, or his approach to deliverance. I differ from him on a few points, as I explain in Book 7. However, I agreed with him on many things and greatly admired his courage and integrity. He was willing to be a pioneer and to teach things which others feared even to mention.

However, because he was a pioneer, he had no mentor and it was, therefore, all the more understandable that he would make some mistakes. Nevertheless, Derek Prince was willing to go ahead anyway, regardless of what people thought of him, *because he was not trying to impress people,* but only to be faithful and to tell the truth. That being so, he could not be intimidated by criticism or ridicule. I believe that one of the reasons why his teaching ministry was so enormously blessed by God was because he only ever tried to please God, not men. We would all do well to follow his example in that.

Be wise about your knowledge
Show it off to very few of infrequently

148

Let them consider you stupid — that wise.

The unrestrained pursuit of human logic, purely by itself, can lead you to some absurd conclusions and to adopt false, unbiblical beliefs.

Sound logic, reasoning and deduction are needed if we are to handle God's Word properly. Those are all God-given abilities. However, if we rely upon these excessively we can end up making some bad mistakes. So, it is valid to draw appropriate inferences from a passage and deduce that if X is true, then Y must also be true. There is a place for deductive thinking, but we must not take it too far, such that our logical conclusions are allowed to *prevail over passages of Scripture,* which expressly contradict them.

Neither can we allow our natural, human logic or deduction to take us *further than the Bible goes,* or to make a point *more strongly* than the Bible states it. A classic example of this kind of error is the way John Calvin and some of his followers over-emphasised or exaggerated what the Bible says about the sovereignty of God. So, it is valid to say that God is in *overall charge* of the whole universe, and that nothing can happen unless He *allows it to happen.* It is also true that, in various ways, God *causes certain things to happen.*

He intervenes, alters the course of history, appoints people to positions, remove others, and makes various other types of choices. All of those things are clearly true, *because the Bible says so.* However, where many Calvinists go wrong is to over-emphasise what the Bible says about God's sovereignty and election and to go further than it goes. In addition, they ignore, or tone down, *what the Bible also has to say* about our freedom to choose whether to obey God and whether to do His will.

Some Calvinists therefore end up believing that if God is sovereign, then absolutely everything that ever happens must be *caused* by Him, not merely permitted. By taking their fallible human logic too far they wrongly conclude that that must be so, because, if it was possible for any of us to resist or refuse God's will in any way, then that would mean He was not genuinely 'sovereign', i.e. as they wrongly define that term. They also wrongly assume that the very concept of sovereignty, as they define it, is incompatible with there being any free choice at all on our part.

In doing all of this they not only wrongly define 'sovereignty', by basing its meaning on their own logic, rather than on what the Bible actually says. They also ignore what the Bible explicitly says, or clearly implies, about *man's freedom to choose.* That includes the freedom to defy God and to disobey Him. Our doing so is all part of what God permits and it does not actually contradict or diminish His sovereignty at all, when the word is defined biblically. That's because what the Bible means by the concept of God's sovereignty is able to accommodate human free will.

There is no inconsistency between these two concepts because, in His sovereignty, God has chosen to give us the *freedom to make choices* and those choices are real, not imaginary or illusory. He really does allow us to decide certain things for ourselves, *even if that means defying Him* and *not* doing His will. Those who make this error of exaggerating the meaning of sovereignty can end up believing that absolutely everything that happens must be God's will, even sin. They therefore believe that He not only allows things to happen, but positively *causes* them.

For the more extreme Calvinists, this assumption extends to literally everything, however trivial, including the mistakes a secretary makes while typing. Even those tiny errors are believed to have been ordained by God from eternity past and to have been deliberately caused to happen, and *even forced to happen*, by Him. Once you get to that stage it is hard to distinguish such thinking from the *fatalism* which is taught within Islam. For Muslims, everything that happens is said to be Allah's will and thus completely impossible to avoid, alter or resist.

But that is not how the God of the Bible operates and, more to the point, that is not how He describes Himself. That kind of theological error comes when we allow our limited human reasoning to become over-extended, such that it takes us *beyond what God's Word says*. We can become so persuaded by our own man-made logic that we are blinded by it and trapped by the conclusions to which it leads us. Then we allow those conclusions to override any counter-balancing points which the Bible also makes, many of which are expressly stated, and which are not based on any reasoning on our part.

Accordingly, instead of holding two valid biblical doctrines in *healthy tension and believing both at the same time*, as we are meant to, many of us underemphasise, or even abandon, one doctrine and exaggerate the other. Such reasoning is not wisdom. It takes us away from truth and obscures God's Word, rather than illuminating it. We must therefore take great care to avoid such unbalanced or over-extended thinking and also seek God's help to point out to us any areas where we may have fallen into such errors.

Our greatest faults are often just our greatest gifts or qualities being misused.

If you closely examine your worst character failings or sins you may well find that they are your greatest gifts or qualities being misused. So, to give an obvious example, if you have the gift of a strong and muscular physique you could use that to bully and intimidate others. Thus, the physical strength that God meant you to use in His service, is being used, instead, to serve yourself. It then becomes a means by which you can sin and, the more strength God gives you, the more effectively you can sin with it.

150

Or if God gives you a very creative and imaginative mind you could use it to become a more effective and plausible liar. Likewise, if God gives you the advantage of a naturally bold temperament you could use it to enable you to carry out major crimes, which you would never have dared to attempt if you had not been given that gift of boldness. The list could go on and on. Another problem is that your own giftings can also cause you to look down on others who do not have those particular gifts.

For example, if God gave you the gift of a quick and decisive mind it could become the cause of you despising those who cannot think as quickly as you, or who cannot make decisions as fast as you can. So, if you did not have that gift, you may well have avoided the sins of impatience and irritability. If you were to examine any historical figure and look at their most significant failures or disasters the likelihood is you would find this principle in operation, because most of us don't attempt major things, or take substantial risks, in areas where we are relatively weak or ungifted.

We tend to do so only in areas where we know we have a comparative advantage. So, for example, Adolf Hitler had very strong gifts in the areas of lateral thinking, boldness and decisiveness. He also had an amazing memory for facts and figures, and the ability to take calculated risks. He therefore made a number of highly original decisions which meant overruling his Chiefs of Staff. In the early years of World War Two, and the years leading up to it, he amazed his generals when he consistently turned out to be right and his gambles paid off.

Of course, in part, this was also because he was demonically guided. Yet it is beyond doubt that he also had major personal giftings, which he was able to use to great effect. However, Hitler went wrong, and began to make some huge errors, when his confidence in his own undeniable talents became too great. He began to overreach himself, went too far, took ever greater risks, and listened less and less to his advisers. So, at least in part, he went wrong, and failed in the end, because of his misuse of, and over-reliance upon, his own greatest qualities.

Have you ever wondered what great things Hitler could have achieved if he had employed his abilities in pursuit of good rather than evil? He had exceptional God-given talents which were put into him to enable him to serve God's purposes, but he chose to use them for evil instead. He could not have done even a fraction of that evil if he had not got those giftings and strengths. So, in your own life, it is likely that you have done the most harm, and sinned the most, in those areas where you have the *greatest* natural abilities, not where you have the *least*.

Reflecting on this may help us to change our ways. Instead of focusing only on our areas of relative weakness, where we lack natural giftings, we can begin to look as well at our areas of natural strength. Then we can ask ourselves probing questions about how we are using those qualities, for whose purposes, and at whose direction. Moreover, it is in the areas of our greatest relative strength that we are most likely to rely on ourselves and act independently of God.

Few of us will disobey God by doing something that He has not called us to do if it means launching forth into some venture for which we know we are not qualified. However, we might very well do so if we do have those strengths and are well aware of the fact. Therefore, we need to exercise the most self-control, and ask for God to restrain us the most, in those areas where we are most at risk of relying on our own giftings. That is where we are most likely to do things that seem good to us, but which God never told us to do.

The wiser we get, the more aware we will become of our own areas of weakness, but also of the even greater hazards that come from our strengths. We will then give more time, thought and prayer to seeking to address the problems that our gifts and strengths can cause. We will also begin to ask God to *hold us back* in those areas, if we are acting wrongly, and to prevent us from misusing those gifts or from going our own way.

It's not about what you WANT but what you NEED.' F.J.F

Expect Evil.!
Unsurprised by the wickedness, cruelty, deceit, vileness, ... evil of man you don't have to respond with: Shock, disappointment, depression, devastation, anger, heartbreak, ... disappointed
Foreseeable, Anticipated, Predictable

CHAPTER 6

HOW CAN WE GET WISDOM?

Give your servant therefore an understanding mind to govern your people, that I may discern between good and evil, for who is able to govern this your great people?"

1 Kings 3:9 (ESV)

And all the kings of the earth sought the presence of Solomon to hear his wisdom, which God had put into his mind.

2 Chronicles 9:23 (ESV)

A wise man will hear and increase in learning,
And a man of understanding will acquire wise counsel,
Proverbs 1:5 (NASB)

[13] How blessed is the man who finds wisdom
And the man who gains understanding.
[14] For her profit is better than the profit of silver
And her gain better than fine gold.
Proverbs 3:13-14 (NASB)

[5] Acquire wisdom! Acquire understanding!
Do not forget nor turn away from the words of my mouth.
[6] "Do not forsake her, and she will guard you;
Love her, and she will watch over you.
[7] "The beginning of wisdom is: Acquire wisdom;
And with all your acquiring, get understanding.
[8] "Prize her, and she will exalt you; She will honor you if you embrace her.
Proverbs 4:5-8 (NASB)

Watch over your heart with all diligence,
For from it flow the springs of life.
Proverbs 4:23 (NASB)

Say to wisdom, "You are my sister,"
And call understanding your intimate friend;
Proverbs 7:4 (NASB)

"For wisdom is better than jewels;
And all desirable things cannot compare with her.
Proverbs 8:11 (NASB)

Give instruction to a wise man and he will be still wiser,
Teach a righteous man and he will increase his learning.

Proverbs 9:9 (NASB)

The need to acquire wisdom was the main theme and focus throughout King Solomon's writings

Let's look at some more of the things which King Solomon had to say about the value of wisdom and also how it can be acquired. The whole of the first eight chapters of the book of Proverbs focus on this theme. That in itself indicates how important God feels it is for us to seek wisdom. Even where God tells us something once or twice it is important. Therefore, some doctrines are founded on just one or two verses.

However, where He spends eight whole chapters repeatedly urging us to seek for something, and explaining in many different ways why we should do so, then you can be sure it is really crucial. For now, let's look at part of chapter two of Proverbs. We are told that wisdom is obtained by those who really *want* it and who are willing to *seek for it* earnestly and with persistence:

¹My son, if you will receive my words
And treasure my commandments within you,
²Make your ear attentive to wisdom,
Incline your heart to understanding;
³For if you cry for discernment,
Lift your voice for understanding;
⁴If you seek her as silver
And search for her as for hidden treasures;
⁵Then you will discern the fear of the LORD
And discover the knowledge of God.
⁶For the LORD gives wisdom;
From His mouth come knowledge and understanding.
⁷He stores up sound wisdom for the upright;
He is a shield to those who walk in integrity,
⁸Guarding the paths of justice,
And He preserves the way of His godly ones.
⁹Then you will discern righteousness and justice
And equity and every good course.
¹⁰For wisdom will enter your heart
And knowledge will be pleasant to your soul;
¹¹Discretion will guard you,
Understanding will watch over you,

Proverbs 2:1-11 (NASB)

How King Solomon got his wisdom

Except for Jesus, King Solomon was the wisest man who ever lived. God gave him that exceptional wisdom as a gift, simply because he wanted it so strongly. When he became the King, Solomon made the acquiring of wisdom his top priority, ahead of riches and power. The LORD (the Son of God in a pre-appearance) came to him in a dream and invited him to make a request and Solomon chose to ask for wisdom. That inspired choice pleased the LORD and He granted his request. So, Solomon was given great wisdom *because he had asked for it.*

However, the very fact that he chose to ask God for wisdom instead of riches, power, long life, success, etc, shows that Solomon already had an unusual amount of wisdom at that point. If not, he would have asked God for something else. It is fair to say, therefore, that one of the surest signs of already having some wisdom is the fact that you are seeking for more of it. Conversely, to have no regard for wisdom, and no desire to pursue it, is a clear sign that you are foolish. At any rate, this is the biblical account of what happened to Solomon:

⁵In Gibeon the LORD appeared to Solomon in a dream at night; and God said, "Ask what you wish me to give you." ⁶Then Solomon said, "You have shown great loving kindness to Your servant David my father, according as he walked before You in truth and righteousness and uprightness of heart toward You; and You have reserved for him this great loving kindness, that You have given him a son to sit on his throne, as it is this day. ⁷"Now, O LORD my God, You have made Your servant king in place of my father David, yet I am but a little child; I do not know how to go out or come in. ⁸"Your servant is in the midst of Your people which You have chosen, a great people who are too many to be numbered or counted.
⁹"So give Your servant an understanding heart to judge Your people to discern between good and evil. For who is able to judge this great people of Yours?" ¹⁰It was pleasing in the sight of the Lord that Solomon had asked this thing. ¹¹God said to him, "Because you have asked this thing and have not asked for yourself long life, nor have asked riches for yourself, nor have you asked for the life of your enemies, but have asked for yourself discernment to understand justice, ¹²behold, I have done according to your words Behold, I have given you a wise and discerning heart, so that there has been no one like you before you, nor shall one like you arise after you.

1 Kings 3:5-12 (NASB)

In the next chapter we are told how God answered that request by giving Solomon *"wisdom and understanding beyond measure....."*:

155

²⁹ And God gave Solomon wisdom and understanding beyond measure, and breadth of mind like the sand on the seashore, ³⁰ so that Solomon's wisdom surpassed the wisdom of all the people of the east and all the wisdom of Egypt. ³¹ For he was wiser than all other men, wiser than Ethan the Ezrahite, and Heman, Calcol, and Darda, the sons of Mahol, and his fame was in all the surrounding nations. ³² He also spoke 3,000 proverbs, and his songs were 1,005. ³³ He spoke of trees, from the cedar that is in Lebanon to the hyssop that grows out of the wall. He spoke also of beasts, and of birds, and of reptiles, and of fish. ³⁴ And people of all nations came to hear the wisdom of Solomon, and from all the kings of the earth, who had heard of his wisdom.

1 Kings 4:29-34 (ESV)

King Solomon began to put that gift of supernatural wisdom into operation in one of the first legal judgments that he gave. In those days a King also had to act as a judge and to decide the hardest cases. On this occasion King Solomon had to hear the testimony of two women and decide which of them was a child's real mother. There were no witnesses to support either of them. In fact there was no independent evidence at all. Look at the amazingly simple, but brilliant, way God gave Solomon the solution:

¹⁶Then two women who were harlots came to the king and stood before him. ¹⁷The one woman said, "Oh, my lord, this woman and I live in the same house; and I gave birth to a child while she was in the house. ¹⁸"It happened on the third day after I gave birth, that this woman also gave birth to a child, and we were together. There was no stranger with us in the house, only the two of us in the house. ¹⁹"This woman's son died in the night, because she lay on it.

²⁰"So she arose in the middle of the night and took my son from beside me while your maidservant slept, and laid him in her bosom, and laid her dead son in my bosom. ²¹"When I rose in the morning to nurse my son, behold, he was dead; but when I looked at him carefully in the morning, behold, he was not my son, whom I had borne." ²²Then the other woman said, "No! For the living one is my son, and the dead one is your son." But the first woman said, "No! For the dead one is your son, and the living one is my son." Thus they spoke before the king.

²³Then the king said, "The one says, 'This is my son who is living, and your son is the dead one'; and the other says, 'No! For your son is the dead one, and my son is the living one.'" ²⁴The king said, "Get me a sword." So they brought a sword before the king. ²⁵The king said, "Divide the living child in two, and give half to the one and half to the other."

26 Then the woman whose child was the living one spoke to the king, for she was deeply stirred over her son and said, "Oh, my lord, give her the living child, and by no means kill him." But the other said, "He shall be neither mine nor yours; divide him!" 27 Then the king said, "Give the first woman the living child, and by no means kill him. She is his mother." 28 When all Israel heard of the judgment which the king had handed down, they feared the king, for they saw that the wisdom of God was in him to administer justice.

1 Kings 3:16-28 (NASB)

How we can get wisdom from studying the Bible - especially the writings of King Solomon

That was how Solomon got his wisdom as a supernatural gift, but the question in our case is how can we get it? For us, it is a much slower process. It comes primarily from studying God's Word, memorising it, reflecting on it, obeying it, and applying it over a long period of time. There is no short cut or easy way. It takes a lot of time, effort and determination. However, if we are willing to pay the necessary price, and to keep doing so for long enough, then we will eventually gain a level of wisdom which even the ablest and most educated people in the world cannot match.

That's because real wisdom is not about cleverness, or education, or understanding how this world thinks and operates. It is about *seeing the world the way God sees it and thinking the way He thinks*. We see that illustrated in the lives of the prophet Daniel and his three friends, Hananiah, Mishael and Azariah. These four young Hebrew men were living in the competitive environment of the court of King Nebuchadnezzar, surrounded by the cleverest men in Babylon. However, because they had the Scriptures, they were able to operate at a level of wisdom far above what any Babylonian could manage:

17 As for these four youths, God gave them learning and skill in all letters and wisdom; and Daniel had understanding in all visions and dreams. 18 At the end of the time, when the king had commanded that they should be brought in, the chief of the eunuchs brought them in before Nebuchadnez'zar. 19 And the king spoke with them, and among them all none was found like Daniel, Hanani'ah, Mish'a-el, and Azari'ah; therefore they stood before the king. 20 And in every matter of wisdom and understanding concerning which the king inquired of them, he found them ten times better than all the magicians and enchanters that were in all his kingdom.

Daniel 1:17-20 (RSV)

157

Joseph had a similar experience in Egypt. God gave him wisdom and insight which made him stand out so much that Pharaoh promoted him to be the Prime Minister of Egypt. No Egyptian could match Joseph's wisdom:

37This proposal seemed good to Pharaoh and to all his servants. 38And Pharaoh said to his servants, "Can we find such a man as this, in whom is the Spirit of God?" 39 So Pharaoh said to Joseph, "Since God has shown you all this, there is none so discreet and wise as you are; 40you shall be over my house, and all my people shall order themselves as you command; only as regards the throne will I be greater than you." 41And Pharaoh said to Joseph, "Behold, I have set you over all the land of Egypt." 42Then Pharaoh took his signet ring from his hand and put it on Joseph's hand, and arrayed him in garments of fine linen, and put a gold chain about his neck; 43and he made him to ride in his second chariot; and they cried before him, "Bow the knee!" Thus he set him over all the land of Egypt. 44Moreover Pharaoh said to Joseph, "I am Pharaoh, and without your consent no man shall lift up hand or foot in all the land of Egypt."

(B) How God 'prepared' Joseph in prison with humility...   **Genesis 41:37-44 (RSV)**

Likewise, the Psalmist who wrote Psalm 119 spoke of how his study of God's Word gave him an unusual amount of wisdom, which even put him ahead of his teachers:

97O how I love Your law!
It is my meditation all the day.
98Your commandments make me wiser than my enemies,
For they are ever mine.
99I have more insight than all my teachers,
For Your testimonies are my meditation.
100I understand more than the aged,
Because I have observed Your precepts.
101I have restrained my feet from every evil way,
That I may keep Your word.
102I have not turned aside from Your ordinances,
For You Yourself have taught me.
103How sweet are Your words to my taste!
Yes, sweeter than honey to my mouth!
104From Your precepts I get understanding;
Therefore I hate every false way.
                    Psalm 119:97-104 (NASB)

Moses also told the people of Israel that if they would learn God's Word, *and do it*, i.e. obey what it says, then it would make them a wise and understanding nation and that the Gentiles would see that:

Wisdom isn't what you know but what you DO with what you know.

158

⁵ Behold, I have taught you statutes and ordinances, as the LORD my God commanded me, that you should do them in the land which you are entering to take possession of it. ⁶ Keep them and do them; for that will be your wisdom and your understanding in the sight of the peoples, who, when they hear all these statutes, will say, 'Surely this great nation is a wise and understanding people.'
Deuteronomy 4:5-6 (RSV)

Moses's successor, Joshua was also told, by God Himself, that ongoing, daily study of the Scriptures would cause him to become both prosperous and successful:

⁷Only be strong and very courageous, being careful to do according to all the law which Moses my servant commanded you; turn not from it to the right hand or to the left, that you may have good success wherever you go. ⁸This book of the law shall not depart out of your mouth, but you shall meditate on it day and night, that you may be careful to do according to all that is written in it; for then you shall make your way prosperous, and then you shall have good success.
Joshua 1:7-8 (RSV)

King David also confirms that wisdom, and many other benefits, are to be found in studying God's Word:

⁷ The law of the LORD is perfect,
reviving the soul;
the testimony of the LORD is sure,
making wise the simple;
⁸ the precepts of the LORD are right,
rejoicing the heart;
the commandment of the LORD is pure,
enlightening the eyes;
⁹ the fear of the LORD is clean,
enduring for ever;
the ordinances of the LORD are true,
and righteous altogether.¹⁰ More to be desired are they than gold,
even much fine gold;
sweeter also than honey
and drippings of the honeycomb.
¹¹ Moreover by them is thy servant warned;
in keeping them there is great reward.
Psalm 19:7-11 (RSV)

None of this is unique to Joshua, Moses, David, Daniel or even to the Jews. God has promised that He will give such wisdom to *all* who really want it:

159

⁵If any of you lacks wisdom, let him ask God, who gives to all men generously and without reproaching, and it will be given him. ⁶But let him ask in faith, with no doubting, for he who doubts is like a wave of the sea that is driven and tossed by the wind. ⁷For that person must not suppose that a double-minded man, ⁸unstable in all his ways, will receive anything from the Lord.

James 1:5-8 (RSV)

Given that God says that King Solomon was the wisest man who ever lived, why would any right-thinking person choose not to study his writings and take his advice?

The three books written by King Solomon deserve to be studied over and over again. He wrote Song of Solomon in his youth, Proverbs in middle age, and Ecclesiastes when he was old. If you want to become wise, then they are all well worth the effort of working through them carefully and repeatedly, especially Proverbs and Ecclesiastes. Consider King Solomon's credentials. Here is what the Bible says about his exceptional knowledge and understanding:

²⁹And God gave Solomon wisdom and understanding beyond measure, and largeness of mind like the sand on the seashore, ³⁰so that Solomon's wisdom surpassed the wisdom of all the people of the east, and all the wisdom of Egypt. ³¹For he was wiser than all other men, wiser than Ethan the Ez'rahite, and Heman, Calcol, and Darda, the sons of Mahol; and his fame was in all the nations round about. ³²He also uttered three thousand proverbs; and his songs were a thousand and five. ³³He spoke of trees, from the cedar that is in Lebanon to the hyssop that grows out of the wall; he spoke also of beasts, and of birds, and of reptiles, and of fish. ³⁴And men came from all peoples to hear the wisdom of Solomon, and from all the kings of the earth, who had heard of his wisdom.

1 Kings 4:29-34 (RSV)

Furthermore, this is what the Queen of Sheba thought of Solomon's brilliance:

¹Now when the queen of Sheba heard of the fame of Solomon concerning the name of the LORD, she came to test him with hard questions. ²She came to Jerusalem with a very great retinue, with camels bearing spices, and very much gold, and precious stones; and when she came to Solomon, she told him all that was on her mind. ³And Solomon answered all her questions; there was nothing hidden from the king which he could not explain to her.

⁴And when the queen of Sheba had seen all the wisdom of Solomon, the house that he had built, ⁵the food of his table, the seating of his officials, and the attendance of his servants, their clothing, his cupbearers, and his burnt offerings which he offered at the house of the LORD, there was no more spirit

160

*in her. *⁶*And she said to the king, "The report was true which I heard in my own land of your affairs and of your wisdom, *⁷* but I did not believe the reports until I came and my own eyes had seen it; and, behold, the half was not told me; your wisdom and prosperity surpass the report which I heard.*

1 Kings 10:1-7 (RSV)

In fact, the whole world in his day knew of Solomon's unprecedented wisdom. He was far above the level of any other man:

²³*Thus King Solomon excelled all the kings of the earth in riches and in wisdom.* ²⁴*And the whole earth sought the presence of Solomon to hear his wisdom, which God had put into his mind.*

1 Kings 10:23-24 (RSV)

In the light of what the Bible tells us about the extraordinary level of wisdom and understanding that Solomon had, why would any sensible person *not* want to study what he had to say and learn about the discoveries that he made? You have the opportunity to read the thoughts, and take the advice, of the wisest man who ever lived. Therefore, it is self-evidently worth making the effort to study the Scriptures, and especially the books Solomon wrote. It is the main way to get wisdom.

It is remarkable that, somehow, that obvious fact does not occur to people, or does not interest them, even when it is pointed out. Thus, multitudes of people who claim to be Christians leave this unique resource unused or under-used. In Solomon's own day the whole world travelled long distances to meet him so that they could learn from him. Today we can do that so much more easily by simply reading what he wrote. Yet many of us cannot be bothered, and even those who do read it are often half-hearted about it, reading the Bible infrequently and sparingly, in small doses, rather than devouring it.

Wisdom also comes from associating with wise people. Therefore, deliberately set out to associate with people who are already wise, or at least *wiser than you.* Seek out in particular those who love the Bible, who want to do right, and who are committed to obeying God. Spend a lot of time with them and you will inevitably become like them. What they have is bound to rub off on you, because that is the way we are made.

This second aspect of the process of becoming wise is relatively simple - just find people who are already wise, at least in comparison to you, and spend as much time with them as you can. You will then improve automatically. It will happen even faster if you are actively seeking to imitate them, rather than just passively being in their presence. By making careful choices about whom you spend your time with, you not only gain the chance to copy the attitudes and habits of wise

161

people. It also keeps you away from fools and reduces the chances of you copying their ways. So, there is a double benefit.

Why did Solomon subsequently go wrong and turn towards foolishness?

Solomon had great wisdom but, in middle age, he went astray for a time. Despite all his dazzling brilliance, he made some very wrong choices. The fact that he did so illustrates the point that all of us are a mixture and can still go wrong, no matter how wise we may become. Even a man as wise as Solomon still had some foolishness left in him. At least he had the potential to become foolish. More to the point, he still had a sin nature. It all went wrong for him because he indulged his sinful nature or 'flesh'.

In particular, he took a ridiculously excessive number of wives and concubines, amounting to over 1000 in total. Moreover, many of these were pagans and idolaters and they led him into idolatry, which was Solomon's biggest sin. That brought him onto a collision course with God. Had it not been for the promises that God had made to his father, King David, he would have been deposed from the throne. Instead, God chose to wait and to tear the Kingdom away from Solomon's son, Rehoboam:

¹Now King Solomon loved many foreign women: the daughter of Pharaoh, and Moabite, Ammonite, E'domite, Sido'nian, and Hittite women, ²from the nations concerning which the LORD had said to the people of Israel, "You shall not enter into marriage with them, neither shall they with you, for surely they will turn away your heart after their gods"; Solomon clung to these in love. ³He had seven hundred wives, princesses, and three hundred concubines; and his wives turned away his heart. ⁴For when Solomon was old his wives turned away his heart after other gods; and his heart was not wholly true to the LORD his God, as was the heart of David his father. ⁵For Solomon went after Ash'toreth the goddess of the Sido'nians, and after Milcom the abomination of the Ammonites.

⁶So Solomon did what was evil in the sight of the LORD, and did not wholly follow the LORD, as David his father had done. ⁷Then Solomon built a high place for Chemosh the abomination of Moab, and for Molech the abomination of the Ammonites, on the mountain east of Jerusalem. ⁸And so he did for all his foreign wives, who burned incense and sacrificed to their gods. ⁹And the LORD was angry with Solomon, because his heart had turned away from the LORD, the God of Israel, who had appeared to him twice, ¹⁰and had commanded him concerning this thing, that he should not go after other gods; but he did not keep what the LORD commanded. ¹¹Therefore the LORD said to Solomon, "Since this has been your mind and you have not kept my covenant and my statutes which I have commanded you, I will surely tear the kingdom from you and will give it to your servant

1 Kings 11:1-11 (RSV)

Given the contents of the book of Ecclesiastes, it seems clear that, in his later years, Solomon repented and got right with God again. He had learned what it was like to have great wisdom, but then he wanted to experiment for a while with folly and excess, and to test them to their limits. Although it was totally wrong of him to do that, there are still some valuable things we can learn, *even from Solomon's sins and wrong choices,* all of which he writes about. So, make Solomon's writings a life-long study. They will not disappoint you.

Wisdom is the application (obedience) of God's word

CHAPTER 7

WHAT WISE PEOPLE DO - PART ONE

"Of Issachar men who had understanding of the times, to know what Israel ought to do......"

1 Chronicles 12:32(a) (RSV)

¹ Blessed is the man
who walks not in the counsel of the wicked,
nor stands in the way of sinners,
nor sits in the seat of scoffers;
² but his delight is in the law of the LORD,
and on his law he meditates day and night.
³ He is like a tree
planted by streams of water
that yields its fruit in its season,
and its leaf does not wither.
In all that he does, he prospers.

Psalm 1:1-3 (ESV)

Keep your heart with all vigilance;
for from it flow the springs of life.

Proverbs 4:23 (RSV)

For the eyes of the LORD run to and fro throughout the whole earth, to give strong support to those whose heart is blameless toward him......

2 Chronicles 16:9(a) (ESV)

³⁰ The mouth of the righteous utters wisdom,
and his tongue speaks justice.
³¹ The law of his God is in his heart;
his steps do not slip.
³² The wicked watches the righteous,
and seeks to slay him.
³³ The LORD will not abandon him to his power,
or let him be condemned when he is brought to trial.

Psalm 37:30-33 (RSV)

³ The LORD was with Jehoshaphat, because he walked in the earlier ways of his father David. He did not seek the Baals, ⁴ but sought the God of his father and walked in his commandments, and not according to the practices of Israel. ⁵

165

Therefore the LORD established the kingdom in his hand. And all Judah brought tribute to Jehoshaphat, and he had great riches and honor.
2 Chronicles 17:3-5 (ESV)

He who is slow to anger has great understanding,
but he who has a hasty temper exalts folly.
Proverbs 14:29 (RSV)

He who is slow to anger is better than the mighty,
And he who rules his spirit, than he who captures a city.
Proverbs 16:32 (NASB)

Wise people hate the things that God hates   *d love wht He loves*

Merely *believing in* God does not make us wise. A wise person goes much further than that. He fears God and he also values and pursues those things that God values. His persistent study of the Bible means that his thoughts, beliefs and attitudes are continually coming closer into line with God's. But it goes even further than just agreeing with God, valuing the things that He values, and loving the things that He loves. A wise person also *hates* the things that God hates, such as falsehood and evil:

5 The boastful shall not stand before your eyes;   *God hates a lying tongue*
you hate all evildoers.
6 You destroy those who speak lies;
the LORD abhors the bloodthirsty and deceitful man.
because God wants us to hate those things:
Psalm 5:5-6 (ESV)

The LORD tests the righteous,
but his soul hates the wicked and the one who loves violence.
Psalm 11:5 (ESV)

What is more, God *wants* us to hate those things too:

The LORD loves those who hate evil;
he preserves the lives of his saints;
he delivers them from the hand of the wicked.
Psalm 97:10 (RSV)

A righteous man hates falsehood,
but a wicked man acts shamefully and disgracefully.
Proverbs 13:5 (RSV)

21 Do I not hate those who hate you, O LORD?
  And do I not loathe those who rise up against you?
22 I hate them with complete hatred;
  I count them my enemies.
                                     Psalm 139:21-22 (ESV)

A wise person also conducts himself with holiness and sincerity towards other people. He doesn't use the wisdom of this world, i.e. feral cunning or craftiness, but only God's wisdom:

Now this is our boast: Our conscience testifies that we have conducted ourselves in the world, and especially in our relations with you, in the holiness and sincerity that are from God. We have done so not according to worldly wisdom but according to God's grace.
                                     2 Corinthians 1:12 (NIV)

Let's now look at some more of the specific things that wise people do, or avoid doing:

Wise people live rightly and show their wisdom in their actions, choices and lifestyle.

Wisdom is not only displayed in what people *say*. It is mostly seen in what they *do*, and also in what they *don't do*. Our actions speak volumes and clearly reveal what we are and how far we have got in acquiring maturity and wisdom. So, a wise person will show his wisdom by displaying the fruit of the Holy Spirit in his character, lifestyle, choices, actions and reactions. He will live right and do right:

13 Who is wise and understanding among you? By his good life let him show his works in the meekness of wisdom. 14 But if you have bitter jealousy and selfish ambition in your hearts, do not boast and be false to the truth. 15 This wisdom is not such as comes down from above, but is earthly, unspiritual, devilish. 16 For where jealousy and selfish ambition exist, there will be disorder and every vile practice. 17 But the wisdom from above is first pure, then peaceable, gentle, open to reason, full of mercy and good fruits, without uncertainty or insincerity. 18 And the harvest of righteousness is sown in peace by those who make peace.
                                     James 3:13-18 (RSV)

The fact that a person fears God and lives in the right way so as to please Him, leads to a host of different blessings. God rewards the wise for the way they choose to live. The things they do also lead to Him showing them His approval and giving them His protection and support:

Our own government are breaking their own laws in order to implement these draconian laws

167

Is it wicked to ignore good advice and instead implement that which is detrimental?

¹ Praise the LORD!
Blessed is the man who fears the LORD,
*   who greatly delights in his commandments!*
² His descendants will be mighty in the land;
*   the generation of the upright will be blessed.*
³ Wealth and riches are in his house;
*   and his righteousness endures for ever.*
⁴ Light rises in the darkness for the upright;
*   the LORD is gracious, merciful, and righteous.*
⁵ It is well with the man who deals generously and lends,
*   who conducts his affairs with justice.*
⁶ For the righteous will never be moved;
*   he will be remembered for ever.*
⁷ He is not afraid of evil tidings;
*   his heart is firm, trusting in the LORD.*
⁸ His heart is steady, he will not be afraid,
*   until he sees his desire on his adversaries.*
⁹ He has distributed freely, he has given to the poor;
*   his righteousness endures for ever;*
*   his horn is exalted in honor.*
¹⁰ The wicked man sees it and is angry;
*   he gnashes his teeth and melts away;*
*   the desire of the wicked man comes to nought.*
                              Psalm 112:1-10 (RSV)

he will bless those who fear the LORD,
both small and great.
                              Psalm 115:13 (RSV)

¹Blessed is everyone who fears the LORD,
* who walks in his ways!*
² You shall eat the fruit of the labor of your hands;
* you shall be blessed, and it shall be well with you.*
                              Psalm 128:1-2 (ESV)

These rewards and blessings will often come in this life, although God never guarantees that. But, even if they don't all come before we die, what is guaranteed is they will come at the Judgment Seat of Christ. A wise person is well aware that God rewards and exalts those who live righteously. That fact motivates wise people to make right choices, avoid sin and do what God wants. A recurring theme in the Bible is that wisdom is primarily expressed through our character, attitudes, values and lifestyle choices, not our intellectual abilities.

We can also show wisdom in the practical things we do, i.e. the skill and expertise we use in our work, because a person who is skilled and competent in their work is considered wise in God's eyes. Never make the mistake of thinking that only intellectual types can be wise. If someone is not academic or bookish, but excels in their practical work, and if they do their tasks with diligence, God would consider them wise, at least in regard to their work. That is crucial, because it takes up half our waking hours.

An example of this was Hiram who came from Tyre. King Solomon engaged him to work on the construction of the Temple. He knew how to work with bronze and how to design and make beautiful pieces of equipment and furniture for the Temple. This point is so important to God that He devotes nearly a whole chapter of the Bible in 1 Kings 7 to describing the bronze pieces that Hiram made. This was God's overall view of him:

[13]Now King Solomon sent and brought Hiram from Tyre. [14]He was a widow's son from the tribe of Naphtali, and his father was a man of Tyre, a worker in bronze; and he was filled with wisdom and understanding and skill for doing any work in bronze. So he came to King Solomon and performed all his work.
1 Kings 7:13-14 (NASB)

The way God draws attention to Hiram, and classes him as wise, ought to encourage anyone whose main talents are practical rather than academic, which applies to 75% or more of the population. In the U.K. there is an attitude of snobbery which causes some to look down on manual work, even if it is done by craftsmen. That is not God's view. If you have been given mainly practical or craft-related abilities, then give thanks for them and seek to become as skilled as possible. Then you will be considered wise in God's eyes in the way you do your work, which matters very much to Him.

My own Dad was a manual worker all his life, first as a farm labourer and then as a coal miner, except for seven years in the army where he was also a truck driver. In every type of work that he ever did he excelled. He was graded as a 'first class shot' with a rifle and when he left the army his discharge certificate said he had given *'Exemplary Service'*. Also, in his farming work, and when he later grew vegetables, he did all things well. Everything he grew was successful. He taught me things all the time when I worked with him on his allotments. I also picked up a lot just by watching.

Even in something as ordinary as shovelling coal, a surprising amount of skill is involved. My Dad could shovel coal for hours in the mine without tiring. Partly that was due to fitness, but mainly it was because of good technique. He spoke of how to use a shovel with the right movement, posture and rhythm, to maximise efficiency. I say all that to emphasise how important practical skills are in God's eyes. He wants all of us to aim to become wise, whatever jobs we may be in, not just those who are in academic professions.

Wise people are careful whom they confide in and are not quick to trust people.

Wise people are sensibly slow and cautious before being willing to trust other people. Unwise people tend to assume that everyone is the same as themselves. That is, they impute their own character to others. However, their reasons for doing so are very different:

a) Naive/simple people tend to be sincere and they often make the grave error of assuming that other people are all equally sincere. Thus, they are prone to confiding in others too readily and are excessively open and transparent.

b) Wicked people, being devious themselves, tend to assume that everybody else is equally devious, even if they aren't. So they don't confide. They are cagey and careful with everyone.

Thus, both groups, the simple and the wicked, make the same assumption, i.e. that all other people are like themselves. Either way, it is wrong. Wise people make neither of the above mistakes. They themselves are sincere, but they know that 90+% of other people are not. Therefore, they have learned not to assume that other people are sincere, whereas the wicked have always known that and weren't under any illusions to begin with. But the wise only tend to realise it later in life, due to bitter experiences of other people's unfaithfulness, disloyalty and dishonesty.

So, wise people are realistic and careful. They pick and choose the people with whom they can speak freely. Even then, they open up slowly and only let their guard down at all after they have made sure that the other person really is trustworthy. They don't rush in or assume that a person is to be trusted, even if they appear, on the face of it, to be genuine. They know that it takes a long time to properly establish what another person really is. First impressions and appearances can be very deceptive, such that a person's falseness only becomes apparent later on:

The sins of some men are conspicuous, pointing to judgment, but the sins of others appear later.

1 Timothy 5:24 (RSV)

Even after another person's trustworthiness appears to have been tested and established, wise people still disclose sensitive information slowly, and in stages,

170

and only where it is essential. They only reveal the minimum, rather than saying all that they know. They have usually learned this from past experiences of being let down. I myself was let down, or even betrayed, by one person after another whom I had hastily assumed to be trustworthy. Eventually I learned to be much more cautious, even though I had thought I was being fairly cautious to begin with.

I have had an unusually high exposure to untrustworthy people because I ran a business and employed a lot of staff, up to 80 at any one time. I therefore encountered more people at close quarters than the average person does. I also got to see them at their worst, i.e. the way they were at work, where people's sins, faults and bad habits are revealed by pressure and by being in close proximity with others for long periods. Therefore, my approach now is to keep most of my thoughts to myself, especially when I am with people who seem to be eager to know what I'm doing or planning. *"Pressure Test"*

You need to be particularly wary of anybody who ever *asks you to confide in them*. Wise, godly, blameless people will not do that, but the wicked frequently do. It's a very bad sign and one that you need to watch out for. See it as your cue to clam up and say nothing more. In short, never confide in anybody who *wants* you to do so. That is especially important if they ask you outright, or even if they are just hinting that you should confide in them, however subtle their hints may be. That desire, in itself, disqualifies them and should set off an alarm in you.

Trusting other people quickly is not a sign of goodness, but of naivety, which is a fault, not a quality. We must not trust anybody until sufficient evidence has been gathered to justify it, which takes a long time. When a person does *not* trust other people, it is not necessarily a sign that they are bad. They may actually be being wise, though not always. The wicked are also reluctant to trust people, but not because they are wise. They operate in a different way and are *suspicious* rather than cautious, and for different reasons, i.e. *because* they are wicked themselves, and fully assume that others are too.

There is even a third group of people who are reluctant to trust others, but they are neither wise nor wicked. They are just naive people who have been *damaged* by others so many times that they are now constantly wary, like a wild animal is. But they are like that without ever having worked out why, or having given it any serious thought. Therefore, observing whether a person is cautious in what they reveal about themselves is a useful litmus test. It can indicate that they are wicked, or wise, or that they are merely a simple/naïve person who has been wounded by others.

It all depends on their *reasons* and on the way they display their caution. So, when you come across a person who is unusually slow to trust others, you have to dig

171

deeper to discover their reasons for that wariness. Only then can you gauge whether they are doing it because they are wise, or wicked, or just naïve but wounded. Your assessment will also need to be guided by other aspects of their speech, actions and character. An example of this is a man, whom we'll call *Jason*. He naively told the whole truth to a family court when in a child access dispute with his ex-wife.

He had become a Christian after they split up, but was not saved some years earlier when he married her and when they had a son, who was now about seven. She had gone in the opposite direction spiritually and had married a Muslim and she had been given care and control of the child. Jason had only limited access, which she obstructed further as she became increasingly hostile to his Christian faith. She hit back at him by being difficult over access and, even worse, by trying to poison his son's mind against him.

Jason made an application to enforce his rights to access and to increase them, so he could see his son more often and try to counteract the lies she was telling the boy. This all happened before I knew Jason and before I had a chance to advise him. He was therefore naïve and made the mistake of being very open about his Christian faith when speaking to his own lawyers and, even more unwisely, in his dealings with the court. He told them plainly that he was a committed Christian, and that his wife was denigrating both himself and Christianity when speaking to their son.

He also pointed out that she had become a Muslim and was seeking to bring their boy up as a Muslim, which he opposed. In his naivety, Jason imagined that the court would act impartially and that the judge would respect his Christian beliefs and take them into account. He also assumed that the judge would not unfairly favour Islam. However, it turned out very badly. The judge did not respect him, or his beliefs, at all and became hostile, seeing Jason as the problem for disturbing the boy's Muslim upbringing. Predictably, the politically correct judge respected Islam, but not Christianity.

I could have warned Jason that that would almost certainly happen if I had known him at the time. I later told him that he should have said nothing about his own Christian faith and should not have mentioned how he felt about his ex-wife's new Muslim faith. It was virtually inevitable, given the modern UK legal system, that any such arguments would go badly for him. Thus, a policy of silence and keeping his beliefs to himself would have been far wiser. He should have expected the court to despise his beliefs, as it was far more likely to do that than to be supportive, or even neutral.

Thirty years ago things may well have been different, but not today. Having said all that, let me give another counterbalancing example of a situation where outright openness about your Christian faith could well be a wise policy. I refer to the position when you are applying for jobs and the question arises as to whether to mention that you are a Christian and that you go to church. People have asked me whether to put this on their CV and whether to be open about their faith and their church activities when in a job interview.

Perhaps surprisingly, given the points made above concerning Jason's naïve openness, I have generally advised people to be straightforward about their faith *when applying for jobs,* because you do not currently work for that employer. Therefore, even if he hates Christianity, he cannot do anything to harm you, other than reject you. But if he does hate Christianity, as so many do, then rejecting you would actually be a big favour. The alternative would have been for you to only discover his hostility to Christianity *after* you begin working for him, which would be vastly worse for you.

Given that so many employers are hostile to Christianity, and that you don't know who they are, but wish to avoid them if you can, being open on your CV makes sense. It gives your potential future enemies a reason to identify themselves and to reject you at the outset. That then helps you to make sure that you and they never actually work together. If you make 20 job applications, and if even 10 of the employers were hostile to your faith, you would still have the other 10 applications to pursue. They would all then, by definition, be employers who are *not hostile* to your faith.

Although it might seem that you are losing half of your opportunities by being open, you aren't really, because you would never have been happy at those firms anyway. Neither would you have prospered, unless you had been willing to compromise and fit in with their standards. But that would be even worse than being persecuted. Therefore, with job applications, a higher level of openness is appropriate to maximise your chances of avoiding a hostile employer and of finding one who is at least neutral.

When I used to sift through CVs when recruiting, the ones who said they were Christians generally got an interview, unless they were clearly unsuitable for other reasons. From then on, however, they had to progress solely on their merits. But even if 5-10% of employers are positive towards Christianity, not merely neutral, there is actually scope for you to gain something from your transparency. It could cause some doors to open which might otherwise have remained closed.

Another reason for being open on your CV is that it is important to be open about your faith and not ashamed of it when you join a new firm. The easiest way to do that is to put it on your CV as it will soon get around, because people talk. That is an advantage as it means you don't need to be quite so brave when you begin in the job, by explicitly announcing that you are a Christian. Many find that

173

Wisdom is taylored of appropriate in the situation to that person — not universally applicable difficult and therefore never get around to it, which causes them, and others, to lose out. The best thing in a new job is to start as you mean to go on, by being open on your CV, right at the start.

Wise people do not trust others until they have weighed them up properly. The Bible does not tell us to trust people.

I was consulted some time ago by a Christian friend who wanted advice. He had gone into business with a man he did not know and had paid a lot of money to him, as well as signing papers redirecting some of his own future income stream to that man. The other man had initially been charming, but once the papers had been signed, he cut my friend off and removed him from the business. The other man had got what he wanted, which was the money. It was only at that late stage, when the damage had already been done, that my advice was sought.

Sadly that is often the case. I then said *"Why did you do it? Why did you trust someone you didn't yet know?"* He replied "*Well, I wanted to be 'Christian' about it and trust people, like the Bible says*". I then said "*Where did you get the idea that the Bible tells us to trust people?*" That question surprised him. He had just assumed that trusting others was a Christian trait and a good quality, but he then said "*Well, I don't know. It's just what you always hear in church*".

Even as he said it, he suddenly realised that, in the whole Bible, we are never once instructed to trust people that we do not know, or to be quick to trust others in general, even if we *do* know them. On the contrary, the Bible repeatedly tells us to do the exact opposite and to be cautious, take our time, and reserve judgment until we know people properly. It particularly warns us about smooth or charming people, because they are even more likely to be false:

*²³ Like a coating of glaze over
earthenware are fervent lips with an evil heart.
²⁴ A malicious man disguises himself with his lips,
but in his heart he harbours deceit.
²⁵ Though his speech is charming,
do not believe him,
for seven abominations fill his heart.
²⁶ His malice may be concealed by deception,
but his wickedness will be exposed in the assembly.*
Proverbs 26:23-26 (NIV)

Although we are not to fear people, we are supposed to be wary of them. Jesus Himself commanded us to be so:

¹⁶ *"Behold, I send you out as sheep in the midst of wolves; so be shrewd as serpents and innocent as doves. ¹⁷ But beware of men, for they will hand you over to the courts and scourge you in their synagogues;*

Matthew 10:16-17 (NASB)

Wise people judge other people mainly by their fruit, i.e. what their lives produce, not solely by their words.

We are therefore told *in the Bible to assess other people by their fruit, i.e. by what they do*, and what their lives *produce* not only by what they *say*. There is no quick way of measuring fruit. It has to be done over months, and even years, not hours or days. That said, we are also commanded to check the accuracy of what people teach in church, even if we know them well and even if they are famous. Perhaps the best example of how we should handle other men's teaching is seen in Acts 17:11, about Luke's assessment of the Christians in Berea.

Luke praises them because when apostle Paul spoke in their church they checked everything he said in the Bible to see if it was correct. They didn't just accept it at face value. Even Paul's teaching had to be checked out, and they were right to do so, even if he had been well known to them. That is how we should all be, not only about doctrine and teaching, but about all relationships and transactions. Take plenty of time to assess *all* other people. Measure their deeds and their fruit carefully and check the accuracy and faithfulness of their teaching.

You may have heard it said that you should "*think the best of everyone*" and "*trust everyone until they do something to cause you to withdraw your trust*". That is very unwise advice and is the wrong default-setting. We should in fact do the very opposite and assume people are *not* to be trusted until they do *a series of things*, not just one thing, which prove that they can be trusted. The misguided policy of assuming that every new person we meet is 'trustworthy', until they are proved not to be, possibly comes from misapplying a valid idea.

That is that we should assume that people are *likeable* and *friendly* until they are proved not to be. That is an entirely different assumption and is both reasonable and helpful. It will also assist us in forming friendships because, if we assume that people are not going to be friendly, then we will automatically be unfriendly to them, and vice versa. However, that is a quite separate, and very different, policy from the one I am advocating, because most people *are* likeable and friendly, but most people are not trustworthy.

It is commonplace for a person to be entirely likeable, and yet still not be trustworthy, because these are two entirely different concepts. We must never equate them, or mistake one for the other, or we will go very wrong. I have often

175

considered people very likeable, for example at job interviews, and even afterwards when they worked for me. Yet they were anything but trustworthy. We should imitate Jesus' approach when dealing with people. He had infinite discernment and could see what was in men's hearts.

He therefore knew whether they were true or false, sincere or insincere. In this next passage Jesus is questioned by a group of Pharisees. They were respectable and scholarly men who occupied senior positions in the community. Despite all that, Jesus did not trust this delegation that had been sent to question Him. He knew they had malice in their hearts and that their real motive was to try to trip Him up and get Him into trouble:

15 Then the Pharisees went and plotted how to entangle him in his words. 16 And they sent their disciples to him, along with the Herodians, saying, "Teacher, we know that you are true and teach the way of God truthfully, and you do not care about anyone's opinion, for you are not swayed by appearances. 17 Tell us, then, what you think. Is it lawful to pay taxes to Caesar, or not?" 18 But Jesus, aware of their malice, said, "Why put me to the test, you hypocrites? 19 Show me the coin for the tax." And they brought him a denarius. 20 And Jesus said to them, "Whose likeness and inscription is this?" 21 They said, "Caesar's." Then he said to them, "Therefore render to Caesar the things that are Caesar's, and to God the things that are God's." 22 When they heard it, they marveled. And they left him and went away.

Matthew 22:15-22 (ESV)

One of the ways that Jesus was able to discern the falseness of this particular group of Pharisees was that they were *flattering* Him. We must always be especially wary of anyone who flatters us. If they really thought that He was "*true*" and that He .... "*teach(es) the way of God truthfully*....." then why were they disagreeing with Him and trying to catch Him out? Their own words proved their falseness, because they contrasted with their actions. At any rate, the point is that Jesus did not trust them. Therefore, He would not give them a full answer and cleverly dodged their trick question.

We will not have the same perfect discernment that Jesus had and we certainly don't have His cleverness and His ability to think instantly of the ideal answer to give to every trick question. However, we can at least seek to move in that direction. We must therefore begin to watch out for falseness in others and not trust anybody with our innermost thoughts and plans until it has been proved, by many different means, and over a long period of time, that they can be trusted.

In this next passage we see Jesus again refusing to answer what sounds, on the face of it, like a reasonable question. It came from a group of the Chief Priests, Scribes and Elders, the senior religious leaders of that time. They asked Jesus by what authority He was doing the miracles. Jesus could have just answered them, but He chose instead to ask them a question first, i.e. whether the baptism of John the Baptist was from God or just John's own idea. Jesus already knew that they did not accept John, or his teaching about repentance, and He wanted to expose that:

27And they came again to Jerusalem. And as he was walking in the temple, the chief priests and the scribes and the elders came to him, 28and they said to him, "By what authority are you doing these things, or who gave you this authority to do them?" 29Jesus said to them, "I will ask you one question; answer me, and I will tell you by what authority I do these things. 30Was the baptism of John from heaven or from man? Answer me." 31And they discussed it with one another, saying, "If we say, 'From heaven,' he will say, 'Why then did you not believe him?' 32But shall we say, 'From man'?"--they were afraid of the people, for they all held that John really was a prophet. 33So they answered Jesus, "We do not know." And Jesus said to them, "Neither will I tell you by what authority I do these things."

Mark 11:27-33 (ESV)

If the Jewish religious leaders in this passage had chosen to answer Jesus truthfully He would have given them an answer to their question. But they didn't answer Him, so He didn't answer them. In the same way we need to test other people and find out whether they are sincere and genuine before we tell them anything about our own thoughts and plans. What Jesus did that day was wise and to have done otherwise may not have been.

God promises to give us wisdom, but only if we really want it very strongly.

God wants us to pursue wisdom very earnestly, not just half-heartedly. The instruction to seek for it whole-heartedly is given over and over again in the Bible, as in these few examples:

*Apply your mind to instruction and
your ear to words of knowledge.*
Proverbs 23:12 (RSV)

*Buy truth, and do not sell it; buy wisdom,
instruction, and understanding.*
Proverbs 23:23 (RSV)

*Incline your ear, and hear the words of the wise,
and apply your mind to my knowledge;*
Proverbs 22:17 (RSV)

177

An intelligent heart acquires knowledge,
and the ear of the wise seeks knowledge.
Proverbs 18:15 (ESV)

The mind of him who has understanding seeks knowledge,
but the mouths of fools feed on folly.
Proverbs 15:14 (RSV)

Wisdom cannot be gained easily or quickly. It comes slowly, and only to those who want it badly enough to work hard for it and to pay whatever price is needed to get it. That price is paid in terms of continued effort, diligence, obedience and persistence. Only a person who really wants wisdom very intensely would be willing to pay such a high price, and to continue to pay it, for long enough. Decide now to become such a person. Start to value wisdom that highly and to seek for it that fervently:

¹My son, if you receive my words
and treasure up my commandments with you,
²making your ear attentive to wisdom
and inclining your heart to understanding;
³yes, if you cry out for insight
and raise your voice for understanding,
⁴if you seek it like silver
and search for it as for hidden treasures;
⁵then you will understand the fear of the LORD
and find the knowledge of God.
Proverbs 2:1-5 (RSV)   — female? 'she'

In Proverbs chapter 8 wisdom is 'personified'. That is 'wisdom' speaks within the chapter as if it was a person and was urging you to pursue him diligently and love him with all your strength. In this verse wisdom promises to love those who love 'him', and that 'he' will be found by those who seek him diligently. That is no coincidence, because Wisdom really is a person and that Person is Jesus. Indeed, one of His many titles is *"the Wisdom of God"* and thus it is literally true that to pursue Wisdom is to pursue Him:

I love those who love me,
and those who seek me diligently find me.
Proverbs 8:17 (ESV)

Ask God directly and regularly for the understanding you will need to become able to do his will and abide by His Word. Don't just wait passively for such understanding to materialise of its own accord. Seek for it actively and also ask God for it persistently:

178

Give me understanding, that I may keep thy law
and observe it with my whole heart.
Psalm 119:34 (RSV)

There is even a sense in which God deliberately hides certain truths so that they are available to be found, but only by those who make a sufficient effort to search for them:

It is the glory of God to conceal things,
but the glory of kings is to search things out.
Proverbs 25:2 (ESV)

God hides some things in the Bible in the way that coal is hidden under the ground at various different depths. Some is on the surface and easy to get. Some is 10-50 metres down. Some is 500 metres down. Some is a mile underground. Finding and extracting that coal brings glory to those who mine for it. Likewise, God hides knowledge and understanding within the Scriptures. His hiding of it glorifies Him, whereas our finding it glorifies us, and brings great benefits.

Although we need to make the effort to seek for knowledge and understanding of God's Word and of His will, we also need to ask Him to help us in doing that. It is our duty to incline our own hearts towards God's Word, but there is also a valid place for praying that God will help us to incline our hearts. Likewise, you have a duty to turn your own eyes away from vanities, i.e. useless, fruitless, worldly things which lead a person astray.

Yet, we should also ask God to help us turn our eyes away from such vanities. The responsibility is not entirely ours. But neither is it entirely up to God to achieve these changes in us. It is a 'joint venture' and involves willing cooperation between a sincere and repentant disciple, who truly wants to change, and a loving God who earnestly wants to help him to change. Here is the Psalmist asking for God's help in this area, just as we should:

[36] Incline my heart to thy testimonies,
and not to gain!
[37] Turn my eyes from looking at vanities;
and give me life in thy ways.
Psalm 119:36-37 (RSV)

179

Wise people do more than just listen. They also obey God's Word and put it into practice.

It is not enough just to read God's Word as a purely academic exercise. We also need to *obey* it by putting it into practice in our daily lives and by actually doing the things we are commanded to do:

Whoever is wise, let him understand these things; whoever is discerning, let him know them; for the ways of the LORD are right, and the upright walk in them, but transgressors stumble in them.

Hosea 14:9 (RSV)

[5]Behold, I have taught you statutes and ordinances, as the LORD my God commanded me, that you should do them in the land which you are entering to take possession of it. [6]Keep them and do them; for that will be your wisdom and your understanding in the sight of the peoples, who, when they hear all these statutes, will say, 'Surely this great nation is a wise and understanding people.' [7]For what great nation is there that has a god so near to it as the LORD our God is to us, whenever we call upon him? [8]And what great nation is there, that has statutes and ordinances so righteous as all this law which I set before you this day?

Deuteronomy 4:5-8 (RSV)

We must be determined to abide by, and to keep on abiding by, God's Word. We must always keep it in mind, not just now and then, or in church meetings. We must continually remind ourselves, *and our children*, of what God has said and done, and especially His commands to us:

"Only take heed, and keep your soul diligently, lest you forget the things which your eyes have seen, and lest they depart from your heart all the days of your life; make them known to your children and your children's children—

Deuteronomy 4:9 (RSV)

Therefore you shall keep his statutes and his commandments, which I command you this day, that it may go well with you, and with your children after you, and that you may prolong your days in the land which the LORD your God gives you for ever."

Deuteronomy 4:40 (RSV)

Oh that they had such a mind as this always, to fear me and to keep all my commandments, that it might go well with them and with their children for ever!

Deuteronomy 5: 29 (RSV)

32 You shall be careful to do therefore as the LORD your God has commanded you; you shall not turn aside to the right hand or to the left. 33 You shall walk in all the way which the LORD your God has commanded you, that you may live, and that it may go well with you, and that you may live long in the land which you shall possess.

Deuteronomy: 5: 32-33 (RSV)

5 Know then in your heart that, as a man disciplines his son, the LORD your God disciplines you. 6 So you shall keep the commandments of the LORD your God, by walking in his ways and by fearing him.

Deuteronomy: 8:5-6 (RSV)

11 "Take heed lest you forget the LORD your God, by not keeping his commandments and his ordinances and his statutes, which I command you this day: 12 lest, when you have eaten and are full, and have built goodly houses and live in them, 13 and when your herds and flocks multiply, and your silver and gold is multiplied, and all that you have is multiplied, 14 then your heart be lifted up, and you forget the LORD your God, who brought you out of the land of Egypt, out of the house of bondage,

Deuteronomy: 8:11-14 (RSV)

12 "And now, Israel, what does the LORD your God require of you, but to fear the LORD your God, to walk in all his ways, to love him, to serve the LORD your God with all your heart and with all your soul, 13 and to keep the commandments and statutes of the LORD, which I command you this day for your good?

Deuteronomy: 10:12-13 (RSV)

Remember also Jesus' sobering words when speaking of those who claim to be His followers but who do not obey what He says:

21 "Not everyone who says to Me, 'Lord, Lord,' will enter the kingdom of heaven, but he who does the will of My Father who is in heaven will enter. 22 Many will say to Me on that day, 'Lord, Lord, did we not prophesy in Your name, and in Your name cast out demons, and in Your name perform many miracles?' 23 And then I will declare to them, 'I never knew you; depart from Me, you who practice lawlessness.'

Matthew 7:21-23 (NASB)

The most alarming feature of what Jesus said above was that these people look and sound like followers of His and can even seem very impressive, and have spectacular ministries. Yet Jesus still rejects them and states that He *never knew them*. That must imply that they were never real Christians at any point, despite all appearances. That has to cause us to stop and ask ourselves whether we are

181

truly sincere. Are we genuinely obedient to God's Word to the best of our ability? Or, do we just pick and choose what to believe and what to obey?

If we persistently refuse to listen to God, he will eventually refuse to listen to us.

In addition to all of the many other reasons why we should listen to God, take His Word seriously and obey it, there is this further sobering thought. That is that if we ignore His voice, and persistently disobey our conscience and the Bible, then a point will eventually be reached where God 'hands us over'. That means that He leaves us to get on with whatever we choose to do, and to suffer the consequences of our own foolishness and rebellion. He may also cease to listen to us when we do get so deeply into trouble that we belatedly seek His help. Proverbs chapter one speaks of this and you must never act in such a way as to cause this to happen to you:

²³ If you turn at my reproof,
behold, I will pour out my spirit to you;
* I will make my words known to you.*
²⁴ Because I have called and you refused to listen,
* have stretched out my hand and no one has heeded,*
²⁵ because you have ignored all my counsel
* and would have none of my reproof,*
²⁶ I also will laugh at your calamity;
* I will mock when terror strikes you,*
²⁷ when terror strikes you like a storm
* and your calamity comes like a whirlwind,*
* when distress and anguish come upon you.*
²⁸ Then they will call upon me, but I will not answer;
* they will seek me diligently but will not find me.*
²⁹ Because they hated knowledge
* and did not choose the fear of the LORD,*
³⁰ would have none of my counsel
* and despised all my reproof,*
³¹ therefore they shall eat the fruit of their way,
* and have their fill of their own devices.*
³² For the simple are killed by their turning away,
* and the complacency of fools destroys them;*
*   Proverbs 1:23-32 (ESV)*

However, this terrible end can be so easily avoided if we will simply *listen* to what God says and obey it:

but whoever listens to me will dwell secure
and will be at ease, without dread of disaster."
Proverbs 1:33 (ESV)

Consider also this stark warning given by Azariah to King Asa and the people of Judah. He told them not to forsake God or else He will forsake them, i.e. by stepping aside and handing them over to face the consequences of their actions:

¹ The Spirit of God came upon Azariah the son of Oded, ² and he went out to meet Asa and said to him, "Hear me, Asa, and all Judah and Benjamin: The LORD is with you while you are with him. If you seek him, he will be found by you, but if you forsake him, he will forsake you.
2 Chronicles 15:1-2 (ESV)

Although it is a clear warning, the passage also contains a promise, in that if we seek God we will find Him, in the sense that He will allow Himself to be found and even ensure that He is found by us. So this is an explicitly clear statement, in both directions, and must be taken seriously and acted upon. Indeed, once you know all of this, as you now do, how can you possibly justify, ever again, not seeking God, or choosing to ignore or disobey His voice?

That same point applies whatever way He might choose to express Himself, i.e. whether it is through your conscience, or His written Word. Don't take any chances over this. It is a deadly serious issue. Therefore, resolve to listen to God's voice at all times, and always to obey it quickly and willingly. Don't ever put yourself into a position whereby God considers it necessary to stop speaking, or listening, to you.

Wise people know that they need to change, and they actively seek to do so

One obvious fact about ourselves, which few people know, and even fewer take seriously, is that we need to *change*. Not only is change plainly needed, but we are also explicitly commanded to do so, over and over again, all over the Bible. Most of us don't even notice those commands in the Bible, or we think they don't apply to us. Or we complacently assume that we have already changed, or that the changes will occur automatically and that we need not do anything to cause them to happen.

Only those who are wise, or becoming wise, can see that God commands us to change and that they therefore need to do something to make that happen. The wicked, fools, and often even the simple, see no need to change and are therefore taking no steps to do so. Only the wise give this any thought. They examine themselves and criticise their own character, attitudes, habits and priorities to

The mark of a wise mind is the willingness to change

identify areas in which they are lacking or are at fault. Unwise people are complacent and self-righteous and see no need for any improvement, let alone repentance.

They don't actually say it out loud, or even to themselves, but their working assumption is that whatever they think, feel, say or do is obviously right. They think it represents the norm, and that there is nothing wrong with it. Thus they see themselves and their own standards as the model or yardstick by which to measure everyone else. They also see themselves as 'good' people and they think that bad people, bad attitudes and bad behaviour, are only to be found amongst *other people* or groups, not in themselves. A wise person can see that such self-righteous assumptions are ridiculous.

He therefore willingly examines himself to identify, remove and correct his own sins, faults, errors, weaknesses, deficiencies, bad habits or wrong attitudes. A fool won't do any of these things and will resent anyone who suggests that he should, or who tries to do it for him by correcting him or offering advice. Therefore, unless a person is wise, he will be blind and deaf to his own faults and will remain so, even if people point them out to him. This condition can affect people even if they are talented and highly successful. We are *not* just looking at unsuccessful low-achievers.

Even famous people at the top of their professions can still be extremely unwise, and entirely blind to faults in themselves, which everyone else can see clearly. An example from military history is Field Marshal Bernard Montgomery, or *'Monty'*, the most famous British general in World War Two. He was an extremely clever man and a highly efficient and imaginative planner. He also had the gift of being able to inspire those who served under him. Yet, in one area of his life he was blind to the point of crassness.

He was arrogant about his enormous ability and also tactless and insensitive in how he spoke to and about others. An example of this is the appalling way he spoke to the media during the *'Battle of the Bulge'* in the winter of 1944. The Germans launched a surprise counter-attack in the Ardennes on a huge scale and pushed the American army back a long way, almost driving a wedge between the Allied forces. In the end, the Germans were stopped, partly by the Americans, but also by British forces under Montgomery.

On 20 December 1944, Eisenhower gave Monty command of American forces, including US 1st Army under General Hodges and US 9th Army under General Simpson. The battle then turned in the Allies' favour, partly due to Monty, but also to the information now coming in from deciphered German messages. These had not been available to the Americans as the Germans had initially maintained radio silence. Monty used the deciphered *'Enigma'* information to move the

American and British forces to exactly where they needed to be to halt the German advance.

This information gave him a huge advantage, which had not previously been available to the American generals Hodges or Simpson. Then, at a staff meeting, Monty humiliated Hodges in his hour of shame by asking for an update from a junior British officer and pointedly ignoring General Hodges himself, even though he was present. Hodges was a shy and sensitive man and this slight was felt very deeply. To make matters worse, on 22nd December, Monty reported to his superiors: *"We have tidied up the mess and got two American armies properly organised"*.

The next day, he said: *"I do not think 3rd US Army will be strong enough to do what is needed. If my forecast proves true, then I shall have to deal unaided with both 5th and 6th Panzer armies. I think I can manage them, but it will be a bit of a party"*. These arrogant remarks caused deep offence and harmed relations between British and American forces for a long time. Ironically, it turned out that the US 3rd Army, under General Patton, was wheeled around brilliantly. They intervened with great success, such that Monty did not, in the end, have to *"deal unaided"* with the 5th and 6th Panzer armies.

To further compound the series of insults, Monty then said at a press conference in January 1945: *"As soon as I saw what was happening in the Ardennes, I took certain steps myself to ensure that if the Germans got to the Meuse, they certainly would not get over that river. The battle has been most interesting, I think possibly one of the most interesting and tricky battles I have ever handled"*. Every American who read Monty's boastful words was disgusted and it was not forgotten.

The point is this was a brilliant man with a hugely successful career who was, nevertheless, a fool when it came to diplomacy and tact. He could not see the effect of his own words on the feelings of others. He also had no ability to see these faults in himself, or why they mattered. Above all, he had no intention to change, or to do anything about his faults. Whether you are successful or unsuccessful, senior or junior, talented or untalented, always be willing to examine yourself, to identify your faults, and to be concerned about them. Above all, be determined to change.

Montgomery was a great man, but these fatal flaws of vanity, pride and boastfulness seriously tarnished his reputation. Yet they could so easily have been avoided, and his place in history made even higher, if he had only set out, early in his career, to root out those faults. Had he done so, his public statements during and after the Battle of the Bulge would have been very different. He could have dealt sensitively with General Hodges and praised the American forces for what they had achieved, which was actually substantial.

They had slowed down the German attack, despite being taken completely by surprise by the strategic stupidity of what Hitler had ordered his armies to do. Hitler threw away Germany's entire mobile strategic reserve, and more besides, on a doomed counter-attack. Therefore, in fairness to Hodges, no reasonable general would ever have foreseen it, precisely because it was so insane. Accordingly, Monty could have given proper recognition to the Americans, for what they did achieve, without lessening the praise due to his own British forces.

Above all, he should have behaved modestly, claiming no credit for himself, and leaving it to others to congratulate him. Had he done so, we would all be praising him today for his tact and diplomacy, as well as for his military brilliance. Contrast Field Marshal Montgomery's attitude with that of Moses. The Bible says he was the meekest man on the face of the Earth, i.e. the humblest, most modest, most self-controlled man and the least boastful or proud:

3 Now the man Moses was very meek, more than all people who were on the face of the earth.

Numbers 12:3 (ESV)

Consider Moses's attitude, even after meeting God face to face, receiving the Law and being made the leader of God's people. He still had a remarkably humble and teachable heart. Note how he speaks to God, asking Him to show him His ways so that he can know Him and find favour in His sight. He also speaks of the Hebrew nation as *God's* people, not his own. He had no illusions about himself and no self-importance. In his place, many would assume they already had God's favour and didn't need to learn or change. Moses didn't see it that way and he is an example to us all of how to pray:

Now therefore, if I have found favor in your sight, please show me now your ways, that I may know you in order to find favor in your sight. Consider too that this nation is your people."

Exodus 33:13 (ESV)

The need to change is meant to be at the forefront of our minds

The need for each of us to change is a central issue throughout the whole Bible. God continually urges us to repent, listen to Him, obey His commands, stop sinning and grow in character, maturity and wisdom. The need to change is meant to be at the forefront of our minds. Yet, for most of us, the thought never even enters our heads, let alone preoccupies us. To illustrate how central this theme is, consider this series of verses from Jeremiah. The tragic fulfilment of his prophecies need never have occurred if only the people had listened and been willing to change:

In vain have I struck your children;
  they took no correction;
your own sword devoured your prophets
  like a ravening lion
                    Jeremiah 2:30 (ESV)

O LORD, do not your eyes look for truth?
You have struck them down,
  but they felt no anguish;
you have consumed them,
  but they refused to take correction.
They have made their faces harder than rock;
  they have refused to repent.
                    Jeremiah 5:3 (ESV)

But this people has a stubborn and rebellious heart;
  they have turned aside and gone away.
                    Jeremiah 5:23 (ESV)

To whom shall I speak and give warning,
  that they may hear?
Behold, their ears are uncircumcised,
  they cannot listen;
behold, the word of the LORD is to them an object of scorn;
  they take no pleasure in it
                    Jeremiah 6:10 (ESV)

[24] But they did not obey or incline their ear, but walked in their own counsels and the stubbornness of their evil hearts, and went backward and not forward. [25] From the day that your fathers came out of the land of Egypt to this day, I have persistently sent all my servants the prophets to them, day after day. [26] Yet they did not listen to me or incline their ear, but stiffened their neck. They did worse than their fathers.
                    Jeremiah 7:24-26 (ESV)

"Thus says the LORD of hosts, the God of Israel, behold, I am bringing upon this city and upon all its towns all the disaster that I have pronounced against it, because they have stiffened their neck, refusing to hear my words."
                    Jeremiah 19:15 (ESV)

You have neither listened nor inclined your ears to hear, although the
LORD persistently sent to you all his servants the prophets,

Jeremiah 25:4 (ESV)

Jeremiah later wrote the book of Lamentations after the disaster had occurred and
the people of Judah had been taken into exile. In that book he then includes this
verse, urging the people to test and examine their ways and to return to the LORD.
That is exactly what each of us need to do:

Let us test and examine our ways,
and return to the LORD!
Lamentations 3:40 (ESV)

You may only have a short period of time left before you face the Judgment
Seat, so don't waste your opportunities to change.

The Bible says *"the fear of the LORD is the beginning of wisdom"*. One reason
for that is that fearing God causes you to focus on the Judgment and on what will
be said and done to us on that awesome day. But even if you are young, your
death could come unexpectedly early, perhaps even today. If so, you might have
only a short period of time left in which to change and to become the sort of person
that Jesus feels able to praise and reward at the Judgment.

Surely it is obvious, once you start to think about it, that you ought to be examining
yourself and also looking for criticism, correction, and even rebuke, from other
people, and from God's Word, to help you to see your faults. When the Bible
criticises certain actions or attitudes, instead of assuming that it is obviously
speaking about other people, and doesn't apply to you, stop and ask yourself: *"Do*
I do that? Does this apply to me? Is this an area where I need to change?"

Although it is plain that we ought to ask such questions when we read the Bible,
very few of us actually do. But it is not only in the pages of the Bible that we
should be seeking to make discoveries about our own faults, bad habits and sins.
We should also become open to hear about these from other people and to allow
others to tell us things which we might not *like* to hear, but which we *need* to hear.
Again, it is obvious that we should be open and receptive to criticism, but very
few of us actually are.

That is not to say that we need to enjoy being criticised, or find it easy. That
would be unrealistic. It is simply that we need to be *willing* to receive it and to
make it clear to certain people (not everybody) that they have *permission* to point
out our faults. You even could ask them to do so. It is rather like taking cod liver
oil as a vitamin supplement. Probably nobody actually likes cod liver oil, but

188

some people recognise the benefits it brings and are therefore willing to drink it. They even request it from others, in order to benefit from it.

One of the biggest obstacles to making discoveries about your own faults is the tendency to justify yourself. A person who does that is more concerned about proving to himself, or to others, that he is not guilty, or does not have the fault in question, than in actually finding out whether he is guilty or does have that fault. Consider the lawyer in Luke 10. He sought to justify himself, rather than truly listening to Jesus and then finding out *whether*, and if so *how*, Jesus' words applied to him:

> **But he, desiring to justify himself, said to Jesus, "And who is my neighbor?**
> **Luke 10:29 (ESV)**

Rather than speak in that way he could, and should, have spoken as Job did, asking God to enable him to see his own sins:

> **How many are my iniquities and my sins?**
> **Make me know my transgression and my sin.**
> **Job 13:23 (ESV)**

Instead of trying to prove that you are not guilty, or are not at fault, cooperate fully with God, and with those who are close to you and know you well. Allow yourself to be convicted about your sins and to be told where you are at fault. You can sometimes even benefit from the things that are said by your enemies and by those who dislike you. At times, those are the only people who are willing to say unpleasant things to you. Your family, friends and colleagues would not dare, or would be too kind to say it. However, an enemy, or someone who cares nothing for you, may be willing to tell you exactly what they think, without any attempt to spare your feelings.

Such an enemy is not seeking to benefit you, and may just want to let off steam. Even so, if you assess what they say, you may find elements of truth in amongst the criticisms, accusations and insults. You may have to 'spit out the bones' where some of their remarks are exaggerated, unfair, or even false. But you can still accept, and learn from, some of the other things they say, which may be true, or partly true, even if their remarks are made ungraciously and with no desire to help you. Sometimes their comments can contain real insights which others would never have been willing to share with you.

We also need to ask God Himself to speak to us, and even to discipline us, when we are going wrong. God disciplines His children anyway, whether or not we ask Him to. Nevertheless, this divine discipline and correction will be more effective, and will take less time, if we welcome it and even ask for it. A person who is

189

asking for God's correction and discipline is also more likely to recognise and understand it when it comes. They will also learn the lesson less painfully. It is common sense, therefore, that we should invite God to teach and correct us:

Blessed is the man whom you discipline, O LORD,
and whom you teach out of your law
Psalm 94:12 (ESV)

Therefore, why go in the opposite direction, whereby you resist God's discipline? Why even prolong the process? Instead, you could simply say to God: *"Is there a lesson for me here? Are you trying to teach me something through this painful trial or adversity? If so, please help me to grasp it fully, and more quickly, so that the lesson can be ended sooner and need not be extended or repeated."*

Most of the character changes and growth in wisdom that we achieve comes by a long series of small and apparently insignificant steps, rather than huge quantum leaps.

Most people don't have any desire to change in their character or to grow in wisdom. But for the minority who do, and who are pursuing wisdom, there is a temptation to be impatient and to imagine that it can all be achieved quickly, by a few quantum leaps forward. Sadly, that is not how it works. A wise person reconciles himself to the fact that most of the progress he will make in improving his character, or growing in wisdom, will come by the accumulated effect, over many years, of thousands of small and seemingly insignificant steps.

At the time when he takes each step, or learns each lesson, or gains each experience, he moves forward by an imperceptibly small distance. It might be only one hundredth of one percent of the overall journey. Thus, on the face of it, nothing has noticeably changed. He may seem to others, and to himself, to be no further forward. But a wise person knows that *if he persists* he will eventually get there. This applies not only to acquiring wisdom, but to all of the worthwhile things that we seek to achieve in life.

Whilst quantum leaps forward can certainly be made, they are exceptionally rare. I would say that over the last three decades or more I have only made about half a dozen quantum leaps, whereby I have been catapulted forward and my understanding has grown, or the direction of my life has altered, radically overnight. Throughout the rest of the time, for well over 30 years since I was converted, my progress in every part of my life, not just growing in wisdom, has been steady and *incremental*.

If you are at least wise enough to want to become wiser, then you will have to accept that this is how God works, at least so far as growth in wisdom and character development are concerned. Resolve now to keep going, not just for months or years, but for *decades,* in developing a godly character, and in achieving God's objectives for your life. That means right across the board, including marriage, family, career and ministry. If a person is not willing to get to his objective by taking 1000 small steps, he will never get there.

If you yearn for quantum leaps and shortcuts, such that you can make huge progress overnight, you won't be willing to settle down to a life of diligent, step by step, progress. Your unrealistic expectations will prevent you from taking those small steps and will also discourage you when quantum leaps don't happen. Ironically, on those rare occasions when gigantic steps forward are made overnight, they only occur in the lives of people who have already taken hundreds of small steps.

Such dramatic leaps are not a substitute for steady, diligent progress. They are God's reward to those who have been willing to seek Him faithfully and to obey Him hundreds of times already. In other words, quantum leaps are a bonus, given on rare occasions, *to faithful people,* and only when God chooses to give them. You must not expect them or make them your objective. Instead, focus on long term diligence and leave the quantum leaps for God to hand out when He chooses to.

Adopting this patient, persistent, realistic approach will make you undefeatable and you will eventually achieve your goals. There is a quotation from President Coolidge which I like. It speaks of the enormous importance of persistence if you are to be successful in any area of life. That principle applies right across the board, not only in spiritual growth. I rarely quote from anything other than the Bible, but this one is worth including:

"Nothing in this world can take the place of persistence. Talent will not: nothing is more common than unsuccessful men with talent. Genius will not: unrewarded genius is almost a proverb. Education will not: the world is full of educated derelicts. Persistence and determination alone are omnipotent."

President Calvin Coolidge

Wise people take care not to make God their opponent.

Wise people avoid angering God or arousing His opposition. It is as simple as this - if we act wrongly then God Himself will resist and oppose us, but if we do good He will support us:

Seek good, and not evil,
    that you may live;
and so the LORD, the God of hosts, will be with you,
    as you have said.

Amos 5:14 (ESV)

Zechariah also tells us what God does to those who lie and steal, whoever they may be. No distinction is drawn, at least within the passage, between believers and unbelievers. 'Everyone' who lies or steals will be affected by a curse which God sends out and which will pursue them and cause them to be 'cut off' and 'consumed':

¹ Again I lifted my eyes and saw, and behold, a flying scroll! ² And he said to me, "What do you see?" I answered, "I see a flying scroll; its length is twenty cubits, and its breadth ten cubits." ³ Then he said to me, "This is the curse that goes out over the face of the whole land; for every one who steals shall be cut off henceforth according to it, and every one who swears falsely shall be cut off henceforth according to it. ⁴ I will send it forth, says the LORD of hosts, and it shall enter the house of the thief, and the house of him who swears falsely by my name; and it shall abide in his house and consume it, both timber and stones."

Zechariah 5:1-4 (RSV)

We are also told that the LORD is avenging and wrathful on His enemies:

The LORD is a jealous and avenging God;
    the LORD is avenging and wrathful;
the LORD takes vengeance on his adversaries
    and keeps wrath for his enemies.

Nahum 1:2 (ESV)

⁶ Who can stand before his indignation?
    Who can endure the heat of his anger?
His wrath is poured out like fire,
    and the rocks are broken into pieces by him.
⁷ The LORD is good,
    a stronghold in the day of trouble;
he knows those who take refuge in him.
⁸   But with an overflowing flood
he will make a complete end of the adversaries,

Nahum 1:6-8 (ESV)

Thus, one of the many reasons to avoid sin is so as not to make God into our opponent. We see this point expressed in this next passage from Proverbs. It warns us not to steal the land of a poor person (by moving a boundary marker) or to oppress the weak in their use of their land. If we do then God Himself will take up that poor man's cause and plead it against the wrongdoer. He will do so even if that oppressor is a believer, *and even if it is you:*

¹⁰Do not remove an ancient landmark
or enter the fields of the fatherless;
¹¹for their Redeemer is strong;
he will plead their cause against you.
Proverbs 23:10-11 (RSV)

Realising that this is how God operates makes a wise person all the more careful to avoid oppressing or wronging other people. We should not wish to do so anyway, but this added factor dramatically raises the significance of how we treat others. It gives us a further incentive to act justly, especially towards the weak and the poor:

The righteous care about justice for the poor,
but the wicked have no such concern.
Proverbs 29:7 (NIV)

A genuine concern for the interests of others is an important aspect of the fear of the LORD. The wise man does not envy, or imitate, those who seek to gain advantage by doing wrong. One reason for that is that he does not want to be cut off by God, as such wrongdoers inevitably will be:

¹⁷Let not your heart envy sinners,
but continue in the fear of the LORD all the day.
¹⁸Surely there is a future,
and your hope will not be cut off.
Proverbs 23:17-18 (RSV)

See the statements made in the book of Hosea about how God viewed the people of the Northern Kingdom of Israel prior to the invasion by the Assyrians, which God allowed as a judgment upon them. Note what God says of them, and how He responds to the sins of His people, which must be taken to apply equally to us. It serves as a stark warning, which a wise person will take seriously:

Hear the word of the LORD, O children of Israel,
for the LORD has a controversy with the inhabitants of the land.
There is no faithfulness or steadfast love,
and no knowledge of God in the land;
Hosea 4:1 (ESV)

And it shall be like people, like priest;
I will punish them for their ways
and repay them for their deeds.
                              Hosea 4:9 (ESV)

With their flocks and herds they shall go
to seek the LORD,
but they will not find him;
he has withdrawn from them.
                              Hosea 5:6 (ESV)

⁹ Ephraim shall become a desolation
in the day of punishment;
among the tribes of Israel
I make known what is sure.
¹⁰ The princes of Judah have become
like those who move the landmark;
upon them I will pour out
my wrath like water.
                              Hosea 5:9-10 (ESV)

I will return again to my place,
until they acknowledge their guilt and seek my face,
and in their distress earnestly seek me.
                              Hosea 5:15 (ESV)

Whoever is wise, let him understand these things;
whoever is discerning, let him know them;
for the ways of the LORD are right,
and the upright walk in them,
but transgressors stumble in them.
                              Hosea 14:9 (ESV)

A wise person will want to put himself in the right place and do the right things, because any sensible person, knowing how God operates, and what His Word says, would want to do those things which bring God's blessing. He will also want to avoid those things which result in His curses, opposition or judgment:

³³ The LORD's curse is on the house of the wicked,
but he blesses the dwelling of the righteous.
³⁴ Toward the scorners he is scornful,
but to the humble he gives favor.
³⁵ The wise will inherit honor,
but fools get disgrace   *Proverbs 3:33-35 (ESV)*

We have to choose each day whether to act wickedly or righteously. This is what God instructed Moses to tell the Israelites in relation to obeying the Law of Moses. Admittedly, we are not subject to the Law of Moses, because it ceased when Jesus died. Even so, this general principle of the need to seek God's blessing and avoid His opposition is still valid. Although the Law of Moses is no longer in operation, there are many other commandments and principles which still apply to us, such as the command to love one another, the law of sowing and reaping, and the law that all who exalt themselves will be humbled. Here is how Moses expressed this general principle:

26"Behold, I set before you this day a blessing and a curse: 27the blessing, if you obey the commandments of the LORD your God, which I command you this day, 28and the curse, if you do not obey the commandments of the LORD your God, but turn aside from the way which I command you this day, to go after other gods which you have not known.

Deuteronomy 11:26-28 (RSV)

Be careful to heed all these words which I command you, that it may go well with you and with your children after you for ever, when you do what is good and right in the sight of the LORD your God.

Deuteronomy 12:28 (RSV)

15"See, I have set before you this day life and good, death and evil. 16If you obey the commandments of the LORD your God which I command you this day, by loving the LORD your God, by walking in his ways, and by keeping his commandments and his statutes and his ordinances, then you shall live and multiply, and the LORD your God will bless you in the land which you are entering to take possession of it. 17But if your heart turns away, and you will not hear, but are drawn away to worship other gods and serve them, 18I declare to you this day, that you shall perish; you shall not live long in the land which you are going over the Jordan to enter and possess. 19I call heaven and earth to witness against you this day, that I have set before you life and death, blessing and curse; therefore choose life, that you and your descendants may live, 20loving the LORD your God, obeying his voice, and cleaving to him; for that means life to you and length of days, that you may dwell in the land which the LORD swore to your fathers, to Abraham, to Isaac, and to Jacob, to give them."

Deuteronomy 30:15-20 (RSV)

If you face opposition bear in mind the possibility that it might be God Himself who is opposing you

Where we face opposition, one possibility, which must at least be considered, is that God Himself may have raised up people to oppose us. We see this illustrated in the life of King Solomon. He began well, but then degenerated into foolishness, evil and even idolatry. It was mainly because he married foreign women who worshiped false gods and led him astray. God was angry about that and therefore raised up a number of enemies to oppose King Solomon:

⁹ And the LORD was angry with Solomon, because his heart had turned away from the LORD, the God of Israel, who had appeared to him twice, ¹⁰ and had commanded him concerning this thing, that he should not go after other gods; but he did not keep what the LORD commanded.

1 Kings 11:9-10 (RSV)

And the LORD raised up an adversary against Solomon, Hadad the E'domite; he was of the royal house in Edom.

1 Kings 11:14 (RSV)

²³ God also raised up as an adversary to him, Rezon the son of Eli'ada, who had fled from his master Hadad-e'zer king of Zobah. ²⁴ And he gathered men about him and became leader of a marauding band, after the slaughter by David; and they went to Damascus, and dwelt there, and made him king in Damascus. ²⁵ He was an adversary of Israel all the days of Solomon, doing mischief as Hadad did; and he abhorred Israel, and reigned over Syria.

1 Kings 11:23-25 (RSV)

If you are facing unusual or unexpected levels of opposition, consider the possibility that God Himself may be opposing you and also raising up adversaries against you. It could be as a result of some sin or rebellion in your life. If so, God may be using those adversaries to get you to wake up, examine your life, and seek Him. Why make it more difficult for yourself? Why require God to go to such lengths? Why make it necessary for Him to have to impose these revelations upon you? You could simply *ask Him* to reveal anything in your attitudes, speech or conduct which is not pleasing to Him.

He will be sure to answer a request like that, if it is sincerely made, because it is in accordance with His will. Also, do not assume that God would never act in this way towards a real Christian. I am quite sure that He would. At any rate, there is nothing in the Bible to suggest that He would not. In my own life He has sent a number of people to oppose and chasten me, even after I was saved. More importantly, God opposed King David. He sent him many adversaries after he sinned in the episode involving Bathsheba and her husband, Uriah.

Yet David was a genuine believer at all these times, before, during and after his sins. Solomon also died as a believer and was saved and yet, as we saw, God frequently opposed him. Indeed, it may well be that the very reason Solomon came back to God, and recovered his faith, was precisely *because* God had

The fear of God – to seek to please God

opposed him. At any rate, the point is that, so far as we are concerned, we must take care not to make God our opponent. Recognise the possibility that what happened to Solomon, David, and many others, could also happen to you, and may already be happening.

Wise people therefore learn God's principles, how He operates and how He wants us to operate

If we want to be wise, we will also make it our business to learn all the other principles by which God operates and how to apply them. Even if the Bible does not contain any specific advice or instruction which deals with your exact circumstances, the application of these broad biblical principles will always be helpful. We need to familiarise ourselves with them all. We will then be better informed as to how God *generally* operates and how He wishes us to operate. We must also familiarise ourselves with God's many promises, and also the statements He makes about cause and effect. Here is an example:

The reward for humility and fear of the LORD
is riches and honor and life.
Proverbs 22:4 (RSV)

If a person has humility and the fear of the LORD, they will eventually receive riches, honour and life as their reward, either in this life, or in the next, probably in both. A wise person will take that statement literally and seriously, and seek to develop those qualities in order to benefit from that promise. A wise person does not seek *directly* for riches or honour, at least not in this life. He seeks instead for those things which will lead to us being given those rewards. Instead of asking for the reward itself, it is wiser to ask God to help us to develop those *character qualities that He has promised to reward.*

Many are seeking for riches and honour, but very few are seeking the humility or fear of the LORD, which qualify us to receive these. However, if we are wise, we will realise that, in God's economy, the one leads to the other and *put our main focus on the cause, not on the effect.* That is the way God thinks and it is how He wants us to think. Another thing which God has promised to reward is where a person loves and cherishes the Bible and is determined to study it. We are told of the many benefits that will come to those who revere God's Word and desire to obey it:

[7] The law of the LORD is perfect,
reviving the soul;
the testimony of the LORD is sure,
making wise the simple;

197

⁸ the precepts of the LORD are right,
   rejoicing the heart;
the commandment of the LORD is pure,
   enlightening the eyes;
⁹ the fear of the LORD is clean,
   enduring forever;
the rules of the LORD are true,
   and righteous altogether.
¹⁰ More to be desired are they than gold,
   even much fine gold;
sweeter also than honey
   and drippings of the honeycomb.
¹¹ Moreover, by them is your servant warned;
   in keeping them there is great reward.
                        Psalm 19:7-11 (ESV)

Therefore, do as the Psalmist did. Greatly increase your regard for God's Word, until you too take delight in it and actually love to obey it, rather than doing so reluctantly:

I delight to do your will, O my God;
   your law is within my heart."
                Psalm 40:8 (ESV)

Also, be like the writer of Psalm 1 who delighted in the law of the LORD and meditated on it day and night. Look at the benefits which the Bible says will come to such a man:

¹ Blessed is the man
   who walks not in the counsel of the wicked,
nor stands in the way of sinners,
   nor sits in the seat of scoffers;
² but his delight is in the law of the LORD,
   and on his law he meditates day and night.
³ He is like a tree
   planted by streams of water
that yields its fruit in its season,
   and its leaf does not wither.
In all that he does, he prospers.
⁴ The wicked are not so,
   but are like chaff that the wind drives away.
⁵ Therefore the wicked will not stand in the judgment,
   nor sinners in the congregation of the righteous;

⁶ for the LORD knows the way of the righteous,
  but the way of the wicked will perish.
                              Psalm 1:1-6 (ESV)

Note also the stark principle stated by Azariah. He warned King Asa, and all the people of Judah and Benjamin, that God will be found by those who seek Him, but will forsake those who forsake Him:

¹ The Spirit of God came upon Azariah the son of Oded, ² and he went out to meet Asa and said to him, "Hear me, Asa, and all Judah and Benjamin: The LORD is with you while you are with him. If you seek him, he will be found by you, but if you forsake him, he will forsake you.
                              2 Chronicles 15:1-2 (ESV)

Should it not be obvious, to any sensible person that we need therefore to seek for God, and to be with Him, and, in particular, never to forsake Him? Given the frank way in which Azariah puts it, none of us has any excuse for not being aware that it is our responsibility to stay faithful and to be determined to avoid the dire consequences of forsaking God. On a more positive note, Hanani, who was another seer or prophet at the time of King Asa, also said:

"For the eyes of the LORD run to and fro throughout the whole earth, to give strong support to those whose heart is blameless towards him ...."
                              2 Chronicles 16:9(a) (ESV)

If this is what God is doing, then, unless we are fools, it ought to be obvious that we should seek to be blameless. Then we can qualify to receive this "strong support", which God desires to give to those who are blameless. How can any rational person think otherwise? One of Asa's successors, King Jotham, took this principle seriously. He pleased God by his actions, such that we are told: *"And he did what was right in the eyes of the LORD according to all that his father Uzziah had done..."* As a result of his conduct, and right choices, Jotham received God's blessing and became mighty:

So Jotham became mighty, because he ordered his ways before the LORD his God.
                              2 Chronicles 27:6 (ESV)

By contrast, King Ahaz did not do what was right and did not please God. Therefore, God did not support him, but actively opposed him instead and caused him to be defeated by the King of Syria:

¹ Ahaz was twenty years old when he began to reign, and he reigned sixteen years in Jerusalem. And he did not do what was right in the eyes of the LORD,

as his father David had done, [2] but he walked in the ways of the kings of Israel.
He even made metal images for the Baals, [3] and he made offerings in the Valley
of the Son of Hinnom and burned his sons as an offering, according to the
abominations of the nations whom the LORD drove out before the people of
Israel. [4] And he sacrificed and made offerings on the high places and on the
hills and under every green tree.
[5] Therefore the LORD his God gave him into the hand of the king of Syria, who
defeated him and took captive a great number of his people and brought them
to Damascus. He was also given into the hand of the king of Israel, who struck
him with great force.

2 Chronicles 28:1-5 (ESV)

Wise people do not take offence at what the Bible says

It is remarkable how many people take offence at what Jesus says, or at what the Bible in general says. Having been offended or irritated, they then refuse to listen or read any further and they harden their hearts, so as to resist what God is saying. Such offence can be taken over a wide range of issues, but the general result is to cause that person to close their mind. Then they no longer want to know what the Bible says and are prejudiced against it.

A wise person realises the harm that is caused by becoming hard-hearted due to taking offence at, or stumbling over, something that the Bible says. It makes a person less receptive, obedient and motivated and also reduces their love for Jesus. That therefore creates a barrier where there ought not to be one. Jesus Himself warned us not to take offence at Him, precisely because He knew that many of us would do so:

And blessed is he who takes no offense at me.

Matthew 11:6 (RSV)

When people take offence at Jesus they become distanced from Him. In Jesus' own day many of the people who lived in his home town of Nazareth, despised Him, and under-estimated Him, because He was local and therefore familiar to them:

[54] He came to His hometown and began teaching them in their synagogue, so
that they were astonished, and said, "Where did this man get this wisdom and
these miraculous powers? [55] Is not this the carpenter's son? Is not His mother
called Mary, and His brothers, James and Joseph and Simon and Judas? [56] And
His sisters, are they not all with us? Where then did this man get all these
things?" [57] And they took offense at Him. But Jesus said to them, "A prophet is

not without honor except in his hometown and in his own household." ⁵⁸ And
He did not do many miracles there because of their unbelief.

Matthew 13:54-58 (NASB)

Taking offence leads to hardness of heart which leads to a closed mind and finally, to unbelief. Far too many people take offence at Jesus, or at what the Bible says, because it tells them the truth about themselves, or does not fit in with their own customs and opinions. Most of us have become familiar with certain denominational traditions and practices. Then, woe betide anyone who questions those and points us instead to what the Bible says. The person who is devoted to customs and familiar practices is likely to take offence and will resist any challenge to these, even from Jesus Himself:

¹ He entered again into a synagogue; and a man was there whose hand was withered. ² They were watching Him to see if He would heal him on the Sabbath, so that they might accuse Him. ³ He said to the man with the withered hand, "Get up and come forward!" ⁴ And He said to them, "Is it lawful to do good or to do harm on the Sabbath, to save a life or to kill?" But they kept silent. ⁵ After looking around at them with anger, grieved at their hardness of heart, He said to the man, "Stretch out your hand." And he stretched it out, and his hand was restored. ⁶ The Pharisees went out and immediately began conspiring with the Herodians against Him, as to how they might destroy Him.

Mark 3:1-6 (NASB)

Those Pharisees took offence simply because Jesus healed a man on the Sabbath day, which the Law of Moses does *not* forbid. Therefore, Jesus was acting perfectly properly. He was just cutting across their own man-made rules and regulations about what can and cannot be done on the Sabbath. They had, over many years, added layer upon layer of additional requirements and prohibitions which had no biblical basis and were not from God. Jesus obeyed every tiny detail of the Law of Moses, but He deliberately ignored those man-made rules, known as *'the oral law'*.

Therefore, He healed the man right in front of the Pharisees. However, instead of being delighted, or wanting to find out more about Jesus and His teaching, they took offence. They were affronted and thought *"How dare He not honour us and our beliefs and practices? How dare he contradict us, especially in public?"* That was their reaction, rather than saying *"What He has done goes against what I have been used to up to now. Therefore, have I been wrong? How do my thinking, traditions and assumptions need to change to fit in with Him?"*

Such narrow-minded attitudes and reactions were not only a feature of the Pharisees. They are also found in us today. Many of us we need to look for these attitudes in ourselves and remove them. We might not be offended by the same

201

things that irritated the Pharisees, because most of us have not grown up in Judaism. Therefore, we have not been taught to value the so called 'oral law', or the traditions of the Rabbis, more highly than the Bible.

Yet we have still been taught, or have unconsciously absorbed, other equally man-made rules, regulations and beliefs. Thus, a person today might be irritated by what the Bible says about the role of women in the church or within marriage. Or they may object to what it teaches about Israel, creation, adultery, divorce, homosexuality, gender, financial giving or a host of other things. Many people have so thoroughly absorbed the values and beliefs of the secular world on such issues, they are irritated by, and even ashamed of, what the Bible says.

I know one man personally who reacted negatively when someone quoted from one of Paul's letters in a home group Bible study. He said *"Apostle Paul and I don't get on."* He meant that he did not like Paul's teaching, because it contradicted his own personal opinions. It did not occur to him that his reaction was absurd, which it clearly was. How can any right-thinking person say: *"Apostle Paul thinks X, but I think Y, and I believe that Paul is wrong and I am right."*?

If you and apostle Paul, or you and any other writer of the Bible, disagree on anything whatsoever, then it is *you* who is wrong, *not them.* You never have any valid basis for disagreeing with them at all, let alone being offended by what they say. Few people would ever put it into such stark words as that man did. But they still think the same way, albeit more subtly, and the net effect is the same. They ignore what the Bible says and cling instead to their own man-made tradition, opinion or practice.

Jesus confronted the Pharisees about this attitude in the next passage. They were upset because His followers were not washing their hands in the formal way that their own *man-made* oral law (not the Bible) required. Despite all the miracles which they were seeing at first hand, and also the inspired teaching Jesus was giving, all they could focus on was that Jesus and His followers did not abide by their cherished rules and traditions:

¹ Then some Pharisees and scribes came to Jesus from Jerusalem and said, ² "Why do Your disciples break the tradition of the elders? For they do not wash their hands when they eat bread." ³ And He answered and said to them, "Why do you yourselves transgress the commandment of God for the sake of your tradition? ⁴ For God said, 'Honor your father and mother,' and, 'He who speaks evil of father or mother is to be put to death.' ⁵ But you say, 'Whoever says to his father or mother, "Whatever I have that would help you has been given to God,"⁶ he is not to honor his father or his mother.' And by this you invalidated

202

the word of God for the sake of your tradition. [7] You hypocrites, rightly did Isaiah prophesy of you:
[8] 'This people honors Me with their lips,
But their heart is far away from Me.
[9] 'But in vain do they worship Me,
Teaching as doctrines the precepts of men.'"
[10] After Jesus called the crowd to Him, He said to them, "Hear and understand. [11] It is not what enters into the mouth that defiles the man, but what proceeds out of the mouth, this defiles the man."[12] Then the disciples came and said to Him, "Do You know that the Pharisees were offended when they heard this statement?" [13] But He answered and said, "Every plant which My heavenly Father did not plant shall be uprooted. [14] Let them alone; they are blind guides of the blind. And if a blind man guides a blind man, both will fall into a pit."

Matthew 15:1-14 (NASB)

Jesus' response offended the Pharisees but He was unmoved and said that they were just blind guides. That is what we will become too if we put any man-made tradition above the Bible. Some people get angry when the Bible is critical of their attitudes or behaviour, as when Jesus implicitly criticised the people in the synagogue at Nazareth:

And all the people in the synagogue were filled with rage as they heard these things;

Luke 4:28 (NASB)

The mere fact that what is being said is true does not stop people from being angry. On the contrary, the more accurate the statement is, the more enraged they become. This was the case with Herodias, who was cohabiting with Herod Antipas, her half-uncle, while she was still married to Herod's brother, Philip, also her half-uncle. John the Baptist pointed this out and said it was wrong, which it obviously was, in many ways. Nevertheless, Herodias held a grudge from then on until she eventually got the chance to have John killed:

[17] For Herod himself had sent and had John arrested and bound in prison on account of Herodias, the wife of his brother Philip, because he had married her. [18] For John had been saying to Herod, "It is not lawful for you to have your brother's wife." [19] Herodias had a grudge against him and wanted to put him to death and could not do so;

Mark 6:17-19 (NASB)

[21] A strategic day came when Herod on his birthday gave a banquet for his lords and military commanders and the leading men of Galilee; [22] and when the daughter of Herodias herself came in and danced, she pleased Herod and his dinner guests; and the king said to the girl, "Ask me for whatever you want and

203

I will give it to you." [23] *And he swore to her, "Whatever you ask of me, I will give it to you; up to half of my kingdom."* [24] *And she went out and said to her mother, "What shall I ask for?" And she said, "The head of John the Baptist."*
Mark 6:21-24 (NASB)

What John the Baptist said about Herodias was entirely true, but she resented it all the more for that very reason. She is not the only one who does that. Our sinful flesh nature means that we all dislike criticism, *especially when it is justified*. But we ought not to. We should positively *want* to know the real truth about ourselves, even if it is upsetting. A wise person will therefore force himself not to take offence at what the Bible says, even when it is critical of him, or contradicts his opinions, or his much-loved traditions, and even when it shows him to be in the wrong.

Wise people do not mock or despise their political rulers and governments

It has become fashionable to disrespect and mock our MPs, Congressmen, Cabinet Ministers, Prime Ministers, and so on. We regularly see and hear such ridicule in the media which causes additional disrespect, but also expresses the disrespect that people already feel. A wise person will ask himself: *"How does God want us to speak of, and relate to, our political leaders and rulers?"* We can be sure that He does not want us to speak evil of them or to curse them. Even if we need to criticise them, we are still to honour them, whether or not we think they are doing a good job:

"Do not blaspheme God or curse the ruler of your people.
Exodus 22:28 (NIV)

Honor everyone. Love the brotherhood. Fear God. Honor the emperor.
1 Peter 2:17 (ESV)

The word 'curse' in the verse above from Exodus means in the sense of *reviling or insulting*. It does not mean where we simply disagree with a politician and criticise his policies or his conduct. Paul quotes this verse from Exodus with that meaning in the book of Acts:

And Paul said, "I did not know, brethren, that he was the high priest; for it is written, 'You shall not speak evil of a ruler of your people.'"
Acts 23:5 (RSV)

Apostle Peter also gives instruction on how we are to speak and act in relation to our political rulers:

204

¹³ Be subject for the Lord's sake to every human institution, whether it be to the emperor as supreme, ¹⁴ or to governors as sent by him to punish those who do wrong and to praise those who do right. ¹⁵ For it is God's will that by doing right you should put to silence the ignorance of foolish men. ¹⁶ Live as free men, yet without using your freedom as a pretext for evil; but live as servants of God. ¹⁷ Honor all men. Love the brotherhood. Fear God. Honor the emperor.

1 Peter 2:13-17 (RSV)

How many of us give even a moment's thought to how God wants us to speak about our political rulers and also those in authority over us at work, or the police, councils, courts etc? God wants us to respect and honour *all* of those rulers. They have all been put into those positions *by God Himself*. He creates governments, and every other form of authority, to keep order and restrain wickedness. He wants us to cooperate with such rulers and to show them honour, even while we campaign against their policies. To do otherwise is to oppose God Himself:

¹ Let every person be subject to the governing authorities. For there is no authority except from God, and those that exist have been instituted by God. ² Therefore he who resists the authorities resists what God has appointed, and those who resist will incur judgment. ³ For rulers are not a terror to good conduct, but to bad. Would you have no fear of him who is in authority? Then do what is good, and you will receive his approval, ⁴ for he is God's servant for your good. But if you do wrong, be afraid, for he does not bear the sword in vain; he is the servant of God to execute his wrath on the wrongdoer. ⁵ Therefore one must be subject, not only to avoid God's wrath but also for the sake of conscience. ⁶ For the same reason you also pay taxes, for the authorities are ministers of God, attending to this very thing. ⁷Pay all of them their dues, taxes to whom taxes are due, revenue to whom revenue is due, respect to whom respect is due, honor to whom honor is due.

Romans 13:1-7 (RSV)

Moreover, God wants us to pray for our rulers at all levels of seniority:

¹First of all, then, I urge that supplications, prayers, intercessions, and thanksgivings be made for all men, ² for kings and all who are in high positions, that we may lead a quiet and peaceable life, godly and respectful in every way. ³ This is good, and it is acceptable in the sight of God our Savior

1 Timothy 2:1-3 (RSV)

God may also hold *us* responsible for what *our leaders* do. That may sound unfair but, at least in democratic countries, they are only in those positions *because most of us voted for them*. It may also be that it is *our failure to pray* for our political leaders that leads to them enacting such ungodly laws. For example, would David Cameron, have pushed through the "*gay marriage*" legislation if the churches had been faithful in their proclamation of the Gospel and had taught the Bible properly?

More to the point, would he have done it if enough Christians had prayed for him to have wisdom and to do God's will? We in the churches might blame our former Prime Minister for what happened, and we would be right to do so, as the idea came directly from him and his wife, not from the Conservative Party. However, it may be that God *also* holds the British people, and especially the churches, blameworthy alongside him and the other politicians who voted for it. Indeed, He possibly blames us even more than them.

There is also another logic at work, which is that *we get the politicians we deserve.* So, since 1992, we in the UK have elected governments which have gone ever farther away from God's standards. Today's politicians cannot even begin to compare in stature with the great men we have had in our history. One reason why we now get these awful leaders is because we have not been a faithful church in general and have not prayed for our governments in particular. Consequently, we got David Cameron and the Americans got Hussain Obama, the first Muslim president.

A few decades ago, men of such dismally low calibre would not have been able to get elected at all, even as MPs or Congressmen, given their perverse beliefs. Now such misguided and wicked men are leading whole nations. The point is, however, that God may hold us accountable for the decisions our politicians make, which our bold witness and earnest prayers could have avoided. For example, God brought judgement on the people of Judah as a whole because of the wicked things done *in their name* by the evil King Manasseh:

² And when they ask you, 'Where shall we go?' you shall say to them, 'Thus says the LORD:
"Those who are for pestilence, to pestilence,
and those who are for the sword, to the sword;
those who are for famine, to famine,
and those who are for captivity, to captivity."
³ "I will appoint over them four kinds of destroyers, says the LORD: the sword to slay, the dogs to tear, and the birds of the air and the beasts of the earth to devour and destroy. ⁴ And I will make them a horror to all the kingdoms of the earth because of what Manas'seh the son of Hezeki'ah, king of Judah, did in Jerusalem.

Jeremiah 15:2-4 (RSV)

Instead of ridiculing, or even just ignoring, our political leaders, we need to actively support them where we feel we can. If we cannot, in good conscience, support them, we can at least pray for them, even while opposing their policies.

Acts:
" We must obey God rather than men "

206

But to mock them, as our comedy programmes do, is contrary to what God wants. Moreover, it is often unfair, as some politicians are more hard-working and committed to what they believe in than many Christians are. I can speak from personal experience, as I used to be a Borough Councillor and also the Chairman of a Conservative Association, helping to organise the local party and elections etc.

I found that many of the people involved in politics were sincere, dedicated, public-spirited and unselfish. That rarely gets reported in the media, but it is real. However, there would be even more of them, and they would be in higher positions, if we were more faithful in praying for our political leaders and if more Christians joined political parties and became active, or at least voted. Instead, most Christians play no part in politics, in the misguided belief that we are not supposed to.

Wise people reject the world's values, principles and practices and are careful as to whom they spend time with.

This world is run by Satan at present and operates according to his values and principles. Therefore, this world will inevitably be hostile to Jesus and to all who follow Him:

[18] "If the world hates you, know that it has hated me before it hated you. [19] If you were of the world, the world would love its own; but because you are not of the world, but I chose you out of the world, therefore the world hates you. [20] Remember the word that I said to you, 'A servant is not greater than his master.' If they persecuted me, they will persecute you; if they kept my word, they will keep yours also. [21] But all this they will do to you on my account, because they do not know him who sent me. [22] If I had not come and spoken to them, they would not have sin; but now they have no excuse for their sin. [23] He who hates me hates my Father also. [24] If I had not done among them the works which no one else did, they would not have sin; but now they have seen and hated both me and my Father. [25] It is to fulfil the word that is written in their law, 'They hated me without a cause.'

John 15:18-25 (RSV)

Wise people will therefore shun the values of this sinful world system and all that it stands for. We cannot have one foot in each camp, i.e. God's kingdom and Satan's kingdom. We have to choose which one to be in. Any form of compromise will make us behave in foolish or even wicked ways. Consider what happened to the northern Kingdom of Israel in the time of King Hoshea. The people were engaging in idolatry and were imitating the sinful sexual practices of

207

the surrounding nations, rather than following God's commands. Their compromise with the world led to disaster and they came under God's judgment:

⁶ In the ninth year of Hoshea, the king of Assyria captured Samaria, and he carried the Israelites away to Assyria and placed them in Halah, and on the Habor, the river of Gozan, and in the cities of the Medes. ⁷ And this occurred because the people of Israel had sinned against the LORD their God, who had brought them up out of the land of Egypt from under the hand of Pharaoh king of Egypt, and had feared other gods⁸ and walked in the customs of the nations whom the LORD drove out before the people of Israel, and in the customs that the kings of Israel had practiced. ⁹ And the people of Israel did secretly against the LORD their God things that were not right. They built for themselves high places in all their towns, from watchtower to fortified city. ¹⁰ They set up for themselves pillars and Asherim on every high hill and under every green tree, ¹¹ and there they made offerings on all the high places, as the nations did whom the LORD carried away before them. And they did wicked things, provoking the LORD to anger, ¹² and they served idols, of which the LORD had said to them, "You shall not do this." ¹³ Yet the LORD warned Israel and Judah by every prophet and every seer, saying, "Turn from your evil ways and keep my commandments and my statutes, in accordance with all the Law that I commanded your fathers, and that I sent to you by my servants the prophets."

¹⁴ But they would not listen, but were stubborn, as their fathers had been, who did not believe in the LORD their God. ¹⁵ They despised his statutes and his covenant that he made with their fathers and the warnings that he gave them. They went after false idols and became false, and they followed the nations that were around them, concerning whom the LORD had commanded them that they should not do like them.¹⁶ And they abandoned all the commandments of the LORD their God, and made for themselves metal images of two calves; and they made an Asherah and worshiped all the host of heaven and served Baal. ¹⁷ And they burned their sons and their daughters as offerings and used divination and omens and sold themselves to do evil in the sight of the LORD, provoking him to anger. ¹⁸ Therefore the LORD was very angry with Israel and removed them out of his sight. None was left but the tribe of Judah only.

2 Kings 17:6-18 (ESV)

Unsaved people speak and act as they do because their minds have become darkened and their thinking is futile. That, in turn, is the result of their hardness of heart and callousness, which causes them to refuse to repent. Instead they plunge ever further into indulging their sensual passions:

17 Now this I say and testify in the Lord, that you must no longer walk as the Gentiles do, in the futility of their minds. 18 They are darkened in their understanding, alienated from the life of God because of the ignorance that is in them, due to their hardness of heart. 19 They have become callous and have given themselves up to sensuality, greedy to practice every kind of impurity.

Ephesians 4:17-19 (ESV)

Paul tells us that we must not 'walk' as they do, but "*put off (our) old self*" and "*...be renewed in the spirit of (our) minds...*". When we "*put on the new self*" it means we choose to do what is right, not the sinful things which our 'flesh', or old self, wants to do. It also means refusing to think in the way that the people around us think:

20 But that is not the way you learned Christ!— 21 assuming that you have heard about him and were taught in him, as the truth is in Jesus, 22 to put off your old self, which belongs to your former manner of life and is corrupt through deceitful desires, 23 and to be renewed in the spirit of your minds, 24 and to put on the new self, created after the likeness of God in true righteousness and holiness.

Ephesians 4:20-24 (ESV)

In Colossians, Paul is equally stark about the thinking and standards of the unsaved world when he says:

He has delivered us from the domain of darkness and transferred us to the kingdom of his beloved Son,

Colossians 1:13 (ESV)

A wise person sees the enormity of the gulf between the way this unsaved world thinks and operates and how we, as Christians, are meant to live. We have to choose every day, in almost every way, to be different from the people around us. We must set our minds on doing what God wants, and on thinking as He thinks, rather than trying to fit in with the values and practices of this lost world. A wise person will also avoid going to places, or being with people, or getting into situations, which might lead him into sin, or cause him to be influenced, or to be drawn into bad relationships.

Therefore, a wise person does not just resist temptation. He also avoids the places, people and situations which are likely to produce temptation. Many unwise decisions and sinful actions can be avoided by simply being careful about where you go, with whom you spend time, and what you get involved with. Merely being with, or even nearby, such people or places can make you more likely to fall into sin, just as playing with hot coals, makes you more likely to get burnt than if you kept away from them:

209

²⁷ Can a man carry fire next to his chest
   and his clothes not be burned?
²⁸ Or can one walk on hot coals
   and his feet not be scorched?
                        Proverbs 6:27-28 (ESV)

Many sins, hazards and bad influences can be avoided by merely joining different clubs or circles of friends and by going to different places, or even by going at safer times of day. I patrolled a town centre as a police officer and I can tell you that the chances of getting into a violent incident are a hundred times higher at 1.00 am than at 1.00 pm. Likewise, the chances of you doing well at university are vastly higher if you choose friends who are serious about their course than if you hang around with a group of idlers, or with those whose focus is on endless 'socialising'.

On the same point, if a young person wants to stay solid as a disciple, and not be led astray into worldly pursuits, they should join the Christian Union and a youth group at church and be active in both. That is vastly better than joining some rugby club which is likely to draw you into social activities which will harm your spiritual growth. Don't wait for things to actually go wrong. Look ahead and foresee what is *likely* to happen in these groups or places. Then choose those which offer the greatest probability of meeting sensible people and the lowest chance of meeting fools. Then you maximise your own chances of being influenced for the good, not the bad.

Wise people have nothing to do with superstition, horoscopes, fortune telling, witchcraft, or anything of the occult.

The world is also steeped in superstition and has a fascination for fortune telling, witchcraft and the occult in general. The word 'occult' means *hidden*. God has withheld certain things from us as He does not even want us to enquire into them, just as you would keep medicines away from small children. So, to use God's terminology, if you saw your three year old trying to open a bottle of bleach, you might say: *"No – that is occult!"* What you would mean is: *"That is dangerous and I have hidden it from you, and forbidden you to touch it, for your own protection."* These are classified by God as *"the secret things"* and He has commanded us to stay away from them and to be content with what He has revealed to us:

"The secret things belong to the LORD our God, but the things that are revealed belong to us and to our children forever, that we may do all the words of this law.

                                        Deuteronomy 29:29 (ESV)

King Manasseh was probably the wickedest king that Judah ever had. Yet, when God criticises him, He focuses primarily on his idolatry and his involvement in the occult, more so than on any of his other sins, thereby showing how important those sins are in God's eyes:

⁵ And he built altars for all the host of heaven in the two courts of the house of the LORD. ⁶ And he burned his son as an offering and used fortune-telling and omens and dealt with mediums and with necromancers. He did much evil in the sight of the LORD, provoking him to anger.

2 Kings 21:5-6 (ESV)

God therefore forbids us to have anything to do with any aspect of the occult. That includes any form of superstition, horoscopes, fortune telling, tarot cards, ouija boards, palm reading, consulting mediums or any other such thing. The list is very long because there are all sorts of off-shoots and variations, which all come under the broad umbrella term 'the occult'. These expose us to danger even if we aren't aware that they are forbidden, just as a child who drinks bleach will suffer harm even though he did not know it was dangerous. There are many passages like this which warn us against the occult:

⁹ "When you come into the land that the LORD your God is giving you, you shall not learn to follow the abominable practices of those nations. ¹⁰ There shall not be found among you anyone who burns his son or his daughter as an offering, anyone who practices divination or tells fortunes or interprets omens, or a sorcerer ¹¹ or a charmer or a medium or a necromancer or one who inquires of the dead, ¹² for whoever does these things is an abomination to the LORD. And because of these abominations the LORD your God is driving them out before you. ¹³ You shall be blameless before the LORD your God, ¹⁴ for these nations, which you are about to dispossess, listen to fortune-tellers and to diviners. But as for you, the LORD your God has not allowed you to do this.

Deuteronomy 18:9-14 (ESV)

Someone might argue that this is said within the Law of Moses, which we are not under, and therefore that the occult is no longer forbidden. However, the same prohibition is repeated elsewhere, including within the New Testament. More to the point, the Canaanites were not under the Law of Moses either. Yet, their occult activity was still classed as wickedness, because it is inherently wrong. Therefore, the occult is off limits for the entire human race, not just Jews or Christians.

Therefore, if you want to become wise, have nothing to do with any aspect of the occult, witchcraft, idolatry, fortune telling or superstition of any kind. The parts of the future which we are allowed to know about are set out for us in Bible prophecy. Everything else is forbidden. It is interesting therefore that so many people, even in the churches, have no interest in Bible prophecy, which makes up about 30% of the Bible, but have a deep fascination with the occult. They long to find out about the future via illegitimate sources like horoscopes, fortune tellers and mediums, but ignore all the legitimate information about the future, which God does want us to know, which is set out in the Bible.

The tragedy is that when they make such enquiries anything they are told will be a lie, either because the fortune teller is a fraud, or because the information comes from a demon. There are no other places it can come from. Another problem is that if we ever get involved with the occult we are also opening a 'window', allowing demons access to our lives and giving them power over us. This is one of the main ways in which people become *'demonised'*, whereby a demon gains access to their life, to one extent or another. They may even be able to enter into the person and live within them.

No right-thinking person would ever want that. Yet it is very likely to happen to us if we ever have any form of involvement in the occult. A related issue is 'accursed' or 'devoted' objects, such as lucky charms, amulets, rabbits' feet, crystals, St. Christopher medals, or any other item connected to superstition or the occult. These need to be got rid of completely from your body, home, office, car or anywhere else, even if they are hidden away in an attic, as is frequently the case. Sometimes people know it is wrong, but they don't want to part with it. So they often hide the object away, rather than display it.

If that is your situation, it is all the more vital to get rid of such objects. The very fact that you are reluctant shows they have some hold over you. Indeed, the demons in your life are probably doing all they can to persuade you not to part with the objects. But look how seriously God takes this. In this passage God tells Joshua to instruct the people to get rid of any 'devoted things' which they have taken from the Canaanites and kept in their homes. This was the reason for their defeat at Ai as He would not support them unless they got rid of the devoted things:

[10] The LORD said to Joshua, "Get up! Why have you fallen on your face?[11] Israel has sinned; they have transgressed my covenant that I commanded them; they have taken some of the devoted things; they have stolen and lied and put them among their own belongings. [12] Therefore the people of Israel cannot stand before their enemies. They turn their backs before their enemies, because they have become devoted for destruction. I will be with you no more, unless you destroy the devoted things from among you. [13] Get up! Consecrate the people and say, 'Consecrate yourselves for tomorrow; for thus says the LORD, God of Israel, "There are devoted things in your midst, O Israel.

You cannot stand before your enemies until you take away the devoted things from among you."

Joshua 7:10-13 (ESV)

In this next passage Joshua is even more emphatic about the need to get rid of all *'foreign gods',* otherwise God would *"turn and do you harm and consume you....."* These are widely defined and include all occult objects, charms, idols, or symbols of superstition. Therefore, if in doubt, get rid of it:

[20] *If you forsake the LORD and serve foreign gods, then he will turn and do you harm and consume you, after having done you good." * [21] *And the people said to Joshua, "No, but we will serve the LORD." * [22] *Then Joshua said to the people, "You are witnesses against yourselves that you have chosen the LORD, to serve him." And they said, "We are witnesses." * [23] *He said, "Then put away the foreign gods that are among you, and incline your heart to the LORD, the God of Israel."*

Joshua 24:20-23 (ESV)

It may be that you have not known until now that there is anything wrong with the occult. Thus you might have got involved, even in the distant past, with horoscopes or fortune telling or mediums or something else. If so, the first thing you need to do is *repent of it now*, however long ago it was. Also ask God to cleanse you of the effect or consequences of that sin in your life. You may also need deliverance from demons. In that case, please refer to my books 7 and 9 which look in much closer detail at what demons are, what they do, and how we can get rid of them.

Wise people get their ideas and beliefs from the Bible, not from the world, or from what people say.

Even if they are part of a church, most people get their opinions and beliefs from the media rather than from the Bible. That's hardly surprising when you consider that the average Christian in the West spends only minutes per day in the Bible, if even that, but many hours online and on Twitter, Facebook, TV or radio. Much of what they absorb is worldly and of questionable value at best. They gorge themselves on what the world says, but are on starvation rations when it comes to the Bible.

It is inevitable therefore that the world will have a greater influence than the Bible. A wise person sets out to do the exact opposite. He minimises the influence that the world has on him and maximises his exposure to God's Word. As a starting point, why not swop the amounts of time you spend watching TV, or on the internet, or on social media for the amount of time you spend in your Bible? Choose to abandon a lot of that and, instead, spend one to two hours per day, or more, on:

a) reading the Bible

b) reading good Christian books and commentaries. NB. You will have to be very discerning, as much of what is sold in Christian bookshops today, or on Christian websites, is either heretical or of little or no nutritional value. See the Approved Ministries section of the Real Christianity website which sets out some ministries and Bible teachers which I feel able to recommend.

c) listening to good Christian teaching on CD or MP3 etc. Again, you will have to be discerning.

If you do these things, and keep on doing them, your life will be transformed. Some people have told me that the idea of spending two or more hours per day on such things is unrealistic. But why is it? At the time of the Reformation, and in the days of the Puritans and non-conformists in the 16th and 17th centuries, and of the early Methodists of the 18th century, people went to extraordinary lengths to study the Bible and to hear good preachers.

The same is true in parts of the developing world today, where there is a much greater hunger for the Bible. That is how a wise person should be. Too many nominal churchgoers, and even real Christians, allow their minds to be saturated with godless, worldly, humanistic material. Therefore, they find themselves unconsciously adopting all sorts of unbiblical opinions and beliefs, without even realising:

a) that they are doing so

b) that those ideas are wrong

c) that they are unbiblical

d) where they got them from

e) why it matters what we think anyway

CHAPTER 8

WHAT WISE PEOPLE DO - PART TWO

A man's discretion makes him slow to anger,
And it is his glory to overlook a transgression.
Proverbs 19:11 (NASB)

In everything a prudent man acts with knowledge,
but a fool flaunts his folly.
Proverbs 13:16 (RSV)

Listen to counsel and accept discipline,
That you may be wise the rest of your days.
Proverbs 19:20 (NASB)

...... They cast lots also for his son Zechariah, a shrewd counsellor......
1 Chronicles 26:14(b) (ESV)

Prepare plans by consultation,
And make war by wise guidance.
Proverbs 20:18 (NASB)

The plans of the diligent lead surely to advantage,
But everyone who is hasty comes surely to poverty.
Proverbs 21:5 (NASB)

[13] The conclusion, when all has been heard, is: fear God and keep His commandments, because this applies to every person. [14] For God will bring every act to judgment, everything which is hidden, whether it is good or evil.
Ecclesiastes 12:13-14 (NASB)

for a righteous man falls seven times, and rises again;
but the wicked are overthrown by calamity.
Proverbs 24:16 (RSV)

"....and by the fear of the LORD a man avoids evil."
Proverbs 16:6(b) (RSV)

......Nevertheless, the heart of Asa was wholly true all his days.
2 Chronicles 15:17(b) (ESV)

Whoever is wise, let him understand these things;
whoever is discerning, let him know them;
for the ways of the LORD are right,
and the upright walk in them,
but transgressors stumble in them.
Hosea 14:9 (ESV)

Wise people don't follow any crowd or crave for people's approval.

Wise people aim to do what is right, even if that makes them the odd one out. The Bible often refers to us as sheep because we share so many of their foolish characteristics. One of those is the desire to do whatever the people around us are doing, whether good or bad. God specifically warned the Israelites not to follow the practices and ways of the people of Egypt, from whom they had escaped. He also warned them not to imitate the ways of the Canaanites, but to take care to abide by His Word:

¹ And the LORD spoke to Moses, saying, ² "Speak to the people of Israel and say to them, I am the LORD your God. ³ You shall not do as they do in the land of Egypt, where you lived, and you shall not do as they do in the land of Canaan, to which I am bringing you. You shall not walk in their statutes. ⁴ You shall follow my rules and keep my statutes and walk in them. I am the LORD your God. ⁵ You shall therefore keep my statutes and my rules; if a person does them, he shall live by them: I am the LORD.
Leviticus 18:1-5 (ESV)

Human beings have a deep longing to be accepted and popular. That desire makes most of us into followers and conformists. The problem is that fitting in means we have to compromise and imitate those around us, rather than do what God says. Doing the right thing will often bring us into conflict with others. Even so, we must never follow a crowd if what they want to do is wrong, or if what they say is untrue: *herd mentality, social pressure/proofing*

"Do not follow the crowd in doing wrong. When you give testimony in a lawsuit, do not pervert justice by siding with the crowd"
Exodus 23:2 (NIV)

A cowardly leader or manager will also let himself be intimidated and pressurised by those under him and do things which he knows to be wrong just for a quiet life. Pontius Pilate, the Roman Governor, presided over one of Jesus' trials and he knew Jesus had done nothing wrong and that He was the rightful King of the Jews. Pilate therefore wanted to release Jesus and knew that that was the right thing to do. Yet, he did not do it, because he feared the Jewish leaders and also the crowds who were shouting for Jesus to be crucified: *feared the crowd*

13 Pilate summoned the chief priests and the rulers and the people, 14 and said to them, "You brought this man to me as one who incites the people to rebellion, and behold, having examined Him before you, I have found no guilt in this man regarding the charges which you make against Him. 15 No, nor has Herod, for he sent Him back to us; and behold, nothing deserving death has been done by Him. 16 Therefore I will punish Him and release Him." 17 Now he was obliged to release to them at the feast one prisoner. 18 But they cried out all together, saying, "Away with this man, and release for us Barabbas!" 19 (He was one who had been thrown into prison for an insurrection made in the city, and for murder.)

20 Pilate, wanting to release Jesus, addressed them again, 21 but they kept on calling out, saying, "Crucify, crucify Him!" 22 And he said to them the third time, "Why, what evil has this man done? I have found in Him no guilt demanding death; therefore I will punish Him and release Him." 23 But they were insistent, with loud voices asking that He be crucified. And their voices began to prevail. 24 And Pilate pronounced sentence that their demand be granted. 25 And he released the man they were asking for who had been thrown into prison for insurrection and murder, but he delivered Jesus to their will.

Luke 23:13-25 (NASB)

We can't even say that Pilate gave way because he was in fear for his life. He cannot have been, because he had a large number of Roman soldiers under his command. Therefore, he was in no personal danger. He was just swayed by the pressure of public opinion as the crowd was baying for Jesus' execution and he wanted to avoid their disapproval. So, for those paltry reasons, he issued a death sentence against a man whom he *knew to be innocent*. We know that, because Pilate himself had just said that he had found no guilt in Him.

He was therefore guilty of a gross neglect of his judicial duty, based on selfishness and the wish to avoid hassle for himself. Yet there is nothing unusual about what Pilate did. Countless politicians, managers, officials, headmasters and church leaders regularly do the very same. It is entirely normal for people to fail in their duty and choose the line of least resistance rather than face the flak that comes to those who do what is right, but unpopular. A wise person recognises his own fear of public opinion and knows that his flesh nature causes him to follow other people and fit in with their standards.

He also knows that it will lead him astray if he does so. Therefore, he exercises self-control and forces himself to do what is right, even if it means standing alone. That is hard enough to do when dealing with the unsaved, unbelieving people

217

around us. It is even harder when the people whose example we must not follow are in the Church, or claim to be. They may well even be the leaders. Even so, your conscience, and God's Word, may be telling you that what they are saying and doing is wrong.

A real Christian, if he wants to be wise, must be willing to check everything and everyone against the Bible and refuse to follow any leader or group that is going in the wrong direction. He must also be courageous enough to pay the price for that conviction, no matter how much it may cost, or how unpopular it may make him. We must seek only for the praise of God, not for the praise of other people, because trying to get their approval will only cause us to make bad choices and go the wrong way:

42 Nevertheless many even of the authorities believed in him, but for fear of the Pharisees they did not confess it, lest they should be put out of the synagogue: 43 for they loved the praise of men more than the praise of God.

John 12:42-43 (RSV)

Wise people seek God's Kingdom first and are serious about staying on the 'narrow path'.

Jesus told us to seek His Kingdom first, ahead of anything else:

But seek ye first the kingdom of God, and his righteousness; and all these things shall be added unto you.

Matthew 6:33 (RSV)

If we do seek His Kingdom first we are much more likely to make right decisions and to get our other priorities in the right order. We must seek it here and now, by operating each day in accordance with His principles and commands. It also means focusing on the life that is to come, after we have died or been raptured and enter into His Kingdom in a much fuller way. Both of these aspects of seeking His Kingdom are valid, i.e. in the present and the future. Jesus also spoke of the narrow gate and the narrow way or path and said that those who choose the wrong way, which will be the majority, will be locked out of the Kingdom:

13 "Enter through the narrow gate; for the gate is wide and the way is broad that leads to destruction, and there are many who enter through it. 14 For the gate is small and the way is narrow that leads to life, and there are few who find it.

Matthew 7:13-14 (NASB)

²³ And someone said to Him, "Lord, are there just a few who are being saved?" And He said to them, ²⁴ "Strive to enter through the narrow door; for many, I tell you, will seek to enter and will not be able. ²⁵ Once the head of the house gets up and shuts the door, and you begin to stand outside and knock on the door, saying, 'Lord, open up to us!' then He will answer and say to you, 'I do not know where you are from.' ²⁶ Then you will begin to say, 'We ate and drank in Your presence, and You taught in our streets'; ²⁷ and He will say, 'I tell you, I do not know where you are from; DEPART FROM ME, ALL YOU EVILDOERS.' ²⁸ In that place there will be weeping and gnashing of teeth when you see Abraham and Isaac and Jacob and all the prophets in the kingdom of God, but yourselves being thrown out.

Luke 13: 23-28 (NASB)

Jesus did not use words loosely. He said what He meant and meant what He said. In the verses above He is making it very plain that:

a) We have a choice as to whether to go to destruction or to life, i.e. to end up in the Lake of Fire or to have eternal life in God's presence.

b) Most people do not choose life and thus they go to destruction. Therefore, being on the side of the majority is generally not a good idea.

c) Some people are not even aware (or concerned) that they are on the wrong path and they will only find out the truth when it is too late.

As with most of the things Jesus said, modern-day Western churches tend either to water them down or ignore them. However, if we want to become wise, we will pay close attention to Jesus' words. Whatever He is saying, whether about seeking His Kingdom first, or choosing life rather than destruction, a wise person will take Jesus' words extremely seriously. Only a fool would ignore them, especially His warnings.

The same is true of the whole Bible, even where it comes via one of the prophets or apostles. It is all equally God's Word. Therefore, when Jesus warns us of the eternal consequences of the daily choices we make, a wise person will not brush it aside. He will listen reverently and keep it very much in mind. The truth of Jesus' words, that *few* people enter by the narrow gate or choose the narrow way, is illustrated by the fact that most people, even in churches, don't take seriously what He said.

We can see that just by looking around us in the churches and by hearing what people say and what they focus on. It is also demonstrated by what they *do not say*, and what they *do not focus on*. The narrow gate is not easy to go through and the narrow way is not comfortable to travel on. They both involve difficulty,

219

No mention of...
No reading of...

trouble and opposition. However, a wise person still chooses the narrow way regardless, firstly because he knows it is right, and secondly because it is worth it:

²⁸ And Jesus said to them, "Truly I say to you, that you who have followed Me, in the regeneration when the Son of Man will sit on His glorious throne, you also shall sit upon twelve thrones, judging the twelve tribes of Israel. ²⁹ And everyone who has left houses or brothers or sisters or father or mother or children or farms for My name's sake, will receive many times as much, and will inherit eternal life. ³⁰ But many who are first will be last; and the last, first.

Matthew 19:28-30 (NASB)

Those who choose to enter, and remain upon, the narrow path, and to focus on and invest in the Kingdom of God, will build up treasure for themselves in Heaven:

¹⁹ "Do not lay up for yourselves treasures on earth, where moth and rust consume and where thieves break in and steal, ²⁰ but lay up for yourselves treasures in heaven, where neither moth nor rust^l consumes and where thieves do not break in and steal. ²¹ For where your treasure is, there will your heart be also.

Matthew 6:19-21 (RSV)

Conversely, those who focus on this present world and on pursuing power, fame, wealth, comfort and prestige here and now, instead of seeking the Kingdom of God, will find when they die that they will lose everything. And it will be lost eternally:

¹⁶ Be not afraid when a man becomes rich,
when the glory of his house increases.
¹⁷ For when he dies he will carry nothing away;
his glory will not go down after him.
¹⁸ For though, while he lives, he counts himself blessed
—and though you get praise when you do well for yourself—
¹⁹ his soul will go to the generation of his fathers,
who will never again see light.
²⁰ Man in his pomp yet without understanding is like the beasts that perish.

Psalm 49:16-20 (ESV)

Wise people realise the great danger of sexual immorality.

Possibly the greatest danger we face as disciples is sexual temptation. A number of Christian students I knew at university fell away from the faith due to getting into sexual relationships. The temptation is great, especially for young people, and it is even worse now than in the 1980s. There is now such widespread immorality, plus the expectation that everyone else will be promiscuous, that it is difficult to avoid being led astray. However, we must do all we can to avoid such danger, because, sexual sin is a sure route to spiritual disaster.

That is partly because it is a sin against one's own body, which is a temple of the Holy Spirit. It is also because of the *soul-ties* which sexual intercourse creates, so as to connect us with the other person, with very long-lasting consequences, which we might not expect. Therefore, the Bible repeatedly warns us against getting into sexual sin of any kind. Consider these passages from Proverbs about a man being led astray by the enticements of an immoral woman. However, the warning is equally applicable to women being led astray by men:

23 For the commandment is a lamp and the teaching a light,
*   and the reproofs of discipline are the way of life,*
24 to preserve you from the evil woman,
*   from the smooth tongue of the adventuress.*
25 Do not desire her beauty in your heart,
*   and do not let her capture you with her eyelashes;*
26 for a harlot may be hired for a loaf of bread,
*   but an adulteress stalks a man's very life.*
27 Can a man carry fire in his bosom
*   and his clothes not be burned?*
28 Or can one walk upon hot coals
*   and his feet not be scorched?*
29 So is he who goes in to his neighbor's wife;
*   none who touches her will go unpunished.*
30 Do not men despise a thief if he steals
*   to satisfy his appetite when he is hungry?*
31 And if he is caught, he will pay sevenfold;
*   he will give all the goods of his house.*
32 He who commits adultery has no sense;
*   he who does it destroys himself.*
33 Wounds and dishonor will he get,
*   and his disgrace will not be wiped away.*
*   Proverbs 6:23-33 (RSV)*

6 For at the window of my house
*   I have looked out through my lattice,*
7 and I have seen among the simple,
*   I have perceived among the youths,*
*   a young man without sense,*
8 passing along the street near her corner,
*   taking the road to her house*
9 in the twilight, in the evening,

at the time of night and darkness.
10 And lo, a woman meets him,
   dressed as a harlot, wily of heart.
11 She is loud and wayward,
   her feet do not stay at home;
12 now in the street, now in the market,
   and at every corner she lies in wait.
13 She seizes him and kisses him,
   and with impudent face she says to him:
14 "I had to offer sacrifices,
   and today I have paid my vows;
15 so now I have come out to meet you,
   to seek you eagerly, and I have found you.
16 I have decked my couch with coverings,
   colored spreads of Egyptian linen;
17 I have perfumed my bed with myrrh,
   aloes, and cinnamon.
18 Come, let us take our fill of love till morning;
   let us delight ourselves with love.
19 For my husband is not at home;
   he has gone on a long journey;
20 he took a bag of money with him;
   at full moon he will come home."
21 With much seductive speech she persuades him;
   with her smooth talk she compels him.
22 All at once he follows her,
   as an ox goes to the slaughter,
or as a stag is caught fast
23   till an arrow pierces its entrails;
as a bird rushes into a snare;
   he does not know that it will cost him his life.
24 And now, O sons, listen to me,
   and be attentive to the words of my mouth.
25 Let not your heart turn aside to her ways,
   do not stray into her paths;
26 for many a victim has she laid low;
   yea, all her slain are a mighty host.
27 Her house is the way to Sheol,
   going down to the chambers of death.

Proverbs 7:6-27 (RSV)

If you need any further persuading of the danger of sexual immorality, consider what happened in the book of Numbers when Balaam advised Balak, the King of

Moab, how to undermine the Israelites. Balak had offered Balaam money to curse God's people, but Balaam refused to do so, because God met him and forbade it. However, Balaam found a way to get round this.

He advised Balak to entice the Israelites into sexual sin with the Canaanites, and also, of course, into idolatry. The people fell for this trick and large numbers of them began to engage in the worship of Baal, and other forms of idolatry, all of which involved having sex with prostitutes who served Baal. This resulted in God bringing a very severe judgment on His people, including a plague, such that 24,000 were killed by God's intervention:

¹ While Israel lived in Shittim, the people began to whore with the daughters of Moab. ² These invited the people to the sacrifices of their gods, and the people ate and bowed down to their gods. ³ So Israel yoked himself to Baal of Peor. And the anger of the LORD was kindled against Israel. ⁴ And the LORD said to Moses, "Take all the chiefs of the people and hang] them in the sun before the LORD, that the fierce anger of the LORD may turn away from Israel." ⁵ And Moses said to the judges of Israel, "Each of you kill those of his men who have yoked themselves to Baal of Peor."
⁶ And behold, one of the people of Israel came and brought a Midianite woman to his family, in the sight of Moses and in the sight of the whole congregation of the people of Israel, while they were weeping in the entrance of the tent of meeting. ⁷ When Phinehas the son of Eleazar, son of Aaron the priest, saw it, he rose and left the congregation and took a spear in his hand ⁸ and went after the man of Israel into the chamber and pierced both of them, the man of Israel and the woman through her belly. Thus the plague on the people of Israel was stopped.⁹ Nevertheless, those who died by the plague were twenty-four thousand.

Numbers 25:1-9 (ESV)

A wise person will take all of these warnings to heart and seek God's help to avoid falling into sin. A fool, or even a simple person, does not see the danger. Or he does not see why it matters. Or perhaps he is overly sure of himself and sees no possibility that he could fall into this sin. Whatever the reasons may be, anyone who engages in sexual sin will pay a heavy price, both in this life and the next. Therefore, be wise and pay close attention to God's many warnings about this.

Do not pursue a promiscuous lifestyle and do not watch or participate in anything, however small, brief, or infrequent, which is not godly and pure. In particular, keep well away from internet pornography of any kind. Have your PC, laptop and phone set to block all such material, as it is utterly poisonous. Those who allow it to get its hooks into them tend to become addicted. Do not let that happen to you and, if it already has, get help to break away from it completely.

223

Wise people know their days are numbered.

We only have a short life span on this earth, whether we are wise or wicked:

¹ "Man who is born of a woman
is few of days and full of trouble.
² He comes out like a flower and withers;
he flees like a shadow and continues not.
*   Job 14:1-2 (ESV)*

Man is like a breath;
his days are like a passing shadow.
*   Psalm 144:4 (ESV)*

Whoever we are, this life is only for a short time and the possessions we gather are only briefly held by us, after which they will go to someone else:

The years of our life are threescore and ten,
or even by reason of strength fourscore;
yet their span is but toil and trouble;
they are soon gone, and we fly away.
*   Psalm 90:10 (RSV)*

¹⁴For he knows our frame;
he remembers that we are dust.
¹⁵As for man, his days are like grass;
he flourishes like a flower of the field;
¹⁶for the wind passes over it, and it is gone,
and its place knows it no more.
*   Psalm 103:14-16 (ESV)*

⁴"O LORD, make me know my end
and what is the measure of my days;
let me know how fleeting I am!
⁵Behold, you have made my days a few handbreadths,
and my lifetime is as nothing before you.
Surely all mankind stands as a mere breath!
⁶Surely a man goes about as a shadow!
Surely for nothing they are in turmoil;
man heaps up wealth and does not know who will gather!
*   Psalm 39:4-6 (ESV)*

For he sees that even the wise die;
the fool and the stupid alike must perish
and leave their wealth to others.
*   Psalm 49:10 (ESV)*

224

This earthly life span of 70-80 years is not what really counts. It is just a preparation or testing-ground for the next life, in Jesus' Millennial Kingdom, and then in eternity. What matters is using whatever time we have now to please God and grow as disciples. Then we can gain His approval and rewards at the Judgment Seat of Christ. That is what this life is really all about. No matter how good or wise we may be, we all have to die, unless we are part of the generation which gets caught up in the rapture. Then, once we are gone, we will quickly be forgotten:

[14] The wise man has his eyes in his head, but the fool walks in darkness; and yet I perceived that one fate comes to all of them. [15] Then I said to myself, "What befalls the fool will befall me also; why then have I been so very wise?" And I said to myself that this also is vanity. [16] For of the wise man as of the fool there is no enduring remembrance, seeing that in the days to come all will have been long forgotten. How the wise man dies just like the fool!
Ecclesiastes 2:14-16 (RSV)

None of us know how long we have got left to pass God's tests. We could die tonight. Therefore, we need to focus every day on living to please God, not to earn salvation, but to receive His praise and reward for how we serve Him, and for the fruit we bear, after being saved. Our time on this Earth is like a fleeting shadow and none of our possessions will remain forever. Therefore, treat every day as if it was your last day before the Judgment and your final opportunity to gain a reward and to lay up treasure for yourself in Heaven:

......Our days on the earth are like a shadow, and there is no abiding.
1 Chronicles 29:15(b) (ESV)

Teach us to number our days aright,
that we may gain a heart of wisdom.
Psalm 90:12 (NIV)

Once we realise that every day could be our last it will help us to prioritise correctly. Then we will be better able to live in obedience and turn away from temptations, not *in order to be saved*, but *because we have been saved*. So, we need to focus on the fact that this world is going to end, either before or after we ourselves die, and seek to help as many other people as possible to be saved before then. We can't save the world, or the planet itself, but we can help individuals. Such an attitude will keep our minds focused on the right things rather than wasting our time on things that do not matter.

Are you prepared for death, judgment, eternity? To meet your maker

225

Wise people generally live longer. Wisdom, knowledge and the fear of the LORD are a protection to them.

Despite being ready to die at any moment, the wise tend to have a longer life span than the wicked. Consider the relative lengths of the reigns of the Kings of Judah, some of whom were good, in comparison with the Kings of Israel, all of whom ended up wicked. Their different standards of faith and behaviour affected their life spans, as the Kings of the Southern Kingdom lived much longer on average than the Kings of the Northern Kingdom. Many passages speak of the longer average life expectancy, and better health, of the righteous as compared to the wicked:

For the protection of wisdom is like the protection of money, and the advantage of knowledge is that wisdom preserves the life of him who has it.
Ecclesiastes 7:12 (ESV)

[10] The fear of the LORD is the beginning of wisdom,
And the knowledge of the Holy One is understanding.
[11] For by me your days will be multiplied,
And years of life will be added to you.
Proverbs 9:10-11 (NASB)

[12] The righteous flourish like the palm tree
and grow like a cedar in Lebanon.
[13] They are planted in the house of the LORD;
they flourish in the courts of our God.
[14] They still bear fruit in old age;
they are ever full of sap and green,
Psalm 92:12-14 (ESV)

The fear of the LORD leads to life,
So that one may sleep satisfied, untouched by evil.
Proverbs 19:23 (NASB)

Although a sinner does evil a hundred times and may lengthen his life, still I know that it will be well for those who fear God, who fear Him openly.
Ecclesiastes 8:12 (NASB)

In this next passage we are told that those who *"consider the poor"*, i.e. those who are kind and generous towards the needy, will be specially protected by God, not only from enemies, but from illness too, and will be healed when they get sick, such that they are kept alive:

226

¹ Blessed is the one who considers the poor!
 In the day of trouble the LORD delivers him;
² the LORD protects him and keeps him alive;
 he is called blessed in the land;
 you do not give him up to the will of his enemies.
³ The LORD sustains him on his sickbed;
 in his illness you restore him to full health.
                    Psalm 41:1-3 (ESV)

Wise people also survive longer in a job or business, partly because they are better prepared and better positioned to face difficult times. It is also because, when they face crises, recessions or other risks or problems, God lifts them up and rescues them, whereas He does not do so for the wicked:

for a righteous man falls seven times, and rises again;
but the wicked are overthrown by calamity.
                    Proverbs 24:16 (RSV)

God also sides with the blameless man and vindicates him, but He opposes and exposes the wicked:

²⁰ "Behold, God will not reject a blameless man,
 nor take the hand of evildoers.
²¹ He will yet fill your mouth with laughter,
 and your lips with shouting.
²² Those who hate you will be clothed with shame,
 and the tent of the wicked will be no more."
                    Job 8:20-22 (RSV)

Wise people realise they are not the centre of the universe and don't allow themselves to be ruled by self-interest.

The more you put God and other people at the centre, and yourself at the edge, the wiser and happier you will be. You can never be happy if you take centre-place in your own universe. One reason is that others will not cooperate with you. They want that central place for themselves. In my law firm the way the best staff ran their files was to keep the client at the centre, always putting his interests first, with the firm in second place and themselves in last place. Such staff always did well and had satisfied clients.

By contrast, the worst staff always put themselves first. They were the ones who ended up having discontented clients and doing badly in their careers. Self-centred employees won't choose any course of action which would involve

227

additional difficulty or pressure for themselves, or require them to admit an error. We had several bad staff like that and none of them ever survived long term. They all failed in the end and many had to be removed. Ironically, one of the reasons why such selfish staff behaved as they did was to promote their own interests. But it never worked for them.

They always ended in failure, whereas the unselfish ones always succeeded. When the wise staff put their clients first and themselves last, both the clients and I would inevitably notice. I then promoted and rewarded them precisely because they were not making themselves the priority or seeking to promote themselves. It was *my* place to promote staff, not theirs. Likewise, it is God's place to promote us, not ours. Therefore, choosing not to put oneself first is actually enlightened self-interest and the surest way to promotion, both in this life and the next.

Moreover, wise people don't automatically assume that they are in the right. They accept correction and are open to being shown to be in the wrong. The wiser a person is, the more they will realise the power of their sinful flesh nature and their own capacity for self-deception. Also, the more easily they can see their own faults and bad habits. Therefore, when a wise person faces disputes or difficult situations, or when he is corrected or rebuked by a boss or senior colleague at work, his first thoughts will be along the lines of:

a)   am I acting wrongly, selfishly or unfairly here?

b)   who is really in the right on this issue, me or the other person?

c)   what does God think about this situation?

d)   what does God want me to do?

e)   am I being carnal or reacting to this correction or dispute in a fleshly way?

An incident occurred recently when my wife and I were on holiday in the Lake District. It illustrates, what it is to be self-absorbed, whereby a person sees themselves as being at the centre. We stayed in a large old mansion which had been split up into apartments. There was a warden whose job it was to look after all the apartments and guests. Parking was limited, and we were allocated a space at the rear. On the day when we were setting off to go home, another visitor had parked his car badly, in a position which did not block us in, but prevented the warden getting past.

The warden then drove up and stopped immediately behind our car. This prevented us from driving off, even though our car was packed up and ready to go. The warden then got out of his car, leaving it parked right behind us, and went off to find the visitor who was preventing him from driving forwards to where he wanted to go. I got out of our car and said to the warden that we were about to go and asked if he could just *reverse* back a little first, in order to let *us* out.

However, he brushed *our* concerns aside and said he was going to find the owner of the car that was preventing *him* from driving forwards. He just said dismissively "*I won't be long*" and walked off towards the apartments. The warden was so absorbed with himself and his own concerns that our needs were a matter of complete indifference to him. I don't think his mind was even capable of registering the thought that *he* was blocking *us* in. He could only think in terms of somebody being in *his* way. Anything other than that did not matter enough even to allow the thought to form prior to dismissing it.

The point is, however, that we were paying guests, whereas he was just an employee of the company. Thus, it would have been obvious to a right-thinking person that he should reverse his own vehicle first, *for a mere moment*, to allow us to get out. Then he could address his own problem of being unable to go forward. Indeed, even if he had been a fellow guest, and not the warden, it would still have been obvious that he should not keep someone else waiting while he firstly tried to solve his own problem.

However, that was not how he saw it. From his self-centred perspective, it was an outrage that a motorist had blocked *his* way. The fact that he himself had blocked *our* way was neither here nor there. That is the essence of self-centredness. It enables a person to face two identical situations and to be animated by the one, but indifferent to the other. The only difference is that the one situation affects himself, whereas the other only affects someone else.

After some minutes, the warden emerged from the apartments together with the owner of the badly parked car who then moved it, enabling the warden to drive forward at last. However, even after that period of time, in which he might have taken the opportunity to reflect on how he was holding us up, the warden never apologised. He never even acknowledged that he had delayed our departure. He was either oblivious to that fact, or indifferent to it.

A wise person is more concerned to avoid wronging another person, or treating them unfairly, than he is about avoiding being wronged himself. It actually makes logical sense to think that way. If we are wronged there are no eternal consequences for us. We will not have to answer for it at the Judgment Seat of Christ. We may even be vindicated there. However, if in our haste to defend our own self-interests we wrong another person, we will have to answer for it.

A self-absorbed person is so pre-occupied with themselves that they can become forgetful of other people's needs, or even their existence. Instead, we need to become so single-minded about serving God, serving others and pursuing the

229

'Great Commission' of making disciples, that we become forgetful of ourselves and of our own anxieties and preferences.

The pursuit of something far bigger than ourselves makes us willing to relegate our own interests in order to benefit others. Self-absorption makes us into a fool, but focusing on God, and on other people, makes us wise. I am not saying that we should *think less of ourselves*, in the sense of running ourselves down or belittling ourselves. I mean that we should simply *think of ourselves less,* in the sense of less often, less intensely and less selfishly.

Wise people are also willing to be corrected and to listen to advice

If the prospect of the Day of Judgment becomes real to you, then you will be able to see why it makes sense not to use your elbows when dealing with other people. One day you will have to answer for it face to face with Jesus, so it would be better to change now.

Therefore, a wise person is not merely *willing* to be corrected now, and to have his own wrong ideas, bad attitudes and selfish behaviour exposed. He positively *wants* to be corrected, because he knows he will benefit from it. Consider how King David and King Solomon put this:

Let a righteous man strike me
- it is a kindness; let him rebuke me
- it is oil for my head;
let my head not refuse it.......
             Psalm 141:5(a) (ESV)

A rebuke goes deeper into a man of understanding
than a hundred blows into a fool.
             Proverbs 17:10 (ESV)

Paradoxically, the wiser a person becomes, and the more knowledge and understanding he has, the more he will question himself, accept correction, and listen to advice. Wise people realise that they cannot safely rely on their own ability or judgement and that they need other people to assist them in the vital process of self-examination and self-improvement:

Better is a poor and wise youth than an old and foolish king,
who will no longer take advice,
             Ecclesiastes 4:13 (RSV)

Self correction requires the help of others!

230

Listen to advice and accept instruction,
that you may gain wisdom for the future.
Proverbs 19:20 (RSV)

Sometimes advice and correction comes from gracious people and is given politely. Other times it comes from ungracious people and is given rudely. Either way, it is best to listen to it and to weigh it up open-mindedly. A wise person will listen to good advice, and act upon it, even if it is given harshly or by someone with whom they are not on friendly terms, as when King David listened to the advice of Joab, one of his generals, even though he spoke very bluntly. David was grieving over the death of his son, Absalom and Joab was sharply critical, but David did not allow himself to get offended. He knew that he was wrong and that Joab was right. Therefore, he listened and changed course:

5 Then Jo'ab came into the house to the king, and said, "You have today covered with shame the faces of all your servants, who have this day saved your life, and the lives of your sons and your daughters, and the lives of your wives and your concubines, 6 because you love those who hate you and hate those who love you. For you have made it clear today that commanders and servants are nothing to you; for today I perceive that if Ab'salom were alive and all of us were dead today, then you would be pleased.

7 Now therefore arise, go out and speak kindly to your servants; for I swear by the LORD, if you do not go, not a man will stay with you this night; and this will be worse for you than all the evil that has come upon you from your youth until now." 8 Then the king arose, and took his seat in the gate. And the people were all told, "Behold, the king is sitting in the gate"; and all the people came before the king. Now Israel had fled every man to his own home. 9 And all the people were at strife throughout all the tribes of Israel, saying, "The king delivered us from the hand of our enemies, and saved us from the hand of the Philistines; and now he has fled out of the land from Ab'salom.

2 Samuel 19:5-9 (RSV)

Sometimes it is only those who are rude, or even hostile, towards us who are willing to tell us the real truth about ourselves or our situation. Our friends are usually too polite to be really blunt. They therefore won't point out the deeply ingrained faults that we are sensitive about, or even blind to. So, harsh, rude people, and even our enemies, can actually have a valuable role to play in correcting us. Even better though is the rebuke of a wise man:

It is better for a man to hear the rebuke
of the wise than to hear the song of fools.
Ecclesiastes 7:5 (RSV)

231

Like a gold ring or an ornament of gold
is a wise reprover to a listening ear.
Proverbs 25:12 (RSV)

Best of all is to receive God's correction and reproof. We should not only be willing, but eager, to receive that:

[23] *Search me, O God, and know my heart!*
Try me and know my thoughts!
[24] *And see if there be any wicked way in me,*
and lead me in the way everlasting!
Psalm 139:23-24 (RSV)

[17] *"Behold, how happy is the man whom God reproves,*
So do not despise the discipline of the Almighty.
[18] *"For He inflicts pain, and gives relief;*
He wounds, and His hands also heal.
Job 5:17-18 (NASB)

Blessed is the man whom you discipline, O LORD,
and whom you teach out of your law,
Psalm 94:12 (ESV)

Examine me, O LORD, and try me;
Test my mind and my heart.
Psalm 26:2(NASB)

Teach me your way, O LORD,
that I may walk in your truth;
unite my heart to fear your name.
Psalm 86:11 (ESV)

Though open to correction, a wise person will not passively submit to being falsely accused or let himself be cursed or violated.

Although a wise person is willing to listen to sincere criticism, and does not take offence when he is validly rebuked, he also knows when it is a false accusation. Sometimes the person criticising you is malicious and is trying to damage you. They might be spiritually mixed up and emotionally damaged themselves and they want to dump their resentments and anger onto you. If so, then instead of being open, you need to put up an 'umbrella' to prevent their poisonous words being sprayed all over you and seeping into you.

232

Or one could think in terms of the metaphor of *'fiery darts'*, which Paul speaks of, against which we need to raise the *'shield of faith'*. As for whether to listen receptively, or to defend ourselves, it all depends on who is talking to you, what their nature is, and what motivates them. Some people are just downright malicious, and their accusing words can operate as curses. They can get through your 'skin' and poison you if you let them speak into your life. In the past, when I had less discernment, I allowed false, malevolent people to violate me by their venomous words, which I naively listened to.

The problem is it isn't easy to know who the malicious people are, especially if you are inexperienced in handling them. But you can at least be aware that such people exist and be on the lookout for them. This problem can particularly arise where you are involved in a dispute and accusations and insults are aimed at you. At such times it is wise to keep your distance, maintain your 'guard', and to limit such people's ability to get to you. You might even ask someone whom you trust to look at any letters or emails before you read them, or even *instead* of you reading them.

You could also refuse to meet with them, or at least without a witness present who will support you and help you to deal with the toxic things that may be said. A friend of mine was once involved in a dispute with someone who was very mixed up and emotionally unstable. That person was therefore lashing out with wild, unfounded accusations and wounding remarks. When yet another inflammatory email arrived, I suggested that she print it off and show it to me first, rather than just open it and read it immediately on her own. We then read it together, side by side.

I was therefore able to counsel her, there and then, and to instantly refute the false accusations and insults and reassure her of their falseness. I did that right at the start, before the 'fiery darts' had any chance to get through her skin and cause damage. She found that screening process very helpful and it prevented her being violated by the other person's outpouring of bile. If such letters or calls keep on coming, you might choose not to read them at all, or refuse to meet up, or to take the person's phone calls. Then you can keep all of their poison away from you entirely.

There are times when such defensive measures are essential for your own protection, and it is not wrong. It does not mean that you are behaving wrongly, or being a fool for not being willing to hear their accusations. That is only the case when you are *in the wrong*, or are *insincere*, and are refusing to listen to a *sincere* person who is *in the right* and is seeking to correct you. But if the other person is insincere, or even malicious, there is no longer any duty to listen to them.

Don't let them get 'under' your skin - or - 'in' your head.

233

Indeed, it may be very unwise for you to do so, as you would be allowing them to harm you. To passively let them unload their accusations onto you would be like standing still in the path of a farmer's slurry spreader and letting it spray its load all over you. You have no duty to submit to such abuse or to make yourself an outlet for other people's rage or venom. They must solve their own problems, without using you as a punch bag.

Wise people have *the love of the truth*. They 'interrogate' or 'interview' themselves to find out whether they are right, rather than just assuming it.

A wise person is so concerned not to do wrong to others that he will interrogate himself to establish who is really right, or "in the right". He won't just assume it to be himself, or take it for granted that his own cause obviously has merit. Neither will he assume that his own interests and needs automatically come ahead of those of other people. He will be slow to form a conclusion about who is right and wrong and will avoid lashing out or acting on impulse.

Our flesh nature is very strong, and the habits of selfishness and self-justification are deeply ingrained. We will therefore never do right naturally or instinctively. Every right choice, or right action, is always contrary to the wishes of our flesh nature. We therefore have to impose it on ourselves by insisting that our new man prevails over our old man. That will never happen by itself, but it is far more likely if you have '*the love of the truth*'. That means you love the truth for its own sake and would rather know the truth, even if it proves you wrong, or shows you to have behaved wrongly.

However, most people do not love the truth. Therefore, they hate to be challenged, questioned or corrected. They view it as an impertinence and feel outraged if it is suggested that they are wrong in their beliefs or conduct. In fact, I have often encountered such defensive and resentful reactions from church leaders when I have attempted to raise some point concerning their teaching. For example, I once spoke to a leader who had just given a talk on the book of Jonah. I felt he had misunderstood both the book and the prophet and that he was missing the point.

I went up to him afterwards privately, one to one, and, very quietly, tried to explain how I saw it, but he had no interest at all and didn't want to know. It seemed to me that if he had just spent time studying that book, he ought to have been interested in it and open to hear more, even if I was wrong. Indeed, if he truly felt that I was wrong then, surely, he would want to hear from me, if only to correct me for my benefit and to clarify what he really meant. One might imagine that would be the common reaction in such situations, but it rarely is.

234

However, he was completely uninterested and was unwilling, or perhaps unable, to answer my points. He could have replied: *"I hadn't realised any of that. I'd like to hear more about it."* Or he could have said *"Actually, you may have misunderstood me. Let me clarify what I meant."* But he did neither. He just looked irritated, had nothing to say, and wanted to change the subject. I imagine he was motivated by a mixture of pride, insecurity and laziness. He probably also felt that he was '*clergy*' and ought not to be challenged or corrected by a mere '*lay person*'.

However, I think that, above all, it was because he did not have the love of the truth. Therefore, when faced with a chance to learn something, he chose not to learn it, simply because it could involve a loss of face, though only in his mind, not mine. Thus, he would prefer to remain wrong, rather than get the truth, whereas a wise person would rather learn the truth, even if it did mean a loss of face. That said, why should it mean that? What is wrong with being corrected or having someone fill a gap in your knowledge? Why should that embarrass you?

It only does so if our attitude is wrong to begin with and we love our own image more than the truth. A wise person sets out to find the truth even if it means he has to change his mind publicly, such that people can see his error. A prime example of that kind of integrity is the Bible teacher *Chuck Missler* of *Koinonea Institute*. Over the years he redid a number of his teaching series when he discovered errors or gaps in his own understanding. He redid Matthew's gospel three times. But that doesn't diminish Chuck Missler. It enhances him, at least in the eyes of right-thinking people.

Therefore, make a decision to develop the love of the truth. Seek the truth even if it means that your current opinion, or your conduct or attitude, will be shown to have been wrong. Why would you want to preserve the *appearance* of having been right when you now know you were actually wrong? It will all come out anyway at the Judgment Seat of Christ. (See my Book 4.) Therefore, why not prefer to let the truth come out now, so that your opinions, attitudes or conduct can be corrected, even if that has to be done in public? It will do you no harm and a lot of good.

There are many benefits that come from being challenged and corrected. Therefore, a wise person will actually pray that God will expose his errors, so he can become more aware of them. Why not pray something along these lines: *"Lord, please point out to me any mistakes in my logic, or errors of fact, or gaps in my knowledge, or anything else of which I am unaware. Speak to me through the Bible or other people and let me know where such errors are. Please also let me see my own sins and character faults as clearly as other people can see them."*

Sadly, that is not what most of us actually pray. Instead, we tend to fight hard to maintain our dignity and to *appear* to be in the right, even after we know we were wrong. I believe that the leader I spoke of earlier had simply downloaded another man's sermon from the internet, complete with overhead projector images. It was plain that he had done little or no genuine study of the book of Jonah for himself. He was just reading out an entire sermon which was not his own work. Therefore, he was not actually *able* to engage in a meaningful discussion with me.

He knew that if he had spoken with me he would have been exposed as having done no real study of his own. Therefore, rather than learn the truth, he chose to avoid exposure, even in a private one to one conversation which would have gone no further. At that moment, I believe he was being a fool. He was trying to save his own face, rather than find out whether his teaching was right or wrong. Strictly speaking, a person who does not love the truth does not actually *want* to be wrong. Neither does he want to believe lies.

He would probably prefer the truth, *but only if it does not cost him something*, or involve any inconvenience. That is the attitude of a fool, and yet it is how most of us operate. If a person persists in maintaining their own opinions, rather than accepting what God says, there will come a point when God will '*hand them over*' or '*give them over*'. That means He will step back and leave them to get on with pursuing their own foolish opinions, and even engaging in sinful behaviour, rather than listening to Him. That is a very dangerous position to be in:

[11] "But my people did not listen to my voice;
Israel would not submit to me.
[12] So I gave them over to their stubborn hearts,
to follow their own counsels.
                    Psalm 81:11-12 (ESV)

Wise people take care not to be *"wise in their own eyes"*.

A wise person realises that such wisdom as he does have is very limited and that he needs God's help and guidance every day. He does not trust himself, or rely on his own knowledge, ability or judgment. Instead, he gradually learns to rely on God and to seek His help rather than being what the Bible calls "*wise in your own eyes*". That expression means having an over-confident belief in your own ability to understand situations and to decide what to do:

[5] Trust in the LORD with all your heart,
and do not rely on your own insight.
[6] In all your ways acknowledge him,
and he will make straight your paths.

⁷Be not wise in your own eyes;
fear the LORD,
and turn away from evil.
                    Proverbs 3:5-7 (RSV)

Woe to those who are wise in their own eyes, and shrewd in their own sight!
                    Isaiah 5:21 (RSV)

Do you see a man who is wise in his own eyes?
*   There is more hope for a fool than for him.*
                    Proverbs 26:12 (RSV)

He who trusts in his own mind is a fool;
but he who walks in wisdom will be delivered.
                    Proverbs 28:26 (RSV)

Before destruction a man's heart is haughty,
*   but humility comes before honor.*
                    Proverbs 18:12 (ESV)

Pride goes before destruction,
*   and a haughty spirit before a fall.*
                    Proverbs 16:18 (ESV)

A man's pride will bring him low, but he who is lowly in spirit will obtain honor
                    Proverbs 29:23 (RSV)

Jesus strongly rebuked the people of the towns of Chorazin, Bethsaida and Capernaum on the edge of Lake Galilee. They had seen and heard Him in person and yet they still did not repent or believe. They were wise in their own eyes and also self-sufficient and therefore they did not see their own need or realise that they lacked anything. Conversely, the humble people were able to believe Jesus' words very easily because they had that humility and sense of dependency that children have. It is only to such infants, both literal and metaphorical, that God reveals the truth:

At that time Jesus said, "I praise You, Father, Lord of heaven and earth, that You have hidden these things from the wise and intelligent and have revealed them to infants.
                    Matthew 11:25 (NASB)

Apostle Paul also spoke on this theme, pointing out that *"the wisdom of this age is folly with God"*. He meant that what we think of as wisdom is often just man-made thinking which does not come from God and does not reflect His thinking.

237

Therefore, it is futile and if we adopt such beliefs and views we would be fools. Instead, we must adopt God's thinking on every possible point. If we do we shall actually *be* wise, even though those around us will *regard* us as fools for holding views so very different to theirs:

[18] *Let no one deceive himself. If anyone among you thinks that he is wise in this age, let him become a fool that he may become wise.* [19] *For the wisdom of this world is folly with God. For it is written, "He catches the wise in their craftiness,"* [20] *and again, "The Lord knows the thoughts of the wise, that they are futile."* — *ultimately nihilistic self destruct.*

1 Corinthians 3:18-20 (ESV)

Wise people willingly humble themselves

Given that so many benefits and blessings are promised to those who humble themselves, common sense dictates that we should all do so. God repeatedly denounces pride, arrogance, and haughtiness. Therefore, it can only be described as foolishness if we refuse to humble ourselves. Let's look at just a few examples beginning with this well-known verse in which God promises to hear the Jewish people, and to heal their land *if they will humble themselves*:

if my people who are called by my name humble themselves, and pray and seek my face and turn from their wicked ways, then I will hear from heaven and will forgive their sin and heal their land.

2 Chronicles 7:14 (ESV)

Note also what James, the half-brother of Jesus, says about how God deals with those who will humble themselves:

But he gives more grace. Therefore it says, "God opposes the proud but gives grace to the humble."

James 4:6 (ESV)

Humble yourselves before the Lord, and he will exalt you.
James 4:10 (ESV)

Jesus Himself makes the point even more explicitly and establishes a law that all who humble themselves will be exalted, whereas all who exalt themselves will be humbled:

For everyone who exalts himself will be humbled, and he who humbles himself will be exalted."

Luke 14:11 (ESV)

238

The point is that God hates pride and distances Himself from all who are haughty. Yet He has regard for the lowly:

For though the LORD is high, he regards the lowly,
  but the haughty he knows from afar.
                    Psalm 138:6 (ESV)

Therefore, we should all be eager to humble ourselves and take every opportunity to do so. However, the question then is *how exactly should we do it?* Due to our sin nature, humility doesn't come naturally to us. Therefore, it involves a deliberate choice to do the opposite of what our flesh wants, like holding a cork underwater. It means forcing yourself to do what your proud, selfish nature doesn't want to do. Jesus told the apostles that anyone who wants to be great must become a servant. That means focusing on the needs of others, and on meeting their needs, rather than our own:

[42] And Jesus called them to him and said to them, "You know that those who are considered rulers of the Gentiles lord it over them, and their great ones exercise authority over them. [43] But it shall not be so among you. But whoever would be great among you must be your servant,[44] and whoever would be first among you must be slave of all. [45] For even the Son of Man came not to be served but to serve, and to give his life as a ransom for many."
                    Mark 10:42-45 (ESV)

None of this will come naturally. The mere fact that we may have become a Christian does not mean that we lose our flesh nature. It does not go away and has to be denied its own way, or 'crucified', by regularly denying ourselves, serving others and repenting willingly when we are wrong or in sin. God's willingness to respond graciously when we humble ourselves applies to everyone, no matter how bad they are, or what they have done, even the wicked King Ahab of Israel, upon whose descendants God pronounced judgment via the prophet Elijah:

[17] Then the word of the LORD came to Elijah the Tishbite, saying, [18] "Arise, go down to meet Ahab king of Israel, who is in Samaria; behold, he is in the vineyard of Naboth, where he has gone to take possession. [19] And you shall say to him, 'Thus says the LORD, "Have you killed and also taken possession?"' And you shall say to him, 'Thus says the LORD: "In the place where dogs licked up the blood of Naboth shall dogs lick your own blood."''
[20] Ahab said to Elijah, "Have you found me, O my enemy?" He answered, "I have found you, because you have sold yourself to do what is evil in the sight of the LORD. [21] Behold, I will bring disaster upon you. I will utterly burn you up, and will cut off from Ahab every male, bond or free, in Israel. [22] And I will make your house like the house of Jeroboam the son of Nebat, and like the house of

239

Baasha the son of Ahijah, for the anger to which you have provoked me, and because you have made Israel to sin. [23] And of Jezebel the LORD also said, 'The dogs shall eat Jezebel within the walls of Jezreel.' [24] Anyone belonging to Ahab who dies in the city the dogs shall eat, and anyone of his who dies in the open country the birds of the heavens shall eat."
[25] (There was none who sold himself to do what was evil in the sight of the LORD like Ahab, whom Jezebel his wife incited. [26] He acted very abominably in going after idols, as the Amorites had done, whom the LORD cast out before the people of Israel.)

1 Kings 21:17-26 (ESV)

When Ahab realised this, and reflected on his own sin, even he chose to repent and humble himself. When he did so, God's heart was touched. He therefore chose to delay the judgment on Ahab's family line so that it would only come after Ahab's death:

[27] And when Ahab heard those words, he tore his clothes and put sackcloth on his flesh and fasted and lay in sackcloth and went about dejectedly. [28] And the word of the LORD came to Elijah the Tishbite, saying, [29] "Have you seen how Ahab has humbled himself before me? Because he has humbled himself before me, I will not bring the disaster in his days; but in his son's days I will bring the disaster upon his house."

1 Kings 21:27-29 (ESV)

Whoever you are, this law about humbling and exalting operates automatically, and in both directions. Therefore, wise people will choose to humble themselves whenever they can, and they will avoid exalting themselves. Then they can fully rely on God to exalt them in due course. When a person humbles themselves, God is so pleased He intervenes in their lives to guide them and give them wisdom:

He leads the humble in what is right,
and teaches the humble his way.

Psalm 25:9 (RSV)

When pride comes, then comes disgrace;
but with the humble is wisdom.

Proverbs 11:2 (RSV)

Humbling oneself also causes God to hear our prayers and to be willing to use us in His service:

because your heart was tender and you humbled yourself before the LORD when you heard what I spoke against this place and against its inhabitants that they should become a desolation and a curse, and you have torn your clothes and wept before Me, I truly have heard you," declares the LORD.

2 Kings 22:19 (NASB)

All these things my hand has made,
and so all these things are mine,
says the LORD.
But this is the man to whom I will look,
he that is humble and contrite in spirit,
and trembles at my word.

Isaiah 66:2 (RSV)

Humbling ourselves is also the only way to enter the Kingdom of God:

Truly I say to you, whoever does not receive the kingdom of God like a child will not enter it at all."

Luke 18:17 (NASB)

God also wants us to avoid conceit, and to be willing to associate with the lowly:

Live in harmony with one another; do not be haughty, but associate with the lowly; never be conceited.

Romans 12:16 (RSV)

There is actually no point boasting about ourselves or our abilities or achievements. The only thing we should ever 'boast' about is God. We must not promote ourselves or desire to be well-known or approved of. Neither should we ever praise ourselves or seek the praise of others:

Let another praise you, and not your own mouth;
a stranger, and not your own lips.

Proverbs 27:2 (RSV)

The only commendation that really counts is when God commends us:

[17] "Let the one who boasts, boast in the Lord." [18] For it is not the one who commends himself who is approved, but the one whom the Lord commends.

2 Corinthians 10:17-18 (ESV)

Therefore, a wise person realises that it is in his own interests to humble himself, take the lowest place, and shun all boasting and pride. In this life, and in the next life, that is a guaranteed route to success. As the late Derek Prince famously put it, *"the way up is down".*

241

Wise people don't take to heart the unfair or critical things that other people say.

Wise people know that whatever is said about them, however harsh or unkind it may be, they themselves have said the same, or worse, about others in the past. Moreover, those who insult or abuse us are only here for a short time and will soon be gone, so try not to place much importance on the untrue or unfair things that others say:

²¹Do not give heed to all the things that men say, lest you hear your servant cursing you; ²²your heart knows that many times you have yourself cursed others.

Ecclesiastes 7:21-22 (RSV)

⁷"Hearken to me, you who know righteousness, the people in whose heart is my law; fear not the reproach of men, and be not dismayed at their revilings. ⁸ For the moth will eat them up like a garment, and the worm will eat them like wool; but my deliverance will be for ever, and my salvation to all generations."

Isaiah 51:7-8 (RSV)

Wise people know that, despite all God's blessings, they are still subject to the randomness of time and chance, just like everyone else.

The general principle set out in Scripture is that a wise person will succeed, prosper, live longer and enjoy protection. However, that is not an absolute rule. The only certainty is that such people will prosper and be rewarded *in the next life*, when they are resurrected. In this present life, there are no guarantees. We all have to face the random events, both good and bad, that time and chance bring, both to the righteous and the wicked, the wise and the foolish. Therefore, we are all subject to the ups and downs of life, no matter how wise we may become:

¹ But all this I laid to heart, examining it all, how the righteous and the wise and their deeds are in the hand of God. Whether it is love or hate, man does not know; both are before him. ² It is the same for all, since the same event happens to the righteous and the wicked, to the good and the evil, to the clean and the unclean, to him who sacrifices and him who does not sacrifice. As the good one is, so is the sinner, and he who swears is as he who shuns an oath. ³ This is an evil in all that is done under the sun, that the same event happens to all. Also, the hearts of the children of man are full of evil, and madness is in their hearts while they live, and after that they go to the dead.

Ecclesiastes 9:1-3 (ESV)

¹¹ Again I saw that under the sun the race is not to the swift, nor the battle to the strong, nor bread to the wise, nor riches to the intelligent, nor favour to those with knowledge, but time and chance happen to them all. ¹² For man does not know his time. Like fish that are taken in an evil net, and like birds that are caught in a snare, so the children of man are snared at an evil time, when it suddenly falls upon them.

Wrong place at wrong time   *Ecclesiastes 9:11-12 (ESV)*

Wise people know their limitations and they still find life baffling sometimes.

Wise people know that, however hard they try, they will never know everything, and they are keenly aware of how much they *do not* know or understand. Some things are just beyond us, however wise we become:

O LORD, my heart is not lifted up,
 my eyes are not raised too high;
I do not occupy myself with things
too great and too marvelous for me.
            Psalm 131:1 (RSV)

¹⁶When I applied my mind to know wisdom, and to see the business that is done on earth, how neither day nor night one's eyes see sleep; ¹⁷then I saw all the work of God, that man cannot find out the work that is done under the sun. However much man may toil in seeking, he will not find it out; even though a wise man claims to know, he cannot find it out.

            Ecclesiastes 8:16-17 (NIV)

Even the wisest of people find life baffling at times, so we will never understand everything or know at all times what to do. God has chosen only to provide us with a limited measure of wisdom, no matter who we are. Wise people come to terms with this and are reconciled to having to live with an element of uncertainty and inadequacy. That keeps them dependent on God to provide, day by day, the wisdom they lack. Even if that is never given to them, they press ahead anyway and don't consider God to be at fault for requiring them to live in a world that is subject to such limitations.

They do what they know to be their duty, even when they are confused or unsure about what God is doing and why. Ironically, therefore, the wiser a person becomes, the more they realise that they *lack* knowledge and understanding. Even Solomon, who had more wisdom than any other man, could not achieve total wisdom, no matter how hard he studied. Even for him, there was still frustration, vexation and a sense of failure and futility at times. In fact, the more wisdom he acquired, the more it added to his concerns and sorrows in some ways:

243

¹²I, the Teacher, was king over Israel in Jerusalem.¹³I devoted myself to study and to explore by wisdom all that is done under heaven. What a heavy burden God has laid on men!¹⁴ I have seen all the things that are done under the sun; all of them are meaningless, a chasing after the wind.¹⁵What is twisted cannot be straightened; what is lacking cannot be counted. ¹⁶I thought to myself, "Look, I have grown and increased in wisdom more than anyone who has ruled over Jerusalem before me; I have experienced much of wisdom and knowledge." ¹⁷Then I applied myself to the understanding of wisdom, and also of madness and folly, but I learned that this, too, is a chasing after the wind. ¹⁸ For with much wisdom comes much sorrow; the more knowledge, the more grief.

Ecclesiastes 1:12-18 (RSV)

Although we have a measure of understanding, God puts a limit on how much we can grasp. He will not allow any person, however wise they may be, to have complete knowledge or understanding:

He has made everything beautiful in its time; also he has put eternity into man's mind, yet so that he cannot find out what God has done from the beginning to the end.

Ecclesiastes 3:11 (RSV)

There is also an element of chance, and even of futility, which came as a result of Adam's fall. God has built this into the way life operates. No matter what we do to plan or prepare, and no matter how wise we become, there will still be random, meaningless events and disasters. Things will not always work out the way they should, or as we expect. Consequently, the best people don't always win, because the outcome of life is also affected by *time and chance*, as well as by hard work and ability.

If we can recognise this, and learn to live with it, rather than rail against it, we will avoid some of the vexation that life brings. In the book of Job, his friends make a series of comments about his appalling situation and give him a great deal of advice. Quite a lot of what they say would have been good advice, and even right theology, if it had been given on a different day, to a different man, in different circumstances. However, Job's situation was a strange one and it didn't fit their own experience, or their theology.

Thus, the things they had to say, although generally true in many other people's situations, were not true of Job or of his specific circumstances. Job's friends could not see the whole picture as God saw it. Therefore, God was angry with them for criticising Job when, on this particular occasion, there was far more to it than they realised. Thus, they were wrong in what they said about Job, even though most of what they said was generally right and would have applied to many other people:

[7] It came about after the LORD had spoken these words to Job, that the LORD said to Eliphaz the Temanite, "My wrath is kindled against you and against your two friends, because you have not spoken of Me what is right as My servant Job has. [8] Now therefore, take for yourselves seven bulls and seven rams, and go to My servant Job, and offer up a burnt offering for yourselves, and My servant Job will pray for you. For I will accept him so that I may not do with you according to your folly, because you have not spoken of Me what is right, as My servant Job has."

Job 42:7-8 (NASB)

A lesson to draw from the mistakes made by Job's friends is that even as we grow in wisdom, and even if we know the whole Bible, there will still be times when the complexity of the issues we face is beyond our capacity to understand. God has not chosen to share all His knowledge and understanding with us, as he pointed out to Job. Therefore, in pursuing wisdom, we need to be realistic about how much of it we are going to obtain, even in the long term:

[2] "Who is this that darkens counsel
By words without knowledge?
[3] "Now gird up your loins like a man,
And I will ask you, and you instruct Me!
[4] "Where were you when I laid the foundation of the earth?
Tell Me, if you have understanding,
[5] Who set its measurements? Since you know.
Or who stretched the line on it?
[6] "On what were its bases sunk?
Or who laid its cornerstone,
[7] When the morning stars sang together
And all the sons of God shouted for joy?
[8] "Or who enclosed the sea with doors
When, bursting forth, it went out from the womb;
[9] When I made a cloud its garment
And thick darkness its swaddling band,
[10] And I placed boundaries on it
And set a bolt and doors,
[11] And I said, 'Thus far you shall come, but no farther;
And here shall your proud waves stop'?
[12] "Have you ever in your life commanded the morning,
And caused the dawn to know its place,
[13] That it might take hold of the ends of the earth,
And the wicked be shaken out of it?

245

14 *"It is changed like clay under the seal;*
And they stand forth like a garment.
15 *"From the wicked their light is withheld,*
And the uplifted arm is broken.
16 *"Have you entered into the springs of the sea*
Or walked in the recesses of the deep?
17 *"Have the gates of death been revealed to you,*
Or have you seen the gates of deep darkness?
18 *"Have you understood the expanse of the earth?*
Tell Me, if you know all this.

Job 38:2-18 (NASB)

3 *Then Job answered the LORD and said,*
4 *"Behold, I am insignificant; what can I reply to You?*
I lay my hand on my mouth.
5 *"Once I have spoken, and I will not answer;*
Even twice, and I will add nothing more."

Job 40:3-5 (NASB)

Although it is right to pursue wisdom, we must never imagine we have acquired it all, or are fully able to apply it. If we do, we will end up applying it wrongly, or at the wrong time, or making pronouncements which go too far, or are based on incomplete knowledge. Then we will be wrong overall, as Job's friends were, even though much of what we say could be correct in itself or in principle. Job's friends obviously had a lot of genuine understanding and knew more than most believers today. They were sincere and earnest too.

Their error was to presume to pronounce with excessive confidence on matters which went beyond their capacity to understand. They also assumed that just because they knew a *general* principle about how God operates, that must mean that God *always* operates in that way, with *all* people, and in *all* situations. Quite possibly Job's friends went wrong because they expressed their own opinions and beliefs without ever asking God for specific wisdom relevant to Job's situation. There is no evidence in the text that any of them ever made such a prayer.

Instead, it seems that they just unleashed what they had to say without ever praying something along these lines: *"Lord, this situation appears to be very complex. What should I say to Job? Or, should I say nothing at all at present? Please guide me and prevent me from misrepresenting you, or misapplying the limited knowledge that I do have".* Such a prayer would have been well worth making and would be a good prayer for us to make too. Job speaks in that way to God at the end of the book of Job when he realises his own smallness and his very limited understanding in comparison to God's:

246

¹ Then Job answered the LORD and said,
² "I know that You can do all things,
And that no purpose of Yours can be thwarted.
³ 'Who is this that hides counsel without knowledge?'
Therefore I have declared that which I did not understand,
Things too wonderful for me, which I did not know."
⁴ 'Hear, now, and I will speak;
I will ask You, and You instruct me.'
⁵ "I have heard of You by the hearing of the ear;
But now my eye sees You;
⁶ Therefore I retract,
And I repent in dust and ashes."

Job 42:1-6 (NASB)

Wise people are not insecure or envious. But if somehow they still are, they recognise these traits as faults, seek to deal with them, and refuse to be influenced by them

In my long experience of both workplaces and churches, I have come to the view that a large proportion of the population are insecure in one or more ways. That insecurity causes profound problems and much unhappiness. People seek to defend themselves from imagined threats, or they compete with others when there isn't actually any competition. They then knock others down to avoid being out-done in these imaginary contests. The tragedy is that those problems could be avoided if the person concerned was to learn:

a) to be content with his own abilities, talents, possessions and calling and not crave to be someone else, or to have what others have

b) to be content for other people to have different, or even better, abilities talents possessions and callings than himself and not to resent the fact that those people have what they have, or seek to knock them down, or take away what they have.

The sin we are looking at here is *envy*. It is terribly damaging and causes untold misery to all concerned, both the one who envies, and the one who is envied. The essence of envy is:

a) wanting to have what has not been given to you, is not yours, and is not meant to be yours

b) wanting others *not to have* what has been given to them, and which is theirs.

247

Envy is a very serious sin but it is important to distinguish it from *jealousy* which is not a sin at all. Many people assume that it is just another word for envy, but it isn't. Jealousy means wanting to get back from someone else something which is *rightfully yours* and which they have *wrongfully taken from you*. Thus, if you see another man walking down the street with your wife, whom he has stolen away from you, and if you want to get her back, then that is to be jealous. You are being jealous for your own wife, and that is *not a sin*.

If instead you saw a man walking along the street with his own wife and you wanted her that would be envy. You would be wanting something which is not, and never can be, yours. In that context, insecurity involves fearing that some other man will take your wife away from you, or that she might wish to go with him or is planning to do so. Envy and insecurity extend far beyond the issue of wives. People feel insecure about themselves, and envious of others, in just about every way you could imagine. Thus, in the workplace, but also in churches, there are many people who:

a)   believe they are not sufficiently able or talented, or that they have been given fewer, or lesser, gifts than others, such that their own achievements are insignificant by comparison, and even worthless.

b)   even if they are talented and have been given important roles or duties, and even if they know that, they can never stop fearing that someone else may come along later who has more to offer or is more talented. They fear that that person could do a better job, or take their job, or their opportunity for promotion, or outshine them in some way.

That nagging anxiety can ruin a person's own life and cause them to act sinfully towards others who might pose a 'threat'. In my Book 6 I tell the story of 'Tracey', a secretary who became a menace in my law firm. She caused terrible damage to others by lying to them, and about them, all because she felt insecure and wanted to advance her own career prospects by undermining others. Please see Book 6 for the whole story, plus other stories of people I have known who behaved in wicked ways due to being insecure.

The tragedy of such insecurity is that it is all entirely unnecessary. A lot of it is caused by the lies whispered into people's minds by demons, which they wrongly assume to be their own thoughts. Please see my Books 7 and 9 for an explanation of what demons are capable of. They operate skilfully, and covertly, to undermine us and to cause us to harm ourselves and others.

Nobody ever needs to feel insecure. If we think as we ought to think, and see ourselves, the world, and our position within it as they really are, then everything becomes much clearer. We are not actually meant to be competing against other

248

people. From God's perspective, that is not what life is about. We must certainly do our best to bear fruit, to be 'overcomers', and to do God's will. But we are not being measured by how we compare to others in our abilities, or in what we achieve in *comparison to them*. The Judgment Seat of Christ will not include any such comparisons.

What talents other people had in this life, and whether they did better than you, will not be on the agenda when Jesus assesses you. He will measure you by reference to *what you did with what you were given*. Whether your talents were great or small will make no difference to the outcome. You don't need, therefore, to do better than others, or to prevent them from outshining you. Each of them will be judged on a stand-alone basis, in exactly the same way. Thus, your achievements won't be mentioned in their judgment, any more than their achievements will be mentioned in yours.

Once the reality of this sinks in, it is life-changing. You suddenly realise that you can be a great success, and hear the words *"Well done, good and faithful servant,"* even if every other person in your church of workplace had more talent and ability than you and ends up being promoted to a higher position and a bigger ministry during this life. Imagine that you work alongside Fred Smith, Joe Bloggs and Jack Jones, or that they are part of your church, and that they each have different roles.

Suppose each of them has more natural ability than you, more ministry gifts, more spiritual gifts, are better known than you, and have risen to a higher level of leadership. Or, perhaps, imagine that you are not in a leadership position at all, whereas all of them are. None of that matters in the slightest to Jesus, and His view is all that ultimately counts. He is the one who will judge us and His assessment of us will stand for all eternity as the final word on how well each of us did.

Many people aim to do better than others, or to prevent others doing better than them. But Jesus actually wants each of us to *want others to do well and to help them to do so.* Imagine that as a result of your encouragement, support and mentoring, Fred, Joe, and Jack all end up rising higher than you and doing 'better', so far as you and others can tell, in the work of the ministry. Jesus might still praise you more than them, reward you more, and allocate you a higher place in His Kingdom, on the basis that *you helped those servants of His* to do better than they otherwise would.

Many people are unaware that the extent of our help for others, and our unselfishness in encouraging them to achieve things for Jesus, is one of the criteria by which He will judge us. Therefore, they misguidedly cause themselves to score 0/100 on this vital criterion because they did not realise this was something they were expected to do, or that they would ever be assessed on that basis. How sad is that?

Therefore, the very steps they take to hinder their 'rivals' and to undermine and discourage them, with the aim of doing better than them, will actually only reduce their own 'score' at the Judgment Seat. It could also cause them to lose the rewards which they would otherwise have been awarded and to be given a lower position in the Kingdom. Therefore, a wise person will not try to compete with others in their ministry, or in their walk as a disciple, and will instead:

a) be content with whatever talents they have been given, small or large, and thank God for them

b) be relaxed about others having more talent than them, or being able to do things they cannot do

c) encourage others to go further, achieve more, and do better, regardless of whether they end up doing 'better' than himself

d) see himself as part of a worldwide *team* of Christians, all of whom are *playing on the same side*, seeking to reach the lost, to make disciples, and to be salt and light to a fallen world, rather than competing against each other.

When you see things this way it suddenly makes sense that you should be content with your own gifts and talents, whatever they may be. Then you can encourage all other Christians to fulfil their potential, without feeling that their success would diminish you in any way. A person who is wise enough to see this is able to embark upon 'the ministry of encouragement', which is possibly one of the best ways of being highly rewarded at the judgment.

They will see it as their aim to lift others up, not to knock them down and will want others to do their best for the 'team', even if they are seen to be doing better than themselves. The ministry of encouragement is vitally needed within the Church, and is also a source of great pleasure and satisfaction for those who engage in it. Yet it is very rarely sought after or practised due, in large part, to this problem of insecurity and envy. Please refer to my Book 7 in which I refer to this in more detail.

A wise person is open to see the sin, and the faults, in himself and will want to take every opportunity to repent and to change.

If God was a doctor, the main medicine He would prescribe to His patients would be repentance. It would be dispensed on a regular basis and in large doses. It is central to the whole Gospel message, which is why the public ministries of both

John the Baptist and of Jesus began with the word *'repent'*. It was also virtually the first word which Peter said too, when preaching his first sermon after the resurrection. It would be difficult to overstate the importance of repentance or to 'over-prescribe' it to yourself as a remedy.

A wise person will take every opportunity to repent, not only at the start of his Christian life when he is first converted, but on a regular basis thereafter. Repentance is also a vital ingredient if we want to grow and mature as a disciple, not only in order to be saved to begin with. Ongoing repentance is what we are all meant to be doing, *throughout our entire lives*. You will never reach a stage where you outgrow that and no longer need to do it, or at least not until you die.

> *12 "Yet even now," declares the LORD,*
> *"return to me with all your heart,*
> *with fasting, with weeping, and with mourning;*
> *13 and rend your hearts and not your garments."*
> *Return to the LORD your God,*
> *for he is gracious and merciful,*
> *slow to anger, and abounding in steadfast love;*
> *and he relents over disaster.*
> *14 Who knows whether he will not turn and relent,*
> *and leave a blessing behind him,*
> *a grain offering and a drink offering*
> *for the LORD your God?*
> *15 Blow the trumpet in Zion;*
> *consecrate a fast;*
> *call a solemn assembly;*
> *16 gather the people.*
> *Consecrate the congregation;*
> *assemble the elders;*
> *gather the children,*
> *even nursing infants.*
> *Let the bridegroom leave his room,*
> *and the bride her chamber.*
> *17 Between the vestibule and the altar*
> *let the priests, the ministers of the LORD, weep*
> *and say, "Spare your people, O LORD,*
> *and make not your heritage a reproach,*
> *a byword among the nations.*
> *Why should they say among the peoples,*
> *'Where is their God?'"*
>
> *Joel 2:12-17 (ESV)*

Wise people do not allow their hearts to become hard. They take steps to soften their own hearts.

A hard heart prevents a person hearing the voice of the Holy Spirit and from accepting and responding to what the Bible says. It is a very widespread problem and does not only apply to those who are embittered towards God. It is also found in ordinary people, *including believers*, who are:

a) complacent

b) indifferent

c) sceptical and unbelieving

d) irreverent

e) presumptuous

f) unrepentant

g) slow to respond or obey

h) determined to stick with their own opinions and traditions rather than what God says.

Any of us can become hard-hearted. It is a condition which makes us resistant to what God is saying to us and slow to grasp it. Even the apostles were sometimes remarkably slow to understand what Jesus said:

¹¹The Pharisees came out and began to argue with Him, seeking from Him a sign from heaven, to test Him. ¹² Sighing deeply in His spirit, He said, "Why does this generation seek for a sign? Truly I say to you, no sign will be given to this generation." ¹³ Leaving them, He again embarked and went away to the other side. ¹⁴ And they had forgotten to take bread, and did not have more than one loaf in the boat with them. ¹⁵ And He was giving orders to them, saying, "Watch out! Beware of the leaven of the Pharisees and the leaven of Herod." ¹⁶ They began to discuss with one another the fact that they had no bread. ¹⁷ And Jesus, aware of this, said to them, "Why do you discuss the fact that you have no bread? Do you not yet see or understand? Do you have a hardened heart? ¹⁸ Having eyes, do you not see? And having ears, do you not hear? And do you not remember,

Mark 8:11-18 (NASB)

If you continue hardening your heart and refusing to listen to God, a point may be reached where He *refuses to listen to you*. If so, He effectively *hands you over* and leaves you to take the path that you have chosen for yourself, however foolish or wicked it is. That is what God did with the Jews when they *"made their hearts diamond-hard lest they should hear the law...."*

¹¹ But they refused to pay attention and turned a stubborn shoulder and stopped their ears that they might not hear. ¹² They made their hearts diamond-hard lest they should hear the law and the words that the LORD of hosts had sent by his Spirit through the former prophets. Therefore great anger came from the LORD of hosts. ¹³ "As I called, and they would not hear, so they called, and I would not hear," says the LORD of hosts,

Zechariah 7:11-13 (ESV)

Have you ever considered how many astonishing statements the Bible makes which we allow to wash over us without taking them seriously or changing our lives in response? Due to our hardness of heart we can become immune to the Bible, as if we were coated with oil which causes God's Word to run off us like water off a duck's back. It is not only unbelievers who are like that. It affects believers too, including genuine Christians. The writer of the letter to the Hebrews addresses this issue and remember that he is writing *to and about believers*, not the unsaved:

⁷ Therefore, as the Holy Spirit says:
"Today, if you will hear His voice,
⁸ Do not harden your hearts as in the rebellion,
In the day of trial in the wilderness,
⁹ Where your fathers tested Me, tried Me,
And saw My works forty years.
¹⁰ Therefore I was angry with that generation,
And said, 'They always go astray in their heart,
And they have not known My ways.'
¹¹ So I swore in My wrath,
'They shall not enter My rest.'"
¹² Beware, brethren, lest there be in any of you an evil heart of unbelief in departing from the living God; ¹³ but exhort one another daily, while it is called "Today," lest any of you be hardened through the deceitfulness of sin. ¹⁴ For we have become partakers of Christ if we hold the beginning of our confidence steadfast to the end, ¹⁵ while it is said:
"Today, if you will hear His voice,
Do not harden your hearts as in the rebellion."
¹⁶ For who, having heard, rebelled? Indeed, was it not all who came out of Egypt, led by Moses? ¹⁷ Now with whom was He angry forty years? Was it not with those who sinned, whose corpses fell in the wilderness? ¹⁸ And to whom did He swear that they would not enter His rest, but to those who did not obey? ¹⁹ So we see that they could not enter in because of unbelief

Hebrews 3:7-19 (NKJV)

The writer of Hebrews (apostle Paul in my personal view) wanted his readers to listen to the voice of the Holy Spirit and not let their hearts become hardened. Moreover, he put the responsibility for preventing that upon *them*. It was *their own duty* to become soft-hearted and to avoid hard-heartedness. That is not something that happens to you randomly, or by accident. You *bring it upon yourself* by lots of small decisions to ignore or disobey the Bible, or your conscience, and to go your own way instead. It usually does not involve any spectacular acts of rebellion.

Mostly it comes from a series of small choices, each of which leaves us a little bit harder and a little bit less sensitive to our consciences, or to the Bible. Unless you take decisive action to repent and change your attitude, you will sink into a much deeper hardness of heart, which is very dangerous. A wise person does not assume that this hardening process could never happen to him. Nor does he fail to take it seriously. He takes active steps to 'tenderise' his own heart by regularly humbling himself, repenting, and forgiving others, so as to remove any bitterness. He also asks God to expose and deal with any remaining hardness of heart.

Where we see hardness of heart in ourselves, or even where we suspect it to be there, we should ask God to expose it. Ask Him to do whatever it takes to reveal the hardness and to help us to soften our hearts and become responsive to His voice. That is a prayer which is well worth making and which God will delight to answer. The benefits which will flow from it are enormous. Yet how often have you done this, or heard anybody urge you to do so?

We all need to ask God to help us to see our own hardness of heart and to tackle it. If we do that then God's will may sometimes be such that we need to make difficult decisions, or do painful and costly things, to obey Him and develop as disciples. On such occasions the price is worth paying because it will tenderise us and help us grow in maturity. Persistently softening our hearts and humbling ourselves causes us to become like small children in our attitudes towards God. At least in this sense, God wants us to have that childlike heart-attitude:

13 And they were bringing children to Him so that He might touch them; but the disciples rebuked them. 14But when Jesus saw this, He was indignant and said to them, "Permit the children to come to Me; do not hinder them; for the kingdom of God belongs to such as these. 15Truly I say to you, whoever does not receive the kingdom of God like a child will not enter it at all."

Mark 10:13-15 (NASB)

In the light of what Jesus says, taking the lowest place is actually enlightened self-interest. It may sound counter-intuitive, but that is how we rise up in His Kingdom. Conversely, grasping for seniority, status and recognition in this life brings us lower down in God's eyes.

Wise people know what will eventually happen to the wicked and are not discouraged by their apparent success or 'invincibility'.

The wicked are not going to be there permanently. A fool or a simple person will not realise this and will therefore be discouraged, but a wise person will not because he has a more accurate, and longer term, perspective on the fate of the wicked:

⁶ The stupid man cannot know;
the fool cannot understand this:
⁷ that though the wicked sprout like grass
and all evildoers flourish,
they are doomed to destruction forever;
                    Psalm 92:6-7 (ESV)

The Bible deals with the problem of why the wicked seem to do so well and why God's judgment on them is delayed. They prosper, and even seem to be invincible, while they continue doing evil. That is how it *appears to us,* because we don't have God's long term perspective about time and eternity. A wicked man being in power for 12 years, as Hitler was, seems a long time to us. Others have lasted even longer than that.

It is not only the great dictators that we are speaking of here. The same is true in our own personal lives at a local level. Wicked people can and do prosper. They get promoted. They become rich. They get elected – and re-elected. They exert great influence. Conversely, those who do what is right are often obstructed and unrecognised and can seem unsuccessful in the world's eyes. In view of this, it is easy to become discouraged.

Some even feel tempted to join in with the wicked in the hope that cooperation may bring us a quieter life. But we must hold on to what the Bible says about the inevitable long-term destiny of the wicked. They really will *all* fail and be brought down in the end, at the very least, by death. After that they will face God's judgment, which is the ultimate long-stop and it limits their power and influence. Even King David struggled with this issue and addressed it in the Psalms:

¹ Fret not yourself because of evildoers;
be not envious of wrongdoers!
² For they will soon fade like the grass
and wither like the green herb.
³ Trust in the LORD, and do good;
dwell in the land and befriend faithfulness.
⁴ Delight yourself in the LORD,
and he will give you the desires of your heart.

255

⁵ *Commit your way to the LORD;*
trust in him, and he will act.
⁶ *He will bring forth your righteousness as the light,*
and your justice as the noonday.
⁷ *Be still before the LORD and wait patiently for him;*
fret not yourself over the one who prospers in his way,
over the man who carries out evil devices!
⁸ *Refrain from anger, and forsake wrath!*
Fret not yourself; it tends only to evil.
⁹ *For the evildoers shall be cut off,*
but those who wait for the LORD shall inherit the land.
¹⁰ *In just a little while, the wicked will be no more;*
though you look carefully at his place, he will not be there.
¹¹ *But the meek shall inherit the land*
and delight themselves in abundant peace.
¹² *The wicked plots against the righteous*
and gnashes his teeth at him,
¹³ *but the LORD laughs at the wicked,*
for he sees that his day is coming.
¹⁴ *The wicked draw the sword and bend their bows*
to bring down the poor and needy,
to slay those whose way is upright;
¹⁵ *their sword shall enter their own heart,*
and their bows shall be broken.
¹⁶ *Better is the little that the righteous has*
than the abundance of many wicked.
¹⁷ *For the arms of the wicked shall be broken,*
but the LORD upholds the righteous.
¹⁸ *The LORD knows the days of the blameless,*
and their heritage will remain forever;

Psalm 37:1-18 (ESV)

²⁷ *Turn away from evil and do good;*
so shall you dwell forever.
²⁸ *For the LORD loves justice;*
he will not forsake his saints.
They are preserved forever,
but the children of the wicked shall be cut off.
The righteous shall inherit the land
and dwell upon it forever.

Psalm 37:27-29 (ESV)

³⁴ *Wait for the LORD and keep his way,*
and he will exalt you to inherit the land;

you will look on when the wicked are cut off.
35 I have seen a wicked, ruthless man,
spreading himself like a green laurel tree.
36 But he passed away, and behold, he was no more;
though I sought him, he could not be found.
37 Mark the blameless and behold the upright,
for there is a future for the man of peace.
38 But transgressors shall be altogether destroyed;
the future of the wicked shall be cut off.

Psalm 37:34-38 (ESV)

20 Can wicked rulers be allied with you,
those who frame injustice by statute?
21 They band together against the life of the righteous
and condemn the innocent to death.
22 But the LORD has become my stronghold,
and my God the rock of my refuge.
23 He will bring back on them their iniquity
and wipe them out for their wickedness;
the LORD our God will wipe them out.

Psalm 94:20-23 (ESV)

In spite of all appearances, it is the wicked who are failing and who will one day be punished. No matter how it may appear now, they have no long term future and are doomed to fail. That being so, a wise person will always ally himself with God's people, and shun the wicked even if, at present, that appears to be costly, or even hopeless:

For a day in your courts is better
than a thousand elsewhere.
I would rather be a doorkeeper in the house of my God
than dwell in the tents of wickedness.

Psalm 84:10 (ESV)

In the end we shall all see the stark contrast between God's judgment of the wicked and His handling of the righteous:

16 Then those who feared the LORD spoke with one another. The LORD paid attention and heard them, and a book of remembrance was written before him of those who feared the LORD and esteemed his name. 17 "They shall be mine, says the LORD of hosts, in the day when I make up my treasured possession, and I will spare them as a man spares his son who serves him. 18 Then once more you shall see the distinction between the righteous and the wicked, between one who serves God and one who does not serve him.

¹ "For behold, the day is coming, burning like an oven, when all the arrogant and all evildoers will be stubble. The day that is coming shall set them ablaze, says the LORD of hosts, so that it will leave them neither root nor branch. ² But for you who fear my name, the sun of righteousness shall rise with healing in its wings. You shall go out leaping like calves from the stall. ³ And you shall tread down the wicked, for they will be ashes under the soles of your feet, on the day when I act, says the LORD of hosts.

Malachi 3:16-4:3 (ESV)

Wise people know that they could fall into sin, or even fall away, and they are not complacent about the potential to become unfaithful in later life

There are many examples in the Bible of people who began well, but then fell away. I can also think of many such examples amongst the people I know. They start out well, and even continue well for a while, acting wisely and remaining true. But, over time, perhaps due to the complacency and over-confidence that can come from success, they slacken off. They then become less honest, choose less wisely, and act less faithfully. Eventually they can reach a stage where they have fallen away completely and their Christian walk has become shallow or non-existent.

In some cases it occurs due to the death or departure of a godly mentor who was a significant influence in their younger years. They only remain faithful while they still have that godly person as a guide or 'pillar'. But when they have to stand alone, relying only on God's Word and their own conscience, they begin to do what is easy or expedient, rather than what is right. A classic example of this is the life of King Joash of Judah. Please see 2 Chronicles, chapters 22-24 for the full account.

Joash became king when he was only about 7 years old. He only survived to that age because he was rescued as a baby by his aunt, Jehoshabeath, and her godly husband, Jehoiada, who was a priest. If they had not hidden him away for six years he would have been murdered by the wicked 'Queen' Athaliah, his own grandmother. She killed the whole royal family when her son, King Ahaziah, died. She then reigned in his place as a usurper for six years until the chance came to assassinate her and put the young boy, King Joash, on the throne:

¹⁰ Now when Athaliah the mother of Ahaziah saw that her son was dead, she arose and destroyed all the royal family of the house of Judah. ¹¹ But Jehoshabeath, the daughter of the king, took Joash the son of Ahaziah and stole him away from among the king's sons who were about to be put to death, and she put him and his nurse in a bedroom. Thus Jehoshabeath, the daughter of King Jehoram and wife of Jehoiada the priest, because she was a sister of

258

Ahaziah, hid him from Athaliah, so that she did not put him to death. ¹² *And he remained with them six years, hidden in the house of God, while Athaliah reigned over the land.*

2 Chronicles 22:10-12 (ESV)

¹ *But in the seventh year Jehoiada took courage and entered into a covenant with the commanders of hundreds, Azariah the son of Jeroham, Ishmael the son of Jehohanan, Azariah the son of Obed, Maaseiah the son of Adaiah, and Elishaphat the son of Zichri.* ² *And they went about through Judah and gathered the Levites from all the cities of Judah, and the heads of fathers' houses of Israel, and they came to Jerusalem.* ³ *And all the assembly made a covenant with the king in the house of God. And Jehoiada said to them, "Behold, the king's son! Let him reign, as the LORD spoke concerning the sons of David.*

2 Chronicles 23:1-3 (ESV)

¹¹ *Then they brought out the king's son and put the crown on him and gave him the testimony. And they proclaimed him king, and Jehoiada and his sons anointed him, and they said, "Long live the king."* ¹² *When Athaliah heard the noise of the people running and praising the king, she went into the house of the LORD to the people.* ¹³ *And when she looked, there was the king standing by his pillar at the entrance, and the captains and the trumpeters beside the king, and all the people of the land rejoicing and blowing trumpets, and the singers with their musical instruments leading in the celebration. And Athaliah tore her clothes and cried, "Treason! Treason!"* ¹⁴ *Then Jehoiada the priest brought out the captains who were set over the army, saying to them, "Bring her out between the ranks, and anyone who follows her is to be put to death with the sword." For the priest said, "Do not put her to death in the house of the LORD."* ¹⁵ *So they laid hands on her, and she went into the entrance of the horse gate of the king's house, and they put her to death there.*

2 Chronicles 23:11-15 (ESV)

For many years, King Joash reigned in Judah and made wise decisions as he sought to cleanse the nation of idolatry. He did all that because he had the wise advice and godly influence of Jehoiada, his aunt's husband, who was a pillar in Joash's life:

¹ *Joash was seven years old when he began to reign, and he reigned forty years in Jerusalem. His mother's name was Zibiah of Beersheba.* ² *And Joash did what was right in the eyes of the LORD all the days of Jehoiada the priest.*

2 Chronicles 24:1-2 (ESV)

However, when Jehoiada eventually died, Joash had to reign without his influence. Joash then began to come under the influence of ungodly men and ended up abandoning the house of the LORD and serving false gods and idols instead. Even when God sent prophets to warn Joash, he would not listen:

15 But Jehoiada grew old and full of days, and died. He was 130 years old at his death. 16 And they buried him in the city of David among the kings, because he had done good in Israel, and toward God and his house. 17 Now after the death of Jehoiada the princes of Judah came and paid homage to the king. Then the king listened to them. 18 And they abandoned the house of the LORD, the God of their fathers, and served the Asherim and the idols. And wrath came upon Judah and Jerusalem for this guilt of theirs. 19 Yet he sent prophets among them to bring them back to the LORD. These testified against them, but they would not pay attention.

2 Chronicles 24:15-19 (ESV)

Joash fell away so completely that when Jehoiada's own son, Zechariah, tried to warn him about the wicked things he was now doing, Joash ignored him and listened to his new advisers, who conspired against Zechariah. He even gave the command for Zechariah to be stoned to death:

20 Then the Spirit of God clothed Zechariah the son of Jehoiada the priest, and he stood above the people, and said to them, "Thus says God, 'Why do you break the commandments of the LORD, so that you cannot prosper? Because you have forsaken the LORD, he has forsaken you.'" 21 But they conspired against him, and by command of the king they stoned him with stones in the court of the house of the LORD. 22 Thus Joash the king did not remember the kindness that Jehoiada, Zechariah's father, had shown him, but killed his son. And when he was dying, he said, "May the LORD see and avenge!"

2 Chronicles 24:20-22 (ESV)

Some people will listen to advice when they are starting out in their career or ministry. But they become proud and overly self-reliant when they grow older feel and they have 'arrived'. It may occur when they qualify in their profession, or gain promotion, or become the manager or leader and begin to rely on themselves, or *'lean on their own understanding'* as the Bible says. They then cease to listen to advice, or to pray for guidance, or to obey God's commands. One example of this is King Rehoboam, Solomon's son. We are told that when he was younger he *'dealt wisely'*:

22 And Rehoboam appointed Abijah the son of Maacah as chief prince among his brothers, for he intended to make him king. 23 And he dealt wisely and distributed some of his sons through all the districts of Judah and Benjamin, in all the fortified cities, and he gave them abundant provisions and procured wives for them.

2 Chronicles 11:22-23 (ESV)

260

However, when he grew older, and his rule became established, he came to think that he knew how to be King and felt strong and confident. He then became unfaithful and *"abandoned the law of the LORD"*:

When the rule of Rehoboam was established and he was strong, he abandoned the law of the LORD, and all Israel with him.

2 Chronicles 12:1 (ESV)

I have been giving all this detail about Joash and Rehoboam because there is a danger that we could go wrong in the same way. We must therefore keep examining the level of our own faithfulness, integrity and obedience as we grow older. Don't imagine that age or experience in themselves, or even promotion and success in one's career or ministry, will necessarily bring wisdom. They may, to some extent, but they may also produce pride, arrogance, self-sufficiency and the cutting of corners on issues of integrity.

If so, you are actually just becoming a fool as you grow older, or even wicked, rather than growing in wisdom as you might imagine yourself to be doing. The best way to avoid the dangers of growing proud, complacent or unfaithful, or of even falling away entirely, is to focus your mind on three key objectives. These three things, if diligently and persistently pursued *for your whole life, not just for a while,* will keep you on the 'narrow path' and prevent you from backsliding or losing your integrity. The three things you need to do are:

a) fear the LORD

b) humble yourself

c) love the truth – which means to genuinely *want* to know the truth, even if it shows you are wrong or does not suit your interests

I define each of these things more fully elsewhere in this book, but also in my other books. Developing each of these traits, and making them into established habits, will preserve you. Even if you begin to stray away from the narrow path for a while, one or other of these three policies will draw you back to it, if you apply them genuinely and seriously.

(The danger of thinking: you've arrived)

The habits of the godly

Wisdom is to be like God - think, respond, love, hate ... as He does
"Be imitators of God"

You don't become 'Like' God by disobeying - not reflects God
Which is "The Lie" - reverse/inverse - pervede.
The Testing Tree - the challenging tree designed to show us to
fear God - consequence of death. God is fearsome, dangerous
A & E should have challenged the serpents claim/wickedness
but instead succumbed to it. A & E should have overcome
evil with good - Not become evil, wicked... but responded
in a godly wise manner - awake to war/wickedness -
to be like God is to obey God, reflect them - not appease them.

Serpent appeals to emotion - at a idoltrous image of God who
won't punish sin - to not fear God He's a pussy cat (misrepresent)
A & E where supposed to conquer satan by doing good - obey
God - as image bearers - instead they were overcome by evil.

CHAPTER 9

WISE PEOPLE LOVE THE TRUTH AND THEREFORE REJECT POLITICAL CORRECTNESS

There is a way that seems right to a man,
but its end is the way to death.
                    Proverbs 14:12 (ESV)

My people are destroyed for lack of knowledge"....
                    Hosea 4:6(a) (ESV)

"....and a people without understanding shall come to ruin."
                    Hosea 4:14(b) (ESV)

But he who is noble devises noble things,
   and by noble things he stands.
                    Isaiah 32:8 (RSV)

And Saul said to Samuel, "I have sinned; for I have transgressed the commandment of the LORD and your words, because I feared the people and obeyed their voice.
                    1 Samuel 15:24 (RSV)

And he said to man,
 'Behold, the fear of the Lord, that is wisdom,
and to turn away from evil is understanding.'"
                    Job 28:28 (ESV)

Make me to know your ways, O LORD;
teach me your paths.
                    Psalm 25:4 (ESV)

Righteousness exalts a nation,
   but sin is a reproach to any people.
                    Proverbs 14:34 (ESV)

"And you, Solomon my son, know the God of your father and serve him with a whole heart and with a willing mind, for the LORD searches all hearts and understands every plan and thought. If you seek him, he will be found by you, but if you forsake him, he will cast you off forever.
                    1 Chronicles 28:9 (ESV)

Most people fit in with whatever the majority currently thinks, rather than simply accept what God says.

Most of us get our beliefs, attitudes and opinions from the media and the people around us. But isn't it obvious that before forming an opinion about any major issue, whether it be Israel, abortion, euthanasia, capital punishment, the roles of men and women, homosexuality, 'gay marriage', gender, pornography, sex outside marriage and so on, we should first of all find out *what God says* about those things? In fact, shouldn't we just find out His view on *every issue* and then immediately adopt that view for ourselves? What God says ought to be our starting point, but it should be our *finishing point too*.

The only exception would be those issues upon which He has not made any pronouncement. Then it is legitimate to form our own views. But even then, we should still be guided by what God has said *in general terms*, or by what He has said about *other issues or principles* which indirectly touch upon what we are now considering. The problem is that is not how most of us operate, even within churches. We either make up our own minds for ourselves or we absorb the views expressed in the media, or by politicians, or by people we know.

However, very few of us ever take the essential step of trying to find out *what God has to say* on that issue, let alone feel obliged to adopt His view as our own. But surely, if a person is a genuine Christian, the obviously right approach is simply to *find out what God's view is and then automatically agree with Him*. How can anyone argue against that, if the point is put as starkly as that? But the problem is the point is not made at all, starkly or otherwise. At any rate, it is not how most of us operate in practice.

Only a fool can read what God says but then disagree with Him and maintain their own opinion instead.

Even if God has set out His view on an issue, and even if we are aware of it, many of us still consider ourselves to be entitled to form our own opinions on that issue. In other words, some of us feel free to *'disagree'* with God and to maintain our own opinion, *even after hearing what He says*. Once we stop to think about this, it is blindingly obvious that that approach is absurd. But, as we saw, the problem is that most of us don't stop to think about it.

Many don't even bother to find out what God thinks in the first place, and it does not even occur to many of us that we should. It would be interesting to hear anybody try to explain how their own opinion could be more authoritative than what God says. The moment you hear the idea stated, you know it is ridiculous. Perhaps that is one reason why we don't question ourselves. It is more

264

You are free to disagree with God but will bear the cost

comfortable, as well as requiring a lot less effort, if we don't bother to examine our basis for thinking what we think, or for believing what we believe.

Recognise the wrongness of this approach. Then find any issues where you and God currently disagree and simply abandon your own opinions and adopt His in their place.

We need to recognise this foolish tendency in ourselves and learn a new way of forming beliefs and opinions. Above all, we need to be willing to abandon any belief as soon as we realise it is contrary to what God says. That sounds simple enough, but the problem is that few of us actually do it, even in the Church. Most people keep whatever social, political, or even religious, views they held before they became Christians. Therefore, few of us will abandon an opinion, and take up another one, simply because *it is what God says*.

Therefore, if you do, you will be swimming against the tide, even within the churches. Nevertheless, be willing to be the odd one out. Reject the received 'wisdom' of this world and, in particular, all forms of political correctness. Instead, find out what God says on every issue and then immediately get your thinking into line with His. This won't make you popular, and you'll be seen as a misfit, but it is self-evidently the right approach.

To 'disagree' with God, just so that we can be accepted and approved of by the people around us, is plainly idiotic. We might achieve a kind of peace by taking that approach, at least for a while. But it will be deeply damaging to us in the longer term, not least because we will find ourselves coming under God's curse for calling evil things good and good things evil. That is something which He strongly condemns. We will then be opposed by Him as a result, which is essentially what it means when God pronounces a 'woe' on a person:

20 Woe to those who call evil good
 and good evil,
who put darkness for light
 and light for darkness,
who put bitter for sweet
 and sweet for bitter!
21 Woe to those who are wise in their own eyes,
 and shrewd in their own sight!
                    Isaiah 5:20-21 (ESV)

What authority, wisdom, power or right — do I have
to disagree with God ?
Who are you to question God ?

265

Wise people resist political correctness, whereas the wicked promote it. The simple and fools go along with it passively.

I am not that old, but I have a memory of political events going back to when I was a child in the 1970s. Since that time, due to the erosion of Christianity in the West, biblical values, language and principles have become far less evident in politics and in our institutions, workplaces, schools, hospitals and courts. Our society is now much more influenced by secular humanism than by Christianity. That overall package of unbiblical values and beliefs is called *political correctness* and the ground that it has captured over the past 30-40 years is staggering.

If a person was transported in a time machine from the 1970s to today they would not be able to believe how drastically things have changed and would be astonished by things which we now regard as commonplace. This change in the public's beliefs and attitudes is the result of a deliberate satanic strategy. The thinking of most of the Western world has been diverted onto another perverted path which rejects all biblical values and promotes the direct opposite *on every count*. That is why we can be sure there is nothing accidental about it.

An intelligent mind was needed to coordinate thousands of organisations, universities, media outlets and governments, all over the world, and to pull all the necessary strings to bring about this social transformation in just a few decades. The essence of political correctness is for a small and strident minority to create a set of beliefs, values and principles which are the *opposite of what God wants*. They then force the rest of us into adopting their way of thinking by peer pressure, ridicule and intimidation.

The majority of the population now accept these alien ideas, or at least remain silent about their disagreement. By contrast, only 25 years ago most people felt free to express their own opinions in public. Now they shrink back for fear of who may be listening and what they might do. For example, with so called 'gay marriage', multitudes privately oppose it and know it to be wrong but, in public, they feel forced to say they support it. At any rate, they won't speak against it, or even appear to be neutral about it, for fear of being called '*homophobic*', which is portrayed as something reprehensible.

That word, in itself, is an example of the victories our opponents have won in the battle over the language. To be '*phobic*' actually means to have an *irrational fear*, not a well thought-out and soundly-based *objection*. Nevertheless, a person who opposes homosexual activity is now automatically labelled as 'homophobic'. The impression is then deliberately given that they have an *irrational fear of something good*, rather than a *well-founded opposition to something bad*. We must strenuously resist being pressurised into using other people's politically correct words and phrases.

266

Resolve always to use your own words instead. Never submit to being told what you can and cannot think or say, or to be forced to say things which you know are untrue, just in order to fit in and be accepted. The success of political correctness as a manipulative control strategy depends on the whole population being pressured and intimidated into saying things which they already know to be false, but to keep on saying them anyway. Your own words then put you into a straitjacket. *For them it doesn't have to make sense - if they can get you to say 2 + 2 is 5 they will - you've surrendered your reason.*

But it is even worse than that because, when you give in to pressure and agree to say politically correct things, it also adds to the pressure that is put on *others*. Those who seek to control us through political correctness rely heavily on our cowardice. If, however, we were to show courage instead, and we refused to submit to their bossy and intrusive rules as to what we are allowed to think and say, their whole policy would unravel. Then their ideas would be exposed for the deceitful, illogical, even ridiculous, nonsense that they are. *CV19*

Therefore, the first step in the battle to defeat political correctness is to simply *stop cooperating with it and stop submitting to it*. As soon as you do that you will be set free. Then you will be able, perhaps for the first time in years, to be completely yourself and to do exactly what God wants you to do, instead of what others expect of you. Moreover, you will also stop putting added pressure on other people through your own acquiescence and your parrot-like repetition of the views of the PC establishment. *Stop using their language*

Have the courage to stand up to political correctness, even if you are the only one. Others may be emboldened by your bravery.

It is no use you waiting for others to show courage first, so that you can then follow them. They are waiting for you! Therefore, *you* must be courageous first and insist on your own freedom of thought and expression, no matter where you are, or who is with you. In this way evil can be resisted. But if we are passive, and sit back doing and saying nothing, it will defeat us. As Edmund Burke said:

"All that is required for evil to triumph is for good men to do nothing."
                                                        Edmund Burke

Therefore, if you are good, or want to be good, then stop caving in to these bullies. Stand up and be counted. Be brave and set an example to those around you, thereby bolstering their courage. Note also the wise words of President Ronald Reagan, one of the greatest presidents ever:

"Evil is powerless if the good are unafraid."
                                        Ronald Reagan

267

I therefore refuse to use the word '*homophobic*' because I don't accept the premise on which it is based. That is to say that I do not have any *fear* of homosexuality, or of homosexuals. The critical views that I express are only of their *actions*, and are due to my opposition to the practice of homosexuality, not from any fear of it, or of those who do it. Likewise, I use the word 'homosexual', not '*gay*', because I am simply not willing to be manipulated into using words that I don't accept and don't want to use.

In any event, the word 'gay' is a misnomer because, as the Radio Four Rabbi, *Lionel Blue*, once said, "*most homosexuals are sad, not gay*". The same technique is used in the debate over abortion. Those who promote it know that it would not help their cause if they were to call themselves '*pro-abortion*'. So, they give themselves the far more attractive and marketable label, '*pro-choice*'.

That phrase is a pure euphemism, and is designed to obscure, not reveal, their position. Yet, it displays an excellent grasp of tactics. On the same basis, they refuse to use the label '*pro-life*'. Instead, they call their opponents '*anti-choice*'. In messing about with the meaning of words and phrases in this way, so as to mislead those who are not alert to their schemes, they are fulfilling the prediction made by Winston Churchill, which was remarkably prophetic:

"The fascists of the future will call themselves anti-fascists."
Winston Churchill

Our opponents are keenly aware of the power that carefully crafted phrases have to shape our thinking. Their approach is therefore utterly dishonest but, in propaganda terms, it is highly effective, especially amongst those who do not take the time, or make the effort, to think for themselves. Of course, if we all thought carefully about the words that other people use, we would quickly see the absurdity of all of this. But, again, that is the problem - the vast majority of us don't ever stop to think, or to examine the meaning of words, or to discern the agenda of those who insist on their use, or their non-use.

We are therefore easily influenced by these manipulative tactics, and allow other people's slogans, euphemisms and propaganda to shape what we believe. Political correctness is imposed on us by human beings, but the strategic thinking behind it is Satan's. He invented it and it is coordinated by his demons. That is obvious, because there is no way that political correctness could have taken over the thinking of whole continents, in such a short time, if it was of solely human origin.

The straitjacket of political correctness has been accepted unthinkingly by fools *but also by the simple*, including a huge number of naïve Christians. Only those who are determined not to conform, and who insist on getting their beliefs from the Bible, rather than the world, will refuse to comply. Sadly, they are very few

268

and are hugely outnumbered within the media, and in our institutions, especially amongst those who reach the top. Even so, you must resolve to be one of that brave minority who refuse to conform, not only for your own sake, but also for the benefit of those others whose courage will be strengthened by your example.

Wise people reject relativist thinking and values.

A key ingredient of political correctness is *'relativism'*. That is the view that nothing is inherently right or wrong and that there are no moral or ethical absolutes. Instead, it is assumed that *"all things are relative"* and that everything depends on your personal perspective or circumstances. At first sight it sounds like a reasonable approach, even a *'tolerant'* one, to use another of their perverse buzzwords. However, relativism is the opposite of how God thinks. He does not operate on the basis of what is *expedient, convenient* or *fashionable,* but in terms of what is *right or wrong.*

He also takes an *absolute* stance about such questions every time. If a thing is true, then it is true and if it is false, then it is false, *regardless of who you are*, or where you live, or what your circumstances are. So, if God says homosexual activity is wrong, which He does, then it *is* wrong. Moreover, it is wrong for *everybody*. It does not become right for someone else just because they believe it to be right. Likewise, if Islam, Hinduism, Buddhism and Sikhism are false religions, which they are, then they are false for *all of us*, in *all places*, and at *all times*.

They can't be false for you, but true for someone else. Neither can we say that any of them are true at the same time as saying that Christianity is true. The various religions of the world are all contradictory sets of beliefs. We therefore have to choose one, or other, or none. What we cannot validly do is to simultaneously believe *more than one* of them, let alone all of them. That is totally obvious, or at least it should be, to any honest and reasonable person.

Yet it is not obvious to millions of confused, woolly-minded, dumbed-down liberals who have been taught to think in *relativist* terms. To them, a set of mutually exclusive and contradictory ideas can all be accepted at the same time. Indeed, they don't find any difficulty in doing so. Such thinking is self-evidently ridiculous and 100 years ago, or even 50 years ago, the vast majority of people, even fools, would have conceded that. But not now.

There has been such a catastrophic dumbing-down in the West, that it is now entirely normal to believe two or more contradictory ideas all at the same time. Such muddled thinking may appeal to our own foolish generation, but it was not how our parents or grandparents thought and it must never be the way that a

Christian thinks. At any rate, no wise person would ever think that way, or fail to recognise it as nonsense when he hears someone else speaking in that way.

Wise people don't accept the modern definition of 'tolerance'.

The new meaning of the word 'tolerance' is not what you would imagine it to be, or what it used to be. It has taken on tones of Orwellian double-speak and now means the direct opposite of what it ought to. In the past, a 'tolerant' person was someone who, while having clear beliefs of his own, and being aware of where and why he disagrees with others, nonetheless gives them the freedom to believe what they want. He feels free to disagree with them, but remains courteous while doing so. However, that is not what tolerance now means to our PC generation. The new definition of a *tolerant* person is one who:

a) accepts other people's beliefs in the sense of assuming that all of them are *also true*, alongside, and at the same time as, his own

b) never says that any belief that he holds is *exclusively true*, i.e. the *only* truth, or *the* truth

c) never says that any other person's belief is *wrong,* unless, of course, it is biblical, which is treated as an exception, and can therefore be said to be wrong

d) is only intolerant of people who claim that what they believe is the exclusive truth, i.e. that it alone is true, and thus that any contrary belief is, by definition, wrong.

This absurd new definition of tolerance creates no difficulties for most of the population, because they do not have what the Bible calls *'the love of the truth'*. Therefore, they have no strong beliefs about which they would ever feel under a duty to make a stand. It only presents a problem to one group, namely *real* Christians who believe the Bible is absolutely true and that Jesus is the *only* way to salvation. Nobody other than a committed Christian has difficulty with this modern notion of tolerance because only genuine, biblical Christianity makes the claim that it is the only way for us to be saved.

All other religions, plus false, apostate, watered-down, liberal, ecumenical forms of Christianity, or what I call *'churchianity'*, are relaxed about other people's beliefs. They feel no need to insist that there is only one way to get to God. They don't even believe that themselves, let alone feel obliged to say it to others. Therefore, this new and perverse definition of tolerance is usually only a problem for real Christians, for whom the truth is paramount. It creates profound issues of conscience for them, but not for others.

At the time I was writing this, a proposal was being put forward in the UK by *Sajid Javid MP*, the then Communities Secretary, that all public sector employees and office holders should be required to swear an *'equality oath'* or else be disqualified from holding any public office or even from working in the public sector at all. This would affect vast numbers of people including council staff, councillors, public sector employees and Members of Parliament, but also those employed in the National Health Service, the armed forces, the police and so on. It would catch millions of us in its net.

The idea came from a report written by *Dame Louise Casey* in relation to her review of *'integration and extremism'*. Because she is rampantly politically correct, her approach is to treat *all* forms of supposed *'extremism'* as wrong, not just those which emanate from Islam and involve rapes, beheadings, paedophilia and the pursuit of Jihad. Therefore, she also wants to target those Christians who are so *'extreme'* as to believe the Bible, and to take it seriously, such that, for example, they oppose the Government's policies on gay marriage or gender, or publicly criticise Islam.

She considers those beliefs to be just as extreme, and therefore just as anti-social, as the beliefs of those who blow up aeroplanes or set off suicide vests. Thus she, and those like her, are more concerned about those who *criticise* Islam than they are about those who follow its teachings by engaging in Jihad, or rape, or by grooming vulnerable children for sex. The Government have no adequate plans to tackle any of them, or at least not with any zeal. They are only motivated to restrict the people who speak out *against* Islam or tell the truth about it, or who expose the inadequacies of the Government's policies.

The same applies with homosexuality, gay marriage, gender confusion, and many other such weird and perverse things which the UK Government now believes are *"in line with British values"* and which therefore need to be protected by this draconian *'equalities'* legislation. Hopefully the Government will fail to get this law through the House of Commons, but even if they do fail, or are delayed for a while, this is plainly the direction in which their minds are thinking. Therefore, they may seek to reintroduce it again later when the wind is blowing more strongly their way.

It is only genuine Christians who are seriously harmed by new politically correct rules and requirements because only they are committed enough to refuse to comply

If this repressive legislation does come in, it will only harm one group, namely genuine Bible-believing Christians. That is because a person from any other religion, or a lukewarm, wishy-washy, compromised 'churchgoer', doesn't mind what he is required to say, or what anybody else believes, unless of course it goes against political correctness. Therefore, such a person would not bother to contradict anybody anyway, or refuse to say something that they are trying to force him to say, as he doesn't have enough conviction to be motivated to take a stand on anything.

Thus, the distorted new definition of tolerance and, in particular the proposed equality oath, will hit genuine Christians very hard, but it won't affect anybody else, because only committed Christians will refuse to swear an oath saying they accept gay marriage, or agreeing that there are multiple genders, or promising not to criticise Islam, and so on. Followers of false religions, atheists, and liberal churchgoers will just sign the equality oath without a qualm, because they don't have 'the love of the truth' and therefore don't care what they sign.

As for Muslims, they probably won't be asked to sign anything anyway, because most officials won't dare to confront them. In any case, deliberately lying to an infidel is not considered to be a sin in Islam, due to their doctrine called 'taqiyya' which permits it. Consequently, most Muslims would just swear the equality oath anyway, without having any intention whatsoever of abiding by it. Therefore, genuine Christians, *and only them*, will lose their jobs. Nobody else will, and the supporters of the new oath are well aware of that fact, which is precisely why they are pressing for it.

It will be like the late seventeenth century when, from 1661 to 1688, the *Test and Corporation Acts* meant that anyone who was not an Anglican, and who was therefore not willing to accept Anglican doctrines, could not hold any public office. Neither could they serve in the army or navy, or be an MP, lawyer, magistrate etc. That was an evil time in British history, during which genuine Christians were frozen out and had to go into business on their own or try to make a living in some other way.

However, even if the proposed equality oath does not become law, we are already subject to increasing levels of pressure and persecution by the general imposition of politically correct values and beliefs and the insistence that we submit to it all or go out of business. This is already happening now, and on a rapidly growing scale, and it is one reason why I decided to stop practising law. An example of this persecution is what happened to the evangelical hotel-keepers, Peter and Hazelmary Bull. They ran a guest house in the UK which was also their own home.

They had always had a clearly stated policy that only married couples could stay in their hotel, not unmarried couples or, more recently, homosexual couples. Then two militant homosexuals, who had no genuine wish to stay at the hotel, but just wanted to attack Mr and Mrs Bull, asked to book a double room. When this was refused they sued, claiming they had been *discriminated against* on the basis of their sexual orientation. The two homosexuals won their case. It was held that the Bulls had acted unlawfully, by not letting them stay in their hotel/home, in which the two men may have engaged in homosexual sex.

That would have gone against the Bulls' consciences, which is why they had always had that policy of only accepting married, heterosexual couples. They did so to prevent both adultery and heterosexual fornication, even before homosexuality became so fashionable. Their case went all the way to the Court of Appeal which, sadly, found against Mr and Mrs Bull by a majority of 3:2. The fact that the Court was so divided shows how controversial this is and that there is, therefore, every reason to continue to fight over these issues.

Two outrageously unjust cases involving street preachers who were treated appallingly by the UK police

In another case some years ago, Harry Hammond, an old man, was preaching in the open air when some homosexuals began to heckle him. He had a sign in his hand which said that homosexuality is sinful and that what is needed is repentance. Some homosexuals in the crowd then *physically attacked him* and knocked him to the ground, injuring him.

Amazingly, when the police arrived *they arrested him, not his attackers*. Moreover, they then prosecuted him, not them, on the basis that he was guilty of a so called '*hate crime*'. His attackers were not charged with any offence, even though it was a clear physical assault upon him, by any reasonable standard. The police chose not to prosecute the two homosexuals for assaulting Mr Hammond.

Of course, if the facts had been the other way round, and two *heterosexuals* had assaulted a placard-wielding *homosexual*, it would inevitably have led to a prosecution. Moreover, it would have been classed as an aggravated assault, because antipathy towards their sexual orientation would have been seen as the motive behind it.

However, the police and the Crown Prosecution Service were not willing to apply the same thinking in reverse, so as to protect Mr Hammond's stance on sexual orientation. Sadly, Harry Hammond died before his case reached the Court of Appeal. So he died with a criminal conviction, as if he was a wrongdoer, whereas he was actually a godly man and wholly innocent. I feel sure that, at the Judgment Seat of Christ, he will have his name publicly cleared and receive a major reward, on the basis of what Jesus said:

¹¹ *"Blessed are you when men revile you and persecute you and utter all kinds of evil against you falsely on my account.* *¹²* *Rejoice and be glad, for your reward is great in heaven, for so men persecuted the prophets who were before you.*
Matthew 5:11-12 (RSV)

Happily, in the later case of John Craven, another street preacher, public vindication came much earlier. He was preaching on John 3:16 when two homosexual teenagers *asked him* what he thought of gays. He said it didn't matter what *he* himself thought and that what really mattered was what the Bible says. He then quoted from the Bible. He did not do it publicly, via his microphone. He had switched that off and was, by then, speaking privately and quietly, just to the two homosexuals. All he said was that homosexuality is sinful but that, *"whilst God hates the sin, He loves the sinner."*

They responded by making a show of kissing each other in front of him and insulting him with crude gestures. Greater Manchester Police then *arrested Mr Craven, not them*, and alleged that what he had said to the two young men was *"insulting"*, that it was *"harassment"*, and that it had caused them *"distress"*. Yet, all he had done was to politely and privately answer the question which *they had put to him* and also to quote from the Bible. To compound that injustice, for almost 15 hours, the police then denied him food and water, and even access to medication for his rheumatoid arthritis.

There was absolutely no need for any of that mistreatment, even assuming he had done anything wrong, which he hadn't. It was contrary to all normal procedure. Of all the people I have ever arrested, or that I have seen being dealt with by my former colleagues, not one of them was ever denied food, water or medicine. It was never necessary or justified, just as it was not in Mr Craven's case. The police were uncharacteristically harsh with Mr Craven and they would never have acted in that way with a burglar or a drug dealer, or even a terrorist.

In my professional view, both as a lawyer, and a former police officer, the police made a deliberate exception in his case. They went out of their way to treat him severely, because they wanted to intimidate him, and also to deter anyone else from speaking as he did and especially from preaching and quoting the Bible in the street. It was probably also a flesh reaction, arising out of their own anti-Christian bias, because the UK police are now a very left wing and socially liberal institution on the whole.

Many officers, even if they themselves aren't personally left wing or PC, have concluded that *acting as if you were* politically correct is the only way to get promoted in today's police forces. It is totally unlike how it was when I was a police officer from 1983-1986. In those days the police had a strong sense of natural justice, and of right and wrong. Therefore, political correctness was

274

something which only happened in a few left wing London boroughs, and which the wider public laughed at. But nobody is laughing now.

However, in the end, Mr Craven's case had a much more pleasing outcome than Mr Hammond's. The Greater Manchester Police were sued in the civil courts by his lawyers, supported by an excellent organisation called *The Christian Institute*. Mr Craven was claiming wrongful arrest, false imprisonment and breach of human rights. When the case was only a few days from trial, the Police caved in and settled the claim out of court, agreeing to pay £13,000 in damages and more than £50,000 in legal costs.

They clearly expected that they were going to be soundly defeated at trial. It was very gratifying to see the police getting their 'come-uppance' and that they got it so publicly. We can all take encouragement from his legal victory and be emboldened to speak the truth, politely and lovingly, even when in public. The police wanted to intimidate people, and to discourage others from preaching in public, or from criticising homosexuality, but their tactics seriously backfired on them on that occasion.

Some examples of the politically correct ideas that have been accepted unthinkingly by most of our generation and even by many Christians

1. Abortion

For nearly 6000 years, ever since the Creation, every nation on Earth has agreed that abortion is self-evidently wrong. It is totally obvious, and our own conscience tells us that, regardless of what the law now says. We also know instinctively that to kill a child is even worse than to kill an adult and that the younger the child, the worse the crime is. However, in 1967 in the UK, and then in 1973 in the USA, abortion was legalised, based on the extraordinary assumption that the unborn child is not a human being, even though we all know, deep down, that it is. Indeed, what else could it be?

This is a classic example of how political correctness works. People choose to be blind and deaf to obvious facts because they want to feel comfortable about doing wrong. Thus, the West is now carrying out abortions on an industrial scale. The UK alone has killed over 8,000,000 since 1967. In America it is over 58,000,000. The people of ancient Judah killed their own children too, by offering them as sacrifices to demon gods like Baal and Molech. But instead of millions, they only killed hundreds, or at most thousands. Yet, note how intensely God felt about the wickedness of what they did:

Dehumanize

275

³ and say, 'Hear the word of the LORD, O kings of Judah and inhabitants of Jerusalem: thus says the LORD of hosts, the God of Israel, "Behold I am about to bring a calamity upon this place, at which the ears of everyone that hears of it will tingle. ⁴ Because they have forsaken Me and have made this an alien place and have burned sacrifices in it to other gods, that neither they nor their forefathers nor the kings of Judah had ever known, and because they have filled this place with the blood of the innocent ⁵ and have built the high places of Baal to burn their sons in the fire as burnt offerings to Baal, a thing which I never commanded or spoke of, nor did it ever enter My mind;

⁶ therefore, behold, days are coming," declares the LORD, "when this place will no longer be called Topheth or the valley of Ben-hinnom, but rather the valley of Slaughter. ⁷ I will make void the counsel of Judah and Jerusalem in this place, and I will cause them to fall by the sword before their enemies and by the hand of those who seek their life; and I will give over their carcasses as food for the birds of the sky and the beasts of the earth. ⁸ I will also make this city a desolation and an object of hissing; everyone who passes by it will be astonished and hiss because of all its disasters.

Jeremiah 19:3-8 (NASB)

Note also what the Psalmist said, centuries earlier, about how God viewed the wickedness of those who killed their own children. He responds to it with very severe judgment, handing them over to their enemies:

³⁷ They sacrificed their sons
and their daughters to false gods.
³⁸ They shed innocent blood,
the blood of their sons and daughters,
whom they sacrificed to the idols of Canaan,
and the land was desecrated by their blood.
³⁹ They defiled themselves by what they did;
by their deeds they prostituted themselves.
⁴⁰ Therefore the LORD was angry with his people
and abhorred his inheritance.
⁴¹ He gave them into the hands of the nations,
and their foes ruled over them.

Psalm 106:37-41 (NIV)

That is how God chose to deal with the people of Judah, and Israel as a whole, for the comparatively small numbers of children they murdered. Therefore, how much more strongly must He feel about the atrocities being carried out today, on such a massive scale, in our hospitals and abortion clinics? Those who promote abortion have been careful to invent new words and phrases to describe it. Their aim in doing so is to obscure the truth and to prevent us seeing how wrong it is.

They also want to tell us, and themselves, that it is not *"killing a child"*, but merely *"terminating a pregnancy"*.

However, if you were to shoot one of your colleagues at work, nobody would call it *"terminating a career"*. Also, instead of referring to a *child,* doctors and others speak of the unborn child as a *foetus,* or even as a *"product of conception"*, a truly Orwellian phrase. How would you feel if your boss ceased calling you a member of staff and called you instead *"a product of employment"* or a *"product of contract formation"*?

The clear purpose of contriving such absurd new words and phrases is to *deliberately dehumanise the child*. They are trying hard to distract your attention, and also their own, from what is being done. They also want to make it appear less real, both to you and to themselves. We must therefore go out of our way to resist that manipulation and to *insist on using the correct words*, even if we are the only person doing so.

I used to be a member of the Research Ethics Committee of a large hospital. I was invited to join it because I was a lawyer. One of the issues that came up before us was a research project on contraception. The researcher came to present their project before the committee and became very agitated when I used the word *"child"* to refer to an unborn baby. She didn't like that at all and sharply corrected me.

It mattered to her very much and she really wanted me to stop saying *'child'*. However, I refused to be told how to speak and I told the committee that I try to avoid using words like *foetus, embryo* or *zygote* because their implications matter to me. For the same reason, the implications of the word *'child'* really mattered to that researcher. If not, she would not have objected so fiercely to my choice of words.

When we consider the issue of abortion, or any other issue, we must think about it in a consistently biblical way and use biblical words and principles wherever possible. If we are not aware of any biblical words for the thing in question we should at least express ourselves in plain English, using clear, honest, ordinary, everyday words. By contrast, the usual starting point for supporters of abortion is to argue along these lines, based on these principles, and using these weasel words:

a) Abortion is an issue affecting the woman's *'own body'* and every woman can do *anything she chooses* with her own body.

b) Nobody has any right to interfere with that woman's right to choose, least of all male politicians.

277

However, their argument is based upon a false premise. The woman's body is *not* entirely her own. In fact, it does not actually belong to her at all. *It belongs to God*, as does everything and everybody else in the entire universe, including men's bodies, for the simple reason that He created us. Therefore, a woman is not free to do anything she wants to do with the child's body, *or even her own body*, because, neither the child's body, nor hers, actually belong to her. That is how God sees it, as these verses demonstrate:

The earth is the LORD's and the fullness thereof,
the world and those who dwell therein,
                                        Psalm 24:1 (ESV)

For everyone belongs to me, the parent as well as the child—both alike belong to me…….
                                        Ezekiel 18:4(a) (NIV)

Who has first given to me, that I should repay him?
Whatever is under the whole heaven is mine.
                                Job 41:11 (ESV)

[19] Do you not know that your bodies are temples of the Holy Spirit, who is in you, whom you have received from God? You are not your own; [20] you were bought at a price. Therefore honour God with your bodies.

Christian only

                                1 Corinthians 6:19-20 (NIV)

[10] For every beast of the forest is mine,
the cattle on a thousand hills.
[11] I know all the birds of the hills,
and all that moves in the field is mine.
[12] "If I were hungry, I would not tell you,
for the world and its fullness are mine.
                        Psalm 50:10-12 (ESV)

imago dei
Image of God

The heavens are yours; the earth also is yours;
the world and all that is in it, you have founded them.
                                Psalm 89:11 (ESV)

Another reason why God owns us is that Jesus *bought us back again* from Satan, the ruler of this world, by His death on the cross. That means that God doubly owns us because He made us and He also bought us back. Accordingly, He has every right to tell us what we can and cannot do, whether with our own bodies, or anyone else's. Therefore, in forbidding abortion, He is not *interfering*. There is nothing illegitimate about Him pronouncing on this, or on any other issue. It is

He who has all the rights. We don't have any rights at all, so far as God is concerned. Neither do we own anything.

The Bible never speaks in terms of *rights*, but only *responsibilities*. Therefore, the whole pro-abortion argument starts from the wrong place, is based on wrong assumptions, and is conducted using bogus principles and flawed logic. The starting point should not be ourselves, or what we claim to own, or our own supposed 'rights' or 'entitlements'. We should always begin, *and end*, with God's commands, instructions and pronouncements. That is how we ensure that we start from the right place on abortion, and on every other issue, and also how we make sure that our thinking is soundly-based and biblical thereafter.

Another illegitimate argument which is routinely used in support of abortion is that it is necessary, *"to save the mother's life"*, where complications arise in pregnancy. They maintain that if the doctors have to choose between saving the life of the mother or the child, it is legitimate to get rid of the child to save her life. They don't only use this argument to deal with situations in the very late stages of pregnancy, or during the birth itself, but all the way through. Thus, they even speak in terms of aborting the child at an early stage to avoid purely theoretical risks to the mother which *might arise later*, but which have not, as yet, actually arisen.

In this way they try to get maximum value from their argument, by applying it even where no danger or complication has yet occurred. However, the claim is entirely false and insincere. Although many women died in childbirth in past centuries, that is no longer the case, or at least not in the West, where the abortion industry exists. There are still some deaths in childbirth in the developing world, but they don't practise abortion anyway and therefore don't need to use this bogus argument about the danger to the mother. But don't just take my word for it. This is what was said by C Everett Koop, the Surgeon General of the United States in the 1980s:

"Protection of the life of the mother as an excuse for an abortion is a smoke screen. In my 36 years of pediatric surgery, I have never known of one instance where the child had to be aborted to save the mother's life. If toward the end of pregnancy complications arise that threaten the mother's health, the doctor will induce labor or perform a Caesarean section. His intention is to save the life of both the mother and the baby. The baby's life is never wilfully destroyed because the mother's life is in danger."

C Everett Koop

God's judgment is surely bound to come upon the Western nations because of their policies on abortion. Moreover, it would seem clear that His judgment will be more severe on us, in the semi-Christianised European nations and in the

United States, Australia, Canada etc, than it will be on countries like Japan and China which have little or no Christian heritage. They are doing the same wicked things as we do, but I believe they are going to be held less accountable because they have not had the privilege of the centuries of Christian teaching that we have had.

Until the 19th century, the Gospel was largely unknown in Asia. Therefore, given our comparative advantages, we in the West ought to tremble at the prospect of God's coming judgment, even for abortion alone, let alone for our many other sins. Indeed, His judgment has already begun, because He will not leave it all to be dealt with on the Day of Judgment.

For example, the financial crisis endured by the Western nations since 2008, plus the crises over healthcare and pensions, are directly related to the abortions we have carried out. I say that because we are missing millions of people, aged from zero to their late forties, who would now be working and paying taxes if we had not aborted them. Their absence is one of the main reasons for our social and financial problems, which are a kind of grim justice in themselves.

Let's now look at some other issues and identify similar errors, lies and absurd beliefs which have caused our society's thinking, and even the thinking of many Christians, to become so unbiblical.

2. Opposition to discipline in schools

In 1987 the British Government allowed a free vote in the House of Commons on whether corporal punishment should be banned in schools, i.e. the use of the cane or slipper, and our MPs foolishly voted to ban it. Ever since then there has been a drastic decline in discipline in our schools. The change was made based on the misguided idea that the *'child is at the centre'*, and *'has rights'*.

The campaigners argued that all corporal punishment is automatically and inherently *"child abuse"*, regardless of how or why it is done. However, such thinking is the exact opposite of what the Bible says. It clearly tells us that physical punishment is appropriate, and indeed absolutely essential, if children are to be properly disciplined. Therefore, due to choosing politically correct ideology instead of biblical wisdom, Britain's schools have seen a collapse of discipline, behaviour and respect.

That, in turn, is one reason why academic standards in the UK have declined so dramatically. Successive governments since the 1980s have chosen to hide that decline by a policy of deliberate grade inflation. Until 2012, exam results were not just held at the same level, despite the fall in real standards. They were fiddled to such an extent that average grades actually improved by about 1% every year.

That blatant dishonesty went on for over 25 years, even though real standards, when measured objectively, were actually falling steadily throughout that entire period.

3. Opposition to parents disciplining and smacking their own children, even within the home

Despite the obvious decline in discipline and academic standards, the politically correct are completely blind to the harm that was done by banning corporal punishment in schools. Therefore, once they had achieved that, they set about trying to ban *all* smacking of children *anywhere*, even by their own parents *and even within the home*. However, smacking is actually God-ordained and is seen by Him as an essential part of bringing up children.

In the warped thinking of the liberals, it is the child who is at the centre, rather than God, or the parents. Therefore, they conclude that to smack one's own child at all is abuse, in and of itself, no matter how justifiably or responsibly it is done. The vast majority of parents disagree with that *in private*, but are intimidated into silence when in public. If those who are seeking to ban all smacking succeed, it will be an even bigger disaster than what has already happened in our schools.

Sadly, many liberal churches are actively involved in supporting that misguided lobbying and they even imagine themselves to be doing God's will. They are so steeped in rights-based thinking that they assume that that is how God thinks, whereas it is actually the reverse of how He approaches issues. Therefore, Christians need to take a bold stand and be willing to speak up openly to resist the tide of humanist thinking on this issue.

In fact, there is a desperate need for *more* discipline for our children, not less, and it needs to be physical. Mere verbal correction, or other non-physical sanctions, will never be enough to discipline a child properly, especially young ones, aged between two and twelve. During those early years the correction needs to be simple enough for the child to understand. That is not just my own subjective view. *It is what God says*, clearly and repeatedly. If you disagree, then you are disagreeing with God, not me, because His views are as follows:

He who withholds his rod hates his son,
But he who loves him disciplines him diligently.
Proverbs 13:24 (RSV)

Discipline your son while there is hope,
And do not desire his death.
Proverbs 19:18 (RSV)

Train up a child in the way he should go,
Even when he is old he will not depart from it.
Proverbs 22:6 (RSV)

Foolishness is bound up in the heart of a child;
The rod of discipline will remove it far from him.
Proverbs 22:15 (RSV)

The rod and reproof give wisdom,
but a child left to himself brings shame to his mother.
Proverbs 29:15 (ESV)

[1] "Children, obey your parents in the Lord, for this is right. [2] Honor your father and mother (which is the first commandment with a promise), [3] so that it may be well with you, and that you may live long on the earth. [4]Fathers, do not provoke your children to anger, but bring them up in the discipline and instruction of the Lord."
Ephesians 6:1-4 (NASB)

4. Opposition to parental authority and to the very role of parents

The PC lobby are now going even further and are undermining the very idea of parents being in authority at all. They object to the very concept of parental authority, in itself, regardless of how it is exercised. People who hold such views claim to be *pro child* and to be promoting the interests and welfare of children, but they are actually doing the opposite. That is what comes from rejecting God's wisdom and replacing it with men's ideas and with what Paul calls *doctrines of demons*. By that phrase Paul means false ideas and doctrines that demons have whispered into men's minds to lead them into error.

As a mark of the absurdity of modern thinking in this area, much of which comes from the European Union, it is being seriously proposed in Scotland that the state should appoint a 'guardian', referred to as a *'named person'*, for every child. That legal guardian would *not* be one of their parents. On the contrary, the whole idea is that that state appointed guardian will represent the child *against its parents* and 'protect' it from their antiquated, illiberal, politically incorrect views. One of the aims of these so called 'guardians' would be to prevent any parent from disciplining their own child.

The State could then bring legal proceedings to take the child into local authority care if the parents were to smack them. The likely next step is to stop parents home-schooling their own children and thereby passing on their own Christian beliefs. Adolf Hitler saw the vital importance of influencing the minds of young children. He therefore made home-schooling illegal in Germany because it hindered him in brainwashing children with Nazi ideology. He wanted the State to take the place of parents so that he could instil his own ideas into the minds of children.

Western governments now seek to do the same. Therefore, for example, many members of the British government want to make it compulsory for children as young as five to be shown DVDs about sex. If that was not appalling enough, these videos will also promote homosexuality, 'gay marriage' and 'transgenderism'! They also want to make it *illegal to withdraw your child* from these lessons, whereas it has always been the case that no school could force any child to attend any lessons which are about sex or religion.

Like many other Western politicians, those who are behind this are so determined to impose their liberal dogma on our children that they are willing to do whatever it takes to get their own way. Indeed, elements within the British government are also proposing to take the same approach with the issue of creation and evolution. It is now being proposed that teaching creation should be made illegal, even in private schools, and even for those who are home-schooled.

The point is likely to be reached where children may be taken into council care if their parents oppose the Government's perverse laws about teaching, just as people are already forbidden to adopt, or even to foster, children if they are not politically correct. That is why, before being allowed to foster or adopt a child, people are now asked what they think about gay marriage etc and if they give the 'wrong' answer they are rejected.

That may soon be the position even with our own children, with the State seizing them if our views are not politically correct or are excessively Christian in the opinion of social workers. Indeed, it is already starting to happen in Canada, whose Prime Minister, Justin Trudeau, is perhaps the most wicked leader of any Western nation.

Contrary to what our law now says, a child is not, and never should be, at the centre of anything. Putting him there will only spoil him, not benefit him. We need to resist this tide of political correctness about children's so-called rights and emphasise instead the parents' duty, *and right*, to bring up their own child in the way that God says they should. That plainly includes smacking. It also involves sheltering the child from any sinful activity, or from any false teaching which goes against God's standards, even if that comes from the State itself.

283

5. Disrespect for the elderly in general and support for euthanasia in particular

Over the last few decades, there has been a steep decline in the level of respect and honour that we show to the elderly. We see it all around us and in the media. Old people are not valued and, very often, they are not properly cared for. That has become apparent in recent years with the cascade of shocking disclosures about old and dying patients being neglected, and even abused, in hospitals and nursing homes. Therefore, we are now frequently doing the very opposite of what the Bible commands, which is that we must *honour* the elderly.

"You shall stand up before the gray head and honor the face of an old man, and you shall fear your God: I am the LORD".

Leviticus 19:32 (ESV)

Instead of caring for every old person properly until they die, an alarming proportion of staff in hospitals and care homes are mistreating elderly patients. However, the problem doesn't originate in our hospitals and care homes. The terrible things happening in some of those places are really just a symptom of a much deeper problem in the hearts and minds of the British population. The doctors and nurses who behave in those ways (by no means all of them) are simply reflecting the way that the wider British community has come to see the elderly.

Much of British society now has a disregard, and even a contempt, for the old. The worst hospital staff reflect that wider callousness, which is endemic within a growing proportion of the general public. The elderly are not only neglected. Active steps are actually being taken to try to legalise *euthanasia*, i.e. bringing forward the deaths of the old. That is not technically legal at present, though I expect it soon will be, for economic reasons if nothing else. The fact that, since 1967, the UK has aborted over eight million babies means that the distribution of our population is now seriously skewed. cv19

There are at least eight million people 'missing' from the United Kingdom due to having been aborted. They would, by now, have been aged between zero and 49 years old. However, that doesn't even take into account the many millions of children, and also grand-children, that those aborted babies would have gone on to have themselves, if they had been allowed to live. Therefore, adding all of these numbers together, we in the UK are probably missing about *fifteen million people*.

So, not only the absolute numbers, but also the *proportions* of the British population are not as they should be. That is to say there are relatively *too many old* people and *too few young* people. More to the point, there are far too few people of *working age* to pay the *taxes* we need. For that reason alone, it is

disproportionate

becoming necessary, in many people's opinions, to solve our financial problems by disposing of the elderly.

The pressure for that is only ever going to increase as our society's average age continues to rise. We shall eventually reach a point where there will be only one tax payer for every pensioner, which is completely unsustainable financially. Therefore, some doctors are already taking practical steps to hasten the death of the elderly, even without officially calling it euthanasia.

They refer to it as putting the patient on a *'pathway'* whereby they cease to provide medical treatment. Some do this without the patient's consent or knowledge and simply stop giving them food and water. The obvious objective is to *cause* death, an outcome which can hardly be a surprise, given that all food and water is denied to them. But the doctors hide behind the technicality that this does not legally amount to euthanasia, as they say they are not *directly causing* death, but merely taking no active steps to *prevent* it.   'First, do no harm'

There may, perhaps, be a time and a place for not feeding someone who is in the very final hours or days of life and is unable to eat. However, in creating this distinction between causing death and merely choosing not to prevent or delay it, they are being disingenuous, as withholding food and water inevitably causes death. Those who advocate this approach will keep on pushing the boundaries further until we eventually have an overt policy of compulsory euthanasia. In fact, even if we don't currently call it by that name, it is effectively what we already have in some places.

Therefore, in many hospitals, we now have a de facto policy of euthanasia, which is being put into practice by those doctors who are currently willing to operate in that way. Moreover, their numbers are growing. All of this is a very long way from what God wants, which is for the elderly in general, and those who are sick and dying in particular, to be honoured and cared for. Any human being, whatever their age, is made in God's image. That fact alone gives them an infinitely important status and makes them inherently worthy of honour, even if God had not expressly commanded it, which He has.

They also have the gift of life which God gives, and which *only He can take away*. Therefore, it is not ours to take, even from a person whom we know is already dying. The only exception is for murderers, whom God has said *should* be executed. However, that exception is made in order to *uphold* the sacredness of human life, not to undermine it. Therefore, a profound change is urgently needed in the way that we view the old and the dying. We need to view them as God does and to adopt policies and procedures, right across the board, which reflect a biblical approach to their care.

As with all the other issues we have looked at, we need to get our attitudes, values, practices and policies *from the Bible*, not from the increasingly warped thinking of our society, which is diverging ever farther away from a biblical world-view. At any rate, that is what the churches ought to stand for, and to speak up for, irrespective of whether we ever succeed in changing public opinion, or Government policy, and implementing what the Bible teaches.

6.   Homosexuality and gender confusion generally

The Bible is unmistakeably clear in saying that homosexual activity is wrong. It says so just as plainly as it says that adultery and fornication between men and women are wrong:

You shall not lie with a male as with a woman; it is an abomination.
Leviticus 18:22 (ESV)

If a man lies with a male as with a woman, both of them have committed an abomination; they shall surely be put to death; their blood is upon them.
Leviticus 20:13 (ESV)

[24] Therefore God gave them up in the lusts of their hearts to impurity, to the dishonoring of their bodies among themselves, [25] because they exchanged the truth about God for a lie and worshiped and served the creature rather than the Creator, who is blessed forever! Amen. [26] For this reason God gave them up to dishonorable passions. For their women exchanged natural relations for those that are contrary to nature; [27] and the men likewise gave up natural relations with women and were consumed with passion for one another, men committing shameless acts with men and receiving in themselves the due penalty for their error.
Romans 1:24-27 (ESV)

Likewise, *'transgenderism'*, or any other form of confusion about your gender, is an abomination. It is not a lifestyle choice, as we do not actually have a choice in this at all. We have no say in the matter, as our gender is given to us at conception and is fixed forever. To deny it, or seek to change it, is not only sin, but utterly silly, because it simply cannot be done. Moreover, to try to act like a member of the other sex, or to dress in their clothes, is also an abomination in God's eyes. That is not what I say. It is what He says Himself:

A woman shall not wear a man's garment, nor shall a man put on a woman's cloak, for whoever does these things is an abomination to the LORD your God.
Deuteronomy 22:5 (ESV)

286

However, our society, and even much of the Church, is increasingly being mentally reprogrammed to accept such perverse and unbiblical things. Alarmingly, in a recent survey, a majority of American Christians i.e. those who claim to be Christians, said they support homosexuality. *Social engineering*

Initially, campaigners only sought to change society's view to the extent that homosexual acts would no longer be treated as a *criminal offence*. However, having succeeded in that, they wanted to go further. Their aim now is to *prevent even the expression of any disapproval* of homosexuality by silencing anyone who dares to speak the truth about it. They have now largely achieved that too.

Therefore, having been emboldened by the success of the second stage of their long campaign, they are seeking to go even further. They are no longer content with our silence. The mere absence of our disapproval is not enough for them any longer. They now want *to compel us to positively approve of what they do* and to express it openly, whenever they tell us to do so, and with words of their choosing. *To get you to downgrade, submit your rationality - embrace the lie it called truth*

Accordingly, few things will now produce more rage than saying that homosexual activity is wrong. Consequently, very few preachers are now brave enough to say it. But we must hold absolutely firm to what God says, no matter what our society says, or does, to us for speaking the truth. However, in saying that homosexual activity is sinful, we are not to look down on the people who commit those sins. Homosexuals are just sinners, as we all are. *- Her, check ....*

We therefore have no right judge them, in the *'kreetace'* sense, as prohibited by Matthew 7:1, which means to usurp Jesus' role as Judge or to assume any superiority over other people. I say that because the criticism is often made of those who oppose homosexuality, gay marriage or gender confusion that they are being *judgemental*. But that is not usually the case. It is simply that we must call sin by its right name, and say what God says about it, whether we are dealing with homosexuals or heterosexuals.

In doing so we *are* of course judging, but only in the *'diakrino'* sense. That means to weigh up, assess or classify people, so as to know who or what we are dealing with, and whether or not they are a valid teacher, or can be trusted. That is something which the Bible actually *requires* us to do, unlike the *kreetace* form of judging, which the Bible *forbids* us to do.

See my audio teaching series on Matthew's gospel, and also my audio series on forgiveness, for more detail on the distinction between these two very different Greek words for two very different forms of judging, both of which are translated as 'judge' in English. Therefore, even over the meaning of the word *'judge'*, there is much confusion, which wrongly silences many people.

7. Ecumenism

Ecumenism became fashionable in Western churches after World War Two. It involves the belief that all the churches should come together and be *united*. However, it is based on a very misguided and unbiblical definition of 'unity'. What they are looking for can only be achieved by each of us abandoning any important doctrinal beliefs which might *create division between us*. Their view is that by such wholesale compromise we can then achieve unity. This comes from a distortion of the legitimate idea that God wants Christians to be *united*, which of course He does.

However, the unity that God wants for us is that which comes *from all of us believing the truth*, i.e. from knowing and accepting true biblical facts and having *accurate doctrine*. It has nothing to do with abandoning, or even adjusting, our beliefs to fit in with whatever is currently the majority view, even within churches, let alone amongst the unbelieving world. Ironically, in order to achieve this kind of shallow, artificial, unbiblical unity, the ecumenical movement urges us to get rid of two things that God very much wants us to keep.

Those are, firstly, our commitment to *truth* and, secondly, the maintenance of *accurate doctrines*. False, man-made unity, based on luke-warmness and compromise, actually destroys the real unity that God wants for us. Genuine unity can only be based on truth and sound doctrine. Otherwise, it would consist of nothing more than the fact that we are all engaging in the same kinds of error and apostasy, or at least that we are not objecting to each other doing so. But that is not unity. It is just an agreed sharing of error.

8. Israel and the Jewish people

This is a vast subject, but I am only going to deal with it very briefly here because I intend to address it more fully within later books which will be about prophecy, Israel, Islam, the end times, and other related issues. For now, let it suffice for me to say that Israel and the Jewish people are deeply loved by God. Indeed, they are *"the apple of His eye"*, i.e. the pupil of His eye, about which He is acutely sensitive and protective:

For thus said the LORD of hosts, after his glory sent me to the nations who plundered you, for he who touches you touches the apple of his eye:
Zechariah 2:8 (ESV)

Israel is special to God because, nearly 4000 years ago, He made a promise to a man called Abraham that He would form a nation out of him, through which the whole world would be blessed. That nation is the Jewish people. God also promised Abraham that He would give his descendants a land of their own which would be theirs *forever*. That land is Israel. These promises which God made to Abraham, and which He later repeated to his son, Isaac, and to his grandson, Jacob, are central to the whole Bible and to all of God's dealings with the human race and to His future plans for the establishment of God's Kingdom on this Earth.

This Kingdom will be based in Jerusalem, from which Jesus will reign, as King of Israel, after He returns. All of this is made explicitly and unmistakably clear throughout the Bible, in which the word 'Israel' occurs 2563 times. Yet, largely due to Satan's deliberate intervention, so as to deceive vast numbers of people about God's plans, these facts are largely unknown, even in the churches. Indeed, a very false and damaging teaching has spread through many denominations to the effect that God has *"finished with the Jews"* and that *"the Church has replaced Israel"*.

Nothing could be further from the truth, because God has expressly, and repeatedly, said that He will never forget, abandon, forsake or replace His Chosen people, the Jews, and that He will ensure that they return to their land and dwell in it forever. So that, in a nutshell, is God's position but the world, and a large proportion of the churches, either don't know it, or deliberately reject it. Therefore, instead of loving, blessing and supporting the Jews, as God has commanded us all to do, there is widespread animosity and even hatred towards them from all over the world.

That has been the case consistently for nearly 4000 years and it is called *'anti-Semitism'* because Abraham and the Jews descend from the line of *Shem*, one of the sons of Noah. However, this consistent, uniform, ongoing hatred and violence towards the Jews is no coincidence. It is whipped up by Satan himself, who is well aware that the Jews and Israel are central to God's plans for the future of the Earth, and to his own personal doom. Therefore, he has made opposing them central to his own plans.

That is why, for example, the United Nations spends an absurdly disproportionate amount of its time discussing Israel, a tiny country with very little land and only 8 million people, and why it is always condemning it and lying about it. It also explains why, for 4000 years, the Jews have been persecuted, most recently by the Nazis and now by the Muslims. But that persecution and hate are also coming from hundreds of millions of private individuals, all over the world, who have believed the blatant lies told about Israel.

By the way, there is another less well-known phrase which people are increasingly using to justify criticising Israel and the Jews. That is *"anti-Zionism"*, but it is a dishonest and weasel-worded phrase because it is actually hiding its true meaning and purpose, which is just to provide a more respectable cover for opposing Israel. The word *'Zion'* refers to Mount Zion in Jerusalem but it has also come to stand for Israel itself and it is used in both senses in the Bible and also amongst modern Jews today.

As a further development of the word, when Jews refer to *'Zionism'* or to themselves as being *'Zionists'*, what they mean is that they support the right of Jewish people, all over the world, to return to the land of Israel and to live there permanently, buying houses and raising families in the land which God gave to them forever. So, to refer to yourself as being *'anti-Zionist'*, and to pretend that that is somehow not *anti-Semitic*, is simply playing with words to disguise your real meaning and intentions.

Moreover, to be an anti-Zionist is, by definition, to be anti-God and to be opposed to *His purposes*, because He is the original Zionist. I say that because he has clearly and repeatedly stated that *He* wants the Jews to return to Israel, and to inhabit all of the Promised Land and that He is going to *cause them to return*. Therefore, do not be deceived by this phrase, which the world, and even a great many Christians, use because it is simply anti-Semitism by another name.

Please refer to the book that I am planning to write on Israel for a much fuller discussion of these issues. However, for now, let me simply say that almost everything that is said about Israel in the mainstream media is a lie. So is probably about 80-90% of what is said on social media. Therefore, if you want to know the truth you are going to have to search for it and be very discerning, even within churches, many of which are just as rabidly anti-Jewish as the secular world is.

Obviously, the place to begin is the Bible itself, which spells out God's plan for Israel and the Jews, and for their future, none of which has changed and all of which is going to be fulfilled. But also go out of your way to love and bless the Jewish people, and not to hate, accuse or criticise them. To be blunt, you would be a fool not to do as God has commanded us because God Himself has sworn to bless those who bless Israel and the Jews and to curse those who curse them. That is why Israel's enemies always come to a grisly end:

"...cursed be everyone who curses you and blessed be everyone who blesses you"

Genesis 27:29(b) (ESV)

"...blessed are those you bless you, and cursed are those who curse you"
Numbers 24:9(b) (ESV)

Pray for the peace of Jerusalem!
"May they be secure who love you!"
Psalm 122:6 (ESV)

Wisdom as: Practical Righteousness

For the nation and kingdom
    that will not serve you shall perish;
    those nations shall be utterly laid waste
                    Isaiah 60:12 (ESV)

....whoever stirs up strife with you
    shall fall because of you
                    Isaiah 54:15(b) (ESV)

For the LORD has chosen Jacob for himself,
    Israel as his own possession.
                    Psalm 135:4 (ESV)

Therefore all who devour you shall be devoured,
    and all your foes, every one of them, shall go into captivity;
those who plunder you shall be plundered,
    and all who prey on you I will make a prey.
                    Jeremiah 30:16 (ESV)

For the LORD has a day of vengeance,
    a year of recompense for the cause of Zion.
                    Isaiah 34:8 (ESV)

There isn't space here to go into all the details, but do yourself a big favour and, from now on, resolve to swim completely against the tide of public opinion by making sure that you:

a) find out the truth about Israel and the Jews and about God's love for them and also His plans for their future

b) love the Jewish people in every way you can

c) support Israel – and do it publicly, not just in private

d) speak up for Israel in your church, amongst your friends, and on social media

e) pray for Israel and the Jews

f) reject the lies told about them, and the hate felt for them, in the secular world and in many misguided churches, and let it be known that you are doing so.

9. Islam – the so-called *"religion of peace"*

Again, as with Israel above, I am only going to mention this hugely important topic very briefly because I will deal with it much more fully in chapter 16 below, and also in my future books. However, Islam is another one of those topics about which the mainstream media, and the vast majority of politicians, are consistently lying, to the point of absurdity. I say that because there are daily atrocities committed by Muslims all over the world, and also explicitly clear statements made in the Koran, the hadith and the sira, which repeatedly and unmistakeably instruct Muslims to engage in jihad and, in particular, to do so by beheading. Yet we are still constantly told that *"Islam is a religion of peace"*.

That lie would be farcical if it was not so tragic and if it was not so widely repeated and believed. This is, therefore, perhaps the most blatant lie that we are told, and which political correctness aggressively requires us to accept. However, the following things are not only true of Islam, *but required by it*, as core teachings. Moreover, they are all things which Mohammed himself did personally and told his followers to do:

a) Violence – it is central to Islam, i.e. authentic Islam, not the supposed 'misrepresentation' thereof, that it must be spread by invasion, fighting and murder. The express aim is to force people either to become Muslims or be put to death – usually by beheading, but by various other means too, including burning, boiling alive, and even gouging out of eyes.

b) Rape – again this is a central part of true Islam, and it is what Mohammed not only taught, but did. So too did his followers, on a consistent basis, even in front of the women's husbands! Therefore, the rapes we keep hearing about on social media, though rarely on mainstream media, which imposes a blanket of silence about this, are completely normal activities for genuine Muslims. They are exactly what the Koran instructs them to do.

c) Paedophilia – sadly, this too is entirely normal within Islam and Mohammed himself married Aisha, one of his 11 wives, when she was *six years old* and had full intercourse with her when she was *nine*. However, even before that, he interfered with her sexually, from the age of six. By the way, please don't imagine that these facts are denied by Muslims. They fully admit it and see nothing wrong with it. How could they, given that it is all clearly written about in the Koran, hadith and sira? They are not ashamed of it in the least. It is only western liberals who deny that Mohammed did these things, or that his followers do exactly the same today on an industrial scale.

d) Lying – it is a core teaching of Islam that Muslims can, and should, lie to infidels whenever it suits them. This is called *'taqiyya'* and it explains why deception is so endemic within Islam and why nothing that we are told by Muslims can be safely relied upon, even if they are not terrorists.

e) Conquest by emigration – at the moment we are seeing millions of young Muslim men, all of military age, coming to the West as supposed 'refugees'.

Yet, the vast majority are not from areas where any war is being conducted. In any case, why would they come here to flee an alleged war, but leave their wives, children and mothers behind? It is another blatant deception, which gullible western politicians either cannot see or are too spineless to admit. Actually, this policy of taking over other nations by massive waves of emigration also has a name. It is called *'hijrah'* i.e. *"migration for the sake of Allah"*.

So, each of these young men who have been allowed in to the West, and who are causing so much chaos and crime, will soon seek, and be granted by our feeble governments, permission to bring their entire extended families over here. They will then begin to have enormous families to take over the West by 'out-breeding' the native population. This is not merely my own allegation. It is exactly what Islam teaches Muslims to do and what they have been doing consistently for 1400 years. That policy has helped them to take over in 57 countries and to be well on the way to taking over in many more.

f) Taxing the infidels – i.e. taking money from us, either by halal certificates, or via our hopelessly naive benefits systems, so as to fund Muslim families and mosques at the expense of the infidels. That is one reason why so few Muslims go out to work, even as few as 20% in some places. Many prefer to have huge families and claim state benefits while paying no tax.

I could say a great deal more about Islam, and the lies that we are told *by our own politicians and media*, but please refer to my future books for a much fuller account. I would just add that it is my growing conviction that the coming antichrist whom the Bible speaks about will be a Muslim and that the religion of the antichrist will be Islam.

There are many reasons why I have reached that conclusion, which are too lengthy to set out here. However, with the alarming expansion of the Muslim population that we are now seeing, plus the avalanche of immigration towards the West, and the vast increase in the scale and ferocity of the Jihad ('holy war'), I am convinced that the arrival of the antichrist cannot now be far away. The pieces are falling into place at an astonishing pace.

At any rate, I have written chapter 16, and also include this brief section here about Islam, in a book which is about wisdom, because I do not believe that anyone can claim to be wise if they do not see Islam for what it is but instead naively believe the nonsense we are told about it being a religion of peace. It is not. It is a religion of war and conquest, of rape, paedophilia and repression, and of deception and theft. There is no point pretending otherwise, or at least not if you claim to be wise, or want to become so.

CY19 8

10. Pornography

The changes that have occurred since the early 1960s, with the unsuccessful trial for obscenity of the publishers of the book *Lady Chatterley's Lover*, have transformed Britain. The same explosion of pornography which came from that defeat has also occurred throughout the Western world. In the space of one decade the legal and social measures we had put in place to uphold decency were swept away and things are now shown on TV, and on the internet, which used only to be seen in seedy cinemas in Soho.

There is now so much of it that pornography no longer shocks most of us. That may be seen as acceptable by our lawmakers, but not by God. Therefore, neither should we accept pornography, or consider it normal, however widespread it becomes. There are many ways in which pornography harms our society, including degrading women, and corrupting the minds of men.

Countless men are now drawn to it and they are becoming increasingly unable, or unwilling, to break free of its hold over them. Even more tragically, it is promoting promiscuity between children and also destroying their innocence, which is one of the most wonderful things about childhood, i.e. as God intends it to be. That is to say that God positively wants children not to know anything about such things, and to remain in that position for as long as possible.

For all those reasons, the demons have pulled the strings of our politicians very skilfully, so as to ensure that pornography was first legalised and then widely promoted. Again, such consistent and widespread changes could not have occurred at the same time, all over the world, without the involvement of demons. Perhaps the worst feature of pornography, although one which few people recognise, is that it is a *desecration of the image of God*. I say that because the human race have all been created in His own image.

That means what it says, quite literally. God made us to *look like He looks*, which was an immense privilege and honour for us. He actually allowed us, and also the angels, to share His physical appearance. Therefore, to take the human body, which is made in God's image and likeness, and to use it for pornography, is a terrible desecration. Indeed, it is a blasphemy. We may not see it that way, but God does. It is therefore an insult to Him, quite apart from all of the other dreadful harm that it causes.

11. Promiscuity

Alongside all the above changes, there has also been a vast increase in promiscuity. It is now considered normal, *even in many churches*, for people to have sex prior to, and even outside of, marriage. Therefore, it is no longer even seen as a basis for comment, let alone disapproval, if people live together before their marriage. The idea that there should be faithfulness between husband and wife, forsaking all others, is now considered by many to be unrealistic, old fashioned, and even ridiculous.

At any rate, it is certainly not seen as important and, even in the churches, many cannot see why this matters so much to God. The resultant chaos and misery that we now see in terms of unfaithfulness and divorce obviously harms women and children, but it also damages men. It is the direct and foreseeable end-product of this new permissive attitude to sex, both before and outside of marriage, which our society, and even many of our churches, have adopted.

12. Feminism

It now takes an exceptionally courageous man to tell the truth in public, even in a church meeting, about what God says about men and women and the way in which they should relate to each other and to Him. For any man to speak about women at all, and especially to mention so called *"women's issues"*, is seen as an outrage. It is felt that only women are allowed to say anything about women. Therefore, woe betide any man who intrudes into this area, especially if he dares to say that men and women are not the same, or that they have different God-given roles.

However, the truth is that although God has made men and women equal, they are obviously and undeniably different. Moreover, He made them different deliberately, for a number of very good reasons. Although they are quite definitely of equal value in God's eyes, He wants the husband to be in authority over his wife and for the wife to submit to her husband.

This is all meant to take place in a context of *love, not domination*, and is intended to mirror the relationship between Jesus Christ and His Church. Indeed, the husband has actually been given the harder task. He has to love his wife "*as Christ loves the Church*". That is a very tall order indeed, which none of us has ever fully achieved.

Feminist thinking, which few are now brave enough to contradict, even in private, has led to the very opposite of what God wants. It has promoted hostility, suspicion, contempt, and even hatred, towards men in general. In particular, it rejects the leadership role of the husband. It also promotes anger, stridency and the practice of women seeking to imitate male characteristics. That may seem to be an odd thing for feminists to want, given their dislike of men. Nevertheless, it is a central part of their policy to seek to 'masculinise' women.

At the same time they will seek to feminise men, i.e. to undermine and devalue the whole God-given concept of masculinity and to urge men to think, act, and even dress, like women. Both of these aims are very wrong, because the truth is that God deliberately designed men and women to be different, but also complementary. His aim is to make them a perfect whole when they are joined together in marriage.

The thinking behind feminism is unbiblical and profoundly misguided. It has therefore resulted, unsurprisingly, in terrible unhappiness, not least in the collapse of marriage in the West and the resultant broken homes and fatherless children. Ironically, feminism has probably done its greatest damage to women themselves. Its adherents have responded to their perceived mistreatment with a level of rage that has only ever made them more miserable and has achieved nothing constructive.

Feminism therefore harms children, families, husbands and society as a whole, but probably women most of all. Interestingly, the vast majority of women are now seeing what feminism really is and they are rejecting it in droves. A recent survey shows that only 7% of British women describe themselves as 'feminists'. Yet, that same survey shows that 92% of British women believe that men and women are of equal value and that they should be paid the same wage if they do exactly the same job.

The point is that women themselves can see that those obvious facts are not what feminism is about. That must be so, because if they thought it was just about being of equal value, and getting equal pay, then the same percentage of women would call themselves feminists as there are who say that men and women are equal. In the 1980s and 1990s many women assumed that feminism was indeed about women being of equal value. However, they have since come to realise that it is actually a militant ideology and a nasty, spiteful, sour-spirited movement, led by women who *simply hate men* and want to knock them down.

Most women don't think that way and don't have that aim, even though they feel fully equal and do want to be paid the same. Accordingly, feminism, when correctly defined, is now being rejected by the vast majority. Sadly that 7% who do hate men, and whose hearts are filled with rage, are very influential, mainly because they operate so militantly and loudly. They then seek to impose their warped agenda on us all, including other women, whether we agree with it or not. As with all political correctness, it is not primarily our *agreement* that they seek, but our *compliance*.

One of the biggest errors of feminism is that it devalues the role of *mother*. It especially despises those mothers who choose to stay at home and to care for their own children rather than go out to work and let a nursery or a child minder bring them up in her place. It is central to feminism that a woman can *and should* do everything that men do, including going out to work, rather than caring for their own children. They see that role as demeaning and restrictive and they are not inhibited about saying so, regardless of the feelings of those mothers who freely choose to look after their own children.

Therefore, going out to work instead of bringing up children is not something which feminists merely wish to make possible, *for those who want it*. They push their ideology aggressively and many of them despise those mothers who don't share their beliefs or their priorities. By contrast, women who think biblically will focus first of all on meeting the needs of their children during their crucial formative years, rather than being preoccupied with themselves, or their careers, or anything else that they want out of life.

However, the policies of recent British governments, and especially the Coalition from 2010 to 2015, which was influenced by the Liberal Democrats, has been to push mothers to go out to work as soon as possible and to place their children in nurseries! Few things are sadder than a policy of deliberately seeking to put young children under the care of other people, *instead of their own mothers*, and thus depriving them of that precious time together at such a vital formative stage.

In pursuit of that ideologically driven foolishness, the Coalition Government said they would pay a further £1,200 per annum to working mothers to help with child care fees. But they proposed to give nothing to those mothers who choose to bring up their own children at home. They referred to them disparagingly as having made a *"lifestyle choice"*, as if caring for their own children was inappropriate, and even selfish.

One of the worst aspects of feminist thinking is the way in which it not only fails to honour men, but deliberately seeks to *dishonour* them. The aim is not only to undermine the role of the husband, but to devalue *men in general*. They portray them as inadequate, stupid and worthy only of contempt. This can be seen even in films and TV programmes in which women are now portrayed as strong and independent, with no need for men to protect or rescue them. One often hears of there being a *"war on women"*, as if women are being undermined. In fact, it is largely the other way round, with men and masculinity being attacked and sneered at.

Feminist ideology is particularly hostile to genuine, red-blooded masculinity whereby the God-given qualities and attributes of men are allowed to be fully and properly expressed. Masculinity, as God designed it and intends it to be, is a good thing, not a problem or a fault. God actually wants men to be capable of fighting, including physically, to defend their wives and families, and also to stand up for their country and generally for what is right.

That aggression, and the in-built instinct to fight, is not a defect or a sin. God has programmed it into the 'software' of the male and He wants it to be properly harnessed and allowed to find an outlet, although obviously only at the right times and in the right way. However, that aspect of maleness is now mocked and spoken of as if it had no value. Yet, strangely, whilst criticising these aggressive qualities in men, they promote and advocate them in women.

Therefore, for example, in two different TV series which I watch, the women police officers are usually the ones who fight the villains, and they always win, whereas the men do not, and even depend on the women. Men are often depicted on TV as spineless and feeble and as the butt of the jokes, whereas the female characters never are. That is forbidden because it would *"stereotype women as weak and stupid"*, and would be an outrage.

However, storylines which undermine manliness are seen as acceptable, and even necessary, so as to recondition our thinking. Their portrayal of men is tiresome, and also damaging, because the effect of that propaganda is to undermine men, and maleness. The thinking of feminists is effectively *"If we can only show men how bad and pathetic we think they are, and how much we despise them, they will see our perspective and then change for the better"*. As a policy, that does not seem likely to work, and it certainly hasn't worked so far.

When feminists set out to mock and denigrate men, it does not cause men to examine themselves and embark on a process of self-improvement. On the contrary, it only produces a matching contempt for women. That seems self-evident, given how little respect is now shown in return to women, especially in the area of sex, where many men now see women as objects to be conquered and then cast aside, rather than honoured, cherished and loved.

I fear even more for the future because a whole generation of young people are now being brought up with no concept of what it means to honour the opposite sex, how to do so, or why they should. In the past young boys were taught *'chivalry'* at school and, for example, to stand when a lady entered or left the room, to seat them at the dining table, and to open doors for them. Sadly, that rarely ever occurs today and, if it did, it would be said to be *"demeaning"* and *"patronising"*, and as *"reinforcing gender stereotypes"*.

It has gone so far that it may now be impossible to reverse the rot in our nations as a whole. But we can at least do so in our own marriages and families, and even perhaps within our churches, if others will allow it. We should therefore set out to deliberately swim in the opposite direction to most of our generation and to take every opportunity to honour our husband or wife, especially in public, and never to make jokes at their expense.

Women in particular need to avoid criticising or disrespecting their husbands in front of others, or complaining about them, even privately, to their female friends, because it has such a corrosive effect. It will diminish the woman who does it, and cause her own heart to be hardened, even if her husband never comes to hear of it. Rather than join in with the belittling remarks that so many women engage in, be different. When other women criticise or mock their husbands, go out of your way to praise yours instead and to let it be seen that you honour him and admire his achievements.

You may stick out like a healthy thumb in a fracture clinic, but it will be good for you and for them and may even cause some of them to rethink their own approach. The same applies to men. Never speak disrespectfully of your wife or girlfriend and always speak up for her if she is criticised. Honour her in every way, even if you are the only one of your male friends who does so, and even if they think less of you for doing so. Their opinion of you doesn't really matter, but hers does, very much indeed, and God's opinion of you matters even more.

13. The abolition of the death penalty

It is a peculiar anomaly that liberals support abortion for innocent unborn children, but oppose the death penalty for murderers. One might imagine that their approach to both issues would be consistent. But it isn't. They do not even recognise the life of an unborn child, let alone ascribe any value to it, but they strenuously defend the lives of heinous criminals.

On both counts they have ended up saying the exact opposite of what the Bible says, which ought not really to surprise us, given that their beliefs are 'doctrines of demons'. As an example of how muddled the West has become, the European Union is warning Turkey not to execute murderers or else they will not allow them to join the EU. Yet that is just about the only thing which Turkey is getting right.

What then is God's stance on the question of whether convicted *murderers* should be executed? We are told this very clearly in the book of Genesis. Also bear in mind that this command about capital punishment *is not part of the Law of Moses*. It was given to Noah long before then and is, therefore, applicable to *all of mankind, not just Israel*. Moreover, unlike the Law of Moses, this command has never been suspended or revoked. Therefore, this is what God still has to say *to every human being*, whether they are Jewish or Gentile:

⁵And for your lifeblood I will require a reckoning: from every beast I will require it and from man. From his fellow man I will require a reckoning for the life of man.
⁶ "Whoever sheds the blood of man,
by man shall his blood be shed,

for God made man in his own image.

Genesis 9:5-6 (ESV)

Nevertheless, let us also look at what the Law of Moses had to say about capital punishment. Even though we are no longer under the Law of Moses, it clarifies God's thinking on this issue and its principles are still of relevance to us:

"Whoever takes a human life shall surely be put to death

Leviticus 24:17 (ESV)

[29] *"And these things shall be for a statute and ordinance to you throughout your generations in all your dwellings.* [30] *If any one kills a person, the murderer shall be put to death on the evidence of witnesses; but no person shall be put to death on the testimony of one witness.* [31] *Moreover you shall accept no ransom for the life of a murderer, who is guilty of death; but he shall be put to death.* [32] *And you shall accept no ransom for him who has fled to his city of refuge, that he may return to dwell in the land before the death of the high priest.* [33] *You shall not thus pollute the land in which you live; for blood pollutes the land, and no expiation can be made for the land, for the blood that is shed in it, except by the blood of him who shed it.* [34] *You shall not defile the land in which you live, in the midst of which I dwell; for I the LORD dwell in the midst of the people of Israel."*

Numbers 35:29-34 (RSV)

Although the death and resurrection of Jesus has fulfilled the Law of Moses and brought it to an end, that does *not* mean that the death penalty has been abolished. The command to put murderers to death was given to *all of mankind*, long before the Law of Moses was given. Moreover, Jesus has not subsequently cancelled it either.

In Romans, Paul discusses how rulers and governing authorities *"bear the sword"* in order to do God's will. Therefore, when murderers are put to death, it is done with God's full approval, to *"execute His wrath on the wrongdoer"*. Paul explicitly confirms, in the New Testament, that God endorses the death penalty:

[1] *Let every person be subject to the governing authorities. For there is no authority except from God, and those that exist have been instituted by God.* [2] *Therefore he who resists the authorities resists what God has appointed, and those who resist will incur judgment.* [3] *For rulers are not a terror to good conduct, but to bad. Would you have no fear of him who is in authority? Then do what is good, and you will receive his approval,* [4] *for he is God's servant for your good. But if you do wrong, be afraid, for he does not bear the sword in vain; he is the servant of God to execute his wrath on the wrongdoer.*

Romans 13:1-4 (RSV)

NB Germany et Hitler - should he have been opposed? Or introducing ungodly laws today. not for our good

300

Every human being is made in the image of God. For that reason, and for other reasons too, every human life is sacred. One reason why God ordained the death penalty for every murderer was precisely in order to uphold the sanctity of human life, not to undermine it. It makes a clear statement that nobody has the right to *murder* any other person. If they do so, then their own life is justly forfeited. That stark response demonstrates the seriousness of murder and shows how precious every human life is to God. So, it is not *killing* that God forbids, but *murder*, because He clearly spells out situations in which it is lawful to kill, whereas murder is unlawful killing.

It is for the very reason that human life is so sacred that the life of a murderer has to be taken away from him. That might sound counter-intuitive at first sight, but it actually makes perfect sense if you think it through. Of course, it also serves as a *deterrent* and as a *punishment,* both of which are valid additional reasons for the death penalty. However, let's be clear. The main purpose of the death penalty is neither punishment nor deterrence. It is primarily *to uphold the sanctity of human life* and to send out a clear message about its infinite value.

It is no coincidence, therefore, that when capital punishment was abolished in the UK in 1965 it quickly led to the passing of the Abortion Act in 1967. Our legislature made a clear statement in 1965 that, in the UK, human life is no longer sacred. We then followed that up, only two years later, by making it lawful to kill an unborn child. The one decision led to the other by a clear chain of logic, albeit a perverse and unbiblical one.

Had we done what God wanted, then we would have done *the exact opposite on both points*. That is, we would have retained the death penalty for murder, but continued to forbid abortion. Both of those policies would have upheld the sanctity of life and would also have been entirely consistent with each other. However, we chose instead to undermine the sanctity of life on *both* fronts and we are already paying a heavy price for that now as God's judgement falls on the UK and on the West as a whole.

Wise people fear God and seek only for His approval for what they think and say, not for the approval of other people.

The Bible promises many blessings and benefits to those who fear the LORD:

The fear of the LORD is the beginning of wisdom;
all those who practice it have a good understanding.
His praise endures forever!
                                        Psalm 111:10 (ESV)

God also commands us not to fear the reproach or disapproval of other people:

7"Hearken to me, you who know righteousness, the people in whose heart is my law; fear not the reproach of men, and be not dismayed at their revilings. 8For the moth will eat them up like a garment, and the worm will eat them like wool; but my deliverance will be for ever, and my salvation to all generations."

Isaiah 51:7-8 (RSV)

One of the many benefits of the fear of the LORD is that it greatly reduces our desire to be approved of by others. That craving for people's approval gets us into a lot of temptations and problems, and makes us willing to say all kinds of nonsense in order to be seen as politically correct and therefore to be accepted. Wanting the praise of men may even cause us to deny Jesus rather than be openly identified as one of His followers:

42Nevertheless many even of the authorities believed in him, but for fear of the Pharisees they did not confess it, lest they should be put out of the synagogue: 43 for they loved the praise of men more than the praise of God.

John 12:42-43 (RSV)

By contrast, note the approach taken by apostle Paul. He saw pleasing God and pleasing men as *mutually exclusive alternatives*, such that you can please one, or the other, but not both. Realising that fact can set you free and enable you to give up trying to please the people around you. Instead, just decide to please God from now on, regardless of what others may say, and always be determined to think and speak the truth, not what society and the media consider to be right:

Am I now seeking the favor of men, or of God? Or am I trying to please men? If I were still pleasing men, I should not be a servant of Christ.

Galatians 1:10 (RSV)

Wise people do not vote at elections on the basis of mere slogans and 'soundbites'

Ours is probably the stupidest generation in all of world history, at least within the Western democracies, if not the rest of the world. The western nations have rejected God, and embraced all sorts of wickedness and folly, such as evolution, abortion, homosexuality, promiscuity, divorce, gay marriage, feminism, pornography, transgenderism, political correctness, the appeasement of Islam, and even the myth of global warming or 'climate change'. All of these false beliefs have caused our generation to become dumbed down to an extent that has never been seen before.

302

It is, in part, the result of God handing our generation over and leaving them to get on with whatever evil nonsense they want to think and whatever wickedness they want to engage in. One also sees this dumbness in our generation's handling of debate and political decision-making. In the past, even when most people left school at age 14 or earlier, or did not even go to school at all, there was far greater wisdom and straightforward common sense than we now see.

In elections, past generations only voted after carrying out a thorough examination of the facts, arguments and issues and after weighing up the views of the candidates. One only has to look at old newspapers and election literature and manifestos to see that, even in the 1970s and 80s, let alone the early twentieth century. People would go, in large numbers, to political meetings where they would listen to detailed arguments and debate the issues. They would also read avidly to get the fullest possible understanding. That kind of diligence has now largely disappeared.

Today, the majority of people, especially those in their twenties and thirties, vote on the basis of mere slogans and vastly over-simplified 'soundbites'. I do not primarily blame the politicians for that dumbing down, or for our unwillingness to study the issues or hear sustained debate. Our leaders know that we are a stupid generation and that any political party which tried to talk sense to us, or which went into detail about complex issues, would lose heavily in any election. They know that the attention span of a modern voter is measured in seconds, not minutes, and certainly not hours.

Thus, they only give us what they know we want, which is *short, catchy slogans*, regardless of whether they are true, or balanced, or reflect reality, or address the substantive issues. Most of us like the message to be couched in bright, simple, colourful images and, ideally, in pictures rather than words. Then we are not even required to think, let alone engage in any arduous study. In short, we are being treated like idiots, for the very good reason that most of us *are idiots*, at least in comparison to previous generations.

Look for example at the childish, dumbed-down arguments presented by both sides in the 2016 Referendum in the UK over the issue of the EU, though far more so by the Remain camp, who were also dishonest and aggressive. It was amazing to see the simplistic nonsense that was being posted on social media, not just by the public, but by the political parties. People were deciding which way to vote on the most trivial points, rather than on any genuine and thorough understanding of the real issues. It was as if the debate was being conducted in a primary school, amongst 10 and 11 year olds, not an adult electorate.

The myth of man-made *'global warming'*, one of the biggest, but most widely believed, lies in history — *cv19*

There isn't space in this crowded chapter to deal adequately with this huge subject of alleged man-made *global warming*. However, I wanted to at least flag the issue and to urge you to investigate it properly, with an open mind, and to re-think it if you have, hitherto, believed it. I should also mention that the supporters of this theory have recently changed its name to *'climate change'* because, ironically, for the past two decades, there has not actually been any *global warming at all*. Even they are forced to admit that.

Therefore, to avoid embarrassment, a more flexible name was given to it so that now, whatever happens, whether it is hot or cold, wet or dry, calm or windy, it can all be attributed to carbon dioxide and other alleged 'greenhouse gases', such as methane. Thus, what we used to call *weather*, the subject which we in the UK spend 30% of our lives talking about, is now seen as proof of this theory, no matter what may be happening. Yet, we were already talking about the weather in Shakespeare's day, and even when the Romans invaded, before any industrially produced carbon dioxide existed.

Interestingly, when I was at school in the late 1970s, and even up until the mid-1980s, the 'consensus view' of much of the supposedly scientific community was that we were actually about to enter into another *ice age*. That was literally what we were taught. Then, in the mid-1980s, that view was quietly dropped and replaced by the idea that man's activities were causing the planet to heat up, hence the phrase 'global warming'. This new view was then pushed aggressively and anyone objecting to it is now called a *'denier'* and accused of not thinking 'scientifically'.

Whenever anyone refuses to accept this belief, or suggests that there is no evidence for it, the global warming lobby simply says that their belief is now *'settled science'*. They then add that *"the time for questioning it has passed"*, and that we should all accept the *'consensus view'*, without further debate. But science is not about consensus views. What other people think, and whether or not they are in the majority, is totally irrelevant. *due diligence*

Science is not about majority votes. It is about identifying truth and error, based on properly conducted experiments and enquiry. So, for example, it used to be the consensus view amongst scientists that the Sun orbited around the Earth, yet that was completely untrue. In the beginning, only one man challenged that view, but he was right, and the consensus was wrong. I believe the same applies today. That said, it is not only one man who disagrees. Multitudes of scientists reject the theory of man-made global warming.

Forget what the conceses view is — what does the evidence say

304

In fact, although the media have given this zero coverage, more than 30,000 scientists, over 10,000 of whom have PhDs, have signed a public petition confirming that they reject it. So, it doesn't actually sound like much of a consensus after all. As for why so many politicians, and so much of the media, are so aggressively pushing the global warming/climate change ideology, I believe the main reason is that it lends itself very conveniently to the *one world government* agenda. Therefore, pushing this theory helps them to gain greater levels of control over every aspect of our lives.

It means an ever-increasing role for the government and greatly increased regulation. Those are essential prerequisites for a one world government of the kind that they seek. Accordingly, be willing to question what you are told in the media, or at school or college, or even by governments, about alleged global warming. Be ready to challenge all of it, to think about it for yourself, and to test the evidence, rather than simply going along with whatever you are told.

Wise people can control their own temper so as debate controversial issues without reviling others.

When did you last hear even a discussion, let alone a debate, on issues such as Bible prophecy, Israel, spiritual gifts, the roles of men and women, demonology, deliverance, divine healing etc? In most churches such topics are felt to be too sensitive and controversial to be mentioned. Thus, they aren't even taught at all, let alone debated within or between churches. This is a shame, as we lose so much as a result. It also brings disgrace on the body of Christ.

Therefore, we need to learn, or rather relearn, how to engage in discussion and how to debate courteously, with good manners and self-control. That requires a determination to focus only on the *issues*, not on attacking or belittling the *person* who is disagreeing with us. Sadly, that kind of aggression is now the standard approach on social media, where insults are traded and harsh language is routinely used. A wise person refuses to engage in such *'ad hominem'* debates, where the *person* who is speaking is attacked rather than addressing the *issue itself*.

That brutish, uncivilised approach is now the standard default setting for much of the debate that occurs on social media and also the mainstream media, and even within churches. By contrast, a wise person speaks with courtesy and self-control, without any loss of temper, or even raising of the voice. That said, this is a lot easier said than done, especially if those around us don't reciprocate and are therefore ill-tempered with us, or seek to silence us, whenever our argument can't be defeated.

305

Again, silencing your opponent, and preventing him from making his argument, or from being heard at all, rather than responding intelligently to the points he makes, is another standard technique today. We see it all the time in universities where the natural assumption, when a visiting speaker is coming, is to try to ban him. Or, if they can't do that, they will 'shout him down', so that he can't be heard, rather than just try to answer him with reasoned responses. So, instead of trying to *win* the debate, their aim is to *prevent* any debate from happening.

Nevertheless, whether or not others cooperate with us in this, each of us must go to great lengths to maintain our own self-control and to persist in trying to operate calmly and graciously. We must do so even if we are the only one who has that aim, which we might well be. Therefore, don't write people off if they disagree with you, or assume that they are stupid. Don't get angry either, even if they get angry with you. Stay calm. Be patient. Keep to the issues and avoid being drawn into trading insults or point-scoring. *Provoke you to respond like them irrationally*

Make the effort also to lower the volume of your voice when others are raising theirs. That last tactic, in itself, can be very helpful. It was a tip I was given in the police for defusing tense situations. Strangely, the more quietly you speak, the more authoritative you will sound and the more people will calm down and listen to you. However, if you raise your voice, you won't be heard, because others will immediately raise theirs and they will usually be able to out-shout you.

Don't esculate of provoke in return.

A wise person has regard to the real purpose of any discussion or debate. That is not to sound clever, or impress others, or even to be seen to win. The aim is, or should be, either for you to teach something to someone else, or for you to learn something from them. As soon as you start competing with others, or seeking to prove your superiority, or merely to show that you were right, rather than addressing the issue, you are moving into operating in the flesh. If so, that can't please God or achieve anything of value.

[4] *in order that the righteous requirement of the law might be fulfilled in us, who walk not according to the flesh but according to the Spirit. [5] For those who live according to the flesh set their minds on the things of the flesh, but those who live according to the Spirit set their minds on the things of the Spirit. [6] For to set the mind on the flesh is death, but to set the mind on the Spirit is life and peace. [7] For the mind that is set on the flesh is hostile to God, for it does not submit to God's law; indeed, it cannot. [8] Those who are in the flesh cannot please God.*

Always expect the worst:

Romans 8:4-8 (ESV)

Expect Evil, Expect stupidity, provokation, insults, deceit

Why wouldn't you expect it — you live in a fallen world where most have a fallen condition of their god is their belly & eyes & their master is Satan himself

CHAPTER 10

WISE PEOPLE THINK IN TERMS OF DUTIES, NOT RIGHTS OR ENTITLEMENTS — but responsibilities

[19] And this is the judgment: the light has come into the world, and people loved the darkness rather than the light because their works were evil. [20] For everyone who does wicked things hates the light and does not come to the light, lest his works should be exposed. [21] But whoever does what is true comes to the light, so that it may be clearly seen that his works have been carried out in God."

John 3:19-21 (ESV)

Whoever is wise, let him understand these things; whoever is discerning, let him know them; for the ways of the LORD are right, and the upright walk in them, but transgressors stumble in them.

Hosea 14:9 (ESV)

[17] If anyone's will is to do God's will, he will know whether the teaching is from God or whether I am speaking on my own authority. [18] The one who speaks on his own authority seeks his own glory; but the one who seeks the glory of him who sent him is true, and in him there is no falsehood.

John 7:17-18 (ESV)

For everyone belongs to me, the parent as well as the child—both alike belong to me......

Ezekiel 18:4(a) (NIV)

[19] Do you not know that your bodies are temples of the Holy Spirit, who is in you, whom you have received from God? You are not your own; [20] you were bought at a price. Therefore honor God with your bodies.

1 Corinthians 6:19-20 (NIV)

[6] And he said to them, "Well did Isaiah prophesy of you hypocrites, as it is written,
'This people honors me with their lips,
but their heart is far from me;
[7] in vain do they worship me,
teaching as doctrines the precepts of men.'
[8] You leave the commandment of God, and hold fast the tradition of men."
[9] And he said to them, "You have a fine way of rejecting the commandment of God, in order to keep your tradition!

Mark 7:6-9 (RSV)

- Fear of God - submission to Him
liberates you from the views
of trusty man.

307

The Christian walks in the
way of Wisdom: the ... of G
not the "way that seems right to a man"
But: Counter culture, Counter intuitive
Christians are 'contrarians' of the world.

The overall 'Human Rights' agenda – what it is and how it arose

This is a very big subject, and one to which few of us have ever given any real thought. I am referring to the widely-held belief that human beings are born with a number of inherent, automatic rights or entitlements, which cannot be taken away, or even questioned. At first sight, that sounds like it must surely be a good thing and that Christians ought to support it. However, at the risk of being considered awkward, I must challenge it. I would put it to you that, in fact, when viewed biblically, we have *no inherent rights at all.* by virtue of being

We have been taught to think that we do, especially since the Second World War, but that is not how God thinks. At any rate, the Bible does not speak of any such rights. Instead, it only ever speaks of *duties and responsibilities*. The Bible takes a completely different approach. It is *God-centred* rather than *man-centred* and that makes all the difference. Many profound implications flow from these diametrically opposed ways of thinking and we shall explore some of those differences below.

My conclusion, as both a lawyer and a teacher of the Bible, is that any legal or social system which is based on the assumption that we have rights, as opposed to duties and responsibilities, will lead to unjust and, above all, unbiblical, consequences. As to where rights-based thinking began, the first traces of it arose in the French Revolution of 1789. That was occurring at about the same time as the American Constitution and Bill of Rights were also being formed. As part of that violent upheaval in France, a misguided and unbiblical document was written entitled the '*Declaration of the Rights of Man*'.

This set out a wholly new basis for a French Constitution. In the third article it states: *"The source of all sovereignty resides essentially in the nation; no body, no individual can exercise authority that does not proceed from it in plain terms."* However, anybody who remembers what Jesus said to His disciples after His resurrection will know that the above statement cannot be true. In Matthew 28:18 He said: *"All authority in Heaven and on Earth has been given to me"* and it is God's Word, not the Declaration of the Rights of Man, which we must believe.

If, instead, we believe the Bible, then the implications are very different. For a start, all authority comes from God, not the State, and it is He, not us, who has all the rights. It is absolutely true that God gives us *freedom*. But He does not give us any *inherent* rights that we can claim are ours *by birth,* without having to earn them, or qualify for them, by meeting His conditions. Moreover, although God does give us free will and freedom of choice, those are *not absolute*. They are subject to various constraints, boundaries and prohibitions which He imposes, without ever consulting us or seeking our permission.

You have the 'mind of Christ'
think like God thinks!

Wisdom: Think & Respond as God does
" Imitation of God" th

SO - Those who say they have 'Christ consciousness'
yet flatly contradict God's word & way

308

How the English legal system used to operate before it was contaminated by rights-based thinking

The biblical way to view our position is that we are *free to do anything unless it is prohibited* by God's Word, or by our conscience, or by the many duties that we owe to our fellow men. Thus, in the Garden of Eden, Adam was free to do anything at all, other than eat fruit from one particular tree. In the English legal system, which developed what is known as the *'common law'*, we always used to think along those lines.

That was primarily because, for centuries, our legal system was constructed on biblical principles. However, the arrival of rights-based thinking has changed all that. Let us look firstly at how things used to be dealt with. In 1958, in his book *'The Approach to Self Governance,'* in which he discussed the merits, or otherwise, of the new developments in legal thinking since the end of the war, *Sir Ivor Jennings* wrote:

".....in Britain we have no rights; we merely have liberty, according to the laws; and we think - truly believe – that we do a better job than any country which has a Bill of Rights or a Declaration of the Rights of Man."

Likewise, in Halsbury's Laws of England, Volume 8(2) Constitutional Law and Human Rights (4th edition 1996) which was written just *before* the Human Rights Act, 1998 was passed, it states:

"Although the rights of the individual lie at the heart of common law they are not 'human rights' in the modern sense: in constitutional law, the individual is a subject of the Crown, not a bearer of rights."

The traditional position of the English legal system, as it stood prior to the Human Rights Act, was put very well by *Sir John Laws* in his judgment in *R-v- Somerset County Council* [1995] 1 AER 513, 524. In that case he identified two major constitutional principles:

a) the common law rule that private individuals can do everything which is not forbidden and

b) the general principle forbidding a public body from doing anything which is not allowed

That may look confusing at first sight, but it is actually a simple concept, albeit a radical one. He meant that the general default-setting, or starting point, is that *every individual* has freedom to do everything, except where that is expressly curtailed by some specific law. By contrast, the general default-setting for *public bodies*, such as governments and councils, was that they do *not* have freedom to do anything, unless permission to do so is granted to them.

Therefore, public bodies were required not to act, but to keep out of things, and they had no basis for interfering in our lives at all unless they had been granted a *specific authority to do so*. This approach maximised the liberty of every individual, and minimised the powers of public bodies, precisely because our legal system, at that time, was not based on rights and did not even think in those terms.

How we ended up with the Human Rights Act

Let's now examine where our modern concept of 'human rights' came from and how we got these new and very different laws. In the immediate aftermath of World War Two the governments of the United Kingdom and the United States pressed for the newly formed United Nations to make a declaration about supposedly fundamental human rights. This resulted in the '*Universal Declaration of Human Rights*' which was adopted by 48 members of the United Nations in 1948.

What they had in mind as the backdrop to this declaration was the array of brutal atrocities which had just been committed by the Nazis and the Japanese. In particular it was a reference to the Nazis' attempt to wipe out the Jewish race. We gave that policy the name 'genocide'. That was the kind of behaviour which the members of the United Nations were seeking to prevent ever happening again. Sadly, the way they went about trying to do that led to far wider ramifications, which they never envisaged.

It is a classic example of the '*law of unintended consequences*'. Three years later, in 1951, the United Kingdom ratified the *European Convention on Human Rights and Fundamental Freedoms*. It went further than the United Nations had gone and specified a series of other things which it maintained were also fundamental human rights. The British Government were signatories to this, but did not give full effect to it within the United Kingdom until after the passing of The Human Rights Act in 1998.

There is no room in this book to examine each of these alleged human rights and the case law arising from them. We shall therefore confine ourselves to speaking of the concept of rights as a whole, the implications and consequences of this overall approach, and the attitudes that it tends to produce. At first sight, these so called rights sound like they must be good for us. At any rate, it doesn't seem that they could do us any harm. However, I contend that both those assumptions are wrong.

310

Even within the churches, we now have a whole generation which is steeped in rights-based thinking and takes it for granted that that must be the correct approach

Accordingly, many British people, including Christians, automatically assume that the Human Rights Act is a good thing. It is taken for granted that to stand up for human rights must surely be what God wants and that no reasonable person could ever be opposed, at least to the broad concept of rights as a matter of principle. However, I would argue that the whole human rights agenda does not actually represent God's approach, values or thoughts at all.

Indeed, it is, in many ways, the very opposite of how a biblically-based legal system would operate, because the very idea that we have inherent, inalienable rights, of any description, is based on *humanist beliefs and human reasoning*. Therefore, it does not reflect the way God thinks about these issues. To explain why I make that bold claim, the best place to start would be to say that God has never actually given any of us *any rights at all*. You can search the whole Bible, but you won't find any rights being given to us.

In fact, if you want to be blunt, *we do not even have a right to live at all*, let alone to do so to any particular level, or to receive any minimum standard of care, behaviour or treatment from others. Our very lives are in God's hands and are only provided to us for as long, or short, a period as *He* chooses, entirely at His own discretion. Indeed, we ourselves, our very bodies, are His property and so is everything that we think we own. I discuss that point more fully in chapter 9, on political correctness.

God is therefore under no *obligation* even to keep us alive. Or, viewed from the other direction, you could alternatively say that we have no legitimate *right* or entitlement to be allowed to continue living. God is free to end our lives Himself, or to allow them to be ended by someone else, whenever He chooses. We would have no basis for complaint, whatever He might do with us, take from us, or choose not to give us. The same applies to our property, homes, careers, and so on.

A young woman who did not like my views on human rights

I was speaking to a young woman recently who has grown up since the passing of the Human Rights Act 1998. Like many of her age, she has been thoroughly saturated in rights-based thinking, such that it has seeped into all of her values, attitudes and expectations. Therefore, she was chafing when I said that the Bible does not give us any rights, but only freedom, subject to a number of prohibitions, duties, boundaries and responsibilities. She got out her phone, did a word search in the NIV Bible for the word *'right'*, and came up with this verse from John's gospel which she quoted to me:

> **Yet to all who did receive him, to those who believed in his name, he gave the right to become children of God—**
>
>

John 1:12 (NIV)

as a matter of fact?

She thought this verse disproved my argument and justified her stance. However, what John is speaking about in John 1:12 is not an *inherent, automatic entitlement* that a person is born with. He is referring to what a believer receives *as a result of meeting God's qualifying conditions*. That is His requirement that we *repent* and *receive* Jesus and *believe* in His name. A person who is truly converted and born again will, of course, receive a great many benefits and privileges.

first fulfill the obligation

Those will include the 'right' (or *'power'*, as the KJV and RSV more sensibly put it) to become children of God. However, there is nothing *inherent* in that. One is not *born* with that, as if it was an unconditional or automatic *entitlement*. Such status is only given *to those who respond to the Gospel* and not to those who don't. Moreover, it is only given to them *because* they respond to the Gospel. That is the crucial distinction between the way the Bible speaks and the way a rights-based system operates.

So, in terms of how the Bible speaks, which was the foundation for how the English legal system always used to operate before the arrival of human rights, a person can become entitled to *receive*, or *do*, or *be*, something. That is clearly biblical. We need look no further than Romans, where Paul speaks of how a worker's wages are not seen as a *gift*, but as his *due*, or entitlement. However, it is only because he has *worked*, that he acquires a *right* to his wages, if you want to put it that way. He had no right to any pay beforehand and thus, if he had not worked, he would receive no pay at all:

> **Now to one who works, his wages are not reckoned as a gift but as his due.**
>
>

Romans 4:4 (RSV)

The crucial distinction is that the worker only has a 'right' to wages *because he has met the employer's conditions.* He worked a certain number of hours and thus became legally entitled to wages for that work, under the terms of his contract of employment, just as the employer was equally entitled under the terms of that same contract, to receive his labour. But that payment of wages has nothing at all to do with the modern concept of *inherent* rights.

That means a right to which one is *automatically* entitled, *without having to do anything in return*, merely by virtue of being a human being. If it did have that meaning, then the worker in Romans chapter four would be entitled to receive

312

wages, as of right, regardless of whether he had worked or not, and irrespective of the *quality* or *duration* of his work.

Any legal system which is founded upon the man-centred notion that human beings are born with a number of inherent and undeniable rights is starting from the wrong place. What then *should* our law assume, and on what *should* it be based? The short answer is that it should be God-centred. Therefore, it should reflect the way that God thinks and operates, as is set out in the Bible, not the way that sinful and misguided human beings think.

The biblical approach is the very opposite of rights-based thinking

The biblical approach is that no inherent or automatic rights are conferred by God upon anybody at all. Instead, the Bible takes a radically different approach. It begins from the starting point that every person is *free*, and has freedom of choice, *but that they also owe a series of duties* mainly to God, but also indirectly, at a secondary level, to our fellow human beings. For example, every one of us is under a primary duty to worship God and to obey Him. That puts God very firmly at the centre and, equally firmly, it removes us from the centre.

Then, at a secondary, or subordinate, level, we are also under a duty to love our neighbour and to do to him as we would wish him to do to us. So, our neighbour benefits, though only *indirectly*, from the fact that we are under a duty to obey God's commands. But our duty towards our neighbour does not arise because of any merit on his part. Neither is it due to, or based upon, any inherent entitlement. Our duty to treat him well arises *because God says so,* not because of anything our neighbour has done to deserve it.

On that basis, the reason we may not kill people, or mistreat them in a host of other ways, is because *God forbids us to do so.* Strictly speaking, therefore, it is not that those other people have a *right to live*, or even a *right not to be killed or mistreated.* The correct way to put it, if we wish to approach this biblically, is that *we* have a *duty* not to kill or mistreat them. Or you could say that we are *not free* to kill or mistreat them. In other words, it works in the exact opposite direction to that of any legal system which is founded upon human rights.

The biblical way of viewing things is that we must obey all God's commands, and not do anything which He has forbidden. A legal system constructed along those lines *puts God at the centre and makes Him important*, rather than *us.* Conversely, any system based on human rights elevates man, puts man at the centre, and makes man important. More to the point, it makes *oneself* important. Most rights-based systems do not even recognise that God *exists at all*, let alone acknowledge any duty to obey Him.

313

The concept of human rights promotes pride and a general emphasis on self. It also feeds our sinful flesh nature and panders to it, which is the opposite of what God wants. Accordingly, any Christian who wants to think about law, politics and social policy in a biblical way needs to consider very carefully the source or origins of their thinking. They must ask whether it is man-made, and reflects the flawed ways in which *we* think, or comes from God and reflects the perfect ways in which *He* thinks.

Likewise, we need to ask *who is exalted by it*, and whether it puts *man or God at the centre*. Any set of laws or public policies which is based on biblical thinking will always be expressed in terms of words like *duty, obligation, responsibility, stewardship* and, of course, *freedom*. Above all, it will speak in terms of *right and wrong*. It will not contain anything about rights or entitlements, except where those arise as a consequence of our fulfilling the conditions of some contract or covenant.

The damaging implications, unintended consequences, and even absurdities, of rights-based thinking

This distinction is not just theoretical hair-splitting about abstract, philosophical concepts. It makes a real and practical difference. Indeed, the ultimate outworking of any rights-based system is that it will inevitably result in injustices, and even absurdities. For example, at the time of writing this, the UK Government is proposing to introduce a system of age checks to prevent children getting access to online pornography. Most people would view that as a very sensible and necessary step to take to protect our kids from harm.

However, a United Nations official has warned the UK that any such measures would be a "breach of human rights". He means that any requirement for people to verify that they are 18 or over before viewing pornography would be a breach of their *right to privacy*. But who says that anyone has such a right? At any rate, who says that children have such a right, especially when seeking to view harmful material contrary to their parents' wishes? God certainly doesn't. He has told us to *"train up a child in the way that he should go....."*

But we can't do that if we aren't allowed to impose any rules or standards on children, or even to ask them to prove they are 18. One sees that same absurdity regularly in reported court cases. The application of the Human Rights Act in a criminal case, or civil dispute, results in the wrongdoer being protected, and even rewarded, and the interests of the victim, witnesses, or public being ignored. At the very least, they are considered to be subordinate to the wrongdoer's supposed 'rights'.

314

As a result of the London bombings of 7 July 2005, even the then Labour Government's enthusiasm for the Human Rights Act cooled down. They discovered, as subsequent governments also have, that they cannot deport suspected, or even *convicted*, terrorists. It is claimed that they might face the risk of torture, or of degrading and inhuman treatment, if they were returned to their own countries. Therefore, to avoid that potential risk to them, it is held that we must let them stay in the United Kingdom. Indeed, in one recent case, the court refused deportation because it was claimed that the cell in which the offender would be kept, if he was deported to his home country, would be too small and would not be comfortable! *A law without consequence will be broken without a second thought*

Consequently, the wrongdoer is protected from that perceived risk of torture, or even discomfort, whether real or otherwise, but innocent members of the public are knowingly *put at risk* in order to make that possible. However, no equivalent hand-wringing takes place over the prospect of putting the general public at risk, or endangering the witnesses who cooperated with the police by providing evidence. Their interests, and even their safety, count for little or nothing because a rights-based system has no real place for them, or at least no prominent place.

But if the prosecution do not have enough *admissible* evidence, or evidence which they are *willing to make public*, then they cannot convict the suspect either. Therefore, in many instances, he can't even be imprisoned in the UK, let alone deported. Given that we cannot convict them, and cannot deport them, we then have no other option but to let them go free. Having done so, the absurdity is further compounded by the galling fact that we then have to provide them with ongoing social security benefits, and even housing, to which they are also entitled – as of right.

Indeed, we even have to provide them with legal aid to fund their applications to resist our own attempts to deport them. Even Tony Blair, the man who inflicted the Human Rights Act upon us, spoke of his frustration at these unintended consequences of his legislation. As he put it, mainly in relation to Islamic terrorism, "*the rules of the game are changing*". He therefore began to wonder, at least to some extent, about the value of the Convention and even of the Human Rights Act itself.

Many Home Secretaries have expressed similar concerns since then, although with equal inability, and unwillingness, to do anything about these problems. When those undesirable consequences occur, as they so often do, it is not a coincidence. They arise foreseeably, and even inevitably, because a rights-based system does not think in terms of *good and evil* or *right and wrong*. Neither does it think of *justice* as requiring criminals and victims to be treated differently, as they each *deserve* to be treated, in view of their actions.

315

It is not designed to think in those terms and therefore makes no attempt to do so. Those concepts are not even recognised by, and do not easily fit within, any such system. That is why rights-based systems do not differentiate adequately, or at all, between offenders and victims, or even between wrongdoers and witnesses. They see them all as essentially equal. Indeed, if anything, where their interests come into conflict, the human rights agenda consistently puts the welfare of wrongdoers ahead of that of the victim, the witnesses, or the general public.

A rights-based criminal justice system struggles to accommodate the concept of punishment

A rights-based system also has difficulty in accommodating concepts like *punishment* or *retribution*, as it does not even think in those terms. Many people who work within the criminal justice system today are somewhat embarrassed by such words and even object to them. They consider them outdated, or even primitive, concepts and are uncomfortable about any policy or practice where the aim is to punish. Thus the very idea of punishment, which is an essential aspect of justice, *and which the Bible clearly endorses*, is toned down or even rejected as invalid.

By contrast, the aim of *rehabilitation of the offender*, which is a valid, albeit a secondary, part of any biblically based criminal justice system, is then made central. But that is not its proper place. Moreover, rehabilitation is changed from being an *objective* on the part of the *justice system,* to being a *right* on the part of the *wrongdoer*. But he has no such right, at least not in any biblically based system. Rehabilitation is an aspect of God's *grace*, i.e. His *undeserved favour*, albeit that it is delivered via human governments and agencies.

To convert it into a right is to seriously distort the proper position. For one thing, it would cease to be grace because that is, by definition, *undeserved*. However, someone might ask what the alternative is. Should we say that we are in favour of torture? Of course not. All that is needed for us to make torture illegal is *simply to ban it*. That is how the objective can best be achieved, not by declaring that each of us have a 'right not to be tortured' or, even less, a right never to be *put at any risk* of being tortured, which is an argument that is now routinely used when we seek to deport criminals and terrorists.

That approach, whereby the things that we deplore, such as torture, are simply *prohibited*, may sound similar to creating a *right not to be tortured*. However, there is a profound difference which is principally seen in the respective *outcomes*. If we simply make it *a crime to torture people*, rather than creating *a right not to be tortured*, we achieve the objective, without any of the unintended

316

consequences. It is these undesirable side effects of a rights-based approach that create the problems.

Simply banning torture, or any other activity that we wish to prevent, creates few, if any, knock-on effects to the detriment of victims, witnesses, the public, or taxpayers. However, that apparently slight adjustment of turning it from a prohibition into a right creates a mass of unintended problems. We then have to try to tackle all the implications of what we have declared a person's rights to be. All sorts of other people then have to be disadvantaged, or even put at risk, to enable those supposed rights to be observed.

None of that occurs when we think, as we always used to, along the much simpler lines of banning what is not in the public interest and leaving everything else well alone. The way the unbelieving world thinks on this subject will influence your own thinking unless you actively resist being squeezed into the world's mould. Rights-based thinking has already extended its pernicious influence way beyond the realms of criminal law and the civil justice system. Once you begin to look out for it, you see its consequences all over the place.

The entitlement culture which rights-based thinking creates

One could say that in Great Britain we are developing a *'culture of entitlement'*. I have witnessed this trend at first hand as an employer. Employees, especially those in their teens or twenties, are increasingly entering the workplace with an inbuilt sense of having rights. It is typical for them to have at the forefront of their minds what they can expect to *get,* as opposed to what they are expected to *give.* They are also concerned not to have to work too hard, or for too long, or not to have to do more work than their colleagues do.

A person who has been brought up to think in terms of entitlements may ask what his job involves, but he does so primarily to make sure that he does "*no more than he has* to," or "*no more than others do.*" By contrast, a worker who thinks in terms of duty will ask himself "*How can I make sure I pull my weight and do no less than I should, and preferably more than is expected of me?*" I may possibly meet the legal definition of an 'expert witness' on this point, given how many people I have employed over the years and the breadth of perspective which that has given me.

I have seen enough employees at close quarters, as a boss, and before that as a colleague, for my conclusions to have some statistical reliability. At any rate, my overall assessment of the *average* British worker, with some shining exceptions, is that they are deficient. Many are like spoilt children. Indeed, for some, that is literally what they are. They put themselves at the centre and think primarily, or

317

even solely, of what they can expect to *get from* their job, not what they can *put into it.*

That is why so many British employers, especially in the hotels and hospitality sectors and also in seasonal jobs like fruit picking, prefer to recruit their staff from Eastern Europe where the culture of entitlement has not yet taken over. When I go to hotels and restaurants, I frequently find that staff from Eastern Europe (unless they are Muslims) *work harder* in relative terms, do *more* work in absolute terms, operate to a *higher standard,* have a better *attitude,* and show better *manners.*

They also have a better overall understanding of the concept of '*service*', than native British workers who have grown up in the UK and been to British schools. The contrast is stark. Of course, no politician will publicly admit any of this. Neither will any employer, as saying openly what I have just said, would put himself at risk of an action for discrimination. So, employers who recruit from abroad will say that they only do so because there is a "*labour shortage in that sector*", not because foreign workers are 'better'.

There is an element of truth in the claim that they can't find enough British staff, but that is not because our population is too small. It is largely because some British people would rather be unemployed than apply for certain jobs. Many are not willing to do "*dirty work*" or to "*demean themselves*" by taking a manual job or a job cleaning in a hotel or serving in a restaurant. However, even that is not the whole truth. Even where native British workers are willing to apply for such jobs, many employers still prefer workers from abroad because they do not have a culture of entitlement.

An example of a young man with an entitlement mind-set

I once recruited a young man aged 19 to work in my law firm. He wanted to be a 'legal clerk', and also to be trained up in the IT department. In his very first week in the job we had to move some furniture from one office to another. The whole task would take about 30 minutes. I was actually doing this myself, assisted by the IT manager. So, we were both senior people in the business but we were, nevertheless, moving furniture, and quite happily.

I then said to the young man who had just joined the firm: "*Can you come and give us a hand carrying this furniture to the other end of the office?*" I said this with the full expectation that he would join in willingly. But he didn't. He said that moving furniture was "*not part of my job description*" and that he "*should not be asked to do it*". I was amazed by his view of himself, and of what he should, and should not, be asked to do. That attitude was so deeply ingrained in him that he was even willing to argue with his new boss in his first week in the job and to refuse, point-blank, to assist.

He did not see himself as doing anything wrong, or even unusual. As he saw it, an illegitimate request was being made and he was standing up for himself. He felt that moving furniture was beneath his dignity and that it was demeaning to be seen doing manual labour in front of other staff. Yet the extraordinary thing is that the IT manager and I, who were both senior to him, were already tackling the very same task. We didn't feel demeaned, or that manual labour was "*beneath us*", but he did.

Even when this irony was pointed out, he still did not alter his view. Unsurprisingly, that young man did not get through his probationary period. I parted with him later that week, because of his appalling attitude. I then got a phone call from his Dad, taking his side and remonstrating with me, even when I explained what had happened. He too felt that his son had done nothing wrong and "*should not have been asked to do manual work*". He pointed out that it was "*not in the job description*" and that it was "*wrong for him to be asked to do it.*"

I told him that moving furniture wasn't in the IT manager's job description either - or mine for that matter. But that argument did not cut any ice with him, any more that it had with his son. So far as he was concerned, his son was being "*taken advantage of*". This story illustrates the extent to which the culture of entitlement is creating a generation of pampered prima donnas or '*snowflakes*' as they are now called. However, it is by no means confined to the workplace.

It has radiated out across many other areas of British society. That is why I have spent so much time focusing upon this issue of human rights, or rights-based thinking, which some might regard as an obscure subject. It has now become for us a major new aspect of worldly thinking, which past generations never had to deal with. Thus, it is worth making the effort to understand what this new philosophy is, where it comes from, and how we can avoid adopting such misguided beliefs, or being influenced by them.

Most important of all, we need to ensure that the culture of rights, or even the language of rights, does not creep into our churches or our theology. It is not consistent with our being called to a life of s*ervanthood* and, even more so, to the need for us to '*die to self*', '*pick up our cross daily*', and '*crucify our flesh nature*'. No disciple can achieve any of those things, all of which we are commanded to do, if we confer upon ourselves a wide range of imaginary rights which God has never given us.

Entitlement: My due, what I deserve, owed
I should not be challenged, questioned...

319

CHAPTER 11

WISE PEOPLE SEEK TO BECOME EXCELLENT AND FAITHFUL WORKERS

Do you see a man skilful in his work?
* he will stand before kings;*
* he will not stand before obscure men.*
*   Proverbs 22:29 (RSV)*

Whoever works his land will have plenty of bread,
* but he who follows worthless pursuits will have plenty of poverty.*
*   Proverbs 28:19 (ESV)*

Like an archer who wounds everyone
* is one who hires a passing fool or drunkard.*
*   Proverbs 26:10 (ESV)*

Know well the condition of your flocks,
* and give attention to your herds,*
*   Proverbs 27:23 (ESV)*

The hand of the diligent will rule,
* while the slothful will be put to forced labor.*
*   Proverbs 12:24 (ESV)*

"Do not love sleep, lest you become poor.......
*   Proverbs 20:13(a) (NASB)*

Most people hugely underestimate the importance of their job in God's eyes and the part it plays in their growth as a disciple

In 36 years as a Christian I have never heard a single sermon on work, or on the role our job plays in both revealing and developing the quality of our character. Neither have I ever heard any leader say how important our job is to God. Doesn't that strike you as odd, given that we spend one third of our lives working, which is actually half of our waking hours, because eight are spent in sleep? You might imagine it would be obvious that our job is vitally important, and that God really cares about how hard we work, how faithful we are to customers and colleagues, and whether we honour our bosses.

321

Yet, somehow, none of this is ever spoken about at all, let alone focused upon. One reason for it being so widely ignored is that most church leaders have either never had a normal secular job at all, or it was many years ago. Therefore, they don't feel confident in teaching about work, the workplace, client care, or handling colleagues and bosses. Another reason is the widely held view that Christianity is about what you do in church meetings, not what you do the rest of the week, least of all at the workplace.

Few would ever say that explicitly, but it is deeply embedded in many people's minds. However, that is not how God sees it. Our job is of vital importance to Him. It is one of the ways, if not the main way, that He exposes us to different types of people, experiences, challenges and pressures, to help us to grow in character and maturity as disciples. Sadly, my subjective opinion of the *average* worker, at least in the UK, is that they are not faithful or committed. They have only a limited work ethic, little understanding of the concept of service, and are resentful of, and even hostile to, their bosses.

One sees and hears their negativity as they express their dissatisfaction and unhappiness about their job and how they dislike their own boss, and bosses in general. I saw a Facebook post in which the writer was scathing about bosses. It was oozing with contempt and also spoke as if all bosses are tyrants, not just some, and as if all employees are abused and downtrodden. I responded to suggest that if each worker was to examine himself, improve his own standards, and identify the faults in himself, instead of complaining about his boss, then he may well end up becoming the boss himself.

The person thought my comment was ridiculous, as if it was obvious that only bosses have faults, never employees. Someone might ask what the harm is in having an embittered attitude towards bosses, even if it isn't justified. The answer is that it undermines your performance as an employee and prevents you from being the kind of worker that God wants you to be. It also spills over into every other part of your life as well. Therefore, even if some of your grievances are well founded, it is still harmful for you if you become sour as a result of holding on to them.

A far better response, even if you truly do have a bad boss, is to look for another job. But, in the meantime, make sure that you provide excellent and faithful service while you are in your current job. That will not only please God, it will also benefit you and help you to grow in self-control, endurance and maturity. That said, I have learned from experience, and from my own mistakes as I now look back, that one should be very slow to conclude that one has a 'bad boss'. It is possible that you do, but it is at least equally possible, if not more likely, that some or all of the fault is yours, not his.

I can think of some stern sergeants and inspectors who put me through my paces when I was young. They returned my paperwork to me for amendment, sometimes repeatedly, and told me off for my errors. However, as I now reflect on those men, with the benefit of over 30 years of experience, and having been a supervisor, boss and employer myself, I see them differently. If my 21 year old former self was to come and work for me today I would have a few salty things to say to him myself that he may not like. In fact, I would probably correct him more robustly than my old bosses corrected me.

Do not assume, automatically, that you are in the right and that any criticism of you is unfounded

We therefore need to guard against complacency, self-righteousness and the automatic assumption of being in the right. Those attitudes come so naturally to us. Very few people, when faced with a boss who is criticising or correcting them, will think to themselves: *"I need to improve and stop causing problems for my boss, such that he is not put to further inconvenience, or financial loss, and no longer has the unpleasant task of having to correct me."* A more common response, however, would be something along these lines: *"Who does he think he is to tell me off and to find fault with my work for no reason?"*

Therefore, if you want to become an excellent worker, which we all ought to want, but very few of us actually do want, one of the first steps is to stop resenting your employer. Force yourself to begin to value and appreciate him, whatever his deficiencies may be, or seem to be. If you feel he has some faults, or is making wrong decisions, the chances are you don't fully or properly understand all the facts. If you knew everything that he knows about what is really going on, his actions and decisions would probably make a lot more sense and you would no longer view them in the same way.

Therefore, when a manager does something which makes no sense to you, or even seems unfair, don't leap to the conclusion that they are acting wrongly. Very often a manager cannot reveal all the background facts or give the staff all the evidence they have. For one reason or another, the facts may have to be kept confidential, even where that silence causes the manager's actions to be misunderstood. Therefore, give bosses the benefit of the doubt. At least delay coming to a negative conclusion about them until you know a lot more about the situation and the wider facts.

Over the years I realised that one of the many tests God uses is to put us in positions of stress and difficulty in the workplace and to see how we react. He wants to see how we will treat customers, colleagues, and especially bosses, when we are under pressure, and whether we remain faithful and respectful towards them. Of all these tests, perhaps the hardest is being required to give honour and loyalty to a boss who, *in your subjective opinion,* is not showing honour or loyalty *to you.*

I put the above words in italics because it is very difficult to be objective when you are in a stressful situation, or are being criticised. It is really hard to see yourself, and your own attitude and behaviour, as others do, and as they really are, rather than as you imagine them to be. We are all naturally self-centred, and even self-absorbed, as a result of our sinful flesh nature. Therefore, our automatic reflex reaction, unless we force ourselves not to do so, is to see ourselves as being in the right. We then justify ourselves in a millisecond, rejecting all blame, and resenting anyone who criticises us.

It is therefore seen as a given that anyone who is criticising us must obviously be:

a)   a horrible person

b)   hostile to us for no valid reason

c)   out to get us

d)   wrong in what he says, and even an idiot

e)   someone whom we should resent and defend ourselves from

Of course, it may be that someone who is criticising you really *is* some or all of those things. It would depend on all the facts. But those facts would first need to be carefully investigated and then reflected upon objectively, and with an open mind, not merely assumed. However, in the specific context of the workplace, the likelihood of a boss being a bad person who is out to get you for no good reason is low. At any rate, it is far less than the 100% certainty which most employees assume it to be when their performance or attitude is criticised.

A wise person, although tempted to justify himself when criticised, will try to overcome that tendency. He will force himself to stand back and weigh up the situation objectively and to assess *whether* he is in the right, rather than assume it automatically. He will also reflect open-mindedly on any criticisms, so as to weigh up whether there is any truth in them, and if so how much truth, and what he can learn from those remarks. Moreover, he will do this even if the comments were not made graciously by a kind, sensitive, tactful boss, but bluntly and rudely by an unkind, ungracious one.

The truth or otherwise of a criticism is not to be determined solely by the manner in which it was said, but by the intrinsic merit, or lack of merit, of the points being made. Sometimes, only a harsh, unkind, unfriendly person is willing to say blunt things to us. Our friends, and even the kinder, gentler bosses, will not do so. Therefore, the fact that the remark feels wounding, and is said by an unkind boss, who may even have intended it to be hurtful, does not, in and of itself, render the criticism invalid.

Of course, it may be invalid. It could be a lie, or a deliberate, unfounded, malicious attack on you. But the point is that no assumption should be made, *in any direction*, until you have forced yourself to weigh the criticism and to examine the evidence, both for and against, with ruthless objectivity. In this way a wise person can learn valuable lessons about his own weaknesses, bad attitudes and faults, *even from his enemies*. He can even do so from those who hate him and who are not seeking to help him at all, but only to knock him down.

Although such people often lie and exaggerate, they do not always do so. Sometimes even their words may contain a grain of truth, from which you can learn. You would probably never have received that lesson from your friends, or even from a kindly, supportive boss. That is why I eventually learned to give thanks even for unkind, harsh bosses, or senior colleagues, who have, in some ways, been unfair to me. God has used them to show me things about my own weaknesses and faults which nobody else would have been willing, or able, to show me.

Seek to learn lessons from every type of boss, good or bad, and to pass all of the tests that God sets for you

If you want to grow in maturity generally, and also in your skill, faithfulness and reliability as an employee, then recognise, and seek to pass, the various tests that God sets for you in the workplace. Realise *what* God is testing, and *why* He is testing it. Cooperate willingly as God uses bosses, colleagues and clients, plus the general demands and pressures of the workplace, to refine your character, increase your maturity, and expose and remove your faults. Once you begin to reflect upon it, God's approach and technique as your ultimate 'line manager' makes perfect sense.

If you lack resilience or endurance, what better way is there for God to address those faults than by putting you into a tough situation, or a dysfunctional team, or by giving you a strict boss, such that you are put under pressure? The demands which are made of you will expose your deficiencies and cause you to grow. It is obvious once you stop and think about it, but most of us never do stop and think about it. We have absorbed an image of God as a soft, cuddly figure who would never put us under any pressure and would always want us to be sheltered and to feel comfortable.

In fact, God is infinitely loving, and wants the very best for you, but He also wants you to grow as a disciple. That can't be achieved without exposing you to a long series of tests, pressures and stresses, which you would never willingly inflict upon yourself. God knows that you would always dodge such trials unless you were forced to face them. You might therefore be praying earnestly for Him to give you a 'better' boss, who will be 'nice' to you. But God may be thinking that what you actually need is an even stricter boss who will be firmer with you. Therefore, a wiser prayer would be:

"LORD, please give me the type of boss that I need, rather than the type that I would like to have. Then please let him continue to be my boss for as long as is necessary to enable me to change, to pass your tests, and to learn the things that I need to learn."

Whether or not you pray that sensible prayer, or choose instead to complain about your boss, the reality is that God will probably send you a number of strict, demanding, and even harsh bosses. He does it on purpose, not to punish you, but to refine you. He knows you need such bosses, whether you know it or not, and whether you ask Him for them or not. So, you are inevitably going to get such bosses, at least from time to time, regardless of whether you ask for them, or realise the vital role they play in your life, and even if you ask *not* to have them.

However, there is still a major advantage to be gained from asking God to send you a challenging boss who will require you to change. That sensible attitude, and willingness to cooperate, will make the refining and maturing process easier. It will also make it shorter than it would be if God had to impose it on you, against your wishes and contrary to your prayers. In other words, no matter how much you dislike it, God is determined to change you and to see you grow and mature.

Therefore, you might as well cooperate willingly, and even thankfully, with the inevitable, rather than keep up a futile fight against it. There may be pleasant seasons when God will let you have a kind, gracious, considerate boss, from whom you can learn how things *should* be done and how a business ought to be managed. You need to give thanks whenever you have such a boss, even if it is only for a while. They are useful role models for you, as well as being a privilege and a blessing while they last.

That said, few people ever do give thanks for good bosses, or even recognise them as being such. At least they don't tend to do so at the time, but only after they, or the boss, have moved on. Therefore, it is an even rarer person who is wise enough to give thanks to God for a strict, demanding, or even harsh boss, *while they are still working for them.* Yet we should give thanks for them because, if we can bring ourselves to listen willingly and fully cooperate, such bosses can do us a lot of good by:

Pray for God go towards the fire 326

a) revealing, tackling and removing those faults in us which neither we, nor a gentle boss, would ever have dealt with

b) at the very least, giving us a 'reverse role model', i.e. showing us how things should *not* be done, how a business should *not* be managed, and how other people should *not* be treated. Seeing such things demonstrated in practice, almost like a laboratory experiment, can be really useful and you can learn from their errors without having to make them yourself. Therefore, never under-estimate the value of those "negative" lessons. There have been many men whom God has used in my career to help me to see what I must *not be*, and how I must *not act*. *How we associate 'truth' with positive - neue - negative.*

Some might ask if there is any point in addressing their own bad habits and faults if their current boss and colleagues have such a low opinion of them that they would not be willing to alter it, even if they were to change. You may feel that you have made such a bad start in a job, or given such a bad impression, that those around you will never alter their view of you. Even if that is so, seeking to change yourself is still worthwhile. Ultimately, you are not doing it for their sake, or to win their approval. It is for your own sake, so that you can become a success and be a better worker, and a better person, in future.

It may be that the only people who will ever think more highly of you will be your *future* employers and colleagues in your *next place of work*, after you have moved on. But for that to be so, you need to change *now*, in your *current job*, even while you are with people who may not be willing to re-assess their view of you, no matter how excellent you become. You have to be realistic about this. Remember also that your key objective is not to change the opinions of your current employers. It is primarily to change *yourself* and your own attitudes, habits and methods, regardless of whether anyone notices. *My ultimate for his higher*

Your aim therefore must be to actually become an excellent employee, even if those with whom you currently work have a fixed view of you which they will never be willing to change. If you think in this way you can make good use of the next few months, or even a year or more, while you are addressing your faults and changing your attitudes and habits, *before you move elsewhere*. Then you will be better placed to be a success when you move on to your next job, where people won't know you, and where you can build a new reputation.

If you were to move jobs immediately, before you have actually changed your ways, the next employer would be likely to form the same negative impression of you as your current one has formed. Then you will have lost the opportunity to make a genuinely fresh start there. Therefore never think that there is no point in changing. Also never hold back from the process of change, just because others cannot see your improvements, or won't acknowledge them. To do so would

327

make you the prisoner of other men's opinions, which you must never allow yourself to be.

Let us now consider more closely the kind of faults, bad attitudes and bad habits which a great many workers have about their job, their clients or their boss, and which God wants a Christian to get rid of. I am probably in a position to give what the law calls 'expert evidence' on this subject as I have been in various jobs and businesses and at every level, from the bottom to the top, and every stage in between. That breadth of experience over three decades means I can see the issues and problems of the workplace from just about every angle.

There cannot be many situations that I have not faced, or types of worker, colleague, client or boss that I have not worked under or alongside, or whom I have not managed. It is rare for any Christian leader, writer or Bible teacher to have such breadth of perspective, because most have never had a secular job or run a business, or at least not for long. They usually go into so called "full time ministry" in their early to mid-twenties and never get to see any secular workplace from then on, if indeed they have ever seen one at all.

The nearest thing they have to a workplace from then on is the churches they serve in, or rather rule over, as is so often the case, and as I discuss in Book 8. I will now set out, and briefly explain, a non-exhaustive list of some of the main sins, faults, weaknesses and bad attitudes which a great many workers have. However, very few even recognise these faults in themselves, let alone seek to remedy or remove them. In my experience, the most common faults are as follows:

Fault 1 - Laziness

Most people assume that laziness is only one of the minor sins, at most, if indeed it is even a sin at all. However, that is absolutely not God's view. He has a lot to say about it. In fact, the Bible has more to say about laziness than about drunkenness, or many other things which most of us would assume to be more serious matters. Here are some examples:

Now we command you, brethren, in the name of our Lord Jesus Christ, that you keep away from any brother who is living in idleness and not in accord with the tradition that you received from us.

2 Thessalonians 3:6 (RSV)

A slack hand causes poverty,
but the hand of the diligent makes rich
Proverbs 10:4 (ESV)

In all toil there is profit,
  but mere talk tends only to poverty.
                  Proverbs 14:23 (ESV)

The sluggard does not plow in the autumn;
  he will seek at harvest and have nothing.
                  Proverbs 20:4 (ESV)

30 I passed by the field of a sluggard,
  by the vineyard of a man lacking sense,
31 and behold, it was all overgrown with thorns;
  the ground was covered with nettles,
  and its stone wall was broken down.
32 Then I saw and considered it;
  I looked and received instruction.
33 A little sleep, a little slumber,
  a little folding of the hands to rest,
34 and poverty will come upon you like a robber,
  and want like an armed man.
                  Proverbs 24:30-34 (ESV)

She looks well to the ways of her household,
  and does not eat the bread of idleness.
                  Proverbs 31:27 (RSV)

Through sloth the roof sinks in,
  and through indolence the house leaks.
                  Ecclesiastes 10:18 (RSV)

Therefore, begin to examine yourself with rigorous objectivity and ask whether you are genuinely a hard worker who gives their full energy and attention to their work. Or, are you actually at some point along the 'laziness spectrum', such that you don't work wholeheartedly, with 100% effort and commitment, or at least not always? Don't be too quick to find yourself not guilty. Any genuine answer would require real self-examination, over a sustained period of time, not a quick, snap response.

However, even if you conclude that you are *less lazy* than your colleagues that does not mean that you aren't lazy. It just means, if indeed it is even true, that you may be less lazy than them. But that is nothing to be proud of. You might as well congratulate yourself for lying or stealing less often than they do. God doesn't merely want His people to be less lazy than unbelievers. He wants us not to be lazy *at all*. So do employers. You therefore need to become a hard worker in absolute terms, not merely relative to those who are even lazier than you.

329

That said, if you are going to arrive at a correct assessment of your own work ethic, you will probably also need to change your definition of the word *'hard'*. In my experience, many people consider themselves to be a hard worker when, by my definition, or even by the standards of the average person, they are nothing of the sort. Therefore, some radical rethinking and redefining will be needed for most of us if we want to become genuinely hard-working in objective terms, and by the proper, biblical definition.

Fault 2 - Low standards and lack of attention to detail

Again, this is a fault which most people either don't know they have, or refuse to admit, or don't care about, even if they do admit it. I am referring to the fact that many workers do low quality work. They cut corners, miss things and don't bother to check for errors. They are too quick to say *"It will do,"* rather than do the job again, redraft a report, or double check a piece of work. God does not like that attitude. He wants you to be a diligent worker, with high quality standards, and to pay close attention to the condition of your 'flocks' or, in modern terms, your patients, customers or clients:

Know well the condition of your flocks,
and give attention to your herds,
Proverbs 27:23 (ESV)

One of the key tests of a worker is how well they do a task when they know nobody is watching and that nobody will ever check what they have done. For example, how well do they paint the back of a shed which they know nobody is ever going to see? Unless a person has that quality control mechanism solidly built into them as a value or habit, they will be satisfied with low standards. They will then do as poor a job as they are allowed to get away with.

They can only be made to work to an acceptable standard by putting supervisors in place to monitor their work and force them to do so. They have no inbuilt desire, within themselves, to ensure that their work is of a good standard. They do it only because they must, and *because someone is watching,* not because they *want to,* of their own free will.

But the truth is that there is always someone watching. God Himself sees every piece of work you ever do, even as you paint the back of a shed. Indeed, He watches such things closely and takes a keen interest. Therefore, always do your very best work, even if nobody is watching, and even if nobody will ever check it because, so far as God is concerned, you are doing it all for Him:

330

And whatever you do, in word or deed, do everything in the name of the Lord Jesus, giving thanks to God the Father through him.

Colossians 3:17 (ESV)

Don't just assume, as most do, that you are a good worker. Ask yourself honestly whether the quality of your work would be any better if a supervisor was nearby, or if you knew they would check your work later. If it would, then ask yourself why because, by rights, it should make no difference. You should appoint yourself as your own supervisor, insisting on the highest possible standards from yourself, regardless of whether anybody else will ever see, or find out, or punish you. Your objective should not be merely to avoid getting into trouble, but to do the best work that you can do, because:

a) You are being paid a wage to do so.

b) The customer has paid your employer for a proper service or product and is therefore entitled to it.

c) You have a contractual duty to your employer to work to a high standard – whether or not he ever finds out.

d) God is watching and checking *everything you ever say or do*. Moreover, He will one day reward or rebuke you for the way in which you did it. (See my Book 4 on The Judgment Seat of Christ)

None of those reasons are anything to do with your boss, or the customer, ever finding out that your work was of a poor standard and punishing you. Admittedly, that may happen, but your apprehension about that ought not to be necessary to motivate you to work properly. It is only needed because of the Fall, when Adam brought sin into the world. What Adam did on that terrible day made it necessary for employers ever since to check up on their workers and force them to maintain high standards, and to work in a trustworthy manner.

If you want to become a faithful disciple, then use the workplace to help you to grow. Aim to make it unnecessary for your employers to supervise you, at least in terms of making sure you work hard and pay attention to detail. It will always be necessary, even with an honest, hard-working employee, to give training and check for *errors* while they learn the *skills* needed to do the job. That is entirely different. It is no sin to make mistakes, or not to know things, or to have not yet developed the skills and experience we need. Even Jesus had to increase in wisdom and stature as He grew up:

And Jesus increased in wisdom and in stature and in favor with God and man.

Luke 2:52 (ESV)

Fault 3 - Unfaithfulness to bosses, clients and colleagues

It is not only in terms of the quality of our work, or our attention to detail, that we need to be faithful. God also requires us to be faithful in every other way, to our employer, our colleagues and also the clients or customers whom we are ultimately serving. He wants us to show complete faithfulness right across the board, and to behave justly, fairly, loyally, decently and honestly at all times. Indeed, He wants us to be faithful always, and with everyone, whether we are at work or not.

Yet, the contract of employment, or *'master-servant relationship'*, as it used to be called as recently as the 1970's, creates wider duties and higher expectations of faithfulness than those which apply generally. It therefore follows that higher standards are required of you at work than in everyday life because, in your contract, you have agreed to do many things which you are not obliged to do elsewhere. However, most of us give little or no thought to the implied 'duty of good faith' in our contracts. Therefore, genuinely faithful people are few and far between:

> *Many a man proclaims his own loyalty,*
> *but a faithful man who can find?*
> *Proverbs 20:6 (RSV)*

Some examples of faithful workers from the Bible are Barnabas and Silas who worked with Paul. Barnabas began as Paul's boss but, as Paul's stature grew, it became clear that God was raising Paul higher than him. Barnabas accepted that gracefully and humbly and became Paul's assistant instead. The way in which Luke writes of their exploits in the book of Acts reflects their change of roles. He begins by saying *"Barnabas and Saul"* but later says *"Saul and Barnabas"*. Few men would be capable of working for someone who used to work for them. Their pride would not permit it.

Later there was a difference of opinion over whether to allow Mark to resume working for them after he had deserted them. Paul did not trust Mark after that and refused to have him back. But Barnabas still saw a potential future ministry in Mark and wanted to give him another chance. In the end he separated from Paul, who refused to work with Mark, and took Mark to work for him. It ended well and Mark went on to be a major success. He was even given the honour of being allowed to write one of the gospels. That may never have happened if Barnabas had not remained faithful to Mark.

When that breach occurred, Paul chose Silas to be his main assistant, in place of Barnabas, and they went on to travel together from then on. In the book of Acts and the letters we see repeated references to Silas, who stays by Paul's side through all of the horrendous persecution that he later faces. Silas therefore ends up getting arrested with Paul in Acts 16:19, when they were dragged into the market place, beaten with rods and put in prison. Even so, Silas stayed with Paul and he did so again when they went to Thessalonica, where there was another riot by those who opposed Paul.

He then had to escape with Paul at night to flee to Berea, and then on to Athens, where they were, yet again, abused and rejected. Throughout many such harrowing experiences, virtually everywhere they ever went, Silas always stayed with Paul. He continued working for him, supporting him, and keeping him company, as Paul faced his many trials and afflictions. Would you have been willing to accept a job as Paul's assistant, given the awful working conditions and the continual suffering and persecution it involved?

More to the point, would you have been willing to *stay in the job* and not resign and seek an easier position with an employer who is less unpopular? We know from how Mark and others deserted Paul that it was not an easy job, to put it mildly. Very few people were willing to do it, and especially to stick at it. I have a strong suspicion that, when the Millennial Kingdom begins, Silas may well be assigned a very high place, as a reward for his extraordinary faithfulness to Paul, and for all that he endured in order not to let him down.

Another example of faithfulness is Baruch, the assistant and secretary to the prophet Jeremiah, who was almost as unpopular as Paul and faced similar persecution and imprisonment as he carried out the tasks God gave him. Yet throughout it all, Baruch was constantly by his side, serving him, supporting him and sharing all the same dangers. But no letter of resignation was ever handed to Jeremiah by Baruch. He stayed faithful and even went to the Temple, at Jeremiah's request, (in Jeremiah chapter 36) and spoke there in Jeremiah's place.

He had to go because his boss had been banned from entering the Temple as he was so unpopular with the authorities. Reflect on the risk that Baruch was taking. He went to the Temple and read out Jeremiah's words publicly, *"in the hearing of all the people"* despite the obvious danger to himself, and also the unpleasantness of being insulted while doing so. That act of obedience took tremendous moral courage and loyalty, for which I am sure Baruch will be rewarded in the coming Kingdom. Even so, the Bible records it very briefly, with no fanfare. It simply says:

And Baruch the son of Neriah did all that Jeremiah the prophet ordered him about reading from the scroll the words of the LORD in the LORD'S house.
Jeremiah 36:8 (ESV)

A fictional example of faithfulness to an employer is *Sam Gamgee*, Frodo Baggins' gardener in *The Lord of the Rings* by *JRR Tolkien*. My favourite character is not Frodo or Gandalf or Aragorn, or any of the other mighty figures. The one I most admire, and wish to emulate, is Sam Gamgee. He is the best example I can think of in literature of what it means to be an utterly faithful servant. Sam is completely devoted to Frodo and 100% committed to serving him and staying by his side, no matter what dangers Frodo faced.

He even goes with him into Mordor, when they faced what seemed to be certain death. At all times Sam put Frodo's needs first, giving him most of the food and water, keeping watch over him as he slept, and defending him from every danger. If you haven't seen the film or read the book I would urge you to do so. If you do, keep an eye on Sam. He is never the star of the show, but you will see in him a vivid illustration of what faithfulness is. Ask God to help you to become like that, but even more so, like Silas, Baruch and Barnabas, in your dealings with your own boss and the company you work for.

However, don't make the mistake of thinking that you only need to be faithful to those who are faithful to you, or only to the same extent as they are towards you. The degree to which other people are faithful to you, or whether they are kind or unkind, gracious or ungracious, polite or impolite, has no bearing on *how you must treat them*. Thus, even if your boss is rude, ungrateful, inconsiderate, and demanding, you must still remain faithful to him, whilst ever you continue to be employed. You cannot simply do back to him whatever he does to you.

That does *not* mean, however, that God expects you to carry on permanently working for your current employer. It may or may not be a good idea to move on to a new job, but you are free to do so, without that being in any way unfaithful. Your faithfulness has to continue *for as long as you work for that employer*, but there is no duty to stay indefinitely if they treat you badly. Indeed, even if you are treated well, I generally advise any ambitious person to move to a new job, or a new role with the same firm, every 2 – 3 years. That way you maximise the experience you get and that is not wrong.

There is a diminishing marginal return in terms of what you learn if you stay forever in the same company, especially if you keep doing the very same job. Every time you get a new role, or change your employer, there will, for a time, be a steep increase in the gradient of your 'learning curve'. Then it flattens out again after about two years. Therefore, by all means develop your career and strengthen and broaden your CV by moving around. Simply make sure that you are always utterly faithful to each employer *while you are still working for them*.

Fault 4 – Not truly caring about their work, or the fate of their client, patient or customer, to the point where it really matters to them

Most employees that I have worked alongside or supervised had only a moderate level of diligence. They did not truly *care* about what happened on their files or what the outcome would be for their client. They therefore found it far too easy, in my view, to go home at night without feeling any concern for the client's welfare, or whether they were doing enough for him, or taking the right steps. Such issues always troubled me deeply. I identified so closely with every client that it pained me to think of letting them down or failing to do all that I possibly could for them.

I really wanted them to win, or to get justice, and I was willing to go the extra mile, and indeed several extra miles beyond that, to get them the very best outcome. As a result, I did a lot of thinking in my own time, even while I was driving or bathing or walking the dog. By doing so, I regularly came up with ideas and solutions to problems which I would never have thought of if the client's case had not mattered so much to me. Whereas others found it easy to switch off and forget the client, I never could. I treated them all as if they were my relatives and was determined to do the very best I could for them.

I am not saying this to boast, but merely to try to explain what it means to *really care* about a client, patient or customer. That attitude is now so rare that many find it hard even to understand the concept, let alone do it. Even more would instantly, but wrongly, imagine that their own level of interest, and the care and attention they give, *are* deep and genuine, and of the kind that I advocate. But they would only think that because they set the bar far too low. Thus they are congratulating themselves when they should, instead, be aghast at their own lack of care.

A stark example of what I am speaking of arose when I went to visit a friend in hospital one Sunday evening. The hospital was already operating on a skeletal staff basis because it was the weekend. Thus there were few nurses on duty. Yet, during my visit, I saw seven of them gather to chat at the nurses' 'station' in the corridor by the edge of the ward. There was only one nurse on duty per section, so, as they chatted, they were neglecting seven whole sections, each of which had several seriously ill patients.

I watched with growing dismay as this wilful neglect continued and began to time it by my watch. That is how I know it went on for 45 minutes, during which not one of those nurses ever checked on, or attended to, *any* of their patients. In case you are wondering, this was not their dinner break. Their breaks were staggered, precisely in order to avoid all the nurses being away from the patients at the same time. So, this entire episode took place *in work time*, while they were supposed to be *caring* for those patients.

I cannot imagine leaving my post of duty to chat with colleagues while leaving ill people unattended. One could only be capable of it if one's heart was callous and indifferent. That does not meet the definition of 'care' by anybody's standards, not just mine. The hearts of those seven nurses were cold and hard and I pity their patients. During those 45 minutes they could each have attended to their patients many times, if only to give them a cup of water or adjust their bedding. But they all did nothing.

Moreover, my friend, who had been in that ward for some days, said that what happened that evening was not unusual. The nurses regularly behaved in that way. It was part of the very culture of the hospital. In my own experience of visiting relatives in hospitals I have often seen similar examples of neglect, if not for so long a period at one time. However, even if that is the prevailing culture, and even if everybody else is neglecting their patients, that is still no reason for *you* to do so.

Your duty, in such a situation, if you were a nurse, would be to stay with your patients, to miss out on the impromptu group chat, and to get on with caring for the patients. That remains the case even if you are the only one doing so. In the past, when standards of care, and staff discipline, were higher in hospitals, it would also have been your duty to report that collective act of neglect to management. However, it would probably not be wise to report it today because the attitude, even of managers, has become so perverse.

Therefore, they would probably just punish you, for being a 'whistle blower', and take no action against the other nurses who neglected their patients. The reason is that in many workplaces, and especially the British NHS, the managers themselves don't care, or at least a large proportion of them. That is why so many NHS whistle blowers, instead of being thanked, are victimised and driven out. They draw attention to uncomfortable facts which those managers already know about, *but don't care about*, and which they prefer to cover up, rather than tackle.

Fault 5 - Dishonesty

In my Book 2 I have written a number of chapters on the issue of *truthfulness* which is one of the key character qualities we each need to develop if we are to grow as disciples. Please refer to those chapters for a much more detailed discussion of the subject of honesty and integrity in general. However, let's look briefly at this in the context of the workplace, where it is a major problem. In all sorts of ways, employees regularly lie to each other, their supervisors and bosses, their clients and customers, and even to themselves.

It is not only telling outright lies, but also general deviousness, manipulation, evasiveness, insincerity, dodging responsibility and being two-faced. We have all come across these things in others, because the reality is they are to be found in almost all of us. If you examine yourself with brutal frankness, you will probably admit that you are not always 100% honest in everything you say and do. Unless you have taken steps to increase your honesty, it is likely that you will still be lying, to one extent or another. For most of us it is only a question of degree.

My advice is to go on a radical programme of retraining, whereby you cut out absolutely *all* lying, cheating, deviousness, manipulation or two-faced-ness of any description. Resolve to be 100% honest, and sincere with everybody, at all times, and to develop a reputation for *absolute integrity*, such that everybody at work knows that you are completely unbendable, incorruptible and 'unbribable'. Let them also see that your word is your bond, that what you say is exactly what you mean, and is always true.

However, don't just glibly tell yourself that that is already your position. Unless you are very unusual, it won't be, given how compromised and corrupt the general population now is, even amongst those who claim to be Christians. Therefore, decide that you will seek *to become* one of those rare 'Nathanael' types who never lie and can always be trusted. In the short term cutting out lying will be difficult, and even costly. All sorts of dodges, excuses and devious schemes will no longer be available to you to get you out of tight corners.

However, in the long run, it will benefit you if you develop a reputation as a person of absolutely unbreakable truthfulness and integrity. That said, whether or not that approach ever benefits you is not the issue. The point is that it is right, and that total honesty is what God wants each of us to have. Given that *He* wants that, what need is there to consider whether *we* want it? It should be self-evident that that is the right approach, both at work and elsewhere, even if we gain nothing from it, and even if it is costly and painful.

Fault 6 - Unreliability

As a business owner who employed many staff over the years, one of my biggest headaches was that so few people can be relied upon to do what they are asked to do and to do it on time. There have only been a handful of staff upon whom I could completely rely. With them I could assign a task, project or responsibility and then relax and leave them to get on with it while I did other things. With most people, however, one simply cannot do that, or at least not safely. There is the

337

distinct possibility that they will let you down in some way, or forget something, or not turn up, or somehow fail in their duty.

I think the main cause of this is that there is an insufficient seriousness about taking responsibility. Doing the task properly is simply not as important to most workers as it should be. However, if you want to be an excellent employee, who stands out from the others, then develop the character quality of reliability. Aim to become the kind of person who takes every task or duty really seriously and neglects nothing. Make diary entries and other careful arrangements to ensure that nothing is ever overlooked or mishandled.

Then other people can entrust things to you and completely relax, knowing that you won't let them down and that they don't need to constantly check up on you. The most reliable person I have ever known was my own Dad. If he agreed to do a thing he would always take it immensely seriously and take great care over it, even if it was the tiniest little task. I never saw him forget anything, or fail to turn up, or be late. He was totally dependable, and everybody knew that and that they could bank on it completely.

Therefore, start to retrain your mind to take all duties extremely seriously, however small they may be. The smallest details can spoil a project if they are overlooked or neglected. Also develop procedures to *supervise yourself.* If you do then, eventually, bosses will realise that they don't need to supervise you themselves, as you are already doing it for them. For example, one habit which I developed early on in my career as a lawyer was to do a complete check of all my filing cabinets and my diary every Friday afternoon.

I checked every single file against my do-list to make sure no tasks were missing from the list. But if they somehow were, then I would add them to the do-list or, better still, do the task there and then. So, from about 1.00 pm to 3.00 pm I would trawl through all of my filing cabinets, my in-trays and my filing tray. I also examined my diary for the coming weeks to see what hearings, court directions, meetings, or other deadlines lay ahead. I had a dread of opening my diary on a Monday morning to find something I had forgotten about, and for which I had failed to prepare.

I chose to do this self-supervision exercise on Friday afternoons because I would be tired by then. It was therefore a good use of lower quality time, when I was not at my best in terms of energy. By doing this simple procedure I effectively became my own supervisor from an early age. That made the task of my bosses much easier, at least in that respect. I recommend that you do something similar, whatever job you have. Scan the horizon for the days and weeks ahead and scrutinise each of your tasks, projects, cases, files or clients to see whether you have missed, forgotten or neglected anything.

In my own case I almost always found some things, whether small or large, that had somehow been overlooked during the week. This 'safety net' therefore saved me from many mishaps over the years. It is one of the reasons why, in my entire legal career, I never had any negligence claim made against me, or even against anybody who ever worked under me. Every year when I renewed our professional indemnity insurance policy, I got a certificate from the insurers which read *"No claims notified against this firm."* That is exceptionally unusual, and I was always very proud of it.

Sadly, despite all my urging, most of my staff did not follow my example and try to become their own supervisor. A handful did, but they were the exception. Therefore, in recognition of the reality of human nature, and of most people's unreliability, I put in place a system whereby every file in the firm came to me to be checked at pre-arranged intervals. I would scrutinise each file myself and see what the file handler was doing and how well they were progressing. For some staff I needed to write detailed instructions about what to do next and also point out things which they should already have done.

For others, whose files were well handled, I could just write *"Well done. Press on."* Nothing more was needed for the best staff. They gave me few problems. But some of the others were an ongoing headache. I soon came to know which category each person came into and our computer was set up to get files brought to me at widely differing intervals. For the least reliable staff it would be every 4 weeks, or even weekly on their worst files. But, for the more reliable staff, it would be 6 weekly, 8 weekly or even 13 weekly, because I could be more relaxed about them.

If I had a boss like me, using such a system, I would see it as a matter of professional pride to be one of the 13-week people, not one of the 4-week ones. I would also want to make sure that my supervisor would not need to say anything, or point out any errors or omissions, when they did see my files. Yet, most of my staff did not seem to have any such concerns and did not appear to mind being seen as being amongst the least reliable and least trusted members of staff. That would have made me feel utterly ashamed, but it did not seem to have that effect on them.

Fault 7 - Not seeing themselves as a servant and having no real understanding of the concept of service

Employment law used to be called *'the law of master and servant'*. That name was changed in the 1970's because of the growing unwillingness of the public to be referred to as 'servants' or to think of themselves as such. In the UK it is now seen as a degrading expression. But why should it be? If Jesus referred to Himself

339

as *"one who serves,"* why should we feel demeaned by being spoken of, or spoken to, as a servant? It can only be demeaning if, due to your own pride, you think that serving others is beneath you. If so, then you are at fault and your attitude is wrong.

This is far more than just a matter of what words to use. The underlying heart attitude is the real problem. A person's pride causes them to want to be served rather than to serve, and certainly not to be spoken of, or treated, as a servant. As a result of this attitude adjustment over recent decades, it is now very difficult to get really good service anywhere. When you do get it, it is a delight, but the problem is it is so rare. Employees in all sorts of businesses, and at all levels, simply do not see themselves as servants. They do not even have any real understanding of the very concept of 'service'.

I tried to drill the concept of service into my staff, but I was largely fighting a losing battle as the attitude I was seeking to build in to them is now so profoundly alien to UK culture. It did not fit with their view of themselves or others. The analogy I used was to say that their 'astronomy' was wrong. That is they saw themselves as the 'Sun', at the centre of the solar system, and all the other people in their lives, whether clients, colleagues or bosses, as being in orbit around them. Instead, we must always see the customer, client or patient as being the Sun, with ourselves orbiting around them.

That distinction may sound pedantic, but it has major implications and taking that approach actually changes everything. Any employee, or indeed any person in any context, who sees themselves as being at the centre of their own universe will never be a success. In particular, they will never develop the mind-set or heart-attitude of a servant, which God wants each of us to have. It is also, by the way, what every client, patient or customer wants us to have if we are dealing with them.

However, it is very rarely what they get, at least not in any genuine way, because so few of us are even *willing* to serve others, let alone *eager* to do so. The desire of the average worker is simply to make a living and to do so with the minimum of stress, hassle and hard work for himself. Those are most people's key objectives and they tower above the needs of the client, customer or patient. If those things ever come into conflict, the average worker's own self-interest will come first every time, without any need to think it over.

340

Fault 8 - Reluctance to endure any difficulty, hardship or pressure at work and seeking excessively to avoid these, irrespective of the effect on others

The average employee does not see it as any part of his role to face difficulty, hardship or pressure. They will go to great lengths to avoid or postpone these, so as to make life easier for themselves, without any thought for what the consequences might be for their clients, colleagues or employer. It is seen as self-evidently right for them to do all they can to make their own job easier for themselves. The impact on others is either not considered at all, or it is seen as being obviously less important than looking after number one.

So, if someone comes to them with a request for help, or advice, or service, their first thought will be of what that request might mean *for their own workload*, or even whether they feel *in the mood* for doing such a task. Then they will fob that person off or say it can't be done, or isn't needed, or that they have come to the wrong place and need to ask someone else etc. People who operate in this way either see it as their right to do so, or they don't care whether it is justified or not, as they fully intend to do it regardless.

Their approach is based on a wrong set of assumptions and attitudes. The employee puts himself and his own needs and wants at the centre and makes them primary such that they take precedence over every other person, duty or consideration. Therefore, few employees, when faced with a difficult situation or choice at work, will think to themselves: *"Doing X would be easiest and quickest for me, but doing Y is better for the client, and/or for my colleagues or employer. So I will put myself and my own needs second and do Y instead of X".*

I am not speaking of being willing to put yourself in physical danger, or break the law, or do absurd things which might harm yourself or your family. Clearly, those things would be wrong and refusing to do them would not amount to putting yourself first or neglecting anyone. Such refusals are wholly justified. I am speaking of situations when what the employee is choosing to dodge or postpone would be merely uncomfortable, stressful or hard, not dangerous or illegal. Such an employee simply doesn't see it as part of his role to be inconvenienced or to be put into uncomfortable situations.

Therefore he will not allow such things to happen if he can possibly avoid it. That is the attitude which I am condemning. It is selfish, unfaithful and a breach of one's clear duty as an employee. When the average UK worker faces an unpleasant task, his mind is focused on the implications *for himself*, not for the client, customer or patient. If their interests would be best served by him staying late, or working through lunch hour, or rewriting a report, or facing up to someone on the client's behalf, or redoing a shoddy piece of research, he is unlikely to do it. It would not suit his own convenience.

He will not put any of that into express words when deciding not to do those things. The decision-making process is all done unconsciously and automatically. It operates in line with his long established default-settings, whereby what is easiest, quickest and least stressful for himself is the obvious choice. Examine yourself as frankly as you can and ask whether any of this resembles you. Would you put yourself to inconvenience, or do something you are afraid of, or that you have never done before, for the sake of the client/customer, or for your colleagues or boss?

Or would you instinctively try to find some way to avoid doing so? If so, how would you seek to justify that? Or have you never even felt the need to ask yourself such hard questions? If you haven't, then it is most unlikely that you are a really excellent worker. All such people will have already addressed this issue and will now force themselves to choose the path which best suits the client or their firm, not the one which suits themselves, or puts them to the least trouble.

Admittedly, they may not have begun their working career with that unselfish approach, but they will have developed the right attitude over the years. They will therefore be continually imposing those values and priorities upon themselves even when, deep down, they would still prefer to avoid such pressures. The very fact that this approach is a sacrifice is what makes such workers so commendable when they, nevertheless, put the patient or client first, and themselves last.

Fault 9 - Unwillingness to be open about mistakes, or to ask questions, or to admit that they don't know things

I have consistently found that the best staff were the ones who admitted their errors, asked for advice, and openly admitted that they didn't know things. Partly that was because they were more confident and were not plagued by insecurity in the way that the less capable employees were. But there was more to it than that. It was also linked to the employee's level of pride, selfishness and lack of integrity. A faithful, honest, unselfish worker will say:

"I have just made a mistake on this file or task or project. I need to point it out to my supervisor today, so they have the earliest possible chance to intervene and to advise me on how to redeem the situation and protect the client's/customer's/patient's interests. The need to do that comes far ahead of my own feelings, or pride, or what people might think of me. If I must endure some embarrassment now for the sake of the client, then so be it."

However, a proud, selfish, unfaithful, dishonest worker will say to themselves:

342

"I have made a mistake here, but I will hide it and hope nobody ever notices, as I don't want anybody to think less of me, or to put me to any extra effort to resolve the error. Maybe the client's interests will be harmed by my covering this up, but that's tough. Nobody can expect me to face embarrassment, or to inconvenience myself, for their sake."

The first approach is obviously better for the client and the firm. However, what many staff do not realise is that, in the long term, it is also better for themselves. If you hide your mistakes, or choose not to admit your ignorance, or to seek advice when you need it, then the following things will happen over the years:

a) You will make more mistakes than the honest, humble, unpretentious employee. He will learn a lesson each time he makes an error and will find out what he ought to have done, whereas you won't. Thus, two or three years later, he will have learned many such lessons and will have become a far more competent, experienced, reliable worker than you.

b) Bosses will notice you making mistakes anyway, perhaps not immediately, but a few weeks or months later, when your error 'explodes' in your face. It will then be revealed, despite all your efforts to conceal it. Or it may come out when the client himself complains. But, by then, it will be a far more serious matter and may even be impossible for your boss to remedy, because the 'concrete' has set. Thus, you won't, in the longer term, succeed anyway in keeping a reputation as a person who makes no mistakes. You will just be seen as a person who hides them. There is actually no such thing as an employee who makes no mistakes. We all do. That is a large part of how we learn and it is futile to pretend otherwise.

c) You will steadily develop a reputation as a worker who cannot be trusted with responsibilities, and especially with new, complex, unfamiliar tasks or files, of the type where mistakes are most likely to be made, or on which advice is most likely to be needed. Thus, even assuming your boss is willing to continue to employ you at all, he is likely to restrict you to simple, familiar tasks that you have done many times before. Then you will learn fewer things, and make even less progress in your career, because your bosses *won't trust you* to be open with them. Conversely, the honest, transparent, unpretentious colleague will be trusted more and more and will therefore be given bigger, higher, better tasks to do. He will also be promoted again and again, whereas you will remain at the bottom, where you belong.

I will now give an example of a situation which arose when I was much younger and worked as what is called an assistant solicitor for a large national law firm. I was one of the lawyers working on a big case for a major commercial client and we had arranged a meeting involving me, a senior colleague who was an associate, one of the partners in the firm, and several senior managers from the client company. We had all gathered to hear our barrister, a top London specialist, give us his advice on the merits of the case and as to the way forward.

Of all the lawyers in the room I was by far the most junior, and the clients were also many years older than me and they all had impressive job titles. So, it was a fairly high-powered meeting. The barrister then began to address us on the case and, in doing so, he used a particular phrase, which I now forget, but it sounded complicated and I had no idea at the time what it meant. I looked around the room, but nobody else seemed to be puzzled and they all seemed to be having no difficulty understanding him. At any rate, nobody asked him what it meant.

He therefore continued to speak and I just listened for a while, without asking him what it meant, in the hope that the meaning of the phrase might become clear to me as he went along, or from the context, or that he might even explain it at some point. But it was no good. A few minutes later I was none the wiser and so I raised my hand, in front of that eminent gathering, and said to the barrister, *"Excuse me, but would you please explain the meaning of that phrase which you are using".*

As soon as I said that, one of the clients, a senior director, said *"I'm so glad you asked that. I have no idea what it means but I didn't like to be the only one to ask."* I looked around the table and it then emerged that they were *all* in the same position. Not one of them had any idea what the phrase meant, not even the Partner, who was my boss or the Associate who was my senior colleague. So, this barrister had been speaking to a room full of lawyers and senior businessmen without anybody admitting that they didn't know the meaning of the phrase until I put my hand up to ask.

They were all too proud, or too insecure, to admit their ignorance in front of the whole meeting, in case anyone might think less of them or even laugh at them. Yet the lawyers were all charging a high hourly rate, and they owed a duty of care to the client company we were acting for to make sure they knew what they were doing and what was going on. To allow oneself to remain ignorant of the barrister's meaning during that crucially important meeting, for which the client company was paying a fortune in fees, was, in my view, a serious breach of their professional duty.

The managers and directors themselves also owed a duty to their own company, to do their very best and to act in its best interests. But those considerations evidently cut no ice with any of them. At any rate, none of them were willing to risk being embarrassed just in order to do their jobs properly and to fulfil their duties to the company which they worked for. Given the choice, they opted to stay quiet and to save face rather than to be honest about what they didn't know.

In my view, that was not only proud, cowardly and foolish, but also unethical. To this day, I wonder what would have happened, and how the remainder of the case conference would have been conducted, if I had not stuck my hand up and asked.

I learned an important lesson that day, which is that it is actually the ablest, most confident, and most knowledgeable person who is likely to ask questions in a meeting, not the least able, or the one who knows the least. Therefore, quite apart from it being your duty to ask, it is actually more likely to impress others, if you are brave enough to ask, than it is to cause them to look down on you. You might imagine that they will laugh or sneer, but the chances are, in reality, that if you don't know what's going on, or what is meant, then the others don't either. So, from that day onwards, I never felt afraid to ask a question again, whoever else was present, and have never held back from doing so.

Let me give you another example, this time of a tragic situation where a proud, selfish nurse actually caused an injury to someone I know. It arose due to her unwillingness to admit her own lack of knowledge and experience, or to seek advice. She was dealing with a patient who had a major abdominal wound following surgery. He had to have what is known as a 'vac', and dressings had to be applied to the wound at regular intervals to protect it and keep it clean and free of infection. The vac worked by applying suction pressure to the wound area.

Taking the vac off and putting it back on was a delicate task. It required a specially trained nurse, or at least one who had seen it demonstrated a few times. One day the vac, and the dressing beneath it, needed to be replaced. Instead of calling for a specialist nurse to apply it, this inexperienced nurse, who had had no training with vacs, tried to do it herself, for the first time ever, and without supervision. The patient himself, who had seen it done many times by specialist nurses, knew exactly how to do it.

He even gently pointed out to the nurse that she was doing it wrongly, and that she needed to apply a special film dressing to the wound first. But she was too proud to be instructed by a patient, even though she could see that he obviously knew far more than her about the vac. Indeed, the very fact that he knew more than she did irritated her and her pride was inflamed by it. So, she pointedly ignored him but did not seek help from any supervisor either, or call in a specialist nurse to do it for her. She just pressed ahead with her own incompetent attempt.

Shortly afterwards, due to her recklessness in doing something which she did not know how to do, the wound developed what is known as a 'fistula'. That is a hole, whereby the contents of the intestines begin to leak out. It occurred due to the wound being subjected to excessive suction pressure. This fistula proved to be a very serious setback and caused much pain and suffering. Yet it could have been so easily avoided if she had simply had the humility to take advice, even from the patient. Better still, she should have gone to a supervisor. Or she could have called in someone else to do it for her, or with her, rather than plough ahead in her pride.

That nurse then walked away from that situation and I expect she will have denied all responsibility for it afterwards, even to herself. Thus, she would not even have learned something from the tragedy. Sadly, many such proud, unteachable employees work in our health service in the UK, and in every other trade or profession too. It is all so depressingly common and yet so totally unnecessary. Choose not to be like that nurse. Make it your policy to *willingly humble yourself* and to take all the advice you can get, without any regard for your pride.

When writing this I was asked what one ought to do if the boss is bad or vindictive. That is what if he is the sort of person who would respond unfairly or harshly to any admission of a mistake or lack of knowledge, such that being open with him would put you at risk? I recognise that such bosses do exist, who would punish openness rather than reward it. However, that is not common, because even bad bosses want their business to run well and can see the advantage of staff who are open with them.

So, they might be rude or ungracious when you admit errors or seek advice, but it is unlikely that they would sack you for that, or even think less of you. Such apprehension is largely based on the employee's imagination and they would not actually get into trouble for being open. But even if it is not imaginary, it is still better to take the risk and be open, given all the advantages that flow from being so. In any case, if your boss really is so stupid as to punish openness and reward secrecy, you are probably in the wrong job anyway. If so, start looking for another job and a better boss, who values openness.

Fault 10 - Failing to give honour to their bosses and even directly dishonouring them

It is very common for employees to dislike their bosses and to disparage them in private conversations. Some see this as justifiable, and even necessary, as an outlet for stress and tension at work. Many also see it as their right to despise their boss and to speak freely to undermine him behind his back. Yet, where would such a right come from? If you feel such contempt for your boss, you should not be working for him at all. If nothing else, such disrespect is in breach of the implied duties that are contained within your contract of employment.

Nevertheless, many employees speak ill of their bosses when they are not there. Some even show disrespect and contempt when they *are* there. Anyone who operates in that way is not pleasing to God and will suffer harm as a result. It is important to your future success as an employee, and perhaps one day as a boss yourself, that you learn how to respect and honour those who are currently your bosses. If you don't it will have an impact, not only on how you are seen now by bosses, but on your own future career.

A resentful, disrespectful employee will never learn or grow as much as one who honours their boss. Besides that, the *"law of sowing and reaping"* means that whatever you do to your bosses on the way up will, one day, be done to you if you ever become a boss yourself. God will make sure of that because He has stated that *"whatever a man sows, that he will also reap"*. I can testify to the truth of this in my own career. When I was a young police officer, and later as a young lawyer, there were some bosses whom I felt were incompetent, lazy or untalented and therefore I did not respect them.

I often felt that they had less ability than me. In part, my assessment of them was accurate, though not entirely so, and, to that extent, I was unfair to them. I learned later that their roles were far more complex and difficult than they had seemed to me when I was a mere onlooker from below, before I had to do their jobs myself. I also found in later years that I sometimes received the same kind of criticism and disrespect that I had shown to my old bosses, and even more so. Therefore, if you are in a junior position now, do not join in when others talk about bosses or snigger about their errors, problems or faults.

Go out of your way to be different. Stand aside from the crowd and show honour to those who are senior to you, even when it may not seem to you to be deserved. The reason for honouring a boss is not because he necessarily *deserves* it, but because it is *inherently right* that you should. It is also because of the beneficial effect upon yourself of learning how to honour those who manage you. Such honour is rarely given, at least in the UK, where many employees take a perverse delight in tearing down those who are above them.

Decide now that you will be different and that, no matter what sort of boss you have, whether good or bad, capable or incapable, fair or unfair, you will force yourself to show him honour and respect. This will please God. He sees all work as being done, ultimately, for Him, and He has put those bosses in charge of you, if only for a season, for you to learn from them. You will also grow more, and learn more quickly, precisely *because* you are honouring your boss as it is hard to learn anything from anyone when you feel contempt in your heart towards them.

If you cultivate this attitude of honour you will learn far more from every type of boss, both the good and the bad, the impressive and the unimpressive. That is important, because God will ensure that you get exposure to every type of boss, both to learn how things *should* be done, and also how they should *not be*. One of the best ways in which you can honour a boss, and help them, whilst also

347

benefitting yourself, is to pray for them. Make it your regular practice to do so, regardless of how that boss treats you, or what you think of them.

Do so simply because God has put them into that position as your boss, at least for a while, and because it is therefore your duty to support them in prayer. I don't mean that you should simply pray that the boss will treat *you* better or make *your* life easier. It is OK to pray for that, from time to time, but what I mean is that you should pray *for that boss himself, for his benefit not yours*, and for God to bless, guide, help and protect *him*. Such unselfish prayers will please God, and benefit the boss, and also the business.

However, the very fact that you regularly pray in that way will also change you. Your heart attitude will steadily alter and you will begin to see the whole situation differently, and *as God sees it*, rather than solely from your own self-absorbed perspective. Moreover, pursuant to the law of sowing and reaping which we saw above, God will respond to your prayers by one day causing someone else to pray for you, and perhaps many of them, because you will most certainly reap what you sow, not only in this way, but in every other way too.

By the way, *don't tell your boss* that you are praying for him, and don't tell your colleagues either. Just do it, quietly and faithfully, and keep it to yourself. Let God be the only one who knows. That way you won't be misunderstood or considered to be either a religious weirdo or a creep, or as being out to get something for yourself. Moreover, the more your boss upsets you, the more you should pray for him. Do that instead of moaning about him. Then wait and see what God does as a result, not only now, but also in years to come.

Fault 11 - Lack of interest, self-motivation and enthusiasm

Many staff are willing to work hard on something that interests them, or when they can see the point of it, or where it will be noticed or attract praise. But they will not do so on tasks which are dull, dirty, or inconspicuous, or whose purpose is less clear. That attitude will blight your career if you don't root it out. You need to show enthusiasm and interest, and be self-motivated no matter what the task is, or who it is for, or whether your work will ever be recognised. Therefore, no matter what the task is, *decide to be interested in it*, and to do your best, even if it is not naturally interesting.

When I had just turned 16 I got a summer job at a large textile mill. I had to empty waste bins of various types of scrap yarn and fabric and pack them into large containers. The man whose regular job this had been was off sick long term. A huge backlog of waste material had therefore built up in number 2 mill. The management only asked me to just keep up with the inflow of new additional

Please / P
Honour / H
Respect / R
Obey / O
Glorify / G

God

Submit
Depend

waste and to prevent the backlog from getting any bigger. That was all they expected of me. However, when I saw the mountain of waste stored in No. 2 mill, I actually felt inspired by the challenge.

I therefore set about trying not only to prevent it increasing, but to reduce it and even to remove it entirely. On the face of it, emptying waste bins and clearing away piles of fabric is not inherently exciting. However, I decided to make it into a race and I set myself ambitious targets to get my main work finished early in the day and then to spend the rest of each day getting the backlog down. I kept at this remorselessly, from June to September. Then, on my very last day at the mill, before I returned to school to start 6th Form, I completely emptied No. 2 mill of the last remnants of the backlog.

The huge storage area then stood totally empty. I got a tremendous sense of satisfaction, and even triumph, from achieving that. But nobody had ever expected, or asked, me to do it. I just wanted to, for my own sake, so as to do my very best. Then, to my great surprise, the Production Director, who sat on the main board of that large company, came over to see me. He had heard about me and was intrigued as to how I had got it all done so fast. He also questioned me about my exam results, which had just come out. Then he offered me a position for the future as a trainee manager at Carrington Viyella!

He did so based primarily on the attitude I had shown in working so tenaciously, and entirely on my own initiative, to clear away all that waste. It may seem very mundane, but he could see what it signified. I thanked him for the offer, but said I was planning to become a lawyer. So that job never materialised, but it could have, and would have done, if I had wanted it. It shows that promotion opportunities can arise in the most unexpected ways, if you work hard all the time, and also that there are far more people watching, and taking notice, than you realise.

Fault 12 - Being content to settle for mediocrity rather than seeking to become the very best they can possibly be in terms of skill, knowledge and experience

This is linked to the last point, but also stands alone as a separate issue. I am referring to how many staff have such a poverty of ambition and aspiration when it comes to the development of their own skills, knowledge and experience. I often felt dismayed at the attitude of many of my staff. They had no hunger or thirst to learn more, or to stretch their own experience, or to gain exposure to new, different, and more difficult files or projects. This was even the case when they were starting out in their careers, at a time when they surely ought to be at their most ambitious.

By contrast, when I was training as a police officer, and later as a lawyer, I took every opportunity to ask for the hardest files and cases. I always wanted to get exposure to new and unusual cases involving different situations and issues, so as to maximise my experience and expand my CV. I volunteered for tasks and cases which others didn't want, precisely in order to be able to learn more, learn faster and increase my repertoire. I also used to impose additional voluntary study upon myself in my own time, and asked to go on every available training course.

I was also always reading, including whole text books – lots of them, which I devoured from cover to cover. I was still doing that, even when I was in my late forties, and had advanced a long way in my legal career. I basically never stopped educating myself. Over a sustained period of time that approach had a profound effect, as it was bound to do for anyone, not just me. It enabled me to get far ahead of many of my contemporaries, who were so much less ambitious. Their main aim was just to have an easy life and to go home on time.

For example, when I was a trainee solicitor I volunteered for as much advocacy work as I could get, not only on my own files, but on my bosses' files too, to save them the effort. This meant I got a bigger, broader exposure to court work than my colleagues, and helped me to become better at it. Also, when I qualified, I volunteered to do advocacy in front of High Court judges. They could be extremely intimidating, but I wanted to learn as much as possible. I also volunteered for Employment Tribunals, and conducted a complex two-day trial by myself immediately after I qualified.

My opponent at that hearing was a senior barrister in his forties who was also a part-time judge. So it was scary, but I still wanted to do it, even though it was hard and stretched me to, and beyond, my limits. I wanted to be the best that I was capable of being and not to miss any opportunity to learn. I remember also, when I was a trainee solicitor, some of our commercial clients had problems with Gypsies camping on their land. None of my colleagues wanted to take those files on, but I volunteered. It meant learning how to make a new and unusual form of application for possession.

I also had to go to the Gypsy camps in person to speak to them, and to drive wooden stakes into the ground with eviction notices attached to them in order to get them out. My colleagues considered that unpleasant work, and also intimidating. But I felt it added to my experience and was good for me, which it was. Therefore, don't be passive and don't ever settle for being average or mediocre. Aim as high as you can go. That doesn't mean you need to be the best, as that may not be possible. We obviously can't all be the best. But we can all be the best that *we personally are capable of being*.

That is a very different objective and one which we should all aim for. That said, very few people do. Therefore, if you decide to be one of that small minority, you will go far and do well. You may even end up actually being the best even if, in natural terms, you were not the most talented or gifted to begin with. That is because you will make the most of your abilities, whereas your colleagues won't. Neither will they be willing to pay the necessary price to achieve it. Therefore, they will only ever operate at 50% or less of their capacity and will never reach their full potential.

Fault 13 – Lack of initiative or inventiveness and giving no thought to how the systems and procedures of their job could be altered or improved

I have often been amazed at the inefficient or even absurd procedures which employees will operate, quite robotically. They continue to do so without ever questioning *why* things are done in that way or thinking of better, easier, quicker or cheaper alternatives. A really inefficient, even silly, procedure might have been put in place years ago by some past supervisor, or even by a "lowly" employee. Now, everyone operates in that way, quite slavishly, without ever thinking about it or questioning it, or showing any initiative at all.

The accepted current procedure could involve the metaphorical equivalent of going seven ways round an octagon. Yet nobody says *"Why do we do it this way? Why don't we just change direction and go one way round the octagon, instead of seven ways?"* Whatever task you are doing, especially if it is at a low level, such that managers don't get involved in it themselves, or don't even see it being done, there are likely to be many ways in which it could be handled more efficiently. Surprisingly few employees ever give the procedures or systems any thought, or spend any time thinking of how those could be improved.

Yet that person might be doing that task once or twice a day, or even twenty times a day. If instead they began to question themselves about it, and to ponder on it, they would probably think of something, however small, which would make the procedure better for themselves, the business and its clients. As for why employees give no thought to such things, or don't offer their ideas to management even if they do think of any, there are various possibilities:

a) They may be inherently unimaginative people who are not gifted with any creativity or problem-solving skills. However, this explanation must be rare because in most cases the task is done so often, and the inefficiencies are so obvious, that almost anybody who cared could eventually identify them, even if they aren't gifted.

351

b) More likely it is because they have switched off mentally while at work. They then operate as an unthinking automaton, just following procedures while their mind is elsewhere, day-dreaming.

c) Then again, it may be that they have actually suggested changes or improvements in the past, but they found that those were not appreciated, or were not implemented. So, they no longer bother to speak up.

d) They may be excessively deferential, such that they feel it is not their place to offer ideas to managers or, even less, to criticise procedures. So, they say nothing.

e) In some cases there is a sense of resentment, or even malice, such that they are actually aware of how things could be improved, but they are simply not willing to help management. Thus, they keep quiet as a form of spite, thinking to themselves *"Why should I help them?"*

If any of these factors apply in your own case, then set them aside. Begin to examine your own job daily, searching for possible ways in which you could do it better, quicker, cheaper and more effectively, so as to benefit all concerned. The very process of doing so will not only yield useful ideas. It will also *change you*. In particular, it will help you to develop the *habit* of looking for ways to improve things. Everybody ought to be doing that, but the truth is that most of us aren't.

If you adopt this approach, and keep doing it for long enough, you may end up a supervisor or manager yourself. In my own law firm I used to offer a £50 tax free reward to any member of staff who came up with an idea, or who could point out to me *anything at all*, however small, which was bad or wrong or inefficient or wasteful in any of our procedures or systems. Surprisingly few took me up on it, even though I was eager to pay the bonuses.

Therefore, one thing I did, and which I wish I had had time to do more of, was to do the staff's jobs myself occasionally, even if only for an hour or two. When I did, I would often see inefficiencies in the procedures they used which appalled me. I would then immediately change the procedures or systems. I would recommend that approach to any manager. Try to go on reception, or drive the vans, or go on the telephones, or the production line. Then see what people actually do, and *how they do it*, and many ideas for improvement will come to you.

Fault 14 - Unwillingness to be corrected, criticised or rebuked, even when it is done constructively, and also resenting, or even hating, any boss who seeks to do so

The Bible says *"if you rebuke a fool, he will hate you"*. I have consistently found that to be true, especially within the workplace. Even though my criticism was always given constructively, and politely, with the aim of helping them to improve, many staff resented it. The main cause of that reaction was their pride. They considered it an outrage for anybody to correct them and they had no desire to improve, or to serve clients better, or to become more skilled. They just wanted an easy life and to be left alone to continue to operate at their current level, without anybody wanting them to change.

However, without constructive criticism from colleagues or bosses you are much less likely to learn about your faults and weaknesses. We tend to be blind to those in ourselves, and cannot see them, unless someone else points them out. It may be deflating, or even wounding, when they do, especially if the person giving the criticism is not kind or gracious. But it is still for your benefit. Therefore, force yourself not only to listen willingly, and to apply the criticisms that are given, but even to *appreciate* those who give them.

Moreover, if someone does give you constructive criticism, or if they just complain to you about your conduct, attitude or performance, try really hard not to excuse or justify yourself, or even to explain, *until after they have completely finished speaking*. Let them get the whole thing 'off their chest' without you saying anything, and without even allowing your face to look surprised, aggrieved or indignant. You may not realise it, but the human face 'speaks' very clearly, even when you don't say a word with your mouth. Therefore the person who is trying to correct you will instantly pick up the signals and see that you resent what they are saying, or are irritated, or that you are not really listening to them *and are actually just thinking of what you want to say in reply*.

Don't do that. Not only does it prevent you from genuinely listening, it also makes the other person feel (often quite rightly) that there is no point in trying to talk to you because you aren't receptive to any correction. Therefore, don't say anything. Just listen attentively, nod and show recognition at appropriate times and, above all, *don't argue, 'answer back', or seek to justify yourself*. The time for that, if at all, is when they have been fully allowed to make their point, and when you have completely understood and seen why it matters *from their perspective*. Then thank the person for sharing it with you and give a genuine apology. Make sure that all of that has been fully and properly done before you even begin to give your side of the story.

If you have not yet been a boss yourself, you may have no idea how hard it is, and what a sacrifice it can be, to risk giving constructive criticism. Anyone who does so knows it will probably be resented rather than appreciated, even if it is totally valid. The reality is most staff like bosses who leave them alone, make no demands of them, and don't expect them to change or grow. They will then dislike any bosses who attempt any of those things. Therefore, be different and force yourself not to be so proud or foolish as to operate in that way. Don't merely be willing to be criticised. Positively seek for it.

Invite bosses and senior colleagues to point out anything that they think requires improvement. Reassure them that you really do want to hear it, and will value it, and not take offence. That is necessary because most colleagues have learned, from painful experience, that such comments provoke antagonism. Therefore, even bosses tend to refrain from offering any criticism, for the sake of having an easier life themselves. But it is not actually in your long-term interests for your bosses to stay silent, if you want to become as good at your job as you can possibly be.

Fault 15 – Being discontented with their wages, hours, terms and working conditions and feeling envious and resentful about what others have, or earn, or are allowed to do

One of the most damaging heart attitudes that a person can develop in the workplace, or anywhere else, is to be *discontented*, especially if it is accompanied by envy or resentment. Discontent reduces a person's motivation and also makes them clash with colleagues and become dysfunctional within a team. Focusing on what others have, as compared to you, is not constructive and does not spur you on to greater achievement or better quality work. On the contrary, a discontented person will usually reduce their work rate to match their own jaundiced perception of what they get from the employer.

Therefore, if they think the employer pays them too little, or provides unsatisfactory terms and conditions, they will persuade themselves that reducing the level of their effort is justifiable. However, even if your assessment of the fairness of your pay and conditions is objective and accurate, which is unlikely, you would still be better off adopting a satisfied frame of mind and feeling grateful for everything you do have. By so doing you will keep up your own motivation levels, be a good team member, relate better with colleagues and bosses, and give off a more positive demeanour.

Moreover, even if your pay is not generous, or is even unfair, the best way to get it increased is by impressing the employer with your positive attitude and high work-rate. But such attitudes and responses are unlikely to come from a negative,

354

embittered person. Therefore, do yourself a favour and stay positive, even if you aren't being treated fairly. If need be, in the end, you can always move to another employer. But even that is easier to achieve if, in the meantime, you can avoid becoming sour towards your current employer.

Resentment will not only reduce your motivation and output in your current job. It will also seep out through your face and voice at any job interviews you have. Whatever is going on inside you will inevitably come out, even if you try to hide it. As Jesus said: *"Out of the abundance of the heart, the mouth speaks"*. Therefore, to avoid developing a poisonous heart attitude, and having it spill over and become evident to others, cultivate an attitude of contentment. Force yourself to count your blessings and to express them, especially to yourself, and try very hard never to be negative.

Fault 16 - Unfaithfulness to colleagues, such that they let others down, fail to pull their weight and even engage in gossip

Human beings are sinful and inherently self-centred. Therefore, a person's main focus is usually upon what they can get *from* others and on *how others treat them*. However, if you want to become a mature disciple, and also a good employee and colleague, you must reverse that. Your aim must be to make sure that *you* are faithful, fair and loyal *towards others*, rather than being pre-occupied with whether they display those traits towards you. Such a profound change of approach requires deliberate effort and will never occur automatically or merely by the passage of time.

To achieve it you have to persistently redirect your thoughts, attitudes and priorities. That way you can ensure that you are giving and contributing properly to others, rather than trying to make sure that you are receiving enough from them. This unselfish approach to life is so alien to our sinful nature, and also to British culture, it has to be a discipline which you impose upon yourself until it eventually turns into a habit. You need to make it your goal to ensure that you are never contributing less than you should.

It must become a matter of professional pride never to let your colleagues down, use them, take advantage of them, or speak disloyally about them. Avoiding all of that needs to really matter to you. But it will never be achieved unless you *make* it happen because such attitudes will not develop by themselves. Sadly, the average employee doesn't see it that way and is not pursuing such a policy. Therefore, he will call in sick when he is not actually ill and give no thought to the extra burdens their absence imposes on colleagues. Or they will not make a full effort in their work and leave it to others to get the job done.

Even worse, they will gossip about colleagues and act deviously or manipulatively to obtain advantages for themselves at the expense of others. All of this is wrong in itself, but the operative point is that it will also prevent you from being the kind of worker that God wants you to be. Aim therefore to become the most loyal, faithful, reliable, discreet and trustworthy worker in your place of work. That won't be hard because few, if any, of your colleagues will be competing with you for that title. Indeed, the thought will never occur to them and if it was suggested to them, they would consider it absurd.

Fault 17 - Automatically assuming themselves to be in the right and to be the most important person in the room

This is an endemic problem. Whenever any issue or dispute arises, people have programmed themselves to assume, automatically, that they are in the right and that the other person is in the wrong. Thus, if a conflict arises, or if there is a scarcity of resources, such that it has to be decided who should get what, and who must do without, or wait until later, the average person sees himself as obviously:

a)   right on the facts

b)   in the right as to the merits of the argument

c)   the most deserving person in the company

d)   the most important person in the company

This ingrained self-centredness and introspection causes each party in a dispute to see the situation entirely from their own perspective. There is little or no recognition of the needs, rights or importance of others and no serious thought as to *whether* they themselves are actually in the right. That is assumed as an absolute given. As they see it, the only task is to *prove* to others that they are in the right, not to *find out* for themselves *whether* they are.

A whole group of people can therefore engage in an argument over resources, roles, status, duties, etc, without any of them ever questioning themselves as to whether they are right and/or whether their own claim or case is more or less valid than the other person's. This is the cause of much tension in the workplace. Therefore, if you stop seeing yourself and your own needs and wants as central, you will become a much more useful member of any team, and a far less frequent cause of conflict.

Fault 18 - Being unable to see themselves as they really are, and as others see them, but only as they imagine themselves to be

This perennial problem is linked to the above point. Very few people are able, or willing, to see themselves objectively, as they really are, and as others see them. They therefore persist in seeing themselves through a subjective and highly flattering lens. Their own faults, weaknesses and selfish ways become invisible to them, whereas other people's are seen in sharp focus. This is the natural condition of the human race, and the Scottish poet, Robbie Burns, famously wrote about it in his poem '*To a louse*':

"O would some power the giftie gie us to see ourselves as others see us."
                                                                              Robert Burns

The only 'cure' for this blindness is to force ourselves to examine ourselves more objectively. That includes interrogating ourselves as to what we are really doing, whether we are being fair or unfair, selfish or unselfish, honest or dishonest about a given issue or situation. In the absence of such rigorous cross-examination of oneself, one will always remain blind. Therefore, don't wait for an accurate view of yourself to arise naturally by itself. It never will.

You must set about producing it deliberately, by a conscious decision, and over a sustained period of time. Become one of those extremely rare people who are capable of stepping to one side and scrutinising themselves objectively, as if they were someone else, or as if the piece of work had been done by someone else. Then you will be much less prone to deluding yourself as to what you really are, or how good the work was, or who was at fault.

Fault 19 - Having no understanding of duty or responsibility and instead thinking exclusively in terms of rights and entitlements

This attitude is a widespread problem which goes far beyond the workplace, but also has a real impact on the kind of workers we become. Our generation has become more self-absorbed than any other generation in history. There is now very little grasp of the meaning of duty. Few even know what it is, let alone take it seriously or feel bound by it. The average person is preoccupied with their real or imagined rights and the *'entitlement culture'*, as we saw in chapter 10. They won't put themselves out to fulfil any sense of duty to others. Indeed, the very concept is alien to them.

This contrasts starkly with the generations which fought World Wars 1 and 2. In 1914 there was an extremely clear and widespread understanding of duty. Even in that horrific war, Great Britain felt no need to conscript any men into the armed forces until well into 1916. Until then, we relied solely on volunteers. Yet there was no shortage. They were utterly unlike our own pampered generation which thinks overwhelmingly in terms of rights and entitlements, with virtually no concept of duty, or of honour either.

Therefore, swim against the tide of our generation and its *"me first"* values. Train yourself to identify your duties and to embrace them rather than avoid them. Be the sort of worker whose main focus is on what they are *obliged to do* for their firm, colleagues, clients and bosses, not on what they are *entitled to receive* from them. Many will think you are naïve, or even a fool, for thinking in such public-spirited terms. But do it anyway. Be determined to be different and refuse to be defined or limited by the self-serving standards of the age we live in.

Fault 20 - Cowardice - mainly morally, but also physically

Few people view cowardice as a fault or a sin. Many assume that the desire to avoid risk, pressure or unpopularity is entirely normal. They also feel that it is legitimate to do whatever is needed to protect themselves and to keep away from people, places or situations which they are afraid of. However, that is not how God sees it. He takes the view that cowardice is a very major sin. Indeed, in the list of sins of those people who are heading into the Lake of Fire in Revelation chapter 21, cowardice is the first one named, implying that it is highly significant:

But as for the cowardly, the faithless, the polluted, as for murderers, fornicators, sorcerers, idolaters, and all liars, their lot shall be in the lake that burns with fire and sulphur, which is the second death."

Revelation 21:8 (RSV)

I think cowardice is included in that verse because it is actually a form of selfishness whereby your duties to others are seen as less important than your own self-preservation, or the avoidance of things that you fear. Cowardice causes a person not to do things which they should do, and to do many other things which they ought not to do. It all comes from deciding not to control and overcome their own fears. Thus cowardice is not only a major sin in itself. It also leads one indirectly into various other forms of sin, neglect, unfaithfulness and disobedience.

Within the workplace, cowardice is a major issue. It causes people to fail in their duty and to do all sorts of wrong things as a result of giving in to their fears, rather than choosing to face them. Therefore, let's get this really straight, so there can be no misunderstanding. The mere fact that you are afraid is *no basis* for assuming that you are entitled to avoid what you fear. There are many times where your

358

clear duty is to face your fear head on, and do whatever is scaring you, rather than run away from it. Moreover, you must do it *while you are still afraid*.

You might be acting for a client and it becomes necessary to do something you have never done before, or don't know how to do, and you are afraid to try. Instead of doing what *you want*, and avoiding the challenge, do what *he needs* and face up to it. It could be that your client needs you to go and negotiate hard with an opponent whom you find intimidating, and whom you would prefer to avoid. If so, force yourself to go. Make yourself engage in those negotiations and do your very best for that client, rather than sacrificing his interests for the sake of avoiding what you fear.

Few people admit, even to themselves, what they are really doing when they avoid danger or difficulty and choose the easy option. The truth is it amounts to selfishness. You are putting your own desire to avoid being scared ahead of your duty to the client, or to your colleagues, boss or the firm as a whole. Whoever you are letting down, *your fears do not excuse your cowardice* or justify you in choosing not to do what you fear. It is actually the fear which gives you the opportunity to display courage. Indeed, there cannot be courage without fear, because all courage involves facing and overcoming your fear.

I recognised this problem early in my working career and resolved that I would never make any decision, take any action, or avoid any action, based on my own fears. Of course, I still had fears, as everyone does. But I decided that I had to treat these fears as being entirely irrelevant when deciding *what I must do* on behalf of my client or my boss or my firm. They, and their needs, had to come first. Therefore, my own fears had to be ignored, overcome, or endured.

At any rate, I knew I could not allow them to have any influence over me. I would urge you to take that same approach, not only in the workplace, but everywhere in life. Do what you *should* do, not what you *want* to do, and do it regardless of whether you are afraid. In other words, never excuse yourself from any valid duty just because you are afraid. Once you begin to face up to your fears in this way, and refuse to be ruled by them, they will start to shrink, and might even disappear entirely.

The demons' standard tactic is to whip up fear in you, so as to get you to do what is wrong, or to fail to do what is right. But when they see that you have resolved to rule out any consideration of what you fear when making your decisions, a large part of their power over you is removed. You then become free. If so, you have won a major victory, which will have far-reaching consequences, in every area of your life, in particular in turning you into an overcomer.

Fault 21 - Unwillingness to start at the bottom

Whether due to pride, arrogance or laziness, many people want to start their career half way up the ladder, rather than from the bottom. However, the only way to learn a job properly, or to really understand a business, is to get your hands dirty and do the real job on the shop floor together with the other workers. That is the best way to learn how their jobs are meant to be done, which is a huge advantage if your aim is to manage or supervise them one day.

Thus, if you want a career in retail management for example, make sure you get plenty of experience on the shop floor, doing all the basic tasks, so that you really know the 'brass tacks' of how a shop operates. Years later, when you are the Store Manager, or the Regional Manager or even the Managing Director, nobody will be able to pull the wool over your eyes. In the past it was normal to start at the bottom, but there is a greater reluctance today to do so. I would urge you to take the opposite approach. Positively seek to gain such experience rather than trying to skip it on your way up the ladder.

Fault 22 - Unwillingness to take extra work home voluntarily, or to work late, or to do anything outside of their stated contractual terms, or to do anything which isn't measured or targeted

It is, of course, wrong to be a 'workaholic' and to spend your whole life at work, such that you neglect your spouse or children. However, a far larger number of people go to the other extreme, whereby they are reluctant to do anything, however small, which is not strictly part of their agreed contractual terms. They leave work bang on time, refuse to take a briefcase home, and won't study in their own time or consider work-related matters when they are not at the office.

One needs a sense of balance and proportion, but that is not to be found at either end of the spectrum. However, in my opinion, you need to be nearer to the willing and flexible end of that spectrum than to the unwilling and inflexible end. A good worker is not a *'clock watcher'*. Neither is he a *'terms and conditions watcher'*. He is therefore willing to do extra things, which are not in his contract, even at short notice, and even without pay, when the needs of the client, or of the firm, require it.

Of course, it may be different for a shift worker with strictly set hours. But if you are salaried, or a trainee, or if you have any supervisory responsibilities, be willing to be flexible when the need arises. Above all, do not be obstructive or resentful about it. By adopting such a positive and willing attitude you will provide a far better service and rise higher in your career. You will also be much happier in your work while you are doing so.

Another issue, which is a vexed problem for managers and supervisors, is that there is a strong tendency for staff to only do those tasks which are measured and targeted by the company. Then other things, which are not measured, or which can't be measured, are neglected, done badly, left until later, or not done at all. Many employees take the view that they will only do those tasks which will result in them being noticed, acknowledged or rewarded and not those which are less visible or which the management are not actively measuring.

From a manager's perspective this attitude presents a major difficulty, and one which is not easy to solve if you are dealing with staff who do not have high levels of personal integrity and self-discipline and who are not strongly client-focused. The problem for the manager is as follows:

a) If nothing is measured or targeted, then some of the staff will do very little work. In particular, they will avoid the difficult, unpleasant, unenjoyable tasks.

b) If, however, only certain tasks are measured, and only key objectives are targeted, then it is likely that only those things will be done, and all the other things will be neglected or left undone. There will be all sorts of perverse incentives to do what looks good in the figures, even though it is not good for the clients or the business.

c) If, however, you then try to solve that problem by measuring and targeting virtually everything then you end up with a working day which, for most staff, and also their supervisors, consists of little else but filling in forms, ticking boxes and examining printouts and schedules, rather than doing the actual substantive work.

As I said, it is vexed problem for managers and there is no easy solution to it, because every option has its own bundle of disadvantages and unintended consequences. Let me give just a few of examples of how measuring and targeting certain specific aspects of a worker's job can cause him to act in a perverse manner and to harm the interests of the clients and the business itself. Some time ago I rang up the Student Finance Company to assist with my children's applications for student loans.

I had to ring a large call centre whose staff were heavily measured and targeted. I then said to the girl who answered the phone, *"Hello, I am ringing to ask two questions"*. To my surprise, as soon as I said that, *she hung up on me!* I later told that story to someone I know who works in a large public sector organisation and he said that the reason she would have hung up is that her employer was targeting her *on how quickly she can complete each call.*

If she took too long *on one call* she would be penalised but, if she could get each of her calls finished in less than a specified number of minutes, she would be rewarded. So, to avoid penalties and maximise her chances of rewards, she simply hung up on anybody who sounded as if they had a complex question, or anyone who had more than one question to ask. Of course, that was not what the Student Finance Company wanted, but it was the actual result, albeit unintended, of their arbitrary and ill thought-out measurement procedures.

Another example arose when I was buying a particular type of laptop which the shop near where I live did not have in stock. So, they rang another branch of their shop in another town, which had got one in stock, and told them to courier that particular laptop to me. I then paid for it and waited for it to be delivered. However, it did not turn up and when I rang the shop to ask why it had not arrived, I was told that an employee in the other shop had subsequently sold my laptop to another customer there, even though it had already been paid for and was my property.

The reason why he did it was not due to any error or misunderstanding. He had done it knowingly and deliberately, so as to boost his own *personal sales figures*. That resulted in inconvenience for me as the customer, plus it caused damage to that company's reputation. On top of that there was a lot of extra administration for the staff of my local shop as they searched for another laptop for me.

However, none of that will have bothered the employee in the other branch, because none of that was being measured, whereas his own individual sales figures were. That was all that he was interested in. My purchase did not count as a sale by him, but had been attributed to the sales assistant in my local shop. Therefore, his own commercial interests did not coincide with those of the other shop assistant, or of the company which was their employer.

Deadlines & time limits

Let me give another example which shows what can go wrong when employees are excessively or inappropriately monitored and measured. This time it is from my own experience as a police officer in the 1980s, in comparison to how things are dealt with today. When I was on foot patrol back then I used to 'stop' quite a few people at night and check them out, very informally, to see if they were up to no good. I also used to stop an even larger number of cars, both at night and in the day, to see what I might find, such as drunk drivers or no insurance and so on.

In those days I could do all of that quite freely, without needing to fill in any forms, and without any supervisor breathing down my neck or questioning me about *why* I had stopped that particular person or car. Therefore, I was able to catch a lot of offenders on the simple basis that, having stopped so many, I was statistically likely to do so. I used to say *"You have to kiss a lot of frogs to find your prince."*

Now, however, due to hugely increased racial sensitivities and the general climate of political correctness, the police are very closely monitored as to *whom* they stop and what *race or religion* they are, and even their *age, gender, or sexual orientation*. Therefore, in order to counteract the allegation that officers are 'persecuting' particular groups, the police began to impose increasingly stringent administrative procedures to monitor the statistics. They want to ascertain exactly *what types of people* are being stopped and questioned or searched etc and to make sure that no one group is 'over-represented'.

The problem is that the only way that can be done is for senior officers to require constables to fill in a form every time they stop anyone and to record who it was, why they were stopped, what they were suspected of, and on what basis, and also their ethnic, religious, age and gender profile. As you can imagine, that is a lot of paperwork. It also takes a long time to fill it in and it therefore creates even more delay and even greater irritation amongst the very few people who are now stopped.

Unsurprisingly, therefore, the police officers have responded to such over-zealous monitoring by simply not stopping or questioning *anybody*, unless the situation is extremely clear cut. But the problem is that works against the public interest because it means that the guilty are allowed to get on with their criminal activities, largely unhindered. I should clarify, by the way, what I mean when I say I used to 'stop' lots of people. I don't mean that I arrested them, or wrestled them to the ground, or even spoke to them formally. Not at all.

All I did was to start a friendly conversation and see how they reacted. Then I would decide, based on their manner, attitude and demeanour, and also from the context of where and when I came across them, and what else was happening at the time, whether I felt any suspicion and whether to take it any further. So, for example, if I saw a person walking along a street at 3.00 am I would just say hello and strike up a conversation, perhaps about the weather or something equally innocuous. Then I would gauge their reaction, and see whether they were nervous, cagey, or even hostile.

If so, I would begin to question them more probingly. If not, I would walk on and say goodnight. Therefore, from their perspective, they were never actually *'stopped'* as such. They were merely *spoken to*. I used my common sense and only reclassified it as officially stopping them if, in all the circumstances, I felt it was warranted. My bosses were happy with that practical, informal approach because they too operated on the basis of common sense and they knew that it worked.

However, the new generation of uber-PC liberal zealots who occupy the higher ranks of our police forces, and also the Home Office, see things very differently.

Common sense, and trusting the individual officer's judgment, play no part in their thinking. But all they have actually achieved, by trying to stamp out *inappropriate* stops or searches, is to ensure that there are *none at all*, or at least too few to achieve the objective of preventing crime and detecting and apprehending offenders which is, or used to be, what the job was all about.

As an employee, especially if you are currently in a junior position, there is not much that you can do to solve the wider problems described above. But what you can do is to make sure that your own actions, decisions and time allocation are not skewed in those ways and that you act with integrity and faithfulness and do *every part of your job, not just those parts which are measured.*

If you will do that, and do what is right, not just what looks good on paper, then it probably won't be noticed right now or show up in this month's figures. However, it will show up in the long term and managers will eventually notice. But even if they don't, you will at least have done the right thing and you will also learn some important lessons, not only about how the job should be done, but also about how bad staff operate, which will be of great use to you when you later become a manager yourself.

Fault 23 - Being a negative, defeatist *'can't do person'* who can only see obstacles, and reasons why things cannot be done, rather than advantages, solutions and possible ways forward

A remarkable number of workers, at least in the UK, have an entrenched mind-set of negativity and pessimism. They can generally only see reasons why things *can't* be done, not how they *could* be. They are also fixated with what problems and disadvantages lie ahead if a step is taken, rather than the possible benefits or opportunities that might flow from taking it. Such a person within a team, committee or office is a menace. They sap the initiative and imagination out of others, prevent things from happening, and thwart other people's creativity and problem-solving skills.

I call them *'can't do people'* and also *'Eeyores'*, after the gloomy friend of Winnie the Pooh, who is pessimistic about everything. A pessimist is actually a perversion of a useful character type, which is good to have on a team. I am referring to the cautious, reflective, problem-finder, who searches for possible snags and issues that might arise in future. However, they don't do that because they are negative, but only to *anticipate, address and resolve* problems in a constructive way, before they ever arise. That kind of person is actually very positive, and they are of huge value on a team or committee.

364

Their diligent forethought can prevent all sorts of problems from ever materialising at all. However, I am not talking about them. I am referring to those who misuse the talent for looking ahead and anticipating problems. Actually, in most cases they don't have that skill at all. They are just thoroughly negative people full stop, and often take a perverse pleasure from preventing things even being attempted. Everything depends on your motive, and on what your intentions, are when you search for snags and problems that might lie ahead.

If you are doing it with the aim of finding or anticipating potential issues so as to *solve them in advance*, and prevent problems further down the line, then that is healthy. You would be a useful team member. But if you are doing it because you are sour, negative and defeatist, or because you don't actually want the project to succeed for personal reasons of your own, then that is extremely unhealthy. Your team or firm would be better off if you were not part of it. That is a sad thing to say, but it is true of many workers.

People sometimes become like that because they are resentful or embittered about past failures of their own, for which they may have felt they were blamed. Or perhaps it is because they know they are not an imaginative or creative person, of the kind that dreams up new ideas or business proposals. Therefore, they soothe their own sense of inferiority by trying to prove that other people's ideas won't work and shouldn't be tried. They can't raise themselves up, but they can at least bring others down, and they get a perverse pleasure from that, without any regard to the harm they cause.

Another explanation for such habitual negativity is that the pessimist is afraid of failure. Therefore, they will do all they can to prevent themselves from ever being put into challenging situations. If a new project is being discussed, that insecure worker may see aspects of it that might put him under pressure later, or where he could potentially fail. He may then seek to prevent the proposal from ever going ahead by talking it down, presenting objections at the outset, and putting other people off it.

If the whole idea can be killed at birth, the negative person feels he has gained a measure of relief for himself personally and, in a perverted sense, he has. The problem is he has done so dishonestly, without ever stating his real underlying motives. He has also done it at the expense of others and of the firm as a whole. You cannot allow your own insecurities and personal 'hang ups' to influence you. In particular, they must not influence the advice you give to others, the input that you give to committees and teams, or the reports you write.

You have no right to undermine any of them for the sake of indulging your own inferiority complex. When assessing the likely difficulties that may be faced when seeking to implement a proposed idea or project, your attitude should be: *"How can I overcome each of these issues, so as to get this thing to work, even if it means more pressure for me?"* Your reaction should certainly not be *"How can I persuade others not to go ahead with this, so that I can avoid being put under pressure or having my weaknesses exposed?"*

Remember, *you* are not the issue. The firm is, and its clients or customers. Your duty is to help it to get things done, even if those things are difficult and even if they create stress or pressure for you personally. You have absolutely no right to prevent, delay or reduce the things that they need to do or to achieve for the sake of your own convenience, or to get an easier life. If you are tempted to think or act in this way then stop and challenge yourself, not only about the negativity and defeatism, but also the underlying selfishness which causes those features.

If you are facing a team meeting or committee in which someone else is proposing a novel way forward, or a solution to a complex problem, don't take any pleasure from thinking of reasons why his ideas can't work. Try instead to find reasons why they *can* work, and ways in which *you* can help them to work. Then, others will begin to see that your comments provide added value and make their ideas even better and more likely to succeed.

After a while those creative types will begin to seek you out and will want you on their team because of what you add to it, rather than seeking to exclude you because of how you detract from it. Even if you can see genuine issues or potential snags that lie ahead, let your only motive for pointing those out be to help the business. It must never be done to shelter yourself from an increased workload or to put down the other person, whose bright idea it was.

If you must speak against the proposal, then try your best to think of viable alternatives that would work, or of solutions which would solve, or at least mitigate, the problems you are identifying. Also, look for potential opportunities that accompany the difficulty which you face, or that are hidden somewhere within it. It is amazing how often such positive benefits, openings, ideas and opportunities can be found *if you are looking for them*. Therefore, make it your policy to look for them. As our greatest Prime Minister of all time said:

"A pessimist sees the difficulty in every opportunity. An optimist sees the opportunity in every difficulty."

Winston S. Churchill

A classic example of 'can't do thinking' from the Bible is the account of the 12 spies whom Moses sent into Canaan to spy out the land in Numbers 13 and 14. Bear in mind that God had already *commanded* them to go into the land, and had also *promised* that they *would* receive it. Therefore, Moses' purpose in sending in the 12 spies was not to decide *whether* to go in and take the land. The only

Ambigust
Seeing things as they really are but not responding like everyone else
Seeing the world - People (self) - for what it is but not conforming with it

question was *how best to go about it*. It was purely a reconnaissance mission, prior to going in.

I will only quote from parts of it, but you will see the dramatic contrast between the *'can do'* approach taken by Joshua and Caleb and the *'can't do'* attitude of the other ten spies. You will also see, which may surprise some, how strongly God disapproved of the ten spies and their pessimism and defeatism. God was angry, not only at their cowardice and lack of faith, but also at the corrosive effect which their negative words had on the people as a whole. Here is where the story begins:

¹ The LORD spoke to Moses, saying, ² "Send men to spy out the land of Canaan, which I am giving to the people of Israel. From each tribe of their fathers you shall send a man, every one a chief among them."

Numbers 13:1-2 (ESV)

Moses then sets out the objectives of the fact-finding mission and he even tells them all to *"be of good courage"*. Therefore, they had no reason to be afraid:

¹⁷ Moses sent them to spy out the land of Canaan and said to them, "Go up into the Negeb and go up into the hill country, ¹⁸ and see what the land is, and whether the people who dwell in it are strong or weak, whether they are few or many, ¹⁹ and whether the land that they dwell in is good or bad, and whether the cities that they dwell in are camps or strongholds, ²⁰ and whether the land is rich or poor, and whether there are trees in it or not. Be of good courage and bring some of the fruit of the land." Now the time was the season of the first ripe grapes.

Numbers 13:17-20 (ESV)

After 40 days all 12 spies return and give their reports to Moses and Aaron and to all the people of Israel. The negative ten go first. They speak positively of the land itself, but their focus then moves immediately to the *difficulties of taking it*, because of *how large the Canaanites are*. Their fear of the inhabitants of the land takes centre place in their report:

²⁵ At the end of forty days they returned from spying out the land. ²⁶ And they came to Moses and Aaron and to all the congregation of the people of Israel in the wilderness of Paran, at Kadesh. They brought back word to them and to all the congregation, and showed them the fruit of the land. ²⁷ And they told him, "We came to the land to which you sent us. It flows with milk and honey, and this is its fruit. ²⁸ However, the people who dwell in the land are strong, and the cities are fortified and very large. And besides, we saw the descendants of Anak there. ²⁹ The Amalekites dwell in the land of the Negeb. The Hittites, the Jebusites, and the Amorites dwell in the hill country. And the Canaanites dwell by the sea, and along the Jordan." Numbers 13:25-29 (ESV)

367

Then Caleb speaks, and note how totally different his attitude is. He reassures the people that the land *can still be taken* and that they are "*well able to overcome*":

But Caleb quieted the people before Moses and said, "Let us go up at once and occupy it, for we are well able to overcome it."

Numbers 13:30 (ESV)

Even after hearing Caleb's stirring words, the ten pessimists went straight back to trying to convince the people that it couldn't be done, and that the Canaanites are "*stronger than we are*". They even described themselves disparagingly as *'grasshoppers'* in comparison to them:

³¹ Then the men who had gone up with him said, "We are not able to go up against the people, for they are stronger than we are." ³² So they brought to the people of Israel a bad report of the land that they had spied out, saying, "The land, through which we have gone to spy it out, is a land that devours its inhabitants, and all the people that we saw in it are of great height. ³³ And there we saw the Nephilim (the sons of Anak, who come from the Nephilim), and we seemed to ourselves like grasshoppers, and so we seemed to them."

Numbers 13:31-33 (ESV)

Note the debilitating effect which their negative, fearful words had on the people as a whole. Very quickly a mood of gloom and unbelief had spread like wildfire throughout the crowds. The people then began to grumble and to express their own fear and despair:

¹ Then all the congregation raised a loud cry, and the people wept that night. ² And all the people of Israel grumbled against Moses and Aaron. The whole congregation said to them, "Would that we had died in the land of Egypt! Or would that we had died in this wilderness! ³ Why is the LORD bringing us into this land, to fall by the sword? Our wives and our little ones will become a prey. Would it not be better for us to go back to Egypt?" ⁴ And they said to one another, "Let us choose a leader and go back to Egypt."

Numbers 14:1-4 (ESV)

Joshua and Caleb tried again to win the people over and to persuade them that what God had commanded them to do *was possible* and that they *did not need to fear* the Canaanites. But by now the rot had set in too deeply and the people would not listen. Indeed, even hearing a positive message was now so irritating to them that they actually wanted to stone Joshua and Caleb:

⁶ And Joshua the son of Nun and Caleb the son of Jephunneh, who were among those who had spied out the land, tore their clothes ⁷ and said to all the congregation of the people of Israel, "The land, which we passed through to spy

368

it out, is an exceedingly good land. ⁸ If the LORD delights in us, he will bring us into this land and give it to us, a land that flows with milk and honey. ⁹ Only do not rebel against the LORD. And do not fear the people of the land, for they are bread for us. Their protection is removed from them, and the LORD is with us; do not fear them." ¹⁰ Then all the congregation said to stone them with stones. But the glory of the LORD appeared at the tent of meeting to all the people of Israel.

Numbers 14:6-10 (ESV)

This whole episode made God very angry. Those ten negative spies had not been sent to work out *whether* to obey God's command to take the land, but only *how best to do so*. Their fear, gloom and unbelief spread like a contagious disease amongst the people. It meant that the entry into the land was delayed for 38 years, until that generation had died off and a new one had arisen. So, God punished that whole generation, i.e. all those who were over 20 years of age at the time of the Exodus:

²⁶ And the LORD spoke to Moses and to Aaron, saying, ²⁷ "How long shall this wicked congregation grumble against me? I have heard the grumblings of the people of Israel, which they grumble against me. ²⁸ Say to them, 'As I live, declares the LORD, what you have said in my hearing I will do to you: ²⁹ your dead bodies shall fall in this wilderness, and of all your number, listed in the census from twenty years old and upward, who have grumbled against me, ³⁰ not one shall come into the land where I swore that I would make you dwell, except Caleb the son of Jephunneh and Joshua the son of Nun. ³¹ But your little ones, who you said would become a prey, I will bring in, and they shall know the land that you have rejected. ³² But as for you, your dead bodies shall fall in this wilderness. ³³ And your children shall be shepherds in the wilderness forty years and shall suffer for your faithlessness, until the last of your dead bodies lies in the wilderness.

Numbers 14:26-33 (ESV)

However, God punished the ten negative *'can't do'* spies even more severely, because of the unhealthy influence they had had on the people. Rather than merely letting them die off one by one in the wilderness, over the next four decades, God wiped all ten of them out straightaway with a plague:

³⁶ And the men whom Moses sent to spy out the land, who returned and made all the congregation grumble against him by bringing up a bad report about the land— ³⁷ the men who brought up a bad report of the land—died by plague before the LORD. ³⁸ Of those men who went to spy out the land, only Joshua the son of Nun and Caleb the son of Jephunneh remained alive.

Numbers 14:36-38 (ESV)

Fault 24 – Being unwilling ever to say no to clients, colleagues or bosses, or to give them any bad news, or warn of problems ahead

We have just looked at people who are always saying no, or at least thinking negatively, and therefore obstructing those around them. Now we are looking at the other end of the spectrum. That is those who *won't ever say no* and who aren't willing to give *any bad news, or warnings*, or to tell the *frank truth* to clients, colleagues or bosses, even when it is appropriate to do so. The most obvious examples of this that spring to mind are some of my former legal colleagues and, later on, my staff, many of whom were reluctant to be straightforward with clients.

They did not want to give them bad news about their cases, or tell the client that he was in the wrong, and that his opponent was right, or that his expectations for damages were unrealistic. Such staff were cowards. They were afraid of getting an angry reaction from the client, or of being told off or blamed, especially if they had previously given different advice. That is they were too cowardly to say that they had changed their minds, or been wrong, or even that the facts had changed.

Instead of telling the frank truth, their way of dealing with their fear was to cower away and say nothing, at least for the time being, always putting off the evil day to some unspecified later point, which often never came. My own approach was very different. I obviously took no pleasure from clients being disappointed, irritated or angry. But I knew that if bad news needed to be given, or if the hard truth had to be told, or if the client's hopes needed to be dashed, then it is best to do it at the *earliest possible time.*

Also, as unpleasant and embarrassing as it may be, if you are telling the client that your previous advice no longer applies, or even that you now realise that it was wrong, you must tell them. *And you must do it today.* The longer you put it off, the worse it will get. You would only be making a rod for your own back by delaying. Therefore, even though you know the client will be shocked and even angry at the news, perhaps displaying 10 'units' of anger, that reaction will only get worse the longer you put off telling him.

So you are probably swapping 10 units of anger now for 50 or 100 units of anger next month, or next year, if you delay telling him. I am simply stating the downright obvious. There is no conceivable basis for disagreeing with the policy of being frank, and of grasping the nettle at the earliest possible time. However, even though it is obviously the right approach, it is not what multitudes of workers actually do. They prefer to hide from the client, and even pretend to be out of the office, in order to avoid a difficult conversation.

Or they might take his calls, but say nothing as yet about the bad news, or the adverse development in his case, or the diminished prospects for success.

Sometimes even my bosses were too scared to give bad news, when I was an employee, and they would ask me to give it on their behalf. In one sense that wasn't a bad idea, if they were too cowardly to do it, as the alternative was for them to do nothing at all, which would be far worse. I never found it easy to give bad news, and I certainly never enjoyed it, but I knew I had to do it. Therefore, I got on and did it.

I just braced myself and rang the client, or got him to come in to see me. Then I told him straight. Strangely, in all the years I practiced law, nobody ever lost their temper with me. Though shocked or disappointed, they could see that I was telling them the truth and that it was for their benefit to hear the bad news. They probably also knew, from doing their own jobs, how difficult it is to do what I did. In all my years in practice, I never received a complaint from any client for giving bad news, or for telling them their case was weak, or even for saying that it should be abandoned.

This need for frankness and courage does not only apply when giving 'bad news'. It also applies in your general dealings with clients and customers when they are asking you how long something will take, or the prospects for success, or what it will cost, and so on. Even before anything has gone wrong, many staff feel a temptation to try to 'please' the client by giving him an optimistic estimate of the delivery time, or the likely cost. They do so because they want him to be happy with them *today*.

The problem is that although the client may be happy with you today, he is not going to be happy three months later, or six months later, when the case/project/production process etc is not as far ahead as you had promised, and when costs are already larger than you had estimated. The best policy, therefore, is to try to "*under-promise and over-deliver*". That involves a trade-off, but it is a worthwhile one. It means that today, when you give the client your conservative, even slightly gloomy, estimates and predictions, nobody will be patting you on the back or praising you.

However, it also means that several months later nobody will be shouting at you for getting the estimates wrong. What is more, if you are able to deliver ahead of schedule, and for a lower cost than you projected, then they will be delighted with you. It boils down to whether you want the pleasure of approval at the beginning or at the end. Based on over 30 years of experience, I absolutely recommend that you always choose to receive it at the end. That is what clients are most likely to remember, and what lasts longest, and it is also what will bring them back to you with repeat business.

Fault 25 - Being unable to consider tasks simultaneously, but only sequentially. Also, being unable to think laterally, anticipate problems, and ask questions which are not on a single 'train line'

One weakness which I tried to iron out of my staff was the entrenched habit of thinking about issues *sequentially, rather than simultaneously*. If you are running a case or handling a project, there are likely to be several issues arising, tasks to be performed, tests to be carried out, or enquiries to be made. Why would any sensible, efficient person choose to consider or implement each of those *one by one*, such that they only start to look at the second issue after they have completed, or found the answer to, the first? Most of the time there is no need for that step by step approach.

It is entirely possible to be pressing ahead on several different fronts, all at the same time. If you go about it that way far less time is wasted on the gaps in between the tasks/issues/enquiries. I used the analogy with my staff of how they might go about making a British Sunday lunch of roast beef, roast potatoes, mashed potatoes, various vegetables, Yorkshire pudding, gravy etc. It would be absurd to make that lunch *one item at a time*, such that you only put the roast potatoes in the oven after the beef is fully roasted, and then only put the vegetables in to steam after the potatoes are mashed.

No right-thinking person would ever do that. You would coordinate each of the component elements of the overall task so that they were all running in parallel and eventually *cooking simultaneously*. Then they will be ready all at the same time, not one after the other. The analogy may sound exaggerated, but that is what many people do every day in their jobs. When I called employees in to see me about one of their cases, they would often tell me they are "*making enquiry X*". However, they would not say *what else* they thought they should *also* be doing at the moment.

I would then ask about that and they would say that when they get the answer to enquiry X, they then propose to make enquiry Y. When asked what they will do when they get the answer to that, they would say that they will then make enquiry Z. I would then say: "*Why not make enquiries X, Y and Z all at the same time, right now? Then, when you get all the answers back, you will be able, straight away, to make a substantive decision. Or you will be able to progress the case in some other way, without wasting any time.*"

Their inability to think on more than one plane at a time, or to think ahead at all, was so entrenched that I drafted a lengthy document called a *'Case Plan'*. It was designed to help staff to think more laterally, but also to enable them to interrogate and supervise themselves. My aim was also to help them to ensure that as many tasks or enquiries as possible were attended to simultaneously, and/or at the

372

earliest possible stage in the case. That approach is far better than crawling along, step by step, with a lengthy time delay between every action you take.

I also referred to their approach as "*train line thinking*" because people think in one straight line, like a railway track, with 'stations' along the way, where they expect to do things, but with nothing in between, and no way of getting off that one track. Please refer to the Appendix for a blank copy of a case plan for a personal injury litigation file. The general approach that it takes may be adapted to make it relevant to any kind of situation, not just litigation. At least it illustrates the kind of probing, analytical, multi-lateral approach that I am advocating.

The staff would look at that case plan on screen and fill it in for themselves and the boxes would expand for their answers to be inserted. I hoped to be able to re-programme the staff not only to think laterally, but also to address issues simultaneously and to reduce the need for them to receive input and guidance from me. Not everyone is a born lateral-thinker, but the skill can be developed, at least to some degree. In particular, anybody can at least learn to plan ahead, anticipate issues, question themselves, and assemble a list of tasks and enquiries, even if they are not naturally gifted as a planner.

Moreover, it is possible to do much of it now, *all at once*, rather than let the steps that you need to take emerge one by one, over many weeks or months, like a slowly dripping tap. It is not only the legal profession which is plagued by this habit of 'sequential thinking', as if along a single train line, with long gaps of inactivity in between. If you go to see a doctor, at least in the UK, he too is likely to deal with you one step at a time and no more. Thus, he might send you to the nurse or hospital for test X, but he will not even consider, let alone request, tests Y or Z until after he has had the result from test X. *illuminate one by one*

In this way patients in the UK can take months even to be diagnosed, let alone treated. That needless delay is partly because of this *'one step at a time'* mentality, which is so deeply ingrained in many doctors. Of course, another reason for their approach is lack of finance. Their policy guidelines often tell them to do tests one by one, not all together, in case some of the tests might later prove to have been unnecessary. So it is not always, or entirely, that individual doctor's fault. In some cases it is a fault of the system.

However, much of the time, that is not the reason, as it can also be due to lazy, sloppy thinking by the individual doctor, who has no imagination and no sense of urgency. Therefore, he thinks of just one thing to do and sends the patient off to try that, rather than think ahead more intelligently, and laterally. Instead, he could ask himself: "*What else could I be doing, checking or asking for right now, alongside that first step, so as to consider other possibilities, speed up the diagnosis, and get the right treatment started at the earliest point?*"

Try hard to eliminate these bad mental habits from your own way of approaching clients, projects or problems. Recalibrate yourself to think as you ought to, even if it doesn't come naturally to you, and even if those around you don't do likewise. If necessary, choose to be the only one in your firm who takes this lateral-thinking approach, with several 'saucepans' on the hob, all at the same time.

Fault 26 – Reluctance to 'take ownership' of tasks and also seeking to fob off clients or colleagues so as to avoid work

Anyone who has ever been in a hospital, or who has had to ring a large organisation such as an insurance company or government department will have experienced this problem. There are a great many staff whose first instinct when they receive a request for help, or a telephone call from a customer, or even from a colleague, is to try to fob them off with some excuse. Or they will tell them they need to see someone else, or ring someone else. Their aim is not to help that client or colleague, but only to get rid of them, so that they personally don't have to deal with his problem.

Therefore, they send the caller elsewhere, and give him *"the run-around"*, rather than willingly taking responsibility for the task. Often that worker would be perfectly capable of handling it, and they are the right person, or at least *a* right person to speak to. But they will tell you that you need someone else because they simply cannot be bothered with you and don't want to be 'lumbered' with your case. The same issue arises when bosses want to get things done and are looking for volunteers.

Staff will begin to run for cover because they don't want to be given the new or additional duty. They keep their heads down, speak of how busy they are, and try to avoid being asked to help with the problem that has arisen. They see it as valid to defend themselves from being *"put upon"* or *"taken advantage of"* by others and to make sure that they do not get more than their fair share of the tasks. Of course, a person can be so over-burdened that it is impossible, or at least inadvisable, for them to take on any more.

However, in such cases, the right approach is to be open with managers, to *say* that you have too much on and to ask to be given a period of respite. That is entirely appropriate, *if that is genuinely your situation*. However, what is not appropriate is for that employee, even if they are genuinely over-burdened, to seek to solve their own problem by giving clients and colleagues the run-around and fobbing them off to find help elsewhere. That displays not only dishonesty, but also a lack of concern for the needs of the client, or the business, and it amounts to putting your own needs ahead of theirs.

374

Moreover, it is all the more blameworthy because it is not done openly, but covertly, so that the client is deceived into thinking he needs to be ringing someone else. Even if you are over-burdened, it is not that caller's fault and it is not right to make him pay the price of you solving your own problem, whether real or otherwise, of being over-worked. On the whole, however, I question whether it is real because it is generally the *busiest* staff who will volunteer to help in an emergency and who will always take a phone call. It is the staff with the lowest caseloads, who are most prone to dodging responsibility.

So, they might claim to be over-worked, but the reality is usually that it is their colleagues who are actually over-worked, due in part to the reluctance of the lazy staff to take ownership of problems or accept their fair share of tasks. If you do take this selfish and dishonest approach, then good managers will eventually notice. Then you will pay the price for your attitude, as you will find that you are not promoted or given the pay rises that the more willing staff get.

In my law firm there were no set salaries or rigid grades. I paid every individual employee exactly what I thought *they* deserved, based on their own skill, attitude, character and work rate. Therefore, they were all on very different pay levels, even if they had the same length of service. Not every manager takes that approach, but the better ones do. Therefore, you will gain more, in the long term, by being enthusiastic and willing than by dodging responsivities.

Fault 27 - Seeking to make themselves indispensable, but in the wrong way, by selfishly refusing to share their own knowledge, skills or experience with other staff

If you work within a business for any length of time you are likely to develop certain areas of skill, knowledge or experience which other staff do not have. It may relate to any number of things, such as IT or other technical know-how, internal office procedures, or even something as basic as where things are stored or filed. The issue is what you should do when you have such skills or knowledge, especially if the management are asking you to show others what you know.

They may ask you to do that for efficiency reasons, to increase the number of staff who can assist in that area, so that they are not so heavily reliant upon you. I have come across this issue and have seen staff handle it both well and badly. Two employees spring to mind particularly for the selfish way in which they responded to requests to train others and to share their knowledge. In each case, they delayed, gave a variety of excuses, and were reluctant and obstructive. Eventually I gave up and took other steps to provide the training, because I knew they would not give it.

They knew they were the only person in my law firm who knew how to do tasks 'X' and 'Y' respectively. They were also determined to keep it that way, even in defiance of my explicit instructions. They never actually said *"No!"* out loud. They simply dragged their feet endlessly, came up with all sorts of implausible excuses, and never got around to giving anybody the training. When any person was sent to them to be shown how to do it, they fobbed them off, invented reasons for delay, and made sure they were never shown.

Their motive in refusing to give the training was that they considered they had a valuable skill. That skill was made all the more valuable *to them personally* by its uniqueness in our firm. So they felt it gave them *'leverage'* and that they could expect to obtain better pay and conditions, and more job security, if they remained the only person in the firm with that particular knowledge/skill. In both cases it backfired for them. I saw what they were doing and how they were defying me, and harming the interests of the business, solely to further their own interests.

That cold, calculating selfishness appalled me. I also saw it as an act of disloyalty both to me personally and to the firm as a whole. So, when the opportunity arose, I got rid of one of them and let the other go, without making any attempt to persuade her to stay. Nobody is ever indispensable especially if they try to go about things in that devious way. The right approach, if you want to make yourself indispensable, is to do the *exact opposite*. Share your knowledge and train others enthusiastically. In fact, volunteer to do so.

Help to build up the overall strength and quality of the firm by enabling as many as possible of the staff to know what you know and to improve their performance by learning from you. An employee who takes that approach is truly rare. They would probably be the only one in most firms, because the norm is to share nothing. If you operate as I recommend, you are actually more likely, in the longer term, to find favour with management, and gain advancement, especially if it is a well-run business, than if you pursue the usual selfish approach.

Even if the company doesn't appreciate or reward you, and even if they don't keep you on as an employee, you have still lost nothing by sharing your knowledge freely. That healthy, unselfish attitude will steadily seep into all other aspects of your work. That will eventually make you into the kind of person who will inevitably succeed, even if you have to go elsewhere, because of the effect it has on your overall character and approach to work. Therefore, you will certainly get your reward in your next job, even if you don't get it in your current workplace.

Fault 28 – Inability to keep their mouth shut and to maintain confidentiality about private or sensitive information

In most workplaces gossip is rife. The staff, and even bosses, give in to the temptation to reveal private information about the firm, colleagues or other sensitive matters. There is something that our sinful nature finds delicious in the giving and receiving of confidential information. The very fact that it is forbidden gives it much of its appeal.

The words of a whisperer are like delicious morsels;
  they go down into the inner parts of the body.
                    Proverbs 26:22 (ESV)

So the temptation is strong, and most of us are affected by it, but it is very unhealthy. If you want to be trusted enough to be promoted, you will have to learn how to control your tongue, avoid gossip, and keep things confidential. For many that is harder than keeping a box of chocolates on their desk and never touching them. But if you are determined to be the kind of employee God wants you to be, then resolve to do whatever is necessary to overcome the craving to divulge secrets. If you force yourself to do this you will have far less trouble, and so will the company you work for:

For lack of wood the fire goes out,
  and where there is no whisperer, quarreling ceases.
                    Proverbs 26:20 (ESV)

The amount of private and confidential information that comes your way will increase steadily as you rise in rank. Thus, every promotion adds to the problem in one sense. However, you are not likely to be promoted, or at least not to be promoted again and again, if those above you can see that you are a gossip and have no control of your mouth. At best, they will promote you no further. At worst, they may even demote or dismiss you. Most likely of all, they will simply make sure you are kept away from all sensitive or potentially damaging information. They will have to, for the sake of the business.

That one fault therefore has the potential to hold back your entire career. That is how serious it is. Senior managers need people they can trust and keeping secrets is one of the main ways in which such trust needs to be demonstrated. Therefore, be very strict with yourself from now on. If you know something confidential, then remind yourself that that is exactly what it is. Put it away in a separate compartment in your mind so that it can never be discussed, except with those who are authorised to hear it.

People who love gossip get a sense of importance from being able to share private information with colleagues. It makes them the centre of attention, with a group of eager listeners gathered round them in the canteen, or in a series of one to one conversations. If you are to overcome this compulsion to gossip, you must get control of your pride and also tackle any issues of insecurity, or any inferiority complex, that you may have. Be willing to be seen as someone who has no gossip to offer, or even as someone who knows nothing anyway.

That in itself is hard for many because, if you don't gossip, many colleagues will mistakenly assume that you are not important enough to have been told anything. It won't often occur to them that you do know, but simply aren't saying. Nevertheless, brace yourself and accept that some people will misunderstand and think you are unimportant. Don't seek to get your sense of worth in that way in the first place. Get it from being excellent at your job, and from being 100% trustworthy, not from holding forth at the water fountain about the secrets that you find out about in meetings or from typing your boss's letters.

Fault 29 – Allowing success or promotion to go to their head and becoming proud, bossy and intolerable to work with

I have known many people who did well at their jobs, and worked hard, such that they were promoted, only for it to go to their heads. Ironically, it can then become impossible to promote them any further, or even to let them remain in that new role, because of how they change. They can become proud and bossy and start pushing their weight around with those who used to be their colleagues. It is very sad, because it is such an unnecessary bar to further advancement in their careers. Yet it is most certainly a bar, because a wise manager will not allow such people to occupy higher positions.

Therefore, if you ever get a promotion, don't let it go to your head. Don't let it puff you up with haughtiness or self-importance and don't use that new role to show others that you now have power and authority. Those things are given to you to be used, in the right ways, and for the right reasons, not to give you an ego-trip or for you to take pleasure from them. Therefore, if you are given a promotion, or responsibility for some team, project or resource, make a conscious effort to humble yourself. In particular, avoid preening yourself, or showing off, or even the appearance of those things.

That too is important, because those around you may be acutely sensitive, and may be expecting you to become boastful. If so, they are all the more likely to misinterpret your actions and words unless you take care to go very clearly in the opposite direction. A prime example of how a person can change for the worse when promoted is a lawyer I once knew, whom I'll call 'Kelvin'. He was the junior salaried partner in his law firm when I was in that same role in my then firm. We both later went on to set up our own law firms, which we each wholly owned.

He did extremely well and I came across him a few years later, after he had achieved a lot of success. The transformation was appalling. I attended a meeting he chaired which involved lawyers from various law firms who were all on a panel, plus some of Kelvin's own staff. He was insufferably arrogant in his manner, and he deliberately humiliated one of his own staff in front of us. It was painful to witness. Yet Kelvin had been insignificant, and even geeky, when he had been in a junior position in his previous firm. Indeed, that fact may explain some of his insecurity.

From that, he changed into a pompous, boastful bully who pushed his weight around. He is, admittedly, at the top end of the haughtiness spectrum but, even amongst junior staff, the same kind of pride can be seen. I am thinking of a shop assistant, whom I will call *'Daisy'*. I was told about her by someone who worked alongside her. All that happened to Daisy was that she was made a key-holder for the shop. That simply meant she became one of the people who was responsible for opening up in the morning and locking up at night. It wasn't really even a 'promotion' at all, just an added duty.

Yet, when that key was given to Daisy, she was utterly transformed by it. She began to take on airs and graces and to talk down to her colleagues, as if she was in charge of them, which she wasn't. Unsurprisingly, that change of attitude annoyed everyone. In the end, the company sacked her because she developed such delusions of grandeur she became intolerable. So it isn't usually the people who rise from colonel to brigadier who are likely to become proud. If anything, they are less prone to it, because they have already had a number of promotions and have learned how to handle it.

The main problem is when lowly staff receive their first promotion or supervisory responsibility. They are the ones whose heads are most likely to be turned by it and to swell up. So, a lance corporal is more likely to lord it over a private than a brigadier is over a colonel. Therefore, try very hard not to take on any airs or graces if you do get a promotion, or if you achieve success in some other way and begin to be noticed. Try to treat others as you always did. Above all, don't talk down to anybody, or even seem to do so.

That said, at the same time, there is also a need to be willing to move up into your new role and to have the confidence to exert your new authority. But that should only be done in appropriate ways, and when the circumstances require it, not proudly or imperiously. Nevertheless, if you weren't willing to assert your authority at all, for fear of being considered haughty, you would fail in your first

379

duty at that new level. That is that you should actually do the job that you have been appointed to. At times, that has to involve using the new authority that you have been given.

Therefore, making clear decisions, exercising authority, and giving orders, even publicly, are not in themselves manifestations of pride. It entirely depends on the *manner* in which you go about it and the *heart attitude* you display while doing so. Therefore, be confident and decisive, but give your orders politely, modestly and with proper regard to the feelings of your former colleagues. Their feathers may already have been ruffled by your promotion. So, if you want to be given another promotion later, take care not to ruffle their feathers any further by your insensitivity now.

Fault 30 – Procrastination and "allowing the best to become the enemy of the good"

Procrastination, or putting tasks off until later, is not only a problem in the workplace, but wherever in life it arises, and it needs to be fought against. It mainly occurs when the task is difficult, dirty, dangerous or dull, such that the worker doesn't feel like tackling it just now. He prefers to leave it for another day, when he will be *"less busy"* or *"in a better mood"* or when he *"has more information"*. Of course, it is not possible to do everything today. Some things have to be put off, through no fault of yours.

Some tasks even benefit from delay, if the reasons for it are valid, and if that delay is not too long. However, on the whole, the excuses that people make for delay are not valid and it would have been far better to tackle the task earlier, ideally on day one. A common excuse is that by leaving the task until later we will be able to *"make a better job of it"*. We can tell ourselves that we will then be able to write a really good report, or give an excellent presentation, or draft a much more impressive Defence and Counterclaim. However, that is usually an illusion. In fact it is self-delusion.

It is referred to as *"making the best the enemy of the good"* because, in the forlorn hope of doing the very *best* work later on, you end up not doing the *good* work which you could have done at the outset. Very often, the reality is that the task only gets done at the last minute anyway, and in a rushed manner, just before the deferred deadline. If so, even less time is actually given to doing it in the end, not more. Ironically, the quality of work done is then lower, not higher, than if it had been done days, weeks, or even months earlier, when you first began putting it off.

There will, admittedly, be certain times where leaving it until later might produce a better outcome or product, but it will rarely be any more than a marginal improvement. Moreover, it will come at a high price in terms of delay to the client and also the stress that you experience in having that client, and your boss, chasing you for it. Therefore, far from being restful, the period of delay may exhaust and demoralise you, which is in stark contrast to the elation one feels from getting a job done early, and then being able to relax.

I first learned that lesson when I was 10 years old. Our class teacher used to set us a piece of homework every Friday which had to be written over the weekend and handed in on the Monday. It was usually a piece of creative writing. I would often leave it un-started all weekend, while I went out to play or watched TV. Then I finally had to do it on the Sunday evening, when it was not possible to put it off any longer. I still remember how that grim prospect got me down. The essay hung in the air like a dark cloud throughout the weekend.

Then, one particular Friday afternoon, I somehow took the notion to sit down and write the story there and then, as soon as I got home. An hour or so later, having done it, and with the whole weekend still ahead of me, I felt a surge of exhilaration. I have never forgotten that moment. That was the best weekend ever and I had a spring in my step the whole time, knowing that the homework had already been done and was not hanging over me.

Fault 31 – Complaining and moaning, especially where it is done to other staff, because it is corrosive to morale and highly contagious

Controlling our tongue is a major job. It is not only a matter of avoiding lying, gossiping, swearing, cursing and arguing. We also need to avoid *complaining*, which is yet another of those sins which people don't consider to be a sin. Many view moaning as a harmless activity, or at least as not being a sin. However, the truth is it is both sinful and harmful. Indeed, it is actually one of the most damaging things you can do, not only in the workplace, but anywhere, because of the knock-on effects which complaining has, both on you and others, as follows:

a) It alters the way you see your job, your boss, your firm and your customers/clients. The more you moan about them, the darker and greyer will be the *lens* that is over your eyes, through which you see the world. You will eventually train yourself only to be able to see half empty glasses instead of half full ones, only difficulties instead of opportunities, and only things to resent, rather than to give thanks for.

b) It alters the way in which other people, especially bosses, see you. Instead of considering you for promotion, they will increasingly see you as a liability, and even a menace, and with good reason.

c) It alters the way your colleagues see the firm, its customers, their own bosses, and also their fellow workers. They will become contaminated by your negativity, ingratitude, resentment and bitterness. This has a remarkably corrosive effect on them and is also highly contagious. So a negative employee can quickly cause a whole team to become resentful and to start complaining themselves. This then lowers the morale and efficiency of the business as a whole, as well as harming those colleagues and holding them back in their careers.

It is not just my idea that complaining is harmful, and also a sin. That is how God sees it, which is why He objects to it so strongly. Consider how God responded to the complaints of the Israelites in the wilderness and how severely He punished them for it:

22 Then Moses made Israel set out from the Red Sea, and they went into the wilderness of Shur. They went three days in the wilderness and found no water. 23 When they came to Marah, they could not drink the water of Marah because it was bitter; therefore it was named Marah. 24 And the people grumbled against Moses, saying, "What shall we drink?"

Exodus 15:22-24 (ESV)

1 All the congregation of the people of Israel moved on from the wilderness of Sin by stages, according to the commandment of the LORD, and camped at Rephidim, but there was no water for the people to drink. 2 Therefore the people quarreled with Moses and said, "Give us water to drink." And Moses said to them, "Why do you quarrel with me? Why do you test the LORD?" 3 But the people thirsted there for water, and the people grumbled against Moses and said, "Why did you bring us up out of Egypt, to kill us and our children and our livestock with thirst?"

Exodus 17:1-3 (ESV)

1 And the people complained in the hearing of the LORD about their misfortunes, and when the LORD heard it, his anger was kindled, and the fire of the LORD burned among them and consumed some outlying parts of the camp. 2 Then the people cried out to Moses, and Moses prayed to the LORD, and the fire died down. 3 So the name of that place was called Taberah, because the fire of the LORD burned among them.

Numbers 11:1-3 (ESV)

Is this a misapplication of text? The Jews had seen God do amazing things in Egypt - their 'grumbling' was a display of faithlessness ∆

382

Perhaps the hardest task is to recognise that you are complaining *while you are doing it*. To be able to do that, you firstly need to become able to see it for what it is and also to accept that it is wrong, rather than justify it to yourself. Having seen all that, you can then start the process of rooting it out of your thinking and, above all, out of your speech. When there are difficulties or disappointments at work, or where the management's decisions and/or the working conditions, are not as you would wish, force yourself to close your mouth.

Then don't say anything at all about it. Even if what you were planning to say was 100% true, it is still a complaint. Indeed, the complaints of the Israelites in the wilderness were often entirely *accurate*. God never said they were *lying*, but only that they were *complaining*. Therefore, they really were thirsty. There really was no water. There really were no cucumbers, and no onions or garlic either. But that didn't stop God being angry when they complained about those facts.

A justified complaint - unlead to neglisent

So, don't tell yourself that it is alright to say a thing as long as it is true. It isn't if it amounts to complaining, especially if that complaint is about your job, your firm or those who manage you. Therefore, get an 'off switch' fitted to your mouth, so that you can stop yourself from even starting to complain. Or, if you have begun to do so, then learn how to stop yourself, in mid-sentence. Train yourself instead to think and speak of good things, which you appreciate, and for which you can give thanks. *How can you desire excellence of quality of not complain? A complaint is a criticism that's justified.*

If you think that your job is so bad that you would have to search for such things, then go ahead and search. The fact that they aren't obvious to you does not mean that there are no such things. It simply means that *you* have become so negative that you no longer recognise them, even when they are right in front of you. So start to cultivate the habit of giving thanks. Do so privately, to yourself, but also in your prayers. Here are a few examples of things about your job which you could appreciate, and for which you could thank God:

a) that you have a job at all – many people don't

b) that you get paid, at whatever salary level or hourly rate you are on. You can be sure that there are vast numbers of others, at least in foreign countries, who get less.

c) that the difficulties or hard tasks which you currently face will enable you to learn, improve, and gain experience

d) that you have some good bosses or colleagues, from whom you can learn how to do things

e) that you have some bad bosses or colleagues, from whom you can learn how *not* to do things

383

If I knew the exact terms and conditions of your job I am confident that I could make a far longer list of good things, that you could give thanks for. So could you, if you looked at them correctly, with the right attitude, in the way God wants you to, and not as a complainer. Try it. Look at your contract. Look also at your working day, your hours, your conditions, your bosses and colleagues. Begin to identify, and to list, all the good things that others, who do not have your job, don't have and which you would not have either if you did not work there.

That is not to say that there are no bad things about your job, and no bad people in your workplace. How could there not be any? If your job was 100% perfect in every way, what scope would there be for you to learn, or grow, or to make discoveries about your own faults? If you practise this policy of giving thanks on an ongoing basis you will be amazed, even after a few weeks, at how much better everything seems. Nothing may actually have changed, but the way that you *see everything* will certainly be very different, and that is vitally important.

Cultivate appreciation not thanklessness !

All 31 faults set out in one convenient, abbreviated list

Each of these common faults on the part of employees need to be reflected on separately and considered carefully one by one. However, it will also help to see the broader picture if I set them all out together in one list, with just the headings. Why not photograph this list and keep it on your phone, so that you can look at it from time to time and reflect on each of the points?

1. Laziness

2. Low standards and lack of attention to detail

3. Unfaithfulness to bosses, clients and colleagues

4. Not truly caring about their work or the fate of their client, patient or customer to the point where it really matters to them

5. Dishonesty

6. Unreliability

7. Not seeing themselves as a servant and having no real understanding of the concept of service

8. Reluctance to endure any difficulty, hardship or pressure at work and seeking excessively to avoid these, irrespective of the effect on others

9. Unwillingness to be open about mistakes, or to admit that they don't know things, or to ask questions, especially in front of others

10. Failing to give honour to their bosses and even directly dishonouring them

11. Lack of interest, self-motivation and enthusiasm

12. Being content to settle for mediocrity rather than seeking to become the very best they can possibly be in terms of skill, knowledge and experience

13. Lack of initiative or inventiveness and giving no thought to how the systems and procedures of their job could be altered or improved

14. Unwillingness to be corrected, criticised or rebuked, even when it is done constructively, and resenting, or even hating, any boss who seeks to do so

15. Being discontented with their wages, hours, terms and working conditions and feeling envious and resentful about what others have, or earn, or are allowed to do

16. Unfaithfulness to colleagues, such that they let others down, fail to pull their weight and even engage in gossip

17. Automatically assuming themselves to be in the right and to be the most important person in the room

18. Being unable to see themselves as they really are, and as others see them, but only as they imagine themselves to be

19. Having no understanding of duty or responsibility and thinking exclusively in terms of rights and entitlements

20. Cowardice - mainly morally, but also physically

21. Unwillingness to start at the bottom

22. Unwillingness to take extra work home voluntarily, or to work late, or to do anything outside of their stated contractual terms

23. Being a negative, defeatist 'can't do person' who can only see obstacles, and reasons why things cannot be done, rather than advantages, solutions and possible ways forward

24. Being unwilling ever to say no to clients, colleagues or bosses, or to give them any bad news, or warn of problems ahead

25. Being unable to consider tasks simultaneously, but only sequentially. Also being unable to think laterally, anticipate problems, or ask questions which are not on a single 'train line'

26. Reluctance to take ownership of tasks and seeking to fob off clients or colleagues when they call, so as to avoid work

27. Seeking to make themselves indispensable, but in the wrong way, by selfishly refusing to share their own knowledge, skills or experience with other staff

28. Inability to keep their mouth shut and to maintain confidentiality about private or sensitive information

29. Allowing success or promotion to go to their head and becoming proud, bossy and intolerable to work with

30. Procrastination and also "allowing the best to become the enemy of the good"

31. Complaining and moaning, especially where it is done to other staff, because it is corrosive to morale and highly contagious

God is telling us to do good (something that's beneficial) or be punished - not do something evil of detrimental to your health or be punished.

Repentance is the f of G

No f of G because don't see him correctly - How DANGEROUS He is - believe a false view - idol of God as All love, forgiveness, kind,... NOT Holy, Righteous, Just... You don't fear God of shun evil because you don't know how AWESOME he is - believe The lie - of a God whose wimpish, weak, passive, careless... Misleading false image of God - your idol prevents you from f of G. Wrong view of God!

We've equated positive with truth of negative with not true Likewise - we fail to distinguish between Fact & Feeling. we say - "2 feel..." not "2 think..." Emotion have trumped reason. Need to distinguish between the two don't be emotion lead but - reason/evidence lead. The Truth will set you free from emotion power over you Distinguish between feelings & facts - is Vital to be wise.

386

CHAPTER 12

WISE PEOPLE SEEK TO UNDERSTAND MONEY

The generous man will be prosperous,
And he who waters will himself be watered.
Proverbs 11:25 (NASB)

The LORD makes poor and makes rich;
*   he brings low, he also exalts.*
1 Samuel 2:7 (RSV)

[17] Beware lest you say in your heart, 'My power and the might of my hand have gotten me this wealth.' [18] You shall remember the LORD your God, for it is he who gives you power to get wealth; that he may confirm his covenant which he swore to your fathers, as at this day.
Deuteronomy 8:17-18 (RSV)

[24] There is one who scatters, and yet increases all the more,
And there is one who withholds what is justly due, and yet it results only in want.
[25] The generous man will be prosperous,
And he who waters will himself be watered.
Proverbs 11:24-25 (NASB)

[19] He who tills his land will have plenty of bread,
*   but he who follows worthless pursuits will have plenty of poverty.*
[20] A faithful man will abound with blessings,
*   but he who hastens to be rich will not go unpunished.*
Proverbs 28:19-20 (RSV)

[5] The plans of the diligent lead surely to abundance,
*   but every one who is hasty comes only to want.*
[6] The getting of treasures by a lying tongue
*   is a fleeting vapor and a snare of death.*
Proverbs 21:5-6 (RSV)

Wealth hastily gotten will dwindle,
*   but he who gathers little by little will increase it.*
Proverbs 13:11 (RSV)

The reward for humility and fear of the LORD
*   is riches and honor and life.*
Proverbs 22:4 (RSV)

387

Why should fools have money in hand to buy wisdom,
when they are not able to understand it?
Proverbs 17:16 (NIV)

In all toil there is profit,
but mere talk tends only to want.
Proverbs 14:23 (RSV)

Why discuss money at all?   What has it got to do with wisdom or Christianity?

Some people think money is not a polite subject for conversation. However, the Bible has a lot to say about it, as the verses at the start of this chapter, plus those that follow, clearly demonstrate. Moreover, those are by no means the only passages. The fact is that money is important, not only for what it can do, and what it signifies, but also for the hold it can have over people if they make the grave error of loving it. Jesus Himself warned us of this:

[19] "Do not lay up for yourselves treasures on earth, where moth and rust consume and where thieves break in and steal, [20] but lay up for yourselves treasures in heaven, where neither moth nor rust consumes and where thieves do not break in and steal.
Matthew 6:19-20 (RSV)

He then went on to add:

"No one can serve two masters; for either he will hate the one and love the other, or he will be devoted to the one and despise the other. You cannot serve God and mammon.
Matthew 6:24 (RSV)

Even more radically, He also said:

So therefore, whoever of you does not renounce all that he has cannot be my disciple.
Luke 14:33 (RSV)

By 'mammon', Jesus meant money, wealth or possessions generally. If it is wrongly handled and wrongly regarded and, above all, if it is loved or worshiped, money is able to ensnare us and to get control of our hearts and minds. So, there is a very real danger. Yet, at the same time, the Bible has a lot to say about how we should handle money. Therefore, it is clearly not envisaged that money itself is intrinsically wrong, or should not be used, or that it will cease to exist.

Money is an essential part of our lives and we cannot avoid coming into contact with it. The only choices we have are to handle it well or to handle it badly, to have a right attitude to it or a wrong attitude, to own it or be owned by it. So this chapter is about how we can handle, and regard, money in the right way, which will also require us to examine the many different ways in which it can be mishandled or wrongly regarded.

The biblical concept of 'stewardship'

Before we begin to look at the issues of earning, giving, saving, investing and so on, it would be appropriate to look first at the concept of *'stewardship'*. The key to understanding this is to realise that none of us ever truly *owns* anything. At least in this life, nothing is entirely or permanently *ours*, because everything actually belongs to God. It is all His and we are merely temporary *stewards*, or you could say *custodians* or *caretakers*, of *His* property. The position is helpfully stated in these passages:

¹ This is how one should regard us, as servants of Christ and stewards of the mysteries of God. ² Moreover it is required of stewards that they be found trustworthy.

1 Corinthians 4:1-2 (RSV)

As each has received a gift, employ it for one another, as good stewards of God's varied grace:

1 Peter 4:10 (RSV)

Admittedly, apostle Peter is primarily referring to our stewardship of our gifts and talents, particularly spiritual gifts. But the point about stewardship is also of general application and covers everything we have or own, including our own bodies. Even they do not actually belong to us, to be exact, because God *created us*. He therefore considers that He owns us and can do with us whatever He chooses. He can also make whatever requirements He wants in relation to our use of the possessions that have been placed in our care.

His ownership of us is then made even more emphatic than that, because God did not only create us. He also *'bought'* us back, when Jesus died for us on the cross to redeem, or purchase, us from sin and thus to set us free from Satan's grip. These blunt verses therefore tell us exactly where we stand in terms of God's ownership of us, rather than us owning ourselves:

For everyone belongs to me, the parent as well as the child—both alike belong to me. The one who sins is the one who will die.

Ezekiel 18:4 (NIV)

Specific & General applications

¹⁹ Do you not know that your bodies are temples of the Holy Spirit, who is in you, whom you have received from God? You are not your own; ²⁰ you were bought at a price. Therefore honor God with your bodies.

1 Corinthians 6:19-20 (NIV)

King David also makes a helpful comment on this point when he refers to the money which he, and many others, contributed to enable the first Temple to be built. Although it was given by him and by those others, David acknowledges that all of that money came from God and was actually God's own property anyway:

"But who am I, and what is my people, that we should be able thus to offer willingly? For all things come from you, and of your own have we given you.

1 Chronicles 29:14 (ESV)

Accordingly, our starting point in looking at every aspect of the broad subject of money and possessions, and also our time, energy and talents, is that we are *mere stewards*. We *own nothing* and are simply handling *God's property* on His behalf. We will therefore be answerable to Him at the judgment for what we did with everything He ever gave us, whether it be gifts, talents or abilities, or money and possessions, or even our own bodies. We shall each have to give an account of our entire handling of everything during the time of our stewardship, from the moment of our conversion until the day we die.

However much or little you have, and whatever you are doing, God has every right to expect you to act in accordance with His specific commands and also His general values and priorities. That means you must do with 'your' time, energy, money and possessions *what He would want you to do*. You cannot simply please yourself, as if it all belonged to you and was none of His business. It *is* His business, as you will one day find out, even if only at the Judgment.

But it would be far better if you were to discover that fact now. Then that understanding of your true status as a steward, *not an owner*, can colour everything you do, especially with the money and possessions which God has temporarily placed under your care. If so, you will be far better placed to handle them correctly. In particular, you can then make all your decisions on the basis of what *He* would want, and what best suits *His* purposes, for you and others, rather than merely to please yourself.

390

We need, at the outset, to denounce the false teaching on money, and the perverse definition of *'prosperity'*, which is coming from the *'money preachers'*

One of the problems with trying to address the whole subject of money from a genuine, biblical perspective is that there are so many church leaders out there who are addressing it from a *false* and *unbiblical* perspective. However, because their teaching is so worldly, and so in tune with our sinful flesh nature, it resonates with multitudes of people. Therefore, it is currently drowning out those few faithful leaders who try to teach the truth about all of this.

Let me begin therefore by naming just a few of these false teachers, because there are far too many to be able to list them all, or even all the main ones. I am referring to men like Benny Hinn, Creflo Dollar, Joel Osteen, Kenneth Copeland, Robert Tilton and Jerry Savelle and also to women like Joyce Meyer and Paula White, and to all the many others like them who teach the same kind of worldliness. By so doing, they are building up huge fortunes for themselves at the expense of their naïve and gullible followers.

The 'turnover' from their ministries, or rather their businesses, which is a more accurate description of what they do, often runs into millions of dollars. Therefore, being a money preacher is obviously good business. However, it is *not good theology*, because it does not reflect God's heart, or what the Bible says. The main problem with the money preachers, and their *'prosperity gospel'* is that it is based on *the love of money*, which is the very attitude that Jesus warned us *not* to have. Their teaching is all about: *They openly teach the opposite of what Jesus thought*

a)   amassing treasure here, in this life

b)   focusing on money as if it was central

c)   idolising money and wealth

d)   treating God as if He was a vending machine, from whom we get what we want

e)   treating God as if He was obliged to give money to us

f)   focusing on what we can get, rather than on what we can give

g)   seeing the level of your wealth as a direct indicator of the extent of God's approval of you

None of the above aims or attitudes are biblical. They are all false and they arise due to the money preachers either misunderstanding Scripture, or directly inventing doctrines themselves, or having ideas whispered into their minds by demons. The one place they are not getting their teaching and practices from is the Bible. Above all, their heart attitude is not godly and comes entirely from the world, the flesh and the Devil, not from God. So, although money in itself is not evil, and although becoming rich is no sin, the *craving to become rich*, and the *obsessive over-emphasis on money*, is evil.

It is called *'the love of money'* and that is exactly what Jesus warned us to avoid, not to adopt as our practice or make into a doctrine. That said, in the pages which follow, I am going to advocate a number of things which, to the uninformed, or the badly taught, may sound a little bit like some of the things that money preachers say. But that is only because their false teaching is based, at least in part, upon the twisting or perverting of what the Bible *does say*. So, the Bible does urge us to earn, save and invest and to build successful careers or businesses, and to make good profits from doing so.

It even tells us that if we give generously, in accordance with God's instructions, then He will reward us for doing so. Moreover, He may very well choose to give some of those rewards in this world, not only in the next. So, all of those things are valid biblical concepts, *provided they are correctly defined and understood*. However, if they are not, then they become false doctrines, in just the same way as if you wrongly defined sin, repentance, judgment, Hell, salvation or faith, as so many people do.

Most false doctrines are just true doctrines that have been misunderstood, twisted, altered, taken from, or added to, in order to make them false. But one can do all that while still making it sound quite a lot like the truth. We shall therefore try to define and explain various biblical words correctly. We shall also try to strip away the false ideas that have been added to the true doctrines, or which have been put in their place.

What then is the proper, biblical definition of 'prosperity'?

There can be no doubt at all that God intends His people to *'prosper'*, or to be *'blessed'*. He also wants that prosperity to take effect in every aspect of their lives, including spiritually, physically, mentally, emotionally, *and financially*. That is absolutely undeniable. We see this stated unmistakably in the very first Psalm and it is restated many times elsewhere where it speaks of the godly person and says that *"...in all that he does he prospers."*

¹ Blessed is the man
who walks not in the counsel of the wicked,
nor stands in the way of sinners,
* nor sits in the seat of scoffers;*

² but his delight is in the law of the LORD,
   and on his law he meditates day and night.
³ He is like a tree
   planted by streams of water,
that yields its fruit in its season,
   and its leaf does not wither.
In all that he does, he prospers.
                              Psalm 1:1-3 (RSV)

King David also speaks of prospering, shortly before his death, when he gives advice to his son, Solomon, who was to be the next King of Israel. That prosperity is dependent upon being obedient to God's commands, but the point is that David is very clear that this will cause him to *prosper*:

Then you will prosper if you are careful to observe the statutes and the rules that the LORD commanded Moses for Israel. Be strong and courageous. Fear not; do not be dismayed.
                              1 Chronicles 22:13 (ESV)

Likewise, we are told of how King Hezekiah prospered as a result of his obedience and faithfulness:

²⁰ Thus Hezekiah did throughout all Judah, and he did what was good and right and faithful before the LORD his God. ²¹ And every work that he undertook in the service of the house of God and in accordance with the law and the commandments, seeking his God, he did with all his heart, and prospered.
                              2 Chronicles 31:20-21 (ESV)

However, it is clear that even those whom God promises to prosper will also experience difficulties, because King David indicates in Psalm 34 that the righteous will face many afflictions:

Many are the afflictions of the righteous,
 but the LORD delivers him out of them all.
              Psalm 34:19 (ESV)

Therefore, the questions we need to address are:

a) What exactly is meant by *'prosper'*?

b) Is it an *absolute* rule, without any exceptions, or only a *general* principle, which may be subject to variations, such as when the righteous suffer afflictions?

393

c) Does it always have to apply here and now in *this life*? Or is God free to keep His promises by giving some of us prosperity in the *next life*, rather than here?

The answers to (b) and (c) above are that it is indeed a general rule. Therefore, it is clearly subject to exceptions. For example, the 'good thief' on the cross did prosper, but not in this life. At least he did not do so in the way that the money preachers speak of. His reward came later, as has been the case for very many faithful Christians who have faced persecution, and even martyrdom, in this life. For them, the prosperity that God promises, or at least part of it, had to come after their deaths, not before.

Yet God has not broken His word, because He has never promised, as *an absolute rule*, that that prosperity will come here and now. He is therefore entirely free to provide some or all of His rewards to us later, and yet still be true to His own word. As for what exactly the Bible means by the word *'prosper'*, it can and does include financial success and abundance. But it is by no means limited only to that. The best definition I can give is that it means to be where God wants you to be, at the right time, doing what He wants you to do, and in the way that He wants you to do it.

For example, Jesus prospered even on the day of His crucifixion. He was exactly where God the Father wanted Him to be, doing exactly what He was meant to do, at exactly the right time, and with complete success. What He achieved that day can thus be said to have prospered perfectly. It achieved everything it was meant to achieve, and it was a complete victory over sin and Satan. Yet, to those standing around the cross at the time, it did not *look* like success or prosperity. Indeed, it looked like the very opposite.

Worldliness isn't prosperity

He was suffering and even dying. Yet He was doing God's will and perfectly achieving everything that He had set out to achieve. We see the same thing, on a much smaller scale, in the life of Joseph, Jacob's son. He was betrayed and sold into slavery in Egypt by his brothers. He then ended up in prison for many years, due to being falsely accused. However, while he was in Potiphar's house, and even afterwards in the prison, God was prospering him, firstly in the sense that He was causing everything that Joseph did to succeed:

[1] *Now Joseph had been brought down to Egypt, and Potiphar, an officer of Pharaoh, the captain of the guard, an Egyptian, had bought him from the Ishmaelites who had brought him down there. [2] The LORD was with Joseph, and he became a successful man, and he was in the house of his Egyptian master. [3] His master saw that the LORD was with him and that the LORD caused all that he did to succeed in his hands. [4] So Joseph found favor in his sight and attended him, and he made him overseer of his house and put him in charge of all that he had. [5] From the time that he made him overseer in his*

house and over all that he had, the LORD blessed the Egyptian's house for Joseph's sake; the blessing of the LORD was on all that he had, in house and field.

Genesis 39:1-5 (ESV)

[19] As soon as his master heard the words that his wife spoke to him, "This is the way your servant treated me," his anger was kindled. [20] And Joseph's master took him and put him into the prison, the place where the king's prisoners were confined, and he was there in prison. [21] But the LORD was with Joseph and showed him steadfast love and gave him favor in the sight of the keeper of the prison. [22] And the keeper of the prison put Joseph in charge of all the prisoners who were in the prison. Whatever was done there, he was the one who did it. [23] The keeper of the prison paid no attention to anything that was in Joseph's charge, because the LORD was with him. And whatever he did, the LORD made it succeed.

A job well done

Genesis 39:19-23 (ESV)

Words like 'prosperity' and 'success' are therefore relative terms, not absolute ones. Thus we can be prospering or succeeding, so far as God is concerned, even though there are things in our lives that are not as we would wish them to be. So, in all the years that Joseph spent in slavery in Potipher's house, and then in prison, he was still prospering, in the sense of doing all things well. However, it went further than that.

God was also using those years to train and develop Joseph, so as to be ready for the tasks that lay ahead, when Joseph would be used by God to save the chosen people. That process of preparation was also part of what it meant for him to be succeeding or prospering. Therefore, the mere fact that you have problems and even face persecution, does not, *in itself*, prove that God is not prospering you. Such hardship may well be part of God's plan for you, just as it was for Joseph:

Making you wise — that's true prosperity

[4] So Joseph said to his brothers, "Come near to me, please." And they came near. And he said, "I am your brother, Joseph, whom you sold into Egypt. [5] And now do not be distressed or angry with yourselves because you sold me here, for God sent me before you to preserve life. [6] For the famine has been in the land these two years, and there are yet five years in which there will be neither plowing nor harvest. [7] And God sent me before you to preserve for you a remnant on earth, and to keep alive for you many survivors. [8] So it was not you who sent me here, but God. He has made me a father to Pharaoh, and lord of all his house and ruler over all the land of Egypt.

Genesis 45:4-8 (ESV)

Therefore, we need to be careful, in our own lives, not to misinterpret the events and circumstances that we face. If we do, we may fail to see that God is still with

If wisdom is more valuable than gold, silver and diamonds to grow in wisdom/fear of God is true and eternal prosperity.

395

us, and is still prospering us, even where we are going through hard times. By the same token, when viewed from the opposite direction, you must not automatically assume that financial wealth is due to God's blessing, especially if it has come to you through your own dishonesty, or by mistreating others. It may actually have been given to you by the demons in return for your having served *them* faithfully, not for serving God.

Remember also that some of the richest people in the world are utterly corrupt and godless. Therefore, it is Satan, *'the god of this world'*, who is prospering them, not the God of the Bible. Thus, the presence or absence of financial wealth, *in itself*, does not necessarily prove anything, in either direction. Neither does the presence or absence of adversity or persecution. You would need to know more than that to be able to form a reliable judgment, in either case, as to whether or not the person is prospering by God's definition.

The virtue of hard work and of earning as much as you can, subject to not sinning in order to do so

One of the virtues which is regularly promoted in the Bible is that of hard work. Likewise, laziness is condemned regularly, and more so than many other sins that we might assume to be worse. God wants us to work hard in everything we do, including our ordinary paid job. In fact, He wants us to do it as if we were working directly for Him which is, actually, exactly what we are doing:

²³ Whatever your task, work heartily, as serving the Lord and not men, ²⁴ knowing that from the Lord you will receive the inheritance as your reward; you are serving the Lord Christ.

Colossians 3:23-24 (RSV)

Your job or business really matters to God. It is not a departure from your service to God, or from His will. It *is* service to Him and it *is* His will. Therefore, He wants you to put your whole heart, soul and strength into doing well in your work or business and into earning all that you can, provided you can do so without being sinful, unfaithful, dishonest or neglecting some other duty. As John Wesley famously said: *"Earn all you can. Save all you can. Give all you can."*

We shall look at saving and giving shortly but the point, for now, is that there is *nothing at all wrong* with earning a high wage, making a big profit or being successful in general. That may be to state the obvious, but it needs to be said, because there is a widespread school of thought to the effect that wealth, profit and success are somehow inherently sinful, sordid and 'unchristian'.

396

There is a vein of asceticism, or you might call it a 'poverty spirit', or 'poverty attitude', which runs through many British churches in particular. It promotes the idea that there is some kind of virtue in poverty, which there isn't, and that money or wealth are intrinsically evil and squalid, which they are not. It is only the *love of money* which is a root of all kinds of evil, *not money itself*. Money, in itself, is morally neutral. It entirely depends on *how you got it*, what you *do with it*, and whether it has *a hold over you*.

Therefore, eliminate from your thinking any idea that you may have picked up, that there is virtue or glory in being poor, or that God doesn't want you to maximise your earnings (by honest means) or to aim to rise as high as you can in your job, business or profession. Then feel free to work as hard as you can, to earn as much as you can, and to rise as high as you can. But, at the same time, do all of that with a proper sense of balance. That is do not neglect your duties to your wife, children, parents or church as a result of focusing excessively on your job or the pursuit of success.

The vital importance of *'thrift'*, an old-fashioned word which has dropped out of the language and needs to be restored

The great virtue of *thrift* has been largely forgotten. Probably only a minority now know what the word even means, let alone practice it. It is the policy of avoiding or minimising your *spending* so as to live as economically as you *reasonably* can, consistent with all of your other duties and obligations. However, it does not mean lapsing into the errors of asceticism or obsessive penny-pinching. So, a Christian should take all *reasonable* steps to *avoid* spending money, but not unreasonable steps. He will also *reduce* his expenditure by getting good *value* if possible, when he does have to buy things.

Whatever you earn, whether large or small, you should always seek to get your spending as low as you reasonably can. Try to avoid waste and needless expense or extravagance so as to keep as much money as possible left over for saving, giving and investing, and also for other things such as pension contributions. That is a form of saving, but is in a sub-category of its own, because it is very long term. Let me give two examples of what I mean by thrift. Firstly, when I was in business, running a law firm, I made it my policy never to buy a brand new car.

I could easily have afforded to do so, but I always felt that I could not justify it. It did not make sense to me, financially, given that brand new cars depreciate substantially in value on the very day you buy them. Therefore, throughout my entire life, including nearly two decades in business, I never had a brand new car. I always bought them second hand, even if they were only slightly second hand, such as ex-demonstrator cars. That way I got a reduced price to reflect the fact that they were not brand new. That approach always seemed sensible to me and it reduced what I had to spend.

Another example was in relation to the premises I used for my law firm. When I started it, money was very scarce indeed so I chose to operate from cheap rented office space, on a short-term licence rather than a lease, and in an unfashionable industrial park. It was not prestigious in any way. In fact, it was rather shabby. Nevertheless, as the law firm grew, and became more and more profitable, I still chose to stay in that unattractive industrial park and I just kept on renting more and more office space there.

I did look into the possibility of moving to more attractive and prestigious premises on two or three occasions over the years. Those would obviously have been more expensive. However, I concluded each time that it would be better value to stay where I was. So, although I *could* afford it, I never got an impressive building, whereas many law firms do have them, even if they can't afford it. I therefore remained, for 13 years, close to a lot of grimy industrial units, but it saved a lot of money. *Stay within your means - not the Joneses*

It also had the advantage, later on, of making it easier for me to sell up and move out because I did not have the encumbrance of a complicated long-term lease. I did not have any freehold ownership of commercial property to dispose of either, which would have been an even bigger inconvenience when I later decided to get out of practising law. So, as it turned out, choosing to go for value, rather than prestige, had additional advantages over and above the cost saving. For one thing, it meant I did not suffer from the crash in property prices that later happened.

In support of my contention that thrift has largely fallen out of the public's thinking, and even their vocabulary, I would point to the financial crisis of 2008, the dire effects of which are still being felt. That catastrophe arose for a number of reasons, in particular the following features, which have become endemic in western culture. For over 20 years now, a large proportion of the population have been:

a) routinely spending *all* of their income every week or month and considering that to be normal

b) assuming that if they want a thing they *must have it,* whether or not it is truly needed

c) assuming that if they want a thing they must have it *now,* immediately, rather than saving up and waiting to buy it later

d) assuming they must have *expensive,* superior, branded items rather than cheaper unbranded alternatives

Economics!
Cost effectiveness & efficiency

398

Weighing up the
COSTS

e) assuming that it is right and proper, and entirely normal, to *borrow money* to get what they want, even for consumption items, not just for houses, cars or businesses

f) considering it normal to remain *constantly in debt* and overdraft, and also to owe money on their credit cards, rather than pay them off in full each month

So, one of our first tasks is to adopt the policy of thrift and to develop it as a consistent habit until it becomes our default-setting, rather than continuing to let money pour through our hands like water, as so many people do. In addition, learn the art of *budgeting*, whereby you plan in advance what money you have and what is already 'spoken for' in terms of future bills and anticipated expenditure. Work it all out, as best you can, so that there are as few surprises as possible and you don't imagine yourself to have more disposable cash than you really have.

Develop the art of being *content* with whatever money you have, however little that may be, and also with your circumstances, whatever they may be. Then live within your means.

If you want to be happy, and to handle money wisely, you must learn how *to be content* with whatever money or possessions you have, large or small, and also in whatever circumstances you face, whether good or bad. Contentment is essentially a *decision, not a talent*. However, it can also be made into a habit, if you practice it for long enough, and if you are sufficiently determined to make it one. Contentment is very little understood, or spoken about, in today's churches.

However, it ought to be, because it has a direct bearing on many other issues and it certainly has a central part to play in enabling you to become skilled in handling money. So let's firstly define what *contentment* is. Then let's consider how we can achieve and maintain it, no matter what we have, or don't have, or what circumstances we face. Let's begin by looking at some passages from Paul's letters which address this vital issue:

⁶ There is great gain in godliness with contentment; ⁷ for we brought nothing into the world, and we cannot take anything out of the world; ⁸ but if we have food and clothing, with these we shall be content. ⁹ But those who desire to be rich fall into temptation, into a snare, into many senseless and hurtful desires that plunge men into ruin and destruction. ¹⁰ For the love of money is the root of all evils; it is through this craving that some have wandered away from the faith and pierced their hearts with many pangs.

1 Timothy 6:6-10 (RSV)

11 Not that I am speaking of being in need, for I have learned in whatever situation I am to be content. 12 I know how to be brought low, and I know how to abound. In any and every circumstance, I have learned the secret of facing plenty and hunger, abundance and need. 13 I can do all things through him who strengthens me.

Philippians 4:11-13 (ESV)

Note also what King Solomon said:

He who loves money will not be satisfied with money, nor he who loves wealth with his income; this also is vanity.

Ecclesiastes 5:10 (ESV)

Note how low Paul puts the bar, in 1 Timothy 6:8 above, in terms of how little we actually need in order to be content, i.e. food and clothing, and he doesn't mean anything expensive either. We know that, because Paul's ministry resulted in him facing all manner of hardships, difficulties and persecutions, which he summarises in this famous passage:

24 Five times I received at the hands of the Jews the forty lashes less one. 25 Three times I was beaten with rods. Once I was stoned. Three times I was shipwrecked; a night and a day I was adrift at sea; 26 on frequent journeys, in danger from rivers, danger from robbers, danger from my own people, danger from Gentiles, danger in the city, danger in the wilderness, danger at sea, danger from false brothers; 27 in toil and hardship, through many a sleepless night, in hunger and thirst, often without food, in cold and exposure. 28 And, apart from other things, there is the daily pressure on me of my anxiety for all the churches.

2 Corinthians 11:24-28 (ESV)

Would you be willing to swap jobs with Paul and put up with all the hardships he faced? An even harder question is could you bring yourself to be content if you had to endure everything he suffered, and on such a remorselessly ongoing basis? Most of us wouldn't, or at least not without being given the same measure of grace which Paul was given. However, Paul's success in this area wasn't entirely about grace. In Philippians 4:11 above Paul says that he had *learned* to be content.

That is very significant as it means that it took time and effort and that his contentment was acquired in stages, through experience, rather than being given to him at birth, as his huge IQ was. That encourages me. It means I can learn to be content too, and that my level of contentment is a choice and is not limited by the extent of my abilities. Therefore, you and I could be just as contented as Paul *if we choose to be* and if we are sufficiently determined to learn how to do it. Therefore, God wants us to learn how to be content with the money we have.

400

That applies to us all, no matter what our wages are, what house we live in, what kind of car we drive, and even whether we have a car at all, or indeed have anything else for that matter. Contentment is an attitude of mind, and one which you can choose to have, or at least learn to acquire. It can therefore be achieved and maintained by anybody, anywhere, at any time, and in any circumstances, if they want to. It is as categorical as that, provided you have the food and clothing that Paul spoke of. They are the only real necessities we can claim to have.

You can therefore train yourself to be content with your wages, possessions, house, car or whatever else, and also with *not* having them. Then you can be free of the angst and turmoil that rob so many people of their happiness. One small example of this which springs to mind is how, when we were newly married, my wife and I would go out for a walk in the evening. I recall one occasion when we passed a fish and chip shop and we sat on a wall nearby sharing a bag of chips – just chips, with no fish. Yet it was a very romantic 'date' and one which I still remember now.

Years later, when we were much better off, we sometimes went to posh restaurants in very nice places. But the chips (French fries) that we ate together, sitting on that wall, still hold their own as one of our best evenings out. Contentment will also free you from taking part in the 'rat race' and from the envy, jealousy and stress that so many people feel, even in churches, when they see others earning more than them, driving better cars, living in nicer houses, or having better holidays.

I am not exaggerating. Many people's lives are literally made miserable due to the inability to feel happy while ever their friend or neighbour has something which they don't have, or if he has something better. It is so sad, and so completely unnecessary, unhealthy and unproductive. I can think of at least two couples with whom we used to be close. However, they drifted away from us, and became resentful of my wife and me, when our incomes rose higher than theirs due to a series of promotions that we had.

The increasingly large difference in our relative wealth meant nothing to us and never even entered our minds until it became apparent that it had entered *their* minds, and had tarnished our friendship. Therefore, never compare your income or possessions with those of any other person, or feel aggrieved or inferior if they become richer than you are. On the other hand, never feel pleased with yourself, or superior to others, if you have more than them. If any such thoughts enter your mind, then recognise them as the sins that they are and repent of them.

You need to be able to have nice things, and enjoy them, yet without any pride, but also to be able to have cheap things, or even lack things which others do have, and yet feel no discontent. By all means save up to get that nice thing that you want. But while you are doing so, be content with not yet having it. Then, when you do get it, be content. Don't become dissatisfied, or start to want an even better one, if you later discover that someone else has one which is bigger, better or more expensive. Keeping up with the Jones's is a treadmill and you should never allow yourself to get onto it.

The virtue of saving regularly, as a weekly or monthly habit

Saving is closely linked to thrift, and follows on naturally from it. Until recently, it has always been considered wise, indeed essential, for people to save from their income. Firstly, the aim was to build up a reserve of capital to assist them on a 'rainy day', when they hit hard times or had unexpected expenses. It was also seen as the obvious way in which to buy larger items, i.e. to "save up" for them gradually *in advance*. Then you can pay in full, in cash, without any borrowing, when the required sum has been saved.

This is simply to state the obvious, as it is plain that this is how we should operate. Yet, it still needs to be said, because the habit of saving up for large items, which I call *'pay now, have later'*, has largely died out, not only for the current generation of young adults, but their parents too. Only those who are now grandparents were brought up to view saving as a virtue and to develop it as a solid habit. Most of those who are now under 60 have learned instead to spend all they have as soon as they earn it.

They also borrow as much as they are allowed to in order to buy the things they cannot afford from their wages. Their aim is to *"buy now – pay later"*, a revolting slogan which retailers aggressively push at consumers. Whenever I see or hear that in adverts it makes me wince. When I was a small child my parents got me started with the habit of saving by getting me a 'piggy bank' to put coins in. I did that regularly and saving became a settled habit which I have kept all my life.

Perhaps that did not happen for you, and you do not therefore have the habit of saving. If so, then set out to develop it now, however belatedly. The question then arises *how much* should you save, as a proportion of your income? There is no right or wrong answer, as we all differ from each other. Also, our own circumstances go up and down over time. I recommend that you open a saving account which is separate from your current account. Then don't ever touch it except in an emergency, or to buy something large for which you have saved up.

Begin by looking at your income and by planning, as best you can, what your likely expenditure is, after making all reasonable efforts to be thrifty and to cut what you spend to the lowest sensible level. Include within that budget any giving that you want to do. Then work out what money you think will be 'spare' each month and available to be saved. If there is absolutely nothing spare then, unless your situation is very bleak, there is a good chance that you are not being thrifty enough and that you are spending too much.

If so, revisit your budget and see what expenditure can be removed, reduced, or delayed, to create at least something left over for saving. Imagine that each month you have £50 or £100 or £200 spare. You should then set up a standing order so that that sum is *transferred automatically* to your saving account. Arrange for it to go out on, or just after, the day you get paid. Then it will be taken away from you before you are tempted to spend it. In due course you will forget that you ever earned it, because the net sum left in your account will seem to you to be your whole wage.

Don't rely on yourself to remember to transfer it each month, or to have the self-discipline to do so. Impose it upon yourself and arrange for it to happen automatically, without the need for you to do or remember anything. The benefit of this new policy of saving will not be felt at once. On the contrary, even after a few months, it will probably seem to you that the total amount saved is still tiny. You may well be tempted therefore to stop saving and to spend it instead, because you don't seem to be achieving anything worthwhile but you must resist that and press on.

The secret of saving is that the real effect is felt in the *longer term*, not immediately. If you can discipline yourself to leave the money alone, and *not to dip into it*, you will eventually see substantial results. It will also have a knock-on effect in other areas of your finances, and on your self-control and self-discipline generally. You might start off saving a small amount per month, but keep on increasing that as your thriftiness increases and as you get pay-rises and bonuses. When those come allocate it to savings *immediately*, before you even know you have it.

So, if your firm gives you a pay rise of say £100 per month, don't just start to spend it. From the very first day you get it increase your giving and also your saving. That way, some of it is instantly 'spoken for', and taken away from you, before you ever see it. The worst thing is to allow yourself to spend it all and to get used to a higher living standard. What you have never had, you won't miss, so don't let yourself have it in the first place. As with thrift, the virtue of saving requires you to do something that has become alien to our generation.

That is to choose, *voluntarily*, to have a lower standard of living than you could have had if you had chosen to spend your entire income, and even to borrow on top of that. The very idea of choosing to live below your means, *and, even worse, to live below the level of your friends and neighbours,* would seem to many today to be unthinkable. That is why millions of people were so severely affected by

403

the financial crash of 2008. They had no 'fat' to live off when hard times suddenly came.

As for how big you can validly allow your savings to become, my view is that there is no upper limit. I heard one person say that your savings should not be allowed to add up to more than three months wages, or else you are being greedy and are *"not trusting God"*. That is just their own personal opinion and has no basis in Scripture at all. Indeed, it is foolish. The absolute amount you save, however big, is not the issue. The issue is whether you have begun to love or idolise money, such that, for example, you can't bring yourself to give it away.

If that is the case then you have gone too far and have allowed your money to control you, or even to become a god to you. But if that is not the case, and you are quite sure that you don't love money, then go right ahead. Keep on and on saving, even if you end up a multi-millionaire. There is nothing at all wrong with that, however much you amass, *provided your heart stays pure and your giving is always at a generous level*. Note that Abraham, whom God loved, was *"very rich"*. So were Job and many other characters in the Bible:

Now Abram was very rich in livestock, in silver, and in gold.
Genesis 13:2 (ESV)

And the LORD blessed the latter days of Job more than his beginning. And he had 14,000 sheep, 6,000 camels, 1,000 yoke of oxen, and 1,000 female donkeys.
Job 42:12 (ESV)

In fact, we are told that Abraham had 318 male servants who were young enough to fight, not counting the female servants and the older men. We know that, because he gathered the younger men from amongst his employees to go and rescue Lot when he was taken captive. That means that the total number of Abraham's servants must have been a thousand or more. How many businesses do you know with that many staff? At any rate, one thing we can be sure of is that Abraham was a very rich man, by anybody's standards:

[14] When Abram heard that his kinsman had been taken captive, he led forth his trained men, born in his house, three hundred and eighteen of them, and went in pursuit as far as Dan. [15] And he divided his forces against them by night, he and his servants, and routed them and pursued them to Hobah, north of Damascus. [16] Then he brought back all the goods, and also brought back his kinsman Lot with his goods, and the women and the people.
Genesis 14:14-16 (RSV)

Abraham's grandson, Jacob, was also very rich:

Thus the man grew exceedingly rich, and had large flocks, maidservants and menservants, and camels and asses.

Genesis 30:43 (RSV)

King David was also rich in his own right. He provided some of the money needed to build the first Temple, including donations from his own personal wealth:

[3] David also provided great quantities of iron for nails for the doors of the gates and for clamps, as well as bronze in quantities beyond weighing, [4] and cedar timbers without number, for the Sidonians and Tyrians brought great quantities of cedar to David. [5] For David said, "Solomon my son is young and inexperienced, and the house that is to be built for the LORD must be exceedingly magnificent, of fame and glory throughout all lands. I will therefore make preparation for it." So David provided materials in great quantity before his death.

1 Chronicles 22:3-5 (ESV)

To prove conclusively that some of that money and treasure was donated by David personally, not just from 'government' funds, see this verse which states it explicitly:

Moreover, in addition to all that I have provided for the holy house, I have a treasure of my own of gold and silver, and because of my devotion to the house of my God I give it to the house of my God:

1 Chronicles 29:3 (ESV)

The concept of 'investment' and how that differs from saving

Investment is a form, or sub-category, of saving. But it differs from saving in some important ways:

a) Saving is generally done through cash held in banks.

b) Money in a bank can only rise by the interest earned on it, and the compounding effect thereof. That said, as interest rates today are so pathetically low by historic standards, the scope for growth is negligible. Thus even with the interest added on, money kept in a bank is unlikely to keep up with inflation, so its real value actually falls over time. By contrast, an investment in the form of shares, unit trusts or investment trusts has the potential to grow in capital value, quite apart from any income in the form of dividends which are *also* payable on them. Thus, investments generally rise in real terms, over the longer term.

405

c) However, the value of an investment can also go *down*, as well, and in absolute terms, not only in real terms. You could therefore buy a share in a company at £3.00 per share and a year later it could be worth £2.00 or £1.00 or even nothing at all if the company fails. Having said all that, the general rule, provided you are willing to invest *long term*, is that shares tend to rise by more than inflation.

To be ready to start investing you really need to have already been a saver, in money terms, for some time, such that you already have some cash stored up for a 'rainy day', have already got used to living below your means, and have developed a long-term perspective. You need to think in terms of years, and even decades, not just months. If that is your position then you may be ready to try investing in the stock market. Ideally, do it indirectly, through unit trusts and the like, rather than directly into specific shares, because that will then spread the risk more widely.

If you want to try this then probably the best and safest way to do it, if you are a novice, is to go to a British company which I admire called *Hargreaves Lansdowne PLC*. They are brokers and financial advisers, and on a very large scale. They can help you to choose one or more unit trusts and to set up a fund within which to hold them. You can buy units or shares in a lump sum of say £1,000 or more. Or you can set up a plan whereby you invest a small sum every month which they then invest into a number of unit trusts of your choice.

Don't get involved in gambling, especially online. It is extremely addictive and destroys people's lives.

Gambling has always been a vice, and has destroyed many people's lives, even in the days when it was illegal and/or strictly regulated. However, in recent years, the anti-gambling laws have been drastically relaxed. Therefore, betting shops have sprung up everywhere, and they are allowed to advertise, and the menace of gambling has grown hugely. The worst part of it has been the development of online gambling via the internet. That is now a massive problem, which governments have chosen to do little or nothing about.

Therefore, by one means or another, but primarily online, the lives of countless individuals, and also of their families, are being wrecked by gambling. It is not only highly addictive in itself. It also leads to a range of other problems as people become increasingly gripped by the addiction. They then resort to lying and stealing to get the money they need to continue gambling. The best way to ensure that you never become addicted to gambling, and that it does not destroy your wealth, family, career and health, is to never even try it.

If you never begin, then you can't go too far. And if you never do it at all, then you can't do it too much, or too often. Therefore resolve, for your own sake, and your family's sake, that you will not gamble at all. Stay away from it completely, especially online gambling. I have seen people's lives destroyed by it and have heard, anecdotally, of many others. Therefore, never set foot in any betting shop and never go on a betting website. Also, never click to open any of the adverts which those despicable companies pour onto people's Twitter or Facebook accounts, hoping to ensnare them.

I would not go so far as to say that gambling, in itself, is inherently sinful or that it is always wrong. Therefore, for example, I would not view it as a sin to take part in an annual office sweepstake on Grand National day when each worker picks the name of a horse out of a hat for a wager of perhaps £1. To do that is not sinful, in and of itself. However, if you were to start to go to betting shops or, even worse, to bet online, then you would be stepping onto a very steep, very slippery slope, which could easily cause you to fall very badly.

Thus even to expose yourself to the potential risk of becoming addicted is unwise, especially if gambling has already become important to you, such that you find you are thinking of it more and more. If that even remotely describes you, then having anything further to do with gambling *would* then be sinful. At least that is my personal view. However, there is also the issue of the example that you set for others. Therefore, even if you are sure that you yourself have enough self-control to gamble moderately and responsibly, what will others think, and do, if they see you gambling?

Your example may cause them to imitate you, and get involved in gambling themselves, only to find that they do not have as much self-control as you and cannot stop at one or two bets. They may keep going until they have nothing left, as so many do with tragic consequences. If so, you could, quite unwittingly, be the cause of another person's downfall. On top of that, your own custom, however small or infrequent, would be helping that betting shop or gambling website to remain open, which is contrary to the public interest as they are such a stumbling block for so many.

The habit, and even the 'ministry', of giving

In dealing with this concept of giving I am going to have to work hard. Firstly, I need to explain what the Bible *does say* about giving, which many have never heard. But, secondly, I also need to identify and disprove the many false things which the Bible *does not say* and which are just man-made teachings. Those unbiblical teachings come from the *'money preachers'* with their false *'prosperity gospel'* and their perverted *"name it and claim it"* teachings about faith. They make God into a divine vending machine who must give us whatever we ask for if we put in the right money and press the right buttons.

I shall also need to address the misguided teaching about *tithing*, especially tithing to one's own local church, which is taught by very many churches, even the better ones. However, in addition to all that, we shall also have to address the reluctance that many people feel to give at all, or to give properly, i.e. *generously*. Such reluctance is usually due to their own stinginess, but also to never having heard any genuine biblical teaching on giving. As a result, they do not even know that God commands us to do it, let alone why He commands it.

So, in approaching this complicated, badly taught and badly misunderstood subject of giving, our aim must be to find out what the Bible actually says. Then we must distinguish that from the man-made traditions which have been developed over the centuries and which people wrongly assume reflect what the Bible says. We shall also need to examine closely what our *motives* should, and should not, be when we give, because many people give, but with very wrong and selfish motives. Alternatively, many others refrain from giving, with equally wrong and selfish motives.

Let's begin by looking at what the New Testament says about how, and why, Christians should give, as distinct from the model of giving that was laid down for the Jewish people in the Law of Moses. Let me firstly point out that the Law of Moses is no longer in operation, not just for the Gentiles, but even for Jews. The entire Law of Moses ended when Jesus died, *including what it said about giving*. Therefore, we are now governed by what the New Testament says on the subject which, although it still commands us to give, does so on a quite different basis.

However, please do not suppose that I am therefore advocating that we should give less than a tithe. Although the standard for our giving is now less precise, it does not necessarily envisage that we will give less in quantity, or as a proportion. We are now commanded to give *"generously* and, for some of us, that could well mean giving *more than 10%*, whereas for others, who are less well off, it could mean giving less. Apostle Paul addresses the subject of giving in 2 Corinthians chapter 9, in the context of organising a collection to help the believers in Jerusalem who were experiencing a famine.

He makes it clear that it needs to be given *"as a willing gift, not as an exaction"*, and also that each one must give *"as he has decided in his heart....."* Thus, it is plain that it is up to us to decide how much to give. However, it is also plain that our giving should not be small, or done stingily, because Paul also speaks of us sowing *"bountifully"* and *"freely"* and, above all, of our being *"generous in every way"* and of how *"God loves a cheerful giver"*. Accordingly, our giving might need to be more than 10%, as how could it be called 'bountiful' or generous if it is expected to be 10% or less? It is one of the most important passages on this subject, so please consider it carefully:

⁵ So I thought it necessary to urge the brothers to go on ahead to you and arrange in advance for the gift you have promised, so that it may be ready as a willing gift, not as an exaction.
⁶ The point is this: whoever sows sparingly will also reap sparingly, and whoever sows bountifully will also reap bountifully. ⁷ Each one must give as he has decided in his heart, not reluctantly or under compulsion, for God loves a cheerful giver. ⁸ And God is able to make all grace abound to you, so that having all sufficiency in all things at all times, you may abound in every good work. ⁹ As it is written,
"He has distributed freely, he has given to the poor;
his righteousness endures forever."
¹⁰ He who supplies seed to the sower and bread for food will supply and multiply your seed for sowing and increase the harvest of your righteousness. ¹¹ You will be enriched in every way to be generous in every way, which through us will produce thanksgiving to God. ¹² For the ministry of this service is not only supplying the needs of the saints but is also overflowing in many thanksgivings to God. ¹³ By their approval of this service, they will glorify God because of your submission that comes from your confession of the gospel of Christ, and the generosity of your contribution for them and for all others,
2 Corinthians 9:5-13 (ESV)

What are the New Testament principles of giving, as taught by Apostle Paul?

A number of important features emerge from the above passage, and from the New Testament as a whole. Therefore, let us look at them more closely. In particular, they do not match the teaching that is given in so many churches about tithing to your own local church, i.e. giving your church 10% of your income. Even less does Paul's teaching accord with the teachings of the corrupt money preachers. The principles and practices which I believe are taught or demonstrated within the New Testament as a whole are:

a) The giving which Paul asked them to do was *not to their own local church.*

b) Paul did not specify any *figure or percentage* for each of them to give.

c) He gave no reason to suppose that he felt he had any *basis or authority* to state a particular figure, or even to suggest one, even if he had wanted to – which he didn't.

d) The giving was only to be done by those who were *willing* to give, and only to the *extent* that they were willing. In other words, it was entirely voluntary and was exclusively for those who wanted to give. There was *no compulsion* whatsoever, because God loves a *"cheerful giver"*.

e) Nevertheless, there is also a clear general principle that God will still bless those who are generous, just as He did in the Old Testament. He will cause *grace to abound* to them, so that they have *sufficiency in all things*.

f) Indeed, God will not only repay, on a like for like basis, those who give cheerfully and generously. He will actually *multiply* their seed for sowing, increase the harvest of their righteousness, and cause them to be *"enriched in every way"*.

g) In other words, there is still a clear principle of *multiplication* within the New Testament model of giving, such that God will give us back far more than we gave Him. Then we will end up *abounding*, which means having an abundance. That means having more than we need, not merely enough. In fact, we will be *overflowing*.

h) The purpose of the giving which is spoken of in 2 Corinthians 9 was for *"supplying the needs of the saints"*, i.e. providing relief for the ordinary church members, *not for paying the salaries of full time local leaders*.

i) If we only give a little, then we will only receive a little from God. In other words, we will *reap sparingly*. But if we give generously, i.e. sow bountifully, then we will also *reap bountifully*. That means plentifully and, in particular, it means receiving more than we need, such that we are left with an excess, or an abundance. With that we can, in turn, be generous again, thus continuing the cycle of our generosity and God's response to it.

How is the Old Testament pattern of giving, as per the now obsolete Law of Moses, similar to, and different from, the New Testament model?

Moses was used by God to give the Law to the Jewish people. It covered a very broad range of issues, legal, practical, social and liturgical. In amongst all of that was what it had to say about giving, and also about tithing for the upkeep of the Temple, the Aaronic priesthood and the tribe of Levi in general. However, the Old Testament pattern of giving was further explained and commented upon by the prophets. We shall now look at two of those in particular, namely Haggai and Malachi.

410

Let us look firstly at what Haggai had to say when most of the people were neglecting to contribute financially to the rebuilding and restoring of the Temple. They were looking after their own needs and wants instead. In response to their disobedience, and lack of generosity, God then sent a drought which hit their agriculture and reduced their income and wealth. So, the real cause of their poverty was actually God's response to their failure to give as they should have:

¹ In the second year of Darius the king, in the sixth month, on the first day of the month, the word of the LORD came by the hand of Haggai the prophet to Zerubbabel the son of Shealtiel, governor of Judah, and to Joshua the son of Jehozadak, the high priest: ² "Thus says the LORD of hosts: These people say the time has not yet come to rebuild the house of the LORD." ³ Then the word of the LORD came by the hand of Haggai the prophet, ⁴ "Is it a time for you yourselves to dwell in your paneled houses, while this house lies in ruins? ⁵ Now, therefore, thus says the LORD of hosts: Consider your ways. ⁶ You have sown much, and harvested little. You eat, but you never have enough; you drink, but you never have your fill. You clothe yourselves, but no one is warm. And he who earns wages does so to put them into a bag with holes.
⁷ "Thus says the LORD of hosts: Consider your ways. ⁸ Go up to the hills and bring wood and build the house, that I may take pleasure in it and that I may be glorified, says the LORD. ⁹ You looked for much, and behold, it came to little. And when you brought it home, I blew it away. Why? declares the LORD of hosts. Because of my house that lies in ruins, while each of you busies himself with his own house. ¹⁰ Therefore the heavens above you have withheld the dew, and the earth has withheld its produce. ¹¹ And I have called for a drought on the land and the hills, on the grain, the new wine, the oil, on what the ground brings forth, on man and beast, and on all their labors."

Haggai 1:1-11 (ESV)

Then, in the book of Malachi, we see that the people of Israel were again disobedient by their failure to give as the Law of Moses required. Even insofar as they did give, they still dishonoured God by offering blind, lame or sick animals for the sacrifices, rather than giving of the very best of their flocks. As a result, they came under God's curse, just as Moses had warned them that they would:

⁶ "A son honors his father, and a servant his master. If then I am a father, where is my honor? And if I am a master, where is my fear? says the LORD of hosts to you, O priests, who despise my name. But you say, 'How have we despised your name?' ⁷ By offering polluted food upon my altar. But you say, 'How have we polluted you?' By saying that the LORD's table may be despised. ⁸ When you offer blind animals in sacrifice, is that not evil? And when you offer those that are lame or sick, is that not evil? Present that to your governor; will he accept you or show you favor? says the LORD of hosts. ⁹ And now entreat the favor of God, that he may be gracious to us. With such a gift from your hand, will he

411

show favor to any of you? says the LORD of hosts. [10] Oh that there were one among you who would shut the doors, that you might not kindle fire on my altar in vain! I have no pleasure in you, says the LORD of hosts, and I will not accept an offering from your hand.

[11] For from the rising of the sun to its setting my name will be great among the nations, and in every place incense will be offered to my name, and a pure offering. For my name will be great among the nations, says the LORD of hosts. [12] But you profane it when you say that the Lord's table is polluted, and its fruit, that is, its food may be despised. [13] But you say, 'What a weariness this is,' and you snort at it, says the LORD of hosts. You bring what has been taken by violence or is lame or sick, and this you bring as your offering! Shall I accept that from your hand? says the LORD. [14] Cursed be the cheat who has a male in his flock, and vows it, and yet sacrifices to the Lord what is blemished. For I am a great King, says the LORD of hosts, and my name will be feared among the nations.

Malachi 1:6-14 (ESV)

This promise of God's blessing for obedience, and the warning about His curse in response to disobedience, is set out in graphic detail within the 68 verses of Deuteronomy chapter 28. It begins with a promise of blessings in verses 1-14. Let us look at verses 1 and 2 which make the basic point:

[1] "And if you faithfully obey the voice of the LORD your God, being careful to do all his commandments that I command you today, the LORD your God will set you high above all the nations of the earth. [2] And all these blessings shall come upon you and overtake you, if you obey the voice of the LORD your God.

Deuteronomy 28:1-2 (ESV)

These are then followed by 12 more verses which spell out what blessings will come upon the people if they are obedient to God. Note that these plainly include promises of financial prosperity, material success and good harvests:

[3] Blessed shall you be in the city, and blessed shall you be in the field. [4] Blessed shall be the fruit of your womb and the fruit of your ground and the fruit of your cattle, the increase of your herds and the young of your flock. [5] Blessed shall be your basket and your kneading bowl. [6] Blessed shall you be when you come in, and blessed shall you be when you go out.
[7] "The LORD will cause your enemies who rise against you to be defeated before you. They shall come out against you one way and flee before you seven ways.
[8] The LORD will command the blessing on you in your barns and in all that you undertake. And he will bless you in the land that the LORD your God is giving you. [9] The LORD will establish you as a people holy to himself, as he has sworn to you, if you keep the commandments of the LORD your God and walk in his

ways. [10] And all the peoples of the earth shall see that you are called by the name of the LORD, and they shall be afraid of you. [11] And the LORD will make you abound in prosperity, in the fruit of your womb and in the fruit of your livestock and in the fruit of your ground, within the land that the LORD swore to your fathers to give you. [12] The LORD will open to you his good treasury, the heavens, to give the rain to your land in its season and to bless all the work of your hands. And you shall lend to many nations, but you shall not borrow. [13] And the LORD will make you the head and not the tail, and you shall only go up and not down, if you obey the commandments of the LORD your God, which I command you today, being careful to do them, [14] and if you do not turn aside from any of the words that I command you today, to the right hand or to the left, to go after other gods to serve them.

Deuteronomy 28:3-14 (ESV)

Then, from verses 15 to 68, Moses sets out all the curses which will come upon the Jewish people if they do not listen to God and do not obey Him. These will affect every aspect of their lives and they are too numerous to include them all here. But, as these sample verses show, they quite clearly include curses which will affect the people's income, wealth and agricultural output:

"But if you will not obey the voice of the LORD your God or be careful to do all his commandments and his statutes that I command you today, then all these curses shall come upon you and overtake you.

Deuteronomy 28:15 (ESV)

[38] You shall carry much seed into the field and shall gather in little, for the locust shall consume it. [39] You shall plant vineyards and dress them, but you shall neither drink of the wine nor gather the grapes, for the worm shall eat them. [40] You shall have olive trees throughout all your territory, but you shall not anoint yourself with the oil, for your olives shall drop off.

Deuteronomy 28:38-40 (ESV)

[43] The sojourner who is among you shall rise higher and higher above you, and you shall come down lower and lower. [44] He shall lend to you, and you shall not lend to him. He shall be the head, and you shall be the tail.

Deuteronomy 28:43-44 (ESV)

[47] Because you did not serve the LORD your God with joyfulness and gladness of heart, because of the abundance of all things, [48] therefore you shall serve your enemies whom the LORD will send against you, in hunger and thirst, in nakedness, and lacking everything. And he will put a yoke of iron on your neck until he has destroyed you.

Deuteronomy 28:47-48 (ESV)

413

The principle of voluntary giving, even in the Old Testament. This was quite separate from the tithe and the same principle has been carried over into the New Testament.

In addition to the *tithes* required by the Law of Moses, the Old Testament also contains the practice of *voluntary giving* over and above what was mandatory. This kind of giving was different in that it was left entirely up to each individual to decide *whether* to give and *how much* to give. God wanted there to be a genuine desire to give, of the person's own free will, with no compulsion and no prescribed amount or fixed percentage. Indeed, they were free to give no gift at all if they preferred not to give. Many passages reflect this, but let's just look at a few of them in the book of Exodus:

¹ The LORD said to Moses, ² "Speak to the people of Israel, that they take for me a contribution. From every man whose heart moves him you shall receive the contribution for me.

Exodus 25:1-2 (ESV)

⁴ Moses said to all the congregation of the people of Israel, "This is the thing that the LORD has commanded. ⁵ Take from among you a contribution to the LORD. Whoever is of a generous heart, let him bring the LORD's contribution: gold, silver, and bronze;

Exodus 35:4-5 (ESV)

²¹ And they came, everyone whose heart stirred him, and everyone whose spirit moved him, and brought the LORD's contribution to be used for the tent of meeting, and for all its service, and for the holy garments. ²² So they came, both men and women. All who were of a willing heart brought brooches and earrings and signet rings and armlets, all sorts of gold objects, every man dedicating an offering of gold to the LORD.

Exodus 35:21-22 (ESV)

The gifts that were being given in the above passages were for the making of the Tabernacle and all of its fittings. These were made from the gold, silver, bronze and other precious items that the people voluntarily chose to give, entirely of their own free will, and in whatever sum or quantity they wanted to give. Nobody was compelled and nobody was told what to do, or even advised whether, or how, to give. It was left entirely up to them to decide.

Note also Moses's attitude when the people responded so generously that it became apparent that enough had already been collected to complete all the work on the Tabernacle. Instead of letting the people carry on giving, Moses told them to stop, because he had already got enough. Can you imagine any of today's corrupt money preachers ever saying that?

³ And they received from Moses all the contribution that the people of Israel had brought for doing the work on the sanctuary. They still kept bringing him freewill offerings every morning, ⁴ so that all the craftsmen who were doing every sort of task on the sanctuary came, each from the task that he was doing, ⁵ and said to Moses, "The people bring much more than enough for doing the work that the LORD has commanded us to do." ⁶ So Moses gave command, and word was proclaimed throughout the camp, "Let no man or woman do anything more for the contribution for the sanctuary." So the people were restrained from bringing, ⁷ for the material they had was sufficient to do all the work, and more.

Exodus 36:3-7 (ESV)

Therefore, this principle of voluntary giving by *"everyone whose heart stirred him"* was already well established in the Old Testament era. It reflects God's own heart of willing generosity. Therefore, even then, it was how He wanted people to give, after they had met their obligations under the Law of Moses. Therefore, the New Testament model of giving, which is simply to give generously and to be free to decide *whether* to give, *how much* to give, and *to whom* to give, is already modelled for us in the Old Testament.

In other words, you could say that when the Law of Moses came to an end, and the obligation to tithe ceased, the duty to give generously, freely, spontaneously, and in accordance with the desires of our own hearts, remained. The way in which Moses handled the voluntary collection for the construction of the Tabernacle exemplifies how we should now operate, and the heart attitudes that we should have, when we give now, in the New Testament era.

Why did the prophet Malachi tell the Old Testament Jews that they were "robbing" God?

With these principles, promises and warnings in mind, let's now look again at the book of Malachi. The prophet tells the people that God says they are *'robbing'* Him. He means that they are not paying their tithes and offerings as they should and that, consequently, they are under God's curse, just as Moses said would happen:

⁷ From the days of your fathers you have turned aside from my statutes and have not kept them. Return to me, and I will return to you, says the LORD of hosts. But you say, 'How shall we return?' ⁸ Will man rob God? Yet you are robbing me. But you say, 'How have we robbed you?' In your tithes and contributions. ⁹ You are cursed with a curse, for you are robbing me, the whole nation of you.

Malachi 3:7-9 (ESV)

Then God says, through Malachi, that if the people will pay their full tithes and offerings then He will *"open the windows of heaven for you and pour down for you a blessing until there is no more need"*. God also promises to *"rebuke the devourer"* for them, by which He means that He will stop giving instructions for their crops to be reduced or ruined and will, instead, allow them to have abundant harvests. He even urges them to *"put me to the test"* by giving properly and seeing what He would then do in response:

10 Bring the full tithe into the storehouse, that there may be food in my house. And thereby put me to the test, says the LORD of hosts, if I will not open the windows of heaven for you and pour down for you a blessing until there is no more need. 11 I will rebuke the devourer for you, so that it will not destroy the fruits of your soil, and your vine in the field shall not fail to bear, says the LORD of hosts. 12 Then all nations will call you blessed, for you will be a land of delight, says the LORD of hosts.

Malachi 3:10-12 (ESV)

A closer look at the model for giving under the Law of Moses and the New Testament model

There are some similarities between how God dealt with the Jews under the Law of Moses, and the way He now responds to Christians, and also Messianic Jews, who give, or fail to give, in accordance with the New Testament model. There is clearly still a promise that God will pour out His blessing on those who give obediently, with a willing and generous heart. There is also the withholding of that blessing, or you could call it the imposition of God's curse, which still comes upon those who do not give at all, or who do not give generously.

Therefore, the money preachers do actually have a point when they speak of God blessing those who are generous, and of Him multiplying whatever people give and, at some point, giving it back to them, greatly increased. That is there are some half-truths in what they say. However, there are also some fundamental mistakes, or rather deliberate perversions, in their teaching, which are as follows:

a) The Law of Moses provided for a large part of the giving to be used to support the Temple, to pay wages to the priests, and to support the tribe of Levi. The New Testament model does *not* do that. There is no mechanism or procedure anywhere in the New Testament for *local* elders to be paid. The only ones who received financial support were the *missionaries,* i.e. those who were *sent* away from home, and thus were unable to get a job, or to support themselves. The other *local* elders, who stayed at home, were not paid anything by the churches of which they were a part.

416

b) The money preachers are today urging people to give money *to them*, i.e. to the money preachers themselves. By contrast, Paul was asking the people, *providing they were willing*, to give money *to the poor in Jerusalem, not to himself*.

c) Far from asking for money for himself, or even for any of his team, apostle Paul generally declined to accept financial support, even when it was offered, let alone ask for it. It would be even more unthinkable for Paul to pressurise or manipulate people into giving to him. Instead, Paul chose to support himself entirely, by living frugally and thriftily and by working part time with his own hands as a tentmaker. Paul didn't earn a fortune in this way, but he made enough to get by, so as to avoid needing any support from the people to whom he was ministering. Here are some verses which show Paul's approach to supporting himself financially: (NB) *Jesus is supported (and disciples) by the women*

¹ After this Paul left Athens and went to Corinth. ² And he found a Jew named Aquila, a native of Pontus, recently come from Italy with his wife Priscilla, because Claudius had commanded all the Jews to leave Rome. And he went to see them, ³ and because he was of the same trade he stayed with them and worked, for they were tentmakers by trade. ⁴ And he reasoned in the synagogue every Sabbath, and tried to persuade Jews and Greeks.

Acts 18:1-4 (ESV)

³³ I coveted no one's silver or gold or apparel. ³⁴ You yourselves know that these hands ministered to my necessities and to those who were with me. ³⁵ In all things I have shown you that by working hard in this way we must help the weak and remember the words of the Lord Jesus, how he himself said, 'It is more blessed to give than to receive.'"

Acts 20:33-35 (ESV)

and we labor, working with our own hands. When reviled, we bless; when persecuted, we endure;

1 Corinthians 4:12 (ESV)

For you remember, brothers, our labor and toil: we worked night and day, that we might not be a burden to any of you, while we proclaimed to you the gospel of God.

1 Thessalonians 2:9 (ESV)

⁶ Now we command you, brothers, in the name of our Lord Jesus Christ, that you keep away from any brother who is walking in idleness and not in accord with the tradition that you received from us. ⁷ For you yourselves know how you ought to imitate us, because we were not idle when we were with you, ⁸ nor did we eat anyone's bread without paying for it, but with toil and labor we worked night and day, that we might not be a burden to any of you. ⁹ It was not because we do not have that right, but to give you in ourselves an example to imitate. ¹⁰ For even when we were with you, we would give you this command: If anyone is not willing to work, let him not eat.

2 Thessalonians 3:6-10 (ESV)

In that final verse above, Paul refers to himself as having the right to be financially supported. However, he chose not to exercise it, in order to set an example. Paul only had the right to be supported because he was *a missionary*, i.e. one who is *sent*, not a *local* elder. Despite that fact, Paul chose not to exercise his right. It was far more important to him to prove the genuineness of his motives by refusing support and therefore to set a good example to others. Moreover, Paul's standard of living was what most of us would view as subsistence level.

He had enough to eat, and some clothes to wear, and he generally (not always) had somewhere to sleep, albeit usually in borrowed lodgings. He was not living in luxury or earning millions of dollars a year, as the worst of the money preachers now do. How utterly different are their hearts, and their motives, from Paul's. He was genuine, humble and totally unworldly, whereas they are fraudulent, self-serving manipulators of the gullible and the "rapacious wolves" that we were warned to expect. *Feed off the flock*

Tithing to the local church, and paying salaries to local elders, are not biblical practices. Yet many churches still teach these things, as if they were in the Bible.

If you scour the New Testament there are a number of things you will never see, not even once. They are not even hinted at indirectly, let alone explicitly taught or practiced:

a) Christians tithing to their local church

b) anybody tithing to anyone or anything at all, not just their local church

c) any local church buying, or even renting, any kind of large or special building to meet in. They all just met in homes, barns, school rooms, farm outbuildings etc and spent nothing on buying, renting or maintaining any purpose-built church buildings.

d) any church paying any kind of salary to its own *local* elders. The only people who were paid anything were *missionaries*, i.e. apostles, i.e. those who are *sent*. Even then, they were not supported financially by the people to whom they were evangelising or ministering, but only by the 'sending church', from which they had been sent out.

418

e) any leader of any kind, whether local or sent, urging anybody to give money *to himself* or to *his own ministry*. The apostles only ever raised funds for *other people*, as when Paul collected for the poor in Jerusalem. If it was offered, a missionary would be willing to accept money from those to whom he was sent, and he was entitled to receive it. But they never *asked for it*, let alone demanded it. They left people entirely free to offer help if they wanted to and not if they didn't.

Therefore, in the early Church, where we see Christianity in its best and purest form, i.e. in the book of Acts and the letters, the local leaders all had jobs. Or they were retired men. They were not paid any salary by the local church. Moreover, little or no money was spent on buildings. Thus very little money was ever needed to fund the activities of a *local* church. They spent a small amount on food for when they ate together, but that was about it.

Therefore, any giving they did could go to whoever they wanted, not their *own leader(s) or any building*. That is the exact opposite of what we find today in most churches, where 75 to 90%, of the entire giving is spent on the pastor's salary and the building, both of which were totally unknown to the early Church.

In many modern churches, the people are milked, like cows, to pay for things which are not needed and are *not biblical*. The paid pastor and the special church building are man-made inventions which the first century Christians never had. If it was not for these exploitative policies, churches today could do far more of the things that they *are* supposed to do, namely:

a) give to support missionary work elsewhere

b) give to the poor locally, including within the local church

c) give to the poor, nationally or internationally

d) support their own families and relatives

Most churches today only give a tiny percentage of their budget to any of these valid things, because the vast bulk of the money is spent on invalid things. Supporting their own needy members is not usually even considered to be part of the local church's role because it is not what they have seen done in the past and it is not what they see other churches doing. They mainly go by custom and practice, not by what the Bible says. So, a Christian today should not be giving to pay the wages of local leaders. Those men should fund themselves. Neither should we pay for religious buildings. Instead we should give to the same people and causes that the early Church gave to.

If we did, the spiritual condition of that local church would be transformed. This is not just theory for me. In my own church, neither I, nor any of the other elders, receive *any salary at all*. We do have a collection each week, but only for miscellaneous, one off expenses, and to meet the needs of any church members who might fall into difficulty, or to give to others outside of our church. None of it is spent on a building either, because we meet in homes. This approach takes away all sorts of temptations to dishonesty and manipulation which traditional, unbiblical churches face.

In the New Testament there is no longer any prescribed amount or percentage for our giving because our duty is to give *generously*. We are also completely free as to *whom* we give to. What that means, in each person's case, is for the person themselves to decide. They choose how much to give, and to whom, on the basis of their own conscience and their own personal circumstances, needs and income. Of course, they will be held accountable and judged as to whether they were generous. But there is no 'one size fits all' figure that we all supposed to give and it does not have to include the building or paying the 'pastor'.

Why then should we give? What should our motives be? And what shouldn't they be?

We have seen that we are still commanded to give generously and that God's blessing will come upon those who do. However, His blessing will be withheld, or He will even send His curse, upon those who don't. The *'law of sowing and reaping'* applies to all of us, whether we are Christians or not, and it continuously causes us to reap whatever we have sown, whether good or bad. This is not only in the context of financial giving, but right across the board, affecting absolutely everything that we ever do or say.

Therefore, all of our actions, reactions and decisions have consequences, either good or bad. That is to say that we *bear fruit* of exactly the same kind as whatever we sowed. We need to bear that law very much in mind, not only when deciding whether to give and how much to give, but in every other area of life too. That includes how we treat people, or speak about them, and whether we act righteously or un-righteously. However, the question we also need to address, especially in the area of giving, is what is our *motive* for doing so?

Motive is crucial and makes all the difference as to whether or not our decisions and actions please God and whether or not our giving is considered by Him to be 'generous'. There are all sorts of possible motives, or mixtures of motives, good or bad, worthy or unworthy, selfish or unselfish, reluctant or willing, honest or dishonest. Other people may not know what our motives are. We may not even know ourselves, especially at the deepest, innermost level. However, we will get closer to the truth if we interrogate and cross-examine ourselves rigorously and regularly.

If we do that we may find out what our motives really are, as opposed to what we claim they are. We should therefore be strict with ourselves, avoiding any undue willingness to declare ourselves not guilty of having any wrong motives. So, it is true that good things will happen, and rewards will be given, to those who give generously. It is also perfectly alright to be *aware* of those future consequences, and to *want* them. There is also nothing wrong with being motivated, at least in part, by the prospect of receiving God's blessing and reward for your giving.

The problem occurs where the obtaining of rewards is your *only* motivation, or even where that is given excessive emphasis and comes ahead of the pure, simple, straightforward *desire to give*. You need to give primarily for its own sake, because you *want to*, and because you *take pleasure* from the act of giving itself, and from the good that it does to *others*. Those sincere and unselfish motives need to be there, alongside the hope and expectation of being rewarded for it yourself at some future point.

If your main thought, or even your only thought, is of *what you will get in return*, as with many who give to the money preachers, then your motives are not pure. If so, it may well prevent any rewards from arising. Remember, the reward is for giving *generously*, not merely for the act of giving in itself. So, it also requires a proper motive as well as the physical act of giving. Therefore generosity, by definition, requires that there be a genuineness of motive, and a sincere concern for others. Otherwise, giving is reduced to being no more than a form of investment, motivated by mere self-interest.

Imagine giving a friend or relative a birthday present. You might be aware that he is likely to get you a present on your birthday. He may have done so in the past. You might even look forward with pleasure to your own birthday and the anticipation of what you might receive from him. Nevertheless, your motive when buying your friend a present is not to induce him to buy you something in return. You are doing it, or at least you should be, because *you want to*, and because giving the gift *gives you pleasure,* regardless of what you might receive back later on your own birthday.

That is how we should give to God, because He loves generosity and hates stinginess and mean-spirited reluctance to give. Indeed, He warns us against stingy people and even tells us not to accept things from them because, even if they offer you food, their heart is not with you:

⁶ Do not eat the bread of a man who is stingy;
  do not desire his delicacies,

421

⁷ for he is like one who is inwardly calculating.
   "Eat and drink!" he says to you,
   but his heart is not with you.
⁸ You will vomit up the morsels that you have eaten,
   and waste your pleasant words.
                              Proverbs 23:6-8 (ESV)

We are also told that a stingy man will end up in poverty. That is the other side of the coin, because we know that generosity leads to abundance. Therefore, the principle is valid in both directions:

A stingy man hastens after wealth
 and does not know that poverty will come upon him.
                              Proverbs 28:22 (ESV)

Giving to the poor. What are our personal duties towards them?

We have focused so far on giving to the work of the Church and, in Old Testament times, to the upkeep of the Temple and the support of the priests and Levites. However, there is another group of people who are also to be supported. They are the poor, and especially those who are within the churches, as opposed to unsaved unbelievers out in the world. We are, of course, meant to give to the poor even if they are not within the Church. But it is clear that they are a lesser priority than our fellow believers:

⁹ And let us not grow weary in well-doing, for in due season we shall reap, if we do not lose heart. ¹⁰ So then, as we have opportunity, let us do good to all men, and especially to those who are of the household of faith.
                              Galatians 6:9-10 (RSV)

This verse from Proverbs makes clear that when we give to the poor, God views us as lending money to Him, and He will repay us for that:

Whoever is generous to the poor lends to the LORD,
 and he will repay him for his deed.
                              Proverbs 19:17 (ESV)

Conversely, if we do not help the poor, then we will come under God's curse and, moreover, He will not help us, or listen to us:

Whoever gives to the poor will not want,
 but he who hides his eyes will get many a curse.
                              Proverbs 28:27 (ESV)

Whoever closes his ear to the cry of the poor
will himself call out and not be answered.
Proverbs 21:13 (ESV)

Consider this verse also, in which we see a Jewish figure of speech *"a bountiful eye"*, sometimes also referred to as *"a good eye"*, which simply means to be *generous*. That is why, even today, if a Jewish person stands in a shopping centre rattling a collecting tin or bucket, trying to raise money for some good cause, they will say *"Have a good eye"*, by which they mean *"Be generous"*. At any rate the point is that if we are generous to the poor, we will be blessed:

Whoever has a bountiful eye will be blessed,
for he shares his bread with the poor.
Proverbs 22:9 (ESV)

Even within the Law of Moses, provision is made for the poor to be cared for and given to. Here is a passage addressed to farmers who have agricultural land and crops. They were not permitted by the Law of Moses to harvest all of their crop. They had to leave some of it around the edges of the field. They also had to leave the grapes that either remained on the vine after the picking, or which had fallen onto the ground. Those could not be harvested. They had to be left there for the poor, so that they could come and help themselves to them once the harvesting was over:

[9] *"When you reap the harvest of your land, you shall not reap your field right up to its edge, neither shall you gather the gleanings after your harvest.* [10] *And you shall not strip your vineyard bare, neither shall you gather the fallen grapes of your vineyard. You shall leave them for the poor and for the sojourner: I am the LORD your God.*
Leviticus 19:9-10 (ESV)

That is an interesting passage because the provision requiring farmers to leave some of their crop in the fields, still to be harvested, gave dignity to the poor. It meant that they could come and feed themselves, *by their own efforts*, rather than being given handouts, with no effort or initiative on their own part. In this way the poor retained the habit of work, and fending for themselves and their families. That habit was needed if they were to escape from being poor and to get back into gainful employment, rather than becoming institutionalised beggars on a permanent basis.

Moreover, this help was to be given by *private individuals*, not by councils or governments on their behalf, and it came from their own assets, not taxation. Contrast that with the approach taken today, in most of the western world, with what has come to be known as *welfare*, or even the *Welfare State*. Virtually the

423

whole burden of supporting the poor has been transferred from private individuals and local churches and placed, instead, on the State. That is not to say that the State does not have any valid role in addressing issues of poverty and seeking to bring relief.

It plainly does, but the point is that *so do we*. However, a great many of us, even within the churches, have now come to believe that the whole duty, or virtually the whole duty, for looking after the poor now rests upon the State, not us. Many of us now think that our only task is to vote for the political party which will do that most effectively *on our behalf*. That is profoundly wrong thinking and we urgently need to return to seeing ourselves as being under a personal duty to support the poor, not just to agitate for somebody else to do so.

Another damaging effect of the modern 'Welfare State' is that it tends to create, and then to entrench, an attitude of lifelong dependency, rather than equipping the poor to care for themselves, thus setting themselves free from poverty. It has even become a central part of the thinking of left wing political parties, such as the British Labour Party and the Democratic Party in the USA to create and maintain a larger electorate for their parties by locking people into reliance upon welfare payments and the receipt of ever broader benefits.

In this way those parties seek to keep themselves in office on the basis that those who live permanently on benefits will be more inclined to vote for them. Indeed, it is for that same reason that left-wing parties support large scale immigration, including illegal immigration, as they see it as another way of bolstering their own vote. But the poor are not there to be used, so as help keep our party in office. They are there to be helped *out of poverty* and enabled *to fend for themselves again*, not to be kept in a dependent position forever. As a very great president famously said:

"We should measure welfare's success by how many people leave welfare, not how many are added."

Ronald Reagan

The 'law of sowing and reaping'

We have alluded to this law already but let's now examine it more closely. I have called it a law, rather than a mere general principle or guideline, because it is stated emphatically in Scripture as something which *inevitably* comes into operation *every time we ever* 'sow' anything. That is whenever we do anything, good or bad, including when we give or fail to give. So, it is not just something that *may sometimes* occur. The fact that it is a law means that it *will always* occur. The law of sowing and reaping is stated most clearly by apostle Paul:

7 Do not be deceived; God is not mocked, for whatever a man sows, that he will also reap. 8 For he who sows to his own flesh will from the flesh reap corruption; but he who sows to the Spirit will from the Spirit reap eternal life. 9 And let us not grow weary in well-doing, for in due season we shall reap, if we do not lose heart. 10 So then, as we have opportunity, let us do good to all men, and especially to those who are of the household of faith.

Galatians 6:7-10 (RSV)

The main context of the passage is financial giving, in particular, the support we give to missionaries or teachers, whose ministries prevent them from supporting themselves. However, it is also of general application. Therefore, it comes into effect whenever we 'sow' anything at all, either to our flesh, which means acting or speaking selfishly and carnally, or to the Spirit, which means doing and saying what God wants. Either way, we will receive back, either now or later, or at the very latest, at the judgment, *whatever it was that we sowed*, whether good or bad.

Thus, if we have been generous with others, then God will be generous with us. If not, then He won't. In short, He will ensure that whatever we do, give or say *comes back to us*, like a boomerang. The non-Christian world has noticed this law in operation, merely by observation, even though they don't know the Scriptures, or realise that it is God Himself who is implementing it. They therefore wrongly call it *'karma'*, a concept which comes from Hinduism, which is a false religion.

They define it wrongly and do not know that God is actually behind it all, but the point is that even they have seen that such a law does exist. However, this law of sowing and reaping does not originate with Paul, or even with the New Testament. We see it expressed in the Old Testament too, for example in Psalm 41. That speaks of how God will deal with those who *"consider the poor"*, which means caring for them and giving to them. King David tells us that a number of blessings will be poured out on those who do these things:

1 Blessed is the one who considers the poor!
  In the day of trouble the LORD delivers him;
2 the LORD protects him and keeps him alive;
  he is called blessed in the land;
  you do not give him up to the will of his enemies.
3 The LORD sustains him on his sickbed;
  in his illness you restore him to full health.
Psalm 41:1-3 (ESV)

King Solomon also speaks of how those who honour the LORD with their wealth, i.e. give generously, will be rewarded in return by God, such that He will bless their harvests and provide them with such an abundance that their barns and vats are full:

425

⁹ Honor the LORD with your wealth
  and with the firstfruits of all your produce;
¹⁰ then your barns will be filled with plenty,
  and your vats will be bursting with wine.
                              Proverbs 3:9-10 (ESV)

We also see this law expressed in 2 Samuel chapter 22. In that passage King David enlarges further on how God will respond to those who are blameless, live and act righteously, and keep His commandments:

²¹ "The LORD rewarded me according to my righteousness;
  according to the cleanness of my hands he recompensed me.
²² For I have kept the ways of the LORD,
  and have not wickedly departed from my God.
²³ For all his ordinances were before me,
  and from his statutes I did not turn aside.
²⁴ I was blameless before him,
  and I kept myself from guilt.
²⁵ Therefore the LORD has recompensed me according to my righteousness,
  according to my cleanness in his sight.
²⁶ "With the loyal thou dost show thyself loyal;
  with the blameless man thou dost show thyself blameless;
²⁷ with the pure thou dost show thyself pure,
  and with the crooked thou dost show thyself perverse.
²⁸ Thou dost deliver a humble people,
  but thy eyes are upon the haughty to bring them down.
                              2 Samuel 22:21-28 (RSV)

So, God will deal in one way with the righteous, blameless, loyal, pure, merciful and humble and repay them in like manner for whatever they say and do. But He will act in the opposite way with those who act and speak wrongly. They will equally certainly reap a harvest to match their deeds, but it will be an unpleasant one. We therefore need to remember this law and act upon it now, every day. We must take care to 'sow' the right kind of actions, words, thoughts and attitudes i.e. those of which God will approve. Then we can fully expect that He will respond in like manner, with a good harvest which will benefit us.

That approach is surely just obvious common sense. At any rate, it is far wiser than to act in such a way that God is obliged to judge, oppose, or even curse us, by sending us a harvest of evil. Therefore a wise person does not ignore or forget about this law, or other laws that are similar. He takes it completely seriously and *acts in reliance upon it*, fully expecting God to implement it. How can it possibly be considered wise to do otherwise?

426

Some of my own experiences of financial giving and also of what I call *"the ministry of giving"*

Immediately after my conversion, God began to lead me on a long process of discovery by which I gained an understanding of the importance of financial giving, and of how He will bless us in return for our giving. It began for me when I felt a prompting to give a cheque for £50 to the man who had just led me to faith, a missionary called Dave Brown. He came all the way from Oklahoma to work on my campus in the UK, where I was a first year student. As I pondered giving him a gift I felt excitement, and a real sense of pleasure and anticipation.

I wanted to give him as much as I could afford and £50 was a lot in those days, especially as I lived on a student grant. Only a few days after I gave him that gift, a letter arrived from the Inland Revenue saying they were giving me a tax refund, due to having recalculated my tax for the previous year. It was totally unexpected, and much larger than the £50 gift I had just given. I knew, in my spirit, that God Himself was behind it and that He was 'repaying' me. The conviction that He was doing so grew stronger and clearer over the years that followed.

I therefore gave more and more money away, only to see it come right back to me in all sorts of ways, mainly through a long series of pay rises and promotions and, later, by ever increasing success in business. I eventually became a salaried partner, then an equity partner, and finally the sole proprietor of my own large and highly profitable law firm. God also protected me from very many attacks on my business by employees, opponents, insurance companies, banks and regulators.

I had set up my own law firm specifically in order to pursue the ministry of giving on a much larger scale. That was my motive and the demons knew it and were therefore determined to stop me if they could. But they never succeeded, or at least not fully. God gave me victory after victory, and I write about some of them in my Book 6, and also Book 2. One example was when a large insurance company attacked the wording of my firm's contract with clients. It was called a "Conditional fee Agreement" ("CFA") or *"No Win, No Fee Agreement"* in layman's language.

This was at a time when many such challenges were being made against law firms by aggressive insurance companies, searching for any tiny technical defects they could find in the wording of contracts. They would then seek a court order to state that the whole agreement was therefore technically "non-compliant with the CFA regulations" and thus unenforceable. If so, the insurance companies would not need to pay us any of our costs, even if we had won the substantive case for the client. However, virtually *all our clients* had been given the *same CFA*.

427

Therefore, if any such ruling had been made, I would have been bankrupted overnight, as many other law firms were. I kept my head down and avoided any serious legal challenge to our CFA for five years. Then one big insurer went for me and took it all the way to a court hearing in London. They challenged the wording of our CFA on four grounds. But they lost on all four and my firm was fully vindicated, and even praised by the Judge, as being *"exemplary"*. He then made a full costs order against them and they had to pay the legal costs of the hearing, which came to £140,000 (about $200,000).

Quite apart from the value of the work in progress on our uncompleted files, which would all have been wiped out if we had lost, I had also faced the risk of paying *their* costs. But, in the end, they paid mine, and in full, and I lost nothing. Yet, during those years, many other firms were badly hit or even closed down by those same tactics. It was quite obvious that God had put a shield or hedge around me. He had protected me throughout, not only against that attack, but every other one too, and primarily because He was responding, as per His promises, to the giving that my firm enabled me to do.

In the early days, as a young believer, God would reward me almost immediately, as with the tax rebate when I was 19. I think He did so because He knew that I was immature and that if He delayed at all in rewarding me, I would not see the link between my giving and His response to it. But, as I grew more mature, and the reality of the law of sowing and reaping became clearer to me, God began to make His responses more and more delayed, even by years. Yet, everything I ever gave away was always given back to me, and multiplied, just as Paul said it would be in 2 Corinthians 9:6-7.

God always keeps His promises and He always repays us in full, even if it takes Him years, or even decades to do so. I now know that fact as surely as I know what day it is. That is how real it is to me now. I believe that my giving was always well-meant, and that it was always done sincerely. However, it was not always done *wisely*, or with *discernment*, or in response to hearing God's promptings accurately. Sometimes what I assumed to be His voice prompting me to give to someone or something was actually just my own thoughts.

It was sometimes just me acting impulsively, rashly, and without proper enquiry as to the genuineness and worthiness of the people and ministries to whom I gave. As a result, on many occasions, I gave to bad, insincere people and to unbiblical ministries. However, their unworthiness and unfaithfulness only became known to me later, after I had already given to them. Often it was *their carnal and grasping response* to my giving, whereby they saw me as a 'sucker' and tried to exploit me further, which alerted me to their real nature. I then, belatedly, stopped giving to them.

428

The problems that can arise for that minority of people whose hearts are more generous than their heads are wise

If you have an unusually generous heart then, realistically, there is no alternative but to learn from your mistakes in this way. It is what inevitably happens when your heart is more generous than your head is wise. That mismatch will continue until your wisdom and discernment grow, and eventually 'catch up' with, your generosity. Until then, you will inevitably misjudge people, make unwise giving decisions and give to people and ministries who are not worthy and should not be supported.

Sadly, there are many such ministries and they are increasing all the more in this age of apostasy in which we live. Thus, generosity, by itself, is not enough. You also need wisdom, discernment, shrewdness, and a willingness to exercise self-control and to wait, so as to check people and situations carefully before you give. Then you will reduce the chances of being deceived or manipulated. Therefore, as well as being naïve to begin with, until I learned from many bitter experiences, my generosity itself became a problem to me.

That is not to say that generosity is wrong. Far from it. It is a great quality, which God will reward, even where it is exercised naïvely at times, as mine often was. But it is also true to say that God does not want you to *remain* naïve. He wants you to grow in discernment and in your ability *to weigh up other people's characters*, so that your giving is targeted more wisely, and only to people who are worthy. In part, He wants you to respond to His specific promptings, and not to mistake your own impulsive thoughts and feelings for His promptings, as I so often did.

But when you do get it wrong, God wants you to *learn* from those bad decisions and avoid making them again, or at least make them less often. It is unrealistic to think you can grow in any part of the Christian life, including the wise exercise of generosity, without making mistakes along the way. This side of death, or the rapture, there is no alternative but to make them. Therefore, some of your learning will have to come from your errors and misjudgements. Indeed, I believe God allows (not causes) you to make those mistakes precisely in order that you can learn from them and not repeat them.

Thus, it is a much bigger cause for concern if your generosity is not large enough to cause you to make such mistakes as you grow in wisdom. If you had to choose, it would be far better to be generous, but naïve, than to be stingy and shrewd. However, even better than that is to be generous *and* shrewd. Then both your heart and your head act as they should, balancing each other and responding accurately to God's promptings. You cannot realistically expect to *begin with* both of those qualities fully formed, or indeed with either of them.

429

They both need to be grown and developed over the years, by regular practice, including trial and error, and from learning from your mistakes as you go along. Therefore, seek to develop *both* generosity *and* wisdom, not just one or the other. In particular, seek to grow in your knowledge and understanding of the ways of the wicked, both inside and outside the churches. In that regard, please refer to my Book 6.

I will now give a particular word of warning, which is usually only of relevance to those whose hearts are very generous, and whose heads have not yet caught up by developing a matching level of wisdom. That is that you need to beware of giving people more than *their* character can handle. If you give overly generously to an immature, carnal Christian then, even if he is not wicked, he may well respond to your excessive and unwise generosity in a carnal manner. I have done this many times, especially when I was in business and had far more to give.

I would give to certain people, only to find that it *'turned their heads'* and caused them to want, and then to expect, even more. They even became resentful, and imagined they had a basis for a sense of grievance, when I eventually saw my error and chose not to give to them anymore. Carnal people are quick to develop an attitude of entitlement, and to resent it when that is not met by ongoing giving at the level they have come to expect. Therefore, one sensible policy, which I learned from repeated bad experiences, is that it is wise to avoid giving by regular monthly standing order.

Churches and charities like these very much, and push for them, because it helps them to plan ahead. However, another reason why they like regular monthly sums is that it makes it harder for you to stop giving if your view of that church or charity alters. You may feel too embarrassed, or even too scared, to stop your giving once you have started and they are well aware of that. Therefore, it is much wiser, in my view, to save your money in a *giving account*, which you keep quite separate from your savings account. Then give irregular, ad hoc, one-off gifts from that giving account.

Instead of promising to give £X per month by bank standing order, give spontaneously, as lump sums. Do this in different amounts and at irregular intervals, spaced out by several months, or whenever you choose, *but not monthly*. In this way you prevent any sense of *expectation* or, even worse, *entitlement*, from ever arising in their minds. It is also less embarrassing, and less confrontational, for you to *stop giving,* or to *reduce* it if your view of that church or charity alters, or if you would simply prefer to give elsewhere.

You then give yourself far more freedom of manoeuvre and also maximise the pleasure that you get from giving. That is far better than feeling bound to continue giving, as per the status quo, to people or groups who have gone down in your estimation, or who have even begun to act improperly. The problems that come from giving people more than they can handle generally only arise if you are very wealthy or very generous, as you are unlikely otherwise to give amounts that are big enough to turn people's heads.

That small minority whose generosity greatly exceeds their wisdom, need to *restrain*, rather than increase, their generosity. At least, they must not allow it to run any further ahead of their wisdom than it already is. They must, at certain times, keep their own generosity under strict control and refuse to let themselves give until they have paused, reflected, checked things, weighed people up properly and, above all, *prayed for guidance*. That includes asking God to tell you *not* to give, *or to give less*, if that is His will, rather than just assume automatically that he wants you to give a large sum.

If you are a really generous and *"cheerful"* giver, then you are likely to run ahead of God. If so you will give based on your own spontaneous impulses, and on the pleasure you get from giving, rather than in response to His leading. So, it is a rare problem, but if you are in that sub-category, as I was, then take note and learn to restrain that excessive generosity at times. You also need to put in place some wise safeguards to reduce the problems that flow from your misjudgements when they still occur, as they are bound to.

However, by far the majority of us are not in that sub-category. If so, our generosity does not need to be restrained, but rather to be *increased*, and sometimes to a very great extent. Stingy people may, or may not, lack shrewdness and discernment. But the lack of those attributes is not their main problem in the context of giving. Instead, their problem is *a reluctance to give adequately, or at all*, even to those who are worthy, and even where God is prompting them to do so. The main reason for that is that they simply *don't want to give*, primarily because they *take no pleasure from giving*.

If that is your position, and it is a very common one, then the answer is to begin by giving from sheer obedience, whether you enjoy it or not. That is you would need to make yourself give, even where you don't want to, and take no pleasure from it. As you do this, and keep on doing it, God will steadily change your heart and develop your generosity as a response to your *obedience*. You will then find gradually, over time, that the needs of others become more and more important to you. You will also begin to take pleasure from giving.

That pleasure will grow stronger and stronger as you keep on giving, and you will even begin to look forward to it with relish. That is a heart attitude which you should seek to develop in yourself. But you must also ask God to create it in you, and to increase it, because God says He loves generosity. That being so, how can any person who wants to become wise possibly justify *not* seeking to have a

431

generous heart? It is an essential part of the character of any godly person. Therefore, if you don't already have a generous heart, then set about trying to get one, as a matter of priority, and don't stop until you do.

The folly of going into debt by borrowing for anything other than a house, car or business

In the financial crisis of 2008 banks, companies, and millions of private individuals, were suddenly exposed as being insolvent, due to their reckless approach to risk-taking and especially to borrowing. The banks were then 'bailed out' at public expense, causing the UK Government, and many others, to build up an even more ridiculous level of national debt than they already had. But individuals were not bailed out, there being no way of helping them, except by greatly reducing interest rates. That punished all the savers, the very people who had been acting wisely, and whose savings had prevented our complete collapse.

As far as possible, you really need to avoid borrowing, except for the purchase of a house or car, or for the setting up or expansion of a business. Other than in those few cases, with rare exceptions, such as perhaps urgent healthcare, you should always live within your means. That means you live on your present income, avoid borrowing, and save up for any expensive item, doing without it until you have the cash to buy it outright. If more people had done this then the 2008 crisis, and the 'credit crunch' that followed, could have been avoided.

Ironically, after 2008, the banks went to the opposite extreme. Instead of pushing people to borrow, when they plainly could not afford to repay, they suddenly switched the tap off and would not lend at all, even to those who were fully creditworthy. Thus, even the stronger small businesses were denied help and many went under, due to the sudden cash flow crises which resulted from the banks' overnight change of policy, whereby they reduced overdraft limits, called in loans, and refused to provide new ones.

If those businesses and individuals had been more careful in the years before 2008, borrowing much less, or even nothing, but rather saving up a cash reserve, they would have emerged unscathed. They would even have been ready to take advantage of opportunities to buy shares, houses and other assets which suddenly fell in value. That drop in prices was largely due to the fall in aggregate demand due to other people's sudden lack of cash and inability to buy. I would therefore urge you, as well as saving, to *avoid borrowing* wherever you can. If you absolutely must borrow, it should only be done:

a) carefully, after much thought

b) after doing everything you can to avoid, reduce or delay the borrowing

c) only for suitable purposes which, other than emergencies, such as urgent healthcare, are for buying a house or a car or for use in your business.

Don't borrow for pure consumer items or for weddings, holidays or the like. Those should be saved up for, or done without, or scaled down in size, to match your means. There is a growing trend, despite the credit crunch, for lavish weddings, in prestigious venues, out of all proportion to people's wealth. They do it to keep up with others and meet expectations. However, it is far better to have a wedding which matches your means, and which is low key, or even entirely self-catered, if need be. Why not just have sandwiches and cakes if that is all you can truly afford?

It can all be done very modestly with the help of your friends or church, rather than in a posh hotel, or even a stately home, which then needs to be paid for for years afterwards. The Western nations (though not the Muslim ones) may have abolished literal slavery. However, where people get into debt, they put themselves into a kind of metaphorical slavery whereby their lives become controlled by the people to whom they owe money. Their freedom of action and movement is then so curtailed that it is as if they were the slaves of their creditors. Solomon spoke of this problem:

The rich rules over the poor,
and the borrower is the slave of the lender.
Proverbs 22:7 (ESV)

Having said all that about the folly of borrowing money yourself, it is, nevertheless, right that you should be willing to lend to others if they are in *need*. That does not mean lending money to people for silly or non-essential things, but only when they are in genuine need. Such lending is one part of how we are meant to care for the poor:

[7] *"If among you, one of your brothers should become poor, in any of your towns within your land that the LORD your God is giving you, you shall not harden your heart or shut your hand against your poor brother,* [8] *but you shall open your hand to him and lend him sufficient for his need, whatever it may be.*
Deuteronomy 15:7-8 (ESV)

The vital importance of paying into pensions, even when you are young

This is linked to the subject of saving, but it is a sub-category thereof, because putting money into your pension is a very long-term project. The money cannot be taken out until (in the UK) you are 55 years old. Due to excessive spending, lack of thrift, and addiction to borrowing, an alarming percentage of the UK

433

population are now doing little or nothing to prepare for their retirement, even if they are already in their forties, fifties or even sixties. They have no plan and are relying solely on the state pension to live on.

But, in the UK, that is far too small to enable you to live properly, in the absence of either large savings, or private pensions or both. I would therefore advise a radical rethink of your financial planning and priorities, even if you are only in your thirties, or even your twenties. It is never too early to start putting money into your pension. I started private pensions for my children when they were aged only 9 and 7 respectively, and the capital value of their pension funds have been growing nicely ever since.

In fact, their case helps to make the point that the longer you can leave money invested in a pension fund, due to starting earlier, the less you need to put in to achieve the same final value when you retire. That is because the shares or other assets, such as real property, which the pension holds will very probably rise in real terms, especially if you can leave it there for decades. That will result in a far better outcome than where the money is all put in to the pension in a tearing hurry in your fifties or sixties.

Therefore, however young you are, start a pension plan now, even if only on a very modest basis. If you live in the UK I recommend that you do so through Hargreaves Lansdowne PLC. I have found them to be by far the best pension provider. It is all very easy to do. Just contact them, or some other company if you prefer, and set up a *"Self Invested Pension Plan" ("SIPP")*. This enables you to contribute lump sums or, better still small monthly payments, in line with what you can afford. Some companies impose a lower limit of perhaps £50 per month, but you can check that.

However, if you can't afford the minimum you could instead save up in a bank account until you have enough to pay in a lump sum. Then keep on doing that, again and again, as the years go by. Do also bear in mind that pension contributions are 'tax deductible'. That means that the figure you pay in from your net (taxed) income is *"grossed up"* to your full pre-tax rate. This is achieved by the pension company reclaiming your tax from the Government (if you pay PAYE) or by you doing so yourself, in your next tax return, if you are a higher rate tax payer.

Thus, if you pay 20% tax then it only costs you £80 per month to put £100 into your pension – or £40 to put £50 in. But if you pay 40% tax then, if you put £60 in to the pension, you can reduce your tax bill for that year by £40. You can then either keep that, or put it into the pension the following year, thus reducing your tax bill yet again. Of course, it may not be possible for you to make pension contributions at the moment. You could still be a student, or have a young family,

434

or be struggling to buy your first house. Or you could just have a very low income, or be a single parent.

In such circumstances, pension contributions may be impossible. However, the point at which they do become possible, may be much earlier than you assume, especially if your overall handling of money is not as it should be. If so, review the situation, cut back on spending if you can, and begin a pension, even at a very small level. That will focus your mind on retirement as you view your twice yearly statements and their projections of your likely retirement income. But even if you can only make tiny contributions for years, it is still important to get into this habit, and to give your fund the longest possible time to grow. Also, the very fact that you have one will cause you to make different decisions over the years.

You may choose to increase the monthly contribution each time you get a pay rise or a promotion, or when the kids start school or leave home, and so on. Of course, you must not go overboard with pensions. You still need to be able to live, give financially, pay your bills, save money and avoid borrowing, quite apart from pensions. However, with thrift, proper planning, self-control, and God's blessings in response to your giving, there is every chance that you will be able to start a pension far earlier than most people do. Indeed, many never start at all.

Some might object that paying into pensions and saving generally is *"not trusting God"* and that you should just *"rely on God entirely"*. That is super-spiritual nonsense, based on a misunderstanding of what faith is and what it means to trust God. He wants us to act wisely, and that plainly includes saving for 'rainy days' and also for old age, which is the rainiest day of all. To fail to do so because you claim to be trusting God instead is not faith, or wisdom. It is just presumption.

Why not apply the same foolish thinking to everything else the Bible commands us to do, such as sharing the Gospel and making disciples? Why not do nothing and say that you are trusting God to share the Gospel Himself and to make disciples on your behalf. It is the same logic, and equally misguided. Earning, saving and investing money is not grasping. Neither is it failing to trust. It is wisdom. Above all, it is consistent with the commands and principles that are set out in Scripture.

Even if you can't start a business, try get into a position where you could become self-employed in some way, in case the persecution of Christians worsens

I shall set out some advice for that minority who are suited to setting up and running their own business and look at how to start, and run one. However, even if you don't have the skill or confidence to do that, at least bear in mind the

435

possibility of one day having to go *self-employed* in some way. It could even be on a tiny scale, where it is just you alone, with no staff. I say this because the persecution of Christians is getting much more intense and all sorts of pressures are being put on Christians, by employers and professions, including on issues of conscience.

Many of us will find in the coming years that we either have to leave our jobs or be sacked for not complying with our employers' politically correct rules and demands, especially if we are in public sector jobs. Therefore, it would be wise to begin to give thought, even now, to developing some skill or trade, such as Paul had with his tent making. Then, if you do ever lose your job, or have to resign because of growing persecution, you can at least go it alone as a window cleaner, IT adviser, piano teacher, gardener, caterer, decorator or driving instructor, or doing needlework, car repairs etc.

The list of potential trades is endless. Therefore, you may be surprised to find that you do actually have some marketable skills, however small or obscure, even if you have never considered them to amount to much. If you can develop this skill now and start to practise it, perhaps on a part time basis, so as to gain experience, you will be better placed to know whether you can do it and whether you would be able to produce sufficient income to live on if the need arises.

At least begin to look into this, to take advice, and to make contingency plans. Then, if it does ever come to it, you would be ready to launch yourself in that trade on a self-employed basis. That is far better than leaving it until the crisis is actually upon you, and you have already lost your job, before you even start to give any thought to an alternative way of making a living.

Setting up and running your own business

The advice I shall give here is not aimed at everyone. I personally believe that only about 10-15% of people are suited to run their own businesses and have the necessary character, confidence, personality, skills and experience to do it. However, it may be that you are, or could grow to be, amongst that group, even if you don't currently realise it. Probably 85-90% of people were created by God in such a way that they cannot be the number one person in a business, not even in a small one. They need a boss who can be the spearhead, take the responsibility, and make the final decisions.

That is OK and there is nothing wrong with remaining as an employee until you retire, albeit perhaps as a senior one, with supervisory or managerial responsibilities. You would just not be the ultimate owner or final decision-maker. However, if you are in that minority who *can* do this, or if you think you could be, and are beginning to consider it, I would urge you to look into it open-mindedly. Do so over a lengthy period of time, and don't exclude yourself hastily prematurely, or without proper thought.

I began my working career aged 21, having also had many summer jobs before that. I then grew in seniority, confidence and skill as an employee until I was 33, when I became a 'salaried partner' in a law firm. That is essentially a glorified employee, with the title of partner, but no capital ownership and, usually, no vote on major issues. Then, when I was 34, I became an equity partner, with a one-third share of the ownership of the firm. The next three years, until I was 37, gave me very valuable experience in running a business, as I was both head of Litigation and Managing Partner.

Never go into business with an unbeliever

I learned a huge amount from doing those jobs, both from the things that worked well, and also the mistakes I made. However, the biggest error I ever made was to go into shared equity ownership in the first place with two men who did not share my Christian faith, or my world view, or have the same values or goals. One of them was actually a Freemason, which I already knew to be very wrong before I entered into that partnership. I shut my ears to God's warnings, because I wanted to accept their offer and naively thought I could handle them.

I learned a lot, and did well, and my department grew until it was bigger than the rest of the firm combined. However, it all ended badly. I tell the story in Book 2 and Book 6 and I would refer you to those for more detail. The short version is that I caught the Freemason forging an invoice on the firm's letterhead, in order to get the client to pay him directly, instead of through the firm. I challenged him on this but, instead of supporting me against the Freemason, the Senior Partner joined with him against me.

The two of them then voted to expel me from the firm, essentially for having exposed and challenged the second partner. They also invented or exaggerated a host of false allegations against me to justify not repaying me my one third equity stake. I never got it back because I had to choose either to sue them over a period of 2-3 years, at huge cost, or to set up a new firm of my own. I had not got enough money to do both. So, having commenced legal proceedings, I had to abandon those, which was extremely painful.

I also never got the chance to sue them later, when I was successful in my new firm, not even when I had sold up in order to become a Bible teacher. By then, they had both gone into bankruptcy, which I think was God's judgment upon them for what they had done to me, and to others, over the years. However, the point is that if you are a genuine Christian, as opposed to a nominal churchgoer with no deep convictions, you will face severe problems if you go into shared ownership with unbelievers.

That would still apply *even with people who claim to be Christians, but who aren't as sincere or committed as you.* In either case, but especially with outright unbelievers, there is inevitably going to be a clash in terms of your approach to running the business, recruitment, handling staff and ethical issues generally. There may also be a difference of view as to how much to pay yourselves as owners and how much of the profit to leave in the business as *"retained profit"* (see below). The key point, however, is that there will inevitably be a mismatch of some kind.

You will not fit in with each other, because you have been *mismatched with unbelievers*, which apostle Paul tells us never to be, and not only in the context of marriage. It also applies in any other situation in which there needs to be close working relationships, shared ownership and genuine trust and confidence. Those things simply can't be maintained if your business partners don't have a Christian faith which is as strong and genuine as yours and/or if their vision for the business differs from yours in any important way:

¹⁴ Do not be mismated with unbelievers. For what partnership have righteousness and iniquity? Or what fellowship has light with darkness? ¹⁵ What accord has Christ with Be'lial? Or what has a believer in common with an unbeliever? ¹⁶ What agreement has the temple of God with idols? For we are the temple of the living God; as God said,
"I will live in them and move among them,
and I will be their God,
and they shall be my people.
¹⁷ Therefore come out from them,
and be separate from them, says the Lord,
and touch nothing unclean;
then I will welcome you,
¹⁸ and I will be a father to you,
and you shall be my sons and daughters,
says the Lord Almighty."

2 Corinthians 6:14-18 (RSV)

Paul's words are very clear. They plainly apply to marriage, and to membership of apostate, unbiblical churches with insincere leaders who teach false doctrine. However, the point also applies everywhere else, including shared business ownership, where total trust, an equivalent vision, and the same ethical values, are needed. Indeed, in all of my observations of law firms over 30 years I have also seen bitter conflict arise amongst unbelievers, and *even where all partners purport*

438

to be Christians. They too can be mismatched if they are not on the same 'wavelength' spiritually.

Ideally, don't share equity ownership in a business with *anybody*, even if they are a real Christian

It is very hard for any business partnerships to stay together, even at the best of times, due to there being so many potential areas for disagreement, and so much real or alleged wrongdoing amongst the partners. I have seen countless law firms split up, sue each other, demerge, or fall apart and go bust, primarily due to differences of vision and *inability to trust each other* or work together amicably. So, this is a problem which does not only apply between Christian and non-Christian partners. It applies wherever there is shared ownership, *whoever the partners are.*

It is different in a large public company, where the owners are thousands, or even millions, of anonymous shareholders. The company is then run by its directors and by layer upon layer of managers under them. In such businesses the ownership is much less personal. In fact, there is no real sense of shared ownership at all. Even the Managing Director or CEO is, effectively, just a glorified employee of the shareholders, albeit a very senior one.

So, my *general* advice to anyone considering going into partnership in a small or medium sized business, unless they have *very good reasons* to feel able to put complete trust in their future partners, is to avoid all offers of shared equity ownership, *even with genuine Christians.* That is the case whether the business is in the form of a partnership or a company. I would strongly recommend instead that you go into business by yourself, or perhaps with your wife or husband as a business partner, and that you do not accept anyone else as an *equity* partner.

If you go into business with your spouse, try to arrange it so that only one of you can be sued if the business fails, rather than both of you

However, there is also a quite separate problem with being in business with your spouse, even if you are very happily married, which is that the business could fail and/or you could both be sued. Therefore, my advice is that you should try hard not to put yourselves in a position where *both* of you could become liable at the same time to any creditor, regulator or opponent. They might then choose to sue or prosecute both of you for something that the business does which creates a debt or civil liability, for example a personal injury or some negligence claim.

439

That being so, it may be wise for you and your spouse to keep your assets separate from each other and away from the firm's potential creditors. Then only one of you would be sued, or have to go into bankruptcy, if the business should fail, or if legal proceedings are brought. The way to protect your assets, is for *only one of you* to officially trade, enter into contracts, or borrow from banks. Then, while one spouse runs the business, as its official owner, the assets of *the other spouse* are all kept separately, in their sole name, and outside of the business.

Accordingly, if the one running the business is sued, or goes bankrupt, any assets which are in the hands of the *non-participating* spouse will all be beyond the reach of the creditors of the firm and will therefore be preserved. However, for this tactic to succeed, the separating of the assets needs, ideally, to have occurred *before* any contracts are entered into or any liabilities are incurred. Otherwise the steps you take to protect your assets might be set aside by a court. The best time to do it is before you start the business. But, if that has not been done, then do it now, at the earliest possible time.

If your spouse needs to work in the business, then make sure they are only ever an *employee*, never a *partner*. Then, if the business does ever fail, or if you become liable in some way, only *you* will be liable to pay out, not your *spouse*. Then, he or she keeps all their own assets, other than those which have been put into the firm itself, and you alone will have all the debts and liabilities. In such a situation, those creditors or litigants who are suing you will hit a brick wall. Legally, they can only make a claim against you, and therefore your spouse's assets are safe from them.

In this way, if your business should fail, you would be well placed, as a married couple, to start another business immediately afterwards, because at least your spouse's assets will have been preserved. The next time around you might possibly have your spouse heading it, at least notionally, while *you* operate as a mere employee of your spouse. That is something which you can still do even if you have had to go into bankruptcy. In other words, if you take this approach, an attack on the business can then only bring down one of you, not both, and the one who has been bankrupted can still carry on, albeit as an employee.

If you operate in this way, then creditors or litigants can only seize the assets of one of you at most, plus any assets that have been put within the company itself, and which may have been classified as belonging to it, rather than to either of you, such as plant, machinery etc. But they can't go for those assets which your spouse has been holding, separately from you, and outside of the business. Those are beyond their reach. This is really important, because business failure is a far bigger likelihood than you might imagine and a high percentage of brand-new businesses go bust in the first two years.

440

Some advice about starting your own business

When businesses go bust, it is not usually due to being unprofitable. Many failed businesses were highly profitable. The main cause of their demise is *cash flow problems*, usually due to inadequate planning, excessive borrowing, bad decisions, overly rapid expansion and unwise recruitment. Another cause is taking on excessively large or difficult contracts, before the firm is ready to cope with projects of that size, urgency or complexity. Accordingly, if you are considering starting your own small business, here is some advice I would give:

1. Plan well ahead, preferably long before you actually start the business. Try to anticipate, prepare for, and solve in advance, as many potential problems as you can foresee. The earlier you start to do this, and the more potential problems you can foresee and provide for, the easier and safer your first two years will be, and those years are crucial to your survival.

2. Save up as much money as you can before you begin, even for many years beforehand, so that you can, ideally, survive without the help of banks for up to two years, or preferably more.

3. Before you start the business, reduce your expenditure at home so that the amount you need to 'pay' yourself each month is kept to a minimum. Continue this frugal policy for as long as you can, even after the business has begun, so as to reduce the pressure on cash flow.

4. If it is absolutely essential to borrow money, then see whether you can get loans from family or friends. Even promises of future help, if needed, i.e. informal 'lines of credit', can be very useful. These can be agreed in advance *in case they are needed* during the first two years. Even knowing that these funds will become available later if needed will give you confidence. It will also prevent you needing to go to banks, who are, in any case, of little use, as they are likely to turn you down flat. At least it may delay the need for banks until later, when you can prove that the business is profitable and well managed, and that it only needs cash.

5. Be aware that when they are dealing with new-start businesses, banks are notoriously negative and unhelpful. It has been said that they only lend out umbrellas on dry days, and demand them back in immediately if there is any sign of rain. I have found that adage to be true. Therefore, it is wise to be realistic about how banks operate, even before you begin, so that you aren't caught out.

6. Start small and grow slowly. A solid start, followed by a thorough, patient build up, are the hallmarks of a business that is operating in the Spirit, in

accordance with God's style and principles. However, a business that grows rapidly at the start is very probably a 'work of the flesh'. It would, almost certainly, be operating on the basis of the proprietor's impatience and impulsiveness, because God never rushes any project. He always proceeds at a steady pace, at least to begin with.

7. Be slow to recruit staff and extremely thorough and careful during the selection and interview stages. Only set them on if they have worked with you for a paid trial day, or preferably a whole trial week, so that you can see them in action, actually doing the job. That is totally different from judging people solely by CVs and interviews, however thorough or discerning you may think you are.

8. Even after you appoint someone, tell them clearly that they are *on probation* for a whole year and that they must prove their effectiveness, faithfulness and reliability during that time or they will not be kept on. Be very open about this *and mean it*. Never be afraid to dismiss people who simply don't meet your standards, even where there is no misconduct. Far too many employers keep staff on who ought to be let go, either because they fear confrontation or because the person *"isn't that bad"*. However, you must not keep anybody on just because they are *"not really bad"*. To stay with you they need to be *good, or in fact excellent.* Don't settle for less, however hard it is to find good staff.

9. Limit the size, urgency and complexity of orders that you take on during the first two years, when your firm is small, the staff are few in number, and their skill and experience are not yet fully developed. Be willing to literally turn work away if it is going to be too big, too complex, or too urgent for you to handle. Biting off more than your firm can chew may well destroy the business. This kind of restraint is easier said than done, as large or high value contracts are so tempting. Even so, resist it and control yourself. Deliberately slow down your firm's rate of growth so that it is manageable.

10. Another reason for not letting any single contract be too big is that it is dangerous to allow your firm to become dependent on one customer or, even worse, on one contract, in case it goes wrong, or *they* go bust or become unable to pay. That can leave you with a cash flow crisis, a big hole in your 'order book' and perhaps the sudden need to lay off some of your staff. The risk is far less, and is spread more widely, if you have a lot of small customers rather than a few big ones.

11. Set out from day one to build the capital value of the firm, as far as possible, *by retaining profit* rather than by borrowing, or even by accepting investments from others. The fewer outsiders who have a stake in your business, or any

kind of power or control over it, the better. Ideally you want them to have *no say at all* in what you do. Then you are free to make all your own decisions for yourself, whenever and however it suits you.

12. Likewise, do not accept any equity partners, either at the start or at any stage thereafter. Always keep the entire equity ownership in your own hands, even if that means the firm must stay smaller for longer. If that is the case, then so be it. I can assure you, from painful experience, that remaining small, even permanently, is far better than sharing ownership.

13. Retaining profit means that you might be able to see that, on paper, you have been making a profit of say £10,000 per month in the first six to twelve months. If that is so, you need to make sure that you *actually pay yourself much less than that*, however high or low the profit may be. Ensure that as much as possible of it is left in the business each month. Then the value of the balance sheet rises, but in such a way that borrowing is either avoided or minimised.

14. By deferring spending the profit until later, preferably until many years later, when you sell up and retire, you will be able to survive any lean spell. Such difficult times are likely to occur in the second, or even the third year, especially if by then you have begun to grow the business. That early period is a really dangerous time. The more 'fat' the firm has stored up, the safer you will be, and the more easily you will be able to survive the cash shortages that would finish off other firms which are less cautious.

15. Even in the third, fourth and subsequent years, or even indefinitely, keep on and on retaining profit and not drawing it all. Ideally, you want to get to a place where you have zero debts. If so, no bank can make demands of you, or tell you what to do, or even close you down, when it takes the notion. The more undrawn profit that you retain, the stronger the firm will be financially. Also the more quickly you will be able to take advantage of opportunities for growth, or for re-equipping or investing in the business, when you deem the time to be right. And you won't need the permission of any bank to do so.

16. Show total integrity at all times with staff, customers and suppliers. Keep all your promises and never deceive, manipulate, short-change or double cross anybody, even if you can be sure they will never find out. God sees everything and has said that He hates a crooked measure, or any form of lies or sharp practice. Remember also that He operates in accordance with the law of sowing and reaping, as we saw earlier. Therefore, ensure that all your dealings, with anybody at all, are such that you would *want* them to be multiplied and sent back to you by God, because they will be.

17. Once you have got through the first two or three years, or longer in some cases, the time may well come when you have the opportunity to expand. You may even feel it is appropriate to take some calculated risks in order to grow and to increase your profits. When you do this, you need to ensure that the risks you take are very carefully considered. Nevertheless, be willing to take such risks *if* the odds are stacked sufficiently in your favour, *and* if you have enough retained profit in the firm to enable that expansion or project to fail without destroying the firm.

18. There is a time for everything. The first two to three years are for playing it safe and getting solidly established. But after that the time for risk-taking may come, provided you are not forcing it to happen prematurely. When that time genuinely comes, go for it and do not be afraid. Excessive caution, when it is the time for seizing opportunities, will hold you back and prevent your growth. There are always clouds somewhere in the sky but, *provided the firm is ready*, you must not be excessively risk averse. Don't let the existence of potential dangers, which are always going to be there, stop you from going forward *when the time is right* to do so. As Solomon said:

He who observes the wind will not sow,
   and he who regards the clouds will not reap.
                     Ecclesiastes 11:4 (ESV)

19. Even if your firm grows and succeeds, do not let any of it go to your head. Never allow yourself to become proud, haughty or pompous or to treat people with disdain. Keep your feet firmly on the ground, humble yourself, and treat people the same way as you ever did. Never take on any airs or graces or imagine yourself to be important. Many successful people can handle the pressures of starting a business, and even the problems of failure and struggle, but they cannot cope with success and they allow their character, and their manners, to be affected by it. Never let that happen to you.

20. Likewise, if you do succeed, don't ever allow yourself to fall in love with money. A good way to avoid that is to keep on increasing your giving as your profit increases. In that way, your generosity goes up and up in line with your success, which will help to keep your heart tender and generous. King David put it well when he said:

.......if riches increase, set not your heart on them.
                     Psalm 62:10(b) (ESV)

444

CHAPTER 13

WISE PEOPLE LEARN HOW TO MAKE GOOD DECISIONS

Make me to know your ways, O LORD;
teach me your paths.
Psalm 25:4 (ESV)

⁵ Trust in the LORD with all your heart,
and do not lean on your own understanding.
⁶ In all your ways acknowledge him,
and he will make straight your paths.
⁷ Be not wise in your own eyes;
fear the LORD, and turn away from evil.
Proverbs 3:5-7 (ESV)

A man's steps are ordered by the LORD;
how then can man understand his way?
Proverbs 20:24 (RSV)

Where there is no guidance, a people falls;
but in an abundance of counselors there is safety.
Proverbs 11:14 (RSV)

I call heaven and earth to witness against you today, that I have set before you
life and death, blessing and curse. Therefore choose life, that you and your
offspring may live,
Deuteronomy 30:19 (ESV)

"And to this people you shall say: 'Thus says the LORD: Behold, I set before
you the way of life and the way of death.
Jeremiah 21:8 (ESV)

".......choose this day whom you will serve......"
Joshua 24:15(b) (RSV)

He who meddles in a quarrel not his own
is like one who takes a passing dog by the ears.
Proverbs 26:17 (RSV)

²⁴ By faith Moses, when he was grown up, refused to be called the son of
Pharaoh's daughter, ²⁵ choosing rather to share ill-treatment with the people of
God than to enjoy the fleeting pleasures of sin.   Hebrews 11:24-25 (RSV)

445

6 When they came, he looked on Eli'ab and thought, "Surely the LORD'S anointed is before him." 7 But the LORD said to Samuel, "Do not look on his appearance or on the height of his stature, because I have rejected him; for the LORD sees not as man sees; man looks on the outward appearance, but the LORD looks on the heart."

1 Samuel 16:6-7 (RSV)

Do you see a man who is hasty in his words?
There is more hope for a fool than for him.
Proverbs 29:20 (RSV)

Open your mouth, judge righteously,
maintain the rights of the poor and needy.
Proverbs 31:9 (RSV)

25 Moses chose able men out of all Israel, and made them heads over the people, rulers of thousands, of hundreds, of fifties, and of tens. 26 And they judged the people at all times; hard cases they brought to Moses, but any small matter they decided themselves.

Exodus 18:25-26 (RSV)

You shall not be partial in judgment. You shall hear the small and the great alike. You shall not be intimidated by anyone, for the judgment is God's. And the case that is too hard for you, you shall bring to me, and I will hear it.'

Deuteronomy 1:17 (ESV)

The difficulties which so many people have with decision-making

A lot of people find decision-making difficult, and even frightening. They therefore delay making decisions, or make bad ones. Or, worst of all, they don't make them at all. On the whole, this has been an area of relative strength for me. I have never been afraid of making decisions, or of getting it wrong, or that others might blame me. I served for three years as a police officer and usually patrolled alone. I had to get used to making rapid, on the spot judgments, often without all the facts, and with nobody from whom to seek advice. At first it was hard and stressful.

I still remember that sense of bewilderment when facing wholly new and confusing situations and having to make my mind up, there and then, as to what action to take, if any. To add to the difficulty, it often had to be done in front of the public, so I did not even have the luxury of privacy when making my mistakes. Then in my second career, as a lawyer, I had to hear clients' problems and then nail my colours to the mast by telling them what *I thought* they should do, and

446

putting it in writing too, as a permanent record, which could be brought back later to haunt me.

Again, this was valuable experience. I learned how to stand alone, take full responsibility, and give decisive, unequivocal advice. The alternative, which I was determined to avoid, was beating about the bush, hedging my bets and effectively offering no real advice at all. That is what too many lawyers do when they lack the courage to put their own necks on the line and clearly spell out what *they* think. I was surprised by how many colleagues, and even bosses, dodged responsibility. They were effectively just giving the client a range of options, with pros and cons, and warnings as to what might go wrong, so as to cover their own back.

But, far too often, it was all done without ever actually giving any real or decisive *advice* to that client. He was still left to work it out for himself and make his own decision. Of course, the primary concern of such lawyers was for themselves, not their client. They wanted to make sure nobody could ever blame them or prove that they had given wrong advice. But they did not seek to achieve that by giving good advice, based on thorough research and sound reasoning. They did it by never actually giving any meaningful advice at all. So it was a cop-out and was done to protect themselves, or so they thought.

They had no regard for the fact that they weren't actually providing what the client was paying for, which was to be told plainly *what they thought he should do*. Such lawyers often hid behind clichés about how the position was *"finely balanced"* and how the client needed to *"bear in mind all the options, with all of their respective pros and cons"*. However, what they were really doing was abdicating their responsibility and failing in the first duty of any lawyer, which is *to advise*. You cannot call your words 'advice' if all they amount to is urging the client to think carefully about what *he* is going to choose.

He hasn't paid a lawyer just to give him a series of options. Those are certainly needed, for starters, but he is also entitled to be told which option *that lawyer thinks he ought to choose*. From a very early stage in my career I recognised this problem of my colleagues' wariness about giving clear, unambiguous advice and I resolved never to operate as they did, even though their way would have been a lot easier. I felt my clients were entitled to expect me to have the courage to take a decisive position and to state my opinion boldly, without any fudge or evasion.

By taking that approach, I made a rod for my own back, making my job harder and more stressful. But it was the right choice and my career blossomed as a result, whereas those who opted for the 'safe' approach never got very far. Indeed, they did not deserve to, as they were not providing the most fundamental part of the service they were charging for, namely *advice*. As I rose higher, and ended up managing several teams of lawyers, my day consisted of little else but decision-

447

making. The only difference was that the people who now sought my advice were no longer clients, but lawyers.

It is sometimes very difficult to tell the difference between good and evil and we need God's help to do so.

Sometimes it is obvious that one course of action is right and another is wrong. However, that is not always so, and the higher up you go in management the harder it gets. You sometimes have to choose between options where what is right can seem wrong, and what is wrong can seem right. Or you may have to choose between options which seem very similar and where the distinction is very subtle. I refer to it as telling the difference between pale grey and light grey. Yet the distinction can still be significant, and needs to be identified.

Moreover, if you are promoted to senior levels, you will also have to make many more decisions and ever more rapidly. It can feel as if they are coming at you on a fast-moving conveyor belt and there is not enough time to investigate, check facts and interview people, or to reflect and pray adequately, before you have to decide. Therefore, you may not always feel confident that you can accurately discern which, if any, of the available options is right and whether a proposal is good or bad.

The advice you get from others can also be contradictory, or even non-existent. They too find it hard to separate the relevant from the irrelevant, to correctly identify the issues, and to make sense of it all. King Solomon was well aware of this problem that we all face, especially leaders. Therefore, when he met the LORD in a dream and was offered a gift, he asked for the ability to know the difference between good and evil. That may sound easy, but it isn't, as Solomon had already begun to realise:

Give thy servant therefore an understanding mind to govern thy people, that I may discern between good and evil; for who is able to govern this thy great people?"

1 Kings 3:9 (RSV)

For fallible human beings, right and wrong, good and evil, truth and lies, and the relevant and irrelevant, can closely resemble each other, especially when decisions have to be made at speed, or under pressure. The best place to start is to do as Solomon did. Keep asking God for wisdom, and especially for the ability to distinguish between good and evil. Also ask him to reveal to you any evil that you are unable to see, or which is being hidden or disguised by someone. But also ask God to "direct your steps" day by day. We need to do that because nobody is capable of always making the right decisions and always knowing what to do:

448

I know, O LORD, that the way of man is not in himself,
that it is not in man who walks to direct his steps.
Jeremiah 10:23 (ESV)

Even when they don't have knowledge or understanding wise people are guided by their integrity.

You will never be able to handle every conceivable situation, such that you always know exactly what to do and how to handle all people or issues. Some circumstances can be so complex and thorny that you can be baffled, because there is no way forward that does not create problems of one kind or another. At such times you can, however, be guided by your integrity by asking yourself whether a certain option or route *feels* right to your conscience. Do that when the situation is so complicated that, *in your mind*, you just don't know what to do and your powers of reasoning can't give you the answers you need:

Guided by Good

The integrity of the upright guides them,
but the crookedness of the treacherous destroys them.
Proverbs 11:3 (RSV)

Our integrity or righteousness is therefore like a lamp which lights up our path and shows us the way to go, when, with our minds, we cannot see the way forward. The wicked have to walk in that darkness with no such help, or at least they are not willing to listen to it. Their main 'guidance' comes from the demons who inhabit or accompany them. But they are very treacherous guides who will seek to cause the wicked to stumble and be destroyed if they can:

[18] But the path of the righteous is like the light of dawn,
which shines brighter and brighter until full day.
[19] The way of the wicked is like deep darkness;
they do not know over what they stumble.
Proverbs 4:18-19 (RSV)

Our honesty will also make life's choices simpler and clearer. By refusing to be diverted onto any dishonest course we are kept on the straight and narrow road, which God wants us to be on, because all of the dishonest options are automatically excluded. That reduces our options, and makes it easier to choose, because only the honest options remain on the table:

[24] Put away from you crooked speech,
and put devious talk far from you.
[25] Let your eyes look directly forward,
and your gaze be straight before you.

449

²⁶ Take heed to the path of your feet,
  then all your ways will be sure.
²⁷ Do not swerve to the right or to the left;
turn your foot away from evil.
                          Proverbs 4:24-27 (RSV)

The righteousness of the blameless keeps his way straight,
  but the wicked falls by his own wickedness.
                          Proverbs 11:5 (RSV)

Integrity will also guard and protect us in another sense, because God will personally intervene to protect those who walk in integrity, whereas He will not do so for the wicked. On the contrary, He will oppose them and even cause them to be cut off and destroyed:

⁷ he stores up sound wisdom for the upright;
  he is a shield to those who walk in integrity,
⁸ guarding the paths of justice
  and preserving the way of his saints.
⁹ Then you will understand righteousness and justice
  and equity, every good path;
¹⁰ for wisdom will come into your heart,
  and knowledge will be pleasant to your soul;
¹¹ discretion will watch over you;
  understanding will guard you;
¹² delivering you from the way of evil,
  from men of perverted speech,
                          Proverbs 2:7-12 (RSV)

²¹ For the upright will inhabit the land,
  and men of integrity will remain in it;
²² but the wicked will be cut off from the land,
  and the treacherous will be rooted out of it.
                          Proverbs 2:21-22 (RSV)

Righteousness guards him whose way is upright,
but sin overthrows the wicked.
                          Proverbs 13:6 (RSV)

He who walks in integrity walks securely,
  but he who perverts his ways will be found out.
                          Proverbs 10:9 (RSV)

The LORD is a stronghold to him whose way is upright,

but destruction to evildoers.
Proverbs 10:29 (RSV)

There are times when, with your *mind*, you are simply incapable of working out what is for the best. Yet, if you face each option in turn and ask yourself how it *feels*, and whether your conscience *feels comfortable* with it, you will often get your answer. Your conscience is a reliable guide and it also operates when all your other resources have been used up, or are inadequate.

Your conscience can therefore operate far beyond the range of your knowledge and understanding. That is partly because God can speak to your conscience through your *spirit*, which can process things which your mind doesn't even know about, or can't yet grasp. Therefore, by putting God first, maintaining your integrity, and listening attentively to your conscience, you will find that God will make your path straight, even when you are out of your depth or feel confused or unsure:

⁵ *Trust in the LORD with all your heart,*
  and do not rely on your own insight.
⁶ *In all your ways acknowledge him,*
  and he will make straight your paths.
⁷ *Be not wise in your own eyes;*
  fear the LORD, and turn away from evil.
               Proverbs 3:5-7 (RSV)

So, there might be a business proposal, a job offer, or a possible relationship. It may seem to offer exciting opportunities and you can't *think* of any reason, with your *mind,* why you shouldn't do it. Yet, somehow, it just doesn't *feel* right. When that is the case, make sure you listen to your conscience and do what it says. Never ignore or override it. Far from it, learn to welcome your conscience's intervention. The more you listen to it, the more it will speak to you. But the more you ignore it, the quieter it will become until, eventually, it switches off completely.

Your conscience will be of no use to you unless you are willing to force yourself to listen to it

Your conscience can make available to you a whole new dimension of guidance, which can go beyond your current level of knowledge and understanding. Given that those things will never be complete, at least until after we die, this is a resource which we cannot afford to waste. However, your conscience will not be of much use to you unless you *force yourself to listen to it and then to obey it.* An

451

opportunity may present itself to you which seems attractive and profitable, but it is not what God wants you to do. All sorts of reasons will spring to mind as to why you *should* do it.

Your sinful flesh nature may also have plenty to say in support of the idea and will make sure that its voice is heard. Also, the demons in your life will speak their approval of the idea into your mind, as will the worldly people around you. It may be that, amongst all of that noise, the only voice that is speaking *against* the proposal is your conscience. Thus, it is very easy to find reasons and arguments in support of taking the opportunity that has arisen. Such thoughts will come crowding in. In a situation like that, you must learn to pause and pray along these lines:

*"Lord, this opportunity seems attractive to me. However, please speak clearly to me, through my conscience, as to whether it is actually right. Let me know whether it is what **you** want and help me not to drown out your voice with my own preferences and arguments".*

Our sinful flesh nature is so strong and intrusive, and we are so used to being guided by it, that it is easy to persuade yourself that any attractive or profitable venture is the right option. That is why most of us opt for such things so quickly with little, if any, internal debate. But train yourself to pause and interrogate yourself robustly and to pray as above. Then you are much more likely to hear the quiet voice of your conscience. I would actually go further and pray along the lines set out below, even if I already think that it is right to go ahead with some opportunity or proposal:

"Lord, I have tried to listen to my conscience and I now think I should go ahead with this idea/opportunity/proposal. However, if that is not your will, and if I have somehow got this wrong, please intervene and stop me, or stop the idea/opportunity from going ahead. Please block my path in any way you see fit, if I am doing the wrong thing here."

Such a prayer will please God and should be used even if you have already made a genuine attempt to listen to your conscience. It serves as a valuable supplement, or as a secondary safety net. However, don't pray this *instead* of listening to your conscience, but *in addition* to listening to it. Subject to emphasising that point, I have found that second prayer to be of great value. God has answered it and has blocked my path many times, thereby preventing me from making wrong choices.

I have needed God to intervene in this way even where I have done my best to use all of my knowledge and understanding and have tried to listen to my conscience. I have to confess that I have not always been pleased *while* He was blocking my path. But I was always grateful for it *later,* when the position became clearer. In this way God has delivered me from many bad situations and wrong choices, firstly because I was guided by my sense of right and wrong and, secondly, because I was willing to give God a final power of *veto*. His Word says that we will be delivered or rescued if we walk with integrity:

He who walks in integrity will be delivered,
but he who is perverse in his ways will fall into a pit.
Proverbs 28:18 (RSV)

Obtaining God's guidance, directly on specific issues, but also by learning the general principles by which He operates

There is no doubt that God can, and does, give specific, individual guidance to His people, and in various ways. In my own case, He usually does it by a kind of prompting, whereby He causes a person, situation or idea, or a verse in the Bible, to be 'quickened' or to go 'fluorescent' in my mind or spirit. I feel as though He is impressing upon me to do something, or to take care, or to look into a thing more closely. There have even been a few occasions when God has literally caused me to hear an audible voice, at least inside my head, telling me something. I will give some examples:

a) An audible voice told me that a girl in a prayer meeting, whom I had only just seen for the first time a few minutes earlier, and had never spoken to, was the person I would marry – and she was!

b) An audible voice warned me that a senior employee at work was disloyal to me and was causing problems and, after a full investigation, it turned out they were.

c) When I was 10 years old, I fell backwards from a bus shelter onto the pavement. As I was falling, in what seemed to be slow motion, I heard an audible voice repeatedly urging me "*Lift your head up*". I did as I was told and therefore hit the ground on my shoulder, breaking it. But the point is I sustained no head injury.

d) As I was driving on a motorway, I heard an audible voice telling me repeatedly, in an urgent tone, to slow down and leave a bigger gap between me and the car in front. About 10 seconds later an accident occurred right in front of me, but the huge gap that I had just created enabled me to stop in time. That prevented me, and also the cars behind me, from crashing, as my slowing down had forced all of them to slow down too.

However, direct audible guidance needs to be seen in its proper context. It does happen, but it is very much the *exception rather than the norm*. Moreover, I would never ask God for it. To make such a request is presumptuous, but it is also to lay yourself wide open to being deceived by a demon. If God wants to speak to you audibly, then He will, but it is not something which you should ever ask for or expect. Leave it entirely to Him as an exceptional, and rarely used, form of guidance.

You can pray for His specific guidance, but leave God completely free to decide *how* to give it. Then He can reveal His instructions by whatever means *He* chooses. God will find one way or another to light up our path, show us what to do, and what not to do, and to reveal His will. Therefore, seek guidance on any issues or decisions that you face, but don't tell God *how* to answer you. As a general rule, that is not how we should speak to Him. That said, it is not always wrong. There is a time and a place for laying down metaphorical fleeces, as Gideon literally did.

However, such a request can easily turn into presumption if it is made too often, or too lightly, or without proper reverence. Therefore, I would be wary of specifying how you want God to guide you unless you are in exceptional circumstances, as Gideon was. Even then, only use it to seek *additional confirmation* of what you *already* think God's will is, not to ask for a direct, brand new revelation of His will. The main ways in which God prefers to guide us are by means of:

a) learning His *general commands* that He makes to all of us, and also the *general principles*, set out in the Bible. We might regard these as what the military and the police refer to as 'standing orders' which are meant to be known and applied by *all* personnel at *all* times. Such orders do not need to be said to us individually or re-stated in every different situation we face. Therefore, we don't need to ask God to give us a specific instruction as to whether or not to lie or steal today, or in this particular situation, because He does not want us to lie or steal on *any day*, or in *any situation*.

b) our *conscience*, which becomes even more effective when it is strengthened by a growing knowledge of the Bible. It is a kind of 'smoke alarm' or 'carbon monoxide detector', which operates when a complex issue or choice arises. We may not have enough experience or discernment or knowledge of God's Word to be able, *with our mind*, to work out what is right and wrong. Yet our conscience can give us an inner prompting, or a sense of a check or warning, which can tell us that something would be sinful, even where we don't really know *why*.

454

In such situations you must learn to obey your conscience and to step back, take care, check things carefully, and avoid doing whatever it is that you feel uneasy about. Don't ever ignore or override your conscience just because you don't know *why* the 'carbon monoxide detector' is bleeping. Take your conscience extremely seriously, and obey it every time, even if you don't know why the thing would be sinful. As you do that, God will strengthen it and 'fine-tune' it to make it an even more effective warning system.

But if you ignore it, especially if you do so regularly, your conscience will steadily weaken, and eventually switch off entirely. When that happens your conscience has become *'seared'*. That means it is no longer sensitive, just as skin which has been branded with a red hot iron no longer has any feeling, because all the nerves are dead. If so, that would be a disaster and you must take care never to let it happen to you. The more you study God's Word, and fill your mind with God's general commands and principles, the more well-informed your conscience will become.

In due course, it will not only tell you that something would be wrong, but also *why* it would be wrong and which of God's commands or principles are applicable at that moment. Accordingly, seek to strengthen both your conscience *and* your knowledge of God's Word. Then you are doing everything that you can do to *"be transformed by the renewing of your mind"*, as Paul tells us, not just sitting back passively and leaving the task of guidance entirely to God.

You would be actively playing your own part by becoming as well-informed as possible, with as much understanding as you can gather for yourself, by your own effort. By so doing, you will put yourself in a position where, more and more of the time, you already know, or at least have a fairly good idea, what God's will is. You can then operate on the basis of what you know of His commands and principles, only requiring the help of conscience where there are gaps in your knowledge, or where the lines seem blurred.

Then you can do the right thing without God needing to give direct, specific guidance just for you. That is an integral part of growing up and maturing as a believer, increasingly operating for yourself, based on what you know of God's Word, without always needing God to guide you every step of the way. It is not that God is unwilling to 'pick up the phone' or 'answer your texts' when you are in trouble, or face a crisis, or are unsure what to do. He *is absolutely willing*. We know that for sure, because His Word tells us so:

Call to me and I will answer you, and will tell you great and hidden things that you have not known.

Jeremiah 33:3 (ESV)

If any of you lacks wisdom, let him ask God, who gives generously to all without reproach, and it will be given him.

James 1:5 (ESV)

God can even speak to us through ordinary, everyday things, even signs on the side of vehicles

God is capable of anything, and that includes being able, *if He chooses*, to communicate with us through things which we see or hear, even in our day to day lives, not just in church or when reading the Bible. It could be something on TV or in a conversation, even one between others, which we only overhear. When this has happened to me, *which is only occasionally, not a regular practice*, it has always arisen spontaneously, unexpectedly and by God's initiative, never mine. It is not something that I have ever asked for or tried to contrive.

One example of this is a time when I was feeling very low, even despairing, over a particular situation. Then, quite suddenly, a concrete mixer lorry drove by which belonged to a company called *'Hope'* and the lorry stopped right in front of us, with its logo and company name facing us. As I saw it the word loomed out at me, and came into very sharp focus, whereas everything else went out of focus, just for a moment. That is what I refer to as a thing *'going fluorescent'*. The word hope became very prominent and I simply knew that God was speaking to me through the logo of that particular lorry, on that particular day, and in that particular situation.

That said, some months later things had again become bleak and the same thing happened, entirely unexpectedly and unasked for. Another of these lorries stopped in front of us and I knew, just as before, that God was telling us to hope and never to give in to despair and that He was confirming the earlier message. It was a real help to us to keep going and not to give up. Of course, God could have chosen to speak to us in some other way, but He chose to do so in that way. He is a God of infinite variety, creativity and imagination, and also humour, and He likes to do unusual and different things at times, although *only at times, not as a rule*.

Therefore, don't go looking for this or even asking for it. Leave it entirely to God to decide whether, when and how to speak to you by such unorthodox means. If not, and you start expecting it, or even worse, looking out for it, avidly reading the logos on vans and lorries and trying to see patterns or messages in them, you will be deceived and you will even deceive yourself. Let God decide what to do, or even whether to do such things at all.

456

Meanwhile, you should focus on the Bible and on good Bible teaching and ask God to speak to you primarily through that. Yet, at the same time, do not close your mind to the possibility that God may, on occasion, choose to speak to you in some spontaneous, even quirky, manner and most probably in a way which is unique to you and to your personality, interests and background. If you do close your mind to this, you will miss out on something good and limit God in His ways of speaking to you.

Although God is willing to give specific guidance, it is also true to say that He wants you to learn His principles, and grow in maturity, so that you can decide for yourself

The point is that, although God is willing to give you specific guidance, He also wants you to grow in maturity and wisdom, such that you become increasingly capable of knowing, understanding, discerning and deciding *for yourself*. The more that becomes the case, the less often you will require His specific guidance or intervention. Indeed, there will be times when God will refuse to give you special guidance because He wants you to grow up and to learn how to find the way forward for yourself, as a result of maturing as a disciple and thus learning how to make decisions for yourself.

Such maturity is achieved by developing an extremely good knowledge and understanding of the *whole* Bible, not just those parts which you find easy, interesting or convenient. God therefore wants you to set your heart to study the entire Bible with consistency and diligence, going round it again and again and again. The ideal method is to read it as if you were painting the Forth Bridge, starting again at one end as soon as you finish at the other.

By way of another analogy to explain God's approach to teaching and guiding us, imagine a platoon of soldiers. All of them are raw recruits with little or no knowledge or understanding and no experience of doing their job, especially in combat. Within that platoon there might be a sergeant who has 20 years of experience, and who has seen action in many conflicts. He is shrewd, skilled, battle-hardened and always knows what should be done and how to do it. That sergeant will be entirely willing to answer questions and to give specific advice and guidance when asked, especially in a crisis.

There will also be times when, in the heat of a battle, he will voluntarily approach a young soldier, without even being asked, and tell him exactly where to go, what to do, and how to do it. However, that same sergeant also wants every private to pay close attention in training to all instructions and guidelines and to memorise every 'standing order' and all of the general principles of soldiering and tactics,

457

at least at a basic level. The sergeant's will is that, as far as possible, they should each become *capable of operating independently.*

He wants them to learn how to make decisions for themselves, when under fire, *based on what they were taught in their training.* There is no contradiction there. It is still the sergeant's will to answer specific questions and to give guidance when asked. But it is also his will for his men to become mature, so that their need to ask him for specific guidance becomes less and less frequent. They will achieve that because they have steadily *learned how the sergeant thinks, what he generally instructs, and what he would do in that situation.*

In this way a platoon of raw recruits, who initially know nothing and have to ask questions all the time, can be brought to a state of maturity and readiness, whereby they regularly find that they already know the sergeant's will. Then they can act think and act as he would, without needing to ask his advice at every moment. I have perhaps laboured this, but with good cause, because many Christians make the mistake of thinking that in all things, at all times, they should expect to receive God's specific instructions.

I even heard of a person who asked God what clothes to wear every day when getting dressed. More importantly, I have seen and heard many cases of churches operating on the basis of what they believe to be God's specific instructions to them, which they would claim were given to them by a series of *rhema* words. That is where God speaks directly into the situation, or to the person, rather than through the *logos*, which is God's Word to all of us, as set out in Scripture.

Both forms of guidance are valid, but we are not meant to operate at all times, or even at most times, on the basis of God giving us rhema words, directly to us, for our precise situation. That kind of thinking is unbalanced and that expectation is unrealistic and even unhealthy. It can easily lead to a person, or a whole church, becoming misguided, deceived, and even wacky. Therefore, we are not meant to conduct ourselves in that way.

We are, primarily, meant to operate on the basis of a sound and complete knowledge of *the whole of God's Word.* That means knowing *all* of His commands and principles, and holding them all in a healthy tension, at the same time, like the strands of a tennis racquet. Then they are all balancing and counter-balancing each other and forming, when seen in their entirety, a proper and complete understanding of the *whole* of God's will. This verse helpfully expresses this concept:

The sum of your word is truth,………
Psalm 119:160(a) (ESV)

458

Although every single line of every single verse in the Bible is *true*, it is only the *whole Bible*, taken together, which is *the truth*. An individual verse will give us instruction, but we need to interpret every verse in the wider context of the whole Bible, to gain the fullest, most accurate, understanding of any given verse. So, base your decision-making upon the whole of God's Word, taken together, and held in a proper balance.

When making big decisions or forming important judgments about people or situations, be sure to ask for God's guidance

We are certainly meant to become mature and capable of making many decisions for ourselves, without needing God's specific guidance on every issue or detail. However, God does not want us to go to the opposite extreme either, whereby we never seek His guidance on any issues. There needs to be a sensible balance whereby, when dealing with smaller matters, we decide for ourselves, based on a solid knowledge of God's character, principles and general commands.

But, for bigger issues, such as whether to trust someone, or buy a house, or move jobs, or when choosing a school for your child, always ask God for guidance about it. That request should become a natural part of the process. Ask God to point out anything which you may not have noticed, or about which you might be mistaken or deceived. He will provide such missing 'jigsaw pieces' to those who *ask* Him. It is surprising how many people don't involve Him in any way in the decision-making process, which is a serious mistake. A classic example is the incident when Joshua met the Gibeonites.

They were one of the Canaanite nations, whom God had commanded the Israelites to destroy. The Gibeonites deceived Joshua into believing they were not from Canaan, but had travelled from a far country. They then asked to make a peace treaty with Joshua, which he should not have made, and would not have made, if he had known they were from Canaan. If Joshua had asked God for guidance before entering into the peace treaty, God would have alerted him to the real facts. But Joshua did not seek God's guidance on that occasion and thus the Gibeonites succeeded in deceiving him:

³ But when the inhabitants of Gibeon heard what Joshua had done to Jericho and to Ai, ⁴ they on their part acted with cunning and went and made ready provisions and took worn-out sacks for their donkeys, and wineskins, worn-out and torn and mended, ⁵ with worn-out, patched sandals on their feet, and worn-out clothes. And all their provisions were dry and crumbly. ⁶ And they went to Joshua in the camp at Gilgal and said to him and to the men of Israel, "We have come from a distant country, so now make a covenant with us." ⁷ But the men of Israel said to the Hivites, "Perhaps you live among us; then how can we make a covenant with you?" ⁸ They said to Joshua, "We are your servants." And Joshua said to them, "Who are you? And where do you come from?"

⁹ They said to him, "From a very distant country your servants have come, because of the name of the LORD your God. For we have heard a report of him, and all that he did in Egypt, ¹⁰ and all that he did to the two kings of the Amorites who were beyond the Jordan, to Sihon the king of Heshbon, and to Og king of Bashan, who lived in Ashtaroth. ¹¹ So our elders and all the inhabitants of our country said to us, 'Take provisions in your hand for the journey and go to meet them and say to them, "We are your servants. Come now, make a covenant with us."' ¹² Here is our bread. It was still warm when we took it from our houses as our food for the journey on the day we set out to come to you, but now, behold, it is dry and crumbly. ¹³ These wineskins were new when we filled them, and behold, they have burst. And these garments and sandals of ours are worn out from the very long journey." ¹⁴ So the men took some of their provisions, but did not ask counsel from the LORD. ¹⁵ And Joshua made peace with them and made a covenant with them, to let them live, and the leaders of the congregation swore to them.

Joshua 9:3-15 (ESV)

Having sworn an oath not to fight the Gibeonites. Joshua was unable to do anything about it when the deception was later discovered. Fighting them would have meant breaking his oath. So, the Gibeonites remained and lived amongst the Israelites and they later became a source of sin, temptation and idolatry for God's people, all of which could have been avoided if Joshua had sought God's guidance:

¹⁶ At the end of three days after they had made a covenant with them, they heard that they were their neighbors and that they lived among them. ¹⁷ And the people of Israel set out and reached their cities on the third day. Now their cities were Gibeon, Chephirah, Beeroth, and Kiriath-jearim. ¹⁸ But the people of Israel did not attack them, because the leaders of the congregation had sworn to them by the LORD, the God of Israel. Then all the congregation murmured against the leaders. ¹⁹ But all the leaders said to all the congregation, "We have sworn to them by the LORD, the God of Israel, and now we may not touch them. ²⁰ This we will do to them: let them live, lest wrath be upon us, because of the oath that we swore to them."

Joshua 9:16-20 (ESV)

Make it easier for yourself to receive guidance by becoming the type of person whom God will guide

Guidance is not only given to us because we ask for it, although it is absolutely right to do so. It is also true to say that God gives guidance more often, and more clearly to those whose *behaviour, attitudes and lifestyle please Him*. Indeed, with such people, God is likely to guide and guard them even if they are not expressly asking Him to do so, because He wants to help and instruct to those who think, speak and act rightly. Let's look at some things which the Bible says will result in God giving more guidance and instruction and doing so more clearly. Firstly, He has said that He will guide the *humble*:

> **He leads the humble in what is right,**
> **and teaches the humble his way.**
> **Psalm 25:9 (ESV)**

Likewise, He will instruct those who *fear the LORD*:

> **Who is the man who fears the LORD?**
> **Him will he instruct in the way that he should choose.**
> **Psalm 25:12 (ESV)**

> **The friendship of the LORD is for those who fear him,**
> **and he makes known to them his covenant.**
> **Psalm 25:14 (ESV)**

If we have any common sense, we will look at such verses and resolve to meet the qualifying conditions, so that God will then give us the promised guidance. Thus, *decide* to humble yourself and to fear the LORD, as an exercise of your will, and do not just sit back passively and wait for such heart attitudes to arise spontaneously, of their own accord, as if it was nothing to do with you. Even in a much broader sense, we can seek to become the sort of person whom God will uphold, defend and deliver and on whose behalf He will intervene. Such promises are made to those who *"consider the poor"* and have *integrity:*

> **Blessed is the one who considers the poor!**
> **In the day of trouble the LORD delivers him.**
> **Psalm 41:1 (ESV)**

> **But you have upheld me because of my integrity,**
> **and set me in your presence forever.**
> **Psalm 41:12 (ESV)**

With verses such as these, and there are great many of them, get into the habit of:

a) asking yourself, very frankly, whether you are currently satisfying the qualifying condition which God has specified

b) if you aren't, then resolve to meet God's conditions from now on, so that the promised help, blessing, guidance, protection etc can then be given to you.

It may be blindingly obvious that we should do a) and b), once we stop to think about it, but the problem is that most of us never do stop to think about it. Therefore, God's qualifying conditions are not met and the help, guidance and blessing etc are not given to us. We are to blame because we have merely glanced at God's Word, without taking it seriously or questioning ourselves about it, as we are meant to, and without acting upon it.

Even if you think you know God's will, and have prayed for guidance, ask God to block your path, or close doors, if He thinks you are about to do the wrong thing.

No matter how skilled you may become at making decisions, and even if you pray for God's guidance, there is always the possibility that you will still get it wrong, especially as there is so much deception in the world. A lot of what we think we know is actually lies and misinformation, coming either from people, or demons, or both. Therefore, even if we consider the position carefully, and take advice from others, we could still make a wrong decision because we might be relying on *false data and false people.*

It could be that all the facts appear to be favourable, but one of the people you are dealing with, and whom you trust, is not actually trustworthy. You don't know that when making your decision, but God does. Therefore, even if you have examined all the facts as best you can, and even if you have prayed earnestly for guidance, it is wise to make it your policy, especially when making any large decisions, to pray along these lines as well:

"Lord, it seems to me that I should go ahead with this proposed project or contract. However, if I am actually mistaken, or have been deceived, or if the facts are not actually as I think they are, or if there is some other reason not to go ahead, of which I am unaware, please block my path and close the doors to prevent this from happening."

An example of this was when I was proposing to buy an area of commercial land some years ago, on which to build a new office block for my law firm. I had agreed a price for the land and had made what I considered to be a deal with the owner himself. It was a purely verbal 'gentlemen's agreement' but, if it had been put into writing, I would have signed it. I thought it was a fair deal, and I was

462

pleased with it. However, as it was a major decision, I had prayed beforehand that God would intervene and prevent the transaction from going ahead *if He knew it was a mistake.*

Then, a day later, the seller's agent/advisor rang me. To my surprise, he began to speak as if I had not already agreed a deal, and a purchase price, with the seller. He was now speaking of a higher price than the one I had already agreed. At first I assumed the agent must be mistaken or confused, or that he was unaware of the agreement I had already made with the seller directly. However, it emerged later that he knew exactly what the position was and that he was simply trying to renegotiate the contract and get a higher sale price.

He thought that his client had agreed too low a price and he was now seeking to rectify that negotiating 'error'. I initially thought the agent was acting alone, on his own initiative, without the seller's knowledge. However, it also emerged later that the seller did know, and had expressly authorised his agent to try this trick. However, it backfired badly for him. I simply said that I was no longer interested in buying the land and that I would just stay where I was. So I called the whole deal off.

That surprised the seller because he wrongly imagined that I wanted the land so badly that I would not pull out, even if they were to act deviously. He badly misjudged me in thinking that. More importantly, God had answered my prayer by causing the real character of the seller, and his agent, to be revealed before we exchanged written contracts. As soon as I saw what they were doing, I knew it was an answer to my prayer for God's intervention and that He was telling me to pull out of the deal. I recognised it as a 'red light', or a 'closed door', and thanked God for it. *Red flag*

It was, however, another form of guidance too. God used their sneaky attempt to renegotiate the price, and the agent's pretence that no agreement had already been made, to open my eyes to their *real character*. Therefore, once I realised what kind of men they really were, *I no longer wanted* to do business with them anyway, even if it wasn't a closed door. Other people's character is an important form of guidance in itself. Thus, once I realise that someone is crooked or discover that they have deceived me, even on one small point, I try to do no further business with them.

There is an interesting ending to the story, which is that the seller was then completely unable to find anybody else to buy that piece of land. The financial crisis of 2008 burst upon us in the following year and the commercial property market then went into a sustained slump. I used to drive by the land every day on my way to and from work and the 'For Sale' sign was there for about *six years* before he managed to sell even part of the land. But it then took him another three years or so to sell the rest of it. I also expect that he had to accept a reduced price in order to eventually get rid of it.

So there are two points arising. Firstly, God saved me from buying a piece of land just before a property price crash. Secondly, I think the seller's nine years of inability to sell were also a judgment on him. He set a trap for me, but his own bad character caused him to fall into it himself. If he had behaved honestly, he would have sold the land many years earlier, at a better price, and I would have been the one who was stuck with it after the 2008 crash. Therefore, his own deviousness was what led to disaster for him, whereas my willingness to be guided is what saved me from it.

Being guided by your 'gut feeling', where you just don't feel comfortable about something, even if you don't know why

We have seen how we can be guided by our *conscience*. That tells us when something we propose to do is *morally or ethically* wrong, even if we don't know what specific law or command would be broken if we went ahead. However, when we speak of being guided by our *gut feeling*, we mean something which is similar, but different in an important respect. This form of guidance is not necessarily about whether the step being considered is *morally wrong*.

It is much broader and includes any situation where, without necessarily knowing why, you just don't feel *comfortable* about what is being proposed. Or you could *have a bad feeling about it*, a sense of *unease*, or an intuitive feeling that it is not the right direction to go in, or the step you ought to take. By convention, this feeling is spoken of as being in your *gut*, meaning the belly, and for a good reason, because that is often exactly where that feeling of apprehension or unease is felt.

The late Derek Prince made a suggestion as to why this is so, and I think I agree with him. He said that a person's own human spirit is located within the belly. This theory is tangentially supported by Jesus's words in John's gospel when He refers to the belly, which is how it is translated in the King James Version. Later versions use the word 'heart', but belly is probably a better way to express it:

That's 'Greek' thinking

He that believeth on me, as the scripture hath said, out of his belly shall flow rivers of living water.

Out of a man's heart comes ...

John 7:38 (KJV)

We might feel a sense of alarm or apprehension, or that someone is not to be trusted, without knowing why, or being able to put our finger on the point. If so, it could be that our own human spirit is telling us how it views the situation. Some people place no reliance upon this, or even view it with disdain, because it does

464

not originate within their mind, or because the objection is not precisely defined. If so, they would be acting unwisely, as you should put a lot of weight on your gut feeling and take its warnings seriously.

In Book 7 I look at the component parts of a person, i.e. body, mind, emotions, will, spirit (new man) and flesh (old man). All of those are equally part of us and have a vital part to play in how we operate. The phrase I often use is that they are all entitled to use the pronoun "I". Therefore, it would be foolish of you to insist on listening only to your mind and paying no attention to your emotions or your spirit. They all have their own distinct parts to play, alongside our mind, when we are making decisions. The apprehension we feel at a certain proposal might reflect how our own human spirit itself perceives the situation.

It may also be that God Himself is speaking to us, but *through* our spirit, on this occasion, rather than through our mind. Thus, our own spirit may be receptive to hear what God is saying, when our mind isn't. Therefore, recognise your gut feeling as a legitimate source of guidance, especially in the *negative*, i.e. where it is giving you a *warning*, or voting no, as opposed to being in favour. So, if your mind thinks that person A *can* be trusted or that proposal A is a *good* idea, but your gut instinct is saying *no*, then listen carefully to your gut.

Be willing to 'overrule' your mind, or at least to postpone a decision, while you check the facts and make further enquiries. However, if your mind is telling you that something is *wrong*, based on the evidence, or on God's Word, but your gut feeling is *positive*, then go with what your *mind* says and, even more so, with God's Word. Scripture always comes first and must be listened to, and obeyed, ahead of anything and anybody else.

A classic example of this, is where a person wants to marry, or go out with, an unbeliever. They know in their *mind* that that is wrong, and that God's Word forbids it, but they claim to *feel* that it is right for them, or on this occasion. Most probably it is their *emotions* that are speaking to them, not their *spirit*. However, wherever it is coming from, the fact is they are deluding themselves and they should therefore overrule what they are feeling, whether it is real or imagined. They should instead go with what they know *in their mind* to be God's will, especially if it is an express command, as in this example.

However, in some other context, if your mind can see no danger and no reason not to go ahead with project X, but your gut feeling is one of apprehension, and it is telling you *not to go ahead*, then listen to *your gut, not your mind*. At the very least, put the proposed project on hold while you investigate it more fully, pray about it, and take advice from carefully selected people.

Sleep on it

465

Let me describe another technique which I have found useful, when facing a major or complicated, decision. At times, the pros and cons are so numerous, and so complex, that you can't "get your head around" all of the facts, evidence and arguments. They may point in so many directions simultaneously that you feel thoroughly confused and unsure what to do. At such times I suggest that you put all the facts and arguments to one side, *just for a moment*, and use this technique.

Imagine each alternative, on its own, firstly as if you were going ahead with the proposed step. Then do the same, but as if you were not going to do so. Then ask yourself *how each prospect makes you feel.* Do you get a *sinking* feeling or a *rising* feeling when each alternative outcome is imagined? It could be sacking a difficult employee, signing an important contract, moving premises, leaving the church you are part of, or whatever. The point is that the way you feel *when you contemplate having already done it* is a very valuable form of guidance.

You might not be able to get this kind of guidance from your mind, or even your conscience, because the disadvantage or danger which concerns you, may have nothing to do with ethics and may not involve sin at all. It may be that your spirit, or gut, can see a hazard or a problem, or some other disadvantage of quite a different kind, of which your mind and conscience are unaware, because they both operate on quite different 'wavelengths' than the one on which your spirit operates.

Obtaining guidance by understanding your duties and their hierarchy of importance

Here is another principle which helps when making complex decisions which involve a range of responsibilities and different levels of relationships with various people. It is to think in terms of the *'hierarchy' of duties.* A number of people, situations or responsibilities may all be involved simultaneously, but their interests do not coincide, and so you feel confused. If so, you then have to decide which person, duty or issue must prevail over the others, or what the 'pecking order' of priorities is in that situation.

Imagine you have a small house, and a wife, and perhaps children as well, but then your elderly mother begins to need your help and comes to live with you. The effort, the time spent, and the sleep lost as a result of caring for her may be taking an increasing toll on your wife due to the stress of sharing a small house with her frail mother-in-law, who might also have dementia. It may also be placing a strain on your children, and their studies may be suffering. On top of all that, it may also put pressure on you in your job.

466

It could be that you took her into your home because you feel you owe her a duty of care and want to avoid her having to go into a council-run care home, whose standards may be inadequate. However, the situation may have proved to be far more exhausting, and protracted, than you had expected and the strain on your wife and children, and even on you in your job, may now be intolerable. It may even be affecting your health, or your wife's health. In order to decide what to do about this, you could ask yourself this:

"What duties do I owe here to each of these parties, my wife, my children, and my employer? Also, what duty do I even owe to myself, concerning my own physical and mental health? And, what order do those duties come in, so that I can decide whose interests and needs must prevail and whose must be subordinated, or even set aside?"

This example actually arose, and I was involved in advising the man concerned. He was stressed out, and his wife was even more frazzled. It had built up over about 18 months as the position became increasingly desperate. Yet, he was deeply reluctant to put his mother into a care home, as he felt it was his duty to look after her. So, he felt trapped and could not see what he should do. I counselled him to look as well at his *other duties*, especially the duty he owed to his wife, which came ahead of the duty he owed to his mother.

So, he began to take steps to find a nursing home for his mother. Of course, that was emotionally difficult too. If it had not been, it would not have been a hard decision in the first place. Yet, it was still the right answer, and the decision had to be made. Having made it, his duty then became to find the best care home available and to make his mother's move as easy as he could make it. But his primary duty, which is the one he owed to his wife, had to be seen as primary, and *treated as such*, when deciding what to do.

The same approach needs to be taken in all sorts of situations where you feel torn between one duty and another and where you can see no way forward which does not involve letting somebody down, or being perceived to have done so. Sometimes there have to be unpleasant consequences, or disadvantages, for somebody, or for some project or objective. Somebody has to take second place. If so, your task is to decide *who it will be*. Of course, in the example given above, the outcome would have been different if the wife had only been experiencing minor stress or inconvenience, and if the mother was in a very bad way, or if no care home was available.

All things are relative and every case therefore turns on its own particular facts. The point is that you cannot always entirely avoid negative consequences in life. Therefore, a mechanism for deciding who or what is your priority in a given situation, and who or what must take second place, and even be let down, is

Is God's word ?

467

essential. The only alternative is to spend your whole life avoiding or delaying decisions because you aren't willing to view anyone as being in anything other than first place. But, of course, if everything is in first place, then nothing is really in first place, which is a recipe for ongoing confusion and indecision.

Wise people are objective and face the real facts, even if those are unpleasant. They also prefer advice which is right, not that which makes them feel better.

Even when we do take advice, there is a strong temptation to go along with whichever advice is most to our liking, i.e. least critical, least painful to implement, and most in line with our own desires and our own flesh nature. However, a wise person will force himself to listen to the truth and to do what is right, not what makes him feel better in himself or makes him look better to others.

In the passage below, Rehoboam has just become King of Israel and is taking advice from two different groups of counsellors. The first group is the old men who worked for his father. They advise him to lighten the burdens on the people and to be reasonable and merciful with them. The second group are his friends, young men of his own age, who advise him to be even more demanding, to increase the tax burden further, and to show the people how strong he is.

Their macho approach appeals to Rehoboam, despite being bad advice, because it makes him feel big and boosts his sense of self-importance. So, despite taking advice, he still goes wrong because he lets his flesh have the deciding say. A wise person chooses the right advice, regardless of his ego. Indeed, as a general rule, if our ego is in favour of something, we should be against it. Sadly, Rehoboam did not take that approach and listened to those who fed his pride:

⁹And he said to them, "What do you advise that we answer this people who have said to me, 'Lighten the yoke that your father put upon us'?" ¹⁰And the young men who had grown up with him said to him, "Thus shall you speak to this people who said to you, 'Your father made our yoke heavy, but do you lighten it for us'; thus shall you say to them, 'My little finger is thicker than my father's loins. ¹¹ And now, whereas my father laid upon you a heavy yoke, I will add to your yoke. My father chastised you with whips, but I will chastise you with scorpions.'" ¹²So Jerobo'am and all the people came to Rehobo'am the third day, as the king said, "Come to me again the third day." ¹³And the king answered the people harshly, and forsaking the counsel which the old men had given him, ¹⁴he spoke to them according to the counsel of the young men, saying, "My father made your yoke heavy, but I will add to your yoke; my father chastised you with whips, but I will chastise you with scorpions."

1 Kings 12:9-14 (RSV)

468

When making a difficult decision, which would require you to do something unpleasant, or even dangerous, *if* you were to conclude that certain facts are true, there is a strong temptation to believe that they are, therefore, *not true*. Our hearts are deceitful, as Jeremiah said, and we tend to believe what we *want to believe*. Instead we should objectively assess the facts and believe whatever is shown to be true, *simply because it is true*, regardless of how we *feel about it*.

We must do so even though arriving at that conclusion is inconvenient or distressing. This kind of self-delusion is a widespread problem, due to our sin nature, and because most of us do not choose to cultivate what the Bible calls *"the love of the truth"*. That basically means having an extremely high regard for truth itself, *purely for its own sake*. If you have the love of the truth you will choose to believe whatever is true, even if that would prove that you acted wrongly, or be to your disadvantage, or result in cost, embarrassment or difficulty.

Whether a proposition is pleasant or unpleasant, and whether it would result in convenience or inconvenience *if it is true*, has nothing whatever to do with *whether it is actually true*. The thing is either true or false. How you *feel* about it being true, or what adverse consequences might follow if it is true, are completely irrelevant factors. Moreover, they must be treated as irrelevant while you are in the process of deciding what is true and false and whether or not to believe a thing.

This applies not only to matters of doctrine, but also in our everyday lives, or in our jobs, or when deciding whether claims or allegations are true or false. If you do not recognise this trait, and force yourself to be objective, you will inevitably make bad decisions. That is sad, because such errors are entirely avoidable if we will only face this problem in ourselves. To consider issues with ruthless objectivity, even when they affect ourselves, goes against all the habits we have learned since childhood. Therefore, this policy has to be imposed on yourself, by sheer force of willpower, like holding a cork underwater.

Your flesh nature will continually want you to revert to your familiar default-setting, whereby you believe whatever is easiest, most flattering and least inconvenient. Few people ever try to be objective, or even realise that this is an issue at all. Most of us never give it any thought, because *not* being objective is so completely familiar. I would urge you however to begin, from now on, to examine how you make decisions, and especially how you choose what to believe. Cross-examine yourself about your underlying assumptions and priorities, and as to whether you are being utterly honest with yourself.

Interrupt yourself, even as you are thinking or speaking to yourself, and say: *"You're arriving at that conclusion very quickly! Why are you so reluctant to believe the opposite?"* Then force yourself to look at the issues again, to review the evidence, and to put yourself and your own preferences to one side. Act as if you were a High Court judge trying someone else's case, rather than your own. Train yourself to be ruthlessly objective, and to make yourself arrive at conclusions that you don't like, if the evidence requires it. Then you will become a vastly more effective decision maker.

keep yourself honest! *Follow the evidence NOT the feeling*

Wise people are prudent and don't take unnecessary risks. But they are not ruled by fear either and will take calculated risks when it is right to do so.

When I ran a law firm, I regularly had to make business decisions that could cause the firm to make, or lose, a lot of money. They were calculated risks and taking them was a daily occurrence. We all need to be able to make such carefully balanced decisions, even where they involve risk. That said, wise people do not go looking for any unnecessary risk. Nor do they take excessive risks. Indeed, they try not to take any risks at all unless it is necessary to do so:

A prudent man sees danger and hides himself;
but the simple go on, and suffer for it.
> *Proverbs 22:3 (RSV)*

Risk cannot be illiminated only reasonably controlled—account for it.

One who is wise is cautious and turns away from evil,
but a fool is reckless and careless.
> *Proverbs 14:16 (ESV)*

Risk level
Danger level
Degree of danger

Prudent people therefore take steps to minimise the risks they face. They also arrange their affairs so that even if things do go wrong they have, at least partly, allowed for it, contained it, and made contingency plans to deal with it. However, although we should seek to reduce the risks we face, it is foolish to imagine that all risk can be avoided in life. Neither should you make risk-avoidance your main preoccupation. Many things which ought to be done or said, are not done or said, because the person focused excessively on the perceived risk. *Risk aversive is risky.*

They then allow that risk, whether real or imagined, to tower over all other considerations, including their duty, and even the need to be obedient to God. Sometimes in life the right thing to do is risky, or even dangerous, but it is still right. Therefore, the existence of a risk, in itself, is not a basis for making no decision, or for taking no action. The question is *whether* to take that risk, and it is wrong to assume automatically that the answer is an obvious no. It may or may not be right to take it and we need to be open to both options, after carefully analysing all the facts. *Unnecessary risk*

Therefore, a wise person takes risk into account, and takes all reasonable steps to avoid or minimise it. But he is not *ruled* by the fear of those risks, or by the fear

CV19 - The propaganda is telling people conversely (perversely) they're being brave by being cowards theyre being caring by not caring (forthtruth) theyre being reasonable by being unreasonable (emotionalism). being wise by being fools.

of anything at all. You must never allow fear to be your master. Indeed, fear must not be allowed to play any part in your decision-making at all. If you do listen to your fears, you will make yourself very easy for people, and demons, to control and manipulate by simply planting the thought in your mind of some potential hazard. Their aim is that you will then automatically turn away and do something else instead of what you ought to do.

Most of the people I meet are ruled by their fears to some extent. In many cases, the grip that fear has over them is almost total and they spend their whole lives in fear of this or fear of that, or dreading some potential event. Yet, the things which they fear rarely, if ever, happen. Such bondage arises because they have trained their own minds to fear. It is also because the demons whisper into their minds to create or increase those fears. You have to recognise this power that fear has over you and actively resist it.

Never let yourself be ruled by fear of anything, other than the fear of the LORD. We should always be ruled by that, but not by any other fear. Our decisions should only ever be made on the basis of sound thinking, biblical principles, conscience and duty, even where those lead us to form conclusions which require us to do risky things. Part of a verse from Isaiah is helpful here on the issue of needing to be firm in our faith. If we are, then we can face anything. But, if we aren't, we will become spineless and spend our whole lives running away from things:

"…If you are not firm in faith,
You will not be firm at all."
Isaiah 7:9(b) (ESV)

When making difficult decisions a wise person grasps the concept of choosing "the least undesirable option". He does not long forlornly for a perfect option, with no disadvantages.

As a lawyer I regularly came across clients who, wanted to be given a pain-free, cost-free, risk-free, difficulty-free option which had no disadvantages. I often had to haul them back to reality and explain that their real objective was to choose the *least undesirable option* from a range of undesirable alternatives. Every one of those could involve costs, risks, problems or disadvantages of one type or another. At first they would persist in hankering after a perfect solution but my job, sometimes, was to get them to see that no such option existed. I used to say they needed to *choose which set of problems they would prefer to have*, as opposed to hoping not to have any problems at all.

I likened it to going to a café with a sandwich menu which consisted only of rat, snail, slug and cockroach and choosing which of these was *least objectionable,* because the sandwich they wanted was not on the menu. That illustration often helped them, and they would then begin to look realistically at the options which were actually available and try to choose the one with the fewest, and smallest, disadvantages overall. It is not only in legal cases that such unpalatable choices can arise. Many of us waste a lot of time and energy, and miss opportunities, because we are not willing to choose the least undesirable option on those occasions when nothing better is available.

'Procrastinating for a perfect option/time... or wishful thinking'

Forcing yourself to be a realist, and to grasp nettles, will greatly increase the speed and quality of your decision making. It may even change you from being a weak, indecisive manager into a strong and confident one. I say that because one of the biggest faults a manager or leader can ever have is not that he makes *bad* decisions, but that he makes *no* decisions. Or it can be that he makes them *too late*, when the right moment has passed and the opportunity has gone.

One common reason why a weak manager or leader does this is because he fears being criticised for making the wrong decision. Or he fears being seen to have failed. He will therefore naively hold out for a perfect solution, which won't involve any risk or disadvantage at all, and for which nobody could ever blame him. Such a manager forgets that the far greater crime is to dodge making decisions, or to leave them until it is too late. Indecision may not seem blameworthy to him, but those who work under or alongside him will be well aware of the problems it causes.

However, when you are faced with two options, both of which are *sinful*, then you must choose neither of them

Having said all that, we do also need to distinguish between choosing "*the least undesirable option*" and choosing "*the lesser of two evils*". These two concepts sound similar, but they are *not* the same thing. The former can be both good and wise, even if it is unpleasant, but the latter is not. The clue lies in the word '*evil*'. We have been looking above at situations where all the available options merely involve *disadvantages or unpleasant consequences*. However, if both options involve *sin*, then you must choose neither. Sin is not a mere 'disadvantage' and it is never the correct option to choose.

Therefore, rejecting both of the evils on offer, whether they are the greater or the lesser, is not indecision. It is firmness of purpose and is not based on weakness or cowardice, but on strength and courage. That is why it is so important that we are always guided in our decision-making by conscience and the application of biblical principles. If you are, you will quickly recognise when an option involves something *sinful*, in which case, you must reject it *on that basis alone*. That can

To be Decisive mean literally to 'cut off' all other options

472

eliminate a series of improper options, until we are left with one which is at least not sinful, even if it has *disadvantages*.

However, if *both or all* of the options being offered to you, involve *sin*, or going against your *conscience,* or *transgressing a biblical command or principle*, then you can't choose any of them. This narrows down your options, which is helpful when you look at this correctly. If that happens, it is your cue to go back to the drawing board and to re-examine the whole situation afresh to search for an option which is not sinful because, if the only ones that you can think of are sinful, you are missing something somewhere.

Your excessive desire to avoid other risks or costs which, though difficult, are not sinful, may be skewing your thinking and limiting your imagination. Imposing upon yourself the misguided precondition that the path you choose must not be unpleasant can prevent you from seeing, or being willing to accept, some other option which, though difficult, God wants you to choose. Let this be another form of guidance. Always do what is right, not what is easiest, and do not follow the line of least resistance. Stay on the 'narrow path' which, though hard, is the right path to be on, whereas the comfortable, easy path is rarely, if ever, the right one to take. *Beware the easy path of least resistance ! That is the most dangerous path of all*

Wise people will not allow the fear of anything, other than God, to influence their decisions

The fear of the LORD is essential and brings many benefits. However, we are not meant to fear anything, or anyone, other than Him. For that reason, the Bible commands us 366 times not to fear, by which it means fear of other people or things, not the fear of God Himself, whom we are positively commanded to fear. If you are not yet capable of ceasing to fear people or things, then resolve that, even if you are afraid, you will at least not let yourself be *influenced* by your fears in your *words, actions or decisions*.

That is possible even if we are not naturally bold by nature, because it is a decision of the *will*. Therefore, it does not depend on our *feelings*. Whenever we make decisions it needs to be solely on the basis of facts, logic, biblical principles, duty, God's will, wisdom, conscience etc, *never on the basis of fear*. I resolved many years ago that I would never make any decision based on fear and made it my policy to exclude all such considerations and to treat them as having no relevance. That has made decision-making far clearer, quicker and less complicated.

Instead of agonising over what people might say or do, I only need to work out what is true and false, what is right and wrong, and what my duty is. Excluding fear as a factor did not make decision-making *easy*, but it did at least make it *clearer.* If you let fear influence you, then you will become bogged down and confused. You will then be unable or unwilling to do your duty, or to obey God's commands, or to do what is right. The Bible refers to such fear as a *'snare'*, which is a trap in which animals are caught:

The fear of man lays a snare,
 but whoever trusts in the LORD is safe.
                    Proverbs 29:25 (ESV)

Never fear what other people might say about you, or do to you, even if it inevitable, and would cause serious harm. Even so, do not be afraid. At the very least, never allow any such considerations, to have any *influence* over you, or to play any part in your decision-making:

⁶ The LORD is on my side; I will not fear.
  What can man do to me?
⁷ The LORD is on my side as my helper;
  I shall look in triumph on those who hate me.
⁸ It is better to take refuge in the LORD
  than to trust in man.
⁹ It is better to take refuge in the LORD
  than to trust in princes.
                    Psalm 118:6-9 (ESV)

The wise know they can be deceived by others and that they will be. They also know their own hearts are deceitful, such that they even deceive themselves, and they make allowances for that. *Mitigate self deceit*

No matter how wise you become you will never be beyond being deceived. If you think otherwise, you are deluding yourself. Being deceived is inevitable. So, realistically, your task is to minimise it, not to eliminate it entirely. We should therefore be on our guard to avoid being deceived, but not be surprised when we still are. Also, when that happens, openly admit that you have been deceived, rather than pretend you weren't. Moses warned the Israelites to *take care* that their hearts were not deceived. Therefore, he clearly didn't think they were immune to it, or he would not have said that:

Take care lest your heart be deceived, and you turn aside and serve other gods and worship them;
                    Deuteronomy 11:16 (ESV)

While ever we still have a sinful flesh nature, which we shall all have until we die, our own heart will lie to us, *even if we are wise.* We lie to ourselves about our

474

own motives, our faults and failings, and whether we were right or wrong in the things we have done. Wise people *recognise* that self-deceiving tendency in themselves and *make allowances for it*. They realise how much delusion and self-deception their own hearts are capable of. Jeremiah, one of the greatest prophets in Israel's history, knew that this was even true of himself:

The heart is deceitful above all things,
and desperately corrupt; who can understand it?
                              Jeremiah 17:9 (RSV)

Therefore, not only should we not trust other people; *we should not even trust ourselves*. Our own heart will lie to us whenever it gets the chance. We therefore need to cross-examine ourselves robustly and say to ourselves: "*Come off it - you are in the wrong here*". If we can voluntarily do that to ourselves, we will prevent many problems. It will also reduce the need for God to discipline us.

Everything is going to be judged, and publicly exposed, in the end anyway. Therefore, you may as well be honest with yourself now and get things out into the open, at least in your own thinking. Consider Solomon's conclusion, at the end of all his writings. He knew that even he had to face God's judgment, despite being the wisest man who would ever live, and that every sin will be judged, even those that we keep secret:

[13] The end of the matter;
all has been heard. Fear God,
and keep his commandments;
for this is the whole duty of man.
[14] For God will bring every deed into judgment,
with every secret thing, whether good or evil.
                              Ecclesiastes 12:13-14 (RSV)

You can even be guided by noticing other people's attempts at manipulation or intimidation and you must resist them whenever they do it

You can also get guidance by watching out for any sign of manipulation, intimidation or control being used by anyone, whether against you or against someone else. You could be in a situation where you don't know whether a proposal or idea is good or bad, and you can't see anything wrong with it. But then you may notice that the other person is being manipulative or is seeking to control you or others. If so, you need to be extremely wary. In this way, other people's conduct can actually become a source of indirect guidance for you.

475

You may not know exactly what is wrong with the proposal, or why it is wrong, but the very fact that someone is trying to pressurise or manoeuvre you is, in itself, a warning sign that you must not ignore. An example of this is a man I once employed as a salaried partner. He came for a job interview with me in a very difficult position, having been out of work for two years due to alcoholism, drug addiction, and a nervous breakdown. He was entirely open about this and I felt sympathetic and wanted to give him a second chance in life.

So I offered him a job as an assistant solicitor, on a trial basis, with a temporary starting salary of £25,000 per annum. That was well below the going rate for a senior lawyer at that time, but at that moment, he had been on unemployment benefits for two years, with little chance of finding any other job. Therefore, he accepted it eagerly and he did very well in the job. So, after three months, I voluntarily raised his salary to £35,000, entirely of my own accord, with no request from him.

Six months after that I raised him to £45,000, again entirely of my own accord. After that, I raised his salary, voluntarily again, to £55,000, then £65,000, and then £72,000. I had also made him a salaried partner and added a pension contribution from the firm of £12,000 per annum. That brought his overall pay package to £84,000 (about $120,000), as well as a generous holiday entitlement of six weeks per annum plus bank holidays. The problem arose on a later occasion when he asked to discuss his salary, which I was happy to do. However, the meeting took an unexpected turn when he demanded a large pay rise.

He said, in a strident tone, as if I had been mistreating him: *"I want a pay rise to £100,000 plus £12,000 pension contribution and, if I don't get it, I will be resigning."* I was startled by his words, but even more so by his aggressive tone. He spoke as if I was stingy and had been exploiting him. Yet he was, by then, being paid well ahead of the going rate, at that time, for employed lawyers at his level. So I knew that I was already paying him well. But what bothered me most was that he was *threatening me* by saying that he would resign if I did not do as he demanded. *Thanddevned*

I had resolved many years before that I would never give in to *any* threat, or to *anybody*'s attempt to bully or manipulate me. Accordingly, when he spoke as he did, it was actually helpful, as it opened my eyes and I knew immediately that I needed to refuse. In that sense, I had gained guidance from *his* words and attitude. So I replied: *"In that case, you had better resign."* He was stunned by my firm and instantaneous reply, as he had become so misguided, due to his resentment, and an exaggerated sense of his own importance, that he had assumed I would cave in. *Not indespensible*

He had also misunderstood my generosity in having voluntarily raised his pay repeatedly over the previous years and he had wrongly interpreted it as weakness. So, he was stuck. He had said he would resign if I said no. Therefore, due to his pride, he felt he had to go ahead and do it. Perhaps he still hoped, even then, that I would panic and give in to his demand. But I didn't. I accepted his resignation without any hesitation, and confirmed it in writing, later that day. He had rashly painted himself into a corner and he then had no option but to leave.

The point is that his words, and especially his manner, were a form of guidance enabling me to see him, and his attitude, as they really were, not as I had wrongly imagined them to be. So his aggressive tone and manipulative approach actually helped me to know how to respond in that situation. Moreover, I did not have to figure out whether to give in to *his* threats, on this *particular occasion*, because I had already resolved, many years before, never to give in to *anybody's* threats on *any occasion*.

Another example of obtaining guidance from people's behaviour is a church leader I knew many years ago. I have written about him in Book 6 and given him the name 'Rick'. He was false, carnal and manipulative, but I had begun to see through him and was challenging him about his attitudes and conduct. As part of that process, I had requested a meeting with him in the presence of two witnesses from the trustees of the church, of which I was the Chairman. During that meeting my concerns grew. Yet, I still wasn't absolutely certain of my grounds and was not sure how seriously I should take his misconduct.

However, shortly afterwards, Rick came to my office to confront me one evening. The veil then came off my eyes, when I heard him speak more frankly than he had ever spoken before. He tried to dominate me, because his attempts to deceive me were not working and, from his perspective, desperate measures were now needed. I should add, by way of background, that quite a few of the staff in my law firm were Christians. Many were also members of Rick's church, as I also was at that time, and three employees were from Rick's own family.

To complicate things further, I was also having severe problems with Rick's own wife who worked in my firm as a secretary. She was being increasingly manipulative and controlling with other staff, so I had called her in the week before to warn her as to her future conduct. It was probably at this point that Rick concluded that the position between us was deteriorating and that the cajoling approach he had taken up to that point was not working. So he came to see me one evening and said in an angry tone:

"This firm is part of the church and so I am the God-appointed authority over it. Therefore, any disputes with Christian staff will be handled by me, not by you."

Up to this point I had felt unsure about what to do with Rick, despite all of my many concerns and the abundance of evidence against him. There was a veil over my eyes and my mind was fogged, most probably due to demonic interference, but also due to human witchcraft and mind control. That has the effect of confusing you and making you mentally numb, and unable to think clearly. However, on hearing Rick speak so aggressively, the fog lifted and I was suddenly able to see. I then said to him, more boldly than ever before:

"Actually, Rick, you have no authority over this firm whatsoever. It is nothing to do with you. It is my firm, and God has appointed me, and me alone, to run it and that is exactly what I shall do."

During that conversation, something broke in the atmosphere. My naivety and confusion melted away in a single moment and, from then on, I took a much firmer line. I left Rick's church some time afterwards and also sacked his wife and daughter-in-law. I also told his daughter to move on to some other law firm as soon as her training contract ended, as I did not wish to continue to employ her thereafter. So, I quickly got all of Rick's family out of the firm. But that ability to be so decisive began at the moment when he openly tried to dominate me.

He only took off his mask for a moment, but that was enough to enable me to see what he really was, and how seriously I needed to take it. So, his outburst was a form of guidance in itself and I would have been very unwise to ignore it. Therefore, make it a rule never to let yourself be manipulated, dominated, controlled or threatened *by anybody*. Such things must always be viewed as very serious matters, and must never be tolerated or overlooked. Therefore, such conduct can be the trigger that causes you to wake up, open your eyes, reassess the position, and take decisive action.

Deciding when it is right to be firm and confront people and when it is better to be diplomatic, seek consensus, or even remain silent.

A wise person *'knows the time'*. They know when to do a certain thing, when to do the opposite, and when to do nothing at all. We are told in Ecclesiastes that there is a time for everything:

¹ There is an appointed time for everything. And there is a time for every event under heaven—
² A time to give birth and a time to die;
A time to plant and a time to uproot what is planted.
³ A time to kill and a time to heal;
A time to tear down and a time to build up.
⁴ A time to weep and a time to laugh;

A time to mourn and a time to dance.
⁵ A time to throw stones and a time to gather stones;
A time to embrace and a time to shun embracing.
⁶ A time to search and a time to give up as lost;
A time to keep and a time to throw away.
⁷ A time to tear apart and a time to sew together;
A time to be silent and a time to speak.
⁸ A time to love and a time to hate;
A time for war and a time for peace.

Ecclesiastes 3:1-8 (NASB)

The Bible sets out many *general principles* but, on those same issues, it also gives other *counter-balancing principles* which point in the opposite direction. We then have to work out when to apply one principle and when to apply the opposite one, because they both have times when they are appropriate and times when they aren't.

So, concerning upholding right doctrine, there were times where the apostles felt it was right to be direct and confrontational. Jude speaks of people who cause damage with their false teaching and wrong behaviour. He urges us to stand up to such people and to defend the Church, and the faith, from them:

³ Beloved, while I was making every effort to write you about our common salvation, I felt the necessity to write to you appealing that you contend earnestly for the faith which was once for all handed down to the saints. ⁴ For certain persons have crept in unnoticed, those who were long beforehand marked out for this condemnation, ungodly persons who turn the grace of our God into licentiousness and deny our only Master and Lord, Jesus Christ.

Jude 3-4 (NASB)

Likewise, both apostle John and apostle Paul publicly exposed and rebuked certain people who were causing harm in churches, or who were wrong on important points of doctrine or practice and they were willing to name them, for example Diotrephes, about whom John says he will *"call attention to his deeds"*:

⁹ I wrote something to the church; but Diotrephes, who loves to be first among them, does not accept what we say. ¹⁰ For this reason, if I come, I will call attention to his deeds which he does, unjustly accusing us with wicked words; and not satisfied with this, he himself does not receive the brethren, either, and he forbids those who desire to do so and puts them out of the church.

3 John 9-10 (NASB)

¹⁶ Avoid such godless chatter, for it will lead people into more and more ungodliness, ¹⁷ and their talk will eat its way like gangrene. Among them are

479

Hymenae'us and Phile'tus, [18] who have swerved from the truth by holding that the resurrection is past already. They are upsetting the faith of some.

2 Timothy 2:16-18 (RSV)

[14] Alexander the coppersmith did me much harm; the Lord will repay him according to his deeds. [15] Be on guard against him yourself, for he vigorously opposed our teaching.

2 Timothy 4:14-15 (NASB)

When writing with advice on how to deal with those who *"persist in sin"*, as distinct from those who lapse into sin or error but then respond well and stop sinning when they are spoken to privately, Paul tells Timothy that such people are to be rebuked publicly, i.e. *"in the presence of all"*. Moreover, he explicitly indicates that one of the reasons for doing this publicly is to deter others from doing likewise, or, in other words, that the fear of God might be produced in them so that *"the rest may stand in fear"*. Do bear in mind as well that this passage, though it applies to all church members, is written in the specific context of how to deal with church *elders*, thereby proving that leaders are also to be publicly corrected when they go wrong:

[20] As for those who persist in sin, rebuke them in the presence of all, so that the rest may stand in fear. [21] In the presence of God and of Christ Jesus and of the elect angels I charge you to keep these rules without favor, doing nothing from partiality.

1 Timothy 5:20-21 (RSV)

On at least one occasion, apostle Paul even publicly opposed and criticised Peter:

[11] But when Cephas came to Antioch, I opposed him to his face, because he stood condemned. [12] For prior to the coming of certain men from James, he used to eat with the Gentiles; but when they came, he began to withdraw and hold himself aloof, fearing the party of the circumcision. [13] The rest of the Jews joined him in hypocrisy, with the result that even Barnabas was carried away by their hypocrisy. [14] But when I saw that they were not straightforward about the truth of the gospel, I said to Cephas in the presence of all, "If you, being a Jew, live like the Gentiles and not like the Jews, how is it that you compel the Gentiles to live like Jews?

Galatians 2:11-14 (NASB)

Paul also tells us to watch out for those who cause dissension by teaching false doctrine and to *"turn away from them"*:

480

[17] Now I urge you, brethren, keep your eye on those who cause dissensions and hindrances contrary to the teaching which you learned, and turn away from them. [18] For such men are slaves, not of our Lord Christ but of their own appetites; and by their smooth and flattering speech they deceive the hearts of the unsuspecting.

Romans 16:17-18 (NASB)

On the other hand, it is not always the right time to be confrontational. There are also times when we should not be. For example, in the book of James, we are told *not to speak against one another*:

[11] Do not speak against one another, brethren. He who speaks against a brother or judges his brother, speaks against the law and judges the law; but if you judge the law, you are not a doer of the law but a judge of it. [12] There is only one Lawgiver and Judge, the One who is able to save and to destroy; but who are you who judge your neighbor?

James 4:11-12 (NASB)

Moreover, in Romans, Paul tells us to be *at peace with all men* where possible:

If possible, so far as it depends on you, be at peace with all men.
Romans 12:18 (NASB)

Paul also tells Timothy, shortly before his death, to remind people to *"avoid disputing about words"*. By that Paul means *"mere words"*, i.e. purely academic, fruitless arguments, which are not about serious issues or points of doctrine, but just peripheral matters. In such cases the aim of those who are arguing is not to uphold the true faith, but just to puff themselves up, or to enjoy an argument, or to be seen to have won:

Remind them of this, and charge them before the Lord to avoid disputing about words, which does no good, but only ruins the hearers.

2 Timothy 2:14 (RSV)

[23] Have nothing to do with stupid, senseless controversies; you know that they breed quarrels. [24] And the Lord's servant must not be quarrelsome but kindly to every one, an apt teacher, forbearing, [25] correcting his opponents with gentleness. God may perhaps grant that they will repent and come to know the truth, [26] and they may escape from the snare of the devil, after being captured by him to do his will.

2 Timothy 2:23-26 (RSV)

481

Paul also tells Titus not to get drawn into *unnecessary* controversies over minor, non-essential matters:

But avoid stupid controversies, genealogies, dissensions, and quarrels over the law, for they are unprofitable and futile.

Titus 3:9 (RSV)

There may appear to be a contradiction here, between all of these verses, but actually there isn't. At any given moment, the question of whether we should make peace, or take a firm stand, depends on all the circumstances and on the relative importance of all the issues, principles or doctrines which are at stake. It also depends on who or what might be damaged or put at risk, either by our silence, or by our speaking out. Accordingly, it is not possible to write a categorical set of rules as to exactly when we should and should not speak out, take a stand, confront a person, create a controversy, or risk splitting up a church.

There are times and places when any one of those options may be the only right course of action. However, there are also times when we should, instead, show forbearance and be willing to compromise, conciliate, overlook a matter, turn a blind eye, seek to build bridges and try to keep people together. An example of when it may be right to overlook another man's error, or wrong thinking, is if we are dealing with someone who is weak in the faith, or lacking in knowledge, or who is only a new believer, as addressed by Paul in these passages:

[1]Now accept the one who is weak in faith, but not for the purpose of passing judgment on his opinions. [2] One person has faith that he may eat all things, but he who is weak eats vegetables only. [3] The one who eats is not to regard with contempt the one who does not eat, and the one who does not eat is not to judge the one who eats, for God has accepted him. [4] Who are you to judge the servant of another? To his own master he stands or falls; and he will stand, for the Lord is able to make him stand. [5] One person regards one day above another, another regards every day alike. Each person must be fully convinced in his own mind. [6] He who observes the day, observes it for the Lord, and he who eats, does so for the Lord, for he gives thanks to God; and he who eats not, for the Lord he does not eat, and gives thanks to God.

Romans 14:1-6 (NASB)

[13] Therefore let us not judge one another anymore, but rather determine this— not to put an obstacle or a stumbling block in a brother's way. [14] I know and am convinced in the Lord Jesus that nothing is unclean in itself; but to him who thinks anything to be unclean, to him it is unclean. [15] For if because of food your brother is hurt, you are no longer walking according to love. Do not destroy with your food him for whom Christ died. [16] Therefore do not let what is for you a good thing be spoken of as evil; [17] for the kingdom of God is not eating and

482

drinking, but righteousness and peace and joy in the Holy Spirit. [18] For he who in this way serves Christ is acceptable to God and approved by men. [19] So then we pursue the things which make for peace and the building up of one another. [20] Do not tear down the work of God for the sake of food. All things indeed are clean, but they are evil for the man who eats and gives offense. [21] It is good not to eat meat or to drink wine, or to do anything by which your brother stumbles. [22] The faith which you have, have as your own conviction before God. Happy is he who does not condemn himself in what he approves. [23] But he who doubts is condemned if he eats, because his eating is not from faith; and whatever is not from faith is sin.

Romans 14:13-23 (NASB)

[1] We then who are strong ought to bear with the scruples of the weak, and not to please ourselves. [2] Let each of us please his neighbor for his good, leading to edification. [3] For even Christ did not please Himself; but as it is written, "The reproaches of those who reproached You fell on Me." [4] For whatever things were written before were written for our learning, that we through the patience and comfort of the Scriptures might have hope. [5] Now may the God of patience and comfort grant you to be like-minded toward one another, according to Christ Jesus, [6] that you may with one mind and one mouth glorify the God and Father of our Lord Jesus Christ. [7] Therefore receive one another, just as Christ also received us, to the glory of God.

Romans 15:1-7 (NKJV)

We need to achieve a position of maturity and balance whereby we know all of God's principles and can tell which one is most applicable in a given situation

A wise person is aware of the different guiding principles in the Bible and also knows how, and when, to apply each one and also *how to hold them all in a healthy tension simultaneously*. At least he knows that he is meant to try, even though it can be very difficult to actually do so. A good overall balance is not achieved by applying every principle every time, but by knowing *which* principle, or which opposite and counter-balancing principle, should be applied at any given time.

A man told me of an argument in his church in which he had given way because he *"wanted to preserve unity and avoid any split in the church"*. From what he said, I felt he had possibly made the wrong decision and asked if he had also considered the counter-balancing principle that we are to *contend earnestly for the faith*, and to take a stand, as Paul did when he publicly challenged Peter. I also asked what made him think that preserving unity, and avoiding church splits, was the main objective, given that Jesus told us that He had not come to bring peace, but division:

51 Do you suppose that I came to grant peace on earth? I tell you, no, but rather division; 52 for from now on five members in one household will be divided, three against two and two against three. 53 They will be divided, father against son and son against father, mother against daughter and daughter against mother, mother-in-law against daughter-in-law and daughter-in-law against mother-in-law."

Luke 12:51-53 (NASB)

This does not mean that everything Jesus said and did will always bring division. Nor does it mean that we should always seek to create division, or always be unconcerned when it arises. It means that if we teach and practise the truth then controversy, division, and even hatred, *will inevitably arise*, no matter how much we might try to avoid them. Consequently, although we should want unity in the church, and take all reasonable steps to maintain it, there are limits. A point can be reached where the doctrine or principle that we are upholding is sufficiently serious to justify allowing, or even causing, a split in the church.

Indeed, there are times when the only way that the true Church can be distinguished from the false church is when a division occurs. At such times the true believers can, and should, separate themselves from the false. Thus, an over-emphasis on unity can actually harm the real Church and undermine the Gospel. It is therefore wrong to pursue unity slavishly, or to pay too high a price for maintaining it, as if it was the most important thing. It isn't. Truth is more important than unity and is, in fact, the only real basis for ever achieving any genuine unity.

Conversely, there is another group which does grasp the need for truth, and for faithfulness to the real Gospel, upholding true doctrine, and asserting the authority of Scripture. But they don't realise that there is also a need to try to preserve the unity of the true Church. The error can therefore be made in either direction, as it can on any other issue. There is something about our fallen nature which causes us to be attracted to one school of thought to the exclusion, or diminution, of all others.

We can then elevate that particular principle and understate, or even completely forget about, any other counter-balancing principles. That is the way most of us are and we need to recognise that tendency and take steps to counteract it. So, some of us are the type of person who can easily see the need for unity and for keeping the peace. Others are more naturally drawn to contending earnestly for true doctrine. But very few of us can manage even to be aware of *both objectives*, and of their importance, let alone to seek to achieve both of them *simultaneously*.

Therefore, some people engage too readily in controversy and defend the truth vigorously on every issue, even if it isn't central, and without regard to the disruption it may produce. Others, however, will seek to preserve unity and peace at all costs, without regard to the loss of truth which that approach can cause. No matter how hard it may be, we should at least aim to have a proper regard to *both* of these objectives and principles *at the same time*, even if we don't achieve that balance, and even if people don't respond well to us.

Thus, you could say that we are meant to become *"diplomatic contenders for truth"*. Or, to give it its mirror image, you could say we should aim to be *"honest and doctrinally faithful pursuers of peace"*. Where such a wholesome balance cannot be achieved or where, despite our best endeavours, the controversy is not capable of resolution, then we have a choice. One or other of these two objectives must prevail and which one we choose, in any given situation, will depend on the gravity of the specific issues over which there is disagreement.

In the apocryphal story of the church which split over what colour of carpets to have, the right answer is for you to give way and to let the others have whatever colour they want. Over such a trivial issue, it is more important to preserve peace and unity than to get your own way, even if you are right. However, that is not so if it is a debate as to the nature of the Gospel message, or the authority of Scripture, or an important issue of doctrine such as same-sex marriage. Then a church split is essential if the alternative is for evil to be done or for false doctrines to be upheld.

Thus, if a church has decided that it is going to allow weddings for homosexuals, the members should be willing to leave that church, and to encourage others to leave as well, if they are prepared to do so. Moreover, prior to doing that, they should speak out openly in opposition to the proposals, *even if that causes unrest and ill will*. There should, of course, be no hostility on *your* part. However, you need to be ready for, and be willing to face, the hostility of *others* which will probably arise in response to your principled stand.

We might summarise the right overall balance by saying that we should:

a) be willing to give way on any *non-essential issue*, which is not an important question of doctrine or practice

b) use diplomacy, compromise and conciliation *as far as we can*, provided we do not go further than our conscience, or the Scriptures, permit

c) avoid controversy and conflict *if we can*, but not be afraid of permitting, or even causing, those things, if they are genuinely needed and are unavoidable

d) be willing to engage in confrontation, debate and controversy if those things are genuinely needed, but *not to desire them, or take any pleasure from them*

Hold it together : Integrity (NOT Unrestrained, beyond limits)
Balance as Managing / Governing : keep it together
keep your head.

485

e) not rush to confront others, but begin with tact, diplomacy and persuasion and only go to the stage of confrontation after all peaceful approaches *have been tried but have failed*

f) even so, not be *timid or reluctant* about the prospect of controversy, such that you *leave it too late* to take a firm stand

Four broad issues over which we can never compromise

There are four broad issues over which there can never be any compromise and where there is no room at all for differences of opinion. These are, therefore, situations where we need to take a very firm stand and be willing to leave a church and/or break off fellowship with another Christian:

a) Where the dispute concerns *the identity of Jesus Christ i.e. who and what He is*. For example, if a church is denying that Jesus is both fully God and fully man, that is a clear basis for you to contend with them openly, to "name names", and to leave that church if they will not change their stance. However, if the dispute was only about the precise interpretation of prophecy, or the sequence of prophesied events, then there is plenty of room for individual opinions and disagreement and no need to break off fellowship. Indeed, it would be wrong to do so.

b) Where the dispute concerns *the nature of the Gospel*, such that a church is preaching a 'gospel' which is false or incomplete. For example, where sin, judgment, Hell, the Lake of Fire or repentance are left out of the message, or are minimised, then that church has a false gospel message. That too is a valid basis for speaking out openly, and for leaving that church if they do not listen.

Grace alone

c) Where the dispute concerns *the nature and status of God's Word*. So, if a church is teaching that the Bible is not infallible, or is out of date, or is not divinely inspired, or that one need not obey it, or that God has now "changed His mind", for example on homosexuality, then that too is a basis for breaking off fellowship. However, disagreements as to the meaning of particular passages, whilst all concerned accept that the Bible is God's infallible Word, and must be obeyed, is not such a basis. *No cherry picking*

d) Where there is *clear and serious immorality on the part of a believer* (not an unsaved unbeliever, an enquirer, or an immature new convert) and also *a refusal to repent*, then a church can and should break off fellowship with him. Therefore, if an established fellow Christian, especially a leader, is engaging in sexual sin, or financial dishonesty, or is telling lies, or dominating people,

486

or engaging in the occult, or other serious sins, then we need to break off fellowship.

But we need not do so where the sins are not gross, or where he is a new convert and does not yet know any better. Neither need we do so where the person is repenting and seeking to put things right, especially if they are not a leader. In such cases, that person needs our help. But if they are continuing in their sin, and refusing to listen or to change, we should either leave that church ourselves, or remove them from the church, if we are able to do so. Here is what Paul says:

⁹I wrote to you in my letter not to associate with immoral men; ¹⁰not at all meaning the immoral of this world, or the greedy and robbers, or idolaters, since then you would need to go out of the world. ¹¹ But rather I wrote to you not to associate with anyone who bears the name of brother if he is guilty of immorality or greed, or is an idolater, reviler, drunkard, or robber—not even to eat with such a one. ¹²For what have I to do with judging outsiders? Is it not those inside the church whom you are to judge? ¹³God judges those outside. "Drive out the wicked person from among you."

1 Corinthians 5:9-13 (RSV)

Other than in these four broad areas, we should generally aim to "agree to disagree" and maintain fellowship with a fellow believer or with a church. We should always try hard *not* to break off fellowship with other believers *unless we really have to*. Being realistic, however, there are few, if any, people who consistently know, in respect of every issue and situation, what the right time is and thus, for example, whether/when/how to take a firm stand or give ground.

Yet a wise person at least knows that such questions need to be asked and that, for many issues, there are biblical principles which can point in both directions simultaneously. Conversely, most of us are simple and are only aware of, or only ever emphasise, one principle or another, rather than both or all at the same time, as we should.

Knowing when a discussion about other people crosses the line and becomes gossip, and when we can, and cannot, treat a conversation as 'confidential'

I have added this short section here in response to a question someone raised with me which concerned a dispute which once arose in their church. Person A was being critical of person B, largely due to envy and insecurity, and therefore person A rang person C and asked to have a conversation *about person B,* on the strict condition that the conversation *"must remain confidential"*. Person C agreed to this and it then emerged that person A simply wanted to criticise person B and to

487

see if person C had any further negative information to add. He therefore began by saying *"What is your opinion of person B?"*

The whole thing then escalated, and C found herself drawn in to this and began to be contaminated by A's jaundiced attitude towards B. Her own thoughts towards B then became increasingly negative, harsh, and even poisonous. To be precise, C already had a negative attitude towards B, even before A approached her. In fact, he had discerned that negativity in her, in the carnal, feral sense of discernment. That is why he rang her, and not persons D, E, F or G etc, who were not already prejudiced against B.

Anyway, at a later date, the tension and animosity towards B grew on the part of both A and C, and A eventually left that church. It was only at that point that my advice was sought. I questioned C about her antipathy towards B and she was initially evasive about it and also reluctant to say what she and A had discussed. Her reason for that reluctance was that A had specified at the outset, when he first rang her, that he wanted to talk about B *"in confidence"* and had asked her to agree, in advance, *"not to disclose any of it to anybody."*

These facts emerged in stages, for the very reason that C felt bound by her agreement with A to keep the conversation confidential and to tell nobody else. However, it all eventually came out when I told her that it was not valid, on that occasion, for A to request confidentiality, or for her to agree to it. She then asked me to define what 'confidentiality' is and when it is, and isn't, valid to agree to it.

I told her that what was wrong with the way that she and A had handled their discussion about B was that it was gossip. It was, therefore, inherently illegitimate, such that any agreement to maintain confidentiality was not only invalid in itself, but also compounded the original wrong of engaging in gossip. I then referred her to Jesus' words in Matthew 18:15-17, in which He sets out what I call *"the Matthew 18 procedure"* for dealing with conflicts and disagreements within a local church:

[15] **"If your brother sins against you, go and tell him his fault, between you and him alone. If he listens to you, you have gained your brother.** [16] **But if he does not listen, take one or two others along with you, that every charge may be established by the evidence of two or three witnesses.** [17] **If he refuses to listen to them, tell it to the church. And if he refuses to listen even to the church, let him be to you as a Gentile and a tax collector.**

Matthew 18:15-17 (ESV)

So, there are four distinct stages to the Matthew 18 procedure, which we shall list and discuss below. However, at every stage, even the final one, the aim must always be to at least attempt to resolve matters, to restore relationships and to promote the health of the local church, not to undermine it. That process is not served therefore by gossip, the aim of which is always to tear another person down by spreading rumours or accusations, whether true or false, and behind their backs, rather than to their face.

The problem with gossip is that it is done with the aim of undermining people, not helping them. Therefore, it has the effect of intensifying and entrenching conflict, not resolving it. That was the context in which, and the aim with which, A had rung C. It was also the reason why both the conversation itself, and the agreement to keep it between themselves, were invalid. So, the Matthew 18 'procedure', when properly conducted, operates in the following way, with the following objectives and in the following manner:

Stage 1 You go to see the person whom you believe has wronged you or offended you, or with whom you are in conflict, and you speak directly *to* him, not *about* him. You also do it with the aim of helping him, restoring relations between the two of you, and promoting peace and unity within the local church. If it works, then that is great and it can all be forgiven and put behind you on both sides.

Stage 2 If he does not listen, you must then repeat the exercise but, this time, you take one or two witnesses along with you to hear what is said on both sides. They can help both you and him to understand each other better, to address the issues, and to prove or disprove any allegations calmly and effectively, so as to be reconciled, because that is still the aim. Note also that you are still keeping the dispute and the process of resolution as private as possible, by involving as few people as possible. It is also done with the alleged wrongdoer *present, in the room, hearing everything, as it is said directly to his face, not behind his back.* I have put all of those words in italics because all of that is crucial, and was wholly lacking when A rang C.

Stage 3 If the person still refuses to listen and if his own evidence and his responses to you have not persuaded you, and the witnesses, that it is in fact *you* who are at fault, then you should bring the dispute before the *whole church.* That means that the discussion is repeated, in front of them all, together with all the allegations and counter allegations, and the evidence of both sides. The local church then decides collectively, as a group, who is right and wrong. Of course, when Jesus gave this instruction His assumption was that you are genuine, and are telling the truth, and that your complaint is valid. However, if that is not the case, then you need to accept what the other person is saying, if it is true, and you must repent and apologise if it is actually you who has done wrong.

Stage 4 If, however, the decision of the local church as a whole is that the other person is at fault, and if he will not listen to you, or to them, and thus will not repent, or change, or be reconciled, then the local church, as a whole, needs to

489

expel him from membership of that church. Thus, from then on, he will be viewed as an outsider or non-member. That is of great significance, because God regards the local church as being of very high importance indeed, not least because it provides a spiritual protection, or 'umbrella', to each member.

This four-stage procedure also demonstrates, by the way, that all local churches are meant to be small and intimate. They should be meeting in houses or barns or small meeting rooms, as the early Church did, and involving only about 10-50 people or perhaps 100 at most. If not, how can the Matthew 18 procedure be implemented, because you can't discuss a dispute between A and B in front of hundreds, or even thousands, of people.

That would be completely impractical and, therefore, cannot have been what Jesus had in mind when He gave this command in Matthew 18. See my Book 8 for much more detail as to how the Church was organised, conducted and led in the first century because it was the exact opposite, in just about every way, from how churches are structured and led today.

Some more guidelines on how to treat conversations which you are being asked to treat as confidential

Returning to the question of 'confidential' conversations, and when they are and are not legitimate, let me set out some sensible guidelines. The first is that you can only agree to engage in a confidential conversation and to maintain that confidentiality thereafter, if the discussion is *exclusively about the person with whom you are speaking*, and does not involve others.

So, for example, if they wish to confide in you about a health issue of their own, or a sin they are committing which involves nobody else, such as internet pornography, then you can agree to speak privately and to maintain confidentiality. However, if the conversation is about others, even indirectly, then you cannot agree to confidentiality as it might become necessary to urge A to speak directly to B himself, or even for you to do so yourself if A will not agree to that. Remember that the whole point of discussing issues is to resolve conflicts, not to enjoy gossiping about people.

However, what if A wants to speak to C about the fact that A is being abused, damaged or lied about by B and what if A is afraid of B and feels unable to go through the Matthew 18 procedure with B? In such a situation, which would be rare, A could legitimately speak to C. However, that would only be the case if A's aim was to receive C's help in addressing the issues, protecting him from B, and implementing the Matthew 18 procedure on A's behalf, where A is *unable* to do it for himself. It would not be valid if it is just an excuse to gossip.

Moving back to the original story, A's position and attitude were not valid. He simply wanted someone to gossip with and had no intention of embarking upon the Matthew 18 procedure, or of asking C to do so on his behalf. A just wanted to speak to another negative-minded person and to attack B's reputation. Indeed, not only was he not seeking for reconciliation, he was expressly forbidding C, from the outset, to do anything to bring it about. Thus, A's phone call to C was wrong, as was their agreement to keep it all between themselves, rather than let it be assessed and dealt with openly and honestly, in the way that Jesus intended.

When writing this I was also asked what one is entitled to do if one has already agreed to keep something confidential, but one later realises that that agreement was illegitimate and even malicious, on the part of the other person, or both of you. I am reminded of an occasion I write about in Book 6 in which a woman I have renamed 'Rhoda' invited my wife over to her house for a chat. My wife was taken by surprise when Rhoda began to criticise a young man whom I have renamed as 'Charles'. She then told my wife to keep her comments confidential.

My wife was not on her guard and did not see the problem immediately, but she saw it later that day and spoke to me. I said that Rhoda was wrong to say those things about Charles and also wrong to tell my wife to keep it confidential. I then said that I would tackle Rhoda about it, together with her husband, 'Stephen'. However, they were both totally unrepentant and would not meet with me under Matthew 18 to discuss what they had said about Charles. Neither would they repeat the accusations to him, directly to his face, or do anything constructive to address their alleged concerns.

My wife did not actually agree to keep it confidential, but she did not refuse either. She was not quick enough in thinking on her feet to see the issue at that moment, or to tell Rhoda to stop speaking. However, even if my wife had agreed (wrongly) to confidentiality, it would still be her duty to correct that error afterwards by telling Rhoda to go to see Charles herself, as per Matthew 18, and/or to get me to urge Rhoda to do so. That does not necessarily mean that my wife should go to see Charles, who had been maligned, to tell him of what had been said. That may not always be appropriate.

However, it would be appropriate for her to go to see the elders of the church to inform them of the gossip and also of Rhoda's refusal to meet to discuss it with Charles. That is what I then did, and I tell the story in Book 6. Sadly, it did not turn out well, as the elders were not interested, so I got nowhere. The main reason why the Matthew 18 procedure is not used in churches today, besides the fact that churches are too big for it to be practicable, is that the leaders *don't want to use it*. They often don't care about resolving disputes, or they are afraid to tackle people. Or, in many cases, they like to gossip themselves.

491

Deciding what the 'time' is for your nation and whether God is currently operating in judgment or mercy for the nation as a whole

Let's look at another example of 'telling the time', but in the wider national context, rather than what is happening in your own local church, or amongst the people you know. A relevant question today, in the Western nations, is whether the point has been reached where a nation has gone too far in its sin to be spared from God's wrath. If so, then the nation *as a whole* cannot be turned around. Therefore, only *individuals* can be saved and rescued from God's judgment.

The book of Jonah sets out how God warned the whole city of Nineveh to repent and turn from their sin or face His wrath. Then, just as the prophet Jonah knew they would, the leaders and the wider population repented en masse and God spared them. Jonah's reluctance to go to Nineveh was *not* because he was afraid, as so many preachers wrongly assume. It was because he knew they would repent and, as a patriotic Israelite, he *did not want* that to happen, or for God to show them mercy.

The Ninevites had destroyed the northern kingdom of Israel in 722 BC and Jonah saw them as a threat to the southern kingdom too. At any rate, the point is that that was a time in their history when God's mercy was still available to the people of Nineveh *as a whole.* Jonah knew that, and his issue was that he did not *want* God to spare them. However, about a century later, in the time of the prophet Nahum, things had changed. Nahum therefore prophesied God's impending wrath on Nineveh.

Then, in 612 BC, just a few years later, Nineveh was destroyed by the Babylonians. It may well be that some *individual Ninevites* repented and were saved. However, for *Nineveh as a whole,* it was too late for that. By 612 BC, God's patience had run out and therefore the city of Nineveh could not escape God's punishment, no matter what some of the people did. The people *as a whole* had crossed a line and gone past the point of no return.

Let's now consider another example, from chapters 34 and 35 of 2 Chronicles. It relates to the people of Judah, the southern kingdom. By this stage the sin of the people, and of their leaders, was so bad that God had firmly resolved to pour out His judgment and He was not willing to change His mind. That judgment followed in 586 BC, when the Babylonians invaded Judah and took the people into exile.

In 2 Chronicles 34:22-28, a prophetess called Huldah prophesies the coming disaster and destruction that was going to come upon Judah, as other prophets had also done earlier. What is interesting is that Huldah singles out King Josiah, who was a very godly king. He personally was deeply penitent about the sins of the people, and the sins of some of the previous kings. Josiah therefore repented and humbled himself personally, as an individual, and he also instituted many reforms to remove wickedness and idolatry from the Kingdom of Judah:

¹ Josiah was eight years old when he began to reign, and he reigned thirty-one years in Jerusalem. ² And he did what was right in the eyes of the LORD, and walked in the ways of David his father; and he did not turn aside to the right hand or to the left. ³ For in the eighth year of his reign, while he was yet a boy, he began to seek the God of David his father, and in the twelfth year he began to purge Judah and Jerusalem of the high places, the Asherim, and the carved and the metal images. ⁴ And they chopped down the altars of the Baals in his presence, and he cut down the incense altars that stood above them. And he broke in pieces the Asherim and the carved and the metal images, and he made dust of them and scattered it over the graves of those who had sacrificed to them. ⁵ He also burned the bones of the priests on their altars and cleansed Judah and Jerusalem. ⁶ And in the cities of Manasseh, Ephraim, and Simeon, and as far as Naphtali, in their ruins all around, ⁷ he broke down the altars and beat the Asherim and the images into powder and cut down all the incense altars throughout all the land of Israel. Then he returned to Jerusalem.

2 Chronicles 34:1-7 (ESV)

Huldah points out that although God was pleased with *Josiah personally*, for his own repentance, and also for his reforms, that would not prevent God's judgment from coming *upon Judah as a whole*. The line had already been crossed and the nation as a whole had already gone too far, even before Josiah came to the throne. Therefore, God had irrevocably decided to judge the kingdom of Judah. All that God was willing to do was to spare *individuals,* in particular Josiah himself, from that impending judgment. He was not willing to refrain from judging the nation as a whole:

²² So Hilkiah and those whom the king had sent went to Huldah the prophetess, the wife of Shallum the son of Tokhath, son of Hasrah, keeper of the wardrobe (now she lived in Jerusalem in the Second Quarter) and spoke to her to that effect. ²³ And she said to them, "Thus says the LORD, the God of Israel: 'Tell the man who sent you to me, ²⁴ Thus says the LORD, Behold, I will bring disaster upon this place and upon its inhabitants, all the curses that are written in the book that was read before the king of Judah. ²⁵ Because they have forsaken me and have made offerings to other gods, that they might provoke me to anger with all the works of their hands, therefore my wrath will be poured out on this place and will not be quenched. ²⁶ But to the king of Judah, who sent you to inquire of the LORD, thus shall you say to him, Thus says the LORD, the God of Israel: Regarding the words that you have heard, ²⁷ because your heart was tender and you humbled yourself before God when you heard his words against

493

this place and its inhabitants, and you have humbled yourself before me and have torn your clothes and wept before me, I also have heard you, declares the LORD. [28] Behold, I will gather you to your fathers, and you shall be gathered to your grave in peace, and your eyes shall not see all the disaster that I will bring upon this place and its inhabitants.'" And they brought back word to the king.

2 Chronicles 34:22-28 (ESV)

The most that God was willing to do was to delay the nation's judgment, for Josiah's sake, but not to prevent it from happening at all. Consequently, God held back the judgment on Judah until after Josiah had died. He didn't want Josiah to have to see it as it would have been terribly distressing to him. As it turned out, Josiah died young, at the age of only 39, having reigned since he was 8 years old. Perhaps God allowed his premature death to spare Josiah from having to see the wrath that He was about to pour out on the nation.

Thus it is not always an act of judgment for a person to die before they get old. In this case it could even be seen as merciful. It meant Josiah never saw the horror of what then happened to the people, and to the subsequent kings, when the Babylonians invaded. If we turn to our own day and ask what the 'time' is now, my personal belief is that we in the West have crossed the line and have gone too far in our sin and rebellion for God to be willing to have mercy on our nations as a whole.

In particular, abortion is now conducted on an industrial scale. Plus there is the epidemic of homosexuality, 'gay marriage', gender confusion, the corrupting of children, and the apostasy in the churches. All of these are now occurring on a scale never seen before in history. Therefore, I personally believe that no matter what our leaders do, and no matter even what the churches do, the USA, the UK and the European nations are doomed to face God's wrath. Indeed, I believe it has already begun with the mass invasion of Muslims, supposedly as refugees, but actually as jihadists. *CV19*

The Muslims intend to destroy the West, and all that it once stood for, and to bring it under the control of Islam. Moreover, I believe God might well permit them to achieve that, or to go a long way towards achieving it, as a judgment upon our nations. That is God may well be using the Muslims to judge us, just as He used the Assyrians to judge Israel, and the Babylonians to judge Judah. To have said that even a decade ago, let alone earlier, would have been viewed as exaggerated, or even hysterical. Yet it is now happening before our very eyes.

A tidal wave of aggressive, militant Muslims is pouring in continuously. Yet, much of our population, and most of our leaders, are too blind and deaf to grasp what is happening, let alone what it will lead to. They are too cowardly to resist it anyway. Even the majority of church leaders have no comprehension of how

What if government are purposefully doing so? 494

evil Islam is, or of what it will do to the West. Thus, even the better churches are silent, and the worst ones are actively supporting the influx of Muslims, by whom our nations are being taken over.

Moreover, and this would have seemed even more impossible until it actually happened, the USA has had *a Muslim president* and for two terms! Nobody would have believed that possible. Indeed, many still won't accept that he is a Muslim, even now. Yet, it happened, and Mr Obama spent 8 years systematically destroying America from within. He made a huge number of appointments of Muslims in all areas of the Federal Government, right up to the highest levels. Even the Director of the CIA was a secret Muslim and John Kerry, the Secretary of State, if not a Muslim himself, was strongly supportive of Islam.

Obama also filled the very White House itself with all manner of Islamic signs, objects, carpets, crescent moon ornaments, Korans etc, as well as ordering *all* White House staff to be silent five times per day for the Muslim prayer times! All of that blasphemy was going on at the very heart of the American government and it cannot fail to do great harm, even long after Obama has gone. In addition to that, he also drastically reduced the size, quality and effectiveness of the American armed forces. Therefore, America is now less able to defend itself, or the West, from the advance of Islam.

Christians should certainly pray for our leaders, and also get involved in politics as party members, and even stand for public office. However, even if we do, I believe the decline of the western nations will continue. I hope I am wrong, but I do not expect any large scale revival to come to the UK, USA or Europe. I only have faith for individuals to be saved, here and there. The 'ship' itself is going down, like the Titanic, and only individuals can escape. For our nations, I believe it is the time for judgment, not revival, just as it was for Ninevah in Nahum's day, and for Judah during Josiah's reign.

Wise people are realistic about the *underlying facts* but, at the same time, are optimistic when deciding *what to do about those facts*.

I was recently talking to a person whom I felt was trapped in a really negative, defeatist, pessimistic attitude of mind. This had become so thoroughly familiar to them, as their consistent way of thinking, that they had come to regard it as normal and to assume that there was no alternative. However, this person denied being a pessimist and claimed instead to be a *'realist'*. They wrongly assumed that that meant they could not also be a *pessimist*, as if the two things were mutually exclusive. I challenged that assertion and attempted to define the three terms, *'realism'*, *'pessimism'* and *'optimism'*.

495

a) A *'realist'* is one who forms a correct assessment of the facts of the current situation, i.e. as to what the position is and what resources are available.

b) A *'pessimist'* looks at those same facts, even if he states them correctly, but then deals with them wrongly *by taking a negative, gloomy, defeatist view* as to whether and how those facts can be handled, what they imply, what is likely to follow from them, and how difficult it will be to resolve the problems or reduce their effect. So, as the saying goes, the pessimist correctly sees that the glass is at the half way point, but he automatically sees it as *half empty, not half full.*

c) An *'optimist'* looks at the very same underlying facts but, unlike the pessimist, he sees a way forward, or a way of reducing the effect of the problem, and his mind immediately turns to thinking of how best to tackle those facts so as to produce a good outcome. He also instinctively assumes that such a positive outcome is possible, or even likely.

Therefore, a realist simply *sees the underlying facts as they actually are*, without under-estimating, misrepresenting or denying them. So they can see the full extent of the problem and the scarcity of the resources available. However, the point is that being a realist does not mean that you can't *also* be an optimist or a pessimist as well. That said, not every person is even realistic to begin with. Some are mistaken about the underlying background facts, or even delusional.

Thus, they don't actually see the real position to begin with, even before we look at how they might, deal with, or respond to, those facts. Even worse, some are so deeply pessimistic that they not only misjudge how to deal with the facts, but they also wrongly state what those facts are, or they wrongly define the problem, in the first place. Then they are not even dealing with the real facts, but with a jaundiced, even warped, misrepresentation thereof, i.e. false 'facts' which are not even true to begin with.

However, even if a person is realistic about the background facts, we still have to consider whether they are an optimist or a pessimist as to *what can then be done about those facts.* A person can be completely realistic about the facts, and state them accurately, and yet still be a pessimist overall because, when they look at those facts, they see no way forward and no way of changing them. A pessimist is, therefore, already defeated before he even begins to address the problem. Therefore he often sees no point in even trying, because he is convinced, from the outset, that he will inevitably fail and that there is no hope.

Thus, even if you truly are a realist, that fact, by itself, does not mean that you cannot *also* be a pessimist. You can be one, if you think and act negatively, in the way you approach the facts and also in the assumptions you make as to the

The + - response to the reality 496

prospects of success in tackling them. By contrast, when an optimist, who can equally claim to be a realist, looks at the same facts, he sees options, possibilities, solutions and ways forward. At the very least, he sees ways of mitigating the harmful effect of those underlying facts. Nevertheless, he is just as realistic as any other man as to *what the facts are*.

It is just that to an optimist, who is wearing the *'helmet of salvation'*, which is hope, the story does not *end* with the facts. It only *begins* with them. Thus, in 1940, an optimist such as Churchill could see the very same facts that the defeatists and appeasers could see. He was well aware of the huge size of the German army and air force, and the power, quantity and quality of their weapons. He could also see, as well as anyone, the staggering victories already achieved by the Germans in 1939 and 1940, when they overran Poland, Belgium, Holland and France in a matter of weeks.

However, whereas much of the world, looked on and saw Great Britain's defeat as inevitable, Churchill never did. He saw *the very same facts* as anybody else could see. Indeed, he saw them even more clearly than they did, but those facts did not intimidate him. Neither was he fazed or overwhelmed by them. He knew, or rather he *decided to believe*, that there would, eventually, be some way forward. He did not know in May 1940 *what* that way forward would be, or *how* we would win, but he still believed that we *would*.

He was therefore determined to resist in every way possible until the facts changed. If nothing else, he hoped that Hitler would eventually make some mistakes, or miscalculate, or overplay his hand. If so, then our chance would come, if we could only hold on through the darkest days when others, who saw the *same facts*, but through the lens of *pessimism*, had no hope. Moreover, he was right. Hitler did make errors, and very serious ones, for example he:

a) failed to press home his advantage in May/June 1940 to prevent the evacuation at Dunkirk, despite his generals' advice

b) invaded Russia in June 1941 against his generals' advice and without any adequate thought about the Russian winter that was only five months away

c) delayed the invasion of Russia from April to June due to getting involved in unnecessary distractions elsewhere, such as in Yugoslavia. This robbed his own troops of six weeks of good weather, such that they did not reach Moscow before the winter began

d) declared war on the USA in December 1941 after Pearl Harbor, when he did not actually need to do so. This forced America into the war against him when they might, otherwise, have left Germany alone and focussed only on Japan

The lense of optimism & pessimism

In May 1940, Churchill had no way of knowing *what* Hitler's future errors would be. He was simply convinced that he would eventually make some, and that the tide would then turn. When we, at our much lower level, look at the facts in our own lives, the main question is not whether we are being realistic about what those are. The far larger issue is whether we are being an optimist or a pessimist *about how we will react to those facts* and what we choose to *do about them*. A wise person will always choose to be an optimist, because pessimism is so unproductive, and even paralysing.

It cripples the mind, switches off our creative imagination, and saps our morale, resilience, endurance and willingness to fight. However, whether optimism is wise or not, and whether we find it easy or hard, is academic. A Christian must be optimistic, because we are *commanded* to be so at all times, in how we approach, and respond to, the real facts. We know that because Paul instructs us, in Ephesians 6, to put on, and keep on, the *'helmet of salvation'*. This is not defined within Ephesians, but we are told in 1 Thessalonians, that it represents *hope*:

and take the helmet of salvation, and the sword of the Spirit, which is the word of God,

Ephesians 6:17 (ESV)

But since we belong to the day, let us be sober, having put on the breastplate of faith and love, and for a helmet the hope of salvation.

1 Thessalonians 5:8 (ESV)

Paul means that we must fill our minds with hope, which is best defined as *the confident expectation of good*. If you choose to maintain that hope, even when things go wrong, and the news is all bad, and people let you down or turn against you, it is a powerful protection for your mind. We all need this if we are to withstand the turbulence of life and its many hard knocks, disappointments and failures. If your mind is not firmly surrounded with this 'helmet' of hope, you will eventually be worn down. *The love of many will grow cold*

You may also stop fighting and give in, either as a result of the sustained pressure of life, or its sudden shocks and surprises, or both combined. But the stubborn maintenance of your of hope will keep you going through it all. Therefore, a wise person *chooses to cultivate hope*, even where he doesn't naturally have any, and even where the circumstances do not appear to justify it.

He will *train* his mind to be hopeful, regardless of circumstances, even where that positive attitude goes against the grain of his nature. He does not leave it all to chance, or allow himself to be governed by the random emotions that are generated by the ups and downs of life. For that reason, an optimist will never

Its most often the sheer surprise – the shock that destroy us →

give in, but will fight on indefinitely, always seeking for some way to improve the position, long after others have given up.

The mind-set of the optimist is not caused by the facts being good. It has nothing to do with what the facts are. It is what he chooses *to superimpose upon the facts, whatever those may be.* Thus, an optimist is not ruled by the circumstances that he faces. He rules over them and he *makes things happen* rather than sitting back passively and *letting things happen to him.* I like Churchill's definition of the pessimist and the optimist and the difference in their mentality:

"A pessimist sees the difficulty in every opportunity. An optimist sees the opportunity in every difficulty."

Winston Churchill

When making decisions, face the very worst that could happen, and reconcile yourself to it. Then seek to avoid it or improve on it as an outcome.

What I am suggesting here may sound a bit like pessimism, or even defeatism, but it isn't. On the contrary, taking this approach when you face scary decisions, and where a lot is at stake, will help you to stay calm. Then you can think straight, rather than panicking or giving way to fear. I have operated in this way many times when handling a crisis that could potentially have disastrous consequences. Therefore, I recommend that you do as follows:

a) Calculate in advance what is the very worst that could happen. Work out what people might do to you, or how much it could cost if things go really badly, or if you were to get the decision completely wrong. *Worst case scenario*

b) Then look that potential worst-case scenario straight in the eye and reconcile yourself to it now in the sense of accepting that it could possibly be the consequence of your decision. *Accept as real?*

c) Come to terms with it, as if it was already the case, or was already inevitable. Then brace yourself to face it, endure it, and deal with it

d) Having faced the worst that could possibly happen, and having already come to terms with it, such that you are no longer panicking, try from then on to prevent that bad outcome. Or, at least try to reduce the cost, damage, bad publicity or adverse consequences to the lowest level possible. In other words, try to 'mitigate your losses'. *Now seek to reduce it*

e) At the same time, look for things that you could still do, or escape routes you could still take, if you fail and if the disaster actually happens. Then you are at least partially prepared if the worst does come to the worst.

Plan to set HIT hard. Then plan to respond well. "Expect Evil"

Accept the reality you'll get hit hard + repeatedly otherwise the surprise will kill you

This approach which I advocate is not pessimism, or even negative thinking. It is actually part of what is involved in being realistic because you are looking frankly and objectively at the current situation, as it really is. You are also recognising what could potentially happen if things do go wrong. However, the point is that you are facing it squarely, head on, rather than:

a) pretending that this frightening situation isn't happening and therefore refusing to address it, or to take any preventative or remedial action

b) panicking and taking hasty, unwise actions to try to make sure these bad things don't happen, where such steps may be premature, excessive or inadvisable

c) ceasing to function mentally, due to your fear, like a deer caught in the headlights, unable to think, decide, or act

In my Book 6 I speak of some very serious threats and legal actions I have faced which would have been extremely damaging and costly if they had gone badly for me. Like anybody else, I found those times stressful and I felt fear about what could happen, or what people might do. However, by taking the approach I recommend above, I was always able to function in a crisis, to think straight, face down my enemies, and never give in to intimidation. Both people and demons will use your fear to manipulate you. They want you to become so panic-stricken that you are unable to fight back.

How now can I reduce this possibility?

However, by naming it, and coming to terms with it, *as if it had already happened*, your fear loses the power that it had over you while it was still a shadowy possibility, floating in the air and haunting you with its menace. Once the fear has been faced up to, and accepted, it is robbed of its capacity to intimidate you. Then you are much better placed to fight back and to at least improve the situation. Or you might even achieve a complete victory, whereby the negative outcome is avoided entirely. Either way, your chances of handling it well are maximised if you take this approach and thus avoid being caught in the headlights.

Accept the worst could happen then plan for solution

Always consider open-mindedly whether you are being deceived and be ready to double-check, and triple-check, the things that people tell you

One of the hardest things about decision-making is that the underlying facts, or *alleged facts*, upon which your decision has to be based, are only as good as the people who provided the information. If they are deceiving you, or if they have been deceived themselves, without knowing it, then all or part of the information that you are relying upon could be inaccurate, exaggerated or even invented. Given that deception is endemic throughout most of the human race, the possibility that you are being lied to is not some remote contingency. It is a virtual certainty, at least some of the time.

Therefore, on any given occasion, as you make your decision, the chances are that at least some of the supposed facts upon which you are relying are not true. Thus, they are not actually facts at all. So, the first step is to recognise that this problem of deception and misinformation exists, rather than denying it, or being oblivious to it. That alone will put you substantially further forward. You will at least be forewarned of the potential problem, and thus better able to address it. Of course, at this stage, you are not aware whether you have been lied to, or about what, or by whom.

You have only got the alleged facts, as they have been presented to you, and probably by several people, because the likelihood that only one person is telling lies is low. This adds to the difficulty when you are assessing a large number of things that have been said, and sorting out the truth from the lies, and the reliable from the unreliable. If you are naïve, as most genuine Christians are, then recognising that some of the things you are being told could be lies, may make you feel uncomfortable. Nevertheless, it is a necessary assumption to make if you want to be a good decision-maker.

You can't make accurate decisions if even part of what you believe is untrue. The answer, therefore, is to begin, as a matter of general routine, to check, double-check, and even triple-check, at least some of the things that you are told. You will then find, distressingly often, that things which you had fully assumed to be true are not true at all, and that people you had trusted are not actually trustworthy. You must then act upon those unpleasant discoveries and adjust your assessments of people's claims and allegations and also of their characters.

Also, change your view of the reliability of anything else they may have said in the past, or that they might say in the future. Moreover, it is wise to let it be publicly known that you routinely check things, and that you don't just rely on what you are told. Saying that openly will act as a disincentive, at least to some people, to tell you lies. Please refer to my Book 6 in which I go into a lot of detail about dealing with deception and deceivers and how you can tell when, and by whom, you are being lied to.

Seek to increase the level of your discernment and also ask God to give you the gift of discerning or distinguishing of spirits

I deal with discernment in Book 6. I also deal with the gift of distinguishing between spirits in Book 1, in the chapter on the baptism in the Holy Spirit. Please refer to both of those for more detail. When making decisions we need the ability to work out who is telling the truth and who is not. Therefore, we absolutely must develop the skill of identifying lies and liars, and working out who and what can be trusted. The gift of distinguishing between spirits is different from ordinary discernment. It is one of the *'spiritual gifts'* which apostle Paul lists in 1 Corinthians chapter 12:

to another the working of miracles, to another prophecy, to another the ability to distinguish between spirits, to another various kinds of tongues, to another the interpretation of tongues.

1 Corinthians 12:10 (ESV)

These spiritual gifts are supernatural and, therefore, do not depend on our minds, or our experience, or on learning how people operate. The knowledge is given to us, by the Holy Spirit, and enables us to identify the source of a statement or proposal, i.e. whether it comes from God, or the person, or a demon. This takes us way beyond our own discernment, which we have developed from experience, because the Holy Spirit points us directly to the answer.

Be willing to revisit and reassess your past decisions and judgments, especially if the facts or circumstances alter

If you have made a decision in the past, it must not now be treated as something cast in stone, which can never be questioned or revisited. You should always be open-minded to see whether you still believe what you were told and whether you still think you made the right decision. Be willing to question anything and anybody, even if it was decided long ago and has already been acted upon. Never assume that every past decision or conclusion is reliable.

If you make that assumption you will be slow to spot patterns of deception which may still be affecting your decisions now. I have often reviewed decisions long afterwards, when I have belatedly come to doubt what I believed at the time. Sometimes it was because new evidence arose which called into question that which I had previously relied upon. Unless you are willing to do this you will make it much harder for yourself to correct your past misjudgements. But it isn't only about exposing past lies.

This approach is also necessary where the balance of the evidence begins to alter, as new facts emerge which you had not previously taken into account or which you had under-emphasised. If you regard your own past decisions and judgments as immoveable and unchangeable you put a needless constraint upon yourself. You cannot afford to do that if you want to make reliable decisions now. Therefore, always be willing to question what you have been told in the past, and to reassess the judgments which you have previously formed.

It is very hard to find genuinely good advice and especially mentoring

Advice is particularly important when making a major decision. We need to be willing to listen to advice which is given to us unsolicited, but also to go out and positively ask for it. Of course, it entirely depends on *who* is giving the advice. Not all people are wise, and not all viewpoints are worthy of respect. The reality is that many people, even if they are neither wicked, nor fools, but only simple, have just got nothing worthwhile to say. They aren't equipped to advise you and have nothing to offer, except perhaps factual information, but that is evidence, not advice, and falls into a different category.

What they say has to be assessed on the basis of whether to *believe* it at all, not whether to *respect* it. You should be willing to hear the *evidence* of any person, however small or fragmentary their knowledge may be, provided you firstly weigh it and assess its reliability. But that is very different from being willing to take their *advice*. Accordingly, it is sensible, whenever you are being spoken to on a matter of any importance, to ask yourself the following questions:

a) Is what is being said merely information, or does it go beyond that and amount to advice?

b) Is the information, true and how much reliance can safely be placed upon it?

c) If the person is offering advice, are they generally wise, at least to some extent, or in some area, such that what they have to say is likely to be of value?

d) Even if they are not wise, and even if their advice would not generally be valuable, have they, *on this occasion*, said something which has merit?

If you aren't regularly asking yourself such questions, you are not likely to be effective in weighing up the things that people tell you. People are not all the same and neither is the reliability of their evidence or the quality of their advice. That said, the value of a person's advice, or of their evidence, does not come from whether they agree with you, or even like you. If they are people of substance and merit, their words should be listened to, though not necessarily acted upon, even if they don't support you.

Indeed, if you are facing a significant problem or decision, go out of your way to obtain the perspective of those who are known to disagree with you. If you only ever listen to those who agree with you, or think along similar lines, you will merely reinforce your own existing views. Therefore, deliberately take steps to have your beliefs tested by exposure to contrary views. Have the confidence, and the humility, to listen to those who disagree with you, or even oppose you, and find out if they have seen any angles which you have not noticed.

Or they may have access to information from other people, who might never be willing to speak to you, for the very reason that they know you disagree with them. Accordingly, don't merely wait passively for unsolicited advice or information to be offered to you. People know that advice is often not well received, and that insecure people tend to 'shoot the messenger', so they won't offer any comment until they are asked to. Therefore, make sure that at least some of the input that you get is from people who don't agree with you, or who have a different perspective, even if they are not opposed to you.

That doesn't mean that you should accept any of their advice, or act upon it, any more than you should with those who agree with you. But you should at least listen, especially to people of experience and merit. Let what they say become part of the overall package of information upon which you base your decision. The problem is that silly advice from silly people is always available, but honest, competent advice, from wise people, who know what they are talking about, is very hard to find. Therefore, very often, you simply can't get good advice, even if you are eager to listen.

That has been my problem for many years. I have often desperately wanted advice, but could not find any, or at least not wise advice from wise people, because they are so rare. Something which is even harder to find is a really capable and faithful *mentor*. For 30 of the past 36 years since I was converted, I have not been able to find anybody whom I could go to with really thorny problems and get sound advice. There was a three-year period when I was the Chairman of our Conservative Association, during which I had an outstanding man to whom I could turn.

However, apart from that period, and also my first three years as a new believer, I have always had to make my own way, without any mentor at all. I think that is the norm. Therefore, any competent mentoring that you can get should be seized with both hands because you are not likely to have it for long. I don't think God wants it to be that way, but there just aren't enough wise people around, who would be of any use to you as a mentor. Therefore, God often has to disciple us directly, without any human mentor, because there are simply none to be found in your church, workplace or family.

When making a big decision, write out all the pros and cons and the issues which concern you. By the end, the right answer will often be staring you in the face.

There is a technique which I have found useful when making a big decision, involving multiple issues which may contradict each other or point in different directions. One can feel bewildered by the scale and complexity of the problem

504

and find it difficult to hold all the facts and issues, and the various pros and cons, in one's head simultaneously, or to assess them as a whole. Most of us can only think of one thing at a time so, if there are several issues and complications to face simultaneously, it can be overwhelming.

You may find yourself unable to see the whole picture, especially if it involves legal, moral, theological, political, commercial and personal issues all at the same time. I find it helpful to write down all the facts and issues and all my fears and unanswered questions in two vertical columns, with all those facts which point in one direction on the left, and those which point in the other direction on the right. Usually there will only be two options, i.e. should I or shouldn't I, or is it or isn't it? However, there could be three or more options available. If so, make one list for each option.

When you then look at the columns in the end, you will usually find that the right answer is staring you in the face. One list will either be much longer than the other or it will contain much more serious or important points, either in its favour, or against the alternative. Beforehand you might have had 20 or more pros and cons, plus miscellaneous issues, anxieties or questions, all swirling around in your mind, like flies buzzing around a room. But you could not get a sense of their relative significance, or how they fitted together.

But now, with them all written down in columns, alongside each other, and perhaps with asterisks by the more important ones, you might see that there are 17 points in favour of the proposed action, 10 of which are major, and only three points against it, perhaps none of which are major. So it may be that the obviously right answer is to go ahead. Yet that may have been very far from obvious prior to that point. It will not always be so one-sided. There will sometimes be situations where it is more finely balanced.

However, when I have done this, one side has usually come out clearly on top, by a substantial margin. Then I was no longer confused or unsure. But it isn't only a matter of seeing which side of the argument has more, or bigger, or better, points for it or against it. The very process itself of writing down every relevant fact, issue, question or concern, and deciding how important it is, and whether it supports or opposes the proposal, helps you in clarifying your thinking and making sense of a swirling mass of information.

Also write down exactly what you are afraid of and why. The fear will often disappear or shrink when you do so. Or it will be exposed as imaginary or false.

Sometimes making a decision is harder due to things you fear which prevent you from thinking through the issues, or being able to think at all. You may be 'caught in the headlights' and just sit back, paralysed into indecision and inactivity. Some of those fears may not be clearly defined but are just vague, nagging worries, many of which are not even real, let alone likely to happen. However, even if they are both real and likely to happen, you still should not make any decisions based on what you *fear*. It is neither healthy nor appropriate.

All decisions should be based on a consideration of the facts and issues, your duties, what is right and wrong, what is wise and unwise, and on what makes logical sense. What you are afraid of is of no relevance, or it should not be. Thus any such fears need to be identified and must not be allowed to play any part in your decision. But the problem is that fears can be hard to pin down or identify. Your mind might be influenced by one big fear, or a number of separate fears, without feeling able to specify exactly what they are.

At such times, use a variation of the same list-making technique. Force yourself to write down exactly what it is that you fear might happen, or might be done to you, if you were to go ahead with the thing you are contemplating. As you see these things written down and clearly defined, in plain English, as opposed to floating vaguely in the air like phantoms, you will find that the fear shrinks. It is exposed on the page, rather than being allowed to carry on as an undefined anxiety. The fears no longer seem so significant, or as likely, to happen, as they did when they were free to swirl around in your head, unidentified and undefined.

Now that you see them there, exposed on paper as the self-aggrandising imposters that they are, you can strike a line through them, quite literally, and exclude them from further consideration. Imagine you were considering changing the way things are done in your company to increase output or efficiency and you are anxious as to what 'Fred', one of your senior employees, might do if you were to go ahead with this. You know he feels threatened by the proposal, and that he might react badly. Alongside all the other pros and cons you could literally write down:

"I am afraid that Fred might get upset and may get angry, cause a confrontation, or even resign".

Until you write it down, and see it on the page in black and white, that vague, unspoken worry buzzes around in your mind. It prevents you from feeling any peace and distracts you from focussing on all the real issues in order to evaluate

506

the commercial case for and against the proposal. But when you see those words written there, with your fear clearly defined and staring at you, the errors in your thinking suddenly become clear. For the first time, you may be able to say to yourself:

a) *Whether or not Fred gets upset is entirely a matter for him, not me. If he does, it will be up to him to get over it.*

b) *If, nevertheless, Fred does get upset, and does not deal with it, then I will deal with him and tell him to calm down. But I won't let him trouble me.*

c) *If he doesn't calm down, then I will deal with him more firmly.*

d) *If he causes a confrontation, then so be it. I will deal with him even more firmly. But I will still not allow that prospect to influence me.*

e) *If Fred resigns that is, again, entirely a matter for him and I will not seek to dissuade him from doing so. At any rate, whether he stays or goes has no bearing on what I now decide to do for the good of this office/shop/factory, and I will not allow his potential response to influence my decision.*

You might think I am over-stating the position or setting the bar impossibly high by saying that you must not allow fear to influence any of your decisions. Or it may be that you simply aren't capable of getting rid of the fear and you still feel it. In other words, you may say that policy is unrealistic as it requires more self-control than you currently have. If so, then at least work towards that level. Do the best you can, for now, to face your fears. Refuse to yield to them, and don't allow them to have any 'vote' when you are making decisions, even if you are still afraid.

That is you need to resolve that you aren't going to listen to those fears, even if they don't go away. Whether you are currently able to achieve it or not, this is still the right approach and is what you should aspire to. Therefore at least attempt it, even if you don't fully succeed. Your fears are used by other people, and also by the demons, to exert pressure over you. They want you to do what you should not do, and to fail to do what you ought to do, by using your fears to paralyse you into passivity and delay. You must not let any of that be done to you. Therefore, "*take every thought captive*" as Paul says.

That means you decide which thoughts you will let yourself have, or at least which thoughts you will allow yourself to *act upon*. Make it a clear policy that your fears won't get any say from now on in your decision-making. Also put them in writing to make it easier to identify and exclude them. That does not mean that you cannot take any steps to avoid or reduce some hazard which might occur. You do not have to expose yourself to danger, or even unpleasantness, provided the

507

steps you take to avoid those things do not involve any failure to do your duty, or to listen to your conscience, or to obey God, or to do your job as you are meant to.

We are under no duty to expose ourselves needlessly to danger or trouble. It is just that we must not act wrongly or sinfully in order to avoid them. Neither must we allow ourselves to be manipulated, controlled or dominated by any person, or by a demon, as the price for avoiding what we fear. That is wrong in itself, and also a breach of our duty. It is also too high a price to pay for the easing of your fears. Besides that, if you give in to your fears on this occasion, the people or demons who are behind it will quickly see that and take note.

Then they will inevitably be back, again and again, like a blackmailer who has been paid something. They will then use the same levers to control you again in future. Therefore, never submit to, or cooperate with, any such tactics. You may as well refuse now, have the confrontation, and get it over and done with today. If you don't, it will only have to be done later, unless you want to spend your whole life being controlled by other people, or by demons, using the leverage that is given to them by your fears.

Never be afraid of being wrong or of being blamed. At least don't let such fears paralyse you, even if you can't yet entirely overcome them.

A common fear is of making a wrong decision, or of being blamed or criticised if things go badly. As a result, many people find the very process of decision-making stressful and intimidating. They will often refrain from making any decision at all, or delay it up to and beyond the last minute, because they fear the disapproval of others. But that is to make yourself the prisoner of other men's opinions, such that you cannot act freely, simply because of what they might say about you, or even privately think of you.

How tragic would that be? Yet that is precisely what millions of people do, getting themselves trapped in the 'snare' of the fear of man, such that they live as slaves, not as free men. As with any other fear, the fear of making decisions needs to be faced up to and overcome. The only alternative is to submit to it for the rest of your life. Ironically, if you do, you will become known as an *indecisive* person.

But they are even more despised than someone who makes *wrong* decisions. It would be doubly sad, therefore, to get a reputation for being indecisive, and thus be viewed with contempt by your colleagues or staff, all because you didn't want to be disapproved of for making wrong decisions. You would be losing a pound and gaining a penny. If this applies to you, then engage in a much more

508

wholesome and constructive conversation with yourself, perhaps along these lines:

a) *"If I get this decision wrong, or if people think that I have, and therefore disapprove of me, then so be it. They are entitled to their opinions."*

b) *"But, whether or not there is the potential for some people to disapprove of me, I will not let that prospect influence me in any way in the decision that I now face."*

c) *"In any case, they would disapprove of me even more, and rightly so, if I misguidedly delayed making a decision, or didn't make one at all, just to pander to other people's opinions."*

d) *"I have both the duty and the right to make a decision now, to the best of my ability. Therefore, I am going to make my decision, as soon as I am ready, without any regard for what others may think of me."*

e) *"That way, whoever does or does not approve of me, I will at least approve of myself. More to the point, God will approve of me for not allowing myself to be ensnared by the fear of man."*

f) *"Moreover, whether I get it right or not, I will at least, for what it's worth, be approved of by some people, for being a decisive person."*

g) *"In any case, even if I get this particular decision wrong, I will learn from the mistake and, in the longer term, become a better decision-maker as a result. Thus, even my errors have the potential to help me to grow."*

The worst decision of all is to make no decision.

Therefore, however good or bad your decisions may be, don't make the far greater mistake of allowing yourself to become an indecisive person. The worst decision of all is to make *no decision*. By the way, we need to be clear that not making a decision *is a decision*, and it is almost always a bad one. It is a decision not to decide anything, or not to do so yet. That in itself is a decision, and *usually the wrong one*, because it is rare for the right course of action to be to keep on postponing making your mind up and taking action.

At any rate, it would never be right if the reason for doing so is fear of what people might think of you, or fear of anything else. It can, however, be entirely right to postpone the making of a decision, *provided* your reason for the delay is genuinely because you don't yet have sufficient facts to make the decision. It may be that you are seeking that information as quickly as is reasonably practicable. If, *and*

509

only if, that is truly the case, then fair enough. Your delay in making a decision would then be prudence, not cowardice.

Indeed, in the right circumstances, the willingness to delay making a decision may even be a sign of courage, and also of diligence. It may prove that you are not willing to be rushed into a premature decision just to appease others who are clamouring for an answer. But if that is not your real reason, and it is actually just an excuse to hide your real motive, which is the fear of getting it wrong and being blamed, then we would be back where we started. That reason for delay would be wrong and even disgraceful.

Bear in mind that, in most workplaces, the managers who are the most despised and resented are not those who are brave enough to have a go, but get it wrong. It is those who won't make any decision at all and leave you waiting for weeks or months while they stew around getting nowhere, forlornly hoping the problem will solve itself, without the need for any decision. If your reputation is of concern to you, then that is the reputation that you most need to avoid, and it is well worth making some wrong decisions along the way in order to avoid it.

CHAPTER 14

WISE PEOPLE REALISE THE HUGE IMPORTANCE OF MARRIAGE

To the woman he said,
"I will surely multiply your pain in childbearing;
in pain you shall bring forth children.
Your desire shall be contrary to your husband,
but he shall rule over you."

Genesis 3:16 (ESV)

Let marriage be held in honor among all, and let the marriage bed be undefiled, for God will judge the sexually immoral and adulterous.

Hebrews 13:4 (ESV)

[18] Wives, submit to your husbands, as is fitting in the Lord. [19] Husbands, love your wives, and do not be harsh with them.

Colossians 3:18-19 (ESV)

[1] Likewise, wives, be subject to your own husbands, so that even if some do not obey the word, they may be won without a word by the conduct of their wives, [2] when they see your respectful and pure conduct. [3] Do not let your adorning be external—the braiding of hair and the putting on of gold jewelry, or the clothing you wear— [4] but let your adorning be the hidden person of the heart with the imperishable beauty of a gentle and quiet spirit, which in God's sight is very precious. [5] For this is how the holy women who hoped in God used to adorn themselves, by submitting to their own husbands, [6] as Sarah obeyed Abraham, calling him lord. And you are her children, if you do good and do not fear anything that is frightening.
[7] Likewise, husbands, live with your wives in an understanding way, showing honor to the woman as the weaker vessel, since they are heirs with you of the grace of life, so that your prayers may not be hindered.

1 Peter 3:1-7 (ESV)

A wise person is extremely careful about whom they marry. They go to great lengths to find a godly husband or wife.

After your decision to repent, believe and follow Jesus Christ, choosing the right husband or wife is by far the biggest decision of your life. The consequences that flow from choosing the right person, or the wrong one, are absolutely crucial and their importance would be difficult to overstate. Your spouse can make your life either a joy or a misery and cause you to become either a success or a failure in your career, your ministry and your walk as a disciple. Thus, it is essential that you choose wisely and that you do not base your decision solely on their looks but on their character as well:

Like a gold ring in a pig's snout
is a beautiful woman without discretion.
Proverbs 11:22 (ESV)

Therefore, before you consider marrying anyone, and preferably for many years before you even meet them, you should be praying for God to guide you towards the right person. Also ask Him to guide you *away from* everyone else, i.e. all those who would *not* be His choice for you. Likewise, parents should pray for their children to meet and marry the right person, and to avoid the wrong ones.

You can begin to pray for your children in that way from the very earliest time, ideally from before they are even born, not just when they become adults. What is more, you can also be praying for your children's *future spouses*. Ask in the same way for them to be blessed, protected and helped to develop into a strong Christian. You can, likewise, begin to do this long before you know who they are.

That way, even while their identities are unknown, you can be supporting that future spouse in prayer, all through their own childhood, teens and early adulthood. Look at some of the things which God says about the vital importance of finding the right wife, but note that the same applies to a woman's need to find the right husband, because that is just as crucial:

An excellent wife is the crown of her husband,
but she who brings shame is like rottenness in his bones.
Proverbs 12:4 (ESV)

He who finds a wife finds a good thing
and obtains favor from the LORD.
Proverbs 18:22 (ESV)

House and wealth are inherited from fathers,
but a prudent wife is from the LORD.
Proverbs 19:14 (ESV)

It is better to live in a corner of the housetop
than in a house shared with a quarrelsome wife.
Proverbs 21:9 (ESV)

*Better is a dinner of herbs where love is
than a fattened ox and hatred with it.*
Proverbs 15:17 (ESV)

*Better is a dry morsel with quiet
than a house full of feasting with strife.*
Proverbs 17:1 (ESV)

The first criterion in selecting a husband or wife is that they absolutely must be a Christian, *and a real one.* That is they must be genuinely born again and walking as a sincere and committed disciple, not just a nominal 'churchgoer', or someone who merely believes that God exists. Even the Devil himself believes that, but he would not make a great husband!

Paul makes it clear that it is vital to avoid marrying an unsaved person because, whatever other qualities they may have, they will never share your values, beliefs or priorities. Neither will they be with you in eternity, as they will be separated from you forever and go to the Lake of Fire, unless they later repent. However, you cannot assume that they will do that.

Even the Bible itself, let alone the *'Great Commission'* of making disciples, will mean nothing to them. Therefore, they won't cooperate with what God wants you to do, or be willing to walk on the same *narrow path* that you must spend your life walking on. More to the point, they will make it far harder *for you to do so.* An unsaved spouse will inevitably make your life a misery, render you ineffectual as a disciple, and even cause you to fall away completely. Indeed, such total apostasy often happens, which is one reason why Paul instructs us not to marry an unbeliever:

[14] Do not be unequally yoked with unbelievers. For what partnership has righteousness with lawlessness? Or what fellowship has light with darkness? [15] What accord has Christ with Belial? Or what portion does a believer share with an unbeliever?
2 Corinthians 6:14-15 (ESV)

Despite what Paul said, many people persuade themselves that they are somehow an exception to the rule and that it would be alright for *them* to have a non-Christian boyfriend or girlfriend. They might even try to justify it on the basis that they will be better able to *"witness to them"*, as if dating was a form of evangelism. It most certainly isn't, and should never be viewed as such, regardless of how anxious you might feel about finding a spouse, and no matter how much you have convinced yourself that they are the right one for you.

513

If you are convinced that God wants you to go out with a non-Christian so that you can lead them to Christ, then the simple fact is that you are deluding yourself. This self-deception tends to affect women, more so than men. They can become desperate, not least because the churches now contain a lot more women than men, especially in the younger age groups. It is also because finding a spouse occupies the average women's thoughts far more than with the average young man, partly due to the 'biological clock' which puts a time limit on them having children, but also because a woman's heart has been made by God with a deep longing for romantic love.

However, just as God doesn't want you to marry a non-Christian, He doesn't want you to go out with one either. This is hard to accept, especially for women, who now greatly outnumber men in the churches, but it is absolutely essential to wait until you meet a genuine Christian. He or she need not necessarily be a mature disciple when you first meet them. Indeed, it would be almost impossible for them to be such, especially as they are likely to be young. However, they would need to have become at least reasonably mature before you agree to marry them.

As an absolute minimum, they need to be clearly on an upward 'flight path', such that you know they are maturing, growing as a disciple, studying their Bible and actively involved in church. In short, they need to take Christianity seriously, have a genuine faith, and not be a mere *'churchgoer'*. That makes things very difficult today because so few people go to church at all. Even of those that do, a high percentage are just nominal Christians, not real ones, and they have no serious commitment to Jesus Christ. Indeed, many are largely indistinguishable from the unsaved world.

However, no matter how difficult it is to find a genuine Christian to marry, you still need to hold out for the real thing. Never allow yourself to compromise by settling for a non-Christian, or even a nominal Christian. I can categorically assure you that you would be far better off, and much happier, remaining single, *even for your whole life*, than if you were to marry anyone who is not a genuine and committed Christian, no matter how nice he or she might be. Being *nice* is not the issue. It is about whether they are *saved* and walking as a *genuine disciple*.

Therefore, to be able to choose the right person, you need to be willing, if need be, to remain single forever. If you find the prospect of permanent singleness so appalling that you rule it out as an option, then you are extremely likely to end up compromising. If so, then you would be headed for disaster, not only in your marriage, but in your entire walk as a disciple. It really is that serious. In fact, it would be difficult to over-state the seriousness of this warning.

What if two unbelievers live together, and even have children, but then one of them becomes a Christian?

Let me now deal with a situation which can also arise whereby a couple were both unbelievers when they got married, or when they began to live together as man and wife, even if they weren't officially married, but then one of them becomes a Christian. What should the saved spouse do in that situation? Apostle Paul gives us the answer which is that, provided the unbelieving spouse is willing, then the believing spouse should stay with them and should not leave or divorce their unbelieving spouse:

[10] To the married I give charge, not I but the Lord, that the wife should not separate from her husband [11] (but if she does, let her remain single or else be reconciled to her husband)—and that the husband should not divorce his wife.

[12] To the rest I say, not the Lord, that if any brother has a wife who is an unbeliever, and she consents to live with him, he should not divorce her. [13] If any woman has a husband who is an unbeliever, and he consents to live with her, she should not divorce him. [14] For the unbelieving husband is consecrated through his wife, and the unbelieving wife is consecrated through her husband. Otherwise, your children would be unclean, but as it is they are holy. [15] But if the unbelieving partner desires to separate, let it be so; in such a case the brother or sister is not bound. For God has called us to peace.

1 Corinthians 7:10-15 (RSV)

A situation exactly like this arose recently for me where a woman asked for my advice. She had been living with a man for 30 years and had had two children by him. However, they had never officially got married, in the eyes of the State, with an official wedding ceremony. The woman then became a believer and wanted to have a wedding ceremony so that she could be officially married. However, a particular leader then told her that she should not do this, on the basis that it would amount to her becoming "unequally yoked with an unbeliever".

In fact, the leader went further than that and urged her to leave the man. The prospect of doing that appalled her, even though her common law 'husband' was not a Christian. It was at this point that she emailed me, via my website, seeking advice as to what to do and whether this leader was right in urging her to leave her children's father. I responded by telling her about apostle Paul's advice in 1 Corinthians 7:10-15, as set out above, and said that she should *not* leave him, provided that he was willing to stay with her, which he was.

I also said that the leader in question was making a further mistake in that they were wrongly assuming that she was not married in God's eyes, solely on the basis

515

that she had never had a *wedding ceremony*. I told her that although an official wedding ceremony, where vows are publicly given and received, is entirely appropriate and should be done, their failure to do that during the last 30 years did not mean that they were unmarried, at least not in their case.

I explained that although the official wedding ceremony is very important, and very beneficial, it is not the decisive factor in determining whether a couple are married in God's eyes. What really counts is the sexual act, or the 'act of marriage', whereby the man and woman are joined and become "one flesh". So, having been living as man and wife for 30 years, and having raised a family, God plainly viewed them as a married couple and so Paul's words applied to them, such that she should not leave the man who was, for all intents and purposes, her husband.

I therefore urged her, far from leaving him, to go ahead and have the very belated wedding ceremony which they both wanted but which the leader wrongly believed was forbidden by virtue of Paul's words about being 'unequally yoked'. The point is that those words apply in the case of a man and woman who are *not already married* in God's eyes in the sense described above. Paul's command therefore did not apply to her and so she should act as a *Christian wife* should act where she *already* has a non-Christian husband, rather than as a *single woman* should act who is only contemplating a *future* marriage to an unbeliever.

However, having said all that about the huge significance of the sexual act as being the 'act of marriage', I do not want to alarm or condemn those who have had a sexually sinful past, with one of more sexual partners, possibly a long list, prior to meeting their spouse. If that is your situation then, although it will have produced problems and complications, which may still persist even decades later, I believe you should stay with the man or woman that you are now married to.

In other words, although you may have been sexually joined to others in the past, which is highly regrettable, God can and will forgive and resolve such 'messy' situations. He can wash you *"white as snow"*, and cause all of your past sins, including sexual sins, to be cast into the sea and to be removed from you *"as far as the east is from the west"*. Therefore, the last thing that I want to do is to put anybody on a 'guilt trip', as they say. We are all sinners, with a lot to repent of and recover from, even if we differ in the precise sins or types of sins that we have committed. Even so, the fact remains that past sexual relationships can cause very real problems, including demonic problems, and I examine those issues more fully in my Books 7 and 9.

Lastly, and for the avoidance of doubt, if there is anybody reading this who, for medical or other reasons is unable to consummate their marriage, I am *not* saying that they are not married in God's eyes. Of course they are. God is not only highly

516

merciful and gracious, but also realistic and practical. So, if due to illness or injury that is your position, have no doubt that you are validly married.

The qualities which men need to look for in a wife

As well as being a genuine believer, we see in Proverbs chapter 31 the many other qualities which an excellent wife has, and which we should look for when deciding whom to marry. The woman of Proverbs 31 is godly, unselfish, virtuous, faithful, truthful, trustworthy, kind, industrious, respectful, God-fearing, caring, wise, enterprising, strong and dignified. She also gets involved in all sorts of useful and wholesome activities whilst, at the same time, honouring her husband and being submissive towards him:

10 An excellent wife who can find?
She is far more precious than jewels.
11 The heart of her husband trusts in her,
and he will have no lack of gain.
12 She does him good, and not harm,
all the days of her life.
13 She seeks wool and flax,
and works with willing hands.
14 She is like the ships of the merchant;
she brings her food from afar.
15 She rises while it is yet night
and provides food for her household
and portions for her maidens.
16 She considers a field and buys it;
with the fruit of her hands she plants a vineyard.
17 She dresses herself with strength
and makes her arms strong.
18 She perceives that her merchandise is profitable.
Her lamp does not go out at night.
19 She puts her hands to the distaff,
and her hands hold the spindle.
20 She opens her hand to the poor
and reaches out her hands to the needy.
21 She is not afraid of snow for her household,
for all her household are clothed in scarlet.
22 She makes bed coverings for herself;
her clothing is fine linen and purple.
23 Her husband is known in the gates
when he sits among the elders of the land.
24 She makes linen garments and sells them;

she delivers sashes to the merchant.
25 Strength and dignity are her clothing,
and she laughs at the time to come.
26 She opens her mouth with wisdom,
and the teaching of kindness is on her tongue.
27 She looks well to the ways of her household
and does not eat the bread of idleness.
28 Her children rise up and call her blessed;
her husband also, and he praises her:
29 "Many women have done excellently,
but you surpass them all."
30 Charm is deceitful, and beauty is vain,
but a woman who fears the LORD is to be praised.
31 Give her of the fruit of her hands,
and let her works praise her in the gates.

Proverbs 31:10-31 (ESV)

The qualities a woman needs to look for in husband

The same points apply equally to choosing a husband. He too must be faithful, godly, true, hardworking, kind, caring, loyal, trustworthy, wise, strong, brave etc. However, in addition to all that, he must also be willing to *take the lead* in discipling and pastoring his family and in teaching them about God's commands. That is because, in God's eyes, both within the marriage and the family, the husband is the spiritual head. He will therefore be held accountable for the way his wife and children turn out.

Therefore, for the avoidance of doubt, the husband comes ahead of the pastor of the church, or even of its elders, if it is organised on more biblical lines. Those men have some authority within the church, but they have zero authority over the wife or the children. In those areas the husband is the leader, not them. I need to point that out because, especially in dysfunctional and abusive churches, the opposite is often taught by controlling and manipulative leaders.

So, wherever there is a dispute or difference of view between the leaders of a church and a woman's own husband, she should follow her husband, not them. The only exception to that would be if the husband was doing or saying something which is plainly sinful, or which clearly contradicts the Bible. Then she must follow her conscience. At any rate, this is what a Christian husband should do in his own walk as a disciple, and in the spiritual upbringing of his children, which he must take very seriously:

518

"Only take care, and keep your soul diligently, lest you forget the things that your eyes have seen, and lest they depart from your heart all the days of your life. Make them known to your children and your children's children—
Deuteronomy 4:9 (ESV)

Let us now look briefly at what the Bible has to say about what a good man is like, what he does, and how to identify him. Focusing carefully on such things will help you to see which men are likely to make good husbands and which are not. Consider these passages which describe a faithful, godly, wise and righteous man. Then *look* for such a man for yourself. Or, if you are already married, then help your husband to *become* such a man, by your ongoing prayer, encouragement and support, not just for a day or a week, but throughout your entire marriage, and also the courtship which precedes it:

Many a man proclaims his own steadfast love,
but a faithful man who can find?
Proverbs 20:6 (ESV)

Better to be lowly and have a servant
than to play the great man and lack bread.
Proverbs 12:9 (ESV)

[1] Blessed is the man
who walks not in the counsel of the wicked,
nor stands in the way of sinners,
nor sits in the seat of scoffers;
[2] but his delight is in the law of the LORD,
and on his law he meditates day and night.
[3] He is like a tree
planted by streams of water
that yields its fruit in its season,
and its leaf does not wither.
In all that he does, he prospers.
[4] The wicked are not so,
but are like chaff that the wind drives away.
[5] Therefore the wicked will not stand in the judgment,
nor sinners in the congregation of the righteous;
[6] for the LORD knows the way of the righteous,
but the way of the wicked will perish.
Psalm 1:1-6 (ESV)

[7] "Blessed is the man who trusts in the LORD,
whose trust is the LORD.

519

8 He is like a tree planted by water,
* that sends out its roots by the stream,*
and does not fear when heat comes,
* for its leaves remain green,*
and is not anxious in the year of drought,
* for it does not cease to bear fruit."*
*   Jeremiah 17:7-8 (ESV)*

My own story of how I met, courted and married my wife.

I have emphasised the need to pray to find the right husband or wife and to carefully consider their character and lifestyle to assess whether they are godly enough for you to marry. However, I absolutely do *not* want to imply that romance and physical attraction play no part in choosing whom to marry. They certainly do, and they are *meant to*. God Himself 'invented' romance and He fully intends for it to be one of the things, *but not the only thing*, which guides us to the right person to marry.

It might assist if I tell my own story of how I came to meet my wife and how we ended up getting married. All of these ingredients that I speak of were involved, including physical and romantic attraction. I first met her when I was 19. I was then a brand new believer, only four months saved, and she was aged 18. We met at a prayer meeting. Some may not see that as an obvious place to find a wife but, actually, churches are by far the best place to be looking.

That is where Christians are most likely to congregate and to be in sufficiently large numbers to substantially increase the likelihood of you meeting single people of the right age and, above all, who are genuine believers. Thus you maximise your chances by looking there, rather than at work or school or, even worse, in pubs or nightclubs. Those last two are the worst possible places to seek to meet someone.

Things took an extremely unusual turn in that prayer meeting. As I sat opposite her, I heard a voice, which was audible only to me, saying "*That's the person you are going to marry.*" This was only the second time, up to then, that anything like that had ever happened to me, though it has happened a handful of times since then. I was startled and bewildered and didn't know what to make of it, or what to do about it. So, quite sensibly, I did nothing at all.

I just 'parked' it, and remembered it, but took no action. I didn't see her again until several weeks later, when we met at a weekend retreat conference. That was when I spoke to her for the first time. We had not spoken to each other at the prayer meeting, as there had been no opportunity, or reason, to do so. Then two more years passed, during which we gradually got to know each other better, albeit at something of a distance. However, we did not go out together, even though my interest in her, and my attraction to her, steadily grew.

The first time we ever went out socially, although we still weren't yet 'going out' together, was when we went to a theatre with a group of other students. We sat next to each other there for the first time. When we did, our hands accidentally touched, very briefly, and it was as if I had received an electric shock. I then suddenly realised how strongly I felt for her. She later told me that she had felt the same way and had had the very same 'electric shock' when our fingers touched. So, by this stage, I had:

a) received a direct word from God which, I hasten to add, is *very unusual*, and cannot ordinarily be expected to happen. Neither should it ever be relied upon *by itself*, in the absence of all the other necessary factors.

b) got to know her gradually, within a church context, and in the presence of others, for nearly two years, during which I had formed a high opinion of her character and godliness.

c) realised that I felt a strong romantic and physical attraction to her or, in other words, that I had fallen in love with her.

By this stage I felt very serious about her, so I spoke to the leader of the student ministry that we were then part of and asked his advice about what to do and what he thought about her. My question came as no surprise to him. He had already noticed how interested I was in her and how I took every opportunity at meetings to talk to her and, in particular, to tease her. I had been doing all these things to such an extent that it was obvious to others how I felt, even though I had never asked her out.

His advice to me was that she was a young woman of real worth and godliness and seemed very suitable for me. Even so, he advised me to proceed slowly and carefully. At this stage I did not entirely take his advice, or I did so only for a short time, because I then asked her out and began what I would call '*courtship*', rather than dating. I say that because we did not even start to 'go out' together until we were both serious about each other and saw marriage as a distinct possibility.

I told her that I loved her, and that I felt I would like to marry her. She said she loved me too, but she was rather startled by the mention of marriage at that early stage. So I began to court her, albeit seeing her only intermittently, because I then graduated and got a job elsewhere, whereas she remained a student for two more years. Then, after 12 months of courtship, we got engaged and, a year after that, we got married, the very week after she graduated.

That is what happened to us, but I am *not* saying it is typical, or that everyone should do the same as we did. Nevertheless, our story illustrates how one can go about finding and choosing a spouse, and it includes all of the different factors which are involved in making that vital decision. That process includes praying for guidance, assessing their character, taking advice, and getting to know them over a sufficiently long period of time, rather than rushing into it hastily.

Last but not least, it also involves seeing whether there is a real, and mutual, *romantic and physical* attraction. I want to emphasise those last two points because, although the world wrongly views them as the *only* criteria to go by, we must not make the opposite mistake of thinking that they don't count at all. They absolutely do count. It is just that they aren't the only things to go by when looking for a spouse.

A wise person is faithful to their future husband or wife, even before they ever meet them, and abstains from all sexual activity until their wedding night.

We dealt earlier, in chapter 8, with the issue of sexual sin, both before and outside of marriage, and the terrible damage it does. The fact that sex is a gift which God has *only* given to married couples, and only *after* they are married, used to be widely accepted, even amongst non-Christians. It was a part of Western culture, due to our strong Christian heritage. Now, it is not even widely accepted within churches, let alone secular society, due to the spread of worldliness and apostasy. Tragically, therefore, many married couples, even in churches, have already been sexually active beforehand.

Very often this sin was committed not only with their future spouse, but with others too, sometimes many others. One of the reasons for this is that the vital importance of total faithfulness during marriage, and complete abstinence beforehand, is not being taught in our churches today. Many leaders feel they have lost the 'culture war' and see no chance of persuading their congregations, especially the younger ones, to live by God's standards and to reject the world's. So they just give up and don't even try.

Other leaders are afraid of criticism and controversy, or they fear that people would leave their church, if they were to teach faithfully what the Bible says. So those leaders don't bother either, out of sheer cowardice. Therefore, most leaders today either compromise in what they teach, or they say nothing at all. They then abdicate their responsibility and let people find their own way which, unsurprisingly, is usually the world's way. This is a crucial issue, not only in terms of disobedience to God, but also in the damage caused to marriages, families, churches and communities by marital unfaithfulness.

Therefore leaders must teach straightforwardly, and without any compromise, what God's commands are concerning sex and marriage. Congregations must also ask their leaders to teach on it. Then God's standards must be explained, no matter how much controversy arises, and even if nobody listens. It is a matter of integrity and obedience to God's Word. Therefore, for the avoidance of doubt, let me state the biblical position clearly and unmistakably. God's will is that every person, both men and women, must:

a) abstain from all sexual activity prior to their wedding night, even if they are engaged

b) have sex only with their husband or wife and nobody else

c) once they are married, remain totally faithful to each other, have no eyes for any other person at all, and avoid any sexual activity whatsoever with anyone other than their spouse

d) avoid even thinking of sexual activity with others, whether in their imagination, or by pornography, or by having a 'roving eye' which looks lustfully at the people they see

It really is as simple as that, even if those around us don't agree, and think that the Bible is old fashioned, unrealistic or ridiculous, as many of them do. Indeed, even within churches, many people think all of those things. You therefore have a clear choice to make between accepting God's standards and commands on sex and marriage, or following the values and practices of the unsaved world. I assure you that you will not regret it if you choose to obey God in these ways, whereas you certainly will regret it, at least in the end, if you don't.

I am not only speaking of the Day of Judgment, but also of the terrible damage and misery that marital unfaithfulness causes here and now, in this life. It creates suspicion, distrust, discord and divorce, which then, in turn, produce broken families, with children living apart from one parent. You only have to look at the explosion in the number of divorces in the UK since the so-called 'sexual revolution' of the 1960s to see the truth of this. No serious person can deny that what we now have is creating unhappiness and social damage on a huge scale.

Yet, at least in the UK, divorce and broken families were a rarity before the 1970s, which proves that it does not have to be that way. We could choose to be different. Promiscuity has not made anyone happy. All it has ever done is to cause enormous damage, thereby proving the wisdom of God's commands. The things He requires of us are not just arbitrary rules and restrictions with no basis in logic. They are entirely for our benefit, because we are hugely better off, in every way, if we approach sex and marriage in the way God tells us to, rather than as the world does.

523

Be pure and chaste before marriage and also dress modestly.

You can be faithful to your spouse even before you ever meet them. If you are unmarried it is your duty to keep yourself pure and to wait patiently for the husband or wife that God will one day give you. You might be a teenager, or a university student, or at the start of your career, but you have not yet found a spouse, or a fiancé/fiancée, or even a boyfriend or girlfriend. Or you could be much older, but still be single. It makes no difference. Your clear duty is to be faithful to that unknown person, whom you have not yet met, but whom God may have in store for you.

Your future husband or wife could now be at another school or university, or working in some other company, or attending some other church. Therefore, they are entirely real. You simply have not met him/her yet. Even though you don't yet know their name, you can still be faithful to them now *by waiting for them*. You can ask God to help you to remain faithful to them and also to help your future spouse to stay faithful to you, even before they know who you are, because they are in the same position. You would not want him or her to be unfaithful to you, merely because they don't yet know who *you* are.

Then, once you do meet the person and enter into courtship as a preparation for marriage, you must still avoid all sin and continue to be utterly faithful to each other, and also to God. That means you must abstain from *all* sexual activity, whether partial or complete. Do not allow *any* compromise, either on your part or your future spouse's part, however slight or infrequent it may be. Take care even to avoid situations which could potentially create *temptation* or provide any *opportunity* for sin.

It is wise therefore, wherever possible, to go out together with others, or to public places. In particular, avoid being alone together late at night, especially in bedrooms, or in any other such situation which increases the chances of temptation for either of you. The woman in particular needs to be vigilant. She must also dress modestly at all times, firstly because that is right, but also to avoid causing the man to stumble. I say that because men are primarily aroused through their *eyes*, which is precisely why the pornographic industry, and advertisers, do what they do.

The Devil and his demons understand men very well and know how best to get them to fall. So, as a Christian woman, your task is to work *against* that, not to make it even more difficult for men. Your duty is to assist your future spouse, and also all the other men who see you, to remain chaste and un-tempted. I wonder when I see some younger women in churches, and the suggestive way in which they dress, whom do they think they are they dressing for and why? What audience do they have in mind? Whom are they trying to impress or attract?

524

One thing is quite certain. If a woman seeks to attract a man by dressing or acting suggestively, she is in great danger of attracting the wrong man, whom God never intended for her. At the same time she will be repelling the *right man*, whom He *did* intend for her. How tragic is that? However, the man also needs to exercise great care and self-control and to remove himself from potentially compromising situations. He cannot just leave it to the woman to 'fight him off' or expect her to take sole responsibility for them avoiding sin as a couple.

In fact, I believe that God will actually hold the man primarily, though not solely, responsible for this. It is he who will have the role of leadership when the marriage begins and the time of courtship is his chance to develop that leadership role prior to the wedding. The best way he can do that is by leading the woman towards godliness and purity and away from sin. However, the man in particular has another duty, which may be very difficult for him, especially if he is young and surrounded by worldly companions at school or university.

He needs to make it clear to everyone who knows him that he is *not* sleeping with his girlfriend or fiancée and that *nothing at all* is happening sexually. That is difficult for young men today because there is ferocious peer pressure to conform to the world's standards on sex. Therefore, a young man who does what is right, and who *lets it be known that he is doing right*, is likely to be savagely ridiculed and despised by other young men. That is, admittedly, a high price to pay, but it must be paid nonetheless. In short, he must allow his own reputation to be harmed, in the warped minds of those worldly young men, in order to protect the reputation of the young woman he hopes to marry.

Many young men find this peer pressure intensely intimidating and are therefore afraid to be open about the fact that they are waiting for marriage because they fear being mocked for it. I don't pretend that it is easy, but it is still right and necessary. Moreover, it is good practice for the man in learning how to reject this world's values and standards and to defy its expectations. That is very useful because that same young man will need to be brave enough to stand apart from the crowd in many other ways too as he goes on into his career and also into any ministry that God gives him.

Having found the right husband or wife, a wise person then works very hard at making their marriage a success. They put their spouse ahead of everyone, and everything, except God.

We have seen how vital it is to take great care in choosing the right husband or wife, and not to rush into it. However, your task of building a strong marriage does not end there. Succeeding in your marriage is a lifelong job and, after your walk as a disciple, it is your biggest priority. It comes ahead of you career, your ministry, and even your children. That fact ought to be obvious, but, sadly, it very often isn't. Many couples, even if they are mature Christians, do not realise:

a) how important their marriage is in God's eyes,

b) that it comes ahead of all other things except God

c) that marriage has to be worked at consistently and that it does not succeed automatically, but requires ongoing effort and sacrifice

If this has not been how you have viewed your marriage to date, then adjust your priorities today and greatly increase your efforts. Begin to treat your husband or wife as God intends you to, and indeed as you promised you would in the vows you made on your wedding day, whether or not you realised their full significance at the time. The best thing a man can do for his children, after following God with all his heart and soul, is to love his wife, their mother.

The same is equally true of the wife. The children need to see her honouring and respecting her husband, their father. For one thing, the success or failure of their own marriages, and also of their families, may depend on the example they see you setting. God and your spouse must therefore be put into their correct places, as priorities number one and two in your life – and in that order. Then all the other priorities, including children, career and ministry, will automatically find their right places beneath them in the 'hierarchy'.

If so, then they will be handled properly. But if your career, children, or ministry are ever put ahead of your husband or wife, then everything will end up going wrong and not being what it was meant to be. There is not space in this book to look in full detail at how to make marriage a success, but I do hope to write a whole book on that one subject in due course. For now, however, I would simply make the following brief points:

Some guidelines for how to build a successful marriage

1. Honour your husband or wife in every way you can. Never do or say anything either to them, or about them, that would diminish them in their own eyes, or in the eyes of others, especially your children. In particular, never belittle them, not even in jest. It is your role to build them up, and never to tear them down, especially when you are with others.

2. Remember that cruel, bitter, hurtful words, once said, cannot be unsaid and can be very hard for your spouse to forget, such that they can still be causing damage, even years later. Therefore, stop and think before you speak and take great care what you say, no matter how angry or upset you may be at that

moment. Your anger may fade, but the memory of your rash words in your spouse's mind may not.

3. Also, take note of the fact that, at the Judgment Seat of Christ, everything that has been said in secret, including every harsh word or false accusation, will be *"shouted from the rooftops"*, for everyone to hear. Once you stop to reflect on it for a moment, you will realise that it will have to be broadcast like that, so that justice can be done, and the truth can be made known. Therefore, think much more carefully about what you say, both to and about your spouse:

> *² Nothing is covered up that will not be revealed, or hidden that will not be known. ³ Therefore whatever you have said in the dark shall be heard in the light, and what you have whispered in private rooms shall be proclaimed upon the housetops.*
>
> *Luke 12:2-3 (RSV)*

> *For nothing is hid that shall not be made manifest, nor anything secret that shall not be known and come to light.*
>
> *Luke 8:17 (RSV)*

> *³⁶ I tell you, on the day of judgment men will render account for every careless word they utter; ³⁷ for by your words you will be justified, and by your words you will be condemned."*
>
> *Matthew 12:36-37 (RSV)*

4. Forgive often and keep no record of wrongs. Of all the people in your life, your spouse is likely to be the one that you need to forgive most often, probably daily, for the simple reason that you are with them daily and on the most intimate level. They are also the one person with whom your unforgiveness would be most destructive, both to you and to them.

5. If you are the husband, then be willing to lead, and to take responsibility, not only for protecting your wife and family, but for being their spiritual guide, counsellor and pastor. That is what God wants, but vast numbers of husbands and fathers today are abdicating and not operating as the leader at all. They leave it to their wives to lead, not only in the family, but in the church as well. This is something for which husbands will be held accountable at the Judgment Seat. Therefore, let the reality of that impending judgment sink in and cause you to tremble and let that apprehension affect how you act now.

6. If you are the wife, then not only allow, but encourage, your husband to take the lead. Also, be willing to submit and to follow him, and make it easy for him to lead. Even if he makes mistakes, as he inevitably will, your patience, respect and support, together with your advice and input, will help him to learn

527

from them. He will then become a better leader to you, and your children, as the years go by. Likewise, the wife will also be held accountable, at the Judgment Seat, for how she behaved as a wife and how she treated her husband. Again, the anticipation of being judged on that awesome day should cause every wife to quake with fear, which is exactly what is meant by 'the fear of the LORD'.

7. If you are the husband, then love your wife and be sensitive, nurturing, patient and kind. Also make it your aim to be romantic. Don't ever underestimate the importance of romance, as so many foolish husbands do, even within the Church. As I said, every woman has been created by God with a deep need for romantic love. He made them that way *on purpose*, not by accident. Therefore, to withhold that from them is a form of abuse which will damage them and make them embittered and unhappy.

8. The most usual response from a woman who is starved of love is to begin to rebel against her husband's leadership. A woman won't follow a man, or meet his need to be respected by her, if he doesn't meet *her need* for love, including romantic love. At least she will not do it for long. Therefore, wise up and become a romantic type, even if it does not come naturally to you, such that you have to work at it in the beginning.

9. At the same time, if you are the wife, then *respect* your husband. It is interesting that apostle Paul never tells the wife to *love* her husband. He knows she will already do so automatically, because God has programmed that into her. At the same time, Paul never tells the man to respect his wife, as he knew that it is love, not respect, that women yearn for. Conversely, it is respect, not love, that men yearn for. Nevertheless, very few husbands ever get such respect today, partly due to the rise of misguided 'feminism', which makes a virtue out of belittling men, as if doing so somehow elevates women. In fact, it only degrades them. Feminism is an unbiblical set of beliefs and values which has brought only damage and misery in its wake. Indeed, it is a 'doctrine of demons' which was intentionally designed to harm family life.

10. Therefore, many wives make the mistake of focusing on trying to *love* their husbands, when it is actually her *respect* that he most craves. At the same time, many men do a lot of other things for their wives, including respecting them, when it is actually *love* that they really want, but are not getting. Discovering that husbands and wives are so completely different in these ways, *and that they crave for entirely different things*, will help you to provide what is actually most needed by your spouse. Then you can stop misguidedly trying to give him or her what *you* want, when that is not what *he or she* wants. Here is a very important passage in which Paul addresses these issues:

528

²² Wives, submit to your own husbands, as to the Lord. ²³ For the husband is the head of the wife even as Christ is the head of the church, his body, and is himself its Savior. ²⁴ Now as the church submits to Christ, so also wives should submit in everything to their husbands.

²⁵ Husbands, love your wives, as Christ loved the church and gave himself up for her, ²⁶ that he might sanctify her, having cleansed her by the washing of water with the word, ²⁷ so that he might present the church to himself in splendor, without spot or wrinkle or any such thing, that she might be holy and without blemish.

²⁸ In the same way husbands should love their wives as their own bodies. He who loves his wife loves himself. ²⁹ For no one ever hated his own flesh, but nourishes and cherishes it, just as Christ does the church, ³⁰ because we are members of his body. ³¹ "Therefore a man shall leave his father and mother and hold fast to his wife, and the two shall become one flesh."³² This mystery is profound, and I am saying that it refers to Christ and the church. ³³ However, let each one of you love his wife as himself, and let the wife see that she respects her husband.

Ephesians 5:22-33 (ESV)

11. Never waste a single moment in anger, bitterness or resentment. Do all you can to forgive offences willingly and to end arguments quickly. My wife and I have been very successful in this way, although it took us many years. When we were a young couple, arguments would be frequent and could last for hours or even days. They could also be quickly reignited. But, over the years, we have both made a concerted effort to make arguments fewer and shorter and with ever wider gaps in between. As a result, they are now only very occasional and last only minutes, or even seconds, before they are resolved. That reduction in conflict won't occur by itself. It has to be *made to happen* by a mutual determination to practice ongoing forgiveness and self-control and always to honour each other.

12. Always remember that your husband or wife is a *sinner*, with a *flesh nature*, and that that is what you are dealing with. But remember also that the very same is true of *you*, and is what your spouse has to put up with. Even if God gives you an excellent spouse, they are probably not yet wise, but only simple at best. That is almost certainly true when you first get married. God is not likely to provide you with the woman in Proverbs 31 on your wedding day, already fully prepared earlier by Him, and having no need to grow or mature. And, if you are a woman, He is even less likely to provide you with apostle Paul for a husband.

13. Therefore, even if you are both sincere and committed Christians when you marry, the likelihood is that you are both simple, not wise, and that both of you still have a lot to learn. Therefore, be realistic about what you are, what

Wisdom is to live in line with the word of God

529

your spouse is, and how much you each need to change. Then be patient with each other as that task of changing goes along. Never forget that you and your spouse have not yet even been fully sanctified, let alone glorified. That state of perfection will only occur when we die.

14. Remember also that one of your roles as a husband or wife is to help your spouse to *become* what God wants them to be, but which they currently are not. Moreover, I believe that at the Judgment Seat we shall each be held accountable, at least in part, for how our spouse ends up, not just for what we do ourselves. That is, *we* are partly responsible for how well *they* do and for whether they grow and mature spiritually and become a strong, solid disciple and bear fruit. Thus, there is no point in you bewailing the fact that your spouse has faults, sins and weaknesses, when one of the very reasons why God put your spouse with you was so that *you* could assist God in *His* objective of helping your spouse to change and mature.

15. Therefore, your job is to help your spouse to become everything that God wants them to be and to bear the fruit that He wants them to produce. Thus, if you were to try to criticise your spouse on the Day of Judgment in order to justify your own actions, Jesus might well say to you, *"But I consider you to be partly responsible for his/her spiritual condition. Therefore, the fact that he/she continued to behave in that way, or failed to overcome that weakness is, at least in part, your fault."* Let the prospect of having that said to you sober you.

16. To complain about your spouse's faults, sins and deficiencies would be like a gardener, having been appointed to tend a garden, moaning that it needs several things doing to it, plus regular upkeep. The employer, like God, might then say *"Isn't that what I employed you to do?"* In other words, why would he appoint you to tend a perfect garden, which requires no work, and which is already exactly as he wants it to be? That ideal state of affairs is meant to be the end result of *your* ministry as a spouse and also, of course, of God's own sanctifying work in your spouse's life. It is not the current position, and is certainly never the starting point, but it is what you are meant to be trying to bring about in your spouse's life.

17. One of the very reasons why God put you together was to *help each other to become* what each of you are meant to be and for each of you to fulfil your potential. God therefore wants you to work alongside Him, assisting Him in His larger and wider project of sanctifying and maturing each of you. A partial role in that process has been delegated to you by God. You need to realise that you have that duty and take it seriously. However, it is important to distinguish between how *God* wants your spouse to change and how *you*

might want them to change. This is a particular problem for wives, many of whom marry their husband with the private aim of changing him.

18. That may sound like what I have just been advocating, but it isn't. It is only *God's* plans, intentions and agenda for change that need to be pursued, *not yours*, however right you might consider yourself to be about what your spouse ought to be, do and think. Therefore, instead of working out what *you* think is wrong with your spouse, setting your own objectives for them, and trying to make yourself the agent of change, just cooperate with what God is doing. To alter the previous analogy, you should act like a junior gardener, following and abiding by the plans of the 'Head Gardener', not seeking to superimpose your own plans onto His, let alone in place of His.

19. Therefore, each spouse should seek to discover God's general plans for the development of their own character and their own sanctification. They should also seek to find out what God's specific plans and intentions are for their spouse in terms of career, ministry, personal fulfilment and any other unique activities or goals that God intends for them. These will be identified as you go along by way of God's specific guidance. However, they will often be revealed by looking at your individual gifts and interests, plus any yearnings that each of you may have, which could indicate that God is calling you into certain jobs or ministries.

20. As these are discovered, and as it becomes clearer what God is calling each of you to do or be, seek to support that process rather than to dictate matters or take over. This too is part of the overall process of change or growth. But it has to be about what *God* wants for your spouse, not what *you* think they should be or do, or how *you* think he or she should change.

21. Thus, if your spouse has a dream of becoming something in particular, and if God seems to be in that, and to be confirming it, then you need to give all the help and encouragement you can to help your spouse to fulfil their calling. Again, this must not be done manipulatively, in order to fulfil your own personal goals for your spouse, but only to help them to fulfil *God's goals* for them.

22. The wife needs to realise, and must try hard to remember, that it is her job to *tell her husband* what she is thinking or feeling and not expect him to be a mind reader. Many wives think to themselves, *"If my husband really loved me he would already know that I am feeling XYZ and would not need to be told."* Once you pause for a moment to consider it, the absurdity of that statement becomes apparent. However, partly due to demonic whispering, it is not apparent to a lot of women and it therefore causes a great deal of

needless grief. So, if you think or feel something, then *say it*, in very clear, simple words, and as graciously as you can.

The vital importance of "leaving and cleaving"

This is a more complex issue, and takes longer to explain, so I will deal with it under its own heading. When a couple get married they must both leave their parents behind and cleave to their new husband or wife, not just in terms of the house they live in, but in every sense. Moses says this in Genesis in regard to the man, but it also applies to the wife:

Therefore a man leaves his father and his mother and cleaves to his wife, and they become one flesh.

Genesis 2:24 (RSV)

Instead of this, in many marriages, one spouse or the other, or even both, are still tied to their parents and to their opinions, beliefs and ways of operating. They may also allow their parents to 'speak into their marriage' and to make critical comments about their spouse. A wise parent won't do that anyway, but a foolish or wicked one will, and it can be very damaging and can badly undermine trust. Therefore, keep your parents out of your marriage and don't betray your spouse by discussing private details about them with your parents or by complaining about them. Also, don't insist on maintaining your parents' traditions or habits or on doing things their way. Find your own way, together, between the two of you.

You must also exclude from the marriage any previous boyfriend or girlfriend, or even a previous spouse if you are widowed. This is a rarer problem, but it still happens. Many people still remain partially attached, in their minds, emotions and spirit, to a previous boyfriend/girlfriend or a deceased spouse. If that is so in your case you need to repent of it and to end that relationship completely, even inside your own mind, so that you are 100% committed to your spouse and to nobody else. That is why the wedding ceremony contains the vital words *"... and, forsaking all others, keep thee only unto him (her) so long as you both shall live"*.

You both need to absolutely rule out all consideration of divorce, so that, no matter how upset or angry you may be, it is simply not an option

In the past, when society's attitude to marriage was more biblical, there was a widespread assumption, even amongst non-Christians, that divorce was socially unacceptable and, therefore, not an option. Indeed, until relatively recently historically, it was not even legal to get divorced except on very narrow grounds, most notably adultery, and, even then, there was a high burden of proof. So, in those days, which persisted until the 1960s, it was part of our culture that you *don't* get divorced.

That operated as a powerful constraint and the expectations of the community, or 'peer pressure', caused people to try much harder with their marriages so as to work things out and also to 'tough it out', and endure the problems while doing so. However, those cultural expectations and constraints crumbled away steadily during the 1970s and 1980s until, by the 1990s, divorce had become not only socially acceptable, but even an expectation.

At any rate it is now considered to be entirely possible that a marriage might end in divorce, not only by the friends and relatives, but by the couple themselves. Therefore, very many people enter into marriage with the thought, even if it is only at the back of their mind, that if the marriage 'doesn't work out', then divorce will at least provide a way of escape from it. Then they can start again with someone else, almost as if they were treating this marriage as a 'dummy run', or training exercise, from which they can learn lessons ready for the next time.

I can remember a young woman who was part of the same intake with me when I joined the police in 1983. She was getting married and was planning her wedding and she said to one of the other WPCs, *"I give it five years"*. She meant that her *own expectation* was that the marriage would probably only last five years and would then, in her opinion, be likely to end in divorce. Moreover, she felt no shame or stigma about that, so much so that she was willing to say it openly. It hardly needs to be said that any marriage is doomed to fail if it is entered into with that attitude, even if it isn't said out loud.

That WPC was unusual in terms of her willingness to express her thoughts out loud, but not particularly unusual in having them. Such attitudes are increasingly common, even if they are only latent, unspoken and buried deep in people's minds. The problem is that marriage is difficult, whoever you are. Thus, even if apostle Paul was to marry the woman from Proverbs 31, they would still have their difficult times, at least at the beginning, until they learn how to succeed at marriage.

So, if you want your marriage to last for life, and to be happy, then enter into it with a rock solid inner conviction that, however hard it may be, and whatever problems have to be overcome, divorce is *simply not an option for you*. Even if you did not enter your marriage with that resolve, adopt it now, belatedly, and change your attitude. You need to burn your boats, as the Vikings were reputed to do, so that the soldiers knew there was no way back and that they must therefore conquer or die. That knowledge affected the way they fought and increased their determination.

If you don't have this immovable inner resolve, which is, after all, only what you promised on your wedding day, then you are likely to buckle and give in when the pressures mount, as they inevitably will. You need to have it firmly imprinted into your mind, in bold capital letters, and in a very large font, that this marriage is *for life* and that there is *no way out of it*. Then, when you are in the middle of a row, or are feeling angry, bitter, hurt or resentful, it will affect the way you conduct yourself and also what you say.

Instead of lashing out with cruel, wounding words or complaining to your friends, or, even worse, ringing a lawyer to discuss a potential divorce, you will say to yourself, *"This is the person I will be with for the rest of our lives and so I have got to find a way to resolve this"*. No matter what has been said or done, and no matter how angry you feel, and whether you are in the right or the wrong, the recollection that you are bound together for life will bring you back from the brink of saying or doing something unwise.

Instead, you will force yourself to find some way to forgive, or to repent or apologise, or to change your own conduct, or to be patient with your spouse's conduct. Anything is possible to those who know they have no alternative and no way out. It is remarkable what a difference it makes to accept that fact because "necessity is the mother of invention" in marriage as well as in science and industry. It enables you to find a way forward somehow, as our parents' and grandparents' generations recognised, but which our own generation doesn't.

Therefore, let that solemn vow, which you took on your wedding day, profoundly affect the way you handle all conflict resolution. When there is an argument, let that vow cause you to humble yourself, to control your tongue, to make the first move, to be the first to say sorry, to be quick to forgive and slow to blame, and even slower to accuse. Let the whole conversation be conducted within the rigid framework of the acceptance that this is the person you have got to be with for life, through thick and thin, in good times and bad, in sickness and health and so on.

Let that knowledge affect every part of your thinking, speech, attitudes, actions *and reactions*. I stress that last word because many believe that if they have been wronged, then they are free to do as they wish in return. That is not so. We are still under a duty to control ourselves, and especially to control our tongues, whether we are right or wrong, and whatever wrong has been done to us.

Many of the problems we face in marriage are caused, or increased by, demonic interference and sabotage.

The demons are active in undermining, deceiving and discouraging us in every aspect of our lives, including our marriage, thereby adding yet further to our difficulties. They are also involved in our churches. Indeed, they will operate wherever we will allow them to do so, even if we are trying to prevent them, because they are determined and persistent enemies, as well as being highly skilled, with nearly 6000 years of experience in opposing and deceiving human beings.

Communication is not fully effective, even at the best of times. Perhaps 20-50% of what is said between husband and wife is either not heard at all, or is misheard, misunderstood, or wrongly remembered. This is already the case, quite apart from what the demons do in addition, seeking to make the position even worse. There may be a number of reasons for that ineffectiveness in communications, including:

a) poor listening skills to begin with and a failure to give focused, undivided attention

b) the hearer trying to think of what they might want to say in reply, while the other is still speaking, rather than concentrating 100% on genuinely *listening* to what is being said, without any regard to how to reply or getting ready to defend or justify him or her self

c) the hearer's own pent up 'reservoir' of anger, bitterness and resentment about past events which have never been properly forgiven. These are then brought back 'out of the cupboard', whenever an argument arises, to be used as ready-made ammunition with which to hit back. Or past grievances are silently nursed in the hearer's own mind, even while their spouse is speaking, thus creating another distraction and further reducing their ability to listen.

There may well be other factors too, which will vary from couple to couple. However, on top of all those ordinary problems, there will also be the intervention of demons, whispering into your mind, and also into your spouse's mind, to intensify the existing confusion, misunderstanding and tension, and to create yet more. This makes it even harder to listen to or understand each other because each spouse's flesh nature is revved up and agitated by the demons' whisperings.

That causes each spouse to over-react, or to react badly, and then to inflame the situation yet further by making unhelpful, unkind, unnecessary comments. But they might never have said those things at all were it not for the demon's intervention. Amongst the couples I have counselled such outbursts and loss of temper tend to be more common on the wife's part, although husbands can certainly do it too. A far more common response from the husband, however, is to become silent and withdrawn, to give up on conversation, and become generally uncommunicative. Both reactions are damaging and the demons know that.

Therefore, they are actively involved *on both sides*, seeking to make use of the wife's sinful flesh nature, usually to get her to lose her temper while, at the same time, seeking to use the husband's flesh by getting him to go silent and to withdraw. Ideally, the demons want to get him to give up on communication altogether, especially with difficult or sensitive topics. The demons want each person to lean even more in whatever direction their sinful flesh nature is already causing them to lean. The demons' aim is to maximise the intensity and duration of the dispute and to add to each spouse's 'reservoir' of bitterness and the perceived 'record of wrongs' done to them.

In addition to that, some of the arguments that couples have are over things that the other spouse never meant, or even that they never actually said at all. They were, in fact, whispered into the hearer's mind by a demon. They can very easily deceive you into taking their whisperings on board, as if they were your own thoughts. In that way the demon can create false memories in your mind as to what your spouse said, or what you wrongly thought they meant, and thereby cause you to become more angry, bitter and resentful than you would otherwise have been.

They can do all this by whispering into your mind but with the words being heard by you, in your head, *in your own voice and accent, as if you had thought it yourself.* They will also use the pronoun *'I'*, rather than *'you'*, so that you assume it to be your own thought. They know very well that if they whispered into your mind in the second person, saying *"You......."*, then you would immediately realise that that was not your own thought and that someone else was somehow speaking to you.

However, they can do even better than that in that they can also speak to *you* by imitating the voice of your *spouse*, i.e. while he or she is speaking. When demons do this they carefully ensure that their whispering is heard, in your mind, *as if it was your spouse's voice*, which they can imitate just as skilfully as they can imitate your voice. They will go about it the opposite way round this time by ensuring that it is said in the second person, rather than the first person, i.e. saying *"you"*, not "I", so as not to give the game away.

In this way, couples can sometimes be absolutely convinced that they heard the other one say XYZ, while the other insists they never said it at all and is at a loss to understand how their spouse can have been so utterly mistaken. They are both then likely to blame the other and to assume that the other is being either dishonest or hysterical.

536

The demon would never go so far as to try to plant such thoughts at any length, i.e. saying whole sentences as if they were from your spouse. It would be hard for them to get away with that. But if their interjections are short, and come in the midst of heated arguments, they can be much harder to detect. That way you are more likely to fall for it, especially if it is just a single familiar buzz word or phrase, which you have come to find intolerable, and which the demons know will provoke an explosive reaction because it has become like a red rag to a bull to you.

However, the good news is that no matter how long you have been married, and whether you are doing badly or well, and even if you are both at your wits end, it really is possible to turn it all around. In fact, that can actually be done quite easily *if* you are *both* willing to work at it, and to keep doing so for long enough. But even if it is only you who can see where the marriage is going wrong, and only you who is willing to change, success can still be achieved. It will just take longer. But your spouse will eventually join in, and begin to change, if you are willing to go first and to lead the way, for a while, all by yourself.

Therefore, be willing to be the first to change, the first to apologise, and the first to exercise self-control, even if for weeks, months, or even years, your spouse doesn't join in with you. Keep at it for as long as it takes until they do. Never put a deadline on it or the demons will simply make sure that your spouse does not respond to you within that stated time period. Therefore, make it completely open-ended and keep going *"for as long as you both shall live"*, as you vowed on your wedding day. If you do that then you will find that things come right in the end.

CHAPTER 15

WISE PEOPLE PUT GREAT EMPHASIS ON BIBLE PROPHECY, GOD'S IMPENDING JUDGMENT, AND ETERNITY

"For the Lord GOD does nothing
without revealing his secret
to his servants the prophets.
                              Amos 3:7 (ESV)

……..Jehoshaphat stood and said, "Hear me, Judah and inhabitants of Jerusalem! Believe in the LORD your God, and you will be established; believe his prophets, and you will succeed."
                              2 Chronicles 20:20(b) (ESV)

So teach us to number our days
* that we may get a heart of wisdom.*
                  Psalm 90:12 (RSV)

Blessed is he who reads aloud the words of the prophecy, and blessed are those who hear, and who keep what is written therein; for the time is near.
                              Revelation 1:3 (RSV)

And behold, I am coming soon."
Blessed is he who keeps the words of the prophecy of this book.
                              Revelation 22:7 (RSV)

Where there is no prophecy the people cast off restraint,
* but blessed is he who keeps the law.*
                  Proverbs 29:18 (RSV)

Open my eyes, that I may behold
wondrous things out of thy law.
                  Psalm 119:18 (RSV)

Thy word is a lamp to my feet
and a light to my path.
                  Psalm 119:105 (RSV)

[18] I warn every one who hears the words of the prophecy of this book: if any one adds to them, God will add to him the plagues described in this book, [19] and if any one takes away from the words of the book of this prophecy, God will take

away his share in the tree of life and in the holy city, which are described in this book.

Revelation 22:18-19 (RSV)

".......In the latter days you will understand it clearly."

Jeremiah 23:20(b) (ESV)

Wise people make the effort to understand the prophecies in the Bible

The angel Gabriel appeared to the prophet Daniel and gave him a lot of information about what will happen in the years leading up to the end of this age, the coming of the antichrist and the return of Jesus Christ. (See Daniel chapters 9-12). Gabriel tells Daniel that the visions he has seen, are for "*the time of the end*". Thus, they could not be fully understood in Daniel's own day, but will be in the future, when the end approaches. However, even then, they will only be understood by those who are wise, not by the wicked:

[1]"At that time shall arise Michael, the great prince who has charge of your people. And there shall be a time of trouble, such as never has been since there was a nation till that time; but at that time your people shall be delivered, every one whose name shall be found written in the book. [2]And many of those who sleep in the dust of the earth shall awake, some to everlasting life, and some to shame and everlasting contempt. [3]And those who are wise shall shine like the brightness of the firmament; and those who turn many to righteousness, like the stars for ever and ever. [4]But you, Daniel, shut up the words, and seal the book, until the time of the end. Many shall run to and fro, and knowledge shall increase."

Daniel 12:1-4 (RSV)

[8]I heard, but I did not understand. Then I said, "O my lord, what shall be the issue of these things?" [9]He said, "Go your way, Daniel, for the words are shut up and sealed until the time of the end. [10]Many shall purify themselves, and make themselves white, and be refined; but the wicked shall do wickedly; and none of the wicked shall understand; but those who are wise shall understand.

Daniel 12:8-10 (RSV)

So, the things that Daniel was told by Gabriel would not make complete sense until later, i.e. not until after Jesus had come, and the books of Matthew and Revelation, and others, had been written. Indeed, they will not be fully understood until the very end, when the prophesied events are about to unfold. When the time comes, the people of that day will be given the insight and inspiration that they need to make full sense of the prophecies. We are now much closer to those days that Gabriel spoke of.

540

Therefore it is increasingly open to us to read and understand these prophecies in the Bible. We can do so even now, up to a point. However, as the very end approaches, we will be fully able to do so, provided we are wise enough, and humble enough. In particular we must read the prophetic parts of the Bible with a right heart-attitude and with a correct approach to Bible interpretation. See my Book 3 for a fuller discussion of how to approach the Bible in general and prophecy in particular.

However, the wicked, whether they are outright unbelievers or false religious people, will never be able to understand the prophecies. So, there is a serious warning to us to become wise enough to do so. The need to understand Bible prophecy should matter to us. Indeed, having a heart that sincerely wants to understand the Bible properly, whether the prophetic or non-prophetic parts, is a vital first step to becoming *able* to grasp it. Then you can become one of the people who are capable of seeing what God has revealed to His servants the Prophets:

"For the Lord GOD does nothing without revealing his secret to his servants the prophets.
                                                                                    Amos 3:7 (ESV)

Wise people think of the long term, and of eternity, not just the present

Wise people emphasise eternity and consider it to be of the utmost importance. They also fear it, because it will go on for ever and ever and ever:

Your kingdom is an everlasting kingdom,
  and your dominion endures throughout all generations…..
                        Psalm 145:13(a) (ESV)

If we end up in the wrong place, there will *never* be any way out of it. If that does not scare you, then you haven't understood it. For every genuine believer, eternity will begin with a personal, face to face judgment at which he will be examined and assessed. We all need to fear that Day of Judgment and take it seriously, even if we are saved. However, we also need to long for what lies beyond that Judgment.

There is going to be an eternity without sin, sickness or death and we will be able to see God face to face and live with Him. That has got to be far more important, and far better, than anything we have now. So, eternity should, quite obviously, be our main focus. This physical Earth that we live on now has been promised to God's people. One day the righteous will inherit it, and live upon it again for 1000 years, whereas the wicked will not. Jesus said so, and He meant it literally:

"Blessed are the meek, for they shall inherit the earth".
Matthew 5:5 (RSV)

⁴ Then I saw thrones, and seated on them were those to whom the authority to judge was committed. Also I saw the souls of those who had been beheaded for the testimony of Jesus and for the word of God, and those who had not worshiped the beast or its image and had not received its mark on their foreheads or their hands. They came to life and reigned with Christ for a thousand years. ⁵ The rest of the dead did not come to life until the thousand years were ended. This is the first resurrection. ⁶ Blessed and holy is the one who shares in the first resurrection! Over such the second death has no power, but they will be priests of God and of Christ, and they will reign with him for a thousand years.
Revelation 20:4-6 (ESV)

¹ Then I saw a new heaven and a new earth, for the first heaven and the first earth had passed away, and the sea was no more. ² And I saw the holy city, new Jerusalem, coming down out of heaven from God, prepared as a bride adorned for her husband. ³ And I heard a loud voice from the throne saying, "Behold, the dwelling place of God is with man. He will dwell with them, and they will be his people, and God himself will be with them as their God. ⁴ He will wipe away every tear from their eyes, and death shall be no more, neither shall there be mourning, nor crying, nor pain anymore, for the former things have passed away."
Revelation 21:1-4 (ESV)

Also, look at what Job said. He was speaking about his assurance that one day his Redeemer will stand upon this Earth and that he himself would also do so. Moreover, he is plainly not speaking of Jesus' first coming, because Job refers in the passage to himself as having been resurrected after having died. Clearly, that is still in the future, but it is going to happen on this literal physical Earth:

²⁵ For I know that my Redeemer lives,
and at the last he will stand upon the earth.
²⁶ And after my skin has been thus destroyed,
yet in my flesh I shall see God,
²⁷ whom I shall see for myself,
and my eyes shall behold, and not another.
My heart faints within me!
Job 19:25-27 (ESV)

542

Having an eternal perspective gives us greater resilience and also motivates us to be obedient to God's commands and to seek His rewards

The more we can develop an eternal perspective on life and see the reality of what lies ahead in the distant (and eternal) future, the wiser, and more stable and resilient, we will be. Also, the more our present actions and decisions will be affected by the approach we take to eternity, because, as we look forward to what is ahead, it becomes increasingly real to us. That then influences how we choose to live now:

⁵My deliverance draws near speedily, my salvation has gone forth, and my arms will rule the peoples; the coastlands wait for me, and for my arm they hope. ⁶Lift up your eyes to the heavens, and look at the earth beneath; for the heavens will vanish like smoke, the earth will wear out like a garment, and they who dwell in it will die like gnats; but my salvation will be for ever, and my deliverance will never be ended.

Isaiah 51:5-6 (RSV)

A wise person will give much greater weight and emphasis to what is going to happen to them in eternity than to what may be happening to them now in this life. However difficult our current circumstances may be, they can never be as bad as the Lake of Fire. And, however long our sufferings in this life may last, they are trivial compared to eternity. Once you grasp basic points like those, which most people never even consider, you will become far more willing to give up what you have in this life and even to give up life itself, to gain that eternal life:

²⁵ He who loves his life loses it, and he who hates his life in this world will keep it for eternal life. ²⁶ If any one serves me, he must follow me; and where I am, there shall my servant be also; if any one serves me, the Father will honor him.

John 12:25-26 (RSV)

A person who has grasped the vital importance of eternity, and reflected on how and where he will spend it, will also be much more willing to *"take up his cross",* as Jesus commands, and to follow Him wherever He leads. There is no point in gaining things in this present world only to lose those things, and even our very souls, before we enter the next life:

³⁴ And calling the crowd to him with his disciples, he said to them, "If anyone would come after me, let him deny himself and take up his cross and follow me. ³⁵ For whoever would save his life will lose it, but whoever loses his life for my sake and the gospel's will save it. ³⁶ For what does it profit a man to gain the whole world and forfeit his soul? ³⁷ For what can a man give in return for his soul? ³⁸ For whoever is ashamed of me and of my words in this adulterous and sinful generation, of him will the Son of Man also be ashamed when he comes in the glory of his Father with the holy angels."

Mark 8:34-38 (ESV)

When it comes to money, possessions, power and status, a wise person will realise that those things are only very temporary. He will focus instead on building up treasure for himself in Heaven. This means living in such a way as to do well and be rewarded at the Judgment Seat of Christ. (See my Book 4)

19 "Do not lay up for yourselves treasures on earth, where moth and rust consume and where thieves break in and steal, 20 but lay up for yourselves treasures in heaven, where neither moth nor rust consumes and where thieves do not break in and steal.

Matthew 6:19-20 (RSV)

If we become Christians and, in particular, if we then go on to become mature and genuine disciples, Jesus will give rewards and positions to those who have served Him faithfully and productively. Therefore, those are the things we should focus on, i.e. *what our position will be in His future Kingdom*, not what we have to eat, drink or wear today:

31 Therefore do not be anxious, saying, 'What shall we eat?' or 'What shall we drink?' or 'What shall we wear?' 32 For the Gentiles seek all these things; and your heavenly Father knows that you need them all. 33 But seek first his kingdom and his righteousness, and all these things shall be yours as well.

Matthew 6:31-33 (RSV)

A person whose mind is set on eternity and on God's future Kingdom will have enough understanding and motivation to ensure they enter by the narrow gate and stay on the hard way that leads to life. Most do not choose to do those things, partly because their minds are so focused on the present that they give no thought to their eternal future:

13 "Enter by the narrow gate; for the gate is wide and the way is easy, that leads to destruction, and those who enter by it are many. 14 For the gate is narrow and the way is hard, that leads to life, and those who find it are few.

Matthew 7:13-14 (RSV)

If we focus on eternity, we will also have the motivation needed to endure the extra difficulties and persecutions that will come to us for being faithful disciples and for sharing the Gospel with unbelievers. A faithful Christian life will inevitably arouse other people's hostility and opposition, but it is worth it when one considers what lies ahead of us. I have included a lot of sample passages here

Live with the end in mind 544

to demonstrate how frequently the Bible addresses this theme and to show that I am not over-stating its significance as an issue:

I consider that the sufferings of this present time are not worth comparing with the glory that is to be revealed to us.

Romans 8:18 (RSV)

[16] "Behold, I send you out as sheep in the midst of wolves; so be wise as serpents and innocent as doves. [17] Beware of men; for they will deliver you up to councils, and flog you in their synagogues, [18] and you will be dragged before governors and kings for my sake, to bear testimony before them and the Gentiles. [19] When they deliver you up, do not be anxious how you are to speak or what you are to say; for what you are to say will be given to you in that hour; [20] for it is not you who speak, but the Spirit of your Father speaking through you. [21] Brother will deliver up brother to death, and the father his child, and children will rise against parents and have them put to death; [22] and you will be hated by all for my name's sake. But he who endures to the end will be saved.

Matthew 10:16-22 (RSV)

[26] "So have no fear of them; for nothing is covered that will not be revealed, or hidden that will not be known. [27] What I tell you in the dark, utter in the light; and what you hear whispered, proclaim upon the housetops. [28] And do not fear those who kill the body but cannot kill the soul; rather fear him who can destroy both soul and body in hell.

Matthew 10:26-28 (RSV)

[32] So everyone who acknowledges me before men, I also will acknowledge before my Father who is in heaven; [33] but whoever denies me before men, I also will deny before my Father who is in heaven.

Matthew 10:32-33 (RSV)

[7] But whatever gain I had, I counted as loss for the sake of Christ. [8] Indeed I count everything as loss because of the surpassing worth of knowing Christ Jesus my Lord. For his sake I have suffered the loss of all things, and count them as refuse, in order that I may gain Christ [9] and be found in him, not having a righteousness of my own, based on law, but that which is through faith in Christ, the righteousness from God that depends on faith; [10] that I may know him and the power of his resurrection, and may share his sufferings, becoming like him in his death, [11] that if possible I may attain the resurrection from the dead.
[12] Not that I have already obtained this or am already perfect; but I press on to make it my own, because Christ Jesus has made me his own. [13] Brethren, I do not consider that I have made it my own; but one thing I do, forgetting what lies

behind and straining forward to what lies ahead, ¹⁴ I press on toward the goal for the prize of the upward call of God in Christ Jesus.

Philippians 3:7-14 (RSV)

¹⁷ Brethren, join in imitating me, and mark those who so live as you have an example in us. ¹⁸ For many, of whom I have often told you and now tell you even with tears, live as enemies of the cross of Christ. ¹⁹ Their end is destruction, their god is the belly, and they glory in their shame, with minds set on earthly things. ²⁰ But our commonwealth is in heaven, and from it we await a Saviour, the Lord Jesus Christ, ²¹ who will change our lowly body to be like his glorious body, by the power which enables him even to subject all things to himself.

Philippians 3:17-21 (RSV)

⁴ because we have heard of your faith in Christ Jesus and of the love which you have for all the saints, ⁵ because of the hope laid up for you in heaven. Of this you have heard before in the word of the truth, the gospel

Colossians 1:4-5 (RSV)

¹If then you have been raised with Christ, seek the things that are above, where Christ is, seated at the right hand of God. ² Set your minds on things that are above, not on things that are on earth. ³ For you have died, and your life is hid with Christ in God. ⁴ When Christ who is our life appears, then you also will appear with him in glory.

Colossians 3:1-4 (RSV)

We cannot claim that we have not been warned in advance of the difficulties and opposition that living as a faithful disciple will generate. The Bible is very plain about all of that. However, it is also very clear about the rewards that await us if we do live faithfully. Therefore, we have every reason to maximise our knowledge and understanding of God's Word, including prophecy.

Wise people are alert and waiting for the rapture of the Church.

We are all expected to take Bible prophecy seriously and to work hard to learn how to understand it. However, we are particularly commanded to be *alert and ready* while we wait for the rapture of the Church. That is when Jesus will return to take away all real Christians, though not mere 'churchgoers'. Then He will begin the judgment of the Church, known as the Judgment Seat of Christ. Look at how strongly Jesus spoke of this:

²⁶ Then they will see THE SON OF MAN COMING IN CLOUDS with great power and glory. ²⁷ And then He will send forth the angels, and will gather together His

546

elect from the four winds, from the farthest end of the earth to the farthest end of heaven. ²⁸ *"Now learn the parable from the fig tree: when its branch has already become tender and puts forth its leaves, you know that summer is near.* ²⁹ *Even so, you too, when you see these things happening, recognize that He is near, right at the door.* ³⁰ *Truly I say to you, this generation will not pass away until all these things take place.* ³¹ *Heaven and earth will pass away, but My words will not pass away.* ³² *But of that day or hour no one knows, not even the angels in heaven, nor the Son, but the Father alone.*

³³ *"Take heed, keep on the alert; for you do not know when the appointed time will come.* ³⁴ *It is like a man away on a journey, who upon leaving his house and putting his slaves in charge, assigning to each one his task, also commanded the doorkeeper to stay on the alert.* ³⁵ *Therefore, be on the alert—for you do not know when the master of the house is coming, whether in the evening, at midnight, or when the rooster crows, or in the morning—* ³⁶ *in case he should come suddenly and find you asleep.* ³⁷ *What I say to you I say to all, 'Be on the alert!'"*

Mark 13:26-37 (NASB)

³⁵ *"Stay dressed for action and keep your lamps burning,* ³⁶ *and be like men who are waiting for their master to come home from the wedding feast, so that they may open the door to him at once when he comes and knocks.* ³⁷ *Blessed are those servants whom the master finds awake when he comes. Truly, I say to you, he will dress himself for service and have them recline at table, and he will come and serve them.* ³⁸ *If he comes in the second watch, or in the third, and finds them awake, blessed are those servants!* ³⁹ *But know this, that if the master of the house had known at what hour the thief was coming, he would not have left his house to be broken into.* ⁴⁰ *You also must be ready, for the Son of Man is coming at an hour you do not expect."*

Luke 12:35-40 (ESV)

Jesus is not telling us of these things for mere academic interest, but so that we can make ourselves ready for Him. He tells us to *"Be on the alert"* and He is saying that to us *all*, not just to a special few or to a single generation. He wants *all* of us, in *every generation*, to be aware that we could be the generation whose lives are suddenly interrupted by the rapture. That is when Jesus will return, without any prior notice, and take His whole Church away, i.e. the *real* believers, not the fake or nominal ones, to face His judgment.

Then, *years later,* He will return *visibly* to the Earth to take up His place as King of Israel and Judge of all the whole Earth. That is when Jesus' earthly Kingdom will truly and properly begin. It is because of that fact that the Gospel is sometimes referred to in the Bible as *"the gospel of the Kingdom"*. We are meant to focus on this coming Kingdom which is still in the future. Yet, much of the Church has either never heard of it, or chooses to ignore it.

Instead, the Kingdom that is coming needs to be kept at the forefront of our minds, and also of our presentation of the Gospel message. It is not a mere side issue. See my commentary on Matthew's gospel for more detail on the gospel of the Kingdom. The timing of *the Second Coming*, which begins the 1000 year Millennial Kingdom, will be possible to work out in advance for those who come to believe in Jesus after the rapture. It can be planned for and awaited. However, the rapture which precedes it will be completely sudden and with no specific build up or advance warning.

Therefore, Jesus wants *every* generation to be ready for the rapture *at all times*, because we can never know when it will happen, so we must remain alert all the time. A wise person takes that command seriously, but most people don't, not even real Christians in relatively good churches. To ignore Bible prophecy is foolishness, but it is also disobedience to what we are commanded to do. Even so, the fact is that most people do choose to ignore it.

Wise people live their lives 'judgment focused', always conscious that everything they think, say and do will be judged, and may even be made public.

The coming judgment is very little known and even less spoken about. It should instead be at the forefront of our minds, regularly occupy our thoughts and inspire apprehension, and even fear. Yet, for most of us, it is not an issue. Can you think of any valid reason why it should not regularly occupy your thoughts and influence your actions? Consider the prospect of *your* private conversations being shouted from the roof tops and of all those who need to know being made aware of what you really said about them behind their backs. How does that make you feel?

¹ In the meantime, when so many thousands of the people had gathered together that they were trampling one another, he began to say to his disciples first, "Beware of the leaven of the Pharisees, which is hypocrisy. ² Nothing is covered up that will not be revealed, or hidden that will not be known. ³ Therefore whatever you have said in the dark shall be heard in the light, and what you have whispered in private rooms shall be proclaimed on the housetops.

Luke 12:1-3 (ESV)

Context ?

Perhaps you believe this does not apply to Christians and is only of relevance to the unsaved. However, I cannot see how that can possibly be the case. Note how Jesus says, *to His own disciples*, "whatever *you* have said..." and "what *you* have whispered…… Clearly, Jesus is speaking to and about His own disciples. Therefore, He is including them within the scope of what is going to occur at the judgment and how secret things will be revealed publicly. He is plainly not excluding them, or us, from that. This judgment process could be decades away for you, or it could be very soon.

Maybe it will even occur later today, if you are unexpectedly killed. So, whoever we are, we don't know when exactly we will face judgment. Thus, it would be very foolish to delay any consideration of it until you are older, or even when you face death, on the assumption that that will be in the distant future. The time to be thinking of your death is *now,* while you still have the chance to alter the outcome of the judgment and the rewards (or rebukes) which you get (or don't get). A wise person is prepared for a rapture (or death) which occurs *today,* or at the opposite end of the spectrum, which may not come until he is an *old man.*

Both are possibilities and they each present their own challenges. Therefore, on the one hand, we need to be ready to meet Jesus now, and to face Him as our judge today. But, on the other hand, we may face the harder test of remaining faithful, and constantly ready, for several decades, during which He does not come. If His coming is delayed, we must stay alert, obedient and watchful *at all times.* We must also pray for the strength to cope with a long 'marathon race' and not to be deceived, or become unfaithful, during those years:

And he said, "See that you are not led astray. For many will come in my name, saying, 'I am he!' and, 'The time is at hand!' Do not go after them.
Luke 21:8 (ESV)

[34] *"But watch yourselves lest your hearts be weighed down with dissipation and drunkenness and cares of this life, and that day come upon you suddenly like a trap.* [35] *For it will come upon all who dwell on the face of the whole earth.* [36] *But stay awake at all times, praying that you may have strength to escape all these things that are going to take place, and to stand before the Son of Man."*
Luke 21:34-36 (ESV)

To assist you in focusing more closely on the Day of Judgment, consider this series of verses on how it will operate, and why we all need to take it seriously and even fear it. I certainly fear it, and it makes me apprehensive, and with good reason, because we are *meant* to be apprehensive about the Day of Judgment.

The fear of God, and especially of His judgment, is always presented in the Bible as a good thing, not as something negative or unhealthy. Many of these verses which follow refer to the judgment on the unsaved, but I include them to give a fuller picture of how awesome the whole process will be:

549

Be silent before the Lord GOD!
  For the day of the LORD is near;
the LORD has prepared a sacrifice
  and consecrated his guests.
            Zephaniah 1:7 (ESV)

[14] *The great day of the LORD is near,*
  near and hastening fast;
the sound of the day of the LORD is bitter;
  the mighty man cries aloud there.
[15] *A day of wrath is that day,*
  a day of distress and anguish,
a day of ruin and devastation,
  a day of darkness and gloom,
a day of clouds and thick darkness,
[16] *a day of trumpet blast and battle cry*
against the fortified cities
  and against the lofty battlements.
[17] *I will bring distress on mankind,*
  so that they shall walk like the blind,
  because they have sinned against the LORD;
their blood shall be poured out like dust,
  and their flesh like dung.
[18] *Neither their silver nor their gold*
  shall be able to deliver them
  on the day of the wrath of the LORD.
In the fire of his jealousy,
  all the earth shall be consumed;
for a full and sudden end
            Zephaniah 1:14-18 (ESV)

"Therefore wait for me," declares the LORD,
  "for the day when I rise up to seize the prey.
For my decision is to gather nations,
  to assemble kingdoms,
to pour out upon them my indignation,
  all my burning anger;
for in the fire of my jealousy
  all the earth shall be consumed.
            Zephaniah 3:8 (ESV)

[1] *"For behold, the day is coming, burning like an oven, when all the arrogant and all evildoers will be stubble. The day that is coming shall set them ablaze, says the LORD of hosts, so that it will leave them neither root nor branch.* [2] *But*

for you who fear my name, the sun of righteousness shall rise with healing in its wings. You shall go out leaping like calves from the stall. [3] And you shall tread down the wicked, for they will be ashes under the soles of your feet, on the day when I act, says the LORD of hosts.

Malachi 4:1-3 (ESV)

Do not imagine that being a Christian means that you will never face God's judgment. It will simply be done at a different *time,* in a different *place*, on a different *basis* and for a different *purpose* than the judgment of the unsaved. Nevertheless, it will still take place and it will still be awesome and terrifying, even if we have done well, but especially if we haven't.

When contemplating the impending judgment, a wise person is not quick to consider himself, or others, as being either a success, or a failure, in God's eyes

It is impossible to assess yourself accurately so as to figure out how well or badly you have done so far, or what Jesus' overall assessment of you will be. I am convinced that most of us will get it very wrong and will be surprised, in one direction or the other, when we meet Him face to face and hear exactly what He thinks of how well, or badly, we did. However, that does not mean that we should not examine ourselves here and now. Paul tells us to do so, to see whether we are still in the faith:

Examine yourselves, to see whether you are in the faith. Test yourselves. Or do you not realize this about yourselves, that Jesus Christ is in you?—unless indeed you fail to meet the test!

2 Corinthians 13:5 (ESV)

None of us can accurately weigh up the extent of our own faithfulness and fruitfulness, quite apart from all the other criteria by which we will be judged. We would get it wrong in all sorts of ways and either be too generous, or too harsh, with ourselves, especially when seen in comparison with others. The judgment which Jesus conducts will be infinitely complicated. It will take account of all the many differences in our circumstances, abilities, opportunities and challenges and also the extent to which we were helped or hindered by other people, or opposed by demons, during our time on Earth.

To account for all of that Jesus will have to apply a vastly complex series of multipliers and discounts to increase or decrease our 'score', so as to put us all on a level playing field. That will be needed to ensure that the judgment is scrupulously fair and does not favour those who began with more and had greater privileges and opportunities, or prejudice those who did not. Therefore, we should

551

all be very careful about pronouncing any verdicts here and now and slow to reach any conclusions as to whether we, or others, are doing well or badly.

You just can't do it and if you attempt it you will either feed your pride, or discourage yourself needlessly. The best policy is to make no judgments of those kind i.e. the *kreetace* form of judgement, which we are forbidden to do, but to leave that entirely to Jesus when the day comes. Until then we should examine our consciences and cross-examine ourselves, to establish our real motives and to root out any falseness, pride, hypocrisy or complacency. This is the *diakrino* form of judgement which is appropriate to use, to assess both ourselves and others.

Yet all of that must be done without going to the other extreme, whereby we join in with the demons and become our own accuser and demoralise ourselves instead of growing in motivation and zeal. So, whether you are too generous or too hard on yourself, the demons will be pleased. Indeed, they will look to see which way you are already leaning, and then seek to push you even farther in that direction. They don't mind which direction it is, as both suit their purposes. So, on judgment day, or 'results day' as one might call it, there will be many surprises, in both directions.

Many will be startled by how well they did and many others will be shocked to learn that they did less well than they had assumed. Some who have spent their whole adult life in church leadership may receive little or no reward. Jesus may say that they were cowardly, lazy, unfaithful and did not have the love of the truth, such that they compromised, took the path of least resistance, and were even apostate. Others who were anonymous in this life, and felt insignificant may be richly rewarded and given high places in the Kingdom because they were faithful and true, even though they were never famous.

A classic example of how people can misjudge others is the account of Job and his friends. They see the disasters which have befallen him and leap to the conclusion that God must be displeased with Job and is therefore judging him for his wrongdoings. They also assume their own superiority and see themselves as wise when, in fact, they all get it wrong. God was actually pleased with Job and He only allowed the tragedies and illness to come upon him to show the Devil how *righteous* Job was, not to punish him. Here are some of the unjust accusations they make about Job, which God later says are mistaken:

"Remember: who that was innocent ever perished?
Or where were the upright cut off?
                        Job 4:7 (ESV)

[4] Is it for your fear of him that he reproves you
and enters into judgment with you?

552

⁵ Is not your evil abundant?
There is no end to your iniquities.
⁶ For you have exacted pledges of your brothers for nothing
and stripped the naked of their clothing.
⁷ You have given no water to the weary to drink,
and you have withheld bread from the hungry.
⁸ The man with power possessed the land,
and the favored man lived in it.
⁹ You have sent widows away empty,
and the arms of the fatherless were crushed.
¹⁰ Therefore snares are all around you,
and sudden terror overwhelms you,

Job 22:4-10 (ESV)

For according to the work of a man he will repay him,
and according to his ways he will make it befall him.
Job 34:11 (ESV)

Later God expresses His anger at Job's friends for their inaccurate conclusions and for the unfounded accusations they make against him:

⁷ After the LORD had spoken these words to Job, the LORD said to Eliphaz the Temanite: "My anger burns against you and against your two friends, for you have not spoken of me what is right, as my servant Job has. ⁸ Now therefore take seven bulls and seven rams and go to my servant Job and offer up a burnt offering for yourselves. And my servant Job shall pray for you, for I will accept his prayer not to deal with you according to your folly. For you have not spoken of me what is right, as my servant Job has." ⁹ So Eliphaz the Temanite and Bildad the Shuhite and Zophar the Naamathite went and did what the LORD had told them, and the LORD accepted Job's prayer.

Job 42:7-9 (ESV)

To further prove that He was actually delighted with Job, and not judging him, God restored Job's fortunes. He gave him twice what he had before, except for his children. God did not need to double those because the children who had died were still in existence. They were in 'Abraham's bosom', waiting for Job to be reunited with them when he died:

¹⁰ And the LORD restored the fortunes of Job, when he had prayed for his friends. And the LORD gave Job twice as much as he had before. ¹¹ Then came to him all his brothers and sisters and all who had known him before, and ate bread with him in his house. And they showed him sympathy and comforted him for all the evil that the LORD had brought upon him. And each of them gave him a piece of money and a ring of gold.

¹² And the LORD blessed the latter days of Job more than his beginning. And he had 14,000 sheep, 6,000 camels, 1,000 yoke of oxen, and 1,000 female donkeys. ¹³ He had also seven sons and three daughters. ¹⁴ And he called the name of the first daughter Jemimah, and the name of the second Keziah, and the name of the third Keren-happuch. ¹⁵ And in all the land there were no women so beautiful as Job's daughters. And their father gave them an inheritance among their brothers. ¹⁶ And after this Job lived 140 years, and saw his sons, and his sons' sons, four generations. ¹⁷ And Job died, an old man, and full of days.

Job 42:10-17 (ESV)

We will misjudge other people's contribution and performance if we fail to take into account the obstacles, and the demonic opposition which they faced

Another common reason why we might misjudge another person's 'performance' in this life, in comparison to our own, is that we might fail to take into account the obstacles and demonic opposition which they faced in comparison to what you or others faced. Imagine that person A, during this life, comes up against 100 units of adversity, demonic opposition, and other difficulties, but he eventually produces 50 units of output or achievement for God. At the same time, person B might produce 100 units of output/achievement, but he only encountered 10 units of resistance, adversity and difficulties.

Can you see how God would very probably see A as having done better than B, even though, in objective terms, so far as we could see, A produced or achieved less? The point is that, in proportional terms, A was far more of an 'overcomer' than B. That is crucial, because one of the key qualities that God is looking for in us is that we should be overcomers. See how frequently overcoming is referred to:

Do not be overcome by evil, but overcome evil with good.
Romans 12:21 (RSV)

He that hath an ear, let him hear what the Spirit saith unto the churches; To him that overcometh will I give to eat of the tree of life, which is in the midst of the paradise of God.

Revelation 2:7 (KJV)

He that hath an ear, let him hear what the Spirit saith unto the churches; To him that overcometh will I give to eat of the hidden manna, and will give him a white stone, and in the stone a new name written, which no man knoweth saving he that receiveth it.

Revelation 2:17 (KJV)

And he that overcometh, and keepeth my works unto the end, to him will I give power over the nations:

Revelation 2:26 (KJV)

He that overcometh, the same shall be clothed in white raiment; and I will not blot out his name out of the book of life, but I will confess his name before my Father, and before his angels

Revelation 3:5 (KJV)

Him that overcometh will I make a pillar in the temple of my God, and he shall go no more out: and I will write upon him the name of my God, and the name of the city of my God, which is new Jerusalem, which cometh down out of heaven from my God: and I will write upon him my new name.

Revelation 3:12 (KJV)

To him that overcometh will I grant to sit with me in my throne, even as I also overcame, and am set down with my Father in his throne.

Revelation 3:21 (KJV)

He that overcometh shall inherit all things; and I will be his God, and he shall be my son.

Why so much stress on 'overcoming' if we're raptured?

Revelation 21:7 (KJV)

We will also misjudge other people's contribution or performance if we don't take into account the time when they lived and the circumstances they faced

Another factor which may cause us to miscalculate how well another person has done in God's eyes or how highly He values their contribution, is the *time* at which, or the *circumstances* in which, their work was done. To use a military example to illustrate this point, look at what was achieved by two different groups of men on or near the beaches of France at two different times, June 1940 and June 1944.

On the first occasion, when the British army was retreating from the far larger German army, 50,000 British soldiers were ordered to stay in France and fight to the end, with no hope of evacuation. Their grim orders were to stay behind and protect the beaches so that the rest of the British army could escape via Dunkirk. That group fought valiantly, but were all either killed or taken prisoner. For them, the war was over only a few weeks after it really began. They then played no further part and very few of them ever received any recognition for what they did.

By contrast, the men who went back in and invaded France on D Day four years later have gone down in history as heroes, and rightly so. Yet, if we were to ask

555

which group made the greater contribution to the overall war effort, and thus deserves greater honour, it may well have been the men who stayed behind in 1940 and never got the chance to be evacuated. Their willingness to sacrifice themselves enabled 340,000 *other* soldiers to get away and to form the nucleus of the new, and much larger, British army which was later built around them.

If those men who stayed behind in 1940 had not fought that rear guard action, protecting the evacuation beaches at Dunkirk, the whole war would almost certainly have been lost. So, theirs was arguably a greater victory, as it kept hope alive. Yet, all around the world, it was seen by many as a defeat. The men who fought in that rear guard are rarely even remembered today, let alone given the honour they deserve, whereas those who later invaded Normandy are. In the same way, many of us will be given tasks to perform by God which will not lead to any fame or glory in this life.

They may even be seen as defeats, for example the efforts of the valiant few who have fought, unsuccessfully so far, to reverse the legalisation of abortion. Many of those pro-life campaigners have fought hard for decades, and have paid a high price. Yet they have received little or no recognition and not many would view them as a success. But their apparent failure is mainly due to the time in history at which they had to fight, due to the time at which they lived. Others, who lived at better times in the history of the Church, such as the 18th and 19th centuries in the UK and USA, were able to achieve what seemed to be far bigger.

Yet it may be that a large part of the reason for their greater success was simply the fact of when they lived, and what God was doing at that time, rather than their own merit. Those of us in the West who struggle to preach the Gospel in these bleak days, when very few will repent or believe, may not necessarily be judged to have done less well than those 18th century evangelists like George Whitefield who attracted vast and enthusiastic crowds.

On the face of it, Whitefield seems to have done better than us. But that may not necessarily be Jesus' view when the whole facts are made known and everything is seen in its proper context. That is an encouragement to those who remain faithful in bleak times or places in history, when only meagre visible results are achieved. It is also a warning to those who live in 'better' times, or better places, when the Holy Spirit is pouring out His power and whole nations are in revival.

A final point I would make is that sometimes God subjects certain individuals to sustained and severe testing, for years or even decades, as He prepares them for unusually big tasks that lie ahead. Yet, other people may be tested and prepared for far shorter periods and they are then able to get on with things much sooner and be seen to be achieving things in their teens or twenties. At the same time, some other man is still being tested and prepared, even in his thirties or forties, or later, for a task that is still future and which only God knows about.

If you are the man whom God has allowed to get on with things sooner, don't look down on the man whom God is still preparing for a future task of which you may not be capable. But if you are the man who is still in obscurity, being tested, don't be discouraged. Your hour will come and God may well be pleased with your progress in the years of preparation, even if nobody has heard of you. Let neither man be quick to declare himself either a success or a failure. Consider that to be an open question, and don't even attempt to answer it. It is Jesus's job to decide that.

Wise people do not make this present physical Earth their focus

Instead of being focused on the rapture, the Day of Judgment and the Millennial Kingdom, we are seeing at present an increasingly widespread and obsessive interest, in the physical condition of this planet and its ecology, climate, sustainability etc. There is nothing wrong with caring for the environment. Indeed, it is our responsibility, as part of our stewardship of this Earth, to look after it sensibly. However we are being presented with a barrage of unfounded propaganda about supposed climate change and the alleged role of carbon dioxide emissions in causing so called *'global warming'*.

Concern about this has reached the level of frenzy for many people, even in the churches. This alarmist message is being taught in schools and universities, as if it was proven fact, when it is actually just a very flimsy and entirely unproven theory. As we saw above, the very same people who are now predicting global warming were, until the mid-1980s, predicting a coming ice-age. Now they say the exact opposite, without any mention of their 180° change of mind, let alone an apology for it. *Government science has zero credibility - propaganda*

However, for the moment, the issue is whether we should be making the condition of our atmosphere and of the planet's animal and plant life such a central and urgent concern. Should a Christian be focused on those things and should such issues alarm us and grip our attention, as they do with the unbelieving, secular world? Without needing to get into the science of it, or rather the *alleged* science, we can answer the question more simply by looking at what the Bible has to say about this planet and its future.

We are told plainly that the surface of this physical Earth is going to be *totally destroyed by fire*. The whole world is going to be so thoroughly judged by God that the planet's entire *surface* will be burned up. That is quite separate from the terrible judgment that will also come upon the Earth's *inhabitants* during the Tribulation. Look at what the prophet Isaiah has to say:

¹Behold, the LORD will lay waste the earth and make it desolate, and he will twist its surface and scatter its inhabitants. ² And it shall be, as with the people, so with the priest; as with the slave, so with his master; as with the maid, so with her mistress; as with the buyer, so with the seller; as with the lender, so with the borrower; as with the creditor, so with the debtor. ³ The earth shall be utterly laid waste and utterly despoiled; for the LORD has spoken this word.
Isaiah 24:1-3 (RSV)

Lift up your eyes to the heavens, and look at the earth beneath; for the heavens will vanish like smoke, the earth will wear out like a garment, and they who dwell in it will die like gnats; but my salvation will be for ever, and my deliverance will never be ended.
Isaiah 51:6 (RSV)

For behold, I create new heavens and a new earth; and the former things shall not be remembered or come into mind.
Isaiah 65:17 (RSV)

¹⁵ "For behold, the LORD will come in fire, and his chariots like the storm wind, to render his anger in fury, and his rebuke with flames of fire. ¹⁶For by fire will the LORD execute judgment, and by his sword, upon all flesh; and those slain by the LORD shall be many.
Isaiah 66:15-16 (RSV)

The prophet Zephaniah also speaks of this:

²"I will utterly sweep away everything
from the face of the earth," declares the LORD.
³ "I will sweep away man and beast;
I will sweep away the birds of the heavens
and the fish of the sea,
and the rubble with the wicked.
I will cut off mankind
from the face of the earth," declares the LORD.
Zephaniah 1:2-3 (ESV)

"Therefore wait for me," declares the LORD,
"for the day when I rise up to seize the prey.
For my decision is to gather nations,
to assemble kingdoms,
to pour out upon them my indignation,

all my burning anger;
for in the fire of my jealousy
all the earth shall be consumed.
           Zephaniah 3:8 (ESV)

Apostle Peter puts it even more starkly. He tells us that this present Earth, i.e. its *surface*, is going to be utterly burned away, such that *nothing at all* will be left. There will be no remaining soil or vegetation of any kind after this process of judgment is completed:

[1]This is now the second letter that I have written to you, beloved, and in both of them I have aroused your sincere mind by way of reminder; [2] that you should remember the predictions of the holy prophets and the commandment of the Lord and Saviour through your apostles. [3] First of all you must understand this, that scoffers will come in the last days with scoffing, following their own passions [4] and saying, "Where is the promise of his coming? For ever since the fathers fell asleep, all things have continued as they were from the beginning of creation." [5] They deliberately ignore this fact, that by the word of God heavens existed long ago, and an earth formed out of water and by means of water, [6] through which the world that then existed was deluged with water and perished. [7] But by the same word the heavens and earth that now exist have been stored up for fire, being kept until the day of judgment and destruction of ungodly men.
           2 Peter 3:1-7 (RSV)

Peter goes on, later in that same chapter, to be even more explicit about what is going to happen to this physical planet when God's judgment comes. In particular we are told that there will be a *new Earth*. But the Greek word used for *new* means *renewed*, rather than *brand new*. This Earth that we live on now will be burned clean, or rather its surface will be. Then it will be made as good as new, the way it was when it was first created. God will not replace this Earth with a different planet. He will cleanse it and make it as it once was, before sin came into the world:

[10]But the day of the Lord will come like a thief, and then the heavens will pass away with a loud noise, and the elements will be dissolved with fire, and the earth and the works that are upon it will be burned up. [11] Since all these things are thus to be dissolved, what sort of persons ought you to be in lives of holiness and godliness, [12] waiting for and hastening the coming of the day of God, because of which the heavens will be kindled and dissolved, and the elements will melt with fire! [13] But according to his promise we wait for new heavens and a new earth in which righteousness dwells. [14] Therefore, beloved, since you wait for these, be zealous to be found by him without spot or blemish, and at peace.
           2 Peter 3:10-14 (RSV)

559

If you want to know in greater detail what God is going to do to judge unbelievers and how His wrath will also affect the physical Earth itself, and bring it to a condition of utter ruin, then read the whole of Revelation, in particular chapters 6 to 19. There is going to be a series of cataclysmic outpourings of God's judgment on the unbelieving people of the world and also on the planet itself.

These will bring it to the point of devastation, even before the whole surface of the Earth is later burned up. However, the news is not all bad because, when that process of judgment is all over, God will then restore both the Earth's atmosphere and its land surface. We will then have a renewed Earth, perfect in every way, as it was to begin with, before Adam and Eve sinned:

¹ Then I saw a new heaven and a new earth; for the first heaven and the first earth had passed away, and the sea was no more. ² And I saw the holy city, new Jerusalem, coming down out of heaven from God, prepared as a bride adorned for her husband; ³ and I heard a loud voice from the throne saying, "Behold, the dwelling of God is with men. He will dwell with them, and they shall be his people, and God himself will be with them; ⁴ he will wipe away every tear from their eyes, and death shall be no more, neither shall there be mourning nor crying nor pain any more, for the former things have passed away."

Revelation 21:1-4 (RSV)

Isaiah also referred to the new Earth, long before apostle John did:

"For as the new heavens and the new earth which I will make shall remain before me, says the LORD; so shall your descendants and your name remain.

Isaiah 66:22 (RSV)

As God is going to destroy the entire surface of the Earth with fire, we must not make ecology or alleged climate change our focus

God will destroy the whole of the Earth's surface and its atmosphere with fire. Even before doing that, He will have already destroyed much of it by many other preliminary forms of judgment. However, He will then recreate a perfect renewed Earth which will last forever and never be polluted. What then should our attitude be in relation to the *current* Earth's atmosphere and to the environment generally? Given that God has made us stewards of this Earth, we have a duty to care for it during this current age and not to pollute it or to destroy the wildlife that live on it.

My wife and I go to considerable lengths to care for the birds in our vicinity and feed them regularly with seeds. We also plant a lot of shrubs and trees, especially those which produce nuts and berries of various types, or which host insects for food. We also seek to provide good roosting and nesting areas. Every house we have owned has ended up a better habitat for birds as a result of us living there. To us it is both an interest and a responsibility. Nevertheless, we know that, in the end, every single tree and shrub that we ever plant will be destroyed when God judges this world.

He will wipe it all clean, ready to start again with a renewed Earth in the Eternal State, after the 1000 year Millennial Kingdom is over. Thus, we are not under any illusions that what we are doing now to care for the birds in our area is going to "*save the planet*". That is an impossible and futile objective, as nobody can save the planet from God's judgment. On the other hand, nobody other than God can destroy it either, as the Bible makes clear that *God Himself will destroy it*, not us. Thus, it is foolish to think that we can either cause that ourselves or prevent Him from doing so.

It is even more foolish to make ecology in general, or the control of carbon dioxide in particular, into the focus of our lives, as so many are now doing, even within the churches. A wise person takes seriously the responsibility we have as stewards of the Earth during our time on it. But they also take seriously what the Bible says about the future of this Earth and what *God, not man*, is going to do to it. Every person I have ever heard who is impassioned about environmental issues, and who has made those issues their central concern, seems to have paid no attention to Bible prophecy.

They do not take into account what the Bible says about God's future plans for this Earth. Such wilful blindness is foolish, however well-intentioned it may be. It is based on men's theories and ideas, without any regard to what God explicitly says on this issue. How can it make any sense to focus so much time, energy and money on trying to preserve this planet when God has said He is going to *destroy* it? He will still destroy it, no matter how many trees we plant, and no matter how little CO_2 we emit.

Likewise, how can it be wise *not* to focus upon the new and perfect Earth which God will create when the judgment is over? A wise person will give most of their attention to the eternal rather than the purely temporary. That is what we should do now, instead of becoming wrapped up in the hysteria about alleged climate change. That would still be the case even if it was really happening, and even if the alleged causal link between man-made CO_2 and increased global temperatures were both proved to be true. However, they aren't true, and there is no credible evidence to support either theory.

Indeed, as we saw, there is a worldwide petition, signed by over 30,000 scientists, who state that they *do not* believe there is global warming, or, even if there is, that it is caused by man-made CO_2. No publicity is ever given to that petition by the

561

world's governments or media. They keep saying that "*scientists agree that the evidence is now overwhelming*", without either mentioning the petition, or setting out any evidence in support of their own position. You are supposed to just accept it without questioning it, or even knowing what it is.

Wise people can 'tell the time' as to whether it is a time of judgment and whether God's mercy is still available to the nation as a whole or just to individuals

Nations go through various stages in their history, whereby they are either rising or falling and where God is either using them or abandoning them, and bringing either revival or judgment. Depending on what 'time' it is, God makes His mercy available either to the nation as a whole, or only to individuals within it. I refer to this process of identifying what stage a nation is at, and what God is doing with it, as 'telling the time', i.e. in terms of God's prophetic timetable worldwide and also His intentions towards that nation.

In the late 1990s, in the charismatic church we were then part of, there was much talk of God imminently sending a huge revival to the UK. As I look back, I believe they were mistaken as to what 'time' it was. It was, in fact, primarily a time for God's judgment to be poured out on the UK, not His mercy. Of course, *individuals* could still be saved, even in the midst of that judgment. However, the revival which they expected to come to the UK as a whole was simply not going to happen, due to the extent of the sin in our nation and, even more crucially, the extent of the apostasy in the churches.

Sometimes, within a particular nation, it is a time for evil to prevail. At such times, Satan, his demons, the wicked people within the population, and especially their leaders, are given the chance by God to have their own way and to do what they want to do. One such time was when Jesus was arrested and put on trial. It was done by wicked men, under Satan's guidance. But God permitted it because He had a deeper, wider purpose for allowing the crucifixion to go ahead:

⁵² Then Jesus said to the chief priests and officers of the temple and elders, who had come out against him, "Have you come out as against a robber, with swords and clubs? ⁵³ When I was with you day after day in the temple, you did not lay hands on me. But this is your hour, and the power of darkness."

Luke 22:52-53 (ESV)

An example from Scripture of two different times or eras in the life of a nation can be seen in God's handling of Nineveh. As we saw earlier, in the time of Jonah, God was willing to warn the population of Nineveh. Then, when they repented, He had mercy on the *whole nation*. We might call that a conditional warning about God's judgment. So, *at that time*, mercy was available to the people as a whole, if enough of them would collectively repent. However, just over a century later, at the time of the prophet Nahum, the situation had changed.

It was now a time for judgment, not mercy, and there was no question of Nineveh as a whole being spared from God's wrath. If we look at judgment in the Bible we can see that it comes in various different ways, depending on how far that nation has gone into sin and rebellion and on whether or not God's patience has finally run out. So, at the time of the Judges, 'we see a series of judgments happening in a distinct pattern or cycle, over several centuries.

The people of Israel would degenerate into idolatry and apostasy and then God would bring judgment through the oppression of neighbouring nations. That would cause many of the people to come to their senses and repent. As a result, God would send deliverance by men such as Ehud, Barak, Gideon, Jephthah, Samson and others. But then, the improved conditions would lead to complacency, a lapse back into apostasy and idolatry, and the resumption of God's judgment. Anyone living at the time of the Judges, *if they had discernment*, would be able to see where Israel was in that cyclical pattern.

Later, things reached a much lower ebb in the life of the nation. It led to the northern Kingdom being completely invaded by the Assyrians and the people being exiled. We might call that a *judgment by invasion.* The same occurred later when the southern Kingdom was invaded by the Babylonians and the people were exiled. At that time wise people, if they had listened to the warnings and prophecies of Jeremiah and other prophets, rather than ignoring them, could have seen what was about to happen. Then they could have prepared for it, at least as individuals.

Another form of judgment we see in Scripture is *'catastrophic judgment'* as occurred at the Flood in Noah's day and also in the cities of Sodom and Gomorrah, when the people were all destroyed by fire and sulphur. By contrast, in our personal lives as individuals or churches we can see *'disciplining judgment'*. This is meant to bring us to our senses so that we wake up, repent, and turn back to God. A wise person can discern when such a form of judgment is occurring in his own life and respond to it with repentance.

Another frightening form of judgment, which I believe applies to the UK and the USA today, is what one might call *'abandonment judgment'*. This occurs where God's patience runs out with a nation, especially if it is one which He has previously blessed and given spiritual advantages. It means that God effectively *hands that nation over* and leaves them to get on with the wicked things they have already decided they want to do. He will withdraw His hand of protection, stop sending them warnings, and leave the people to degenerate into decay and eventual collapse.

I believe this kind of abandonment judgment occurred to the UK in the mid-20th century when the nation was judged by God for its rapidly rising sin, the apostasy of its churches, and its betrayal of the Jewish people during the 1920s and 1930's. At that time we had the mandate from the League of Nations to administer 'Palestine', and had also promised in 1917, in the 'Balfour declaration', to establish a homeland for the Jews. But we failed to do so, for fear of offending the Arabs.

As we reach the end of the last days, we will also see what one might call *'apocalyptic judgment'*, when God pours out His full wrath on the whole world for its sin, and rebellion. This will assuredly come and will be on a scale not seen since the Flood. The book of Revelation has a lot to say about this, although it is by no means the only book which does so. Many of the Old Testament prophets, and also many of the other New Testament books and letters, address this coming judgment on the Earth. It will be cataclysmic and will bring death and destruction on a massive scale.

As we read the Bible and observe world events in the news it is clear that the end cannot be far away now, as so many predicted events have already occurred and others are moving into place ready to be fulfilled. Last of all, there will be the two main judgments which will stand for all eternity. The first of these is the Judgment Seat of Christ, at which all saved believers will be judged on the basis of what they did since their *conversion* and the extent to which they bore fruit and were faithful.

They will then be rewarded, or not, or possibly even rebuked, for what they did and didn't do in the time they had and with the talents they were given, whether small or large. Later will come the very final judgment at the Great White Throne, when all unsaved, unrepentant, unbelievers will be judged and then sent to the Lake of Fire.

So, if we ask what the 'time' is at present, at least in the Western world, the UK, Western Europe and the USA, Canada and Australia, I would say that we have already entered into the stage that I call 'abandonment judgment'. By that I don't mean that nobody can be saved, but that these *nations as a whole* cannot be saved. They have simply gone too far, in particular by conducting abortions on an industrial scale, with 8,000,000 babies killed in the UK since 1967 and 58,000,000 killed in America since 1973. That is unprecedented in world history and nobody can say that it is a small matter.

Therefore, as nations, we have crossed a line and there is no way back, *in my personal opinion*, no matter how much we might pray for God's mercy on the UK, USA and Europe. I believe that at this stage in world history these nations are being judged by God and that only individuals can be saved, not the nations as a whole. As countries they will therefore continue to decline morally and spiritually. They will then become increasingly unable even to hear God's convicting voice at all, let alone to turn to Him en masse in repentance and faith.

Only individuals will do so, one here, and another there, but not on any large scale basis, as happened in Nineveh in Jonah's day, though not in Nahum's day. The time we now live in, within the West is one of growing sin, rebellion, folly and apostasy and of a downward spiral into moral bankruptcy and chaos. We also see this illustrated in the astonishing increase in homosexuality and gender confusion, both of which are primarily the *result* of our nations' abandonment of God, not the *cause* of it. Perhaps the most notable feature of that judgment on the West is the increasing *inability* to respond to the Gospel even when it is proclaimed.

That is because God has been taking away from a large proportion of our populations the *very ability to hear.* Therefore, many of the people have become spiritually *deaf and blind*, so they cannot hear or understand, no matter what we say or write to them. However, their hearts are only being hardened by God because they have already been *hardening their own hearts* now for many years. It is like it was in the days when Amos prophesied a *"famine ..... of hearing the words of the LORD."*

"Behold, the days are coming," declares the Lord GOD,
"when I will send a famine on the land—
not a famine of bread, nor a thirst for water,
but of hearing the words of the LORD.
Amos 8:11 (ESV)

CHAPTER 16

WISE PEOPLE UNDERSTAND THE REAL NATURE OF ISLAM

Then Zebah and Zalmunna said, "Rise yourself and fall upon us, for as the man is, so is his strength." And Gideon arose and killed Zebah and Zalmunna, and he took the crescent ornaments that were on the necks of their camels.

Judges 8:21 (ESV)

And the weight of the golden earrings that he requested was 1,700 shekels of gold, besides the crescent ornaments and the pendants and the purple garments worn by the kings of Midian, and besides the collars that were around the necks of their camels.

Judges 8:26 (ESV)

In that day the Lord will take away the finery of the anklets, the headbands, and the crescents;

Isaiah 3:18 (ESV)

[1] O God, do not keep silence;
do not hold your peace or be still, O God!
[2] For behold, your enemies make an uproar;
those who hate you have raised their heads.
[3] They lay crafty plans against your people;
they consult together against your treasured ones.
[4] They say, "Come, let us wipe them out as a nation;
let the name of Israel be remembered no more!"
[5] For they conspire with one accord;
against you they make a covenant
[6] the tents of Edom and the Ishmaelites,
Moab and the Hagrites,
[7] Gebal and Ammon and Amalek,
Philistia with the inhabitants of Tyre;
[8] Asshur also has joined them;
they are the strong arm of the children of Lot.
Psalm 83:1-8 (ESV)

[1] An oracle concerning Damascus.
Behold, Damascus will cease to be a city
and will become a heap of ruins.

567

² The cities of Aroer are deserted;
  they will be for flocks,
  which will lie down, and none will make them afraid.
                              Isaiah 17:1-2 (ESV)

The West's spineless naivety about Islam and wilful refusal to see it for the evil that it is

You might ask what a person's view of Islam has got to do with whether they are wise. My answer is that the actions of Muslim terrorists, pursuant to what the Koran calls the *Jihad*, or "holy war", are by far the biggest threat to peace, freedom of speech, and freedom of religion, in the world today. I am also increasingly coming to the view that Islam will be the religion of the antichrist, whose coming is spoken of in the Bible. Therefore, whether you can see all of that, such that you know the real truth about Islam, is a key issue in determining whether you are wise or naïve.

I would go further and say that whether you are willing to *tell the truth* about Islam, even if you can see it, is an indicator of whether you are a fool, or even wicked. This is nothing new. The Jihad has been raging for nearly 1400 years, ever since Mohammed started it in the early seventh century AD. From then on Islam has, *mainly by violence,* conquered first Arabia and then 56 other nations. Therefore, there are now 57 countries in the world that are ruled by Islam, plus many more that are heading that way, with rapidly growing Muslim populations.

That relentless process of takeover is also partly due to *massive immigration* by Muslims, including bogus *'refugees'*, combined also with a disproportionately high birth rate amongst Muslims in comparison to westerners. This demographic aspect of the takeover also has a name, the *"Hijra"*. That is what Mohammed said should be done, *in addition to Jihad*, to cause Muslims to become the majority in one nation after another, by sheer population growth, until the native population is eventually overwhelmed and submits to living under Sharia law.

However, no matter what happens, liberal westerners continue to think that Islam is being falsely accused and that only a *"tiny minority"* of Muslims support the Jihad. We therefore need to think carefully about Islam and decide who is right and who is wrong, what is true and what is false. Either the liberal view of Islam is correct, or mine is, but one thing is certain - they cannot both be right. Therefore, we need to find the real facts, examine the evidence open-mindedly, and come to a clear decision.

These huge questions as to what Islam really is, what its objectives are, what its followers are doing, whether it poses a threat to us, and what we should do about it, are of crucial importance. Therefore, any person who does not arrive at the right conclusions on such issues cannot be wise. That is all the more true of anybody who gives these questions no thought and thus comes to no conclusions at all. Therefore, determining the real nature of Islam is no minor matter and you cannot excuse yourself from the duty to reflect on it and to make up your mind.

However, your judgment must be based on fact, not on wishful thinking, politicians' lies, or media propaganda. I say that because, right across the western world, feeble politicians, aided by a corrupt media, maintain the fiction of Muslims as *victims*, and of Islam being a great *'religion of peace'*. Such absurd things were not said in the past, when leaders told the truth, and the press reported it. For example, William Gladstone, a tremendous scholar, and our greatest Prime Minister of the nineteenth century, understood Islam very accurately and was not afraid to tell the truth about it:

"The Koran .... is an accursed book. So long as there is this book there will be no peace in the world."

> William Ewart Gladstone
> (Prime Minister of the United Kingdom
> four times between 1868 and 1894)

The origins of Islam are in pagan idolatry and the occult

An interesting passage in Judges chapter 8 refers to *'crescent ornaments'* worn by the Midianites, who were part of what we now call the Arab race. They worshiped the Arabic moon god, whose emblem was the crescent moon. This is highly significant because the Arabs were still worshiping the moon god many centuries later, in AD 610, when Mohammed invented Islam. He merged together parts of Judaism and Christianity, plus the Arabic moon god, whom he elevated to become what is now called Allah. He also kept the symbol of the crescent moon, some of which Gideon had confiscated from the Midianites, nearly 2000 years earlier:

Then Zebah and Zalmunna said, "Rise yourself and fall upon us, for as the man is, so is his strength." And Gideon arose and killed Zebah and Zalmunna, and he took the crescent ornaments that were on the necks of their camels.

Judges 8:21 (ESV)

And the weight of the golden earrings that he requested was 1,700 shekels of gold, besides the crescent ornaments and the pendants and the purple garments worn by the kings of Midian, and besides the collars that were around the necks of their camels.

Judges 8:26 (ESV)

Let us be clear - Allah is *not* an alternative name for the God of the Bible, as so many misguided liberal Christians are wrongly taught. It is actually the name of the very same moon god whom the Arabs worshiped when they were pagans, long before Mohammed founded Islam. Thus, anyone who worships Allah is not merely worshiping God by an alternative name. They are worshiping *a false, pagan god*, and that needs to be said, loudly and publicly, no matter how politically incorrect it may be.

Therefore, Islam is not *"one of the three great Abrahamic faiths"*, to quote that awful politically correct phrase. It is, in fact, a false religion and there is nothing good or admirable about it. Moreover, the symbols within Islam, in particular the crescent moon, are based on the *occult*, not the Bible. One day all such occult symbols and objects are going to be destroyed, when Jesus returns. The prophet Isaiah refers to that time:

In that day the Lord will take away the finery of the anklets, the headbands, and the crescents;

Isaiah 3:18 (ESV)

The Sabbeans in Arabia also worshiped the same moon god, *'Allah'*, who was believed to be married to the sun goddess. They set up an idol devoted to Allah at the Kabah in Mecca, along with 359 other pagan gods whom the Arabs also worshiped. They had, therefore, already begun the practice of praying towards Mecca, where those occultic idols were located, long before Mohammed established Islam, between AD 610 and 632. All he did was get rid of the other 359 Arabic idols and false gods and promote the equally false moon god, Allah, to first place, as the one and only god.

However, that does not mean that he is the God of the Bible, as we are constantly, but wrongly, told. Allah always was, *and still is*, the Arabic moon god and has nothing whatsoever to do with the real God of the Bible. Indeed, he is the very opposite, in every respect, especially in terms of his character and nature. The Bible shows God to be full of love, mercy, grace and kindness, but the Koran reveals Allah to be vicious and cold-hearted, without a shred of love or grace towards anyone, not even his followers.

The true nature of Islam – a list of its main features and practices

There is not space, even in this whole book, let alone this chapter, to set out a thorough account of the history and ideology of Islam and of its corrupt, perverted and violent activities. However, even if we restrict our examination of Islam to the most basic facts, and then apply the plainest, most obvious logic to those facts, the conclusions are inescapable. One is obliged to accept that *Islam itself, i.e. true*

570

Islam, as distinct from the actions of a supposedly unrepresentative minority of its adherents, is all of the following things:

a) a false religion which is contrary to, and inconsistent with, the Gospel.

b) evil and Satanic in origin, created as a result of Mohammed's encounters with a demon, probably Satan himself, who spoke to him and gave him all the doctrines of Islam.

c) violent by its very nature, i.e. when the Koran is *correctly understood*, not only when it is supposedly *'misunderstood'*, as is constantly claimed by western liberals.

d) repressive of and contemptuous towards all women, even Muslim women. They see females as mere property and as having no value, dignity or freedom, to such an extent that it is literally alright to rape them. That is exactly what is being done now on a vast scale, even in Europe, not only in Muslim countries which operate under Sharia law.

e) contemptuous towards non-Muslims, whom they call *'infidels'* or *'kuffirs'*, seeing us as the equivalent of dogs, and thus sub-human.

f) repressive of freedom of speech, and freedom of religion, and determined to deny these freedoms to all of us.

g) committed to *imposing Islam by force of arms,* so as to win control of every nation, until the *entire world* has either been killed or compelled to become Muslim. The conquering of non-Islamic nations is referred to as *Jihad* and is not merely the aim of some fanatical and unrepresentative minority. It is a *core objective* of Islam itself, i.e. *true Islam*, as set out in the Koran and as modelled by Mohammed himself. Therefore, we must never honour him by calling him *"the prophet Mohammed"*, or even *"the Prophet"*, as the servile and cowardly BBC does. He was *not* a prophet and should not be spoken of as if he was. *He was - a false prophet*

h) committed to the use of *deception*, "*taqiyya*", as a means of promoting Islam, supporting the Jihad, and undermining infidels. The Koran teaches that it is *entirely alright to lie to infidels* in order to deceive them into compliance, or to make them complacent prior to attacking them. When liberals believe what Muslims say about the supposed peacefulness of Islam etc, they have no idea that such lies are, *in themselves*, a central part of Islam. They are used as a deliberate tool of war, which explains why so many Muslims are dishonest, as I frequently found when I was a police officer. Telling lies is an *integral*

571

part of Muslim culture and spills over into every part of their lives, not just the pursuit of Jihad.

i)   committed to imposing a status of *servile slavery*, known as *"dhimmitude"*, upon all infidels who are not killed in the Jihad. Islam is willing to permit such infidels to live, but *only provided they pay money* to the Muslims who rule over them. So, non-Muslims are taxed, for example by pressurising companies into paying vast sums to have *halal* certificates and logos for their products. This is being done now in the West, even where Muslims are in a minority. They also bring about the same effect by *claiming state benefits* and often maximise those claims by falsification and deception (taqiyya).

j)   For all these reasons, a high percentage of Muslims claim state benefits, and on a permanent basis, not just occasionally. Indeed, only this week, as I was writing this, it was said that 60% of the Muslims in Europe are claiming welfare benefits. Indeed, even the politically correct German government has said that they expect up to 75% of the migrants who are flooding into Germany to be claiming benefits for many years and possibly *for their whole lives*.

k)   If they do have jobs, many Muslims will try not to pay income taxes. Or they avoid work altogether, have huge families, and claim state benefits for them. Many Muslims are effectively unemployable, due to their anti-social attitudes, and could not get jobs, even if they wanted them, as they are taught that it is *the role of infidels to subsidise them*, either by being taxed as *dhimmis*, or by funding welfare benefits. Therefore, the larger the Muslim population becomes, the greater is the financial burden on the non-Muslim taxpayers, until it becomes overwhelming. Ultimately it will cripple any western economy, as we are now finding.

Extracts from the Koran itself which show that it is western liberals who 'misunderstand' Islam, not the Jihadists

These features of Islam are *not* merely the practices of some unrepresentative minority who *"misunderstand the real nature of Islam"*. That is what a few Muslims say, but it is a lie, as they well know. It is only said to disguise what Islam is really about, to create complacency in the West, and to reduce our opposition to Islam. Yet these lies are willingly embraced by gullible liberals who even see it as a badge of honour to prove they are not *'Islamophobic'* and are not promoting *'stereotypes'* which portray Islam in a negative light.

Rather than ask you to take my word for it, let's look firstly at a number of passages from the Koran which spell out exactly what Mohammed's teachings were on waging a "holy" war and on slaying, beheading, maiming, crucifying, burning, boiling and generally terrorising infidels. Some people will only be able to believe these things if they see, with their own eyes, *extracts from the Koran itself*. Let's look therefore at just a sample of them to prove that I am not making this up and that it is *the jihadists who are the real Muslims*, not the so-called moderates:

Koran 2:191   *"Slay the unbelievers wherever you find them."*

Koran 3:15   *"Soon shall we cast terror into the hearts of the unbelievers"*

Koran 3:28   *"Muslims must not take the infidels as friends."*

Koran 3:85   *"Any religion other than Islam is not acceptable."*

Koran 4:74   *"Whoso fighteth in the way of Allah, be he slain or be he victorious, on him We shall bestow a vast reward."*

Koran 5:33   *"Maim and crucify the infidels if they criticise Islam."*

Koran 8:12   *"I will cast terror into the hearts of those who disbelieve. Therefore strike off their heads and strike off every fingertip of them."*

Koran 8:60   *"Muslims must muster all weapons to terrorise the infidels"*

Koran 8:65   *"The unbelievers are stupid: urge the Muslims to fight them."*

Koran 9:29   *"Fight those who believe not in Allah nor the Last Day, nor hold forbidden which hath been forbidden by Allah and His Messenger, nor acknowledge the religion of Truth, (even if they are) of the People of the Book, until they pay Jizya with willing submission, and feel themselves subdued."*

Koran 9:30   *"The Jews and Christians are perverts, fight them."*

Koran 9:123   *"Make war on the infidels living in your neighbourhood"*

Koran 22:19   *"Punish the unbelievers with garments of fire, hooked iron rods, boiling water, melt their skin and bellies"*

Koran 25:52   *"Therefore listen not to unbelievers, but strive against them with the utmost strenuousness...."*

Koran 47:3-4   *"Those who disbelieve follow falsehood, while those who believe follow the truth from their Lord... So, when you meet*

573

> (in fighting Jihad in Allah's Cause), those who disbelieve smite at their necks till when you have killed and wounded many of them, then bind a bond firmly on them, (i.e. take them as captives)... If it had been Allah's Will, He Himself could certainly have punished them (without you). But (He lets you fight), in order to test you, some with others. But those who are killed in the Way of Allah, He will never let their deeds be lost."

Koran 48:29   "Muhammad is the messenger of Allah. And those with him are hard (ruthless) against the disbelievers and merciful among themselves."

Koran 61:4   "Surely Allah loves those who fight in His cause."

Koran 61:10-12 "O you who believe! Shall I guide you to a commerce that will save you from a painful torment. That you believe in Allah and His Messenger (Muhammad), and that you strive hard and fight in the Cause of Allah with your wealth and your lives, that will be better for you, if you but know! (If you do so) He will forgive you your sins, and admit you into Gardens under which rivers flow, and pleasant dwelling in Gardens of 'Adn- Eternity ['Adn(Edn) Paradise], that is indeed the great success."

Further extracts which come from the Hadith and Sira

The Koran, from which I have been quoting, is supposedly what the angel Gabriel revealed to Mohammed between AD 610 and 632. However, the *hadith* are meant to be the sayings of Mohammed, or reports of what he did, which were recorded and written by his followers. In addition, there is the *sira* (or *sirah* according to some) which is Mohammed's life story or biography.

So, I will quote from each of these as well, to further demonstrate how barbaric Mohammed was. Above all, it will prove that the Jihad, and the rapes, paedophilia and deception displayed by Muslims today, *represent real Islam* and are not a corruption of it, or a departure from it. I will just quote a few sample extracts:

Sahih Bukhari (52:177) Allah's Apostle said, "The Hour will not be established until you fight with the Jews, and the stone behind which a Jew will be hiding will say. "O Muslim! There is a Jew hiding behind me, so kill him."

574

Sahih Muslim (1:30)	*"The Messenger of Allah said: I have been commanded to fight against people so long as they do not declare that there is no god but Allah."*
Sahih Muslim (1:33)	*the Messenger of Allah said: I have been commanded to fight against people till they testify that there is no god but Allah, that Muhammad is the messenger of Allah*
Sahih Bukhari (11:626)	*[Muhammad said:] "I decided to order a man to lead the prayer and then take a flame to burn all those, who had not left their houses for the prayer, burning them alive inside their homes."*
Sahih Muslim (1:149)	*"Abu Dharr reported: I said: Messenger of Allah, which of the deeds is the best? He (the Holy Prophet) replied: Belief in Allah and Jihad in His cause..."*
Sahih Muslim (20:4645)	*"...He (the Messenger of Allah) did that and said: There is another act which elevates the position of a man in Paradise to a grade one hundred (higher), and the elevation between one grade and the other is equal to the height of the heaven from the earth. He (Abu Sa'id) said: What is that act? He replied: Jihad in the way of Allah! Jihad in the way of Allah!"*
Sahih Bukhari 2:35	*"The person who participates in (Holy Battles) in Allah's cause and nothing compels him to do so except belief in Allah and His Apostle, will be recompensed by Allah either with a reward, or booty (if he survives) or will be admitted to Paradise (if he is killed)."*
Tabari 9:69	*"Killing Unbelievers is a small matter to us"*
Ibn Ishaq/Hisham 990	*"I leapt upon him and cut off his head and ran in the direction of the camp shouting 'Allah akbar' and my two companions did likewise".*
Ibn Ishaq/Hisham 992	*"Fight everyone in the way of Allah and kill those who disbelieve in Allah."*

575

The truth about Mohammed himself, and how he *personally* murdered countless people and engaged in both paedophilia and rape

There is not space in this chapter to look in detail at the life of Mohammed. However, any account of the evil of Islam would not be complete without looking, at least briefly, at his own character and at the brutal and perverted things which *he himself did*, not only once or twice in uncharacteristic outbursts, but consistently. He was a murderous psychopath, and also a paedophile. At least he was if you consider having sex with a nine year old child to be paedophilia.

I say that last point entirely seriously, because opposition to paedophilia cannot be assumed today, as many liberals are seeking to change public opinion to make it lawful. Therefore, let's look briefly at some key events in Mohammed's life so you can decide for yourself whether he was a *"holy man"* and the founder of a *"great religion"* or a perverted sadist. It is necessary to form a view of him personally because, if one ever criticises Islam or its followers, one is told that the person or group to which one is referring are *"misrepresenting or misunderstanding Islam"*. *Mo' is Islam*

You will hopefully agree that Mohammed had an accurate understanding of Islam, such that that excuse cannot be used with him. Therefore, if we conclude that he himself was a murderer, liar, rapist, sadist and paedophile then he was not an ideal person to found a major religion, or someone we should see as a role model. I shall therefore set out a series of facts about Mohammed. These would be viewed as controversial by Western liberals, who won't allow a word to be said against him.

However, Muslims themselves would not disagree with any of these facts. They know that all of these things are true *and they aren't ashamed of them*. For example, Muslims do not attempt to deny that Mohammed had full intercourse with a nine year old girl called Aisha. They also know that he 'married' her *when she was six and he was 53*, and that he consummated the 'marriage' when she was nine and still pre-pubescent. But many Muslims *see nothing wrong with that* and do the same themselves.

Likewise, they don't deny that he personally beheaded hundreds of people and ordered the killing of countless others. They see nothing wrong with any of that either, and approve of his actions, and of the Jihad which he began, even if they don't participate in it themselves. So, let's begin to look at what *Mohammed himself* did:

1. Mohammed received his 'revelation' about Islam when a demon physically attacked him in a cave at Hira in AD 610. These visitations continued until AD 632. He concluded in the end that this was an angel but in the beginning

576

he believed, rightly, that it was a demon. However, even after he had changed his mind and decided that it was an angel, this is how he described the event:

"The angel caught me forcefully and pressed me so hard that I could not bear it anymore."

(Bukhari 9:111)

2. Mohammed initially thought that he was either insane, or that a demon was attacking him, and this is how he spoke of it, in his own words. He even considered committing suicide due to his mental distress. This episode is also significant in two further ways which distinguish him, and his 'visitor', from the genuine prophets or other figures in the Bible who met real angels:

   a) No character in the Bible ever thought, at any stage, that the angel who appeared to them was a demon. They *always* knew immediately that they were angels, whereas Mohammed's initial belief, which was correct, was that it was a demon

   b) No character in the Bible who met an angel ever wanted to commit suicide as a result, or even considered it. Yet Mohammed did, further demonstrating that it was a demon who assisted him in establishing Islam and producing the Koran. This is what he said himself:

      "Woe is me, poet or possessed - Never shall the Quraysh say this of me! I will go to the top of the mountain and throw myself down that I may kill myself and gain rest."

      (Ibn Ishaq p.106)

3. Mohammed himself told his followers to rape captured women *in front of their husbands*. Therefore, even to this day, although the liberal Western media won't report it, the fact is that *rape is central to Islamic doctrine and culture*. That is why there are such chronic problems with rape in every country that has ever let Islam in, most notably Germany and Sweden, but also the UK. Sadly, the police in all those countries are zealously politically correct and try hard to hide these crimes, and not to disclose the religion of the rapists. The media also co-operate in that, which is remarkable, because it is not ordinarily in the nature of journalists to cover things up.

4. Accordingly, when Muslims rape women they are not acting contrary to the principles of Islam but doing exactly what the Koran *permits and encourages them to do*. And they are doing the very same as *Mohammed himself did* and told his followers to do. Consider this extract concerning raping women, even in front of their husbands, which Mohammed said *was alright if they were captives*:

577

"Some of the companions of the Apostle of Allah.... Were reluctant to have intercourse with the female captives in the presence of their husbands who were unbelievers......

"So Allah, the Exalted, sent down the Quranic verse: "And all married women (are forbidden) unto you except those (captives) whom your right hands possess."

(Sura 4:24, Abu Dawud 2150 and Muslim 3433)

5. In the final nine years of his life, Mohammed *himself* waged violent Jihad 65 times. Therefore, it is not possible to pass it off as something which his over-enthusiastic followers did, contrary to his wishes, or even after his death. He did it himself, on an industrial scale. Thus, Jihad in general, and the beheading of prisoners in particular, was something which Mohammed personally engaged in, and on a frequent basis. It was central to Islam and to his own life.

6. Mohammed personally ordered his followers to carry out crucifixions, amputations, torture, enslavement, rape, beheadings and the gouging out of eyes. Therefore, when Muslim terrorists do all these things today, far from being 'extremists', who are departing from the true teaching of Islam, they are doing exactly what Mohammed himself did, and what he told his followers to do, on many occasions. Moreover, the Koran, Hadith and Sira confirm in writing that those are the very things which Muslims are *commanded* to do:

"They were caught and brought to him (the Holy Prophet). He commanded about them and (thus) their hands and feet were cut off and their eyes were gouged and then they were thrown in the sun until they died."

(Sahih Muslim 4131)

"The punishment of those who wage war against Allah and His Messenger, and strive with might and main for mischief through the land is: execution, or crucifixion, or the cutting off of hands and feet from opposite sides."

(Koran 5:33)

7. Mohammed *personally* beheaded between 600-900 Jews *in a single day*. Therefore, the beheading of non-Muslims cannot be portrayed as something exceptional or occasional. He did it on a massive scale and he must have enjoyed it, as one would expect of someone who is heavily demonised:

578

"Then the apostle went to the market of Medina and dug trenches in it. Then he sent for [The Banu Qurayza tribe] and struck off their heads in those trenches as they were brought out to him in batches..... There were 600 or 700 in all, though some put the figure as high as 800 or 900.

(Ibn Ishaq p464)

8. Mohammed himself 'married' a six year old girl called Aisha and had full penetrative sex with her when she reached the age of nine! However, even from their 'wedding day' onwards, when she was only six, Mohammed engaged in non-penetrative sex, which many Muslims still practise today with very young girls, *and even babies*, who are too small for full intercourse. They call this appalling practice *'thighing'*. I will leave it to your imagination as to what exactly it involves, as it is too disgusting to describe. This explains why so many Muslim men do the same things to little children today and why so many in the Muslim community see nothing wrong with paedophilia and even justify it openly:

"....the Prophet married her when she was six years old and he consummated his marriage when she was nine years old.....

(Sahih Al-Bukhari 7:62-64 and 65, 88)

9. Mohammed was so obsessed with sex that he would visit his 11 wives and have intercourse with *all of them* in one night. That is not possible unless a man is demonised. This also helps to explain why so many Muslim men are addicted to sex and go completely out of control, raping women, girls, boys, and even men, due to being so fixated with sex. Indeed, their idea of heaven is that each man will be 'given' 72 virgins, with whom he can spend eternity in an endless orgy. How totally different they are from Christians, of any denomination.

At the risk of revolting you further, Mohammed would be seen at the mosque with semen stains on his clothing, which Aisha, one of his 11 wives, would wash off. I am sorry to be so gross, but it is necessary to state the grisly facts to show what kind of man he really was. It also shows that neither Mohammed, nor Aisha, nor his followers, were ashamed of these things, or saw anything wrong with them. Their brazenness explains why so many Muslims today feel no shame about sexual deviancy:

"The Prophet used to visit all his wives in a round, during the day and night and they were eleven in number"

(Bukhari 5:268)

"Aisha had said "I used to wash (semen) off the clothes of Allah's Apostle and he would go for the prayers while water spots were still visible on them."

(Bukhari 1:4; 232)

10. There are 109 verses in the Koran commanding Muslims to fight unbelievers until the whole world is under the domination of Islam, for example these:

"And fight them, until there is no more Fitnah (disbelief in Allah) and the religion will be for Allah alone."

(Koran 8:38-39)

"Fight and slay the pagans wherever you find them, and seize them, beleaguer them, and lie in wait for them in every stratagem of war."

(Koran 9:5)

"Verily, Allah has shown me the eastern and western part of the earth, and I saw the authority of my Ummah (nation) dominate all that I saw."

(Sahih Muslim 2889)

11. Based on Mohammed's teachings, Muslims believe that *all* Jews must be killed before this world can come to an end. This is just one of the reasons why Muslims are so hostile to the Jews, and why they seek to attack them, as in the Arab-Israeli wars, all of which were started by the Arabs, never the Jews:

"The Last Day will not come about until Muslims fight the Jews, when the Jew will hide behind stones and trees. The stones and trees will say O Muslims, O Abdullah, there is a Jew behind me, come and kill him."
(Sahih Muslim 41:6981-6984, Bukhari 4:56: 791)

12. Muslims are held captive within Islam by fear, as death is threatened to anyone who leaves Islam for any reason. Moreover, this practice of capital punishment is done on the personal instructions of Mohammed himself. If it was not for this, millions of Muslims would abandon their religion, but they dare not do so. What does it tell you about Islam that this death threat is the only way to stop people leaving it?

"The Prophet said "if somebody (a Muslim) discards his religion, kill him."

(Bukhari 52:260 see also
84:57; 89:271 and Koran 4:89)

If we obey the Bible we will become a model citizen. If we obey the Koran we will become a Jihadist.

Obviously, not every Muslim does what the Koran instructs and personally engages in Jihad, or rape. I fully accept that. However, a small minority *do* and they become terrorists. By contrast, a Christian who takes the Bible literally will love others and become a model citizen, and if he is a so called 'extremist', then his 'extreme' adherence to the Bible will make him even more of a model citizen. However, a man who takes the Koran literally, and does exactly what it says, will become a Jihadist, a rapist and a paedophile. It is as simple as that, because those are the very things Mohammed did and that the Koran *commands his followers to do*. Thank God therefore that so many Muslims disobey the Koran. If they all obeyed it our situation would be utterly appalling.

Nevertheless, even if those who actively implement Islam, and take its doctrines seriously, are only a tiny minority in *relative* terms, they are still sufficiently numerous, in *absolute* terms, to threaten our security. At any rate, even as a small minority, and whether or not they represent 'real Islam', the jihadists have so far managed to conquer 57 nations, mostly in the Middle East, Asia and Africa. Thus, the so called 'radicals' or 'extremists' within Islam are hardly an irrelevant or ineffective sub-group.

If you want to be wise, therefore, you need an accurate knowledge of Islam, and of its history and aims. It is not the same as understanding the nature and aims of Buddhism or Mormonism. Admittedly, those are both false religions, and they are also Satanic in origin. But neither of them has any chance, or intention, of taking over the world, taking away our freedom, or destroying our societies through violence, as Islam does. In that regard, Islam is unique.

I actually describe it as 'Satan's masterpiece' because, of all the false religions that the Devil has ever founded, Islam is by far the most vicious. It is head and shoulders above all the others in its capacity to harm us. Therefore, if you are complacent about Islam, or even gullible enough to speak up in its support, because you believe the lies it tells about itself, or that the media tells on its behalf, you cannot be wise. It would make you naïve at best and, as we have seen, if you are naïve, then you aren't wise.

Accordingly, this is a subject about which we all need to wake up and become thoroughly well-informed. Once we understand Islam properly, based on truth, not deception or political correctness, then we need to speak out against it, openly and actively, and reject the rubbish we are told. One reason why naïve liberals believe these lies, and repeat them, is that they want to be accepted, by ensuring that any opinion they express is PC and consistent with the prevailing world view, as expressed by the media and the liberal establishment.

Why politically correct people engage in *virtue signalling* concerning Islam and other PC issues

Most of our generation are now so terrified of thinking or speaking differently from others that they will say the most incredible nonsense if that is what it takes to fit in. Another reason why people repeat lies about Islam, and other aspects of political correctness, is that they are engaging in *'virtue signalling'*. That is the practice of saying things to indicate to others that you are virtuous in some way, i.e. as the politically correct define virtue, not as God does.

So, in a misguided world, where holding PC views is seen as good, you can *signal* to others that you possess that virtue by mentioning a view that you hold, or claim to hold, or by denouncing the opposite view. It can be done directly or indirectly. So, by saying you despise Nigel Farage, or Tommy Robinson, neither of whom are racist, but are falsely alleged to be, then you can signal that you are not racist, or 'Islamophobic', or anything else they are (falsely) alleged to be.

Therefore, a 'virtue signaller' expresses support for Islam because, by doing so, he hopes to indicate to others how broad-minded and *sophisticated* he is. The thinking behind it is as follows:

a) People who are 'low-brow' or unsophisticated are opposed to Islam.

b) Therefore, by praising Islam, I will give the impression that I think at a deeper level than others and am sophisticated and 'high-brow'.

c) So, when a jihadist drives a lorry into pedestrians while shouting *"Allahu Akhbar"*, or murders people in a theatre, then, instead of condemning Islam, I will *sympathise with the Muslim community* and express my anxiety about how low-brow people might *"lash out against Muslims in retaliation"*.

d) Then people will admire me for my largeness of mind and notice how much cleverer I am than those narrow-minded types. *How tolerant, inclusive truly open minded & intelligent*

A virtue-signaller's thinking is reminiscent of the story of the Emperor who was deceived into buying a non-existent suit of clothes. A con man, posing as a tailor, told him that the garments were only visible to *the most intelligent and educated people*, with a proper appreciation of art and culture, but *invisible to anybody else*. When the Emperor went to try on his new clothes, which did not actually exist, he did not want to admit that he could not see anything, in case he might be considered unintelligent.

He spoke about the beauty of the design and the wonderful fabric and so did his courtiers, as they did not want to be seen as stupid either. Thus, a fortune was

582

paid for the garments and everyone in the palace outdid each other in their superlatives. However, when the Emperor went out in public 'wearing' his new clothes, a small boy in the crowd saw him, stark naked, and shouted *"The Emperor's got no clothes on"*.

The crowd looked at each other nervously, reluctant at first to admit that they couldn't see any clothes either. But, one by one, they joined in with the boy's laughter until eventually the whole crowd was laughing. This story applies perfectly to Islam, which is actually a religion of war, but is said to be *"a religion of peace"*. That is just as big a lie as saying the Emperor's clothes look beautiful. However, as in that story, people are anxious not to be thought less of for being unable to see Islam's wonderful qualities.

Therefore, they persist in saying that it is a religion of peace, even though all the evidence of their eyes and ears is plainly telling them that it is nothing of the sort. They don't want to admit that, for fear of being called 'right wing' or 'bigoted', or even a 'racist'. Deep down, they know it isn't true, but they would rather maintain an obvious lie than express an unpopular opinion.

They even go further and claim that Islam has produced all sorts of scientific and mathematical advances, especially in algebra. One hears that claim made all the time and yet it is a lie. Of course, *Arabs* have achieved many such things, in the centuries *before* Islam took over in Arabia, and even after that, where those Arabs were *not Muslim*, because it is important to remember that *not all Arabs are Muslim*.

However, Islam itself, and those who follow it, have never produced *any* significant advances in science, maths, or anything else. It is a myth, which is believed without question by naïve liberals, but which has no basis in reality. If it was even partially true, then the 57 nations currently ruled by Islam would not be the impoverished, undeveloped backwaters that they *all* are. The only exceptions are the Gulf States, which have oil. However, that oil had to be extracted *for them* by engineers *from the West* because, even now, the Arabs are incapable of extracting it for themselves.

Therefore, when a person bends over backwards to maintain the fiction that Islam is a religion of peace, despite the daily atrocities, and when the only people they consider to be dangerous are Islam's critics, it is usually due to virtue-signalling. They want to be admired for being able to see what lesser people cannot see, due to not having their sophistication. Such people are self-deceived, but they are also seeking to deceive you.

That said, they do the same with homosexuality, gay marriage, and all the other areas in which they claim moral superiority. For all these reasons people will say things which are plainly untrue, without feeling any unease, because they have another agenda. That has nothing to do with truth and is all about demonstrating that they have the right views, i.e. those of the liberal establishment. What is true or false is irrelevant to them. Their only aim is to impress others and not to be thought to be out of step with the metropolitan elite.

If you take their approach you will never end up believing the truth, as set out in the Bible, or even the plain facts of history. The craving to impress others, or to be accepted by them, will always lead you into error and deception. Therefore, if you want to be wise, think only of whether something is *true or false*, regardless of how many people will agree with you, or how pleased they will be with you for holding that view, or how angry they will be with you for rejecting it.

Cowardly way to impress stupid, wicked cowards

Most of the mainstream media imposes a news blackout on negative stories about Islam and any other things they don't want to report

You might wonder how all these things could be true of Mohammed, and how so many atrocities could be committed by Muslims, and yet the general population be so unaware. It is not that difficult to explain once you realise that most of the mainstream media is *covering up, and refusing to report*, any news which reflects badly on Islam. This is not just the policy of a few journalists here and there. It is the approach taken by most of the mainstream media, with a few honourable exceptions, such as The Times in the UK which first broke the story of the Muslim gangs in Rotherham due to the courage and diligence of their reporter, Andrew Norfolk, and his editor.

Apart from such noble exceptions, this wall of silence is happening in most of Western Europe and the English speaking world. Let me give just a few examples, although I could give more. Take firstly the major riots which took place in France, especially Paris, in February 2017, while I was writing this chapter. Muslim men, *and nobody other than Muslim men*, went onto the streets day after day, rioting, setting fire to cars, attacking policemen, and causing mayhem.

It was not just a small local punch up. It was a vicious, widespread, organised riot. Therefore, it was obviously newsworthy, and one would expect the mainstream media to cover it in detail. Instead, even after the fourteenth day of heavy rioting, barely a word had been said by newspapers, radio stations or TV channels anywhere. Consider the improbability of that arising coincidentally, with no guiding hand coordinating the multitude of media outlets, all over the Western world.

I went on Facebook after the fifth day of rioting to comment on the news blackout. It cannot have happened accidentally, whereby thousands of journalists decided, independently, that they didn't consider the riots to be newsworthy. On the contrary, they all knew the public would be extremely interested, which is why it is obvious that they must have been *instructed* to say nothing about it. Personal choices by individual journalists cannot have caused this. It was plainly imposed from above by the handful of billionaires who control the media.

Likewise, also in February 2017, an enormous march took place in Poland involving patriotic citizens who were concerned at the Islamification of Europe, especially France and Germany. They were making it known to their own government that they do not want Poland to be Islamified and that they therefore do not want any Muslim immigrants or refugees to be allowed in.

By any reasonable standard, that march was newsworthy, in view of the contentious subject matter and the vast numbers of people who took part. Yet, as with the Muslim riots in France, and the gang rapes in Germany and Sweden, very little was written or broadcast about the march by Western journalists. It was mainly on social media that it was seen, as private individuals tweeted and posted about it.

You might argue these events were accidentally overlooked. So, let's look now at a longer term crisis in the UK which has been ongoing for years, but which most of the mainstream media still ignores or camouflages. I refer to the 'grooming' gangs in towns and cities all over the UK, such as Rotherham, Birmingham, Rochdale, Oxford, Telford, *and many others*. In each of these places, *over many years*, with barely any opposition from police or social services, organised gangs of Muslim men groomed thousands of vulnerable girls for sex.

They were often girls in care homes, or from dysfunctional families. Therefore, many did not have parents keeping a close eye on them and were easier to prey upon. In *Rotherham alone* 1400 girls were repeatedly raped by gangs of Muslim men and passed around, like commodities to be traded. However, not all the girls had no families to stand up for them. Many had parents who went to the police and social services, reporting the rapes, and *pleading with them to take action*.

Despite those complaints, the police did almost nothing about it, for years. In many cases the police even tried to intimidate the concerned parents, threatening *them* with arrest, and warning them not to do anything which could be construed as 'Islamophobic' or as stirring up 'racial tension'. They were literally *protecting the rapists from the girls' parents*, rather than the other way around.

In fairness, many junior officers wanted to arrest the offenders, but were told by senior officers not to do so. That in itself proves the police knew of this, or such orders could not have been given. They chose not to act, because of the climate of political correctness in the police and their paranoia about being accused of 'racism' or 'Islamophobia'. There would have been career-ending consequences for any officer accused of those things and they knew that.

There was an equivalent scandal involving social workers at the homes where troubled girls were living under council care. They also knew what was going on, but turned a blind eye to it, so that *only a tiny number of them* did anything to help the girls. They too feared being branded as racist or Islamophobic which would, equally, have meant instant career death.

There was also silence from MPs, councillors, and council officers. Yet they would quickly raise any other issues affecting their constituents. They were only silent about Muslims. One honourable exception I know of, who did try to do something, was Ann Cryer MP from Keighley in Yorkshire. She alerted others in the Labour Party but was ignored, and even dismissed as a racist. That compounds the guilt of Labour politicians because *she told them, and they still did nothing.*

One would imagine that once the *national* news media got to hear of the gang rapes they would see the silence of the *local* newspapers and radio and TV stations as being newsworthy in itself, and report on that. But they too said nothing about any of this until Andrew Norfolk, a reporter with the Times, broke the story of the Muslim grooming gangs in January 2012.

But it was only in 2017, decades after this scandal of grooming first began on a large scale, that the BBC belatedly joined in and produced a drama programme, *'Three Girls'*, plus a documentary, *'The Betrayed Girls'*. These tell some of the story of what happened. However, the BBC only did that *after we already knew what was happening,* thanks to Andrew Norfolk of the Times, plus individuals on social media, not due to the BBC.

Therefore, most of the media, both local and national, said nothing for years. It was not until the story eventually broke in a large way in 2012 that the police were forced to take some token action, very much against their will, and a few more Muslim men were arrested. But they were only a *tiny percentage* of the men who had been involved, and who *still are involved*, in grooming young girls. Most of the men who did it, and who still do it, were not even questioned, and the investigation was made as narrow as possible.

Even then, most of the mainstream media still maintained their wall of silence. They either did not report the arrests and convictions or, if they had no choice but to report them, they gave only the briefest of details and, above all, *made no mention of the fact that the men are Muslims!* That crucial fact is *always* left out, on the occasions when anything is said at all. The very most they do is to list the names of the offenders, which are all Muslim names, but only at the end of the article, where it is much less likely to be seen, never at the top, or as a headline.

The normal saying is that *"dog bites man"* is not news, but that *"man bites dog"* is. That maxim prevails in all cases except where the story contains some element that the media does not want us to hear about. So, to extend the adage, we can now say that "man bites dog" is news, but *"Muslim man bites dog"* would not be. Therefore, Muslims in particular, but also other groups, such as homosexuals and transgenders, cannot now be criticised publicly.

That is why so many people are silent, especially about Islam. Even if they do try to speak out, the mainstream media won't report their words and, increasingly, neither will social media companies such as Facebook and Twitter. They are becoming ever more PC and they aggressively delete posts and tweets, or even close down people's social media accounts, if they dare to criticise Islam. The maxim coined by Voltaire suggests, therefore, that we are now ruled by Islam because, more than any other thing, we are not allowed to criticise it:

"To learn who rules over you, simply find out who you are not allowed to criticise."

'Voltaire' (Francois-Marie Arouet)

Sir Winston Churchill's opinion of Islam from his book *'The River War'* of 1899 and also William Gladstone's even earlier comments

Let's now look at a longer quotation from Winston Churchill about the real nature of Islam. As a young man he served in the army in India, which then included what we now call Pakistan. He also fought against Muslims in Afghanistan, where he personally killed many of them in hand to hand fighting. During those years he studied Islam closely and also had extensive practical experience of it, based on living alongside Muslims, as well as fighting them.

So, he knew exactly what he was talking about and could be classed as an expert. Moreover, the things that Churchill was saying reflected what Islam was like in 1899, nearly *120 years ago*, thereby proving that the Jihad, and all the other violent features of Islam, are *nothing new*. At any rate, this is what was said about Islam by the greatest Englishman of all time, and certainly the greatest statesman of the twentieth century:

"How dreadful are the curses which Mohammedanism (Islam) *lays on its votaries! Besides the fanatical frenzy, which is as dangerous in a man as hydrophobia* (rabies) *in a dog, there is this fearful, fatalistic apathy. The effects are apparent in many countries. Improvident habits, slovenly systems of commerce, and insecurity of property exist wherever the followers of the Prophet rule or live. A degraded sensualism deprives this life of its grace and refinement; the next of its dignity and sanctity. The fact that in Mohammedan law every*

587

*woman must belong to some man as his absolute property – either as a child, a
wife, or a concubine – must delay the final extinction of slavery until the faith of
Islam has ceased to be a great power among men.*

*Individual Muslims may show splendid qualities. Thousands became the brave
and loyal soldiers of the Queen: all know how to die: but the influence of the
religion paralyses the social development of those who follow it. No stronger
retrograde force exists in the world. Far from being moribund, Mohammedanism
is a militant and proselytizing faith. It has already spread throughout Central
Africa, raising fearless warriors at every step; and were it not that Christianity is
sheltered in the strong arms of science, against which it has vainly struggled, the
civilisation of modern Europe might fall, as fell the civilisation of ancient Rome."*

Winston Churchill

**President Thomas Jefferson's opinion of Islam and his determination to fight
against it in the 'Barbary wars' of the late 18th and early 19th centuries**

If you are American, then quotations from former British Prime Ministers might
not be as persuasive as those of former Presidents. So, let's look at some of those,
from the eighteenth, nineteenth and twentieth centuries, and especially Thomas
Jefferson, the third President. Few people know that he was a fierce opponent of
Islam, both before and after he became President. He saw it for what it really is
and was determined to tell the truth about it, and to stand up to it, rather than give
in to its violent and greedy demands.

The background to the story was the activities of Muslim pirates and slave traders
who, between 1530 and 1780 kidnapped and enslaved perhaps 1.5 million
Europeans and Americans. In one case, the entire population of Baltimore, a
village in Ireland, were seized and taken into slavery by Muslim raiders called
'corsairs'. They operated from ships and launched raids on defenceless civilians.
As well as taking white slaves they took hostages and demanded ransom
payments. They also operated as pirates, attacking merchant ships when they were
far out at sea and vulnerable.

The only thing which kept these Muslim pirates at bay was the British Royal Navy
which then 'ruled the waves' all over the world. However, when the Americans
declared independence from us they no longer had Britain's protection, which was
a major problem, because America did not yet have a proper navy of its own.
Therefore, during the late eighteenth and early nineteenth centuries, American
merchant ships were especially vulnerable to Muslim pirates who mainly came
from what we now call Algeria, Libya, Morocco and Tunisia.

All of these were part of the Ottoman Empire, ruled over by Turkey, and were called *"the Barbary States"*, from which comes the little-known phrase, *"the Barbary wars"*. It is little known for the simple reason that it is not politically correct to speak of it. Therefore, you won't hear anything about these early problems faced by the United States. The war they fought is not taught in schools, or mentioned in the media, because it doesn't suit the agenda of the liberal establishment to criticise Islam, or to refer to its long and consistent history of violence.

The liberal left prefers to tell itself that Islamic violence began in 2003, when President George W. Bush invaded Iraq as if, prior to that, there had been 1400 years of peace and quiet. In fact, these Muslim pirates were causing extreme problems 200 years ago and it was a real crisis for the early Americans. The young Thomas Jefferson, together with another future president, John Adams, who succeeded George Washington, went to London in 1785 to negotiate with the Libyan Ambassador, Al-Rahman, from Tripoli. When Jefferson and Adams protested at the actions of the pirates from the Barbary States, they were told by Al-Rahman:

"It was written in the Koran that all nations who should not have acknowledged their (the Muslims') *authority were sinners, that it was their right and duty to make war upon whoever they could find and to make slaves of all they could take as prisoners, and that every [Muslim] who should be slain in battle was sure to go to Paradise."*

Ambassador Al-Rahman had only one solution to offer, which was that the Americans should pay 'protection money' to the Barbary States, just as one would to the Mafia. So, the choice they were given was to live in *'dhimmitude'*, i.e. having the status of *'dhimmis'*, who have to pay to be allowed to live under Muslim rule. That would mean paying 10% of their annual budget to the Muslims or face ongoing piracy, hostage-taking and slavery. Jefferson made up his mind that if ever he was in a position to command American forces, he would wage war on the Barbary States rather than submit to such extortion.

The views of other American Presidents about Islam and how the fight against Islam even influenced the drafting of the American Constitution

The crisis caused by the Muslim pirates also had an impact on the whole of subsequent American history. It even featured in the debates that led to the drafting of the American Constitution in the years after that visit to London. Many of the delegates debating the draft Constitution argued that only a strong federal union could repel the threat of the Barbary States. So, the threat posed by Islam

589

even influenced the setting up of a *federal* structure, rather than having 13 separate states, and provided some of the rationale for taking a federal approach.

It also had a major bearing on discussions of military matters and on the setting up of the United States Navy and the Marine Corps. Alexander Hamilton, another future president, said that without a *"....federal navy ... of respectable weight ... the genius of American merchants and navigators would be stifled and lost"*. Also, James Madison, yet another future president, argued that only a federal union could protect America's shipping from *"the rapacious demands of pirates and barbarians"*, by which he meant the Muslims, as there were no others.

The threat posed by the Muslims in the 1780s also explains why the American Constitution, which only provides for an Army at two-yearly renewable intervals, puts no such limitation on the Navy. The army was seen as being for protection at home, on American soil, but the purpose of the Navy, in the minds of the 'Founding Fathers', was to go out and protect the nation from the scourge of Islam. So, even in the more obscure provisions of the Constitution, the threats posed by Islam lay behind these decisions and shaped the birth of America's institutions.

However, even in the late eighteenth century, there were some Americans, and John Adams was one of them, who thought it was better to pay money to the Muslims than to fight them. Adams said that a war against the Barbary States would be *"too rugged for our people to bear"*. He then added a statement which has proved to be prophetic, and which is still true today, when he said, *"We ought not to fight them at all unless we determine to fight them forever"*.

The point about standing up to Islam is that there will never be any end to it until Jesus returns and destroys it, because Islam is committed to endless violence. Therefore, whether or not we choose to *join* that battle, and defend ourselves militarily, they will continue to attack us anyway, until we have either been killed or conquered. So, it is not a question of us *starting* a war against Islam, as liberals wrongly believe George W. Bush did in 2003. The Jihad began in the early seventh century, when Mohammed started his campaign to take over the whole planet.

Therefore, the war has already been underway for 14 centuries, and it will continue unceasingly, regardless of whether we join in to defend ourselves. Jihadists require no provocation from us and are determined to fight us, and to take over our nations, whether we fight back or surrender. It makes absolutely no difference to them and they will never stop fighting us, either way. Therefore, the only questions we face are whether to fight back and, if so, how best to go about it, because they will never leave us alone to live in peace, whatever we do.

In the late eighteenth century, payments were initially made to the Barbary States, but their demands only increased, until they wanted 10% of the entire American budget. However, even if that had been paid, they would only have insisted on more. Then news came of appalling mistreatment of captured Americans in Algiers and Tripoli and American public opinion began to harden in favour of war rather than appeasement. It was at this point that the United States created a permanent Marine Corps, just before Thomas Jefferson became President.

The task of ordering war and sending those newly assembled Marines to fight back against the Muslims fell to Jefferson after he entered the White House in 1801. At last he was able to do what he had wanted to do ever since his meeting in 1785 with the arrogant Ambassador Al-Rahman who had brazenly told him what Islam was really about and what its true intentions were. So, Jefferson had long sought a pretext for war and it came in 1801 when Libyans from Tripoli seized two American ships. That set off a chain reaction of additional demands from the other Barbary States.

Jefferson's problem was the Constitution prevented him from declaring war, as that could only be done by Congress, the same restriction President F.D. Roosevelt faced in 1941, even after Pearl Harbor. Jefferson dealt with this subtly, by sending the US Navy to North Africa on 'patrol', with instructions to enforce existing treaties and punish any infractions of them. He did not inform Congress of his authorisation of this mission until after the fleet had already sailed and was too far away for Congress to recall it.

However, Jefferson was then 'helped' by the aggression of Yusuf Karamanli, the Pasha of Tripoli, who declared war on America in May 1801 to further his demand for more 'protection' money. That declaration of war enabled Jefferson to get around the restrictions of the Constitution and he responded with a heavy bombardment of Tripoli and of its navy, crippling one of their biggest ships. This led to Congress passing an enabling Act in 1802 which amounted to a declaration of war by America and provided for a permanent presence by the US Navy in the Mediterranean.

The other Barbary States made the mistake of under-estimating this fledgling nation, America, which would one day become a superpower, as Morocco then declared war and the rest of them increased their demands for money. There then followed what began as a disaster, but later turned into a triumph, when the Muslims in Tripoli captured the new American frigate, *Philadelphia*. In response to that, the American heroes, Edward Preble and Stephen Decatur, mounted a daring raid on Tripoli's harbour.

A force of US Marines boarded the captured ship and blew it up to prevent the pirates using it. They also inflicted heavy damage on the city's defences. When

591

the news of this spread, the famous British Admiral, Lord Nelson, called the raid *"the most bold and daring act of the age"*. This early American victory led to a song being written which is the anthem of the US Marines, even to this day, and which begins, *"From the halls of Montezuma **to the shores of Tripoli…."***

The origin and meaning of those famous words are now known only by a very few. However, the song bears vivid witness to the fact that Islam has been America's enemy from the very birth of the nation, and that it already was so before America became Islam's enemy. So, don't blame George W. Bush for starting the war against Islam. That honour belongs to Thomas Jefferson, but even he didn't actually *start* the war. He merely had the good sense to realise that America needed to *join* it, because that war had already been started by the Muslims themselves.

Matters escalated in 1815 when President Madison asked Congress for permission to send Stephen Decatur to North Africa again, to seek to defeat the Muslim pirates more decisively. This time the main aggressor was Omar Pasha of Algiers, but he was taught a bitter lesson when he ended up with his fleet blown to pieces and his grand harbour full of heavily armed American ships.

Algiers was then forced to pay compensation to America, which made a nice change from what had gone on before. He also had to release all the hostages, just as Iran did in 1981 for President Reagan. President Madison's words following that victory were very apt and we would do well to reflect on them today and to adopt the same policy in our own struggle against Islam:

"It is a settled policy of America that, as peace is better than war, war is better than tribute (i.e. paying money to extortionists). *The United States, while they wish for war with no nation, will buy peace with none."*

President James Madison

What Presidents John Quincy Adams and Theodore Roosevelt said about Islam

John Adams, the second President of the United States, had a son, John Quincy Adams, (1767-1848) who became the sixth President. He had an even clearer view of Islam than his father had, as shown in this quotation from one of his essays which was written before he was elected to Congress in 1830:

"….he [Mohammed] declared undistinguishing and exterminating war, as part of his religion, against all the rest of mankind…..The precept of the Koran is perpetual war against all who deny Mohammed is the prophet of God."

John Quincy Adams

Consider this even starker statement made by President Theodore (Teddy) Roosevelt, who was in the White House from 1901-1909, and who is widely regarded as being one of the top five Presidents of all time. Note the clarity of his views, and his willingness to speak his mind and tell the truth, which today's leaders dare not do. Note also how he makes clear that Islam has to be resisted, not only with words, but with *military force*. That is as true today as it ever was. The only difference is that our leaders will not even say it, let alone do it:

"Christianity is not the creed of Asia and Africa at this moment solely because the seventh century Christians of Asia and Africa had trained themselves not to fight, whereas the Moslems were trained to fight. Christianity was saved in Europe solely because the peoples of Europe fought. If the peoples of Europe in the seventh and eighth centuries, and on up to and including the seventeenth century, had not possessed a military equality with, and gradually a growing superiority over the Mohammedans who invaded Europe, Europe would at this moment be Mohammedan and the Christian religion would be exterminated.

Wherever the Mohammedans have had complete sway, wherever the Christians have been unable to resist them by the sword, Christianity has ultimately disappeared. From the hammer of Charles Martel to the sword of Sobieski, Christianity owed its safety in Europe to the fact that it was able to show that it could and would fight as well as the Mohammedan aggressor... The civilization of Europe, American and Australia exists today at all only because of the victories of civilized man over the enemies of civilization because of victories through the centuries from Charles Martel in the eighth century and those of John Sobieski in the seventeenth century.

During the thousand years that included the careers of the Frankish soldier and the Polish king, the Christians of Asia and Africa proved unable to wage successful war with the Moslem conquerors; and in consequence Christianity practically vanished from the two continents; and today, nobody can find in them any "social values" whatever, in the sense in which we use the words, so far as the sphere of Mohammedan influences are concerned. There are such "social values" today in Europe, America and Australia only because during those thousand years, the Christians of Europe possessed the warlike power to do what the Christians of Asia and Africa had failed to do — that is, to beat back the Moslem invader."

Theodore Roosevelt

How Charles Martel of France, and later King John III of Poland, saved Europe from Islam by being willing to confront the Jihadists with military force

As we have seen, today's politicians in the West, though not in more sensible countries like Japan, the Philippines, Hungary and Poland, are not willing even to name Islam as the enemy, let alone use military force to withstand it. That is why western Europe is now being overrun by Muslim immigrants, some of whom are jihadists. However, it was not always so and, quite apart from the Crusades, which some people may know a little bit about, there are also three lesser known wars in which Europe was saved from Islam by the use of military force.

The first was under the leadership of Charles Martel of France in AD 732. The second was under King John III of Poland in 1683 and the third was in Greece in the 1820s and 1830s. Let's look very briefly at these three wars, because they provide a lesson that we urgently need today. Charles Martel, the grandfather of 'Charlemagne', was a Frankish (French) statesman and military leader. As a Duke, and also as Prince of the Franks, he was the de facto ruler of France from AD 718 until his death in 741.

He saw that Islam, which was then just over 100 years old, had already conquered all of Arabia and had then spread rapidly outwards, solely by means of violent Jihad. It had even conquered Spain in AD 711 and was now fighting its way into France, determined to take over the whole of Europe. Matters came to a head in the October of AD 732, exactly 100 years after Mohammed's death, when the Arab armies, led by Al Ghafiqi, were resisted by Frankish forces led by Charles Martel. This battle, which we know as the battle of *Tours* or, alternatively, the battle of *Poitiers*, was won decisively by the French.

Charles Martel then went onto the offensive, pushing the Muslims out of France entirely and effectively ending their ambitions in Europe for nearly a thousand years. However, the key point is that the reason why Charles Martel defeated the Muslims is that he realised they could only be stopped by *military force* and because he had no hesitation about using it. In taking that approach Charles Martel was the complete opposite of today's weak, dishonest, cowardly politicians who won't even criticise Islam, let alone fight it militarily.

The next major battle against Islam in Europe was in 1683 when King John III of Poland defeated the Ottoman Turks at the battle of *Vienna*. He was King of Poland and Grand Duke of Lithuania and, like Charles Martel, he had no hesitation at all about fighting back, with full military force, to defend his own country, and Europe as a whole, from being overrun by Islam. The city of Vienna had been besieged by the Turks for two months.

The siege was ended when the Turks were defeated by a powerful coalition of armies from the Habsburg Empire, the Polish-Lithuanian Commonwealth, and the Holy Roman Empire, all of which were under the command of King John III. This was a decisive turning point in European history, after which the Turks ceased to be such a menace. In King John's war against the Turks, which continued until 1699, the Muslims also lost almost all of Hungary, which they had previously conquered.

However, these were not the only times in history when Islam has been thrown out of a nation which had previously been ruled by it. Such *"de-islamification"* has also been achieved in Spain, Portugal and Greece. In fact, the Greek island of Crete achieved it twice, as we shall see below. There isn't space here to go into detail, but here are the bare facts.

Spain and Portugal began to be conquered by Islam in AD 711, when the Muslim leader, Tariq Ibn-Ziyad landed at Gibraltar, which is now British territory. By the end of his campaign, most of the Iberian Peninsula, i.e. Spain and Portugal, was under Islamic rule. It was then that the Muslims tried to cross the Pyrenees to conquer France, but were defeated by Charles Martel, as we saw above.

Muslim rule in most of Spain and Portugal then continued, despite varying levels of resistance, until it was finally beaten back by the Catholic kingdoms of northern Spain in what has come to be known as the *'reconquista'* or reconquest. This eventually ended in 1492, when the last remaining Muslim-held territory was won back and set free from Islam in the battle of *Granada*. For the avoidance of doubt, I am not endorsing Catholicism, but simply pointing out that those Catholic forces only succeeded in driving Islam out of Spain and Portugal *because their political leaders were willing to use military force.*

Grasping that fact is the key to understanding this whole problem. Islam cannot be defeated by pacifism, or by lighting candles or by millions of us changing our Facebook profiles to show the flag of the latest country to have suffered a jihadist attack. None of that will achieve anything, as is proved by the fact that all those measures are being used to a tiresome extent at present and are utterly failing to stop the ongoing terrorist campaign.

On the contrary, we are simply making it easier for them, and causing them to despise us even more than they already do, by our pathetically weak, passive, feminine responses to each outrage. By contrast, highly effective military action was taken by the Spaniards. Moreover, it did not end with their victory in 1492. Even after that, they continued to resist Islam to such an extent that, in 1567, King Philip II of Spain even made the use of the Arabic language illegal.

He did so because he was deadly serious about the nature of Islam and the threat it posed, and he was absolutely determined to prevent it from ever coming back. But that wasn't all. The Spaniards were also willing to physically expel Muslims from the Iberian Peninsula, i.e. *to deport them* in large numbers, to make sure they posed no ongoing threat.

Imagine if the Spanish leaders had been as squeamish and feeble as ours now are about deportation, or if they had focused on the Muslims' supposed 'human rights', rather than on protecting the freedom, and the lives, of the Spanish and Portuguese peoples. If those leaders had acted as passively and weakly as ours now do, then Islam would inevitably have staged a rapid come-back in the whole Iberian Peninsula, as it now doing in our day.

How Greece was set free from Islam by fighting against the Muslim Turks and how the British poet, Lord Byron, fought in that war

Let's turn now to Greece, which fell under the control of the Muslim Turks, i.e. the Ottoman Empire, in the mid fifteenth century, at about the same time as Spain and Portugal were driving Islam out. By the way, when we say Greece was under Turkish rule, we must be clear as to what that means. It means Greece fell under the domination of *Islam*. We need to say that explicitly because the point is missed otherwise. This persisted until the early nineteenth century when the *Greek War of Independence* broke out, in 1821, after a national uprising was proclaimed.

The Turks fought savagely to suppress the Greeks but, in 1827, a combined fleet of naval ships from Britain, France and Russia destroyed the Turkish fleet at the battle of *Navarino*. This was a decisive turning point in the whole war. Then, in 1828, France landed troops in the Peloponnese to stop the Turkish atrocities and, with their help, the Greek forces were able to regroup and then to advance, seizing more territory from the Turks. After this, the Western powers imposed a ceasefire and, in 1832, Greece was finally recognised as a sovereign state, albeit that the island of Crete was not included.

The story of Crete's resistance against Islam is longer, and far too complex to tell it all here. However, the Turks managed to keep hold of the island of Crete when the Greek war of independence ended. It was briefly liberated during that war but, in 1828, the island was reconquered by the Muslims, though by Egyptian forces, not Turkish. It then became an Egyptian province, albeit that Egypt itself was a vassal state, subject to Turkey, and part of the Ottoman Empire. Then, in 1840, Crete was transferred to be under direct Turkish rule again.

So, Crete had successfully driven Islam out, only for it to come back again. Thankfully, the story did not end there, and we can take encouragement from that, which is why I included this episode. There then followed a long and complicated series of events by which the people of Crete continued to resist the Egyptians and the Turks, and Islam itself. In particular, there was an uprising in 1866 which was eventually put down by the Turks. However, it led to growing international support for the Cretan people, even in America.

The long campaign of resistance did not finally end until 1898 when the Ottoman forces were expelled, and Crete became an independent state, although it later re-joined Greece and became a part of that nation. The reason I mention Crete in particular, is that Crete's story illustrates the crucially important point that *Islam is not invincible*. Therefore, it is always worthwhile resisting it, even if it has already conquered a nation, or *reconquered* it, as in the case of Crete.

Therefore, no matter how much ground Islam may have captured, geographically or politically, and no matter how many Muslims may have moved into a country, it is still worth resisting it and seeking to reverse the tide, even if you have to do it twice, like Crete. It shows that there is always hope for any nation, provided their Governments are not passive dhimmis, but have courage, self-respect, and the will to fight for their citizens' freedom.

It is unlikely that you have ever heard any of this about Greece because it is not taught in schools, just as the genocidal massacre of the Armenians by the Turks in the early twentieth century is not taught either. But even if it has ever been mentioned, it is extremely unlikely that any history teacher would be brave enough, or honest enough, to mention the role played by Islam in the Greek War of Independence. They would probably speak as if Islam had nothing to do with it, or as if the Turks were not Muslims, and as if the nations being ruled over from Turkey were not part of an Islamic *Caliphate.*

Most people are also unaware that the famous poet, Lord Byron, was killed in Greece in 1824 while fighting for the Greeks. But even those who do know that, such as perhaps a few students of English literature, would probably only think that Byron was fighting *for* Greece, whose history and literature he loved. It would not occur to them that he was fighting *against* the Turks and, in particular, *against Islam*. Yet that was the very reason the Turks conquered Greece in the first place, i.e. to pursue Jihad, and the basis for their savagery against the Greeks.

Such facts of history are now edited out, even in so far as any of this is ever taught at all, which it rarely is. My wife actually went to the same school in Scotland that Lord Byron attended. There is even a statue of him. However, she was never taught anything about *why* Byron died or *who*, or rather *what*, he was fighting against. Islam was never mentioned, even at Lord Byron's own former school where, in every other sense, they were trying to commemorate him. It shows how the *'I-word'* and the *'M-word'* just cannot be mentioned these days.

What conclusions can we draw from each of these wars against Islam?

We have looked at a number of countries which, at various times in history, since AD 732, have fought back against Islam, and refused to surrender to it or to regard it as invincible. Therefore, by their example, one can see that the conquest of territory by Islam is neither inevitable nor irreversible. Even where the Jihadists have taken over, they *can* still be kicked out again, provided there is the moral courage, and the political will, to resist them and the willingness to do whatever is needed militarily to defeat them.

That kind of clarity of vision, and strength of purpose, were present in the past, but they are sadly lacking in today's cowardly, politically correct and heavily feminised world. Looking at all the above quotations, and the decisive actions of Charles Martel, King John III of Poland, and others, do you see the consistent pattern? These leaders from the past all understood the real truth about Islam and were *not afraid to speak publicly about it* or to fight it militarily.

How likely is it that all these historical figures were mistaken about Islam and that the weaklings and cowards who govern us today are correct? The truth is just as obvious as it ever was. It is simply that our politicians do not have the courage, or the honesty, to speak about it, at least not in public. They care too much about their careers, and too little about their countries, to risk doing that.

However, it is not just necessary to realise that our armed forces need to fight back against the jihadists. We also need to grasp that that fighting must be done *with full force*, not in a half-hearted manner, whereby we only deploy the smallest number of troops or police, and with minimum weaponry. Neither must we restrict their powers and their rules of engagement. If the Jihadists are to be prevented from taking over in any more nations, because those that already have a Muslim majority are probably lost forever, we must allow our troops to fight with every ounce of their strength. *Devote to Destruction*

That means no longer placing politically correct limitations on our own soldiers, such as those which led to the conviction and imprisonment of the British Sergeant, 'Marine A', for 'finishing off' a mortally wounded jihadist rather than taking him prisoner. That approach, and a host of other such pedantic restrictions, prevent us gaining the decisive and permanent military victories we could so easily get on the battlefield if we allowed our troops to fight with full intensity.

But also at home, in the civilian context, we need to stop being squeamish about resisting Islam. Therefore, we should immediately, and without any apology, deport all jihadists or known sympathisers. Then let them appeal *from abroad, after their deportation, and at their own expense*, not while they remain here, funded by us, via Legal Aid. Likewise, no planning permission should be given

598

for any further mosques and all immigration by Muslims should be ceased, so that the problem is at least not made even worse.

Charles Martel of France and King John III of Poland would scratch their heads in bafflement at the array of legal, political and military limitations we place on our troops and police in fighting back against Islam. They would be even more amazed at how our civilian population is forbidden from even speaking about Islam unless they want to praise it, and how their Facebook and Twitter accounts are shut down if they criticise Islam – though not if they criticise Christianity! If we hope to remain free countries that limp-wristedness has to end.

The false accusation of 'racism' which is used to intimidate others into silence

Another depressing feature of modern political debate is that the accusation of 'racism' is now routinely levelled against anybody who expresses a view on just about anything, not just things which pertain to race. It occurs even where what is being discussed has nothing whatsoever to do with race. This is usually done deliberately, knowing it to be a false accusation, because the real objective of the one making the accusation is to intimidate his opponent into silence.

There is, of course, such a thing as racism. It does exist, and is a sin, and when it arises we must take it seriously. However, its definition has been so extended, and so warped, that it no longer has its proper meaning. Therefore, most of the time, the racism only exists in the mind of the accuser. Real racism, correctly defined, is to think less of a person, or to treat them badly, or unfairly, *on the basis of their race*. It does not mean disagreeing with, criticising, opposing, or refusing to give in to the demands of, a person or group who are of a different race, *where their race is not the reason for your doing so.* *Islam is not a race*

Criticising bad ideas not people

Therefore, if we criticise the policies and actions of the corrupt former President Obama, that is not racism, as so many people claim. It is simply to criticise his *policies and actions* and has absolutely nothing to do with his skin colour. Mr Obama was an evil man, and a committed Muslim, and he did great harm, not only by his own actions, but also through the long list of enemies and traitors he appointed to key positions, many of whom are also Muslims.

Thus, it would be equally appropriate, and equally necessary, to criticise Mr Obama, and to describe him as wicked, *whatever race he was*, just as it is necessary to criticise white politicians who are corrupt and evil, such as Hillary Clinton or John Kerry. They worked with and for Obama, held the same misguided views, and committed the same treacherous acts against the American people. So, why would it be racist to criticise Mr Obama, but not racist to criticise them, when one is objecting to the very same things, which all of them did?

This ought to be seen as a statement of the blindingly obvious but, sadly, it still has to be said, because most people don't realise it. The bogus allegation of racism is now used routinely whenever a person says anything with which the accuser disagrees. He will quickly invent some supposed connection with race, however tenuous, and condemn the other person for being a *racist*. That is convenient because it means the accuser doesn't have to address the substantive issue, for example whether Mr Obama's policy on X, Y or Z is right or wrong.

All of that can be ignored and the accusation of racism serves as the entire argument, so that it alone is relied on to discredit whatever was said. They don't address the actual argument, because it is assumed there is no need to do so once racism has been alleged. That accusation does the job, all by itself. By this twisted logic, anybody criticising Mr Obama is *'obviously a racist'*, there being no other conceivable reason to criticise him. On that basis, nobody need ever answer the substantive point, or respond to the criticism, or defend Obama's policies.

The same approach is taken to anybody who condemns Islam or criticises the words, actions or beliefs of any Muslim. It is claimed that they too must be doing so because they are *'racist'*, even though Islam is *not a race*, but a *religion*. Therefore, to say anything against it, whether rightly or wrongly, has nothing to do with anybody's race, but only their beliefs and practices. There are Muslims on every continent and *from every race* and their Islamic faith is just as false, and just as evil, wherever they live and whatever race they may be.

Those who defend Islam by accusing its critics of being racists are well aware the accusation is false, even as they say it. They nonetheless make it, because they know it is highly effective at silencing people. So, they continue to use that tactic regularly. Linked to the whole problem of bogus allegations of racism are the issues of *immigration* and so-called *'multi-culturalism'*. These two topics have, likewise, been deliberately made so explosive that people are no longer allowed to discuss them openly or to state their real views.

The only view that is considered acceptable, and which will not result in outrage, and accusations of racism, is for you to be in favour of unrestricted immigration. In addition, you must keep on emphasising that you support multi-culturalism. People quickly realise that expressing any other view will result in fierce hostility. Therefore, as people don't like being shouted at, they soon learn not to say anything that will antagonise the *'race police'*, i.e. that growing section of the population who are obsessed with race.

They are all around us, in our workplaces, amongst our friends and even in our churches, and they increasingly see everything in terms of race. But if we want to be wise we need to be able to think clearly, fearlessly and honestly, and *without any restrictions*, about the political, economic, military or religious issues facing

600

our society. That freedom of thought and speech must extend to all issues which, directly or indirectly, touch upon race, and whether in a real or an imaginary way.

There is absolutely nothing wrong with talking about immigration, or about the fact that Muslims have large families, and we must insist on speaking out openly and in public

We must never submit to any of the boundaries or prohibitions that other people seek to impose on us to limit what we are allowed to think or say. Take therefore the issue of immigration. That too has nothing whatsoever to do with race. It is sheer common sense that any country must have rules as to *who* it will let in, and especially *how many*, and that it must be able to enquire as to what skills, trades, qualifications or capital immigrants have to offer. That is self-evident and applies to any country, regardless of its current racial mix or the race of those who wish to move there.

For years, many of us have argued that the UK is letting in far too many immigrants, mainly due to the tragic error of joining the European Union, which insists on free movement of labour within the EU. However, the UK has *also* been letting in very high numbers of immigrants from *outside the EU*, many of whom are *Muslims*, and they bring us all sorts of social, economic, political, criminal and religious problems. What is more, the true extent of that immigration is deliberately disguised by the UK Government by its dishonest policy of only ever speaking in terms of '*net*' migration.

That is an artificial definition which is intended to mislead us as to the true scale of the *inward* migration, or immigration, which is what really matters. The Government therefore takes the figure for those coming *into* the country and *deducts* from that the number of those who *left the UK*. So, for example, in the year to 30 June 2016, the total *net* migration to the UK was *335,000*. However, that figure is a dishonest device which is designed to disguise the fact that, in that year, *650,000* people *entered* the UK and *315,000 left* it.

So, if you were thinking, *as they intended you to think*, that 335,000 immigrants doesn't sound too bad, then think again. You need to see the real numbers, and also realise *what kind of people* are leaving the UK and *what kind of people are entering it,* because we are not comparing like with like. The 315,000 people who left the UK were mainly highly educated and skilled workers and almost all of them were *tax payers*, many at the higher rate of 40%. Furthermore, the vast majority were *not claiming any benefits*.

Therefore, most of those 315,000 who left the UK were native Britons, born and educated in the UK, each of whom were *contributing* perhaps £10,000 to £50,000 per annum to the nation *in tax,* while *taking nothing out.* In stark contrast, the *650,000* who *entered* the UK were, overwhelmingly, *unskilled and uneducated and had zero capital.* Moreover, although admittedly, many of them got jobs, they were mainly *lowly paid jobs.* Therefore, they generate very low *tax receipts* for the UK Exchequer.

However, except for those who do get jobs, who are usually non-Muslim East Europeans, a high proportion of the others end up claiming *welfare benefits* and *remaining on them permanently.* Therefore, one immigrant, especially if he is a Muslim and therefore has a large family, or produces one later, may become a drain on UK taxpayers for decades to come and *so may their children and grandchildren too.*

Due to the extreme sensitivity of this issue, the UK Government is deliberately misleading us into imagining that 'only' 335,000 immigrants entered the UK in 2016, when it was actually 650,000 who came. They also want us to think that those who *left* the UK and those who *came in* were the *same kind of people,* i.e. that it was a *'like for like'* exchange. But it was nothing of the sort. We were generally swapping a taxpayer for a non-taxpayer, and a non-benefit claimant for a benefit claimant and, very often, a non-Muslim for a Muslim.

Therefore, it is not only a question of numbers in absolute terms, but also the *type of person involved.* The key issue is the effect that those coming in are going to have on the *character and cohesion of our society,* not only in 2018, but for generations, to come. When you consider the dramatic difference in the *numbers of children* they each have, the longer term results are even more staggering. You will never hear any of this from the media, or the Government, because they don't want to alert us to what is really happening, but the fact is most Muslims have large families, for various reasons, partly so they can claim benefits for each child.

It is also because they are taught to see population growth as part of the process by which Islam can take over a nation. They know that can be done within two or three generations, even without fighting, if they simply have *2-3 times* as many children as we do and if their *children and grandchildren do the same.* Consider the maths. If a native British couple have two children they will only ever *replace* themselves, at best, with no element of multiplication. Then, if their children do the same they will, likewise, just replace themselves, again with no multiplication.

Therefore, if we imagine a native British couple in 2018, and they have two children, that brings the total number up to 4 people. But 30 years later, in 2048, if we assume that the parents have died by then, and that another generation of children have been born, there will *still be only four people in total.* That is if we ignore the *spouses* whom their children go on to marry, because they are already here in the UK. I am only looking at the *children* who result from those marriages.

However, contrast that with a Muslim family which begins, in 2018, with two parents but goes on to have six children instead of two. Let us also assume that that Muslim couple's six children then go on to do the same, but also that they start their own families when they are only 20 years old instead of 30-33, as is now the norm in the West. On that basis, a Muslim couple can produce five generations in a century, whereas a native British couple will only produce three.

So, let's follow this through, very roughly, and see how many descendants are produced by that one Muslim couple in 100 years, where we assume that each generation has six children, rather than two, and that each generation begins to start a family aged 20, rather than 30-33.

Year	Total number of descendants produced by one Muslim couple	
2018	nil	
2038	6	
2058	36	i.e. 6 x 6
2078	216	i.e. 36 x 6
2098	1296	i.e. 216 x 6
2118	7,776	i.e. 1296 x 6

Remember that the native British couple we looked at earlier went on to *merely replace themselves* in each successive generation. Moreover, even that was only done three times in the century, not five times. Therefore, by 2118, their total number of descendants then living, would still be only two i.e. *if we ignore all spouses*, for both Muslims and non-Muslims, and if we also assume that each generation dies after having children. That is not actually so, in either case, but the example is deliberately over-simplified to make it easier to follow. Nevertheless, you see the general point.

You will also see why statisticians project that the UK will be a *majority Muslim country by the 2050s* and solidly Muslim by the 2070's! You might quibble with the assumptions in my illustration and prefer to recalculate it on the basis that Muslims have children when they are 25, or even 30, and that they only have 5 children, or even only 4. However, even on that basis, the result is the same, in that they still take over eventually. It just takes longer to get there. That said, my assumptions are probably conservative because Muslim birth rates are much higher than ours, not just marginally so. Thus, some Muslim families actually have *more than* six children, not fewer.

Also, my figures do not include anything to reflect the impact of heavy *ongoing immigration* by Muslims, or of conversions to Islam, over and above the effects of their disproportionately high birth rates. Remember that, unlike the native British population, a high proportion of young Muslims have arranged marriages whereby a husband or wife is brought in for them, from Pakistan or elsewhere.

That means that the growth in the Muslim population could possibly be *even faster* than in my illustration. Accordingly, our policy of allowing virtually unlimited Muslim immigration is to sign the death warrant of our own culture, not to mention our freedom of speech and religion. That is why this issue of immigration by Muslims is so alarming, not just a dry academic argument about statistics.

Moreover, given that we are discussing racism at the moment, the point is that to oppose unrestricted immigration and to impose limits on numbers, and to screen for criminal records etc, is *not racist*. Neither is it racist to single out Muslims for special treatment and to have a policy of excluding them while letting others in, such as Sikhs and Hindus. Those religions, though false, are not based on waging war against us until we either submit to them or are wiped out. Some might view that as a technical distinction, but it seems rather important to me.

Thus, we must insist on the freedom to say whatever we want to say about immigration and not to be intimidated into silence by bogus accusations of racism. We must not allow that slur to be attached to us, even indirectly, and we must ignore it when it is made, as it inevitably will be. Above all, we must not apply it to ourselves. Neither should we honour that false accusation by seeking to defend ourselves from it. The assumption that we are *not* racists should be made *automatically* and should be the default-setting.

That should then stand until and unless we say or do something to indicate that we *are* racists – by the *real* definition, not the bogus one. We should never submit to the requirement to go around proving to everybody that we aren't racists. That is one of the most pernicious burdens imposed upon us by the politically correct zealots who make these unwarranted allegations. One of their master strokes has been to create the false impression that our society is engulfed in a tidal wave of racism. Everyone is then assumed to be a racist unless they strive officiously to prove they are not.

604

I therefore reject the whole multi-cultural agenda, laden as it is with these unfounded assumptions about *'endemic racism'* and the need to see racism under every stone and as providing the underlying motive behind every thought, word or deed. We are not actually under any duty to build a *'multi-cultural society'*. Neither should we feel obliged to see that as being better than a British society or a French society or an American or Danish society, or any other for that matter.

Every nation, and every race, is valid and none of them requires the acceptance of a policy of multi-culturalism, or the denial of their own culture, in order to become so. It is also extraordinary how one-sided this approach is. It is assumed that a Nigerian, Mexican, or Pakistani culture is obviously valid and praiseworthy. We are also told that we in the West should admire, preserve, and even 'celebrate' those cultures.

However, if anyone speaks up for *British* culture or, even worse, *English* culture, or says they are proud of it, that is automatically assumed to be invalid and, of course, racist. Therefore, those who see value and merit in the British way of life, and who wish to preserve it, are portrayed as small-minded bigots, xenophobes and racists. Yet those who wish to promote and preserve Pakistani culture, or Zambian culture etc, are seen as entirely right and, in particular, as *anti-racist*.

It was God who created the various nations

Let's therefore look briefly at what the Bible says on the subject of nations, because it was God Himself who created each one, allocating them their own boundaries, and also giving them their own languages. None of this happened by accident. God also causes each nation to be large or small, and strong or weak, and He also raises them up and lowers them down:

And he made from one every nation of men to live on all the face of the earth, having determined allotted periods and the boundaries of their habitation,
Acts 17:26 (RSV)

He makes nations great, and he destroys them;
he enlarges nations, and leads them away.
Job 12:23 (ESV)

God *wants* each nation to have its own language, land and boundaries, but also to have its own culture and customs. He even gave them different skin colours, according to where on the Earth He sent them to establish their respective nations. Or, in other words, He decided where to send them based on their skin colour, so that they would be better suited to the level of sunlight in that place. We see the beginning of this process of population movement and nation building in Genesis chapters 10 and 11.

As a result of the growth of wickedness in Babel, which we now call Babylon, and especially their development of the occult, God decided to split up the whole human race into different nations, living separately, in different places, and with their own languages. Up to this point there had been only one common language. Also, the majority of people had not spread far since the Flood and were all in what we call the Middle East. But God changed all of that:

¹ These are the generations of the sons of Noah, Shem, Ham, and Japheth. Sons were born to them after the flood. ² The sons of Japheth: Gomer, Magog, Madai, Javan, Tubal, Meshech, and Tiras. ³ The sons of Gomer: Ashkenaz, Riphath, and Togarmah. ⁴ The sons of Javan: Elishah, Tarshish, Kittim, and Dodanim. ⁵ From these the coastland peoples spread in their lands, each with his own language, by their clans, in their nations.

Genesis 10:1-5 (ESV)

The Bible sets out all the different nations which developed from Noah's sons, grandsons and great grandsons, each of whom developed into separate nations. They subsequently travelled far and wide to establish separate, distinct countries all over the Earth and they are listed in Genesis chapter 10, which concludes:

These are the clans of the sons of Noah, according to their genealogies, in their nations, and from these the nations spread abroad on the earth after the flood.

Genesis 10:32 (ESV)

God dispersed the people because of their increasing wickedness, their development of the occult and, in particular, their building of the Tower of Babel as a means of idolatrous worship. He also gave them all different languages to reduce their capacity for wickedness by limiting their ability to communicate and cooperate with each other. God's response did not remove wickedness from the Earth, but it did reduce its extent and its effectiveness. However, the point is that it was something which *God Himself did*, rather than being the idea of any man:

¹ Now the whole earth had one language and the same words. ² And as people migrated from the east, they found a plain in the land of Shinar and settled there. ³ And they said to one another, "Come, let us make bricks, and burn them thoroughly." And they had brick for stone, and bitumen for mortar. ⁴ Then they said, "Come, let us build ourselves a city and a tower with its top in the heavens, and let us make a name for ourselves, lest we be dispersed over the face of the whole earth." ⁵ And the LORD came down to see the city and the tower, which the children of man had built. ⁶ And the LORD said, "Behold, they are one people, and they have all one language, and this is only the beginning of what they will do. And nothing that they propose to do will now be impossible for them. ⁷ Come, let us go down and there confuse their language, so that they may not understand one another's speech." ⁸ So the LORD dispersed them from there over the face of all the earth, and they left off building the city. ⁹ Therefore its name was called Babel, because there the LORD confused the language of all the earth. And from there the LORD dispersed them over the face of all the earth.

Genesis 11:1-9 (ESV)

The position is further confirmed by Moses in Deuteronomy. He speaks of how God created each of the nations, divided up mankind, and fixed their borders:

When the Most High gave to the nations their inheritance, when he divided mankind, he fixed the borders of the people according to the number of the sons of God

Deuteronomy 32:8 (ESV)

God wants each of the races and nations to be different and to have their own cultures, rather than all being the same

It follows that God positively wants each nation to be *different* and to have its *own* distinctive culture, customs, traditions, music, dress, and so on. He loves variety and creativity and *doesn't want us all to be the same*. He wants Spanish people to be Spanish and to act, speak, sing and dance in a Spanish way. He also wants Japanese people to be Japanese and to operate in accordance with their own ways and customs. So, the Japanese are meant to be quiet and reserved, but others, such as many African nations, are meant to be more extravert.

The point is that God likes them all, as they are, and does not want them to cease being themselves or to try to be like others. He therefore likes the British sense of humour, French cooking, German music, American enterprise and so on. God wants all of us to be ourselves, to act like ourselves, and to preserve our own nations with their respective styles, manners and cultures. At any rate, He is entirely happy with our doing so, *provided of course that our culture is not sinful*, and He has no objection to us being different from each other.

Of course, that does *not* mean that there is anything wrong with people of different races *marrying* each other. I stress that because a very tiny number of people misguidedly think there is. God just wants to preserve each of the various nations, and for them to remain diverse, because each nation is unique. However, His concept of *'diversity'* is very different from the misguided PC definition of that word which is pushed by the multi-culturalism lobby. God's aim is to have a diverse world in the sense of having lots of nations and cultures, each of which are *distinct and different from each other*, not all blended into one.

The politically correct version of diversity is to insist that the white European nations, plus the USA, Australia, Canada and New Zealand, *and only them*, are inherently *invalid*. It is then said that they should allow unlimited immigration from other cultures to rectify their supposed deficiencies. The biggest of these 'defects' is that they have white skin and, even worse, that many of their own customs and ways are based on Christianity. Liberals therefore denigrate our own British culture, as if maintaining that, or being proud to be British, is somehow wrong.   *White privilege*

Yet, at the same time, they would be outraged if anybody suggested that Pakistani culture, or Algerian culture is wrong, or that immigrants from those countries should integrate and adopt British or French culture in place of their own. Thus, there is a double standard. Our own culture is seen as inherently invalid and we are told that it should make way for the immigrants' cultures. But the culture of any immigrant to the West is automatically deemed to be valid and it is not thought that they should change in any way, or integrate with our culture as the host nation, even after they come to live here.

Once you begin to examine the West's obsession with racism and the agenda of multi-culturalism, it is quickly seen to be nonsense. But that doesn't prevent these ideas from being bowed down to by those who want a quiet life. These false allegations of racism won't go away without a fight. They have to be stood up to. Courageous people therefore need to speak up against it and to show, *publicly*, that they will not submit. That requires courage, but what you say may embolden others and we may then, one day, see a turning of the tide, just as they did in Spain, Portugal, Greece, Hungary, and so on.

For the avoidance of doubt, let me clarify what I mean by *culture*. When I say that God is in favour of us each having our own national identities and our different customs, traditions and cultures, I am *not* referring to *the sinful, idolatrous, and even occultic* things which form part of the cultures of many nations. For example, in Africa and Asia where, historically, the influence of Christianity has been limited, their cultures have been heavily influenced by their *false religions*.

The main ones are Islam, Hinduism, Sikhism, Shintoism and Buddhism, plus the animistic, idol-worshiping, occultic religions that are found in Africa. To the extent that a nation's traditions and culture emanate from their false religious beliefs, those are *invalid, and God does not approve of them*. So, when I say that God approves of our different cultures, I mean the *innocent, non-sinful, non-*

608

occultic aspects thereof, such as what we eat, how we dress, our styles of music, architecture, literature, and so on.

Thus, God is quite happy that British people eat turkey on Christmas day, whereas Germans eat fish, and that the British drink tea but Americans drink coffee. Such traditions are innocuous. However, He is *not* happy that Hindus celebrate Diwali and Muslims celebrate Eid, because those festivals derive from their *false religions* and are idolatrous and blasphemous. I go out of my way to say that because I was asked to clarify what I mean by 'culture' when this book was at draft stage and I hope I have now done so.

A peoples uniqueness of expression of their way of living

Will the antichrist actually be a Muslim, rather than a European, as so many people assume?

There is no space in this chapter to examine this question in any adequate detail because it is a very large issue and would require a lengthy examination of the prophetic Scriptures. It also flies in the face of most of what is taught about prophecy and the assumptions that most Bible teachers and church leaders make. However, I do at least want to flag the issue, because I am increasingly coming to the view that the antichrist will be a Muslim and that the religion he seeks to impose on the whole world will be Islam.

I also believe that the persecution of Christians and Jews in the 'Tribulation', most notably the *beheadings* spoken of in the book of Revelation, will be done by Muslims. Consider this verse and ask yourself what other group, in all of world history, other than the Muslims, has used beheading as a means of murder, to such an extent that it is their trademark? Instead of trying to imagine how some other group might arise in future and introduce such a policy, why not just look at the one group which is *already doing that*, and has been doing so consistently, and on a massive scale, for 1400 years?

Then I saw thrones, and seated on them were those to whom judgment was committed. Also I saw the souls of those who had been beheaded for their testimony to Jesus and for the word of God, and who had not worshiped the beast or its image and had not received its mark on their foreheads or their hands. They came to life, and reigned with Christ a thousand years.

Revelation 20:4 (RSV)

For a much fuller examination of this theme of the coming antichrist, and whether the religion which he seeks to impose on the world will be Islam, please refer to my other writings. In particular, see the commentary which I intend to write on the book of Daniel. See also the writings of Joel Richardson, an author whom I greatly admire, whose books have influenced my thinking in this area. See, in particular, his three books entitled *'The Islamic Antichrist'*, *'Mid East Beast'*, and *'Mystery Babylon'*. _{Bible the mother of the occult is the mother of harlots}

In these he argues that the antichrist will be a Muslim, that the 'fourth beast' in the book of Daniel is a revived Islamic caliphate, and that *'Babylon the great'* or the *'mother of harlots'* referred to in Revelation chapters 17 and 18 is Saudi Arabia. That is the land of the Arabs, who are the descendants of Ishmael and the oldest enemy of the Jews. Saudi Arabia is also the birthplace of Islam, the location of its main shrine at Mecca, and the main exporter of Islam to the world via its massive funding of mosques, Islamic propaganda and jihadism. Indeed, the terrorists who flew planes into the Twin Towers and the Pentagon on 11 September 2001 were Saudis.

If all of that is true, then there is all the more reason for us to stiffen our spines and resist Islam now and, in order to do so, to become better informed about it. However, although I can't go into detail here, I would like to at least make a few brief points to explain my reasoning and to discuss the significance of the antichrist being Islamic and the implications of that prospect for us now.

I also want to challenge the widely held belief that the future antichrist will rule over the whole world, such that there can be no opposition to him except by individuals. That cannot be the case because we read in Scripture of whole nations, indeed whole groups of nations, fighting against the antichrist and against specific nations which he will rule over, *and which are now already Islamic.* That must mean that, at the end, some nations will still be non-Islamic, or at least that they will not have a majority of Muslims within them.

There is no space here to examine this complicated theme properly but look, for example, at Ezekiel chapters 38 and 39, in which there is the prophecy of *'Gog and Magog'*. Those chapters identify each of the nations which will, in the future, come up against Israel to attack it. They are listed with the names they had over 2500 years ago, at the time when Ezekiel wrote this. But the point is they are *all now Islamic* nations:

[1] The word of the LORD came to me: [2] "Son of man, set your face toward Gog, of the land of Magog, the chief prince of Meshech and Tubal, and prophesy against him [3] and say, Thus says the Lord GOD: Behold, I am against you, O Gog, chief prince of Meshech and Tubal; [4] and I will turn you about, and put hooks into your jaws, and I will bring you forth, and all your army, horses and horsemen, all of them clothed in full armor, a great company, all of them with buckler and shield, wielding swords; [5] Persia, Cush, and Put are with them, all of them with shield and helmet; [6] Gomer and all his hordes; Beth-togar'mah from the uttermost parts of the north with all his hordes—many peoples are with you.

> [7] "Be ready and keep ready, you and all the hosts that are assembled about you, and be a guard for them. [8] After many days you will be mustered; in the latter years you will go against the land that is restored from war, the land where people were gathered from many nations upon the mountains of Israel, which had been a continual waste; its people were brought out from the nations and now dwell securely, all of them. [9] You will advance, coming on like a storm, you will be like a cloud covering the land, you and all your hordes, and many peoples with you.
>
> Ezekiel 38:1-9 (RSV)

Briefly, my position is that in the last days the antichrist will arise, and will also gather his armies, from countries which are today *Muslim majority nations*. Moreover, they are all in the Middle East and North Africa. Those nations will then form an alliance or coalition and will invade Israel, as well as persecuting Jews and Christians outside of Israel. This persecution will occur even in nations over which the antichrist does not rule.

Then, after a short but brutal victory over Israel, which will involve terrible persecution of the Jewish people, Jesus will return from Heaven to destroy the antichrist and his coalition of armies. He will do so prior to establishing His Millennial Kingdom. See my chapter above on prophecy, and my forthcoming book on Israel, for more detail. The key point is that if the antichrist is a Muslim, and if the nations he rules over are Islamic, as I believe they will be, then it increases yet further the significance of Islam as an issue. It also makes it all the more important that we resist it now, both as individuals and nations.

But Gog & Magog appear in the Millennia 'after' Christ return

Another crucial point is that, if the antichrist's control does not extend to the entire world, but only to some nations, and to parts of others, then it means there is every reason to resist Islam now, because its victory over us is *not inevitable*. In other words, we are not *all* doomed to come under the heel of Islam, even though many nations will do so. Therefore, the fight against it is not hopeless, or bound to end in defeat.

In short, there is still everything to fight for and every reason to hope, and even to believe, that we may be able to save *our own nation* from coming under Islamic domination. Of course, we cannot prevent the antichrist from coming to power, and from causing the Tribulation, in which multitudes of Christians and Jews will be murdered. The Bible says that that will happen and therefore it will. But what we can at least hope to do is to prevent our own nation from being one of those that are ruled by the antichrist.

If we achieve that then our own nation will be fighting *against* him at the end, rather than being yet another of the Islamic nations that are going to fight for him. Obviously, being one of those non-Islamic nations, which are going to be the object of his hatred and wrath, will not be pleasant. However, it is still a lot better than being ruled over by Islam, and eventually by the antichrist, and therefore fighting for him.

At the very least it will be better in terms of avoiding the terrible judgment that God will inflict upon all those nations, and individuals, who support the antichrist and his religion. Please see my other books and commentaries for a fuller discussion of why I believe the antichrist will be a Muslim and how Bible prophecy points to that, rather than to him being a European, as so many assume he will be.

CHAPTER 17

CONCLUSION AND CALL TO ACTION

All these things my hand has made,
and so all these things are mine,
says the LORD.
But this is the man to whom I will look,
he that is humble and contrite in spirit,
and trembles at my word.
Isaiah 66:2 (RSV)

if my people who are called by my name humble themselves, and pray and seek
my face, and turn from their wicked ways, then I will hear from heaven, and
will forgive their sin and heal their land.
2 Chronicles 7:14 (RSV)

For Ezra had set his heart to study the law of the LORD, and to do it, and to
teach his statutes and ordinances in Israel.
Ezra 7:10 (RSV)

You have commanded your precepts
to be kept diligently.
Psalm 119:4 (ESV)

⁹ How can a young man keep his way pure?
By guarding it according to your word.
¹⁰ With my whole heart I seek you;
let me not wander from your commandments!
¹¹ I have stored up your word in my heart,
that I might not sin against you.
Psalm 119:9-11 (ESV)

Give me understanding, that I may keep your law
and observe it with my whole heart.
Psalm 119:34 (ESV)

How to make the best possible use of this book

We have covered a lot of ground in this book and looked at many topics and issues which most Christians would not associate with the pursuit of wisdom, even in so far as they ever give a moment's thought to what wisdom is or how it is attained.

613

You will hopefully also have concluded that you are currently far less wise than you had supposed, or even that you are not wise at all, but just simple. You will probably realise that there are traces of foolishness too, at least at times, or in certain parts of your conduct and character.

Whatever stage you might currently be at on the 'spectrum' from wicked to wise, choose now to make it your lifelong aim to become wise, and to get rid of any remaining foolishness or naivety that is still present within you. I say lifelong because I don't want to give any false expectations of being able to become a wise person in the time it takes to read this book. It doesn't work like that. The advice I give, not only in this book, but in each of my other books, commentaries and audio series, and the biblical principles on which they are all based, have to be slowly *absorbed*.

Above all, they have to be *put into practice*, and not just for a few days, but over a long time, so that new habits can form and your whole mind can be *'transformed'*, as it must be. Therefore, set out on what is bound to be a long journey and keep going. Aim to get as far as you can get before your journey is ended, either by death or the rapture. Also, seek for wisdom in the broadest possible sense, right across the board, even where that involves looking at topics which you have never previously considered important, or have never thought of at all, such as:

a) God's judgment on your life, i.e. His assessment of the fruit your life produces

b) the eternity that lies beyond that judgment

c) Bible prophecy

d) Israel and the Jews

e) your job

f) money

g) political correctness

h) Islam

i) the errors of 'rights-based' thinking

j) obtaining guidance and making good decisions

k) the role demons play in our lives (see my Books 7 and 9)

l) building a successful marriage

m) the need to change, grow and be 'transformed' by the renewing of your mind

n) the 'love of the truth'

o) fearing God

p) humbling yourself

I have also covered very many other points and issues not only in this book, but also in my other books, when discussing what wisdom consists of and what wise people do. However, I have listed the ones set out above because they would probably not be on most people's lists of what wisdom is about. Therefore, I suggest you broaden your definition to include all of the above, and more. Then seek to become wise, and to eliminate foolishness and naivety, in every conceivable area of your life.

To make the best possible use of this book, I suggest that you do not merely read it once and then put it away. Instead, read it through again, perhaps even repeatedly, because it contains a huge amount of detail and much of it is not what you might expect, as well as being contrary to current orthodoxy and political correctness. Thus it will be hard to absorb it quickly. Therefore, go through it again more slowly, a chapter at a time, and spend a week, or maybe a month, dwelling on that one chapter, pondering it and assessing yourself to see where you need to change.

For example, why not spend a whole month looking at the chapter on work? As you do that, think deeply about each of the main faults I have identified in the average worker. With each of these, ask God to reveal to you whether you have that fault and, if so, how. For Him to really answer you, and to open your eyes to your own faults and wrong attitudes it will take time, just on the issues covered in that chapter, let alone all the others. Therefore, don't rush it. Dwell on that chapter for as long as it takes and meditate upon it until you extract the fullest possible value and see real change in yourself.

Then do the same concerning marriage, money, decision making, and so on. Do that until you have covered all of the book thoroughly, not just at 90 miles per hour as you 'whizz past' each chapter. In fact, to get the fullest possible benefit, get hold of my series of talks on biblical wisdom and listen to those on MP3. Then even more of this will sink in. By listening you will also be able to keep on addressing these issues at times when you cannot read, by using what I call 'second hand' time, while you are already busy driving, cooking, bathing, or walking the dog.

The benefit of listening in this way is enormous and far more information will sink in and be truly understood than if you only read it. It also makes it much easier for you to reflect on what you hear. If we were to try to put into a single

615

phrase how we can most effectively seek to develop wisdom, we could not put it better than what King David said, as he was dying, to his son, Solomon, who was to be the next King. I used this quotation in the introduction, but it is so fundamental to the pursuit of wisdom, that I will use it again here to close this book:

Now set your mind and heart to seek the LORD your God…...
1 Chronicles 22:19(a) (ESV)

APPENDIX

<table>
<tr><td>Supervisor to indicate here how often this file is to be reviewed.</td><td colspan="2"><h1>CASE PLAN</h1></td></tr>
</table>

Name of client:		Fee Earner:	
Adult or Minor:		Previous fee earners if any, in order:	
Ledger No:		LIMITATION DATE:	
Accident Date:		Is Primary Liability OPENLY Admitted? (ie NOT merely without prejudice)	
Date client instructed us:		Are they arguing Contributory Negligence:	
Town/Location of Accident:		Are they arguing re Causation:	
Have you checked on Google earth street view?			

(TO BE USED AND RE-USED THROUGHOUT THE CASE AND TO ACCOMPANY ANY RECOMMENDATION TO ISSUE OR CLOSE)

Has the client ever complained in any way?

---

1. ***BRIEF CIRCUMSTANCES/PARTIES***

a) ***Type of Accident?:*** *RTA, Slip & trip, Work, Holiday, Animal, Other (please state)*

b) ***Facts/circumstances***

c) *Name of **Main** Defendant (give full name and status) =*

---

d) *Other possible alternative/concurrent defendants? (give name, role and brief reason to blame them).*

e) *Have they indicated any defence or expected defence? If so, what? Does it seem valid / true / realistic?*

PROVING OUR OWN CASE

2. *DUTY*

a) *Define the duty or duties – firstly where it comes from and then what it is, (eg general duty under Occupiers Liability Act, and specifically to install and maintain a door closer to prevent the door slamming NB Don't discuss breach)*

b) *Who owes the duty(ies) (are you sure it is the Defendant or could it be someone else?)*

c) *To whom is the duty owed? (is our client definitely in this group or category?)*

d) *In infant cases, have you considered whether the parent(s) themselves could be to blame?*

---

3. *BREACH*

a) *Specify what the Defendant did that he shouldn't or didn't do that he should have. NB No fancy words or section numbers – just set it out in simple basic words eg:*
   a) *The Defendant's employee spilled some vegetable oil on the floor.*
   b) *Employee didn't clean it up and*
   c) *Didn't put up warning sign and*
   d) *Didn't alert our client*
   e) *Defendant had a system which made it likely that oil would be spilled*

b) *Evidence of there being a breach*

c) *Are you sure that it was done / not done by the defendant(s) you are pursuing (rather than by somebody else)*

d) *Do we need any non-medical expert evidence? Who from?*

e) *If so, to prove what?*

4. CAUSATION

a) How/why do you say that the breach(es) you're alleging _caused_ the client's _accident._

> *NB Many of you misunderstand this section. It's not about proving there's a breach or about whether he's really injured. It is asking whether the client would still have been injured, i.e. would not have avoided injury, even if the Defendant had not done the wrong thing you are complaining of or had provided the thing or the training etc that you say was missing. For example if we alleged that there was insufficient training but it is shown that even if he'd had reasonable training this would still have occurred. In other words, it may be that there are breaches, but they didn't cause the accident/incident. Another example – in an RTA the Defendant's car may have had bald tyres. There's a clear duty to have adequate tread and it's a breach (and a crime) not to. But, if the RTA was on a dry day then bald tyres are an advantage. They give more grip, not less. So bald tyres can't have caused the RTA. They would only do that on a wet day. Please apply this same logic to consider causation in your case.*

b) Also, did the accident cause the _symptoms?_ i.e. would he have had some/all of the same condition / symptoms _anyway?_

> *I.e. are there pre-existing illnesses, degenerative conditions, etc or previous accidents or other circumstances that could equally / better explain the injury / symptoms? (OR some of them) Example – A man has got a bad back but his Dad had a bad back and he himself has a history of back pain. Things like that should alert you to check out whether the current symptoms come from a pre-existing condition/propensity and therefore would have occurred anyway even without the accident. Be alert to this possibility and ask the expert to comment on it.*

5. LOSS

a) Do the generals exceed £1,000? What are they realistically?
(ie assuming 100% liability). *(Don't just say "fast track" – give a rough estimate based on current knowledge of symptoms to help us gauge how weighty the quantum is).*

b) OR is it a child/mental patient? *NB (even infants' generals now need to go over £1,000)*

c) What are the special damages? Is the schedule complete? Yes/No

> *Loss of Earnings (consider whether these are reasonable/unavoidable) NB Do you think it's possible that the client has remained out of work longer than his injuries justify? Is he now failing to mitigate his loss by getting a new job and/or returning to his own job and/or lighter duties?*
>
> *NB - Does the client's employer require sick pay to be repaid? (i.e. if they aren't the Defendant).*

Handicap on the labour market?

Travel?

Care and assistance claim?

Medical expenses?

Other?

d) *How real / <u>realistic</u> are each of these?*

e) *Are any of the losses <u>unlawful</u> in any way? (e.g. working without paying tax, immoral earnings, etc?)*

f) *What / where is your <u>evidence</u> for the losses?*

g) *For the losses generally has the client properly mitigated his losses?*

h) *Is any <u>additional</u> medical expert from any other discipline needed? If so, why?*

i) *What <u>efforts</u> have been made to <u>settle</u>? (Have you tried the settlement team?)   Yes/No (If so, what happened?):*

6. <u>*EVIDENCE*</u>

What have you got so far?

a) *Photographs – of what?*

Who took them?

<u>*When*</u> *were they taken?*

Quality / relevance? (i.e. are they good enough to prove breach?)

Do we need more/replacements?

b) *Witnesses*

Name(s)	*What key ingredients they can show/prove for you*	*Statements Obtained?*

NB Set these out in bullet form beside each name

1.   *Yes/No*

2.	Yes/No
3.	Yes/No
4.	Yes/No

NB   Remember you will need to serve <u>witness summonses</u>.

c) *Have you obtained <u>voluntary disclosure</u> of all relevant documents from the Defendant in accordance with the pre action protocol?*

d) *What do the <u>documents show/suggest/prove</u>?   (set out key facts/points)*

e) *Have you checked and understood the documents and considered whether any are missing? If so, <u>what</u> is missing?*

f) *Do any questions or <u>lines of enquiry</u> emerge? (Set them out)*

g) *Do <u>other documents</u> now seem to exist and to be relevant as a result of what you've seen on disclosure? Have you sought to get these?*

h) *<u>What are they</u> – i.e. what are you requesting? (List them).*

i) *Is an Application for <u>Pre Action Disclosure</u> of Documents appropriate here?*

j) *Are there any <u>OPEN admissions</u>? If so, of what and from whom? Are they capable of being retracted? i.e. is this multi track?*
(NB If admissions have been made without prejudice then say so here – because that alters how we treat them, because they can be retracted even in a fast track case. If so, your position could be harmed if you've relied on a WP 'admission' and failed to gather evidence).

k) *Have you done a <u>Notice to Admit</u> Facts?*

l) *Have you served/should you serve requests for further information? If so, what? - set out the requests in brief.*

m) *How <u>strong</u>/credible/consistent is your overall evidence?*

n) *Do you <u>believe</u> the client and why/why not?*

o) *Have we <u>instructed</u> a doctor? (if so <u>when</u> and <u>what type</u> of expert?)*

621

p) *If you've not instructed a doctor yet, set out why not*

q) *Does the medical evidence support the client's injuries?*
    i) *in terms of being real/genuine?*
    ii) *in terms of causation?*

r) *Do you feel you need any other medical evidence/report and if so why? E.g. MRI, x ray, updates, questions to expert, etc?*

---

7. CONTRIBUTORY NEGLIGENCE

a) *Is contributory negligence alleged/likely to be alleged?*

b) *If so, why? What do they say our client did that was wrong/negligent /foolish?*

c) *Even if contributory negligence is not yet alleged, analyse the question of whether there is contributory negligence as if you were being asked to produce an imaginary letter of claim against our own client. (Think in exactly the same way as if he was a defendant and identify the duty, the breach and whether there's causation, i.e. did his own error/foolishness actually cause the accident. Remember, they need to show he did something wrong himself and that it caused or helped cause his own accident? If you can't show this, they probably can't.)*

d) *Having done the above exercise, does the alleged or potential contributory negligence seem real/valid?*

e) *How significant was it? What percentage would the quantum be reduced by and why?*

---

8. OPPONENT / FUNDING / LIMITATION

a) *Is the Defendant insured? (If not can he pay personally?)*

b) *If the Defendant is a business, is it solvent? Will it be able to pay the excess on its insurance? Do you know whether there is an excess and, if so, how much?*

c) *Is the Defendant an insolvent company which has now been removed from the Roll at Companies House? If so, you'll need to get it restored to the Roll before you issue proceedings*

d) Is it an *MIB case?* *(IF SO, NOTE STRICT NOTICE REQUIREMENTS – SEE SUPERVISOR)* NB Note also 9 month limitation period in MIB cases.

e) Do you have the Defendant's correct and full name and category? (eg individual, sole trader, partnership (ie a firm) limited company, charity, Local Authority, Chief Constable, County Council, Secretary of State, etc)

f) What is the attitude/nature/character of the Defendant/TPI? How *determined* are they?

g) If the Defendant is a limited company, is it part of a *group* of companies – if so are you sure you are suing the right one? (Consider suing more than one, or even all, if in any doubt)

h) Have you done a Company search?

i) What *Part 36* Offers are there and when?
   Ours   = £
   Theirs = £

j) Does the difference justify issuing proceedings?

k) Are you giving any / sufficient *discount* ie for contributory negligence and/or losing outright ie for "litigation risk"? (ie on top of, and separate from, the risk of getting quantum wrong).

l) What is your *realistic* valuation of quantum (assuming 100% liability).

m) What has the client authorised as a minimum?

n) What are *the other side alleging* / saying about quantum / mitigation of loss / medical causation?)

o) Do you have *answers* to what they allege? If so, what?

p) What do you need to be able to answer / *rebut* – ie what would you need to prove / disprove and how? i.e. what other *evidence* could you possibly get / use?

q) *Have you given Julie a copy of the limitation date notice (CDN 1) for this case?   Yes / No*

r) *Have you notified her in writing of any notices of changes to the limitation date (CDN 4)?   Yes / No*

s) *Please state the date when the limitation date notice was last <u>checked</u> / reconsidered (i.e. in case things have changed since it was first completed. This should be checked regularly throughout the case especially if the injuries were caused by a process rather than an event – in such cases be cautious and calculate from the earliest possible date i.e. from when that process began, not when it ended):*

t) *NB Have you checked that the entries in the client's medical records tally with when he says the accident was? If it differs, see supervisor re changing the limitation date on the computer.*

---

9. <u>CLIENT CARE</u>

a) *Has the client ever <u>complained</u> or grumbled in any way? (even informally*

b) *If so, what about? And when?*

c) *Have you had contact with the client by letter or phone at least every 4 weeks throughout the case without exception? If not, set out the dates of each contact with to the client*

d) *What <u>fee earners</u> have had conduct of this file – (set out initials and approximate periods of 'ownership' if more than one fee earner).*

e) *Have you filled in a blue form for change of fee earner?   Yes / No*

   Has this been given to Carrie?   Yes / No

---

10. <u>YOUR HANDLING OF THE FILE/YOUR CONCERNS</u>

a) *Is the file a 'bogey' file in any way? (please say so openly and early on*

b) *Do you feel you understand what to do? i.e. are you comfortably <u>within your depth?</u> Yes / No* *c)* *Is there anything you don't understand or are worried about? If so, what?*

d) *How is your relationship with the <u>client</u>?*

e) *Has the file been <u>neglected/drifting</u> at any point – if so when / for how long / why?*

f) *Would you like us to transfer the file to a colleague?*   *Yes / No*

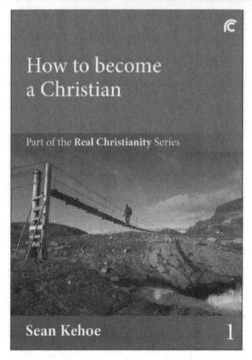

How to become a Christian

Sean Kehoe

Book 1 in the Real Christianity series seeks to explain the full, authentic Gospel, or "good news", as it is set out in the Bible. Tragically, much of the Church has reduced it to *"God loves you and wants you to love Him,"* which is very true, but it isn't the Gospel. It leaves out many essential 'ingredients' such as our sin, God's holiness, His impending judgment, Hell, the Lake of Fire and our urgent need to repent. Each of those things, which we might call "the bad news", have been edited out by most preachers in the hope that it would make the Christian message more attractive and also to avoid offending people. Therefore we have ended up with a false, watered down, man-made gospel which does not bring salvation. Ironically, such compromise does not actually attract people anyway.

Indeed, it is counter-productive, because the good news only makes sense if someone has told you what the bad news is. Therefore, because they have not heard any of that, many see no reason to repent or believe. So, this book frankly explains the real Gospel, firstly for your sake, but also to enable you to witness to others more effectively and authentically. It has been written in the clearest possible way, using plain English and avoiding religious jargon. It can be read by an absolute beginner but will also help mature Christians and leaders who want to understand and share the Gospel more accurately.

All of the books in this series can be ordered online from **www.realchristianity.com**.

Growing in the character of a disciple
Sean Kehoe

Book 2 in the Real Christianity series looks at what happens next, after we become a Christian, and at how we can grow into mature disciples. That involves an ongoing process of change, whereby we are meant to become more and more like Jesus Christ in our character, attitudes and conduct. Another word for this process is 'sanctification', such that we develop lives of obedience, self-sacrifice, humility and discipline. Indeed, the very word 'disciple' has the same root meaning as discipline, because it involves following and obeying Jesus in our daily lives, even when it is very hard to do so. Christian character cannot be formed overnight. It is a fruit which has to be grown and which takes years, or even decades, to develop. This book introduces you to some of the key things that are needed to bring about that growth, but it is very honest about how costly and difficult it is going to be.

The book also looks at four much neglected subjects which are vital if we are to become effective disciples. These are thankfulness, faithfulness, truthfulness and forgiving others. Forgiveness, in particular, is a severely misunderstood subject. The book therefore spends time explaining what forgiveness doesn't mean, and doesn't involve, as well as what it does. That is needed because many people have such a garbled, inaccurate definition of it that they find forgiving others impossible. A proper grasp of all these issues will give you a much stronger start in the Christian life. However, even if you began many years ago, they will now help you to progress farther and faster as a disciple.

All of the books in this series can be ordered online from **www.realchristianity.com**.

Real Christianity

Book 3

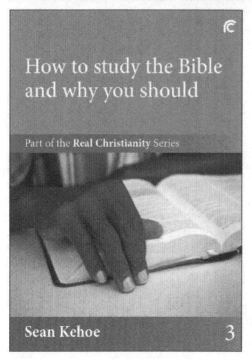

How to study the Bible and why you should

Part of the **Real Christianity** Series

Sean Kehoe   3

How to study the Bible and why you should

Sean Kehoe

Book 3 in the Real Christianity series explains how to study the Bible more effectively. Even in Evangelical and Pentecostal churches, which were once known for their devotion to God's Word, the Bible is now widely neglected, misunderstood and even ignored. To read the Bible properly does require some skill but, more importantly, that you approach it diligently and with the right heart attitude and method. Many of us find it difficult because nobody has shown us how. Even worse, some have been taught wrong ways, which then handicap them. This book looks at the right way to interpret the Bible, known as the 'golden rule'. That is to take the Bible literally unless the words used, or the context, plainly indicate that we should do otherwise, such as where a figure of speech is used.

It also looks at the main errors in people's thinking, which undermine faith and promote unbelief, namely 'scepticism', 'liberalism' and 'allegorism' or the 'allegorical approach'. The author has a very high view of Scripture and would urge you to take it literally and seriously, with a determination to understand it, act upon it, and be changed by it. The Bible is utterly unique. It is God's Word to us. No equivalent book has ever been, or ever will be, written. The author also advises on Bible translations, recommending those which take a literal 'word for word' approach, rather than 'dynamic equivalence', or even paraphrasing, which often take liberties with God's Word. He is convinced that every determined person, provided they can read and write, is able to gain a balanced understanding of the whole Bible for themselves, whoever they are, and regardless of ability or education

All of the books in this series can be ordered online from **www.realchristianity.com**.

Real Christianity

Book 4

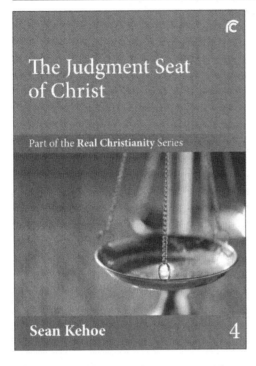

The Judgment Seat of Christ

Part of the **Real Christianity** Series

Sean Kehoe

4

The Judgment Seat of Christ

Sean Kehoe

Book 4 in the Real Christianity series looks closely at a subject which most churches ignore and which is, therefore, very little known or understood. It is the judgment which awaits Christians, at the 'Judgment Seat of Christ'. On that momentous day our whole lives, from conversion onwards, will be evaluated in a face to face meeting with Jesus Christ Himself. He will either reward and congratulate us, or rebuke us and leave us empty handed. N.B. This is not to be confused with the Great White Throne judgment, for the unsaved, at which they will be condemned. One would imagine that this hugely important issue would be taught thoroughly and be a regular topic of conversation. Yet it is rarely even mentioned in most churches.

The author explains what it is and why it matters. In particular, he focuses on what each of us can do now to improve Jesus' assessment of us and to increase the rewards, and praise, which He gives us on that Day. The author also looks very closely at the criteria for this judgment, and identifies at least 29 different issues on which we will be assessed. If we address these things now, while we have time to change, we can alter the outcome of that judgment. We are meant to see life as a test, and to be motivated by the prospect of rewards. Indeed, that is why Jesus Himself told us about them and urged us to seek for them. So, contrary to what many imagine, we are actually supposed to seek for rewards, and also for a high place in Jesus' Millennial Kingdom and in the eternal state thereafter.

All of the books in this series can be ordered online from **www.realchristianity.com**.

Real Christianity

Book 6

How to identify and handle wicked people

Part of the Real Christianity Series

Sean Kehoe 6

How to identify and handle wicked people

Sean Kehoe

Book 6 in the Real Christianity series looks at yet another subject which is rarely even mentioned, let alone taught, in most churches. It is about how to identify and handle wicked people. The author has much experience in this field, and from many angles, having spent three years in the police and then 25 as a lawyer and as a businessman and employer. He also practised in litigation and employment law and was also active in politics for many years. Thus he is able to write about many of the things which the wicked do and how they go about it. His view is that 'the wicked' are far more numerous than most of us imagine, and, crucially, that they include many people who appear to be entirely ordinary. Moreover, he maintains that the wicked are also to be found, in large numbers, *inside churches*, not just among unbelievers.

Indeed, it is often the leaders of churches whom God regards as the most wicked of all, if they become dishonest, manipulative, or unfaithful. That is partly because they have greater knowledge and are thus more accountable, but also because they do such terrible damage to God's people. The book seeks to define this group known as 'the wicked', and then to describe their techniques. It also gives many detailed examples of their malice, deviousness and schemes from real life situations. The aim is to help you identify the wicked earlier, and then to handle them better, both in practical terms, but also spiritually. That is, we not only need to know what to do about the wicked, but also how to pray about, and even against, them.

All of the books in this series can be ordered online from **www.realchristianity.com**.